D0421242

Scenic Art for the Theatre

WITHDRAWN

* 000202732 *

Scenic Art for the Theatre
HISTORY, TOOLS, AND TECHNIQUES

Second Edition

Susan Crabtree and Peter Beudert

ELSEVIER

Amsterdam   Boston   Heidelberg   London   New York   Oxford
Paris   San Diego   San Francisco   Singapore   Sydney   Tokyo

Focal Press is an imprint of Elsevier

Focal Press

Focal Press is an imprint of Elsevier
30 Corporate Drive, Suite 400, Burlington, MA 01803, USA
Linacre House, Jordan Hill, Oxford OX2 8DP, UK

Copyright © 2005, Elsevier Inc. All rights reserved.

No part of this publication may be reproduced, stored in a retrieval system, or transmitted in any form or by any means, electronic, mechanical, photocopying, recording, or otherwise, without the prior written permission of the publisher.

Permissions may be sought directly from Elsevier's Science & Technology Rights Department in Oxford, UK: phone: (+44) 1865 843830, fax: (+44) 1865 853333, e-mail: permissions@elsevier.com.uk. You may also complete your request online via the Elsevier homepage (http://elsevier.com), by selecting "Customer Support" and then "Obtaining Permissions."

Recognizing the importance of preserving what has been written, Elsevier prints its books on acid-free paper whenever possible.

Library of Congress Cataloging-in-Publication Data
Application submitted.

British Library Cataloguing-in-Publication Data
A catalogue record for this book is available from the British Library.

ISBN: 0-240-80462-7

For information on all Focal Press publications
visit our website at www.focalpress.com

04 05 06 07 08 09 10 9 8 7 6 5 4 3 2 1

Printed in the United States of America

On the cover: The shop floor at Scenic Art Studios. Artists at work on *Our Town* (below) and *Never Gonna Dance* (above).

In Memory of Mary Ellen Kennedy

"Don't draw things, draw relationships."

"It's so simple: just put every brushstroke in the right place."

Contents

Preface to the Second Edition

It may seem unusual to publish a second edition of a book about scenic painting. One obvious motivation to write a new edition, which is that new information has come forth to clarify our knowledge of scenic painting, is not present. Little of the act or art of stage painting has changed recently; painting is still just painting after all. No new colors were formulated, nor have different brush types appeared since the publication of the first edition. There are no faddish painting techniques to defend, nor are there exotic materials being introduced into paintbrush handles to gain us milliseconds of time per stroke. The practice of scenic painting has changed very little, in fact. It is likely that Philip de Loutherbourg would adapt well to Joseph Forbes's shop after a week or two, and probably the same would happen in reverse. Certainly both would probably learn something new from each other.

So, then, why would we endeavor to write a new edition of a book about scenic painting? One reason is that we wanted to refine certain parts of the first edition. These are simple changes any writer (or painter) would make if given a second chance at an important project. Surely those who have read or used this book would expect no less.

Another reason we wrote a second edition is that we wanted to make an even better book. While this does not necessarily happen if you are able to repaint a drop, having a second go at a book can be a great way to improve and build upon a foundation. We give our thanks, too, to our publisher, who allowed us the freedom to improve upon the quantity and quality of the visual material of the first edition.

The second edition has many more photos to assist the text and guide and possibly inspire the reader.

There is another motivation for a second edition that is not so much about the book itself but about the art of scenic painting. It is not that there is something new to say about scenic painting, but this book presents new perceptions and an awareness of the art form. No, not new, but perhaps more in depth. We attempted to express the essence of scenic art and being a scenic artist in the first edition. For every technique or tool described, we included an insight into the thoughts and intentions behind the technique. Scenic art is built upon many intangibles, such as knowing when to stop painting and when to simply paint with all your might and soul. We sought to recognize those aspects of the art as part of the first edition.

The second edition of this book is a reevaluation of many of the observations and insights from the first edition. A sense of confirmation is arrived at through the thoughts offered to us by the gifted scenic artists who gave their time to this edition in the interviews included. It can be best described as a revelation, not simply that what we said in the first edition was right, but that what we put forth the first time out was confirmed so eloquently and affirmed so forcefully by these talented people. There are currents of thought and knowledge, of knowing what is appropriate and good in painting, that run through those who do this well for a living. It is this stream of knowledge, or awareness, which we offer to the reader, especially those who may wish to pursue scenic artistry as a way of life.

Acknowledgments

Susan Crabtree and Peter Beudert wish to acknowledge the many individuals who have helped in the preparation of this book. The following individuals provided information and aided us in materials acquisition: Joe Forbes and the staff of Scenic Arts Studio, Cornwall, New York; Rachel Keebler and the staff of Cobalt Studios; Monona Rossol of Arts, Craft, and Theatre Safety, White Plains, New York; Terry McCellan, Bonnie Carpenter, and Alexander Adducci of Northern Illinois University; C. Lance Brockman, University of Minnesota; Martin Durrant, Victoria and Albert Museum, London, England; Barbara Bezat and Alan K. Lathrop, Performing Arts Archives, University of Minnesota Libraries, St. Paul, Minnesota; Nina Couch and Alan Woods, Lee Lash Institute, Ohio State University; Dale Seeds of the College of Wooster, Wooster, Ohio; Tobin Collection of Theatre Art at the Marion Koogler McNay Art Museum; Joe Varona; Michael Anania; Mark Short, Kenmark Inc.; Tobins Lake Studios; Toni Auletti; David Birn; Anne Mundall; John Shack; James Joy; Kay A. Zuris, Public Museum of Grand Rapids, Grand Rapids, Michigan; Van Caplin, Civic Light Opera of Pittsburgh, Pennsylvania; Denny Nelson, Purdy Brush Company; Howard M. Wagman, The Wagman Primus Group; Karl and Don Armbruster; the staff of the United Scenic Artists, 829 New York, Miami, and Chicago; Robert Clack; and Dave Clow.

Susan Crabtree would like to acknowledge firstly the coauthor of this book, Peter Beudert, for his Herculean efforts, and Angelique Powers for her assistance in creating technique examples. Thanks to the following individuals who lent valuable commentary in manuscript preparation: Deb Clow, Rachel Keebler and the staff of Cobalt Studios, and Monona Rossol.

I also want to express my thanks to every scenic artist, scenic designer, and student of scenic art that I have had the opportunity and privilege to work with over the years; you are all in this book.

Peter Beudert lovingly thanks Lynn Beudert for her insight and endless support. He also gratefully acknowledges Clare P. Rowe for her contributions to this publication and her inspirational talents as a scenic artist. Very special acknowledgement is also given to Justine Collins for her hard work of transcribing interviews and managing the text. He is deeply indebted to Pierre Vidal and Mathias Auclair of the Bibliothèque de l'Opéra National de Paris for their assistance over the last few years. Thanks also to the Office of the Provost of the University of Arizona, Albert D. Tucci, Kimb Williamson, Dana Kenn, Robert Schmidt, and Xuzheng He. Special thanks to Peter Wildman for his digital models used in this book.

Part One
The Professional Scenic Artist

Mural detail from the Cabot Theatre at the Broadway Theatre Center in Milwaukee, Wisconsin, designed by David Birn, painted at Cobalt Studios by David Zinn and Rachel Keebler.

Chapter 1

Training and Working as a Scenic Artist

Being a scenic artist is an unusual and highly rewarding career. One thing that makes scenic artistry unusual is the physical scale of the work. Stage paintings are often enormous relative to an artist's canvas. One-thousand-square-foot canvases knocked out in one, two or three days (or even hours) are not the stuff of everyday life, except for the scenic artist. Another thing that makes scenic artistry unusual is the apparent anonymity of the artist to the public. The fact that the apparent "credit" for the canvas goes first to the scenic designer may seem odd. Imagine Michelangelo allowing his staff to paint the ceiling of the Sistine Chapel from his sketches—it's unfathomable. Yet the value of the artist these days is less emphatically on the skill of the artist than the creative idea. It is the norm in theatre that the scenic designer has the public face as the creator when it comes to stage scenery. However, those of us who work in theatre know well that scenic artists are as much a part of the creative process as designers. Just as Broadway producers insist on such gifted designers as Tony Walton, John Napier, and Heidi Landesman (to name but a few), it is inconceivable that any of these great designers would venture into a "painted" design without being assured that only top scenic artists would be available. Great painters like Joe Forbes, Rachel Keebler, Doug Lebrecht, Nancy Orr, Jane Snow, and Mary Heilman are equally in demand for high-venture stage productions as are the better-known scenic designers.

Scenic artistry is profoundly rewarding, too. How many young artists dream of living off their painting? This is what the scenic artist does, for it is a career of painting, plain and simple. That scenic art is also hard labor becomes apparent all too quickly to the young (and old) practitioner. And sometimes this reality is the thing we find hard to overlook. Yet who can deny the rich pleasure of the act of painting? When the canvas is primed and fresh, when the cartoon is ready and the colors mixed, it is exciting to lay down the first color on a drop. There is an immediate reward of a brush pulling on canvas and the proper stroke of paint. Does this not reward us in some profound way?

Most fundamentally, a scenic artist is a highly specialized painter who works on very large-scale and often realistic paintings. Yet this sort of painting is by no means all that scenic artists do. In fact, it is difficult to state exactly what type of painting a scenic artist will be required to do during the course of any given day. All scenic artists are certainly expected to be capable of painting large-scale backdrops, once the principal output of the trade. Contemporary scenic artists are also expected to adeptly paint two- and three-dimensional scenery by employing a wide array of painting techniques. Faux finish techniques on three-dimensional surfaces are as common now as the traditional trompe l'oeil painting that is the foundation of scenic art.

Scenic artists paint on canvas, linen, wood, plastic, foam, and metal as a matter of course. They paint

Figure 1.1 19th-century painting techniques. From the Lyric Opera of Chicago/Northern Illinois University Historical Scenic Collection (Courtesy of The School of Theatre and Dance, Northern Illinois University, Alexander Aducci, Curator).

vertically in front of them and horizontally below them using hundreds of colors, a variety of mediums, and various finishing products, and they are expected to be experts in the use of these materials. They paint with brooms, sprayers, rollers, pumps, sponges, rags, and, of course, brushes. Sculpture and carving are skills expected of many scenic artists, especially in regional theatres (though at the top levels of the craft there are sculptors who do exclusively that). Thus, knowledge of assembling and carving wood, foam, fabric, metal, and other materials is also essential knowledge for the scenic artist, although not the focus of this text.

Scenic artists must be able to not just reproduce what is given them, but to transform it. Usually, scenic artists are interpreting the work of a scenic designer from a very small scale into a large size appropriate for the theatre. The key to the craft is the ability to interpret. Most anyone can learn to trace or mechanically reproduce an image. Scenic artists must interpret visual information received from the designer, not just by surface appearance but also by how that information relates to the overall stage picture. Thus, scenic artists must understand the scenic designer's artistic intentions. This ability to interpret cannot be understated. This is increasingly true as scenic designers who provide the information from which scenic artists must work are themselves working less and less by painting and more and more by digital collage. The bottom line is that scenic artists have to paint scenery with a brush—or something like a brush—and make the image happen no matter what form the information comes in. Good scenic artists must also be able to remain neutral in their own painting style in order to absorb the style of the art they are expected to interpret.

Thousands of people around the world have careers as scenic artists, and the profession has existed since the Italian Renaissance. In fact, scenic painting existed as early as Classical Greece, but it is in the last 500 years that it has flourished and been refined, and practitioners have prospered. The fact that scenic art is a career has two profound implications: one is that a person can make a very good living at it, the other is that it is a business as well as an art form.

It is undeniable that more job opportunities exist in professional scenic painting now than ever before. This is certainly true if one includes scenic artists who work in television, film, and decorative arts. It is also true that there are many more paths by which one enters the profession now then there were in the past, even the recent past. This is most true in North America, where a sprawling private and public university system provides good exposure and, in some cases, excellent training in theatre practice. The traditional training format was an apprentice system, one in which women were rarely admitted. This has changed significantly in the last 100 years, in part as a result of the universities mentioned earlier and the appearance of very specialized private schools and studio training. The American union for theatrical artists, United Scenic Artists (USA), also has recently instituted an apprenticeship program for scenic artists.

No matter how one begins to develop scenic painting skills, it takes time—often a lot of time—to become an accomplished, independent artist. Even after advanced training at a university, it may take years of experience to attain the skills required to proficiently paint one challenging and diverse project after another. Almost every successful scenic artist can point to one or two people in their career who

Figure 1.2
The scenic shop at Cobalt Studios.

took them under their wing and trained them. Though apprenticeship is no longer the only way in to the profession, it is almost always a critical part of a scenic artist's development. There are always extremely gifted painters who seem to understand exactly how scenic painting works even after minimal exposure to the art form. However, the rest of us must keep in mind that being a *good* scenic artist takes time. There is much to learn artistically, managerially, and practically. Another important aphorism to keep in mind is that scenic artists never stop learning. Every encounter with the physical world is another opportunity for the scenic artist to better understand the practice, techniques, and art of the profession.

TRAINING TO BE A SCENIC ARTIST

It takes an enormous amount of experience to become proficient at theatrical painting. This chapter is meant to help beginning scenic artists understand how and where to get this experience as well as why it is so important.

What a Scenic Artist Should Know

Successful scenic artists, like many artists of the theatre, need a wide array of skills and knowledge to serve them in their profession. Of course, good scenic artists must draw and paint very well. Scenic artists also must know their tools—paint and brushes—as well as the surfaces they are called on to paint and the hundreds of products used in painting, staining, dying, sealing, texturing, thinning, extending, or chemically drying paint. Scenic artists also must possess knowledge in the areas of scenic design, drafting, calligraphy, and sign painting. In this profession, where visual images are reproduced on a large scale, such expertise is the foundational skill set.

In addition to these skills, exceptional scenic artists will have acquired a wide base of knowledge to support the visual images and effects that they are asked to create. Knowledge in the areas of art and art history, architecture, architectural and theatrical history, photography, printing, mechanical image reproduction, and geometry and the natural sciences are all part of the body of knowledge that contributes to the day-to-day work of the scenic artist. A keen curiosity and good powers of observation will help put this acquired knowledge to work. Travel and experience certainly contribute to the ability to synthesize one's knowledge of the physical world.

Drawing and drafting are the tools scenic artists use when beginning a scenic image. All convincing images, particularly trompe l'oeil, begin with a sound drawing. The drawing of architecture relies on the rules of *geometry* and *perspective* to guide it. Geometry is essential because it provides a rational, mathematical basis for the visual arts. Most artists need comprehensive drawing and drafting skills as well as a sound understanding of perspective to reproduce a complex image like a perspective street scene. This is especially true when laying out a full-stage drop. Scenic artists painting a drop must be in command of the overall perspective while drawing it out in small manageable pieces. But, beyond drawing, even the simplest wet blend of one color to another must have correct proportion to look balanced. Classical Greek ideals of proportion and form are based on geometric rationality. These aesthetics of proper proportion and ideal form are the core of many of the visual images we see today.

More specialized forms of drawing include *calligraphy, lettering,* and *sign painting,* which shape letters and words, perhaps the most precise set of graphic images in the world. These images are familiar to all viewers, who instinctively recognize good or poor lettering. Scenic artists should thus have a working knowledge of the construction of common serif and sans serif style lettering as well as an understanding of calligraphy and sign painting. Calligraphy and sign painting rely on brush techniques as well as the form of the letters themselves and are specialized skills that scenic artists must at least comprehend.

As noted earlier, scenic artists are dependent first and foremost on their skills as painters. These skills must be based in the fundamentals of *painting* and *color theory* and a variety of *painting techniques.* Sound understanding of color is critical for scenic artists, as they will mix paint colors based on their understanding of how colors interact to achieve their target color. Manipulating the application of color on a painted surface so it appears to be one hue at a distance even though close up it might be a combination of hues is a skill based on understanding color and human optical perception.

Scenic artists also must be well versed in how painting techniques have evolved. Scenic artistry is a profession in which artists might be called on to recapture the soul and substance of art from all eras in history. In one production, a scenic artist may be called on to recreate in a very large scale Rembrandt's *The Night Watch,* whereas in the next production, the challenge might be to create wallpaper in the style of Andy Warhol. Scenic artists must understand the methods whereby these works were originally created to recreate them on stage. Furthermore, they must be able to recreate these images very quickly. Scenic artists cannot reproduce *The Night Watch* with the thickly applied oil-based pigment that Rembrandt used or turn to silk screening as Warhol did. Instead, they must rely on their knowledge of modern mediums and alternative techniques to recreate the same effects quickly while fulfilling the vision of the scenic designer.

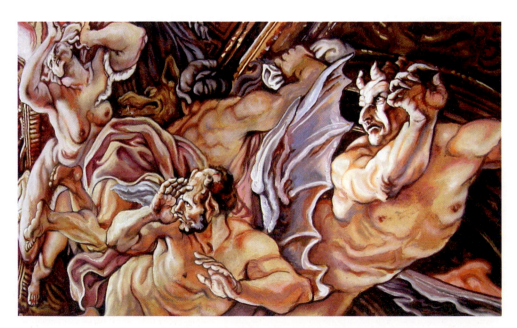

Figure 1.3 A scenic artist must know art history and style. *Chaucer,* Scenic Art Studios.

Knowledge and understanding of the *histories of art*, *architecture*, and *theatre* also are essential to understanding what scenic artists are called on to paint. Scenic artists need to have a thorough knowledge and understanding of the scenic designer's artistic intent behind the use of classic and artistic references in a design so that the intent comes through clearly in the contemporary execution of it. Theatre is tremendously reliant on history and historical references. We work with 400-year-old plays as a matter of course. Although the statement a production makes is obviously contemporary, the elements of

expression often are drawn from history. Many scenic designers describe their work in terms of other artists or artistic movements, even if no direct imitation is involved. Because designers often rely on phrases to evoke a scenic vision, such as "the cool controlled world of Vermeer" or "the dark quality of Romanesque architecture," all the while describing a design for *The Life and Death of King John,* scenic artists had better know what these coded words mean. These references are a way of describing the intangibles of design. Sometimes, the best way to put words to an image is to bring to mind the memory of

Figure 1.4
Scenic artists will be asked to emulate many different painting techniques and styles. *Enchanted April,* Scenic Art Studios.

a well-known image as a vehicle to convey style and intention.

Photography is a useful means to observe the world because it asks the careful photographer to consider light, both natural and artificial, in an objective way. Light reveals all visual images. Understanding and reproducing how surface, form, and atmosphere respond to light is the mark of a proficient painter. The very act of photography helps anyone retain the memory of a place. A stock of photographs can serve as a fabulous personal resource for scenic artists. For example, an album of cloud and sky photos will come in handy for scenic artists painting sky drops and landscapes. This is evidenced by the ubiquitous presence of Judy Juracek's marvelous publications *Surfaces*, *Natural Surfaces*, and *Soft Surfaces* in scenic studios and on scenic designers' shelves. These three publications are rich collections of high-quality photographs of common and uncommon objects and surfaces that designers and artists use in the theatre.

Knowledge in the *technology* of related crafts has direct application to scenic art, particularly with computers and mechanical image reproduction. Copy machines and the computer are now irreplaceable tools for most scenic designers and scenic artists. Complex signage is easily cartooned or actually cut into many commonly used materials with the aid of a computer-guided router, commonly called a CNC (Computer Numerical Control) machine. Stencils of any type can be made in the same way, and a computer will help in the registration process. Digital image manipulation can aid a scenic artist in adapting paint elevations to odd sizes or in creating more mechanical printing "looks" like dot screening. Scenic designers use photocopying and digital imaging extensively to make paint elevations. Large-format copy machines and printers provide a source to scenic artists for finished, or nearly finished, color images for stage use. Ultra-large-format painting machines are widely used for full-stage drops or large painted surfaces. The very presence of these machines forces a debate as to the relevance of the scenic artist versus a machine that paints. One cannot expect that the simple and marvelous human gesture of painting can ever be cost-effectively replaced, but it is a good idea for scenic artists to be fully aware of how such machines work and what sorts of binders, pigments, and application processes they employ.

Natural sciences such as *geology* and *geography* are a means of rationally defining our world. Geology and cartography certainly are removed from the study of painting and theatre, but for an artist responsible for painting representations and aspects of the world we live in, there is no area of knowledge that will not at one time or another prove invaluable. For instance, scenic artists are often called on to realistically paint stone. Thus, the ability to paint marble, limestone, and fieldstone is needed in the scenic artist's repertory. Understanding the science of the structure of the earth will help artists in creating a faux drift marble finish as much as geometry will help them understand architectural shapes. The same can be said of taxonomy, the classification of all organisms; anthropology, the study of the cultural development of humankind; and geography, the study of the earth's features—all areas of knowledge that will be of great value to scenic artists.

The experience of *travel* certainly is an obvious asset for any scenic artist, as it is an important means for understanding the world one lives in. Travel has been, and still is, an important component of higher education for university students. It is revealing the first time one goes to Italy and sees the blue sky there contrasted with the red tile roofs. Once one has seen a vista with these elements in it, the aesthetic relationship of these colors to the Italian landscape makes sense. Add in the recognition one has at seeing umber and sienna in their native state. It is as much a part of their world as the "purple-mountained majesty" is a part of the Americas. So many aspects of the world

Figure 1.5 An example of turn-of-the-century American scenic painting elevation, Twin Cities Scenic Collection (courtesy of the Performing Arts Archives, University of Minnesota Libraries, St. Paul, Minnesota).

cannot be fully captured in a photograph, such as the diminutive size of an old European village or the massive quality of Manhattan building details. Travel is not just leisure time for scenic artists; observing the variety of the world builds integrity into their work. Time and time again, scenic artists are called on to fill in the blanks, make up a detail, or flesh out a piece of trim. Having a personal reserve of experience will make that work all the more interesting and authentic.

The qualities of a good chef are not unlike those of a good painter. Good cooks take individual ingredients and make a mixture that is better than the sum of the parts. In fact, relatively simple ingredients make magnificent dishes, like a cassoulet or a risotto. In the same light, a painting is, after all, just so much paint. Part of what makes painting and cooking similar is the craft behind them. Good cooking starts with solid technical skills: chopping items correctly, making a simple béchamel sauce, using ingredients at the right temperature, and so on. Then one actually cooks each element of a dish in the correct manner—not too long, not too quickly. Then one seasons with restraint to allow the inherent flavors to emerge. It is not magic, just good practice. The same is true of painting; if one takes all the correct steps in order and does them well, the result is sound. I was taught early on that every step of the painting process needs to look good, and that a poorly done step cannot be covered up by better work later. Best to correct things then and there. Good painters, like good cooks, know that painting too much—*overpainting*—can destroy good work just as too much salt can ruin a delicate dish. Part of learning to paint is learning process and practicing restraint when appropriate.

That Special Something that Makes You a Scenic Artist

Ultimately, scenic artistry is basically a visual art. Besides the vast array of technical and organizational skills they must possess, scenic artists must be able to see and interpret the world. The word *seeing* here is distinguished from the word *looking*. Developing painting skills becomes part of every waking moment because these skills are directly related to the skills of observation. Scenic artists must learn how to see the world around them, constantly exercising their observational skills by breaking down every form or vista into the components necessary to translate them into two-dimensional images. How is the depth of

field described in line work? How would the line work be constructed to represent the foreshortening of forms? How can a texture be recreated? What base coat should be used? Which elements would be painted first? What painting techniques would be used? Where would the shades be located? What highlight color would complement the cast shadow and describe the quality of light? If this image were executed in an impressionistic style, what would the palette of colors be? Because scenic artists are first and foremost visual artists, these exercises are preformed numerous times each day—almost unconsciously—because the artists are always seeing and improving their paint skills, whether there is a brush in hand or not.

Scenic artists must be conversant and fluid in many different styles of art. These skills are also reflected in the scenic artist's ability to recognize and understand the skill and stylistic fluidity of other artists. Whether walking through a picture gallery, looking through a book, or observing the work of peers, scenic artists perfect their skills by scrutinizing how other artists have solved cartooning problems, applied color theory, and utilized painting techniques. When scenic artists are in the paint shop, these skills of observation are reflected in their accurate drafting ability, chroma and value consciousness, stylistic fluidity, and ability to recognize the accuracy of essential visual elements in the work on the shop floor.

Formal Training for Scenic Artists

Until the 20th century, training in the art of scenic painting was available only to the sons of established scenic artists and young men willing to work under a long apprenticeship. Often, children began to learn the craft in scenic studios at the age of 12. This changed considerably in the 20th century, principally due to the power of labor unions that humanized working conditions, improved pay scales, and permitted the inclusion of women in the craft. Equally significant is the vast expansion of training opportunities in the theatre through the American university system. There are dozens of university programs in which terminal Master of Fine Arts degrees are available to performers, artists, and technicians of the theatre. Few offer degrees specifically for scenic artists, but many offer training in scenic art. Even more universities have undergraduate degree programs in theatre offering Bachelor of Fine Arts or Bachelor of Arts degree options. These programs prepare students for advanced training or provide ambitious students with enough information to continue their own training as apprentices or full-fledged scenic artists.

University Programs

The population boom in the United States during the 20th century created a large university network, making post-secondary schooling available to millions of students. As noted above, many universities in the United States have adopted practical training for theatre craft into their curricula. The growth of this system has taken place at roughly the same time as the growth of unions representing the theatrical trades. Some of the first influential American scenic designers established the first theatrical training programs at American universities. Yale University established the first training program for scenic designers in the 1920s under the direction of Donald Oenslager.[1] Yale Drama School continues as one of the finest training programs in the country, particularly in the design fields. The basic format of that program has been widely imitated throughout the country, and now over 250 American universities, representing every state, offer advanced training in the theatrical arts. Many of these offer degrees specifically in theatrical production at the undergraduate and graduate levels.

[1]Larson, 1989

Figure 1.6
The scenic shop at North Carolina School of the Arts. Daniel Thobias (left) and Adriane Donlet painting on *The Sleeping Beauty,* designed by Raber Umphenour.

The university setting may be the most logical place to begin training as a scenic artist. In these programs, classes are available in the many disciplines of theatre, such as acting, directing, design, stage management, and technical theatre, which help students understand the work performed by all contributors to a theatrical production. Most programs include theatrical history and critical studies courses, which help create an understanding of dramatic literature and production history. Students of scenic artistry will find that classes in design, technical drawing, and rendering will have a direct application to their craft.

The university also provides other classes that are equally important to the scenic artist. The topics of art, art history, architectural history, painting, photography, the natural sciences, and many other useful fields of study are available to students in this setting. As well as providing an excellent means to explore many topics related to scenic painting, university programs also give students the opportunity to gain practical experience while working on well-organized productions with a professional staff. Only comprehensive theatre programs offer classes specifically in scenic painting. Many university programs have only one class in scenic painting; some have two or more. Beyond these courses in the curriculum, students may enroll in independent studies to continue the study of scenic painting. Students with an interest in scenic artistry often obtain a Bachelor of Fine Arts degree in theatre or theatre production. Many students opt to go on and obtain a Master of Fine Arts degree in scenic design. As of the publication of this book, few institutions, such as North Carolina School for the Arts and Cal Arts, offer a degree that includes scenic artistry and properties painting.

A good university program is an excellent place to begin a career in the theatre. However, some programs may have the opposite effect of discouraging talented artists through overwork or in miserable working conditions. It is therefore important that students, their parents, and advisors know what to look for in a university program. Any student interested in studying scenic art should pay a visit to the college or university before choosing to attend classes there. They should look through the curriculum and inquire about scenic art classes and possible production experience, and meet with the professor teaching the scenic art classes and any staff scenic artists. Interested students should also talk to students already in the program and tour the facilities to determine whether the equipment and space available are conducive to well-painted productions. The following are some points interested students should consider:

- What is your evaluation of the painting and overall production facilities? Are the working conditions comfortable and safe? Is there adequate light and ventilation? Is the shop reasonably neat and inviting?
- What sort of work are students in the program doing? Are they being challenged by their class and production work?
- Is the instructor truly a specialist in scenic painting?
- Is there a paint frame or wooden deck space large enough to handle a full-stage drop? (If not, chances are that drops are not done there very often.)
- Are materials handled and stored properly? (This will be an insight into the general working conditions and attitudes of the program.)
- Is there enough space to conduct a scene painting class?
- Is there enough time in the production schedule to allow for scene painting instruction, or is it taught only by working on productions?
- Are there opportunities to work on productions with professional supervision? Can you see photos of past productions where the design incorporated advanced scenic art techniques?

In addition to asking these questions, interested students should see a school production if they can, or at least look at the scenery in the shop and determine whether the painting looks professional. They should try to get a sense of the production schedule in terms of how the painting is considered in the construction period. If the scenic artist or technical director maintains that most of the painting for a production is done in a weekend, students should look elsewhere.

Specialized Schools or Programs

Serious students of scenic painting may seek to attend a specialized school or studio where theatrical painting is the emphasis of the training. This might be in addition to undergraduate training in theatre or might be undertaken during a career in order to elevate one's painting skills.

From the 1950s until 1988, the Studio and Forum of Stage Design, operated by Lester Polakov, trained scores of scenic artists and designers. This famous studio taught painting, drawing, and design and served as an important meeting place for the New York City design world. But when the studio closed its doors in 1988, it left New York City—the traditional center of scenic production in North America—without a place to study scenic art.

However, this gap began to be filled in 1990, when Cobalt Studios opened in White Lake, New York. Cofounded by Rachel Keebler and Howard Jones, both leading professional American scenic artists and teachers. Cobalt Studios is now operated by Rachel Keebler and provides intensive instruction in scenic painting. It is one of few such studios in the world and is unique in the thoroughness of its program. Cobalt Studios maintains an ongoing offering of courses. Students can attend a concentrated two-year program in addition to the two- to four-day sessions, three-week short courses, and frequent weekend seminars. Cobalt also is a working scenic studio, which provides a unique opportunity for students to work on actual high-profile scenic productions with well-known professional designers. The studio also

serves the professional community as a hub for information about the profession, methods, materials, and techniques.

Scenic artist training also is available in the New York City area at the recently formed Studio and Forum of Scenic Arts. This private studio, owned and operated by Joseph Forbes and Janet Stapleman, offers a two-year training program in scenic painting. The location of the studio, as well as its prestigious faculty, makes it the obvious successor to Lester Polokov's famed studio.

In addition to these programs, the scenic artists' union, United Scenic Artists (USA), occasionally sponsors painting workshops featuring the "old masters" of New York. These are generally available only to union members. Meanwhile, the United States Institute for Theatre Technology (USITT) annual conference often includes some scenic art demonstrations of a very high caliber, although these tend to be no more than one or two days in length.

Many European countries have followed the system, begun during the 18th century, of establishing large centralized art academies such as

Figure 1.7   The shop floor at Scenic Art Studios.

L'Académie des Beaux Arts in France or the English Royal Academy of Dramatic Art (RADA). These institutes offer extremely specialized training in either art (the French Beaux Arts) or theatre (RADA). They are very different from the United States university system in that they are highly specialized and extremely competitive. Both countries have other centers where theatre arts and scenic painting are instructed or where specialized decorative painting is taught. These schools, however, are few in number, competitive, and can be very expensive for foreign students.

Apprenticeships and On-the-Job Training

The experience and training students gain in a university situation does not fully prepare them to work in or run a professional shop. The skills and knowledge expected of a scenic artist are too vast; the confidence the scenic artist must have to perform the job with alacrity generally comes only with seasoned experience. Thus, some form of apprenticeship, either formal or informal, is essential to learning the profession of scenic artistry. Nearly every scenic artist has had a master-apprentice experience in his or her own training, one or two individuals who "showed the artist the ropes" (or buckets in this case). No better training can be obtained than the one-on-one instruction of working with a master scenic artist for an extended period of time. There is rarely a job where you don't come away with something more than a paycheck. Every new project or partnership brings a new technique or a new way of doing things, even if only a new way to stir paint. Every scenic artist you encounter—whether they be fellow students or old pros—will have knowledge to share.

United Scenic Artists has an apprenticeship program for scenic artists in New York City. It is a three-year training program in which the apprentice has the possibility of working in a variety of venues, including network television, episodic television, cable television, scenic studios, and the Metropolitan Opera. The apprenticeship program takes applicants based on availability of work in the region. Entrance to the program is by a three-step process of an examination, portfolio review and interview, and practical skills test. Apprentices work with journeymen scenic artists at a ratio of one apprentice to five journeymen and they are paid at a fractional rate of journeymen scale that increases every four months. The apprentice is

made a full USA scenic artist member at the successful completion of the apprenticeship.

Cobalt Studios devotes approximately half of its curriculum for long-term students to work with actual productions in its studio. In this way, it can offer an apprenticeship in tandem with the scenic art coursework. Many professional scenic artists want to informally instruct assistants and are pleased to share what they know with a novice because they themselves got their start in much the same way. Compensation may be problematic, but as the scenic artist fresh to the professional world acquires and displays skill and confidence, the pay will improve.

The four types of training of a scenic artist listed here—university schooling, specialized training, apprenticeship, and on-the-job training—together form an excellent path toward becoming a scenic artist.

WORKING AS A SCENIC ARTIST

Getting and keeping work as a scenic artist requires considerable time and effort, particularly at the beginning of a career. Very few regular full-time jobs are available in the profession. When starting a career, much of the work available is on a short-term freelance basis, which means that, at first, you cannot turn down many job offers. If your work is good, one job inevitably will lead to another. Most practitioners of the theatrical trades will know someone you may have worked with, and scenic artistry is no exception. Once you have worked well for one company, the word of your performance will precede you to the next job. Employers want to hire known quantities, so get known for the right reasons. If your work is good, on schedule, and within budget, producers, scenic designers, and other scenic artists will seek you out.

When you are contracted to do a job, to work a season, or to deliver a product, the company that employed you is your client. Before you work that first job, take a few moments to consider what a good scenic artist is and what an effective employee or contractor is. One of the best ways to do this is to imagine yourself in your client's place. The client hires a scenic artist with the expectation that the artist will fulfill a function or perform a task. This means a high-quality job done on time with no unnecessary problems or holdups, performed by a person with a professional attitude. A professional

Figure 1.8 Design for chandeliers, *Un Ballo in Maschera* at the Metropolitan Opera, New York City. Sketch drafted by Hal Tiné, painted by Peter Wexler. Photo by Peter Wexler, courtesy of the New York Public Library for the Performing Arts at Lincoln Center, Billy Rose Theatre Collection, Peter Wexler Collection.

attitude is very important. "I have no complaints about the work that artist did but I don't have time for the hassles," paraphrases the reason clients often give for not rehiring talented artists. It is not enough to paint beautifully; you must manage the work well

and perform it professionally. If problems do arise, and they often do, scenic artists should always try to find a solution on their own before making demands on the client. If you need to bring the problem to the attention of the client, you should present it along with one or two suggested solutions. If your engagement has made the client's job easier or has made the contract run more smoothly, there is a strong chance that you will be asked back.

The employer also must have a professional attitude. If you are working as an employee, it is the employer's responsibility to provide you with a work space that is both adequate for the job at hand and safe. The workspace must be large enough to accommodate the project, have adequate lighting, a mixing area, a water source, and heat in the winter, and be safe and secure. If you are working in a bad part of town, you should not have to worry about your personal safety or the safety of your vehicle. If you are working in a warehouse, you should not have to be concerned about working in a toxic environment. Chapter 4 discusses the workspace at length.

The employer also must provide adequate materials to work with and a reasonable time frame for the painting to be completed. If time is short, the employer must provide a means to hire additional assistants.

Figure 1.9 Opening scene with chandeliers, *Un Ballo in Maschera*, at the Metropolitan Opera, New York City. Photo by Peter Wexler.

If one of these work conditions is constrained—not enough time, space, or assistants—the employer must be willing to compensate you for the extra effort you will have to make to get the project done on time. There is a saying in theatre, "We can do it fast, cheap, or good. Pick any two." Obviously, if there is plenty of time and money, the product will be beautiful. If quality is important but there is very little time, then the product will be very costly. If the employer insists the product be done quickly and cheaply, then the quality will suffer.

Many scenic designers, when starting their careers, find that they also must fulfill the function of the scenic artist on the project. This is very common in educational, community, and small regional theatres. For this reason, many scene designers have discovered that scenic artistry is a useful skill in developing their careers. Scenic designers often find that any skills they gain or improve upon as a scenic artist benefit their design skills as well.

Labor Unions

The United States has two large labor unions that establish working conditions and negotiate contracts and pay scale for artists and technicians in the film industry, television, the theatre, and related entertainment industries. These two unions are United Scenic Artists (USA) and the International Alliance of Theatrical Stage Employees (IATSE). The USA was once allied with the much larger International Brotherhood of Painters and Allied Trades (IBPAT). However, USA recently left that alliance in favor of a much more logical alliance with IATSE. In fact, USA is now a single local within IATSE known by its original local number 829. A scenic artist is more likely to become a member of USA, although there are IASTE locals that specialize in representing theatrical scenic painters. Some scenic artists are members of both USA as well as a local IASTE, usually in the area where they obtain most of their employment.

United Scenic Artists

USA is a New York City-based organization that represents scenic artists, scenic designers, costume designers, lighting designers, properties artisans, industrial artists, computer artists, and muralists. USA began in 1896 as a union for scenic artists by separating from a labor organization that represented stagehands. In 1922, the union subdivided to

Figure 1.10   The United Scenic Artists stamp.

recognize scenic artists and scenic designers separately. Since then, the union has branched out to represent the various categories mentioned above. USA also maintains offices in Chicago, Los Angeles, Miami, and New England. Some of these offices were once separate autonomous locals, but the union merged into a single local in the 1990s, retaining the New York City local number of 829. USA has members in every state of the United States, the greatest density of which are in the New York City metropolitan area. Membership in the union is considered by many scenic artists to be one of the gateways into a successful career.

How to Become a Member of United Scenic Artists.
Members are admitted to the USA union through one of three methods: Track A, the Open Examination (Track B), or the apprenticeship program. These means of entry into the USA are not available in all of the four regional offices. The New York City office is the only location where the examination and apprenticeship options are currently available.

Track A is a relatively new attempt to streamline the entry process for experienced scenic artists. Applicants' resumes are screened by a committee before they are accepted into the Track A examination. This examination consists of an extensive interview and portfolio review for which applicants must provide three letters of recommendation from current USA members. A panel of union members then evaluates the applicant's portfolio. Based on certain criteria, the panel decides which applicants should be recommended for entry into the union. Track A exams can be taken in New York City, Chicago, and Miami. Information concerning this examination is also available through the office in Los Angeles. Non-USA members employed in a union-represented scenic studio or producing studio (network television, major opera, and so on) for over 30 days must submit an application for Track A entry.

The *Open Examination* (also known as the *Track B examination*) was the traditional path and once the only path of entry into the USA. This lengthy examination, offered only in New York City, consists of several parts: a general aptitude test, a home project, an interview, and a practical skills test. This famed and feared examination once included a two-day practical examination but the process has been streamlined considerably in recent years. The home project consists of a packet of one to five separate projects that are to be completed and brought to the exam site. These home projects are designed not only to test applicants' scenic art skills but to test their knowledge of art and architecture and their capacity to follow instructions.

The second part is the on-site practical exam, which, until recently, took place over the course of two seven-hour days. It now has been abbreviated to one seven-hour day. In this section of the examination, applicants are provided with instructions and a paint elevation to execute on a 5′ × 5′ flat or small muslin drop, paint, buckets, water, and a mixing area, nothing else. The applicants are responsible for bringing with them any tools that they will need during the examination. At the beginning of the day, the applicants are given instructions on what is to be painted on the flats or drops during the course of the day. The applicants' works are judged by a panel of union members on drawing accuracy, color accuracy, technique, rendering of light and shadow, and overall ability as a scenic artist.

Many applicants do not pass the examination the first time, but they may take the exam as many times as they wish. The exam requires a nonrefundable examination fee and a refundable deposit of one-half the initiation fee.

The *apprenticeship program*, described earlier, culminates the three years of training with automatic USA membership.

The Benefits of Union Membership.

Once admitted, new members pay a one-time initiation fee (higher for Track A) and quarterly dues. In return, the union negotiates wage scales and terms with scenic studios and producers to standardize and maintain wage scales in the industry. The union also establishes basic working conditions and monitors scenic studios and producers to ensure adherence to the union agreement. The union represents its members in cases of unfair labor practices and monitors the activities of nonunion studios and theatres that employ union scenic artists by individual letters of agreement. The USA also acts as a clearinghouse for employers seeking employees, normally for long- or short-term temporary work that is known in the business as *overhire*.

Because so many theatre artisans work on a freelance basis, the union also collects health and welfare contributions from employers hiring union members, which are invested in health insurance and pensions for the members. These benefits are available to union members who have made or have employers who have made contributions to the fund during the course of their careers. The union also provides a small death benefit to the member's survivors.

Gaining membership in the union is an accomplishment and an affirmation of one's talents and skills. Union membership allows scenic artists to demand good compensation for their work as well as good working conditions. The union's compensation rate is excellent and is constructed to benefit the scenic artist handsomely for overtime rates. Union membership also serves as a recommendation of your skills and professionalism to prospective employers and allows you to raise your standard of compensation for work. In addition, the USA maintains an availability list of scenic artists throughout the country. Thus, by reporting into the union office and keeping the union appraised of your whereabouts and work situation, you enable it to contact you regarding jobs in your area. In busy metropolitan areas, such as New York City, Chicago, and Los Angeles, union calls may be a main source of employment for members.

The primary disadvantage to union membership is the cost of joining. Initiation fees are currently $3,500 for Track A and the Open Examination; however, members joining by exam are given a $2,000 refund. Membership fees via the apprenticeship program are $1,700. Additional fees are required upon entry into the union for the first six months of dues and processing fees. USA members also pay to the USA continuing quarterly membership dues and 2 percent of the gross wage earned on employment covered by union contracts.

Currently, there are 22 states considered "right-to-work" states. Employees in these states are not required to join a union or pay union dues to a union

Figure 1.11 *The Tale of the White Snake*, elevation by Xuzheng He, Quan Dong Province Theatre, People's Republic of China.

representing their workplace. Both USA and USITT remain highly active in these states, and the wage rates negotiated by the unions serve as valid and, at times, binding agreements. All right-to-work states have different rules and guidelines that govern union representation and authority. These rules are constantly changing, so keep up-to-date on workers' rights issues where you work.

Union membership is not a guarantee of employment. Individual members must not expect the union to find them work. If you do not happen to live in New York, Los Angeles, or Chicago but in a city where the union has no strong foothold, the union office may not be able to send you out on many work calls. It is also very difficult to find consistent over-hire work outside of the major metropolitan markets in the United States. You must be prepared to continue the task of finding and keeping work on your own.

The International Alliance of Theatrical Stage Employees

The International Alliance of Theatrical Stage Employees (IATSE) also represents scenic artists in some regions of North America for the film industry as well as theatre. IATSE's membership consists of dozens of entertainment industry professionals, including art directors, animators, camerapersons, costume design and craftspeople, film and video lab technicians, motion picture craftspeople, property craftspeople, press agents, projectionists, stage employees, and television craftspeople. Other trades commonly associated with scenic arts skills, such as sculpting, plastering, painting, designing, animation, and sign painting, also are represented by IATSE locals. Local 816, Painters and Scenic Artists, located in Sherman Oaks, California, specifically represents scenic artists in the theatre, broadcast, and film industries.

This local has jurisdiction in 13 states. In addition to scenic artists and painters, members in this local also include those in professions as varied as courtroom artists and computer graphic artists.

The initiation fees, dues, and requirements for membership vary from local to local. All IATSE locals are governed by the International IATSE office in New York City. The officials and board of the international office are elected from the membership throughout the United States and Canada. These officials are elected at the biennial conventions by delegates representative of all the locals.

Employment Options

Several avenues of employment are available for scenic artists. It is not a career in which one would expect to find adequate amounts of work anywhere in the country. A scenic artist may need to choose between living in one of the two dominant metropolitan regions (New York and Los Angeles) where the highest volume of work is found, or to move elsewhere and plan to look for work in a different manner.

Freelance Work in a Major Market

Freelance scenic artists comprise a significant portion of the professional artists working in the United States, and freelance work is the most common sort of work for scenic artists getting their start. So much freelance work exists because many theatres operate on a seasonal basis and are "dark" for several months of the year. These seasons may span the summer months, as in a summer festival or musical season, or the seven to eight months from fall to spring, as is common for many regional repertory companies or universities. Because of these split seasons, beginning scenic artists often have difficulty finding a year-round engagement. Many scenic artists fall into a pattern of dividing up their employment between the same set of companies season after season and having to move their households back and forth between the cities where the companies are based. Some scenic artists enjoy this "gypsy" lifestyle because it gives them the opportunity to see different parts of the country (at least on the trips in between) and to work with and learn from other professionals. Even some professional scenic artists with a permanent position at a scenic studio still work extensively on a freelance basis.

However, as a freelance scenic artist, you may instead want to be based in a major metropolitan area where there is enough demand for scenic artists to keep you employed year-round. Freelance scenic artists work on call for production companies, shops, or individual projects for long or short periods of time. In New York, Chicago, and Los Angeles, theatrical and movie production is an ongoing business (although there are other major metropolitan areas like Seattle and Miami that can keep scenic artists very busy). Once established in such an area, you will get work continually as your reputation as an efficient and talented painter spreads. If you have poor work habits or are unreliable, your reputation will precede you and keep you from getting calls.

While working as a freelance scenic artist, it is important to maintain a current résumé and portfolio, and to always keep your business card with you. Note that when you send your portfolio to a potential employer, *never* let your original portfolio images out of your hands. Many scenic artists maintain two portfolios: one contains the originals in an expensive case and is used only for personal interviews; the other contains color copies mounted on gray or black bristol board in an inexpensive but professional-looking case. This is the portfolio you send to potential employers on request. If this portfolio is not returned to you, all you have lost is the cost of the case and the time it took to put together. While a digital portfolio on a CD/DVD may be convenient, most digital portfolios do not communicate the skill of the artist as well as more traditional formats. When preparing for an interview, tailor your portfolio to the needs of the client. Have a stock of images to choose from and select those that are most appropriate, and then print a new table of contents as needed. Also remember that less is more. Ten or so stunning images will be more impressive than 10 stunning images plus 40 mediocre or unsuitable ones.

It deserves mention that scenic artists often are the most highly paid and sought-after of the skilled professionals in technical theatre. A huge amount of painting is done in theatre, television, movies, and industrials, not to mention commercial display, advertising, museum display, interior decoration, and so on. Scenic artists are in demand for many reasons. Painting is faster than building, and the results are spectacular. Producers find painting very cost effective. Certainly, advertisers and filmmakers find painting a background less expensive than going on location. Skilled painters have been a source for decorative work since the classic Greek theatre. It is unlikely that this demand will change in the near future.

Figure 1.12
Example of portraiture, painted by Xuzheng He for the film *The Quick and the Dead.*

Freelance Work Outside of Major Markets

New York and Los Angeles are the major markets in the United States for scenic artists. Chicago and Miami are secondary markets where one may find work fairly often. The other major American metropolitan markets of Philadelphia, San Francisco, Minneapolis, Seattle, Boston, Washington DC, Phoenix, and Atlanta may offer some work for a scenic artist at some time, but it may be difficult to get into these markets and make a living. For these non-major markets, a scenic artist may look to developing relationships with regional theatres or regional opera companies that may need overhire. You may seek employment in the field of industrials—advertising, exhibitions, and corporate events—but it may be difficult to have a career as a true freelance scenic artist outside New York or Los Angeles. Be prepared to build connections and look for less traditional scenic painting outlets.

Working at a Staff Position at a Scenic Studio or Theatre

A far simpler life than freelancing is to get a permanent job at a scenic studio. One obvious advantage to this option is that you will have a steady paycheck and, in most cases, health insurance. Also, because you are in a consistent work environment, you can store your tools in the shop, drive or take public transportation on the same route to work every morning, and choose to live in a place convenient to the job site. The artistic advantage of working in a studio is that you will have more control over projects in development rather than being called in the last two weeks of a job in progress. The work site can be set up and maintained for the convenience of the people who work there. You can arrange and install your materials and tools in an orderly fashion rather than store them in cardboard boxes piled up around makeshift mixing tables. You can also maintain a stock of mediums, paints, and finishes rather than sending someone out to the store every time you need something or having to scrounge around in an unfamiliar shop.

The hard part is getting such a job. Perhaps 150 full-time theatrical scenic studios are operating in the United States today. More theatre companies than scenic studios exist; however, not all of these need a scenic artist on a year-round basis. Many such theatres use scenic artists only on a job-by-job basis. The large theatrical scenic studios, common in the early part of this century, staffed with dozens of scenic artists, are a thing of the past. Many modern-day scenic studios have only one to four full-time scenic artists on staff, and hire extra scenic artists as needed. The scenic studios that still maintain staffs of several scenic artists are the large scenic studios in the New York City region or the major television networks and film studios.

As your career takes off, you may find yourself being offered more work than you can handle. This may happen particularly if you have a full-time position with a scene shop and your first responsibility is to your permanent employer or because you have a steady flow of freelance work coming in. You may be able to squeeze in a weekend job here and there, but a call for a profitable two-month-long opera job would be out of reach to you because of your previous commitments. Another code of professionalism comes into play when you find yourself having to turn down work. If possible, you should assist the client who contacted you in finding someone who is available for the job. There are two reasons for doing this. First, if you assist the client in locating a scenic artist, that client will be more inclined to call you for another project in the future. Second, once you have attained some measure of success, you should give a hand to other scenic artists just starting out in the business or in a dry spell. These scenic artists will then be more inclined to help you in the future when you are looking for assistance on a project.

Contracting and Self-Employment Business Skills

Regardless of what direction your career may take, you may find yourself in the position of working as a contractor. Many of the responsibilities of the employer to the freelance employee mentioned earlier are the duties of the contractor. A contractor is the person or company that has agreed to execute the work and take care of every aspect of the project from locating the working space and hiring the staff to delivering the finished work to the client. Some variations in the specifics of a contract may exist. For instance, as frequently happens in the case of scenic art contracts, the client may agree to deliver the raw materials, in this case the scenery or drops, to you. The space might be on site or it might be the space of the contractor who is building the scenery. The contract might be structured so that the scenic artist is a subcontractor and the primary contractor is building the set. However the contract is structured, you must be very clear regarding its terms.

The first step to working out a contract is to discuss the scope of work with the client. This discussion should be accompanied by information related to the project's blueline plans, color copies of the paint elevations, and written descriptions from the client outlining what your responsibilities will be. You then need to submit a bid to the client, indicating what your price will be to do the job. When formulating a bid for a job, you must consider the following:

- *Space*—Who will provide the space in which the work will be done? If you provide the space, how much will the rent cost? If you are the owner of the space, what are your costs?
- *Materials*—What will the cost of your materials be? Who is responsible for purchasing and delivering these materials?

- *Labor*—Who will contract the labor? If you, what will you pay employees? Are you paying them on an IRS Form 1099-MISC, as contract labor? Or will you have to withhold and file payments for social security, state and federal income taxes, and Medicare, as well as make the employer's contribution for social security, workman's compensation insurance, and state and federal unemployment insurance? If your employees are union members and you have signed a contract with a union, what percentage of the labor cost do you have to pay to the union's health and welfare plan? Ethically, if your employees are long-term or permanent, you should set up a health care and pension plan if a union does not otherwise cover them.
- *Kit Fees*—What fee should you charge for the use of your tools on the job? If your crewmembers are bringing their own tools to the job, should you give them a kit fee? Do you have to rent or buy any tools or equipment for the job?
- *Samples*—Clients frequently need to see samples of paint finishes before they decide on a contractor. While this practice is more common in bidding on decorative painting and faux finish jobs, it may be requested when bidding on scenic artistry as well. Sometimes, the request for samples and reworking of samples can get out of hand and a scenic artist may feel that he or she is working harder to get the job than actually doing the job. It is common practice to place a limitation of three free samples on this attempt to satisfy the customer that you can do the job. After that, if they need to see more examples, it is customary to charge for the additional samples.
- *Out-of-Town Expenses*—If the work is out of town, look into what your expenses will be for housing, food per diems, and transportation for yourself and your crew. Do you have to ship or rent a truck to transport tools and materials?
- *Insurance*—If you contract work on a regular basis, you may need to start carrying general liability insurance. What will this cost?
- *Accounting*—If you do contract work on a regular basis, your tax returns can be very complex. What will it cost to hire a professional accountant?
- *Taxes*—If you are withholding taxes for your employees, you also have to file quarterly statements. What are these costs?

- *Extra Costs*—Just figuring out a bid can consume a great deal of time. It also takes time and is costly to compose and send faxes, talk on the telephone, handle the billing, and enter costs in a register. Time is involved in collecting the materials and supplies for the job. If the job is not at your regular work site, time is involved in packing up and transferring materials to the work site and bringing them back again. You must also consider the time needed for cleanup after the job has been completed.

If this all sounds a little overwhelming, keep in mind that when you first begin to contract work, it will probably be on a small scale. You and an associate may decide to contract a job that you can do in someone's garage or you might accept a small contract that you can do over the weekend. Working up to large-scale, lengthy contracts can and should be gradual so that you can learn the business. Some scenic artists find that they would rather be employed than be the employer, so that they have time to do the actual painting and do not get bogged down in business details. Contracting your own jobs will give you an appreciation for what your employers have to deal with on a day-to-day basis.

Studio Ownership

Some scenic artists prefer to be their own boss and enjoy the hustle and bustle of organizing the work. Some also find that the most difficult aspect of taking on work is finding the space in which to paint. If you develop an ongoing rapport with enough clients through contracting work, you may need to set up your own permanent shop space. The cost savings of not having to rent a space, move equipment in and out again at the completion of the job, clean it out, and store the supplies and materials may well offset the expense of having to pay rent or mortgage on an ongoing basis. But before taking this step, it's important to remember that the theatre profession can be one of feast or famine. It is essential that before you sign a lease—and most certainly before you sign mortgage papers—you objectively gauge the potential of future work. Certainly before making the decision to set up and operate a permanent shop it is very important to familiarize yourself with professional business practices. This does not mean getting an MBA, but getting some training in small business operations, arranging with the small business organization in your area to meet with a mentor, and developing a business plan are all good ideas.

Many small scenic shops have been opened after two or three very successful months, only to close their doors a short while later. Many owners of scene and paint shops find that they have to diversify their businesses, taking on jobs in display and interior decoration to fill in the gaps in theatrical employment. They also find that they have to learn how to tap into business in other regions when there is not enough work locally. In the beginning, shop owners may find that they spend as much time trying to find contracts as they do fulfilling contracts. Many successful shops have an employee whose full-time position is dedicated to finding work for the shop and writing contracts.

In terms of the day-to-day business of a shop, all of the business items discussed to this point still apply. However, the expense column for the cost of space never goes away. The owner of a shop must always be thinking months and even a year or more ahead, cultivating new clients and matching jobs up with the employment pool. If the shop is successful enough, it will retain good employees on a permanent basis. But it is important to remember that making a commitment to an employee is a very serious responsibility. If you have to lay off someone with little or no notice, you have deprived that person of the chance to look ahead for the next job. Two days after I left a company in the Midwest for another commitment, my friends from there called me to tell me that they had come to work in the morning and the doors had been locked by the Internal Revenue Service. Since this was an area where there were few alternatives, it took some of those people many months and even years to recover the tempo of their profession.

On the other hand, when a shop is on its feet and there are several clients accustomed to relying on that shop for their scenic work, it can be satisfying to be your own boss and to provide employment and good working conditions for others. Scenic studio ownership means conducting a business as well as being a scenic artist. Inform yourself fully of the fiscal responsibilities and risks if you contemplate opening such an enterprise.

Working in the Film Industry

Film work is one of the most lucrative options for scenic artists in the United States. The movie industry is based primarily in Los Angeles and New York City.

As in the theatre industry, employment is found through a scene shop (either on the studio lot or in an independent scene shop that caters to films) or on a freelance basis through film production companies. Work in the scene shops tends to be more steady, although many shops operate by laying off staff and then rehiring them on a recurring basis. The compensation in the shops is good, but working on a freelance basis directly for a film company or contractor to a film company usually pays better. Film production companies are formed for the production of a specific film. Once the film is completed, the company is dissolved. One reason the pay is so high in film work is that the workweek is predicated on overtime just to stay on schedule. A typical workweek in feature film runs 60 to 72 hours. After the initial 40 hours, the crew makes one and a half times their regular rate. The cost of performers, directors, production staff, and studio time is so high that it is less expensive for producers to pay overtime to the film crew or the extra expense to the scene shop rather than to keep the primary people on contract longer or rent the studio for an extended period of time.

The downside to working on films is that the jobs are not steady or predictable. Most films hire their crews very quickly and with little notice. If you happen to have taken a long weekend to go to a family function, you might miss a call that would have resulted in several weeks or even months of work. Frequently, there will be a call for another film in a week or so, but there might not be. Toward the completion of shooting, or the wrap of a film, layoffs begin, usually with little or no warning. The general rule of layoffs is that the last person hired is the first person laid off. So most painters are aware that their employment could be coming to an end, but other than networking with other painters on the job site, there is little or no time to look for the next job. Because of the lack of warning about when the next job will start, it is difficult to plan anything during time off.

Some painters have developed a reputation for working as a *charge painter* on films. The charge painter is the person responsible for organizing and managing the painting on the production. In most cases, the charge painter also rents a kit of tools back to the production company. The charge painter usually is contracted in advance of the production, so people in this position have the luxury of knowing where their next job is going to be at least a few weeks before everyone else. Most charge painters call on a group of people who work with them on a fairly regular basis. Because of this alliance, such people also may have a few weeks notice on where their next job is going to be. If they are good, they can feel fairly confident they will have gainful employment for most of the year.

Working in the Television Industry

The major television networks also support permanent staffs of scenic artists. As with films, Los Angeles and New York City are the largest metropolitan bases for this industry. Television series and soap operas keep many scene designers and scenic artists employed. Soap operas rely on nearly round-the-clock calls to keep up the shooting schedule necessary to produce a new segment five days a week. Many weekly television series are budgeted for one new set per segment, in addition to maintaining the standard sets for the series. Each daytime drama and television series has a small army of set painters, set dressers, buyers, property artisans, grips, and designers to keep up with the shooting schedule.

The explosive growth of cable television has provided work for many designers and scenic artists. Scenic support for cable network feature films, dramas, talk shows, and comedy series has become as extensive as that for network television.

Freelance Work Outside of Theatre and Film

Good scenic artists will soon discover that their training and skill have in great measure prepared them for work in other fields. Beyond the world of entertainment lies a wealth of challenging work for scenic artists. Commercial display, interior decoration, museum display, and restoration all call for highly skilled painters. For some, scenic artistry may be a stepping stone into these professions, and for others these options present an interesting sideline.

Contemporary interior decoration utilizes faux finishes and decorative painting techniques to a large degree. Trained faux finish painters are in high demand in residential and commercial projects. Very skilled painters also may find work as muralists. This may be in addition to services that you can offer as a faux finish and decorative painter, or this profession may become your solid stock and trade. Because scenic artists have become accustomed to covering large

Figure 1.13 Museum installation and aging techniques, Lindberg Gun Shop, "Grand Rapids 1890s," painted contacted by Crabtree Scenic, Buffalo Bill banner painted by Mary Evers, Public Museum of Grand Rapids, Michigan.

surfaces with images and paint techniques, it is easy to make the transition into mural painting, decorative painting, and display work. Many skilled scenic artists have shifted to professions in these areas or bounce back and forth between these professions and scenic artistry. Also, because scenic artists are familiar with working quickly and efficiently, they are often successful in related painting professions.

To work in these professions, scenic artists may need to attain new skills or change their work habits. For instance, scenic artistry tends to be a very messy job since most of the work is done in a paint shop where the mess created from dripped paint and overspray is not an issue. But when working in someone's home or a business, it may be necessary to mask off all the adjacent areas as well as the foot paths to the

A   B

Figure 1.14   Example of mural painting, picnic diorama, diorama backing contracted by Crabtree Scenic, Stone Mountain Museum, Stone Mountain Georgia. **(A)** The diorama mural partially completed in the shop. **(B)** The mural as it was completed in the diorama on site.

utility sink and the door to insure that no damage is done to the premises as the job progresses. It may also be necessary to establish the paint schedule with the client in advance to minimize inconvenience to people living or working there. It is important to determine whether anyone that might be present in the home or business has sensitivity to the chemical vapors from the paint and mediums being used and make adjustments in the schedule or the ventilation if this is the case.

A scenic artist also may have to become familiar with other lines of paint, mediums, and finishes that are more ultraviolet light–resistant than theatrical scenic paint. It may be necessary, as in the case of faux finishes, to become adept at techniques involving oil-based paints and mediums. It is not uncommon in all of the professions mentioned above for the

scenic artist to be working in a new construction or renovation site with other contractors in a variety of trades, from plumbers to carpet installers. Though an environment like this might be familiar to scenic artists, other tradespeople may not be accustomed to working with an artist in their midst. It is not unheard of to come back from lunch break only to discover that the dry wall installer has spattered mud all over a carefully prepped wall because the ceiling had to be taped. Be aware of what the other trades are doing, if there is a contractor on the site; ask how your work can best schedule in with the other trades.

Also very challenging are professions in restorative painting and museum display. In many ways, these professions cross over the two fields because restorers frequently find themselves working on an object or in a building of such priceless beauty that it may as well be in a museum. They may find themselves having to recreate or touch up a surface originally created in antiquity. Museums often employ restorers with the proper expertise to clean and repair damaged or aged paintings. Scenic artists can obtain some of the best training to be had in this profession in Europe, where restoration studios accept apprentices. Once when visiting a small cathedral in Orvieto, Italy, I looked into the aisle where a canvas was under restoration. With elaborate care, a huge canvas had been taken off its frame and laid down on a deck where it was being restored by the artists who were walking on it, their feet wrapped in cotton booties, using bamboo extensions with their brushes just as scenic artists do when they paint a drop on a paint deck.

There are a great many varied challenges in the field of museum display. In the last few decades, museum displays have moved out of their display cases and into interactive, walkthrough exhibits. Diorama painting for displays has become even more challenging as museum audiences expect greater levels of realism. Scenic artists searching for a challenge may find that work in the profession of museum display, with its high standards of excellence and longevity, can be very satisfying.

In all of these professions, there are varying standards and levels of expertise. The artist may start out working on small jobs or as an assistant learning the trade. The profession of restoration is not something entered into without extremely specialized training. Work in all of these areas can be very fulfilling because of the high level of quality and skill required for work meant to be seen much more closely than stage painting. Many artists find it satisfying to work on a project that will last for years, decades, or centuries rather than the average run of a stage production.

INTERVIEW WITH RACHEL KEEBLER, COFOUNDER AND HEAD OF COBALT STUDIOS

Rachel Keebler, a leading scenic artist in the United States, operates Cobalt Studios, one of the few teaching scenic studios in the world. Keebler cofounded Cobalt together with Howard Jones in 1988. She has a BFA from Boston University and has also taught at North Carolina School for the Arts, Temple University, and Hong Kong Academy for the Performing Arts.

Susan Crabtree: Why don't we start with you telling me about what you do at Cobalt Studios and what the focus of the studio is.

Rachel Keebler: I plan the students' experiences there, I plan (with my assistant) the execution of the shows, and I paint. The Studio's main purpose is as a school, and it is also a scenic studio that paints primarily backdrop work. Students come primarily from theatre programs. Some of them come from art schools but all of them have one thing in common: they want to learn how to paint. To be accepted at the school, students have an overnight interview and fill out an extensive application. During the interview, prospective students show their portfolio, question us, and we question them. I'm looking for students with the determination needed to be here, because ours is a long program. The days are long—basically seven hours a day, five days a week—and students are instructed most of that time, whether it is how to put down masking tape, use a brush, or how to size a drop. It's a long haul and to be a student you put yourself in an insecure position, admitting that you don't know certain things. So, students need determination. The two-year curriculum for the scenic artist training program takes students through all the skills an artist needs to do art—most specifically, how those skills are applied in large scale, to scenery.

SC: What characteristics do you want students to have?

RK: I want them to have an artist's ability and an eye for detail. But almost as important may be to have a figurative toolbox of information and techniques that they can call upon to do the second most important thing, and that is to be a good problem solver—to be fast on their feet and be able to come up with new ways to do things on the fly. This also encompasses the concept of looking at every project with a fresh approach.

SC: Tell me a little bit about the student's lifestyle at Cobalt Studios.

RK: Students are encouraged to be and remain individuals, and that's what they do. They don't really do lots of things as a group. When we get up in the morning and have breakfast, everybody has a different breakfast at a different time; we're coming and going and sometimes we barely speak to each other. Everybody goes back to the studio at their own pace—we don't come down as a group. We first outline the schedule for the day and catch up on any information that we need to talk about. Then we split up and do what we need to do for the day.

Figure 1.15   Paint cart to hold roller supplies while Cobalt Studio's Rachel Keebler rolls the paint through the backdrop-sized stencil of letters glued onto bobbinette.

Guest teachers and I don't team-teach; either they teach or I teach. We don't team charge [charge artist] shows; either they charge or I charge it. We have one brain on each item going on and in that way we can have seven major things going on at once, whether it's teaching at one end of the studio and working on a show at the other end or whatever. The students have the experience of having very individualized attention.

Certain class projects are handpicked for the students. Other times they can pick their own projects. For example, for an animal project, they pick three animals from the file and then the teacher picks one of those. If the teacher doesn't think any of the student's choices are appropriate, we'll come up with another. My criteria for projects? The project has to challenge students, it has to be able to be done within a reasonable amount of time, and it has to be direct to the point of what we are teaching. If it's a drapery project, I don't want a little tiny drape and a whole lot of other things around it. I just want drapery. This is one of the hallmark ways we do things and we get good feedback from the students about it.

SC: Tell me a little about the history of Cobalt Studios.

RK: It began with my turning 30. At that point I had already taught at North Carolina School of the Arts

and Temple University. I liked teaching but I never thought about doing it full time. At that point, my father called me and said, "Your mother has an idea. Start the Manhattan branch of the North Carolina School of the Arts." I said it was a good idea but that it shouldn't be in Manhattan, and I knew I couldn't do it by myself. That summer I worked with Howard Jones and I thought that he would be a good person to start the school with since we worked well together and saw eye to eye. I mentioned the idea of starting a school for scenic artists to him. Two weeks later, we had brunch about it, and that was the start of Cobalt Studios. We spent three years drafting a business plan; solidifying our dreams by correspondence (he was still teaching in North Carolina). We decided it should be within two hours of New York City and near the Hudson so it would be easier to get to from New York.

I moved out of the city and nearer the Hudson to put myself in a better position of finding a place for Cobalt Studios. While I was there, I picked up a paper about property in Sullivan County, New York, an area I had never been before. I talked to real estate agents, saw a couple of not very good places. Then we found this place. We had decided to buy the housing and either build or rent the studio in the course of creating the business plan and this place fit the bill.

In fact, the man who typed the business plan for me came and visited the studio four years after we started this place and said it was eerie because it was exactly what we had planned, down to having a greenhouse. A dream come true.

Howard designed a lot of the physical aspects of the Studio and we worked together on designing the curriculum. We decided on a format that included both work and classes—students could expect to spend about 50 percent of their time on class work and 50 percent on commission work. This has changed a bit. Today, students spend over half of their time on class work. Sometimes we have to hire painters so students have time for their class work. We need to make sure we stay on target with our curriculum because it all works in sequence. This is why we don't accept any students midway through the program.

SC: And students live in a farmhouse?

RK: They may live off campus but most of them choose to live in the farmhouse. It's more convenient and a lot cheaper than renting. Students sign up monthly for different chores that they are responsible for, like trash, fire chief, etc., and we have a system by which students and teachers rotate the cooking. One of the students supervises the food. The students stay at the house and we have a good time, but even before and after dinner people go their own way. They'll go to the gym or they'll go to their rooms or do whatever they want to do. It is really not a summer camp. People are responsible for their own happiness. When you have males and females and we're all living in the same house, it's like a family, and sometimes they act like brothers and sisters. Though it is often difficult, there are wonderful benefits of this living situation, both for us and for our students. Part of it is learning how to balance your life with your work. The Cobalt house is really a good "home after home" for them.

SC: How long have you been a scenic artist and what made you decide to get into the profession?

RK: It was a sequence of events, it was not a conscious decision. I'm the daughter of an artist—a potter, my mother—and my father is an engineer-type person who is also an editor of trade journals and went to sales meetings a lot. So I have a parent who has a mechanical mind, my father, and someone who has an artistic mind, my mother, and I'm a combination of these two. As the third of four children, I was left to my own devices in a lot of ways and I had done some scene painting as part of the theatre scene in high school. When it came time to choose a college, I chose one that had my two loves: art and horseback riding—Skidmore College. While I was there I encountered James Leonard Joy teaching (the one year he taught), fresh out of Carnegie Melon, and I got sucked into the theatre. I started spending all my time doing costumes, stage management, lights, and painting, and in time started painting with Jim Joy. He taught in a way that I will never forget: he got the brushes and the paint and stood in front of me and showed me how to paint. The first thing I remember was lining and how to make painted wood paneling. Painting the molding on wood grain he would show me what I needed to do and then would hand me the brush and say "OK now do what I did" and that was the style of his teaching. He always led the way. The training I received from him is the foundation of my professional life. Jim Joy proceeded to take me to many places around the country painting for and with him. I did summer stock, worked in Boston, worked in Kansas City with him, and because of the summer jobs I had while I was in college, after graduation I was hired to work at the Seattle Rep where he was one of the designers. By this time I was working with other people as well, such as John Ezell in Kansas City and with Peter Gould and Larry Opitz at Skidmore. By the end of the first year of college I said to myself "I'm spending all my spare time doing theatre, I should just go to a college that teaches it." So I asked Jim where I should go and he said to Boston University, where the best scenic artist on the East coast, Don Beaman, teaches.

So I packed up my portfolio, went there, interviewed, and got in. I didn't apply anywhere else. I was there for three years and learned a lot about painting from Don Beaman and hopefully absorbed some of the beautiful ways that he puts his paint down. I have learned the most, though, from Jim Joy, as I worked for him because he always asks for the next-to-impossible and always has faith that I will be able to *do* the next-to-impossible (or figure out how to do it). After working in Seattle I moved to New York City and taught in North Carolina and got into the Union. I taught the next fall at Temple University.

SC: So you've been a teacher more or less throughout your career?

RK: Yes, since 1981.

SC: Did you have any training as a designer?

RK: Yes, at Boston University. It's important to have design training as a scenic artist. Once, I was working

Figure 1.16
Detail of scrim painting by Don Beaman,
Camino Real, Boston University.

on a production of *Carousel*. I didn't know the story of *Carousel*—I'd never seen it—but I was painting it for a repertory company in Albany and I was charging. They brought in plywood cutout profiles of trailers for me to work from—no renderings, just plywood cutouts—so I called the Russian designer and asked him what he wanted the trailers to look like. He said, "I want them to look like aluminum trailers in the dark." I then asked him if he could tell me a bit about the scene that they played in. He said, "Oh yes, she is running around in the dark, she's looking for someone in the trailer and she's not finding them and she's very distressed." I imagined it as a dreary set, so I painted it that way and the designer said it was painted just as he wanted. Actually, even Jim Joy has praised me for being able to take painters' elevations over the phone. So being able to figure out a scene would translate into a paint job. Being able to think like a designer can help you to help the designer realize their designs.

It's also good to have design training if you're a scenic artist for the same reasons it is good for a scene designer to take a directing course. You learn about how hard it is and so you realize that it's not easy to come up with the designs that they give you. It's difficult to coordinate the painting, the props, and the building of the scenery; you have to know so much about constructing scenery and you have to negotiate so much. Design training gives the scenic artist the ability to step up and really help the designer. I get tired of scenic artists who say, "Well you didn't tell me that." I maintain that it is as much a scenic artist's responsibility to get the information (not to create it) as it is for the designer to provide it. We just can't sit back and wait! It is important to know about focus on stage as it relates to theatre— the whole concept that most of what designers do is designed to move the focus to the actors. And by extension, most scenic art is controlled to move the audience's focus toward the actors.

When you are in a theatre program you learn about how drops go up and down and how hard it is for floor surfaces to hold paint. You realize that scenery has a function and not just a look. One should always be curious what that function is and what a piece of scenery is required to do on stage. That helps you figure out how to paint it; to choose the right materials and techniques for the needs of the show.

SC: Because every production has a designer that is different, do you have a method of developing a dialog when you are working with a designer?

Figure 1.17
Mastery of trompe l'oeil technique and painted marble in this work by Don Beaman.

RK: I start by keeping my mouth shut and thinking while I'm looking. Say a designer comes in and presents a design. Quietly study everything, concentrate on what you don't know about the whole project; what is unclear or hasn't been presented to you or what the scenery does. It's not necessarily apparent through drawings or renderings what a piece of scenery's functional or visual requirements are so you might need to ask about that. One thing I'm trying to do is to figure out whether what the designer is presenting to me is what they want because I've found that frequently it's not *quite* what they really want. They want this but they really kind of want to have a little more flavor of that or they want it to be the style of a particular artist. I need to find out if there is some intent or desire that is not apparent in the visual material that's given to me, and often times I'll be very direct about it. I'll have the rendering in my hand and I'll say, "Is there anything about this that you would like to have changed that you're not happy with?" This question needs to be asked in a certain way. You have to make sure that they know that you are asking not because you think there is something wrong, but because you want to know. You often get a positive response, with the designer saying, "Yes, actually, this part over here."

Speaking to the rendering in that way is a trick that I learned from Howard Jones about teaching, and that is when you go to look at a student's project

you don't say, "Look at what you did, you made the sky too dark." You say, "When I look at this rendering and I look at the painting, it looks as though the sky is too dark." You don't put it on the creator, you address the item, that you are looking at. It is all about making the paint job right. You should listen carefully and emote the fact that you're there to help the designer realize their art on stage.

SC: Besides Cobalt Studios, what type of training do you think a scenic artist ought to have?

RK: I believe a scenic artist must do summer stock because summer stock does several things. Summer stock is a great place for you to figure out if this is really what you want to do because everything is there. You have schedules, you have deadlines, you have pressure, you have fun, you have camaraderie, you make friends that you keep for the rest of your life, you make contacts that you keep for the rest of your life. A good session of summer stock will get you more jobs, good work, and if you don't like it, you probably won't be a scenic artist. It's trial by fire. Your experience will probably determine whether you continue in this profession or not.

Another thing is that even though there are many levels of scenic art and one can get work as successful scenic painter without it, I think art training is essential. If you don't know perspective, if your drawing is no good, if you can't use your eyes, you won't be asked to do the "art" part of scenic art.

Figure 1.18   Rachel Keebler demonstrates foliage painting techniques at Cobalt Studios.

This may be OK because there are a lot of painters out there and a lot of scenic painting involves more technical skill than artistic skill. A well-trained house painter could have a great career as a scenic painter, you know, because they learn how to work fast and dirty too. So if you want to do the art part of scenic art, you really must have art training.

Cobalt Studios tries to teach, in two years, many people who have not had much art training. Most of our students come from theatre backgrounds and many of them haven't had much art training and it's because of this that Cobalt really gets heavy on the art training part, heavy on the drawing, heavy on the brush work, heavy on mixing colors and developing the ability to see completely. One thing I can point out about being a student here is that it is not an internship program where you just watch or wash buckets. You are expected to listen to the lectures and learn about these things and then you're asked to do them, you're asked to mix paint, you're asked to draw, you're asked to base-coat, and to finish paint, spray things, and to know your light and shadow. It's assumed that you will pay attention and learn every aspect of the business.

SC: What words of wisdom would you offer someone who is going into a career in scenic artistry?

RK: Keep drawing. Be humble but also be responsible for yourself and what you do. Clean up after yourself.

Always be thinking. I would suggest that a scenic artist would recognize their place. You are a part of the machine that puts on a play or puts on an event in the entertainment industry. The production is the machine and as a part of the machine you must have the skill and strength, physically and mentally, to do what this machine needs, or it can grind you up and spit you out.

I also think that a scenic artist needs to be able to admit when they are wrong, and its best if you can laugh about it. Also admit when you don't know something. I learned another important thing from Mary Hielman. She came out to teach scene painting and stressed the importance of giving credit to others—don't be a prima donna. If the stage crew hadn't built it so beautifully, you couldn't have painted it so beautifully. Know your place and notice how to function in a new shop. When we are free-lancers we travel around so much. We really are guests and need to find out who to get information from and who we are working with so we can function.

SC: Looking back over your career, what would you say are some of the most difficult or elusive skills to learn in the profession of scenic artistry; in the area of painting and outside the area of painting?

RK: Knowing what is important *when*. What is important changes from moment to moment and Cobalt Studios epitomizes that. A phone call can change your next two days—is it more important to answer the phone call or to be teaching the lecture? What is the most important thing to attend to now? I've also found that writing skills, not only in setting up Cobalt Studios but also in preparing lectures, have been very good for me. Organizing one's thoughts and being able to articulate and describe are essential.

SC: What are some of the most common misconceptions about the profession of scenic artistry?

RK: That it's the same as designing. That we are totally responsible for how it looks. You say you've painted something and they say what a wonderful design. It's almost as though we are getting credit for the design, instead of for the beautiful execution of the painting. There is a lack of realization that there are two different departments and one makes design decisions and the other one executes them. I think that's the biggest misconception that the public has.

As to the biggest misconception within the business, it is that scenic art is physically easy to do. I know that some people think that the painting is easy to do because they stand around watching scenic artists, and a good scenic artist makes it look easy. But in reality it is very demanding, and there is a lot of brain work to it and often it is physically stressful because you do so many different things from day to day. You're on a scaffolding for four days in a row and you get all stiff and then you're sitting on the floor for two days or you have to work in a hot place for a long time then you have to work in a cold place, the noise level in the scene shop, the fumes, the welding fumes, the welding noises, incredibly high sound levels in those shops—our business requires strength and stamina, intelligence, and guts. (Not necessarily in that order!)

SC: In the last century there have been some significant changes in the way scenic artistry is done. Are there painting techniques or skills that you feel people new to the profession aren't being exposed to anymore?

RK: Not very many because I feel that most people new to the profession are coming in to either community theatre situations or university situations in which lots of the basic, historic techniques are still being used. The major exception is the making of your own paint. I think that's going by the wayside. I'm not sure if that is good or bad but if I were to run a summer stock operation I would still do it with [dry] pigment (see Chapter 6). All the components can be stored dry over the wintertime—you mix up

only what you use, the qualities of the paint force you to paint directly and not mess about, and at the end of the season you wash off the flats and store them and in the spring pull them out and start painting!

At Cobalt we teach the use of the appropriate paint for the job. We teach the spectrum of the types of paint including all canned paints, dyes, dye substitutes, and "pigment paint." There are very few places that have the pigments and use them anymore. In order to really know about paint you do need to know what the basic components are.

SC: Let's talk about digital renderings and what kind of impact you think they might have on scenic artistry.

RK: First of all, I'm happier to get a good computer-generated image from a designer than a sloppy hand-painted rendering. I would say that if anyone is not being taught something that they used to be taught, it's designers not being taught how to paint. Because I believe that being able to draw and to paint enables you to see and remember what things actually look like, I think designers are being short-shifted. Also, because the reproduction of their designs will be accomplished with scenic artists and a paintbrush, it's important that designers know about painting because they are asking others to do it for them. A student told me that the best thing about Cobalt Studios is that it trained her to be versatile. While other artists have a specific style, she is able to do whatever they ask her to. When she does a rendering, she sits down and she paints it as if she were painting a drop. If you can imagine getting that rendering from her as a painter, it has already been figured out in terms of opacity and layering of paint.

I think this has something to do with the importance of using a designer's intent to interpret a rendering, to be able to make it up when it's not there. If indeed the world would totally change and all images would be made full scale by computerized mechanisms instead of scenic artists, this wouldn't be an issue. The shortcomings of the design would just be enlarged, not fixed by a knowledgeable scenic artist. When I talk to computer fine artists who were fine artists before they went into computers, they tell me that the drawing and painting skills they knew before they got into computers contribute incredibly to their ability to create and choose images, and that they find themselves head and shoulders above other computer artists that don't have that art background. Many colleges and universities surely will continue to

Figure 1.19 The road leading to Cobalt Studios

train people to paint. Certainly productions will always need painting. I just don't see the business ever dying. I think that computer generated art will eat into our business but I don't believe it will take over. In fact, it may just stimulate the appetite for scenic art the way videos have stimulated the movie industry.

SC: Over the next few decades, do you think that scenic artists will have to evolve their skills and abilities?

RK: They have already had to, starting in the 60s, when color images from books and magazines became more available for designers to use. At the turn of the century, everybody was painting and the painters had to evolve into being more the "goop and glaze" sort. But there was also a great deal of painting, especially in the 60s before metal and plexi, the dimensional scenery. As far as the art part of scenic art, in the 1960s and 1970s, scenic artists had to start being able to reproduce fine art on stage. It seemed as though designers were losing the ability to step back and say, "It's only theatre and it will look great under light." They haven't been trained that distance, lights, and the focus of a production that goes on in front of their scenery will cause an audience to not examine it as closely as they do. Their lack of familiarity with painting stops them from realizing that things don't really have to be dimensional. It is quite easy to paint a great deal of things to *appear*

dimensional, but they're actually not dimensional and the audience would never know. There is a tremendous amount of scenery that are over-done, and over-built, because many scenic designers don't know those theatrical painting tricks. To me, that is what has been lost or is being lost.

SC: Do you have any favorite scenic art–related stories you would like to share about productions you have worked on in the past?

RK: My most memorable story was my first Union touch-up call. When the union representative called, she asked whether I was afraid of heights. I said I wasn't so I showed up the following Monday morning to work on the job. It was the production of *K2* on Broadway! Another scenic artist that came to help touch up was a journeyman who had not been asked that question and was afraid of heights. He spent the time on top of a huge A-frame ladder that was sitting on the trap room floor. The top of the ladder was at stage level (most of the stage had been removed) so he didn't feel he was high up. I had the wonderful time of being the painter in the bosun's chair repairing the set of *K2*, up above the proscenium and down to stage level. I have to say the most wonderful thing was seeing Ming Cho Lee standing on the lip of the stage with his assistant standing behind him ready to catch him because he had his toes over the edge and he was gesturing toward which part to put more paint on. That was a wonderful experience. I felt very appreciated.

One of the most difficult experiences I had scene painting was working on the Broadway show *The Rink* in a Union scenic studio. The set for *The Rink* was a laminated plywood wall that curved from the front of the stage right proscenium all the way upstage and back to the stage left proscenium. It was a forced perspective view down a barrel vaulted skating rink. The top profile went up and down, and a great deal of the set was made up of the radiating beams of the ceiling. So they put scaffolding in front of it in a curve and they attached Styrofoam to the beams, which we carved, and then we painted it. We were painting with asphaltum up high on the scaffolding. Down below at the bottom of the wall was a scenic artist spraying FEV [French enamel varnish] on it, and in the corner the shop was someone doing rim spray (which is a roofing material in which the operator has to wear a whole body suit and the chemicals come out of a 55-gallon drum and are heated and sprayed on the scenery). We are up high in the scaffolding climbing around like monkeys

Figure 1.20 A display of student work at Cobalt Studios.

trying to get done, and there are all these fumes in the air—it wasn't a good experience, but we got it done.

Another time, I was working at a Union scenic studio on the Broadway show *Doonesberry* together with Tommy Ford, an elderly scenic artist who has an attitude but is an excellent painter, very respected in the business. He's painting and I'm painting next to him on a piece of China silk that has been stretched over a metal frame in the shape of a Chinese dog. I'm painting orange dye and trying to make it beautiful, and Tommy picks up his paintbrush and make a drizzle line right across the middle of my painting. I said, "Tommy, what did you just do? How will I ever fix this?" And he says, "Aww, it will be OK." I said, "No it's not going to be OK." The piece ended up getting cut, so therein lies the lesson: when you have an opportunity to be the most upset about something is really when you should keep your cool.

SC: What do you enjoy most about scenic artistry?

RK: The challenges that come with making functional art on a large scale, while at the same time being a tool the designer's use to realize their art. I love making people happy. I love making the next-to-impossible a reality. I love seeing the light of understanding come on in someone's eyes. I love the variety brought to my life by each new student.

Chapter 2

The Relationship Between the Scenic Artist and the Scenic Designer

No two artists in scenic production are as closely related through their craft as the scenic artist and the scenic designer. The scenic artist has a very unique role among the many skilled artisans who contribute to scenic production. This often (but not always) singles the scenic artist out as the key translator of the scenic designer's work from the drawing board to the stage. Stage design styles vary from degrees of sculptural to two-dimensional "painted" scenery, all of which place different emphasis on scenic art, which might require very little sophisticated painting or quite a lot.

No matter which end of this spectrum, scenic artists are the last craft to contribute to the scenic production process before the set goes to the stage. Often, the scenic artist has a huge influence on the final product. The scenic artist is, at times, the primary artisan to make scenery look like what the scenic designer imagined, and they do so in the same terms that the scenic designer first created their work. The scenic artist and the scenic designer thus share a common language of art.

COLLABORATION BETWEEN THE SCENIC ARTIST AND THE SCENIC DESIGNER

Generally, if you were to place a scenic designer in a scenic studio, he or she would feel most comfortable painting. Many professional scenic artists are also excellent scenic designers. The easy crossover between the two disciplines might be due to the long tradition of stage design being a painter's art. This commonalty is why the scenic artist is able, perhaps more than any other vocation in the theatre, to understand fully and express the scenic designer's work. Of course, the scenic artist is only one member of a larger production staff, all of whom contribute to the goal of fulfilling the scenic designer's vision. But it is the scenic artist who is the last in the chain of planners, engineers, carpenters, welders, sculptors, and other artisans who make scenery.

Although many scenic designers are accomplished painters in their own right, most scenic designers do not practice these skills often enough to efficiently paint large productions. In fact, a United Scenic Artists (USA)-affiliated designer is prohibited from painting in a union shop unless they hold valid union working cards in both categories and are paid to perform both functions by the producer. Even if the scenic designer is a very accomplished scenic artist and is authorized to paint, the constraints of the production schedule will frequently call them away from the paint shop to consult with other departments, designers, and the director of the production. It is therefore critical that scenic artists know as much as possible about the scope of a design and the intent of the scenic designer so that they can help answer questions in the shop in regards to construction. In effect, scenic artists must understand a production design and the scenic designer's intent so well that they can work without the scenic designer's presence.

Assistant scenic designers are crucial members of the design and production process at any level, but in large-scale, high-budget events, they are absolutely indispensable. Assistant scenic designers represent the scenic designer, particularly if a show is spread out to a number of different shops. Top scenic designers normally work on several projects simultaneously, so their assistants execute the drafting and at times the paint elevations along with the designer. The assistant, or associate, will know every bit as much about a project as the scenic designer. The scenic artist may often work most closely with the assistant designer.

As noted in the first chapter, a scenic artist is an artist who *interprets* work, not simply reproduces it. His or her goal is to thoroughly capture the spirit and letter of the designer's creation and adapt it for the scale of performance with the materials selected for that production. The scenic artist's skill in painting must be matched by an innate sense of what looks correct in a theatre space for each production. The scenic artist must also have a firm grasp of the scenic designer's intentions. The scenic designer may have had a very particular image in mind when painting the model and paint elevations. Or the designer may have created the visual image from a gut reaction to the production, toying with the paint palette and working layers over one another until a satisfactory image emerged. The designer may make several attempts before being content with the results. This is part of the scenic designer's artistic process. When it comes time for scenic artists to recreate these images, their efforts must be accurate and purposeful.

Scenic artists must ask themselves a series of questions when undertaking a project: How do I capture the spirit of the designer's work? Is the painting style to be precise and rigid or loose and impressionistic? What materials and tools can I use to emulate the style and effect of the designer's images? In others words, what makes this production style unique? Scenic artists can answer these questions only with a full understanding of the scenic designer's work and visual style. This understanding comes from knowledge of art, artists' styles, architecture, and painting techniques gathered through years of education, experience, and observation.

The Scenic Artist Working with the Scenic Designer

Many scenic designers prefer to have a close collaborative relationship with the scenic artists they work with.

Figure 2.1   A design from elevation to the stage: Design for a ballroom rug, *Un Ballo in Maschera*, Metropolitan Opera, New York City, sketch drafted by Hal Tiné, painted by Peter Wexler, photo by Peter Wexler. Photo courtesy of the New York Public Library for the Performing Arts (at Lincoln Center), Billy Rose Theatre Collection, Peter Wexler Collection.

This collaborative approach may even result in the scenic artist becoming an important part of the design process. Occasionally, when a scenic designer is working with a scenic artist whose skills and talents are well known, he or she may elaborate or expand the design to cater to the scenic artist's abilities.

It is important to recognize that the scenic artist is much more than just a person who enlarges the designer's paint elevations. Their relationship is true artistic collaboration. Like two good cooks creating a complex meal, their sensibilities and tastes complement one another. Comments like "a slash of red"

Figure 2.2   Ballroom rug in scene shop, *Un Ballo in Maschera*, Metropolitan Opera, New York City, photo by Peter Wexler. Photo courtesy of the New York Public Library for the Performing Arts (at Lincoln Center), Billy Rose Theatre Collection, Peter Wexler Collection.

Figure 2.3 Ballroom scene with chandeliers and rug, *Un Ballo in Maschera*, Metropolitan Opera, New York City, photo by Peter Wexler.

Information from the Scenic Designer to the Scenic Artist

The materials the scenic designer uses to communicate information to the scenic artist include paint elevations, painted models, draftings, samples, and references or research. The scenic designer may provide the scenic artist with all or some of these depending on the demands of the painting. These are simply the tools and means of communication available to the scenic designer. It is the responsibility of the scenic designer to provide enough visual information to communicate completely his or her intentions to the scenic artist. No scenic artist should have to do the research of the scenic designer. However, for the sake of clarification of details, it is not uncommon for scenic artists to pull a book off their shelf of reference books or out of their file of images to show to the designer.

Draftings and White Models

The scenic designer communicates his or her ideas to the technical director and the construction staff through a full set of draftings and a scale model or a rendering. The model may be a *white model*, an unpainted scale model. A full set of draftings consists of: a composite ground plan, individual scene ground plans, section, front elevations, and detail and properties drawings. From these, the technical director and construction staff can determine the size, shape, placement, and materials of the scenery to be constructed.

The scenic artist must always be provided with copies of the draftings for even the simplest scenic designs. The scenic artist must have the drafting skills necessary to read plan views of the scenery. These drawings are essential for the scenic artist for budgeting and planning the production. The drawings are used in the painting process to verify the size, shape, and configuration of scenery coming to the paint shop, to draw any contours on the scenery, as well as to help the cartooning process. The scenic artist also uses the ground plan and white model to assist his or her understanding of relative placement of the scenic units on stage. It is important to understand which units "play" together in the same scenes and which units need to take "focus" in the scene.

Paint Elevations and Models

The scenic designer's cartoons and paint elevations or painted models, which may serve as the paint

or "just let it run" need not be defined or measured. On the other hand, finding a common vocabulary is very important. When the scenic designer asks for a "fine spatter of raw umber," the scenic artist should be certain that he or she understands the meaning of that phrase. It may be necessary to do a sample for the scenic designer's approval on a flat or a hidden corner of the set—just in case.

It is essential that the scenic artist and designer communicate frequently, from the initial stages until opening night of the production. This contact may take the form of formal or informal meetings, phone calls, e-mails, or whatever it takes to exchange information. Many scenic designers like to be around the shop while their designs are being painted. This is particularly true when working with a scenic artist for the first time. Many scenic artists prefer to have the scenic designer drop by the shop regularly so that they can be confident that the quality of the work is as the scenic designer had envisioned. Both the scenic artist and the designer have a responsibility to communicate with one another. A routine should be set up to ensure that this happens. It may be difficult if the scenic designer is out of town while a show is being painted, but it is not uncommon by any means. Making frequent phone calls, shipping paint samples, and sending photos via overnight mail or by e-mail are efforts that may seem excessive but will probably save time in the production process.

Figure 2.4
A typical architectural elevation, *Trelawny of the Wells*, designed by Peter Beudert.

elevations, are the primary medium by which the scenic designer expresses his or her scenic vision to the scenic artist. Sometimes the paint elevations have been computer generated since most designers now draft their designs in computer-aided design (CAD) programs. These scale drawings, paintings, and three-dimensional pieces must accurately reflect the line, color, and texture of the painting as well as the style, mood, and subtlety that the designer seeks in the finished scenery. They can be very beautiful examples of painting in themselves. Some scenic designers pride themselves on their meticulous and finely detailed elevations. Sometimes, however, paint elevations are not specific enough and are delivered to the scenic artist with references and a lengthy explanation. Usually, the quality of the paint elevations lays somewhere between these two extremes.

There are no established standards for paint elevations as there are for drafting, but some standard guidelines reflect the norm.[1] Paint elevations must be rendered in an accurate and measurable scale so that they can be easily read and measurements can be transferred. The scale of the paint elevations usually ranges from one-quarter inch to one inch per foot with one-half inch scale being the most commonly used scale in the theatrical industry. Paint elevations should be painted or mounted on rigid white board, which provides a neutral background for the elevation and makes them sturdy enough to survive the rigors of the paint shop. Paint elevations should be clearly labeled and that labeling should match the references of the drafted front elevations or ground plan. A centerline reference is helpful for large units and drops. The color of paints utilized in the elevation should be clear to the scenic artist. Dabs of the actual paint used and placed along the side of the elevation as the elevation is created are very helpful to the scenic artist. Paint elevations are easily scanned or photocopied if multiple copies are needed for the paint staff. Paint elevations are the property of the scenic designer and must be protected from damage in the shop so they may be returned undamaged to the designer when the painting is complete.

For complex figurative work, such as a full-stage backdrop of a street scene in perspective, the scenic designer should supply the scenic artist with an unpainted line drawing, called a *cartoon*. This cartoon is a copy of the line work on the paint elevation just before the scenic designer paints it. Normally the painting process tends to obscure the line work of

[1]Unites States Institute for Stage Technology, USITT Publication, 1992.

Figure 2.5 An elevation of a mountainous landscape backdrop, *Seven Brides for Seven Brothers*, Wichita Music Theatre, designed by Xuzheng He.

an elevation, making it difficult for the scenic artist to determine exactly how the cartoon should be laid out on the scenery. In some cases, the designer may draw the cartoon on the drafted front elevation, but this is often a case of too much information on that sort of drawing. The front elevations are primarily for the construction crew's benefit, and much of the cartoon of two-dimensional images is left off to avoid confusion.

A fully painted model of the scenery can be used in place of two-dimensional paint elevations. The model must be designed to come apart easily for the

Figure 2.6 A close inspection of the elevation reveals the interplay of color and brush technique, *Seven Brides for Seven Brothers*, Wichita Music Theatre, designed by Xuzheng He.

Figure 2.7 A fragment of scene painting from the Lyric Opera of Chicago/Northern Illinois University Historical Scenic Collection (Courtesy of The School of Theatre and Dance, Northern Illinois University, Alexander Aducci, Curator).

scenic artist. This way the scenic artist may use individual pieces of it while working on a specific unit of scenery. These different pieces of the model will be needed at the same time in separate areas of the shop or even separate buildings to serve the various scenic artists working on it. Also, it is difficult to take measurements from an assembled model, carry it around, and protect it from damage while mixing colors. I have seen many carefully crafted scenic models disassembled as carefully as possible by the scenic artists only to be returned to the designer somewhat worse for wear in spite of the care taken to repair these models. If a model also is the working elevation for a production, it must be clear to other departments that, once the scenery goes into the paint shop, the model must reside there as well.

The Digital Elevation.   Digital painting tools are commonly used by scenic designers to create paint elevations and renderings. Designers have been using xerography for decades to create cut-and-paste collage elevations and renderings, so the relatively recent adoption of digital technology is not so radically new. Scanners and color printers are commonly found in scenic designers' studios and are an indispensable part of the design process. Some designers create their entire elevations digitally, never picking up a brush or pencil. This, in theory, should make no difference to the scenic artist when it comes time to commit the design to canvas in full scale. However, there are aspects of this process that the scenic designer needs to carefully oversee to avoid surprises. All elevations, digital or conventional, must accurately represent the information previously discussed: the cartooning must be legible, the color choice must be clear. The same standard applies to digital and conventional elevations that information provided to the scenic artist in a paint elevation must be as unambiguous as possible.

The introduction of digitally generated paint elevations and renderings or models for theatrical design during the last decade has been a point of discussion and disagreement between professional scenic designers and scenic artists. Some scenic artists fear that digitally generated design work does not fully convey the required information to them. Such discussion is best answered by thorough and professionally made paint elevations, no matter the medium. Rachel Keebler put the argument to rest most succinctly by saying: "I like good information when I get it."[2]

Figure 2.8   A digitally generated architectural elevation, *Harvey*, designed by Robert Schmidt.

Digitally generated images are not inherently better or worse than conventionally painted work. All paint elevations need to be accurate and complete.

A scenic designer must have full control over the production of the elevation when working digitally. It is the responsibility of the scenic designer to print the file and tile together the printed pieces of the elevation to make up the correct scale. The scenic designer must never provide an unprinted file or simply e-mail the elevation to a scenic artist unless asked for one. The scenic artist would most likely not have identical printing capabilities to generate that elevation so the color content may shift radically. What if the scenic artist's printer is low on magenta? What if

---

[2]USITT Conference, 2001.

Figure 2.9   A digitally generated drop elevation, *Gross Indecency*, designed by Robert Schmidt.

Figure 2.10   From a digital elevation to the stage, *Gross Indecency*, designed by Robert Schmidt.

they use different paper? It is also highly unprofessional to provide anything other than a printed elevation in the correct scale. One can only ask the scenic artist to paint what is provided to them.

Samples

If some of the scenery or an entire set has a specific paint treatment, finish, or texture, the designer may provide the scenic artist with a full-scale sample in place of a paint elevation. A full-scale sample can often be much more useful than a paint elevation for the scenic artist. Sometimes, these samples are actual pieces of wood, marble, or other material that the scenic designer would like the scenic artist to reproduce as closely as possible. Other times, the scenic designer paints the sample and passes it on to the scenic artist with an explanation of how they were produced. The scenic designer may also work with the scenic artist to generate paint samples so the two can confer about the paint treatment. The creation of the sample might be the method by which the paint technique is created for that particular production. They are very useful when the designer is out of town. The scenic artist may decide to create paint samples to be

shipped to the designer for his or her OK before committing to a given paint technique. This is particularly true in the case of highly textured scenery. The actual making of the sample may determine the materials used for the full-scale scenery and help the charge painter determine the materials to be purchased for that production. A heavily dimensional texture applied to scenery does need to be as light as possible and dry within the time available, thus a sample can help guide the choice of material used for texture as well as the technique of application.

References and Research

All scenic designers work from a base of research as they develop a design. This research serves the designers throughout the process of designing from the first stages of development to the final decision on finish painting. Sharing the research with the construction and painting staff is a very useful means to share their ideas and intent. Research is a very helpful neutral reference point. The research image can help explain the intent of an elevation. It is not uncommon that a paint elevation have parts of it that the scenic designer likes better than others, or parts that

Figure 2.11   Samples created by Cobalt Studios students set to dry before the next layers go on. This is from Donna Wymore's seminar, "Texture and Aging Techniques for Film and TV."

"work" better than others. The research picture may be the best means by which scenic designers can clearly communicate the style they seek. Or, as discussed in Chapter 1, a reference might be the work of a specific artist that is to serve as the stylistic touchstone for a stage picture or painting technique. These references can come in the form of pictures in books and magazines, photographs, photocopies, lithographs, and as many different forms as there are reproduced visual images.

PREPARING TO PAINT FROM THE ELEVATION

In any case, it is unusual that a professional scenic designer's paint elevations and related visual information given to the scenic artist are so complete that they fully describe every detail of the finished scenery. Designers often work in a kind of shorthand to eliminate repetitive parts of the job or, realizing that the scenic artist will grasp their intent, take shortcuts in the completion of the paint elevations. The scenic designer's work frequently is done in a reduced scale, which in itself forces the image to be somewhat simplified. Also, when working through the paint elevations or painting a model, the scenic designer may be more concerned with the overall appearance of the scenery rather than specific paint details. Part of the scenic artist's responsibility might be to fill in the artistic gaps in the elevations and flesh out the details so that the painting is effective for the full-scale scenery. A paint elevation for a three-dimensional unit of scenery might well be rendered two-dimensionally because the scenic designer trusts the scenic artist to flesh out the details onto all surfaces of the unit.

Studying and Preparing the Paint Elevations

The scenic artist needs to "read" and fully understand the paint elevation and all related visual material in preparation for painting. If a crew of several scenic artists is working on a production, one of the crew is the charge painter. The charge painter studies the packet of bluelines, paint elevations, and other material from the scenic designer to ensure that he or she understands how the set is put together. Next, the charge painter should go through the paint elevations and make sure that he or she understands how the paint elevations relate to the bluelines. Often a designer will make notes in the margins of elevations or attach notes to references or samples. The charge painter should read all these notes. All reference material that relates to a specific elevation also should be available for later use by the paint crew. When the elevations are covered with acetate or clear vinyl to protect them, these references and the designer's comments can be mounted on the same board so that they will always be available for consideration while those scenic units are being painted. While looking through the packet, the charge painter will compile a list of questions to ask the scenic designer. Next, the charge painter will discuss this material and related questions with the designer.

Light and the Paint Elevation

When studying paint elevations, it is important to view them in appropriate light since some lighting may cause the appearance of color variance. Color is the specific quality of light reflected by an object that can be measured by wavelength. The type of light used when viewing an elevation has a enormous influence on the color one will see. It is important that the scenic artist view the paint elevations in a light that is as close as possible to stage light. This is particularly important in the paint mixing area, where colors are matched to the paint elevation. It is crucial that the scenic artist be able to clearly view and match color, so that the elevation may be reproduced with the same degree of subtlety. It is essential that the scenic artist understand how scenery appears when it is under stage lighting. Furthermore, it may also be useful for the scenic artist to know if the scenery for a specific scene is seen under specific lighting moods such as moonlight or a blazing Arizona sun. These variations of lighting intensity will affect the painting techniques.

Most scene shops are lit in a completely different manner than the stage where the final painted work is to be seen. Incandescent lighting is very close in characteristics to conventional stage lighting, but not commonly used in scenic studios for economic reasons. Often low-cost lighting is used throughout a scenic studio shop. Standard fluorescent, "daylight" fluorescent, low-voltage fixtures, mercury vapor, high-pressure sodium, HMI, and even sunlight have color temperatures very different from stage light and will change the apparent color of a model or paint elevation (see Chapter 6 for further discussion of color temperature).

The paint mixing area is the one area where incandescent light fixtures should be installed. The paint deck may be lighted differently from the paint mixing area. A scenic artist must be extremely aware of all lighting conditions in regards to looking at the work they are doing. Avoid looking at an elevation or mixed paint or the actual painted scenery without taking into account the lighting conditions.

Reading a Paint Elevation

What the scenic artist must understand from the paint elevations and talking with the scenic designer are the color, technique, texture, style, and the artistic intent sought in the scenic design. It is easy enough for the scenic artist to make assumptions and surmises about the designer's paint elevation, but unless the designer has been questioned about the specifics, there is no way of knowing whether these assumptions are correct. In some cases, the designer may have no strong opinion about how the scenery is to be painted; in other instances, the designer may feel strongly that the painting should be approached in a specific manner.

Color is probably the most evident aspect of a paint elevation. Some scenic designers may include their color swatch boards with the paint elevation packet. The swatch board is a scrap of illustration board on which the paints have been paletted that can give the scenic artist useful clues to how the colors were mixed. In terms of color, the scenic artist should ask very specific questions, such as "Does this shadow have a purple tint?" or "Was this gray mixed with blue and burnt sienna?" More importantly, the scenic artist may want to ask some broader questions about the palette of the elevation. The designer may have chosen a palette that is cool or that is primarily warm. That palette may be based on complementary colors, opposing hues, such as reds and greens or yellows and purples. The palette may be primarily monochromatic, using one color varying only in value and neutrality. Or, the palette may be based on two colors, dichromatic, perhaps based on blue and umbers.

Technique refers to how the paint or texture should be applied. This may not be entirely clear by looking at the paint elevation. For instance, if parts of the paint elevation have been rendered in colored pencil, does this mean that the designer wants colored

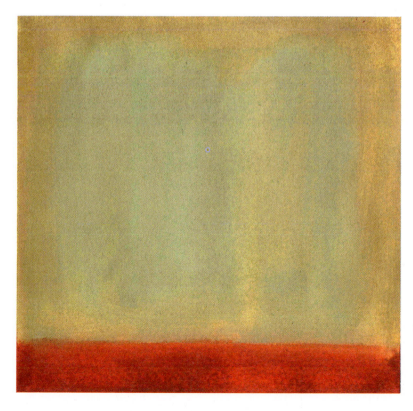

Figure 2.12
Simple color elevations present many challenges when enlarged to full scale, *The Last American in Paris*, designed by Peter Beudert.

pencil–like lines in the painting, or was the pencil used just for the sake of accuracy in the reduced scale of the elevation? In terms of the painting technique, the scenic artist must discuss with the scenic designer the medium itself. Is the paint to be opaque color or is it applied in transparent layers creating variation and depth? A paint elevation that, to the eye, appears to be made up of a multitude of subtle variations may actually have been painted with only five separate hues of transparent colors. These are the questions that the scenic artist must put to the designer.

The technique may also affect the way the scenery is to be approached in the paint shop. If the scenic designer renders the paint elevations using transparent pools of color, then the scenic artist needs to bear in mind that painting of this sort is done most easily in the continental technique: horizontally rather than vertically. The paint will need to be thin and of the right intensity. Obviously, this will involve considerable floor space and drying time. Both of these factors will need to be addressed when the scenic artist is planning time and space. It is crucial for the designer to be aware of what the shop can provide in the time budgeted. The scenic artist should have an understanding of the shop's potential. If the scene shop lacks sufficient floor space or time to leave flats down for a prolonged period, other techniques may have to be considered and discussed with the designer. Some very elegant solutions can come from the necessity of working within time, space, and budgetary limitations.

Texture and *finishes* are issues that must be decided from the onset of a project. Every building material has an inherent texture, and if the scenic designer desires that texture to be altered so that it is either smoother or rougher, the scenic artist must be aware of it from the start. If the texture is something that must be applied before the painting starts, as in the case of a rough-cut wood or fieldstone, then the scenic artist will have to apply the texture before the color. The texture could be just a matter of finish such as a glossy wood paneling or smooth marble. In this case, extra finishing work, sanding, and spackling may need to be done on the scenery before the painting. Like technique, texture, its application and drying time, must be factored into the time frame of the scene shop. How the texture is applied is important. Many options are available for application, such as hopper guns, brushes, grainers, rollers, trowels, and hand work. These techniques produce different results, take varying amounts of time, and have different costs involved. The scenic artist and the scenic designer must decide which techniques would best suit the resources of time, budget, and labor to produce the desired results. (We'll discuss texture tools in Chapter 5 and texturing techniques in Chapter 9.)

Talking with the Scenic Designer

When talking with the scenic designer, it is important to get answers to the questions that the paint elevations themselves do not and cannot answer. Simply talking allows the scenic artist to grasp the paint process the designer used making the paint elevations or envisioned being used on the scenery. It also establishes how various samples and references sent with paint elevations fit in. This interview may entail asking questions as simple as "What did you use as a base color?" "Do you want the overall paint treatment to be opaque or layers of glazes?" "Is this finish gloss or semi-gloss?" or "What process did you use to obtain these results?" It is common sense to try to emulate the designer's painting process, which sometimes is not clear at first glance, to obtain the same results. Many variables are involved in any painting process. During this interview, the charge painter should take detailed notes. If notes are specific to a particular paint elevation, they should be attached to that particular elevation.

Beyond understanding the painting processes, this discussion with the scenic designer is very important in terms of understanding the designer's overall scenic vision. Is it a dark and dreary dungeon in the spirit of Piranesi's prison etchings? Perhaps the entire scene is to have the filmy depth of a Watteau painting. Some scenic designers may communicate ideas at a more pragmatic level. For instance, the designer may simply say, "I first underpainted everything with red." The charge painter should use this interview as the best chance to get the designer's overall impression of how he or she envisions the painting of the design. Because many designers must work on two or three designs at the same time, a personal interview at the beginning of the paint process may be the last time the charge painter and scenic art staff can speak with the designer face-to-face until the scenery is nearly ready to leave the shop. Occasionally, because of conflicting schedules, the charge painter must conduct this initial interview with the designer over the phone and exchange pertinent visual information via delivery services.

Every scenic designer brings a quality called *style* to a production. Style is the invisible glue that aesthetically holds together the scenery. It is absolutely crucial that the scenic artist understand the style the designer has chosen. Also important is that the scenic artist understands that this style in part may be the personal style of the designer. In this, the scenic artist must be neutral and objective enough to conceal his or her own personal style and, for that production, adopt the style of the designer. The chosen style for the production may be a clear historic reference, such as German expressionism or French art deco. The scenic artist must understand and retain this style for every piece in that production. For the charge painter, this means monitoring the work of the entire paint staff throughout the production.

In addition to technique and style, the scenic designer and the scenic artist need to make sure that they understand one another on the artistic content of the design. This area, *intent*, is a primary area where the art of scenic artistry comes into play. The scenic artist needs to fully understand the designer's stylistic intent and be able to recreate it in full scale. This includes understanding where the designer wants the focus within any given scene or recognition of the overall effect of the scenery. This, as with style, is where a good scenic artist becomes invaluable to a scenic designer. It is impossible to express a sense of style or theatricality without understanding the intent behind the style.

INTERPRETING THE SCENIC DESIGNER'S WORK

Interpretation of paintings from small to large, from flat to three-dimensional, is expected of the scenic artist. Interpretation for the scenic artist can mean many things. In many instances it is a rather simple interpolation of scale. It can also include sensitivity towards the visual style of a production and vigilance that the style is consistent. This chapter began with a reminder that the scenic artist and the scenic designer bonded by the art of theatre design in a profound manner. To interpret does not necessarily mean to reinvent. To interpret the work of a scenic designer is to fully understand the intention of the designer and apply it accurately and consistently throughout the length of time of painting. The effort of understanding the designer's intent, concept, and vision for the scenic design should be at the core of every decision the scenic artist makes. Granted, this effort to support the designer's vision is complicated by many other issues, such as time, space, the skill of the crew, and so on. But in juggling all these elements, the core concern of the scenic artist is to come as close as possible to the scenic designer's vision with the resources available.

It is also important to remember that the scenic artist's understanding of the scenic designer's vision may be informed by more than just the visual materials provided. It is always immensely helpful if the scenic artist understands the context of the production.

Figure 2.13   A backdrop paint elevation by Clare P. Rowe for the musical *On a Clear Day*, Music Theatre of Wichita.

Is it a comedy, tragedy, opera, or musical? The designer might instruct the scenic artist along the lines of "This should be a romantic scene because this is where the two lovers finally get together." Even in the absence of this sort of explanation, it is generally useful for the scenic artist to understand the emotional atmosphere and stylistic construct of the performance as well as the directorial approach of the production. For instance, a postmodern design approach may use relatively realistic elements, but in a very different manner than a realistic design would. The scenic artist should be aware that the scenic designer is creating a visual metaphor to support the production concept, not just making a literal environment.

This is not to say that a scenic designer's work needs to be revised by the scenic artist. Many scenic designers are perfectly capable of painting exactly what they want in the elevation. Joe Forbes' description of Tony Walton's designs for *Guys and Dolls* is one such example.[3] It was essential to that production that the team of scenic artists painted exactly what Walton put in the elevation. Forbes knew to reproduce the "hand of the man" for that production.[4] But Forbes, too, knew that Walton based his work on the painting style of Andre Derain, underscoring the importance of knowing the process of the designer.

Other scenic designers may not take the same approach as Walton does when it comes to their paint elevations. The rapid success of *Phantom of the Opera* that allowed for such a high-budget transfer from London to New York caught the scenic designer, the late Maria Bjornsen, by surprise. Some of her elevations for *Phantom* are photocopy collages of research materials that did demand some interpretation on the part of the assistant scenic designer for the scenic studio. By no means was Bjornsen anything less than a gifted artist and designer. There was no question as to the intent of her work, as shown through the elevation and models for *Phantom*.

Thus, scenic artists must know the end result before they begin painting and must be as flexible stylistically as an actor in a repertory company who has a role in an Anton Chekhov play one night and a Christopher Durang play the next. Within the spirit of that style, scenic artists need to improvise a little on sections of the scenery that are not fully described by the paint elevations rather than infuse the painting process with their own style.

---

[3] TCI, August-September 1992, p. 43
[4] Ibid.

Checking Elevations and Draftings with the Scenery

The process of painting a production begins with a thorough organization of the work. Part of this preparation consists of developing a clear understanding of how big the scenery is, what structural form it will come in, and how the scenic artist will actually put the paint on. The charge painter is responsible for checking all the scenery as it is received from the construction staff against the designer's elevations. This is important since painting scenery twice is a very costly exercise. Here is an instance when the scenic artist represents the interest of the designer in the paint shop. If possible, the charge artist should monitor the construction of the scenery so that he or she may be aware of construction techniques or materials that will require extra attention once the scenery reaches the paint shop. Remember: forewarned is forearmed. Usually in advance of the build, the charge painter and the technical director will meet to discuss schedule and construction techniques that will have a bearing on the painting of the scenery. For example, will the units need to be spackled and sanded? Will the units need to be painted on the floor or assembled and vertical? Should the stiffeners be removed before the scenery can be painted? During the building process, the technical director may ask the scenic artist, "Can you paint on this material?" or "Do we need to build a bridge so that you can reach into the center of this unit?"

Once the scenery comes into the shop, there may still be some differences in the way the scenic artist understands the scenic units' design function and the way they have been built. The charge painter may need to consult with the designer or technical director before proceeding. Items such as reveals on doors and windows or floor treatment through doorways are not often clear on the paint elevations. In some cases, the construction staff may need to do some additional work on a particular unit. In other cases, the charge painter may need to call the designer, explain the differences, and ask how he or she would like to deal with discrepancy.

Enlarging the Design to Full Scale

One skill germane to scenic painting is the process of enlarging small drawings and paintings to full scale for the stage. This is part of the scenic artist's interpretive skill, calling on artistic judgment, knowledge of styles of architecture and art, and a sense of what is theatrical. This skill is intuitive and takes time to develop.

Scale

The fact that paint elevations and cartoons are drawn in small scale is an important consideration. The scenic artist enlarges these drawings on the scenery. However, simply enlarging the original work like a copy machine will not result in a complete description of the scenic designer's vision. The lines of a cartoon do not need to become 24 times wider when transferred from one-half-inch scale to full size. That would be an absurd transformation. The scenic artist would naturally try to retain the sense of line when drawing the cartoon. This transition requires interpretation of the designer's work and some significant decisions on the part of the scenic artist. These may include the clarification of small details or of a light source suggested by the painted highlights and shadows. Perhaps the scenic designer made part of the paint elevation fade off into expressive and indistinct blobs of paint. But the scenic artist, working in full scale with large brushes, may need to know exactly what those blobs of paint are. Is the blob a house or a tree? Will the contours of that blob have a sense of the organic or the architectural? The scenic artist may need to complete the picture.

Understanding how the scale of the painting will read in the theatre where the scenery is to be installed is important. In a large theatre, highly detailed objects can be painted in broad paint strokes. The observer will complete the image and believe it to be detailed. Paradoxically, in this situation, highly detailed painting may actually appear to flatten the image. On the other hand, forms created with broad paint strokes may appear overly simplified in smaller theatres. Color is not the same close up as at a distance. As demonstrated by the methods of Seurat and Pissarro, the eye will mix separate colors at a distance. So the surface of a gray stone wall that responds so beautifully to any color of stage light actually, on close inspection, may be a combination of peach, ocher, and Italian blue sprays.

Technique

Selecting the proper paint techniques for a design is a major aspect of the preparation process. The scenic artist must determine how to recreate techniques of the paint elevations made with the small brushes and art tools of the designer. The obvious answer, with larger brushes, is only part of the solution. Brooms, sponges, garden sprayers, feather dusters, and all manner of implements can become paint tools as long as they achieve the desired effect (see Chapters 5 and 9). At this point, the scenic artist combines knowledge of the field of scenic artistry, the designer's advice, experience, and imagination to devise a solution. As you gain experience, you will find that more and more frequently, the answer to interesting problems already will be at hand. However, even the most experienced scenic artist will encounter a new challenge that requires a fresh approach and experimentation with conventional and unconventional tools before finding the right solution.

Character

The key to good interpretive skills is identifying the essential elements and character of a scenic designer's work. These elements could be the line of the drawing or perhaps the sense of the color itself. A scenic artist may have faithfully and laboriously copied every line and mark from the scenic designer's paint elevation, yet the essence of the drawing is missing. Strict adherence to every detail may obscure the spirit of the work. Vladimir Polunin described this phenomenon in his 1927 book, *The Continental Method of Scene Painting:* "Carefully examine it from several points of view to ascertain if the drawing on the canvas represents the same characteristic lines contained in the tracing. If it fails to do so, it is proof that you have allowed the detail to break up the important lines. Correct, always bearing in mind that in scenery it is the general effect that is essential."[5] Remember that the scenic artist is an artist and interpreter of the design, not a mimic. Without the interpretive skills of a scenic artist, a simple sky drop might lose the dramatic quality of style that makes it theatrical.

Making Samples

Sometimes, traditional elevations are not enough to describe the paint treatment. Scenic samples often are an indispensable part of the preparation of painting and may be done by the scenic designer or the scenic artist. When using heavily textured or layered surfaces or when working with nontraditional, unprocessed

---

[5] Polunin, [1927],1980, p. 17

materials, it can be better to work from a sample. This part of the preparation is best done by collaboration between the scenic artist and the scenic designer.

A sample is a full-scale swatch of the finished scenery. This swatch may be a small test flat, a 4′ × 8′ piece of sheet stock, or a piece of the material out of which the scenery is to be constructed. In some cases, the construction staff may have to build a small mock-up of scenery for the sample work. On a sample, you can experiment with different materials, application techniques, distressing techniques, media mix, and finishing techniques. The time taken to work up a sample will save time in the long run by answering questions about the process.

There are no rules about how samples are done or who does them, but some commonsense guidelines may help. The scenic designer should provide some sort of visual image as a starting point and reference to the visual image he or she envisions. This reference may be a photograph, a piece of finished wood, a piece of stone, or even references out of books or magazines. The books by Judy Juracek (*Surfaces, Natural Surfaces,* and *Soft Surfaces*) are excellent photographic resources that many designers use as source material. In some cases, the designer may refer to some common visual image easily identifiable to the scenic artist such as "concrete" or "brownstone." The scenic artist will then create a sample for the designer's approval.

The sample usually is created in the scenic studio. The scenic designer who has presented the scenic artist with a completed sample must be able to thoroughly explain the recipe and techniques used to produce that sample, so that the scenic artist can replicate it, explain the process to others, and budget time and materials for the scenery. One of the great benefits of working-up a sample are the questions that knowing the process and materials can answer, such as "What materials were used?" "How many distinct steps were involved?" "What was the order of these steps?" "What was the drying time between steps?" "In all, how long did the process take and what was the cost per square foot?" The sample allows the scenic artist to determine the feasibility of a process for a given production. Is there enough time and space? Is the process durable to withstand moving and trucking? Will extra labor be required? Can the materials fit into the budget for the production?

In some situations, a sample makes a lot more sense than a paint elevation. Situations that call for a simple paint treatment on specific material are a perfect example of where a sample may be all the information a scenic artist needs. However, it is important not to overlook the need for some sort of elevation or rendering to give an overview of the scenery. Even a simple treatment of wood may vary from light to dark applications depending on where it plays onstage. In many cases, the scenic designer may give the scenic artist a paint elevation describing the value and color variation over the surface of the scenery that is to be used in conjunction with a paint sample. In some instances, the lighting designer may request a sample of one or more paint techniques for their own design process.

Using the Scenic Designer's Research

Concepts and ideas are difficult to express in words. There is never any guarantee that one person's comprehension of a visual idea or concept is the same as that of the person endeavoring to express it. But the scenic artist's need to know and understand the scenic designer's meaning is crucial. Communication and comprehension are at the core of their collaborative relationship. The designer needs to express an overall concept to many different people. Those of us who share in the responsibility of executing the separate pieces of scenery that make a design need to share in the rationale behind it. We all know that a picture is worth a thousand words, but looking at the same image can be wonderfully objective. The designer, by providing the scenic artist with a few key images that epitomize the design concept, a specific texture, or paint treatment, instantly can clarify his or her intent. In some cases, the designer may want the scenic artist to focus on a specific area of reference. All that may be needed in some cases is a color photocopy that has one corner circled in red with a note that reads "These are the type of rocks I want!"

If the paint elevations are not enough information or the scenic designer is not able to fully convey his or her intent through them, then research and specific references may have to fill the gap. Generally, the designer will supply the scenic artist with copies of these sources or, if the reference is well known, tell the scenic artist what it is. For instance, the designer might say, "This is a Tuscan Doric column and capital" or "I want the painting style to be reminiscent of a Renoir oil painting." Most scenic artists are bibliophiles and may well have the reference material in their own libraries. A well-equipped paint shop will have a small library of architecture and ornamentation reference books. The scenic artist who needs more information can ask the designer to supply it, or in some cases, it may be just as easy for the scenic artist to go to the local library or search the Internet and collect the sources.

When Research Takes the Place of an Elevation

In some cases, the scenic designer's references for a production may supersede the paint elevations in part or completely. The designer may give the scenic artist a color elevation of a city street that is descriptive of the line work but is accompanied by a page from *Architectural Digest* and a note that says,

"Here, use these colors and shading." The designer may send a photo of birch trees with an elevation of a foliage drop and indicate that these are specifically how the trees are to be rendered on the drop. In some instances, the designer may lay a color wash over a black and white photocopy or collage by way of a paint elevation. In instances like these, it will be up to the scenic artist to merge these visual images. The musical *Sunday in the Park with George*, which revolves around the painting of *Sunday Afternoon on the Island of La Grande Jatte* by Georges Seurat, is an extreme example. Here, a natural progression takes place from the reference, the work of art itself, to the designer's elevations, and how the scenic artist integrates the two in the painting of the scenery.

A   B

Figure 2.14   Elevation (**A**) and details (**B**) of pointillism technique, *Sunday in the Park with George*, designed by Peter Beudert.

In rare cases, the scenic designer may hand over photographs to the scenic artist in lieu of a painted elevation. Photo-realism or a photographic appearance are valid style choices in their own right. It is not unusual that a scenic artist is called on to paint in an extremely realistic style from photographs. In this case, preparation and the approach to painting is no different than with any other sort of project. This may be a case where the scenic artist turns to mechanical reproduction methods to supplement or replace painted scenery. There are several means by which machines can provide scenic images for the scenic artist. Photographic poster-size enlargements are a relatively affordable option. Wide format printers and plotters are capable of printing subtle image onto a variety of media, including paper and canvas. Full-size drops can be reproduced by mechanical painters directly to canvas, linen, and a variety of materials for a reasonable cost. Simply projecting an elevation or other designer's source material onto a drop or other piece of scenery is a very effective means to facilitate a realistic technique.

In even more demanding situations, the scenic designer actually may ask the scenic artist to complete the painting in the style or spirit of the reference material. I once got a piece of stationery from a designer that had been printed with a cloud motif. The designer's instructions were to "paint clouds like these on the drop." This is not an ideal situation for the scenic artist, as one's interpretation of that direction may actually be very different from the desired effect. The designer may provide a broad concept for the scenic artist to follow, but it was up to the scenic artist to fill in the detail and create the actual image. A designer may have a very elegant sense of design, but painting may not be his or her forte. Designers such as this rely on the scenic artist to understand and carry out the intent of the design, filling in what the designer can imagine but not execute.

Copying Works of Art

The research that the scenic designer has done may appear in a very literal way in the design. It is not unusual to see outright copies of other artists' work on stage. Copying a work of art opens up a new set of challenges. The designer will have to determine if the work must be reformatted to fit into the design. Also, there are amazing variations in the quality of color reproductions in secondary sources. In the case of *Sunday in the Park with George*, the designer was

obliged to send to the Art Institute in Chicago for a color-correct print. Because one of the main themes of the production was Georges Seurat's preoccupation with color, it was inconceivable that the designer and the scenic artist should reference anything other than an accurate reproduction of that painting.

Another consideration in copying a work of art is that often the overall impression of a work of art is different from the real thing. Many people are surprised and occasionally a little disappointed when viewing a famous work of art for the first time. The *Mona Lisa* may seem surprisingly small and dark when viewed in the Louvre for the first time. Ultimately, the scenic artist may need to do some interpretation to adapt the reproduction of a work for stage. What is the vision that motivated the designer or director to select this image? What is the context of this viewing? The concept behind the selection of a particular piece will be revealing.

As the designer for a restaging of Diaghilev's *L'Après-Midi d'Une Faune*, I had to reconstruct the design by Leon Bakst. In reproducing the original backdrop, I was struck by the tremendous variations available in book reproductions. Which one was correct? The key to reproducing the drop was first to choose the version that best represented the vision I had of the music. Then I worked a palette of colors from several different versions that appeared to harmonize with each other. I used palettes from different versions because the printing qualities varied from book to book. Some versions had beautiful, subtle greens where others turned the greens to brown. The versions with the good green tones rendered the background nearly black, others had it rather bright blue. Finally, the description of Leon Bakst's work in Polunin's *The Continental Method of Scene Painting* (pp. 37–82) led me to understand the spirit of the work I had undertaken.

Understanding the Limitations of a Paint Elevation

A scenic artist should be aware that scenic designers use shorthand in making paint elevations, and some details or portions of the built scenery may not be included. Keep in mind some simple facts:

- The scenic designer's elevations usually must describe three-dimensional units in two dimensions, which could mean that something is not shown. Think very carefully about all

Figure 2.15 A sample of design borrowing from a known style. Painting in the style of Fragonard, scenic painting by Susan Crabtree. *The Dialogue of the Carmelites*, scenic design by Francesca Callow, University of Michigan.

surfaces when beginning to paint three-dimensional scenery.

- The elevation may overlook corners or reveals, the areas within openings and under overhangs. The scenic artist will have to decide or ask the designer what to do around the corners of a unit.

- A scenic unit rendered in the scenic designer's elevation may be a different size from the final built shape. Scenic units may change in size during the process from drawing board to the stage for a variety of plausible reasons. Drop sizes can change subtly, so be very observant of the actual item to be painted.

- The change in media from high-quality artists' color on paper to scene paint on the real scenery can present problems. The paint elevation often is done on smooth illustration board. It may not reflect the actual texture of the surface on which the scenery is to be painted or how the scene paint will behave.

- The change in texture from the elevation or model to the scenery can have a tremendous effect. Paint will react very differently from one material to another. The scenic designer has the freedom to work on a smooth surface. The scenic artist, however, needs to get the same effect from multiple surfaces with varying textures. The scenic artist should pay close attention from the beginning to how the units of scenery are built and particularly to what materials are being used. In some cases, the scenic artist can have an influence on how the scenery is built and how surfaces are treated. Careful attention to construction techniques will save the scenic artist from having to deal with materials that will not accept paint evenly.

- Repeating patterns, wallpaper patterns, molding, bricks, and lettering may not register the same on the scenery as in the elevations. The smallest change in the dimension of the pattern or the scenery may throw off the repetitions.

Also, the designer may have simply painted a section of a repeating pattern in the paint elevation and then noted that it should continue. However, when the pattern turns a corner or descends a stairwell, it may not make sense. It may be up to the scenic artist to make the necessary adjustments so that the placement of the pattern looks logical. The scenic artist should be certain of the registration, or alignment, of a pattern on the scenery in its entirety before paint is applied.

WORKING WITH THE SCENIC DESIGNER IN THE SHOP AND ON STAGE

As a production enters the painting phase, collaboration and communication with the scenic designer are essential. Most scenic artists prefer to have the scenic designer in the paint shop as much as possible for feedback in a timely manner, to ensure that the painting is as the scenic designer had envisioned. Before backdrops are folded and scenic units are stacked and stored away, it is best that the scenic designer has a chance to approve the scenic artistry. As the set moves into the theatre, the scenic artist and the scenic designer will collaborate on fine-tuning the painting of the design.

Communicating with the Scenic Designer During the Painting Process

Having the scenic designer on-site is a great luxury for the scenic artist. Generally, the designer will visit the paint shop every day while the set is in production to keep track of the progress or even, if in a nonunion

Figure 2.16 Scenic designer Alan Veas (at right) in conference with a scenic artist at Scenic Art Studios, New York.

shop, pick up a brush and paint. In some cases, the designer simply will want to perform as one of the paint crew, asking the charge painter what he or she wants the designer to do. In other cases, the designer will volunteer to paint a particular unit such as a portrait or a particularly complex piece of scenery. It is preferable in almost all cases to have the scenic designer as close at hand as possible to monitor the progress.

When the scenic designer is out of town while the design is in the paint shop, the designer and the scenic artist should check in with one another at least once every business day. This serves two purposes. For one, it gives the scenic artist a chance to ask the designer questions that arise on a day-to-day basis concerning the painting of the production. Daily check-ins also help keep the designer up-to-date on the progress of the production. The scenic designer therefore must inform the scenic artist of where he or she can be reached on any given day. It may be best to have a preset time of day to check in by phone. The alternative, trying to find a designer who is shopping or in a rehearsal, can be difficult.

Often, the assistant scenic designer serves as the principal conduit between the scenic artist and the designer. The assistant scenic designer can be responsible for making decisions in place of the scenic designer. Most top professional American designers are far too busy to be able to visit every shop where every one of their productions is being painted, so they rely heavily on their assistant or associate designers. The final approval of the scenery is still going to be made by the scenic designer, so there may be changes at the end of the painting or in the theatre.

Just because the separate units of scenery are painted does not necessarily mean the painting has been completed. As the set pieces near completion, the scenic designer or scenic artist (or both) should take time to study the paint elevations or model and look at the scenery in the context of the whole design. Do the set pieces join together visually in an appropriate way? Does the painting technique flow well through one scene and from one scene to another? If changes or additional painting are anticipated, this is the time to do it, not when the set has already been delivered to the theatre.

Finally, the set is delivered and set up on stage, more or less finished. Some touch-up painting will have to be done at this time and a list of notes from the scenic designer may include repainting or adjusting some pieces. Bear in mind that some of these notes

Figure 2.17   Scenic designer Tony Walton (left) at Scenic Art Studios, New York.

may come from the producer, director, costume designer, or lighting designer and are filtered through the scenic designer. For this reason, it is a very good idea for the scenic artist to go to the theatre and examine the set under rehearsal conditions. How can a scenic designer's note truly explain the contrast problem between a gray suit and a gray drop? As a scenic artist, your insight into color may provide the objective eye that a scenic designer needs to decide what to do. Thus the scenic artist can make a significant contribution to a production even after the scenery has left the paint shop.

Finishing Work on Stage

The final phase of finishing a set is a very important time for the designer. As the load-in date looms closer, time will be very tight, particularly if an off-site designer has not had the opportunity to see all elements of the set until it is on stage. Once all the elements are assembled and seen under stage light, the designer may request that some additional work is done to "gel" it together.

This work is done at the scenic artist's *touch-up* on stage. The touch-up is scheduled after the scenery has been fully unloaded on stage and assembled, usually after the stage carpenters have completed most of their work and the scenic designer has had a chance to see the set under stage lights. Ideally, the touch-up should be scheduled at a time when the work lights can be on and the stage is relatively quiet. All too often, this is not the case. Stage time during the technical rehearsal week is very precious. The scenic artist and designer often have to share the stage with the properties department, stage carpenters, electricians, the lighting designer, and sometimes the performers.

Most of the notes that the scenic designer will give to the scenic artist are very standard: "Paint the edge of the flat that is still raw wood." "Spray the wrinkles out of the drops." "There are bolt heads visible on the step facings." Some designers do not even give obvious notes such as these, assuming that the scenic artist will see the problems and take care of them as a matter of course. The notes that the designer is apt to be the most concerned with are those involving the aesthetics of the design. These notes may be more along the lines of, "The distant landscape of the ground row is too sharp. Could you spray it down with some blue gray so that it is more atmospheric?" or "The rocks are flattening out. Work more highlights and shadows into them."

Planning and Doing the Touch-Up

It is time to start planning the touch-up when the painting of the set nears completion. If the paint shop and the performance space are in separate facilities, this usually begins with the charge painter conferring

Figure 2.18 *Fiorello* city drop, designed by Michael Anania, Pittsburgh Civic Light Opera.

with shop assistants about what paints, tools, and materials will be needed in the touch-up kit (we'll discuss the touch-up kit in Chapter 4). The color and paint most integral to the painting on the scenery will need to be included in the touch-up kit. For instance, if the majority of the set is painted with a wood grain technique, then these paints and finishes will need to be included in the kit. If there are three major elements in the set—a house, a deck, and a garden wall—then the primary colors used in these set pieces should be stored after the painting for touch-ups. In some cases, specialized colors that combine color and finish in one bucket may need to be mixed for catching edges and scratches on the scenery. If the designer has seen the set under stage lights and given a list of notes to the charge painter the day before touch-up, then some specific paint and materials may be packed for dealing with certain notes. For instance, the designer may have asked that a sign be painted on the side of a building. If this note is given in time, the charge painter may have been able to prepare a pounced pattern (a perforated drawing) ahead of time.

During the touch-up, the charge painter will assign notes to the members of the scenic art staff. The scenic designer usually is present during the touch-up and even though his or her energy may be divided between many different departments and individuals, the designer will be available for consultation. At some point, either right at the beginning of touch-up or at a technical rehearsal the day before the touch-up, the charge painter should meet with the designer and go through the list of notes together to ensure the charge painter completely understands the designer's notes.

Changes in the Theatre

Typically, changes in the theatre are minor, but occasionally the notes that are given for touch-up include major changes, rather than finessing and fine-tuning. Extra units of scenery may be added at the last minute, or the color of the entire set may need to be changed. A simple note to tone down all the walls of the set can result in hours of work on ladders or scaffolding. On the set of a production of *Fool for Love*, I was given a note that the actress would be thrown against the walls of the set repeatedly and the texture of the walls was too abrasive. Of course, this could have been avoided in the beginning, but sometimes mistakes occur in the design process and the obvious is overlooked. The entire set had to be given a smooth texture skim-coat, after which the walls had to be repainted and aged down again. The stage schedule had to be adjusted to accommodate this change. The charge painter may have to adjust the touch-up schedule and possibly the paint schedule of the next production to accommodate major changes. This may involve scheduling an additional touch-up, hiring extra crew members, bringing a piece of scenery back to the shop for repainting, or building and painting additional pieces of scenery to be sent to the theatre as soon as possible. At this stage in the production schedule, such changes are problematic. When asked to do major changes in such a tight time frame, the charge painter should consider realistically how the change can be done. If more time in the schedule, overtime, or extra crew members are needed, then the charge painter should make sure that these needs are clearly stated to everyone concerned.

If the scenic designer has requested a major change in the painting of the set after it has gone to the theatre, then it must be very important to him or her, the director, and the management or it would not be requested. However, the scenic art staff must not be expected to carry out this work without more time, personnel, or compensation.

EXTRAORDINARY CHALLENGES FOR THE SCENIC ARTIST

The so-called bottom line during the production process is that scenery must be built and painted on time so technical rehearsals may take place and a show can open as planned. Neither the scenic artist nor the scenic designer has the authority to alter this deadline, unless that person also serves as producer. This may place extraordinary pressure on a scenic artist for several reasons. As said before, the scenic artist usually is the last one to work on scenery before a load-in, which means the scenic artist will be particularly vulnerable to delays in the design or construction process. The scenic designer may not have presented the paint shop with enough information or provided it when it is needed. Perhaps construction started late because of poor management or problems on a previous production. A scenic designer may want to make substantial changes in the painting, whereas the producers and technical director are pressuring the scenic arts staff to finish the set and move on to the next production. Part of being a professional scenic artist is learning how to balance the needs and demands of the scenic designer with the reality of the production schedule and resources.

Late Design and Lack of Design Information

The scenic artist needs to know the entire scope of a project before time and costs can be planned. Frequently, a design is priced out and approved, based on the bluelines and a color model. Then, later in the production schedule, the scenic designer may be late in submitting paint elevations or may omit information that the scenic artist needs to stay on schedule. When this happens, it frequently is because the designer is overextended. Often the scenic artist can readjust the schedule after getting assurances from the designer that a necessary piece of information or paint elevation will arrive by a given hour on a given day. If the problems with late work continue, the scenic artist should alert the production management so the problems can be resolved. It should not be the responsibility of the scenic artist to police the designer.

Tinkering

Occasionally, the scenic designer will be insecure or unhappy with the design after seeing it on stage. One of the easiest ways to change a design once it is on stage is to resort to paint. So, in the course of the touch-up notes, the designer will give the scenic artist notes designed to solve these problems. However, if, once these notes are done and the official touch-up day has come and gone, the designer continues to give the scenic artist complex notes contrived to solve design issues, it can be problematic for several reasons. The prolonged touch-up may cut into the production schedule of the next production. If the production comes at the end of a season or is on a single contract, the scenic artist will have committed to letting the paint staff go by a certain day, usually the day after touch-up. So the scenic artist may not have adequate staff to take care of the extra notes. If this is the case, then the scenic artist may need to inform the production management of the problems. If the designer can talk over his or her concerns with the production manager, artistic director, director, or producer, perhaps these concerns can be addressed without belaboring the touch-up.

Replacement of a Scenic Designer

In very rare situations, a scenic designer who has failed to perform to the producer's satisfaction may be let go. This situation will have an impact on every department. The scenic art department, being the last to deal with the scenery, will be set behind the most. When the designer is let go, one of two things may happen. If it is early enough in the process, the producers may decide to hire another designer to submit a design or complete the design in progress. If the dismissal is too close to the opening, the producers may ask a member of the production staff to serve as designer and usher the original design to completion. The scenic artist is an obvious choice to replace the designer because the scenic artist is one of the people best equipped to understand what the design is to look like, based on the preliminary information. However, if this extra responsibility falls to the scenic artist, extra compensation must be made. Having to make the final decisions in the design process is a great responsibility and cannot be shouldered lightly.

CONCLUSION

The scenic designer always will benefit from a healthy collaborative relationship with the scenic artist and vice versa. This is true throughout the entire production and rehearsal process. The scenic artist's role may seem less important after the set leaves the shop, but the scenic artist's intimate knowledge of the technique and color of the painting can prove to be a tremendous asset to the production. The scenic designer sat in a studio choosing chrome green over emerald green for some oddball bounce-light color. Since that time, perhaps no one person could ever begin to realize the unique aesthetic qualities of that set nearly as well as the scenic artist. He or she knows every detail of the set's surface, because this person actually made the image appear. The scenic artist knows how much ultramarine blue really is in that gray color everyone else is upset about—and probably just how to fix it. No other person in the entire production staff actually emulated the designer's hand at work to such a degree. The scenic artist needs to be an extension of the artist that is the scenic designer.

INTERVIEW WITH JOSEPH FORBES, PRESIDENT OF SCENIC ART STUDIOS

Joseph Forbes is the President of Scenic Art Studios located in Cornwall, New York and serving the

New York metropolitan region. He has been a member of the New York City professional theatre for decades as a scenic artist and has painted for virtually every prominent American designer. He has also worked with many great scenic artists of the 20th and 21st centuries.

Susan Crabtree: Tell me a little about your shop and your position.

Joseph Forbes: I am President of Scenic Art Studios. We have been in business for eight years, and our primary market is Broadway musicals. We are the only independent paint studio left in New York and are the inheritors of the old Nolan's Scenery Studios crowd. All the old artists that used to work there work for me now. I came through Nolan's myself—I started there my first day in the business. We have shops located in New York and Connecticut.

SC: How many people do you have working for you on a regular basis?

JF: It varies wildly. I would say we never get below 10 and we go as high as 50. On average it's between 10 and 20.

SC: How many different facilities do you have?

JF: At least two all the time, but when the busy season hits, which we are in right now, we have at least four. It's sort of a unique managerial problem because I am the only one playing this way—everyone else is in a building and can look out a window and keep track. I have to rely more on the people that I hire to take a greater management role and to be self-reliant and self-sufficient.

SC: How is your crew structured so that you don't have to have your hand in every single thing?

JF: I try to put a good charge artist in each facility—someone who is good at organizational issues, who can deal with the carpenters and the welders without creating a lot of tension and can also deal with the designers, keeping them happy and answering their questions. And then I combine that with an artist who just paints beautiful scenery. I don't ask that person to be the politician because for some reason they seldom are the same person. So I basically put one good organizational person and one strong artist together and then fill in from there.

SC: Do you also have lead painters?

JF: The Union has two rates: charge artists and journey artists. I have sort of created a lead artist rate and I pay them charge rate for two or three days of the week so that they are getting a little extra money and recognition.

SC: Do you have shop assistants?

JF: Yes, we have two full-time and then we hire more as we need them. The shop assistants take care of the logistics. They take care of the ordering and the trucking and getting the drops up and down off the floors. The shop assistants we have now, Tommy and Michelle, are both certified flame retarders so they take care of the flame retardant issues and go down to the theatre and flame retard if there is a call for that. The charge artists are the ones who manage the crew.

SC: How long have you been a scenic artist?

JF: Probably 25 years now. I started as a designer and went into scene painting to make money and to support my design habits. It got to the point that I was making so much more money as a scenic artist. Being a professional designer, especially in New York, you're looking at years of being somebody's assistant and doing the drafting and the ugly work before you even get a shot at a Broadway show, unless you are from Yale and are well connected, which I wasn't. It just became economically not feasible for me to keep on designing. I still hold out that thought that someday, someway, somehow I'll find enough time that I can go back and design things because that was really my first love. I've never been driven to be a scenic artist. I didn't come out of school thinking it was my life's ambition. My whole career has been the path of least resistance. Whatever door opened, whatever opportunity presented itself, I took it and that one thing has just led to another. Probably not the best way to organize your life, but there you go.

SC: So would you say in the area of scenic artistry you have any specialties?

JF: I think I have a very good eye. I think I understand what designers want very well. That's what I seem to get the most compliments on. I can interpret what a designer is saying and what a designer is telling me from his renderings and accurately give that to him. I am very good at looking at a drop and seeing if it's right or if it needs to be pushed somewhere or whether the perspective is a little bit off. I would say those are my strengths.

SC: What was your education?

JF: I have a BFA in Scene Design from the University of North Carolina at Greensboro. I studied under Andres Nomacos, then I spent two years at Lester Polokov's studio in New York. That was a fabulous experience for me. I opened the place up and closed it down at the end of the day and in return I got my classes for free. It was a really intense, seven-days-a-week kind of learning situation. It was a fabulous school. There is really no place like it. I am sorry that

Figure 2.19 Painting *A Christmas Carol* at Scenic Art Studios.

it doesn't exist anymore because you were learning from the best people in the business. You were learning from the people who were in your textbooks—they were your teachers. It was really a fabulous education and because I was there answering the phones, there was a constant call for work for artists for designing little off-Broadway shows so I sort of became a clearinghouse for nonunion off-Broadway work and could supplement my income and keep my friends employed. It was a great lifestyle.

Getting in the Union [Untied Scenic Artists] was almost a letdown because I had to give up all the fun I was having. I took the exam and passed it the first time, which was sort of unheard of, and I was fully expecting to not pass it. When I passed I was really unprepared for it. I had to borrow the money for my initiation fee from my parents because I just wasn't ready; and then I joined the union and got thrown into Nolan's the very first day. I went on to spend my

first six years in the business at Nolan's. The time at Nolan's gave me what I needed to be able to do what I do now. I learned how to paint drops correctly, to know how to hire.

SC: What were some of the most important lessons you learned from your mentors?

JF: Hard work is more important than talent. I had certain skills and I could draw but I have never had a *strong* arts background. I didn't take art. I remember when I first came to Lester's, I cheated and went back and looked in the notes he had taken when he interviewed me to see what he had written about me, and he had written nothing—"Needs absolutely everything." That was pretty much the case but I was truly motivated to work hard and really threw myself into it and I think that is what I came away with more than anything else. Hard work and dedication to it will take you a lot farther than having a lot of talent and not really pressing it. Does that make sense?

Figure 2.20 Large sculpture projects like this piece for *Aladdin* are part of the work at Scenic Art Studios.

SC: Absolutely, because that is the way I feel. I never felt that I was brilliant but I have done it so much and love to do it and keep doing it and in spite of everything you get better.

JF: You do. I turn around now to the scenics and ask, "When did we become the old masters?" because now people come and ask us questions like we have all the answers, and I don't remember anyone saying "Congratulations, you are now one of the old masters."

SC: You did, obviously, have training as a designer. How do you think this has enhanced your skills as a scenic artist?

JF: Because of my design training, I can look at the larger issues beyond just scene painting. When I have a show on my floor, I really function as one of the designer's assistants. I can catch carpentry errors, I can catch errors from other departments that really have nothing to do with scene painting and resolve

those issues before they ever become a problem. That has been a big help. In this wild and crazy career of mine I have also worked as an IA [International Association of Theatrical Stage Employees, IATSE] carpenter when I first got out of school with National Scenery Studios for two years. So I have a basis for construction and how things should be built and what is correct and what isn't. The ability to look at the whole package and see issues beyond just the painting issues—that's part of why designers have a comfort level with me, because they know that I will look out for their interests in other areas and make sure that problems don't become problems.

SC: Do you have a formula for dealing with designers or is it different for every designer as far as making sure that you truly understand what they are after?

JF: It really varies with every designer because you really have to take them as individuals and know where they are coming from. With Tony Walton,

I have such a level of communication with him and he is such a wonderful man to work with that what he gives you is to a large degree what he wants. With other designers, what they give you is not really what they want and so you have to tread that fine line and get them to tell you, "Feel free to embellish on this or correct this." It's really just being a good listener and taking time to let them communicate their ideas.

SC: What type of training do you think a scenic artist should have?

JF: I would think any kind of art background but particularly a classical art background. We get far too many artists in here that come out of modern art programs and can spend days telling you how much emotional effort they put into something but do they understand perspective? Do they know the orders of architecture? Those are the kinds of things that don't get stressed in a typical art school education these days and that is really what a scenic artist has to have because so much of what we do is based in the classics.

My standard recommendation is to find a summer stock company that has a good designer who knows how to paint, who relies on paint, that you can go out and in one season paint 15 to 20 drops. I still can't think of a better way to learn it fast. There are a couple of schools that emphasize scene painting, not academic schools but private professional schools such as Cobalt and the Studio for Scene Painting and Design. I end up interviewing a lot of people who say "How do I get into this business?" and that is where I generally start. These are the schools where you can learn, these are they venues where you can go out and work.

So much of learning this job is going out and establishing contacts in the business. I don't really know of any "academic" programs that teach this. I'm not saying that going to college and getting a degree isn't important because I think liberal arts training helps you to develop as an artist. However, I don't think that there is an academic program that will teach you to be a scenic artist per se. I think it is almost a two-step process. I tell people who have been through art schools who have never worked in the business that they are looking at five to seven years more to become a scenic artist. Of doing summer stock, working nonunion, taking classes at night at someplace that teaches scene painting, finding a good scene painting studio where they can learn from people. I also find that most scenic artists want to pass on what they know. I think that we are all aware that we hang on to a lot of arcane knowledge

that is hard to find and so there is a conscious effort to pass it on to people so that it doesn't die.

SC: Do you have any words of wisdom for up-and-coming scenic artists?

JF: Learn from the best. Go work with the best. Come to New York or go to LA. Go someplace where the best are doing the best and learn in that situation, and then once you learned something, if you want to go back and settle in Ohio and think regional theatre, that's great. You'll know what you are doing. I have a problem with academic theatre and what they teach. I graduated from the University of North Carolina and it was a huge shock for me to come to New York and realize that I spent four years learning nothing. I had learned a lot but I didn't know anything about professional theatre and what it really meant to be a scene designer or a scenic artist and I was really starting from scratch. I would say learn from the best because this is a wide-open business. If you are going to school, apply to Yale or NYU— why not? It's not all about grades, there are a lot of intangibles when you start talking about theatre arts and design and scene painting. It's who you are, how motivated you are, and what potential they see in you a lot of times.

My other piece of advice is to find a mentor. I really mark my growth as an artist to two or three individuals who saw something in me and decided invest their time in me and change me. Two or three years down the road I was a different person and I think that the number of mentors that you have in your life determines how far you go and how good you become.

SC: And who were your mentors?

JF: Andres Nomacos at the University of North Carolina was a brilliant artist and a brilliant designer and a very well educated man. Lester Polacoff was certainly a big influence on me. Fred Jacoby at Nolan's. When I started to work at Nolan's he was 70 years old and for some reason he took a liking to me and would tell me tales and show me processes. When he finally retired at 78, he handed me his Russian boar-bristle brush that had one purpose in life, which was to create damask wallpaper, and he gave it to me and said, "I want you to have this because they don't know how to use this here and it will just get destroyed, so you keep it." I still cherish it, and of course the first thing I did was go out and design a show with damask wallpaper so I could use it. Those have been the three people who have helped me most in my scene painting career.

Figure 2.21   Finished scenic units for *Thoroughly Modern Millie* at Scenic Art Studios.

SC: Looking back over your career, what would you say were some of the most difficult or elusive skills for you to learn in the profession of scenic artistry?
JF: Certainly in the area of painting, figure drawing and portraits have always been and still are my weakest suit. That's one of the great things about being a scenic artist—you never master it all, there is always that something that will continue to push you until the day you die. For me that's it, that's always been my biggest fear that someone will ask me to paint a portrait.

It's also really tough to live up to the expectations of the designers. A lot of designers I have such strong relationships with. I'll use Tony Walton as an example. Tony brings so much love to what he does that you can't help but fall in love with him to a certain degree. He is like a father figure to you and the

last thing you want to do is disappoint him. He is the only designer in my professional career that has brought me to tears. He doesn't know that but it's true because I just couldn't do what he wanted me to do and I sensed his disappointment and it just crushed me. That is the biggest fear—trying to live up to expectations, particularly now that we have a reputation of being so good. Designers that I haven't worked with come in the door expecting miracles. Sometimes we succeed and quite honestly sometimes we don't, and that is the most difficult thing for me.
SC: What do you think are some of the most common misconceptions throughout the profession of scenic artistry?
JF: One is that anyone can come in and do this. You get a lot of artists that come from other backgrounds that walk on the floor and say, "Oh, I can do this"

and they are shocked that they don't find immediate acceptance or employment. That there really is an entire book of knowledge that is very specific to what we do and you can't just walk off the street and just do it. You may have all the talent in the world, you may be a brilliant artist, but if you've never starched and floated a drop, you don't know what that is. That's what I tell people. There is a lot more to this than what you see and if you want to become a scenic artist, just learning the techniques and the processes specific to what we do takes a tremendous amount of time.

SC: Do you feel that there are techniques, skills, or aspects of the training in scenic artistry that people are no longer getting exposed to?

JF: Absolutely. I think we've already lost a vast amount of knowledge from just the previous generation and a lot of it is in the change in style and how designers are trained. A lot of the designers coming out of school now don't paint. They are taught to make models and they work in AutoCAD and they use the Xerox copier and they find an image in a book, blow it up, and cut and paste it and hand it to you and that's the drop. The whole "old school" scene painting style is being lost. There are very few places where you still get it. When we get a show that is truly a painter's show, it's a great treat for us. When we have real paint elevations from designers that still paint in the old style, to me that's what it's all about. I don't go to the theatre to see vacuform bricks. Show me a backdrop and get excited, my heart beats faster. To me that's the magic of it.

Also, the amount of work that we have now is so small compared to what it used to be, so we're not training the next generation. When I started at Nolan's 20 years ago, I was never higher than sixth or seventh man hired in terms of the pecking order and I had a full-time job. Now I have trouble keeping two or three lead artists employed full time. There's just not the volume of work and so we're not training the next generation of people. I can't tell you how many times I've had a talented young scenic artist work for me for a couple of months and I see that here is someone 10 years down the road who could be a lead artist and I run out of work, have to lay him off, and they end up in movies and I never see

them again. It's a little discouraging how the number of people who know how to do this is getting smaller.

SC: Tell me how you see the skills of the scenic artist evolving in the next decade or so.

JF: Certainly a couple of my artists are now highly computer literate. We will take designers' renderings and put them on a computer and clean up the graphics and images. Sometimes we will go ahead and have the entire pounce printed on a computer and save all that labor. As time goes by and technology improves, that's a trend that is going to continue. I don't think we're all going to lose our jobs to the computer, but I think that our jobs will become much more computer oriented. Whether or not they will come up with a printing process that can look like the human hand, I'm not sure. I haven't seen it yet. And that's good. I'm glad they haven't found a way to do that yet but I'm sure they will before we're done. It's really just finding applications and using the computer application that saves labor and saves time. I think that will only grow.

SC: Tell me what you enjoy about scenic artistry. What keeps you at it?

JF: It's always been about doing theater and the fact that it's such a collaborative process and you have to work with so many different people and different disciplines. I started out acting and realized I wasn't going to make any money there so I started designing lights, then I built scenery, then I designed scenery. But it has always been about making theatre for me. The only downside to doing what I do now is I miss going into the theatre. I miss standing backstage and actually watching it happen. I think that's the only thing that I miss. I love it when I get called down to the theatre. I love it when I have to sit out in the house with the tech table and discuss problems with the designer—for me that's the best moment of all.

SC: Anything else you want to add?

JF: I'd just say to people trying to get into this business that you have to really want it. You have to chase it. You can't take no for an answer. You have to be able to deal with failure and hard times, but that's part of the charm of it. Being a starving artist and just going out and doing theatre and working with people, that's really what it's all about.

Chapter 3

The Scenic Artist and the Scenic Studio

Many scenic artists work in scenic studios. You find scenic studios on college campuses, as parts of theatres, and in outlying districts of major cities around the world. They vary greatly in terms of quality and facilities and come in many forms and sizes depending on such factors as who or what the studio serves, whether it is union-affiliated, and whether it is part of a theatre complex that determines the characteristics of the studio. However, scenic studios are not the only locations where scenic artists work. For example, a "studio" can be almost anything for scenic artists involved in movie production.

The scenic artist is just one of many employees in a scenic studio—successful shops are made up of many talented craftspeople whose dedication to and enjoyment of the unusual demands of theatre is evident. Scenic studios are therefore often interesting and rewarding workplaces—the work itself is always changing and presents constant challenges to the artisans. Few days seem just like the last. In the next section, we'll discuss the types of scenic studios in which scenic artists might work.

TYPES OF SCENIC STUDIOS

There are many different kinds of scenic studios in the United States. Some are commercial scenic studios that are well outfitted and work year-round. These studios have permanent staff members in all fields (carpentry, metal fabrication, scenic art, and so on) and supplement this staff with additional specialists as needed. Other studios are associated with for-profit or nonprofit theatres and their working season reflects the production needs of their theatre. Some scenic studios come to life seasonally, sprouting up in the summer, occupying pole barns or other alternative spaces. Some shops are assembled for just one or two productions and may have a staff of 3 or 70. What all these studios have in common is that they employ scenic artists. The most common types of scenic studios in the United States are as follows:

1. *College or University-Affiliated Scenic Studios.* These scenic shops are usually noncommercial. In some shops, professional scenic artists are hired on a permanent, seasonal, or temporary basis. These scenic artists generally work with student assistants. Professional scenic artists in these shops may also teach classes or seminars in scenic art. In other university-level scenic studios, scenic artists are drawn from students studying for a degree in technical theatre or theatrical design. These shops are rarely represented by production unions (International Alliance of Theatrical Stage Employees, IATSE, or United Scenic Artists, USA). However, individual employees of these shops may be in a union.

2. *Semiprofessional Theatre Scenic Studios.* These studios often support small theatres, which may

Figure 3.1
Painting for the Feld Ballet at Michael Hagen, Inc.

be commercial or nonprofit and may employ one nonunion artist if at all, chiefly to paint and possibly work on other tasks. Volunteers, interns, and the scenic designer may all take part in the painting process in these studios, which may be active for only part of the year.

3. *Professional Theatre Scenic Studios.* These studios serve commercial or nonprofit professional theatrical associations, regional theatres, or civic theatres and may have a contract with IATSE or USA, or hire USA scenic artists on individual contracts. They may employ one or several scenic artists full-time or on a seasonal basis. The painting staff may be augmented with temporary overhire or by the relocation of existing staff members from other areas.

4. *Independent, Professional, Commercial Studios.* These large for-profit commercial scenic studios may be either union or nonunion. If the studio does not have a union contract but uses USA artists regularly, USA may approach it to sign a blanket contract. The construction staff in these studios usually is covered by an IATSE contract. Union shops have carefully regulated wage scales based on union standards and make contributions to the union health and welfare plans. Nonunion shops may have similar wage scales and company benefits, but the grievance process and benefit plans available to employees of a studio under a union contract will not be available to them. Commercial studios can be of any size; some of the largest scenic studios in the United States are independent commercial studios that build and/or paint for a variety of clients including the theatre, industrial displays and presentations, industrial film, commercial film, and television.

These shops work primarily on a contractual basis with individual clients.

5. *Film and Television Scenic Studios.* Many of these studios operate in major media centers such as New York and Los Angeles. They are covered by IATSE or USA contracts depending on the location and whether the client is in television (usually USA) or film (usually IATSE). Some of these shops are mammoth year-round shops that serve the major networks or the film industry in Los Angeles and New York. Other shops may be year-round operations that work on a contractual basis with individual clients. Still other shops may be temporary or seasonal, serving as the production unit for a specific feature film or television series. The union affiliations of these temporary studios may be complex, but union presence is very strong in film and television.

It can be difficult to sort out the union affiliations of any given shop. A nonunion shop may be in the process of negotiating a union contract at the time you are offered a position or after you accept employment with them. Generally, if you are not a union member in the employ of a shop that is in the process of negotiating a blanket union contract, you will be asked whether you want to apply for your union card. In this case, the initiation fee may be waived. Many scenic artists have received their union card in circumstances such as this.

THE STAFF IN A SCENIC STUDIO

Scenic studios are intricate workplaces where diversely skilled people work towards a common goal. The artisans and craftspeople working in these shops are valued for their speed, skills, and artistic abilities. Because theatrical productions often work on compact time schedules overages and production changes do happen, and some artisans may have to work overtime to get caught up. Overtime is regulated in shops covered by a union contract, so union members are compensated for any time worked beyond an 8-hour day and a 40-hour week.

Scenic studios employ individuals to be department heads of specific areas of scenic fabrication and support. These departments must collaborate with one another since their responsibilities are frequently interdependent. The organization of individual

Figure 3.2 Cobalt Studios student Jessica Papazian mixing color. The elevation is visible as are a test flat and a hair dryer in a bucket.

effort, space, time, and finances is the key to a smoothly running shop, so there are individuals who serve as managers and liaisons among these departments and the designers. The primary individuals and departments involved in the fabrication of scenery for a theatrical production are as follows:

- *Production Management.* This department is responsible for setting and supervising the production budget and schedule.
- *Technical Director.* This person coordinates the efforts of the individual departments involved in the fabrication of the production set.
- *Construction Department.* This department builds the set and is managed by the construction shop manager, who is also called the head carpenter.
- *Paint Department.* This department is responsible for all the texture and paint treatments on the set and is managed by the charge painter.
- *Properties Department.* This department is responsible for the fabrication, acquisition, organization, and installation of all the hand properties and set dressings. This department is headed by the properties manager.

There are no rigid rules concerning the hierarchy of managers and individual departments in a theatrical production or their responsibilities. Frequently, one individual has two or more roles, particularly in smaller organizations. For example, the technical director may also be the production manager or the designer. One person may be responsible for building and painting the set. There are also many other individual positions and departments in a production company that, because they are removed from the fabrication of the scenery, have little or no direct impact on the scenic art department.

The Scenic Designer

The *scenic designer* is usually an outside contractor in professional scenic studios. Some studios and theatrical companies hire staff scenic designers; this may be the case in regional and university-affiliated theatre companies. Only very rarely is the scenic designer also in charge of a scenic studio. Usually this occurs only in small production companies, some university theatres, and when the scenic designer actually owns a scenic studio. In most shops, the scenic designer does not decide who, when, where, or how many people paint the design. That is the job of the charge painter, technical director, and production manager. But it is the responsibility of the scenic designer to provide the production company or scenic studio with all the information they need, on schedule, so that the design can be budgeted and executed according to the production's timetable.

The Production Manager and the Technical Director

The *production manager* is responsible for the entire organization of a theatrical production, from contracting to scheduling and from to final construction to shipping. Production managers are most common in large theatre organizations with multiple productions, contracts, or stages. Smaller theatres or independent commercial scenic studios may not have a production manager at all. When present, their role can change drastically from shop to shop. In large operations they manage the theatre production as a whole, including scheduling production meetings and communicating with producers, designers, directors, cast, and crew. In most organizations, the production manager assigns the overall budgets to the departments and supervises the budgetary flow of a production through the organization. Time management is a large factor in the operation and long-range planning of a scenic studio. Labor is generally the greatest cost. If problems arise, the production manager assists in troubleshooting and reallocating finances. However, it is up to the technical director and production shop heads to handle the details of day-to-day affairs.

In commercial scenic studios, the production manager may have an even larger responsibility, that of bidding on potential contracts. The production manager must manipulate the internal costs of the scenic fabrication while bidding against competitors. He or she may also be owner or part-owner of the scenic studio. Large-scale commercial scenic studios generally have a much narrower focus than a performance-oriented studio. A commercial studio generally deals only with the technical aspects of a production, working as a contractor or among the contractors to the performance company. The performance company may have its own production manager who consults with the scenic studio's management.

Production managers may or may not be specialists in construction. In both commercial and noncommercial studios, the production manager may be involved in the actual construction decisions, depending on that person's area of expertise. A production manager may be an expert in metal work or hydraulics and contribute to the planning and execution of scenery. However, it is extremely rare that the production manager actually works on a regular basis on the shop floor. The production manager's responsibilities always pull that person back to the phone or some crisis. The technical director and the production shop heads normally do the nuts-and-bolts decision making.

The *technical director* is primarily responsible for supervising the constructing and coordinating the schedule of painting the scenery with the charge painter. In smaller and noncommercial studios, the technical director also may oversee costumes and lighting. The technical director's primary functions are to control the financial aspects of construction, to draft or oversee the drafting of construction drawings for the construction staff, and to coordinate the three scenic departments: construction, art, and properties. Before a design is sent to the department heads, the technical director costs out the construction of the design for the production manager to determine its financial feasibility. In costing out a design, the technical director may only be concerned with construction, or he or she may be responsible for coordinating the cost of the design in other departments.

Figure 3.3 Scenic artist Jane Snow working on *Beauty and the Beast* at Scenic Art Studios, New York.

Once a design has been sent to the shops, the technical director supervises finances in the construction shop, and, in some cases, the paint and property shops as well. Financial control translates into two broad categories: money spent on materials and money spent on labor. The technical director's duty is to see that these two commodities are used efficiently and wisely in the departments. He or she is responsible for the production schedule in each department and for assisting these departments in coordinating their efforts. The space in which to build scenery is a third category of expense. The cost of the physical plant that houses the scene shop is frequently an ongoing expense that is factored into the budget by the accounting department or by the owner or directors of the company. However, it is sometimes necessary for the technical director to factor the expense of additional space needed to fabricate the scenery into the budget of a particularly ambitious production.

Scenic construction and scenic painting probably are the most closely interdependent shop areas because they both handle the same physical elements. The scenic artist cannot start work until some of the scenery is constructed. The need for cooperation is therefore paramount in these areas. The technical director must decide the most effective way for these two areas to assist each other. This may mean shifting labor resources to build the bulk of the scenery as early as possible, which would let scenic artists have as much time as possible to paint the scenery. This logical conclusion is not as easy as it sounds and requires careful planning.

Production Shop Heads

The six primary departments of theatrical production are costumes, lighting, paint, properties, scenery, and sound. An individual runs each of these shops. These are the costume shop manager, master electrician, charge painter, properties master, head carpenter, and sound supervisor or technician. Some areas may need to be further subdivided depending on the production. For example, armor, sculpture, drapery, special effects, and various other specialties may demand that another department be added, with its own staff and staff head. They may be attached to one of the six departments listed previously.

Shop managers spend a great deal of time organizing their own areas. However, they also are experts of their professions and are a significant part of the skilled labor in their department. The job of a shop manager is to decide how jobs are to be executed, in what order, where, and to assign staff members to the job. The shop head is responsible for keeping the shop on schedule and within budget. If there is a specific problem concerning the management of these areas, the shop head must ask the technical director or production manager for assistance in resolving the problem.

Paint, Props, and Scenery: A Team of Three Departments

Scenery production encompasses three departments: scenic art, scenic construction, and properties. These three areas are run by separate individuals who work toward the common goal of having high-quality scenery completed and installed by the first technical rehearsal. It is absolutely critical that these areas be well organized so that the scenery is finished in an efficient manner. The department heads for each of these areas (charge painter, properties manager, and head carpenter) work together to sort out day-to-day planning issues. The technical director is involved in many of the larger decisions among these three areas regarding questions of resource management. For example, the technical director must ensure that the paint department receives the soft goods for painting early in the construction process, when space is available in the paint shop. Early in the construction process, the technical director has the head carpenter build or contract the building of all the soft goods. The technical director, charge painter, and head carpenter then allot space and time for painting. The scenic artists can then work on the soft goods while the head carpenter and the construction staff can get started on the other scenery.

The Paint Department Staff

There is a formal structure to the staff within a paint area. USA has several distinct painter categories and pay scales for the types of positions they delineate. Beyond this classification system there are common-sense reasons to have one person in charge artistically and organizationally.

The Charge Painter or Charge Person

The working relationship between painters is fairly common to any shop where two or more painters work together. When painters work together, generally one single painter serves as a liaison between the painters and the designer, organizes the schedule with the technical director, and coordinates between all painters. USA calls this manager the *charge person*. If there is no one painter who is the organizational and artistic leader of the crew, the paint shop is apt to be chaotic and the scenery inconsistently painted.

The Lead Painter

The charge painter may assign a *lead painter* to be in charge of a particular aspect of a project. The scope of a project may be just too large for one person to supervise effectively, so the lead painter is given a portion of the project to supervise. For example, the charge painter may lead on all the soft goods, while the lead painter supervises the painting of the hard scenery. The lead painter may be the individual who paints all the foliage for a show or is in charge of all lettering. The lead painter may or may not be assigned assistants based on the production's needs. Several lead painters may work on a particular production or project, depending on the scope of the production and the skills needed. In a large studio, more than one production may be in the shop at one time. The charge painter may decide to assign a lead painter to those productions.

The Assistant Scenic Painter or Journey Person

Assistant scenic painters work directly with the charge and lead painters, doing much of the painting under the supervision of the charge and lead painters. USA calls a scenic artist at this level a *journey person*. The size of the paint crew depends on the size of the production in the studio. Some productions require a staff of only one or two people. Other productions may require a score of painters. The painters on a crew may have various skill levels, specialties, and experience. The charge painter coordinates and orchestrates the expertise of these individuals on the production.

Shop Assistants or Industrials

Shop assistants maintain the shop and function as a support system for the scenic artists. In a large paint shop, the tasks of preparing scenery to be painted, ordering stocks of paint and materials, running errands,

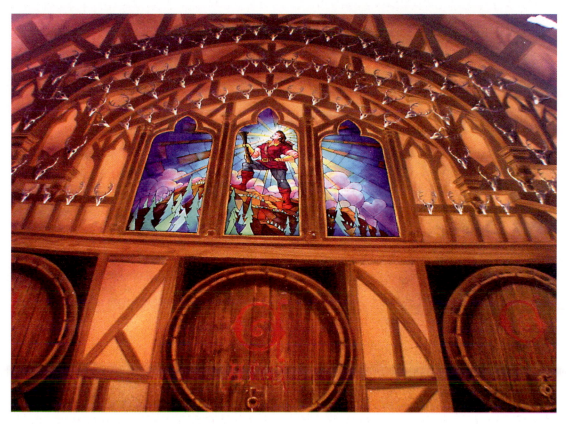

Figure 3.4   A backdrop with translucent windows for *Beauty and the Beast* painted at Scenic Art Studios, New York.

maintaining tools, and simply keeping the shop clean and organized can be immense. Shop assistants accomplish these duties so that the scenic artists can spend more time painting. In some shops, the shop assistant functions as a managerial assistant to the charge painter. In very large operations there may even need to be a shop manager to supervise the shop assistants. The position of shop assistant is a valuable one. Good shop assistants make a huge contribution to a smoothly running shop.

Apprentices or Interns

Apprentices serve as assistants on a production. Depending on their experience, they may work as painting assistants or as shop assistants under the journey person. Although apprentices are in the studio primarily to learn the trade of scenic artistry, this education involves a lot of hard work, and they are usually paid for their efforts. The charge painter and more experienced scenic artists in the shop work with the apprentices in the course of production to help them advance and improve their skills. Not all shops have apprenticeship or intern programs. In many situations, even though there is no formalized apprenticeship program, the more expert scenic artists are mindful of mentoring inexperienced members of the crew. USA guidelines are that there must be no more than one apprentice for every five journey persons.

PAINT DEPARTMENT MANAGEMENT

Management is a large part of the job of a charge painter. It requires constant attention and considerable skill. A charge painter can no more ignore the management part of work than walk away from a half-primed seamless drop to take a lunch break. A charge painter needs to do the following:

- Coordinate the scenic art departments' part in the sequence of construction with the technical director and production manager;

- Maintain adequate supplies of paint and other materials;
- Supervise the output of the crew of painters and shop assistants;
- Coordinate the interaction with other departments of the scenic shop that require paint or a painter;
- Budget all time, space, and personnel scheduling;
- Oversee all expenditures within the area; and
- Serve as a liaison between the scenic designer and the scene studio (see Chapter 2).

The job is even more complicated if a scenic artist is working as a freelance contractor and hiring assistants. Freelance scenic artists may be expected to be totally self-sufficient. Issues of budget, finance, painting space, and equipment become much more complex.

Planning Scenic Painting

The scenery should be finished by the date for load-in to the theatre. This means that by the load-in date, the drops should be in their bins, the flats should be stacked against the wall of the shop near the loading doors, the painted deck should be on a roll or sheet cart, and the touch-up kit should be packed up and ready to go. The reality of the expression "time is money" is obvious when a crew of stagehands is assembled to load in the set and the scenery is still scattered around the paint shop or a drop is still stapled to the paint deck. In most productions, no leniency can be shown to the paint shop concerning the load-in date. In one of the most out-of-control productions I was ever involved in, I saw scenery that had yet to be touched by the painters loaded on the truck. Nothing could be done—the truck was rented, the load-in crew had been called. The scenery had to be finished in the theatre at touch-up. The main factor in this debacle was that the charge painter had realized from the beginning that the production was over-designed and behind schedule. She had explained these circumstances to the production management, but her warnings had gone unheeded. Naturally, the hours we put in during the week before the set loaded in were extensive. This unfortunate situation cannot be laid at the feet of the designer either. She presented the shop with a design that had been approved by the director and production management. The design was sent straight into the shop without having been costed-out by the charge painter and the technical director.

Costing Out a Design

Fortunately, most production management personnel are not so shortsighted. Out-of-control productions can result in a small fortune being paid in overtime wages. Inadequate preparation of a production is the number one reason for emergency situations. In most productions, the technical director and the charge painter are asked to cost out the design before it is released to the shops. When costing out a design, the charge painter must consider three separate issues: time, materials, and space.

Costing out time involves totaling the projected figures for hours of work and comparing this figure with the available nonovertime hours of the charge painter, scenic artists, and shop assistants allotted in the schedule for the completion of the painting. If not enough work hours are available to paint the set, the production management must be alerted that overhire or overtime will be necessary.

The cost of materials is the total cost of paint, finishes, texture, consumables, kit fees, and rental of special equipment that are needed to paint the design. Also added to this figure should be a shop budget to cover the wear and tear on the shop equipment that has to be replaced and repaired on a regular basis.

Charge painter inexperienced in costing out a production should carefully match the square-foot coverage information listed in the directions on cans of paint and finishes with the square footage of the scenery. When costing out labor and materials, a contingency of 15 to 25 percent over the estimate should be added into both projected budgets to cover unforeseen expenditures.

Budgeting space is more involved. Painting scenery takes up a great deal of square footage. The amount of scenery that can be laid out at any one time in the space or that can occupy the paint frame, if there is one, is critical. No number of extra painters will help get the scenery painted any faster if there is not enough space for them in which to work. The amount of scenery that can be laid out at the same time and the length of time it will take to paint and dry must be projected into the time available. If this figure comes up short, more space will have to be rented, which will be an extra expense.

When budgeting time and materials on a design, the charge painter works with the designer and the production staff to determine whether the design is feasible. If limitations are discovered, it does not necessarily mean major cuts are needed or that a

Figure 3.5 A highly organic piece created at Showman Fabricators, Inc.

redesign is necessary. Many times, creative solutions are found that make the realization of a design possible. This is just another phase of collaboration.

Preproduction Planning

The charge painter normally begins to plan a project before any of the other paint staff are given their assignments. Initially, the charge painter studies the bluelines, paint elevations, and additional material from the scene designer, outlining the scope of scenic art on that production. The charge painter then talks with the scenic designer concerning questions he or she may have about the scenic art. This interview is instrumental in clarifying the designer's vision for the scenery (see Chapter 2).

The charge painter's next task is to evaluate the project for materials and labor needs as they fit into the schedule and the space available. The charge painter submits the paint budget to the technical director or production manager for approval. Once the budget is approved, the charge painter usually hires or designates shop assistants to begin preparing the scenery and placing orders for the paints, special materials, and equipment for the production. Commitments are then made to other members of the crew based on the projected schedule for the production. The charge painter does sample work needed at this point, and lead painters may be brought in to do samples and begin work on cartooning. The rest of the crew is hired or assigned as soon as the scenery is loaded into the paint shop and ready for painting.

Frequently, the startup for the paint crew at the beginning of a production or a repertory season is not as leisurely as this sounds. Only a few days may be available between the hiring of a charge painter and the first full day of painting. Skilled personnel

PROJECT: PIECE: BID DATE:				PRODUCER:
LABOR PLANNING/PRECONTRACT OBTAIN MATERIALS DRAWING PUT DOWN/SIZE TRANSF/INK PAINT MIXING BASE PRIME FINISH/DETAIL PICK UP/FLIP UNSTAPLE/FOLD/BOX SPECIAL CUT/NET TRANSLUCENCY STENCILS FLAME RETARD? CLEAN UP TOTAL HOURS $PER HOUR TOTAL$ RATES	CHARGE	SCENIC	SCENIC	**SUPPLIES** PAPER (FLOOR) PAPER (POUNCE) FABRIC MISC. SUPPLIES SIZE/STARCH PAINT SPECIAL COLOR FINISHES FLAME RETARD STENCILS SPEC. TOOLS LEAF GLUE **TOTAL SUPPLIES**
EXPENSES PHONE POSTAGE TRAVEL HOUSING PER DIEM SHIPPING FROM SUPPLIER SHIPPING TO CLIENT	DAYS DAYS DAYS			TOTAL LABOR EXPENSES SUPPLIES OVERHEAD/DAYS SUBTOTAL ADJUSTMENTS SALES TAX FIRST QUOTE BALLPARK **FINAL PRICE**
TOTAL EXPENSES				

The form of the Bid Worksheet used at Cobalt Studios. Each item is entered into a spreadsheet program that can be tailored to the needs of each job.

Figure 3.6   A bid sheet form used at Cobalt Studios.

Figure 3.7
The scenic shop at North Carolina School of the Arts. Rebecca Lancetot drawing a pounce for *The Sleeping Beauty,* designed by Raber Umphenour.

may be difficult to locate. The shop space may not be adequate for the scale of the production. The time frame already may be compressed. It is not uncommon for the charge painter to find they must resolve problems like these from the very start of a production. However, most producers and production companies are aware that committing to a charge painter and crew early and getting the design information to the charge painter long before the scenery comes into the paint shop are good business practices. Building and painting scenery in a crisis time frame simply makes the project more expensive and compromises the quality.

Preparing Paint and Tool Stock

The other aspect of planning that the charge painter should have well in hand early in the production process is the ordering of materials and supplies. This is an area where the charge painter should feel comfortable delegating responsibility. Many charge painters have a lead shop assistant that functions as the shop manager. It is not uncommon for the charge painter to delegate the ordering of materials and supplies, partly or entirely, to this person or one of lead painters on smaller crews. Some larger shops even have buyers or purchasing departments whose responsibility it is to order and procure all the materials the shops needs to function.

Materials Estimation

To organize the orders for a production, the charge painter must calculate the amount of materials needed. Many items are always kept in stock and replaced as needed, such as painting tools, scenic paint, and cleaning supplies. However, productions often need extra quantities of tools and materials. A large set may come through the shop that is painted entirely in sepia colors in a paint application that resembles pen and ink drawings. For this production, the charge painter must order extra quantities of umber and black paint as well as the lining and sash brushes to apply it with. Sets that are heavily textured almost always entail special orders. I once had to order so much drywall compound that it was delivered on a flatbed truck and loaded into the shop with a forklift. Once the materials are in the shop, they must be organized so that they are near the painting crew.

If all the scenery in the production is tied together visually by the same color palette, it makes sense to mix the colors for the entire production at the same time rather than piece by piece. To do this, the charge painter must be fairly sure of the coverage estimate for the design. However, because of the nature of scene painting, it is not always possible to anticipate how much of one color will be needed for a given process unless a unit is being completely covered and square footage recommendations can be relied on.

Miscalculations will happen and so paint swatches and recipes should be documented for remixing. With time, most scenic artists become fairly adept at predicting amounts.

If the set is heavily textured, it may be necessary to buy or rent special equipment to mix the quantities of texture. It may also be necessary to purchase containers to store the quantities or texture in. The mixing of the colors and textures in a production can be very time consuming. It can also be time consuming to procure the materials for painting and texturing and to mix the mediums. The charge painter must consider these issues when creating the schedule.

Preparing Materials Before Painting Begins

Prior to loading the scenery in the shop, the pounces, stencils, and templates may need to be prepped. Once the scenery is in the shop, the time it spends occupying the shop space may be at a premium. If these elements of cartooning and paint treatments are done before the scenery is loaded into the shop, the time the scenery is in the shop can be used more efficiently.

Whether the painters who initially painted the scenery will also be responsible for touch-up varies from shop to shop and from one production to another. Regardless of who is doing the touch-up, it is always a good idea to generate the touch-up kit as you go rather than running around the shop decanting the dregs of paint into small containers at the last minute. Many sets are designed so that they are painted with a tight color palette in specific processes. If some colors are meant to be used as glazes, they should be mixed in concentrate and instructions for thinning and swatches of the thinned glaze should be attached to the can. To avoid spoilage, a little disinfectant can be mixed into the touch-up paints. If the touch-up kit is generated early, it can also be used as a basis for matching and remixing colors.

Creating the Production Book

Constructed scenic designs are sometimes stored and used years later or sent to other performance companies on rental, and multiple copies of sets are sometimes produced for road shows. The charge painter may find that he or she is asked to paint additional pieces of scenery for a set being reused, or to recreate the paints and texture treatments on a piece of scenery that was damaged in storage or shipping. He or she may also be asked to repaint a copy of the set years after the first production using the scenery that initially left the shop. In circumstances such as these, the charge painter repainting the set may not have worked on the initial production. This is why keeping accurate production books are so important.

A *production book* is a log of the information pertinent to the painting, texture treatments, and sculpting that is done for a particular production. It includes the orders placed and copies of receipts, paints swatches, sample cards of paint treatments, photographs of the finished set and the scenic model, bluelines, and copies of the paint elevations. Many times much of the information found in a production book will have been turned into other departments or returned to the scenic designer, so care must be taken to made copies of documents and elevations before they are returned. In some paint shops it is more imperative to keep these records than others. For example, Hudson's Scene Studios in Yonkers, New York, has an entire loft area used for storing productions books, samples, and pounces because it must often replicate or repair scenery for the long-running productions and road shows it works on.

Balancing Time, Space, and Labor

At the beginning of the production, the charge painter must weigh the staff requirements against the time and space available for painting. If the design requires twelve $60' \times 27'$ drops, there will be very specific space demands to execute them. If two drops can be painted side by side, then two teams of scenic artists will need to be hired. If the space is limited to painting one drop at a time, then the time frame for the project will need to be longer and the staff relatively small. Working vertically or horizontally also may have an effect on the time frame of a project. If a paint frame is available to paint drops on while the hard scenery is being painted on the floor, the production may be able to move through the shop swiftly. All these factors help determine how many painters are needed for the project and the amount of time required for the job.

Before deciding on the number of people on the paint crew, the charge painter must look at the volume of scenery to be painted and determine whether it can be painted in the space available in the given amount of time. It is a great luxury to have such a vast amount of floor space in the paint shop that all the scenery for a production can be laid down at once. However, this is rarely the case. Usually, the charge painter must decide how much scenery can be laid out at a given time and in what configuration. Then, the charge painter can begin to plan out how many teams of scenic artists are necessary, how many scenic artists there should be on each team, and how long these teams, if working standard days, need to finish the production.

When planning how to use the available space, the charge painter must take into account whether the paint area is shared with other shops. When space is configured so that the painters and construction crews are in the same space, the head carpenter and the charge painter must coordinate the use of the space. Early in the production, the charge painter may need a lot of square footage for painting soft goods, ground cloths, or Masonite® decking. These space-hungry units typically are painted early in the production because they can be built quickly, painted while more space is available, and do not take up much room in storage. Later in the build, the construction shop may need the greater share of space for assembling and rigging large scenic units. It is imperative that these two departments schedule the use of space early on to determine whether extra shop space must be secured. Storage is another important issue the charge painter and head carpenter must discuss ahead of time. Scenery stored in the paint area will slowly encroach on that space as the units are completed.

When scheduling which scenic units are painted and at what point in the time schedule, the charge painter should first divide the scenery into similar groups and then divide those groups among the teams of scenic artists working on the production. For instance, suppose there are two different scenes, each consisting of a backdrop and hard scenery, one scene primarily painted as marble and the other primarily painted as wood paneling. Given enough space, the charge painter may decide to have two teams of scenic artists working on the scenes simultaneously. To begin, the first team paints the drop for the marble scene on the paint deck while the second team paints the hard units for the wood paneling scene elsewhere in the shop. These two teams would then switch locations in the shop, with the first team moving on to the hard scenery for the marble and the second team moving on to the paint deck to paint the backdrop for the wood paneling scene. This way,

the painting within each setting is consistent and the space in the paint shop is used efficiently.

Many charge painters create a week-by-week chart of the available painting areas in the shop. Into this chart the specific elements or groups of scenery can be assigned along with the teams of scenic artists assigned to paint them. In this way a charge painter can decide whether there is enough space and personnel to complete the painting in the time allotted in the schedule.

The charge painter must judge on a day-to-day basis whether the work is proceeding according to schedule. The week-by-week chart can be used to track the progress of the paint crew and judge whether the schedule is slipping behind. This is one of the most important aspects of a charge painter's job. Estimating the time needed to paint a piece of scenery is a skill that comes with experience. Charge painters need to envision and plan out every step of the painting process and how long each of these steps might take. They must keep in mind, for example, that oil-based paints and finishes take more time to dry than water-based mediums so the space involved is tied up longer. Also, when dealing with toxic materials, they must factor in that more space and time is necessary so that these processes can be isolated from other people working in the shop. They must also factor in such activities as color mixing, preparation, priming, layout, drying, scenery handling, and cleanup. All of these nonpainting activities take quite a lot of time. For instance, stretching and priming a drop can take two people several hours. Usually, a full day of preparation and drying is needed before cartooning and painting a drop can begin.

The charge painter must have a firm idea of how much time is required to paint a production. A production may require more painters than currently are allotted by the production company or more hours than are in the standard workday. The load-in day is the finite time by which the scenery must be completed and generally is not negotiable. If additional staff or shop time is required, the charge painter must advise the technical director or production manager of this well in advance. It is much more difficult to add staff at the end of a project. Asking for more painters at the end can be a sign of poor planning, and money may not be available for overtime. A well-prepared and experienced charge painter can predict well in advance whether resources are adequate to meet the demands of the project.

PAINT SCHEDULE

AREAS	WEEK 1	TEAM	WEEK 2	TEAM	WEEK 3	TEAM	WEEK 4	TEAM
PAINT FRAME	SHOW DROP	ANGELIQUE FRED	SHOW DROP	ANGELIQUE FRED	SKY DROP	ANGELIQUE	DRAWING ROOM PORTAL	ANGELIQUE FRED
DECK SPACE 1	GARDEN DROP	BRUTUS LOUIS IZZY	GARDEN DROP	BRUTUS LOUIS	DRAWING ROOM DROP	BRUTUS LOUIS	DRAWING ROOM DROP	BRUTUS
DECK SPACE 2	POUNCE WORK DRAWING ROOM	CHARGE (FANNY)	GARDEN LEGS – SETS 1 & 2	T.C. IZZY	GARDEN BORDERS SETS 1 & 2	T.C. IZZY	GARDEN WALL & GROUND ROW	T.C.
BAY 1	TRIAL DRAWING ROOM	—	TRIAL DRAWING ROOM UNITS	—	PRIME CARTOON DRAWING ROOM UNITS	CHARGE FRED	PAINT DRAWING ROOM UNITS	CHARGE LOUIS
BAY 2	CONSTRUCT GARDEN	—	PRIME CITY PROFILES	SPIKE FANNY	PRIME CARTOON CITY STREET PROFILES	SPIKE FANNY	CITY STREET PROFILES	IZZY
STAGE	PAINT STAGE DECK	T.C. SPIKE FANNY	—	—	—	—	—	—
MISC.			PREP NEXT PRODUCTION	CHARGE			PREPARE TOUCH-UP	SPIKE FANNY

TEAMS: SHOP ASSISTANTS: SPIKE & FANNY
PAINTERS: LOUIS, FRED, IZZY
LEAD PAINTERS: T.C., ANGELIQUE, BRUTUS

PROJECTS: SOFT GOODS: GARDEN DROP, GARDEN LEGS-2 SETS, GARDEN BORDERS-2 SETS, DRAWING ROOM, SKY DROP, SHOW DROP

HARD SCENERY: GARDEN WALL, GARDEN GROUND ROW, DRAWING ROOM UNITS, DRAWING ROOM PORTAL, CITY STREET PROFILES 1–9, STAGE DECK

Figure 3.8 A Paint Schedule.

Project Planning for the Independent Contractor

A charge painter working as an independent contractor has an even larger job. After learning the time frame and the design particulars from the client's production company, the independent contractor must prepare a bid for the job. Included in the bid are the following costs:

- An appropriate space for painting.
- Crew members, including base pay, social security, workers compensation insurance, unemployment insurance, food and housing per diem, tool or kit fees, and travel expenses.
- All standard equipment normally found in the scene shop (this list may include air compressors, airless sprayers, fans, and even a paint deck).
- Any special equipment necessary for the production that may have to be rented or purchased.

Beyond the obvious physical needs are the additional business overhead needs and expenses that others rarely need to consider, including items such as insurance, shipping, office expenses, accounting expenses, and the time it takes to deal with contracts, payroll, quarterly withholding and tax payments, and workers compensation insurance. These and other

Figure 3.9 Rebecca Lancetot and Rebecca Pancoast in the scenic painting area at North Carolina School for the Arts.

complex financial considerations are a necessary part of independent contracting on a large scale.

Scheduling the Order of Painting with the Technical Director

Ideally, the charge painter and the technical director cooperate on a construction schedule that emphasizes completing units in the order that they most logically should be painted. It is important to paint like units and units common to the same scene together in order to use the paint time and space in the most efficient means possible. The technical director and charge painter also must take into account that texturing processes and sculpting can require enormous amounts of time to execute, thoroughly dry, and seal. These should be addressed at the very beginning of the construction and paint process. In some scenic designs, the properties place great demands on the

production schedule and are considered an important part of the scenic construction. It may be necessary to include the properties manager in preliminary discussions. Much of this communication takes place in production meetings, where information is exchanged between departments.

Setting the Production Schedule

The way in which paint and texture treatments are done may also have an effect on the production schedule. This is information the charge painter needs when he or she plans the production schedule with the technical director.

The production schedule may be set up months in advance of the actual production. Because most shops have finite space and because renting extra space can be expensive, it is important to have an efficient production schedule that uses the shop space to its utmost advantage. For instance, it may be necessary to schedule the drops for a May production to be painted in January when shop space is available.

When planning a production schedule, the charge painter should plan to paint like elements of the set together. For instance, if there are three sets of soft brick legs to be painted that relate to a brick wall backing, those soft goods should be painted simultaneously if space allows, or at least one after another if it does not. If these elements are hard scenic units and involve texture treatments, drying time must be factored in as well. Another matter that the charge painter should consider when discussing the schedule for hard scenery is whether the scenery will be painted down or up and assembled. The charge painter must also determine whether trim, casements, windows, doors, hardware, and fixture must be installed before or after painting. If the scenery is to be painted while it is assembled, there may need to be deliberation about how reveals and seams will be dealt with when the scenery is disassembled for transportation to the theatre.

The paint shop and the construction shop must work together in planning the production schedule. The schedules of both departments must be carefully coordinated because they collaborate in the fabrication of a complex product. One of the goals of a carefully considered production schedule is to move the scenery as smoothly as possible through the construction shop to the paint shop to the theatre. This said, shops can be very hectic places to work. Scenic production moves at a pace that is not found in most other professions. Many so-called planning sessions between the charge painter and technical director take place in five-minute bouts of conversation. But because professionals in the theatre work on countless productions, one after another, they become very adept at anticipating conflicts, communicating with one another, and resolving problems.

As the charge painter plans out the schedule of scenic units as they move through the space, he or she must also schedule the personnel that will be working on the scenery. It may become apparent that there will not be enough personnel to adequately cover all the work to be done without overtime hours or overhire. The technical director and production manager need this information as soon as possible, perhaps even before the final design has been approved, so that they can make adjustments in the design or budget when they have the luxury of choice rather than when they are forced to make difficult decisions.

Special Construction Requirements for the Scenic Artist

Scenery needs to be built to allow efficient painting, and thought should be given to how the scenic artist needs to handle the scenery. Proper construction technique includes allowing the scenic artist to paint all the scenery in the shop as thoroughly as possible. This may seem obvious, but it is a critical part of the construction process. It is also important that the scenic artist keep an eye on the construction process to catch potential problems before the scenery reaches the paint shop. Building even simple scenic units involves many variables. The placement of seams on and between units may greatly influence the paint process. Some designers are extremely precise as to where seams should fall, whereas others pay less attention to these details that can potentially interfere with the appearance of the scenic art. For instance, if there is a predominantly vertical pattern on the walls from a wallpaper pattern, the seams of the walls themselves should be incorporated into that pattern whenever possible. The scenic artist should pay close attention to how units are built, regardless of whether the scenic designer does. The scenic artist also should pay close attention to what scenic materials the scenic designer or technical director has specified for scenic units. Unorthodox materials may require special attention or sampling to search for compatible mediums. During the construction of the scenery, the designer may notify either the technical director or the charge painter about changes in specified materials or treatments. The technical director and the charge painter always should check with one another when any changes occur in construction specifications.

Other issues that the charge artist and the technical director may need to discuss are application of hardware, window and door thicknesses or reveals, and decorative moldings to the scenery. Reveals in doors and windows may need to be detached from the units so that they can be laid out separately for the painters. These reveals can be painted and attached to the units later. Some hardware may be put right in the middle of where the painter needs to make a careful blend. It may be better that the hardware is fitted and then removed for painting. The same can be true of decorative moldings. If the moldings are a different color or paint treatment, it may be better to fit them first, carefully label them, and attach them to the unit after both have been painted. This approach has pitfalls, too. The scenic artist must be prepared for touch-ups over nail and bolt heads and in mitered corners that match up less than perfectly.

The scenery should be ready to paint when it is transferred to the paint shop. Ready means there are no unfilled holes, edges are sanded as needed, there is no unnecessary hardware in the way, and so forth. The scenery also must be structurally sound enough to be handled, painted, and, in most cases, carefully walked on by the scenic artists. The scenery must be accessible to the scenic artist, which may require building custom supports for heavy scenic units or scaffolds erected for the scenic artists to use to access the surfaces to be painted. Often, the technical director and charge artist need to coordinate the schedule of their crews to allow for handling scenery in the paint process. If a unit weighs 1,000 pounds and needs to be moved, who moves it? That is not the job of the painters alone. Some shops prefer that scenic artists do not shift or stack the scenery.

PUTTING A PRODUCTION TOGETHER: ARTISTIC MANAGEMENT AND ORGANIZATION

The charge painter should understand the intent of a production or design. He or she should make a point of reading the script for the production and, if possible, attending the initial full-company production meeting to be clear on the director's concept for the production. By the time of this first production meeting, the scenic artist will most likely be acquainted with the scenic design through consultation with the scenic designer and by studying the bluelines, model, paint elevations, and research materials.

Conveying Stylistic Information to the Paint Crew

It is the charge painter's responsibility to explain the stylistic approach of the scenic design to the rest of the paint crew. This may be done formally at a crew meeting or, as often as not, while chatting around the break table. Many of the scenic artists on the crew are apt to be as experienced and educated as the charge painter, and a little explanation will go a long way. However, the charge painter should take care to ensure that the less experienced members of the crew comprehend the scenic designer's stylistic approach. All the painters on the crew should be fully acquainted with and have access to the bluelines, model, paint elevations, research materials, and instruction about style provided by the scenic designer.

One of the aspects of conveying information to the crew is making sure that everyone is clear on what all the scenic elements are called. In talking with the scenic designer, the charge painter needs to make sure they are both talking about the same set pieces when they are discussing the backing flats for Scene 4, for example. Crew members must also know which set pieces are being discussed when they are sent to paint or pattern these for the carpentry staff. Often the descriptions for the scenery are more prosaic, such as the colonnade or the telephone pole backing. This is fine as long as everyone is on the same page.

Early in the production process, perhaps before the scenery even reaches the paint shop, the charge painter may want to generate or have one of the lead painters generate samples for the production. Generating samples early in the production cycle can be very important because once the samples for paint and texture treatments have been completed and approved by the scenic designer, it may be necessary to order more materials and supplies.

Managing Artistic Personnel

Nuts and bolts advice only goes so far in terms of explaining a well-run paint shop. If a paint shop is running well, it is because the people on the crew are good and the charge painter knows how to use their skills and abilities to the utmost. It is also because the charge painter knows how to keep people happy. Keeping crew members happy and retaining superior staff members involves more than bringing in donuts every Monday morning or taking the crew out to lunch from time to time, although these things help. Good management involves valuing the skills and merits of the individuals on the crew. The charge painter should be sure to express appreciation where it is merited, pass along complements from the scenic designer and production staff, and manage personnel and production problems that arise in a manner that burdens the crew members as little as possible.

Good management also involves delegation and trust. Regardless of the expansiveness of the paint shop or the quality of the materials used, the skills of the individuals on the paint staff are the charge painter's primary resource in effecting well-painted scenery.

When painting a production, there are always some jobs that are more fun and personally rewarding to do than others. Some crew members may be keen to cartoon whereas others may enjoy the process of painting. Many scenic artists have a special skill at which they excel. Even the charge painter is the charge because he or she excels at organization. Usually in every production there are two or three special projects or pieces of scenery. The charge painter should carefully delegate tasks so that each crew member has a chance, as often as stylistic content and schedule permits, to do jobs that are challenging, personally rewarding, and where their talents can shine. Crew members that have strong skills in some techniques should be paired with people that have expressed an interest in developing those skills. The converse is also important. If a crewmember is weak in the area of cartooning, for instance, and avoids jobs involving complex cartooning, it may be useful to pair that crewmember with someone who has first-rate cartooning skills. As they become more comfortable with their skills, they will probably enjoy the skill more and be a more valuable crewmember in the long run.

When delegating assignments to the crew, the charge painter should also trust the crew to do the assignments as asked. The term "micromanaging" comes to mind when describing a supervisor that cannot leave well enough alone. Vast amounts of the information in this book came from people who were working for me. Everyone has different methods of working, and there are many ways and means of reaching an end. The charge painter must organize and orchestrate everyone's talents but must also have the wisdom to stand back and let them do their jobs. The charge painter must also be astute enough to gauge how much autonomy to give each crew member. Some of the scenic artists on the staff may be so experienced that the charge painter can simply hand them the paint elevation of a complex drop along with any information from the scenic designer and say, "Any questions? OK. Think you can have it done in two weeks? Great! Call me if you need anything." Other less experienced scenic artists need more guidance. A less experienced scenic artist might feel more comfortable if the charge painter checked in periodically through the course of the workday giving reassurance if the project was going well and suggestions at points where the scenic artist seemed to be stymied.

Working with Other Painters

Scenic artists work in physically demanding conditions for long hours, creating large, complex, two- and three-dimensional works of art based on visual information from the scenic designer. The charge painter must carefully blend the combined efforts of these many hands as seamlessly as possible and be able to recognize the strengths of each painter and put those strengths to good use to ensure that the whole project has a stylistic continuity.

To synthesize the efforts of the scenic art crew, the charge painter usually divides a project into stylistic units. For example, he or she might mentally put all the wood graining into one slot, the foliage into another, and the lettering into a third as each of these types of painting uses different tools, colors, and skills. The charge painter who assigns scenic artists to different elements of the scenery carefully matches their skills and experience to the projects at hand. Lead painters may be asked to create samples of specific treatments. After approval by the designer, these samples and techniques serve as guides for other members of the crew. As more people are added or shifted to a project, they can refer to the sample work for stylistic continuity.

When assigning scenic artists to execute freehand or loose techniques like foliage or marble, the charge painter should select artists who can see the project through until the end, for the sake of continuity. Some painters may never "click into" the style desired, and the charge painter may need to reassign them or put another painter on the project. It must be added that one of the greatest pleasures of charging a production is watching other experienced artists masterfully paint the units they are assigned. By giving other artists enough psychological space to do their work in their own way, the charge painter stands to increase his or her knowledge. People always respond to trust. It can be a tricky issue to know when to trust an artist to do the job as needed and when to step in and give advice. The best charge painters are also aware of the value of praise. When the scenic designer complements the way a piece of scenery has been painted, the charge painter should always pass the praise along to the scenic artist who did the work. However, if the designer is displeased, the charge painter needs to discover what changes should to be made and endeavor to direct the paint crew to effect those changes without demoralizing them.

Working with Other Production Departments

Theatrical production departments are interdependent because the production itself is the product of all

Figure 3.10 Scenic artists at Scenic Art Studios flip a drop over to the backside for translucency work.

the departments working together. So it should not be a surprise to the scenic artist when the stage director, stage manager, or publicity manager shows up in the paint shop. Usually, people from other departments come to the paint area because painters can do best what nearly every other area needs at one time or another. For example, the publicity department may need a sign painted and lack the means to get it done, or an electrician may need footlights painted gold. In theatre, people generally help each other out with the little things. (Don't forget to ask for extra tickets or an extra light by the mixing table!)

Other departments may be expected to paint their own work for a production. Costume and properties generally have sizable paint areas. But scenic artists should be aware that these departments still may rely in part on the paint shop because the paint shop is probably the best equipped area in which to paint.

The Costume Shop

A well-equipped costume shop will usually have a subdepartment, the crafts department, where hats and accessories are made or altered and where materials and costume items are dyed. The crafts department usually has a dye vat for mixing and heating large volumes of dye. The dye vat is very useful to the paint department because scenic artists frequently are called on to dye soft goods a specific color. When the designer makes such a request, the charge painter must make arrangements with the crafts departments or costume manager to use the dye vat, based on shop demand and schedule. The paint shop may be able to return the favor when the costume shop needs floor space to distress a large quantity of costumes or use the large-volume spray booth in the paint shop.

The Properties Shop

The properties shop has a lot of crossover work with the paint area. Unlike the scenic construction area, the properties shop generally paints the units that it builds. This is true particularly with furniture pieces and small hand props. However, there are exceptions, and some property shops may be understaffed or set up only for acquisition and construction. Generally, a good properties shop keeps its own supply of paint, stains, solvents, and brushes for their own needs. It is unlikely, however, that the properties area will have everything needed for more complex paint jobs. Frequently, members of the properties shop will visit the paint shop to borrow a cup of this or that, a particular tool, or to ask a scenic artist to mix a specific color.

Occasionally the scenic designer designs the properties to be painted in an abstract or stylized manner that matches the scenery, such as a large property designed so that it is the focus of a scene or production. In this case, the charge painter and properties manager must plan props painting together. Occasionally, a production comes along that is particularly extensive in terms of the volume or amount of properties that have to be built. In these cases, the paint department may assist the properties shop by taking over all or a large percentage of the properties painting for that production.

When a charge painter comes into a new organization, it is important to meet with the properties manager, technical director, and production manager to discuss how the painting of properties is handled in that organization. Otherwise, after working hard to get the scenery done, the charge painter maybe surprised by the pile of properties that appears in the paint shop the day before load-in.

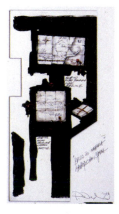

Figure 3.11 Prop documents, *Un Ballo in Maschera*, Metropolitan Opera, New York City, sketch painted by Peter Wexler, photo courtesy of the New York Public Library for the Performing Arts (at Lincoln Center), Billy Rose Theatre Collection, Peter Wexler Collection.

CONCLUSION

The key to staying current with developments in other departments is communication and cooperation. Scenic artists must keep in mind that they do not work in a vacuum and that their job is just one part of the complex and intertwined world of scenic production. In addition to the weekly or monthly production meetings scheduled by the production manager, the charge painter should make it a habit to check in with the technical director, head carpenter, and properties manager on a regular basis. Different organizations have different methods for keeping the lines of communication open, depending on the preferences of the individual department heads. In some organizations, shop heads have lunch together the same day every week. When working as the staff charge painter for the University of Michigan, I informally conferred with the technical director when we went out for coffee during afternoon breaks. This 10 to 15 minutes three or four times a week was very valuable in terms of maintaining a smoothly running shop.

AN INTERVIEW WITH JANE SNOW, SCENIC CHARGE PAINTER AT SCENIC ART STUDIOS

Jane Snow is one of the premiere scenic charge painters in America. At the time of this interview, she was the charge painter at Hudson Scenic Studios in Yonkers, New York. Hudson Scenic is one of the preeminent scenic studios serving the Broadway stage. Snow currently works at Scenic Art Studios in the New York City metropolitan region.

Susan Crabtree: Tell me a little about your position at Hudson Scenic Studios. How many people do you have working for you and how is your crew divided up?

Jane Snow: I'm currently the scenic charge painter at Hudson. We used to be called chargemen, but for obvious reasons they no longer call us that. At Hudson we are per diem workers in the Union [USA] and have a staff anywhere from about 8 to upwards of 50 scenic artists. The categories are divided according to the Union contract, which in our case is called a scenery suppliers contract. Under this contract there are three categories: a scenic charge painter, journeymen, and shop men or industrial members. At Hudson, because we like to delegate the work, we've created other positions that are not in the standard union contract. For example, we have someone who we call second, or second in charge. When I'm away, on a bid session, or in a meeting or on phone calls, this person helps me run the floor.

In between the second and journeymen we've established a position called lead artist. If we have more than one show in the shop, I will delegate a lead artist for each show. They get paid a bit more than journeyman rate. So, instead of just the three categories, here at Hudson, we have five categories. This helps because it's always clear who is in charge of working on a show—who is leading the job. In a profession like scene painting, when you all have to work and play well together, it helps to have some sense of order so that you know that this person is in charge, this person is responsible; this is the person you go to to ask a question. It's not necessarily that way in other scenery shops, but that is the way that I have found it works best here. As scenic artists we are all used to responding to a director or a designer and so having one pair of eyes responsible for each job is immensely helpful.

SC: What is the focus of the work at Hudson Scenic?

JS: Mostly we produce, design, build, and automate Broadway shows. In between the Broadway shows, we take on anything we can get. We do the occasional industrial. We do, very occasionally, commercials. We do a tiny bit of television. It's mostly Broadway and tours of Broadway shows.

SC: Can you give me some titles of productions Hudson has worked on?

JS: The original *Les Mis*, New York *Les Mis*, the New York *Miss Saigon*, the New York *Phantom*. Most recently we've done *Music Man*. We've done *Copenhagen*. We've done *Kiss Me Kate*. We've done the *Lion King*. We've done *Beauty and the Beast*. Neil Mazzella, the owner, is committed to Broadway, he is committed to theatre, which is one of the reasons I came here because I, too, am committed to theatre and I find it much more interesting than any other aspect of scenic art. It is more fun and more varied and more ridiculous than any other. It is unique.

SC: What are some of your biggest challenges in respect to your position?

JS: Dealing with the volume of work and the seasonal nature of it means when it rains it pours—it is a monsoon. We have at times rented two buildings to keep up with the volume of the shows that we are doing and then we will get down to not much at all and I have to lay off artists. That's heartbreaking because you get a flow going with a group of people and the momentum is such that you see great things happen and people clearly love what they are doing. They are having fun and then the work is over and I have to lay them off. That is tough.

The job can also be stressful because as silly as it is, it is a business. When you get those Friday afternoon calls that say, "We are in Iowa and we have just unfolded your drop and the paint is coming off in sheets. What are you going to do about it?" or "Dame Judith has just sat upon your deck and gotten her white linen suit covered in aniline dye." Those things happen and there is absolutely nothing you can do about it. At that point, on that late Friday afternoon or Saturday opening of a show, you say, "I'm sorry. We'll see what we did wrong and try to fix it and perhaps you can put her in her Act II housedress for now." Those are scary moments.

SC: How long have you been a scenic artist?

JS: I've been a scenic artist for 28 years, counting when I started building and painting scenery when I was a kid. Technically, I became a scenic artist when I moved to New York about 15 years ago, but before that I had always painted scenery anyway. It was always one of the things that I loved to do.

SC: So how did you decide on it as a profession? It sounds like you were almost born to it?

JS: Yes, there was really no choice. I started when I was a kid and I was always interested in theatre, but I went to a shabby school that only had three books in the library and it didn't have any extracurricular activities. I always would "eye" the little stage that was in the auditorium thinking that we should put something on. We never did. When I got to junior high I started painting the scenery for the annual school musical.

SC: What was your education?

JS: I have a bachelor's degree in art and theatre from the University of Tennessee. I was fortunate enough to study under a man named Robert Cothran who is a brilliant Yale designer who had landed at the University of Tennessee. He is a brilliant designer and brilliant scenic artist of the old school so I learned to paint on a paint frame. We didn't do continental painting like a lot of universities that have a paint frame, so that's how I learned. I'd done scenic painting, as I said, since I was 14, but he really taught me how to see in terms of being a scenic artist.

SC: What was one of the most important lessons you would say he taught you?

Figure 3.12 Scenic artist Jane Snow carves a statue of St. Jerome for a production of *Faust* at Scenic Art Studios, New York. Shown is the carving process in six steps from (**A**) two pounces of the image, (**B**) the initial block of foam, (**C**) after very rough carving, (**D**) final carving, (**E**) finished surface, and (**F**) final painting.

E F

Figure 3.12 (Continued).

JS: I guess he taught me how to look at things. How to really look at things and analyze them. And Cothran, Mr. C, is a renaissance man, so it is not just looking at the tree and seeing it and analyzing it in terms of its shape, its volume, the texture, and shading and the scale. Then you start thinking about what sort of tree it is and how it grew and what its genus is and how the leaves turn. Do squirrels eat the nuts and how are the trees pollinated? He was just an encyclopedia of all things animal and vegetable and mineral and would talk about these things. And in a wonderful way it would flush out the whole learning experience and animate the object he would discuss.

He is a wonderful teacher and that is so important to learn how to do. To listen and to see in the same way that you listen. Like when you listen to a beautiful piece of music and you're looking at something that is beautiful, you begin to see and listen and look at things differently under a teacher like him.

Of course his technique was superb. He is a master. I wish I could paint like him.

SC: Do you see scenic artistry as a craft?

JS: I do. And that is not to denigrate it. I don't see it as an art. I see theatre as an art but I see scenic painting as a subspecies of theatre and I think it's a brilliant craft. One of the highest crafts there is. I think it is derived from several different arts and crafts and combines them into this specific, strange, esoteric craft of scene painting, which fascinates me. It always has. I remember reading how Michelangelo's apprentices and assistants created pounces. That just thrilled me. I'd never been to the Sistine Chapel but to see it in photographs—the little perforations still in the fresco—call me silly, but it still is really exciting to me. To think this is something that is being carried on and it is as simple and as complicated as that still to this day. In that sense we are still one of the few crafts or arts that carries on that type of work.

Figure 3.13   The shop floor at Showman Fabricators, Inc.

That carries forward those techniques. Time invested in art. That is exciting to me. I may not consider it an art but that doesn't mean that it isn't something wonderful and true and good and to be upheld. I think it's completely honorable to be a craftsperson. It is something that I carry with pride.

SC: How have your design skills enhanced your skills as a scenic artist?

JS: Learning design in school allowed me to understand what happens at a different level in our business—that is, how a designer has to work in our business. How a designer sees, how he or she has to accommodate all the different needs and concerns of a given show. Of course I learned how to draft and how to read drafting. I gained a sense of the study of spatial illusion from the aspect of how an actor, how a human body, moves in space. And that informs how you paint. Often if you are trying to create spatial illusion in painting, studying design helps you because you study three-dimensional form. As a

painter you study it, but you render it in two dimensions, so studying design is very valuable as a scenic artist.

Also equally important to me were my years as a carpenter. I spent as much time being a carpenter as a scenic artist. I learned an appreciation for the craft of scenic carpentry, which I think a lot of scenic artists don't have. That also reinforced my ability to read drawings and to understand the production process. To know what carpenters have to do before the scenery comes to the scenic artist—that, I think, really helps me as a charge painter. I can understand more than many scenic artists about how something needs to get done in terms of it being built. It doesn't frighten me the way it does someone who doesn't know anything about it. I also think understanding lighting is important for students.

SC: Do you have a specialty in scenic art?

JS: I would say portraiture and sculpture. I don't do nearly as much as I should or want to, but when something comes through the shop that I can manage and there isn't a real pressure of time, or it's simple enough that I can knock it out in a couple of days, I take it.

SC: Do you often have time to paint or do sculpture now?

JS: When I first started charging, nonunion in New York, I painted and worked right along with the crew. In the union, being a scenic artist and being a scenic charge painter are two different jobs. One is a craftsman and one is a craftsman who has become a manager. And a manager is concerned with schedules and coordination and communication and phone calls and bids and planning. There is no time to put on paint clothes. I spend almost all my time on the phone or out on the shop floor talking and listening. It actually complicates both jobs if you try to do both. If you put paint clothes on and you're trying to concentrate the way you have to when you're a scenic artist, you can't. The phone is ringing, you're being paged, the carpenter is coming over, the other scenic artists on the other shows need help, the designers have just walked in for three shows—it's just not viable.

SC: What have been some of the highlights in your career?

JS: Just coming to New York was a thrill. My first year in the city was one of the best I'd ever had. It was so wonderful just getting to know the city and finding out that yes, I could make a living as a scenic artist as opposed to doing what I had been doing, which was being a tech. director, a show carpenter, and painting wherever I could. I really didn't know that you could be a scenic artist. There aren't too many places where you can make a living at it.

SC: What types of training would you recommend to someone who wanted to be a scenic artist?

JS: I would say drawing, art history, history, literature, drama, and painting. I really feel a good liberal arts foundation is a good foundation for being a scenic artist as much as it is for being an English major. But if that can't be done, if you have to be self-taught, read and draw and paint and go to museums, go to plays and operas and any kind of live performance. If you want to be a scenic artist tomorrow you have to learn how to use a computer, how to manipulate images, and how to do layout.

SC: Do you have a special philosophy on cultivating people's talents?

JS: I guess the reason I like being in charge is that I know I can create a setting with my organizational skills in which artists can do their job. I've worked in shops where there is so much chaos. The scenery is literally falling down around your ears and it becomes extremely difficult to concentrate the way a scenic artist has to concentrate to do their work. It's bad enough in scenery shops where there is noise, dust, and air pollution of all sorts, from people swearing to trucks unloading, diesel fumes, sawdust, all sorts of things that are toxic and nightmarish. Someone who doesn't know better, on a busy day, could walk through here and think it's Dante's inferno. It's that awful sometimes, and occasionally there are even bad smells, such as when you open a rotten can of blue paint. It's a very difficult job and my pleasure is in creating order for the artists to make beautiful scenery. I want it so they can come in and work in a certain amount of comfort.

Also, I think artists really crave organization and serenity. I think people appreciate that and it makes them happier. Happier people make better scenery. A lot of it is about morale too. I like to laugh, I like to have fun, and sometimes you have to make your own fun.

SC: Do you have a method of developing a dialog with designers who you're working with?

JS: The first thing I try to do with a designer whom I'm not familiar with is to try to listen to their vocabulary and try to understand it. So much about scenic design and art is words rather than pictures—and increasingly so. We still get elevations, but many of the elevations need a great deal of interpretation. Not that many of them are hand-painted anymore. Many of them are the artist's computer generated xerography that we then have to somehow translate into hand-painted scenery. There is a great deal of interpretation that has to be accomplished, and listening to how the designer describes the scenery, listening to the context, including what that designer likes and if there are special paint techniques that the designer is looking for.

Everyone speaks in slightly different vocabularies—even words as simple as color, hue, value, chroma, intensity, what have you. And many designers are not by nature painters. They are more three-dimensional, sculptural designers so they don't have a huge paint vocabulary. So my job is trying to establish what dialect that designer has and listening to that and responding in that dialect. Interpreting based on the dialect and understanding the context of the design, trying to then translate that to the shop floor to the scenic artists who are going to be working on it.

It is good for the artists to be able to hear the designer, and as much as possible we try to bring the designer onto the shop floor, make sure the artists can hear the designer and what they are saying so that it is not misunderstood. Often the designers are not able to talk to every scenic artist so I am the one who is the funnel of the information—I have to translate it, transcribe it, digest it, and spit it out to the scenic artists.

SC: Do you have any key questions that you like to ask designers or does it vary from designer to designer?

JS: It varies pretty greatly. I try to put myself in the position of the scenic artist who does not understand the context, does not know the vocabulary, and I look at whatever the designer has presented and essentially ask, "Do you want this to look like this?" Sometimes they do and sometimes they don't. Sometimes there is a blob on the color Xerox they like and sometimes they want to eradicate the blob or sometimes they want you to fix it up or they say, "No, this is perfect. I love this." This generates the conversation, especially if it is someone you are not accustomed to working with. If you ask a question such as, "I see the contrast here is quite close, Do you want to pop this area up or push it down?" that starts the juices flowing. How you ask the questions also determines the answers you get. For someone who is reticent about paint techniques or a little shy I'll say, "Do you like this color?" and then we begin to establish a little vocabulary about color and hue and value and texture and shape and tone, and pretty soon the object is to try to draw the designer out about what they want to see. "Do you want this to look like this?" That's pretty much it.

Chapter 4

The Scenic Artist's Working Space

A scenic artist's workplace should be set up to allow for efficient painting and safe working conditions. The actual painting tools scenic artists need are frequently their own property and are not supplied by the work site. However, there are some physical characteristics of a workplace, like the floor itself, that are critical to the suitability of a workplace for a scenic artist. Adequate space is one of the most critical elements required for a scenic artist because of the scale of stage scenery. In addition, proper lighting and adequate power service, ample running water and drainage, good ventilation, and approved safety equipment are necessary.

Scene studios are potentially hazardous environments that demand special protection and equipment for those working in them. Toxic paints and chemicals, powerful electrical equipment, scaffolds and ladders, high noise levels, and many other potential hazards are present. For this reason, the materials, equipment, and even the design of the shop itself must meet the regulations of the United States Occupational Safety and Health Administration (OSHA).

Other rules that must be considered are local fire and building codes, environmental protection rules, and toxic waste disposal regulations. This chapter discusses some of the local rules and OSHA regulations. However, no text can cover all these regulations. Instead, OSHA requires employers to determine which regulations are applicable to their particular workplaces and to train and protect their workers. Employers in scene shops rarely meet these obligations. As a result, scenic artists usually must educate themselves about safety and health. To ensure that safety requirements are being met in the workplace, many theatre companies and scene shops employ an industrial hygienist to consult with them about hazards in their physical plants and in their employee's practices. These professional safety and hazard troubleshooters can identify problem areas and suggest solutions. Monona Rossol, author of *Health and Safety Guide for Film, T.V. and Theatre*, has contributed to this book, particularly at the end of this chapter, where she has written a section on safety in the theatrical paint shop. However, a text on safety alone in the workplace along with the OSHA Industrial Safety Handbook should be on the resource bookshelf of every theatrical paint shop.

United Scenic Artists (USA), Local 829, and the International Alliance of Theatrical Stage Employees (IATSE) provide free OSHA training to all 829 and any other theatrical union members who wish to attend. They also offer OSHA compliance consults without cost to all employers of Local 829 members in permanent New York area scene shops and to two major employers in the Chicago area.

THE PAINTING SPACE

For safety and efficiency, scenic shop painting areas should be located apart from construction areas. Construction areas have different lighting and space demands and they usually produce dust and fumes that are unhealthy for painters. On the other hand, scenic painting areas can be hazardous to construction workers. Solvent vapors, spray mists, and other flammable materials are toxic. In addition, some materials can pose fire and explosion hazards around welding or woodworking machinery. However, scenic painting and construction areas also need to easily exchange units with each other, so locating them in different buildings may often create problems.

Unlike construction areas, paint areas do not necessarily need a lot of expensive fixed tools. In fact, for most productions, a paint staff can operate with only good brushes, paint, hand-pressurized sprayers and water. However, efficient painting areas should have even lighting throughout, some areas where light can be focused, running water and sinks, plenty of electrical outlets, counter areas for mixing, basic equipment for mixing paints, handy storage areas for paints and buckets, and good ventilation.

But most of all, paint areas must have space—and plenty of it. Scenic artists must spread out their work. Many individual pieces need to be painted in lengthy sequence and left to dry without being moved. Although rarely possible, the aim should be to have enough space on the floor and paint frame areas to lay out an entire scene at once. While not absolutely necessary, high ceilings are also useful for assembling (or *trialing*) the occasional set that can be more efficiently painted vertically and in its proper configuration. It is not unusual for scenic artists to be expected to paint fully constructed units that are 18- to 24-feet tall. It also helps to have enough space to look at the painting in progress. Many eyes may want to survey the work in progress in a scenic studio—producers, clients, scenic designers, directors, and others may want to have a good view of the painting before it arrives at the theatre. Therefore, some studios have observation decks for this purpose.

The Layout of the Scenic Studio

Previous chapters discussed the flow of the production process. Timing, sequencing, and cooperation also are critical to the construction process, and this interdependence is reflected in the physical layout of scenic studios. The fairly simple pattern of the flow of materials in a scene shop affects how the paint area works in relation to the other shops. Generally speaking, large pieces of raw materials come into the shop through a loading door. These raw materials of muslin, wood, and metal are crafted into larger pieces and assembled into units of scenery. The scenery is then passed on to scenic artists for painting, texturing, and finishing. Once painting is completed, the scenery is stored until it is time to move it on stage or onto a truck for shipping.

To accommodate this pattern easily, a scene shop should have three elements:

1. Enough space to move scenery around easily;
2. Dedicated spaces for the construction and paint shops so that the staffs of both shops can work simultaneously in safety; and
3. Space in the paint area where raw materials and finished scenery can be stored out of the way.

Many shops have severe space limitations. Some productions will even press the limitations of the most spacious shop, forcing the construction and painting to be done in a specific sequence. This is why it is important for the technical director, the construction shop head, and the charge painter to work together to schedule the movement of scenery through the shop.

THE SCENIC PAINTING AREA

Painters need three basic work areas: a painting area, a preparation area, and a storage area for scenery yet to be laid out for painting as well as finished scenery. The painting area can be very simple. Any large interior with a flat wood floor, high ceiling, and good light is a fine painting area. The space can become more flexible and sophisticated with paint frames, more specialized flooring, specific lighting, and even a viewing gallery. The preparation area must have a sink with running water, a mixing table or bench, storage, and good quality lighting. There also may be a spray booth, customized storage areas, offices, locked bays for storing tools, and a separate drafting area for complex drawing projects.

Managing the Paint Space

Minimally, a paint shop needs enough space to lay out a full-stage drop or a full stage of hard scenery with room enough to walk around the units. Any space beyond this minimum increases the efficiency of the shop. The paint process often starts with the dance of moving scenery around from prepaint storage to painting to finished storage. The scenery movement must be choreographed carefully through the shops.

If the construction shop and the paint shop space are combined in one room, the space must be flexible enough to accommodate both in changing configurations. The size, shape, and amount of the scenery certainly will dictate this. The efficiency of a paint shop is related directly to the amount of space available. Time, space, and labor are interconnected. If a production design includes 14 large wall units, all of them textured and colored similarly, the most efficient way for the scenic artists to work would be to address all of these units at the same time. In this way, each step in the painting process is completely finished on all the units at the same time. After the wall units have been stored away, the next phase of the design can be laid out for painting. However, if space is limited and only half of the wall units can be painted at a time, the painting schedule will take longer and special care will have to be taken to ensure consistency between the two groups of scenery. Space and time are interconnected in a paint schedule. With less space, it may be necessary to hire extra painters to finish the scenery on time. However, due to spatial limitations, these painters will not be able to work as efficiently.

Space enough to paint a full-stage backdrop is critical in a paint shop. Without adequate drop layout space, either up or down as described next, a paint area is severely hampered. If there is not enough space in the shop, a rented space may turn out to be cheaper and more efficient in the long run when painting a number of drops. If no space is available for a full stage drop in the studio, the stage itself may be a possibility if the studio is near the theatre and the stage is available. Otherwise, another option is to paint the drop in two pieces, one half at a time. The designer may also decide to cut up a large drop into smaller sections or panels to fit into a small shop space. Later this drop would be used on stage as a single unit or a group of units.

Shop Configuration and Painting Techniques

The construction of the scenic studio dictates the potential painting technique. A paint shop basically consists of a floor and walls, both of which are important as potential work surfaces. These surfaces also represent the two choices a scenic artist has in methods of working: vertically or horizontally. An extensive scene shop will be configured so that scenic artists have the choice of painting in either method.

The Eastern or Vertical Style

Painting vertically, also called working up, painting up, or the eastern style, is a common method and one of the oldest methods of painting scenery. Until the beginning of the 20th century, scenery, for the most part, was two-dimensional. Much of the scenery made by production companies in the 19th century was painted on a frame hung on the back wall of a theatre's stage. Painting in this style requires that either the drop must move up and down in front of the painters, or the painters must move up and down in front of the drop. This technique requires one or two important pieces of equipment. Both solutions require a large wooden frame that the drop is mounted on. The frame either moves (called a *floating frame*) or is fixed (called a *static frame*). A static frame requires a second piece of equipment called a *flying bridge* or scaffolding that a painter can use to reach the entire drop on the frame. Some shops use personnel lifts.

It is illegal to use a scaffold whether built from the floor or suspended unless there is a certificate-holding "competent person" in the shop who is present and who has provided training to every person who gets on the scaffold. There also are fall protection regulations with mandatory training rules for personnel lifts.

Painting up is particularly useful and space-efficient for painting soft goods. The frame provides one large work area, while other pieces of scenery can be painted on the paint deck. Painting up is convenient as painting tools are at hand at all times, and it is easy for the painter to view the work in progress. Painting work directly in front of you is also easier on the back muscles, but painting up makes any washy or wet painting techniques difficult to control.

The Continental Style or Painting Down

The alternative is to work with the scenery laying on the floor, also called working down or the continental style. Working down is fine for nearly all styles of scenic painting, but it requires more caution to avoid spills and when walking on wet areas of the scenery. Painting scenery on the floor involves using

Figure 4.1 Twin Cities scenic studio interior. Painters worked on narrow static paint bridges between floating frames, St. Paul, Minnesota (courtesy of C. Lance Brockman).

long-handled brushes or brushes in bamboo or dowel extensions. Working with extensions is necessary because it is brutally hard on the scenic artist's back and knees to bend over and kneel down all day. The brush extensions take a little time to adapt to, but the skill is developed rather easily. Once scenic artists are accustomed to painting down, they find it is as comfortable as painting up.

How These Styles Developed

At the beginning of the 20th century, American commercial scenic studios and production company scene shops tended to work vertically (see Figure 4.1). Vertical painting once the frames are installed makes good business sense. A scenic studio based on the

eastern style, churning out backdrops, needs much less floor space.

The technique of working down adapted well to studio spaces where height is limited. This sort of low-ceiling studio was common in continental Europe where this style evolved. Continental style permits the painting to be looser and wetter, more like actual watercolor technique. The Austrian designer Joseph Urban brought this technique to the United States in 1911. He brought an atelier of scenic artists with him from Vienna to Boston when he became artistic director of the Boston Opera, and the continental style came with them.[1] The style was

---

[1]Larson, 1989.

Figure 4.2   Scenic artist Kat Sharp painting down (continental style) with extensions at Cobalt Studios. Scrim designed by José Verona for the Miami Ballet Company production of *The Nutcracker.*

sporadically imitated at first, as most American scenic studios relied on the eastern method and older scenic artists resisted the change. However, scenic designers of the early 20th century sought new techniques, and such designers as Urban, Robert Edmond Jones, Lee Simonson, and Norman Bel Geddes designed scenery that relied on continental style. The Adler brothers, who came over with Urban, founded Triangle Studios in New York City and popularized the style. Robert W. Bergman, of Lee Lash Studios, New York, developed many innovative painting techniques for these designers in the 1920s that relied on the continental technique.[2]

Most students of scenic art today start to learn the trade by painting down, now the most common system of painting scenery. A scenic artist can apply paint much more freely and rapidly working down. The drop or the scenic unit can be soaked, sprayed, scumbled, or whatever without fear of the paint running and streaking. Almost all blending techniques are easier on the floor, and it is as comfortable as painting up. Working down also is more convenient because painters can access all areas of the drop at the same time. One painter can finesse the sky while another painter works on foliage at the bottom of the backdrop.

Working in the Eastern Style

Working up generally is limited to two-dimensional scenery, such as drops and flats. One of the hardest aspects of working up is to achieve techniques such

---

[2]Ibid.

as glazes and spatter without drips and running paint. Paint may have to be thickened and blends may need to be sprayed with paint guns. It can be neater, because the scenery is not walked on and there is less chance of spillage. However, a paint drip can run for several feet. Many paint frames are hung to tilt out four to six inches at the top so that most drips fall harmlessly to the floor.

As noted earlier, working vertically requires certain large pieces of equipment to move either the painter or the work up and down. *Paint bridges*, on which the painter stands while working, are expensive permanent pieces of shop equipment, but they allow the painter access to the full width of the drop at once. Bridges themselves also can move up and down, or the frame can move in front of the bridge. Alternately, a drop or unit of scenery can be stapled or nailed to a wall or paint frame and reached by ladders, scaffolding, a lift, or a specialized paint scaffold called a *paint boomerang*. In the case of these last few methods, painters have to move themselves side to side and climb or raise the lift to the levels where they need to work. To paint a house by these methods is fine, but for the complexities of scenic art, these methods of working up are inefficient and can be exhausting.

Paint Bridges and Static Frames   If the painters move, they require a flying paint bridge wide enough to span a frame large enough to accommodate a full-stage drop. Standing on the paint bridge, scenic artists can move themselves up and down to work on whatever section of the drop they need access to and can walk back and forth in front of the drop. The bridge is counterweighted for ease of movement and should be moved by motorized winch, with limit switches at the upper and lower limits of travel for safety. The controls for the winch should be located on the paint bridge with a remote switch. The front of the bridge, facing the work, should be as open as the OSHA regulations regarding fall protection will allow. The bridge must be railed and gated all the way around with toe boards at the edges. Whenever workers are 10 feet above the floor, they must be harnessed and tied off. The back of the bridge should have a shelf to hold paint and brushes that also are tied off so they cannot fall and hit someone below. The bridge also may be outfitted with pneumatic air supply for working with spray equipment.

The flying bridge gives painters access to the scenery, drops, or flats that are attached to a static frame. Static frames are either wood trusses or free-span frame. In the case of a trussed frame, wood battens are added to the frame to match the shape of the soft goods in order to provide a complete nailing surface all the way around the perimeter of the drop. This feature allows any size soft goods to be painted on the frame. Wooden truss frames can leave an imprint on a drop, as the fabric of the drop presses on the truss regularly while being painted. After working on the truss frame for a time, a painter will adapt the pressure of his or her technique and lighten brushstrokes to avoid picking up the pattern of the truss.

Free-span frames have no internal supports to leave an imprint from brushstrokes. The drop is hung off a traveler track, then piped and clamped at the bottom so that it pulls taut. The sides are attached to long boards that move back and forth on tracks mounted behind the soft goods so they can be moved into position at the sides of the drop. These boards can be locked into place and stiffened or chained into place to the outside of the structure to withstand the pull of the drop when it shrinks during priming. Flattage can be painted from a free-span frame system by setting the scenery on the floor or a ledge at the bottom of the frame.

Floating Frames   Floating frames are trussed wooden frames rigged to a head block or sheaves that move it up and down on fixed steel tracks. The frame is counterweighted and may be controlled by an electric winch. The floating frame is used like a static frame, but it moves up and down instead of the scenic artist moving. Scenic artists can reach scenery on a floating frame in two ways. Most common is the floating frame that sinks into a slit in the floor, called the *paint well*, until only the last few feet or so at the top of the frame are exposed. The frame rises up out of the well until the bottom truss of the frame is exposed.

This system requires a well about 50 feet long by 15 to 20 feet deep and a few feet wide. The top of the well narrows to a thin slot, only a few inches wider than the frame, for safety reasons. Generally, these wells have a curb in front to keep errant brushes and buckets topside. This curb also acts as a toe stop for the scenic artists. As tools are occasionally dropped into the paint well, there should be an access door on the floor below for retrieving dropped snap lines and brushes.

Not so common, because it requires nearly 50 feet of ceiling height, is the frame that moves up and

Figure 4.3   Susan Crabtree paining on a free-span frame and flying paint bridge at Tobins Lake Studios, Brighton, Michigan.

down in front of a fixed paint bridge. The painter works on a static bridge or catwalk positioned at mid-height of the room and the frame is raised or lowered so that the painter can reach any part of the drop. This arrangement is much more efficient if there is a paint mixing balcony where there is access to water, storage, and a dumbwaiter lift for paint, so the scenic artist need not spend too much of the day hauling buckets and tools up and down stairs. In all these situations, the control of the frame movement must be convenient to the painters working on the bridge. Floating frames may be operated manually or, more conveniently, by a motorized winch with a remote switch.

In all cases, working up always keeps the work at eye level and within arm's reach. The paint buckets are easy to reach from the cart that artists keep at hand or on a shelf at the back of the catwalk or paint bridge. The paint frame is very useful for working on two-dimensional flattage as well. The limit generally is in the length of the paint well that the frame slips into or the space between the frame and the bridge. Usually, this distance is no more than six inches, so that the painter can stay as close as possible to the work. Painting up in this manner is generally as fast as painting down. Parts of the preparation and layout can be considerably simpler for one person to do when working vertically as gravity will help quickly establish perfect vertical lines essential to good layout.

Working in the Continental Style

Some pieces of scenery can be painted only on a floor. Large three-dimensional units cannot be

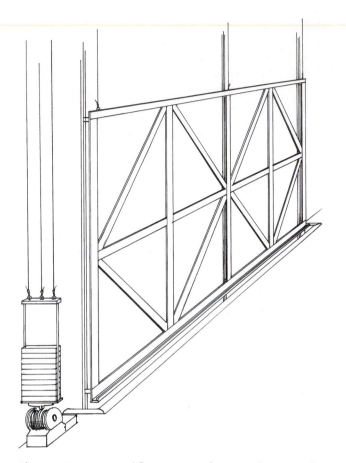

Figure 4.4   Trussed floating paint frame and paint well.

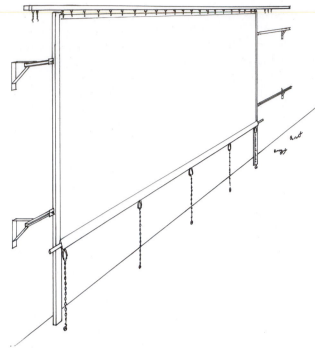

Figure 4.5   A free-span paint frame.

mounted on a frame at all. In most scene shops, the *paint deck* is the primary painting space. A paint deck is frequently made of wood, so that drops can be stapled onto it and other scenic units nailed down. Wooden flooring is expensive, however, and new scenic shops may not be able to afford the cost of installing a wood floor. The materials used to fabricate the paint deck may vary depending on the preferences of the scenic artist or charge painter and what type of floor is in the space to begin with. Preferences also vary as to what sort of protective covering is laid on top of the paint deck.

Paint decks should always be covered with a protective coating; otherwise, over time, the buildup of paint will result in a rough surface that will be imprinted on the drops. Some scenic artists prefer to cover the paint deck with a heavy paper called *bogus paper*. This product comes in four-foot-wide rolls and can be taped together to cover an entire deck. It is sturdy, lies flat, and does not warp too much

when it gets wet. Other scenic artists prefer to work over very thin plastic sheeting called *visquene*. It is important to use visquene that is only 1.5 to 2 mils (.0015–.002 inches) thick. Heavier visquene will retain the wrinkles that were set when it was on the roll. Heavy visquene is also very, very slippery. Unlike bogus paper, visquene should never be layered because it will be slippery then as well. The protective covering on the paint deck will have to be changed out from time to time.

There are also other reasonable alternatives. If the floor of the shop is concrete, a wood frame can quickly be assembled to the size of the drop to be painted. This frame can be set down temporarily to accommodate the painting. However, if the soft goods to be painted are very large, the frame may bow or warp while the drop is stretching during priming. Also, a wooden frame on the floor can be a tripping hazard. A temporary wooden surface of plywood can easily be assembled for use as a paint deck, but frequently the slight warp of the sheets creates seams that are imprinted on backdrop. A wooden deck should be securely attached to a subframe, or, for greater versatility, it may be joined together with coffin locks.

Many scenic artists prefer to paint soft goods on sheets of soft fiberboard, like Celotex® or Homasote®, lain out on a level concrete floor. In a shop where scenic artists and carpenters share space, a temporary paint deck of soft fiberboard can be quickly laid for drop painting and then stored on sheet carts when not in use. Soft fiberboards are easy to staple into and lay very flat. A drop will take on the texture of whatever it is lying over as it is painted, which makes smooth, even flooring surfaces important.

Laying out scenery on the floor is fast, flexible and convenient because nothing needs to be nailed to a frame and no counterweights or winches must be dealt with. Two pieces of equipment are useful when painting down: the paint cart and the bucket basket, or paint carrier. Buckets are never set directly on the scenery or on soft goods because paint may run down the side of the bucket and leave a ring on the scenery.

Once working with extensions, it makes no sense for the scenic artist to continually retrieve and move buckets. *Paint carts*, or paint trays on wheels, are therefore used. At one end of the paint cart is a set of

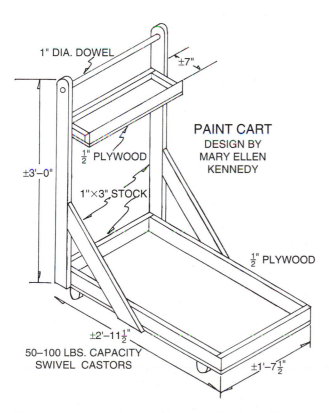

Figure 4.6 A paint cart (designed by Mary Ellen Kennedy).

upright supports with a bar between them at hip height, so the scenic artist can wheel the paint across a drop or around scenery like pushing a shopping cart. Below the push bar may be a tray for smaller items, such as cartooning tools, or to prop up the paint elevation. The lower tray of these carts should be large enough to accommodate at least two five-gallon buckets or half a dozen one-gallon buckets. Bucket baskets are trays large enough for only one or two one-gallon buckets. These have an upright handle at hip height as well but no castors. They are carried from place to place so there is no difficulty with wheels tracking through wet paint. For certain tasks, where just one or two buckets are needed, the bucket basket can be more convenient to use than the paint cart.

Working on a Stage Floor Most theatres come equipped with a large wooden deck that is well suited for painting. This is the stage floor, and it can become a valuable part of the scenic artist's workplace. Yet, important considerations may render the stage floor impractical. Producers and managers make their money from performances. Obviously, if a stage is in use as a paint area, the theatre is unavailable as a performance house. An empty theatre loses money, so a producer may elect to put the painting area in a warehouse instead of tying up the stage for the scenic artist. The alternative is carefully planning the stage availability between productions. This returns to the issue of scheduling covered in Chapter 3.

If available, the stage floor is very good for painting drops. The floor is usually wooden, very level, and free of any supporting columns. When planning to work on a stage floor, do not overlook having lighting installed, as most stages do not keep a complex system of work lights available. All tools and water will have to be brought to the stage. The stage deck and walls should be protected from paint with drop cloths, paper, or visquene.

Lighting and Utilities in the Scenic Painting Area

The light in a paint studio is very important. Scenic artists must have specific light qualities in which to work. It has to be bright enough to see the work clearly and of a very particular quality for theatrical work. Scenic artists must be aware of light intensity and color temperature in the studio and the effects these two qualities of light have on color.

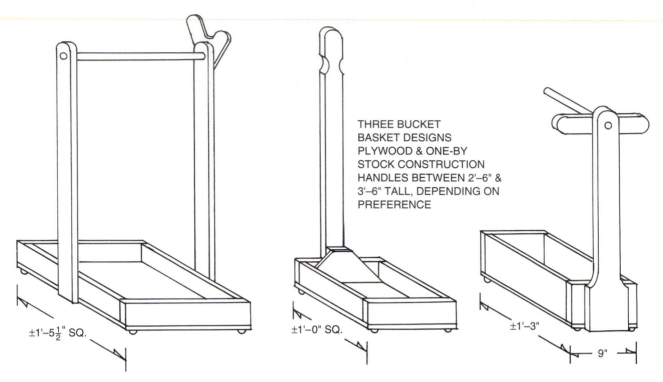

THREE BUCKET
BASKET DESIGNS
PLYWOOD & ONE-BY
STOCK CONSTRUCTION
HANDLES BETWEEN 2'–6" &
3'–6" TALL, DEPENDING ON
PREFERENCE

Figure 4.7 Three types of bucket baskets.

The Effects of Color Temperature

Color temperature is the relative whiteness of light measured in degrees Kelvin. A heat lamp has a very low color temperature, around 2,200°K, and it casts an orange glow. In the real world, color temperatures of light can vary widely from the average home incandescent light (low color temperature, 2,700°K) to noontime sunlight (high color temperature, 6,500°K) and even some higher natural light conditions.

Stage lighting has a very specific color temperature that may not be equal to the color temperature in the scenic studio. This variance can change the apparent color of paint. Scenic artists must be aware of the lighting conditions intended for the finished scenery. For the theatre, this is around 2,800 to 3,200°K. A stage set meant to be seen under theatrical lighting needs to be prepared differently than would a corporate logo meant to be seen in an outdoor setting. This consideration should be addressed in the painting studio.

Ideally, a theatrical paint studio will have a bank of stage lights over the mixing and paint areas to complement the existing light. Although fluorescent light is an economical choice for scene shops, it is a very poor choice for the critical work of color mixing.

Fluorescent lighting will affect color perception because of its higher color temperature. Fluorescent fixtures can be corrected to the same Kelvin range as incandescent fixtures with color-corrective filters. However, some people can still perceive a shift in color when moving between areas lit with incandescent and fluorescent lights, even when color-corrective filters are used on the fluorescent fixtures.

Sunlight is problematic in a scenic studio. As pleasant as it is to have natural light pouring through the windows, the effect on perception of color is unwanted and distracting. Sunlight makes subtle shifts of color hard to detect, bleaches out bright colors, and reflects into the eyes of the painter. The warmth of sunlight also can cause patchy and uneven drying. Windows should be covered with translucent shutters or curtains for any complex painting situation so the sunlight is diffused.

Light Intensity

Light in a scenic studio should be bright and even. Evenly placed lights should illuminate every corner of the paint shop without shadows. Ideally, the lighting should be consistent from the mixing area to the paint area so that colors do not appear to shift in different areas in response to color temperature. The lighting should be placed high enough above scenic artists so that it does not shine in their eyes. Many shops are moving toward interior/exterior tungsten halogen fixtures. These put out a good source of light, are much longer-lasting than incandescent sources, resemble stage lighting in color temperature, and are economical to operate.

Remember to be aware of what light is in play with the mixed paint, elevations, and painted scenery at all times. The paint deck may not have the same light as the mixing area. It is important that both are seen under the same lighting conditions when comparing the painted scenery to the elevation.

Compressed Air

A source of compressed air is very useful for scenic artists, and ideally it should be available in several locations throughout the paint shop as well as in the mixing area. There also should be a supply of short and very long air hoses for working with pneumatic tools, such as pneumatic paint guns and pressurized garden sprayers (see Chapter 5). These guns can be primary tools in the painting process of a particular production. Compressed air also can be used to power pneumatic staplers and air nozzles for cleaning charcoal and pounce dust. Many shops have a compressed air system throughout the complex. In large shops, the source of compressed air is usually a large reservoir compressor, ideally hidden somewhere out of earshot. If a pneumatic system has not been installed in the shop, a portable compressor will provide plenty of power for most painting jobs; however, portable compressors are noisy and not pleasant company.

The compressed air available to carpenters may have a device in the system known as an *oiler*. Oilers mix small amounts of light oil into the compressed air, which is good for pneumatic nailers and staplers. However, oilers are not good for devices that spray paint or spray onto a painted surface. The oil will mix with the paint and leave small discolored spots on the painted surface. Scenic shops should therefore run a separate pneumatic airline without an oiler for the paint area and maintain separate pneumatic hoses that are only used for painting.

Either the airlines or the spray tools in the paint shop need regulators to control air pressure. Most pneumatic tools in the construction shop are operated at pressures far too high for paint tools. A regulator in the paint shop can be set to reduce the pressure to 55 psi for spray guns and 30 psi for garden sprayers to avoid over-pressurizing these tools, possibly causing a messy and dangerous rupture in the hose or tank of the tool.

Fans

Fans are necessary tools in a scenic studio as they are often used for drying paint quickly. Fans are also essential for *floating* a drop, literally lifting a drop off the floor with air pressure. Drops that are stapled to a deck must be floated by forcing air under them in the priming process. (We'll discuss drop preparation in Chapter 7.) Fans can shorten drying time and help keep production on schedule. In some climates and during the rainy seasons in others, they are indispensable. Vladimir Polunin refers to the need for fans in 1916:

> In England, drying takes much longer than on the Continent owing to the moisture in the air and the fireproofing in the canvas. In Paris, a primed cloth will dry thoroughly in half a day in the summer; in Monte Carlo in even less time. In England, during the periods of winter fogs, a primed cloth may not dry for several days, hence heating and drying arrangements are necessary.[3]

> Standing fans are more efficient than window fans to speed drying time. Box fans, used by carpet cleaners to speed carpet drying, force out air close to the floor surface. They are terrific for drying drops.

Electric outlets for fans and other tools should be convenient and easy to reach. Nothing can slow work more than having to look for an open outlet to plug in a fan (see the "Safety and Health Regulations" section later in this chapter).

Other Work Areas in the Paint Shop

The scenic artist's job includes many tasks other than applying paint to scenery. The many steps of drawing preparation and cartooning call for different needs in the work area itself. Beside the primary painting bays, decks, and frames in a paint shop

---

[3]Polunin, [1927] 1980, p. 12.

there are many other areas that need to be designated for specific functions such as mixing, preparing patterns, doing office work, taking breaks, storing paint, materials, tools, and scenery.

The Layout and Pounce Area

A separate work area for cartooning, pouncing, and other drawing projects is very useful in the paint area. Much of the cartooning on the scenery and pounces will be done on the paint deck; however, it is very useful for scenic artists to have a drawing board where they can draft complex images and designs. It is efficient and comfortable if a permanent pounce table is set up in the shop for this sort of work. (We'll discuss pouncing and cartooning in Chapter 8.)

The Office

Every paint shop should have an office area where the business of the shop is conducted. Reference books, catalogues, computers, fax machines, copiers, and other business equipment are kept in this area. This is also where the charge painter manages the paperwork involved in running the shop. The designer's model, paint elevations, and bluelines should be stored in the office in flat storage files. Storage is especially important in shops where more than one design is in production at a time. These materials must be kept sorted out so they do not get mixed up or lost.

Unless a separate room is available, the safety materials belong here as well, including first-aid kits, the OSHA "Right to Know" handbook including Material Safety Data Sheets (MSDSs) and the written Right to Know program, and the telephone with emergency numbers posted prominently near it. The presence of these materials also means that the office must not be locked during any hours where work is ongoing.

The Break Area

The employees of scene shops have a right to a break every two hours and a meal break after every four hours worked. OSHA requires that a clean hazard-free environment be provided for breaks and meals. This rule means that the area must not be contaminated with the same dusts and air contaminants as the work areas. The alternatives are: 1) creating a separate lunch room in which chemical products are not used or stored, 2) designating a part of the office as the break room, or 3) allowing workers to eat off-site.

THE SCENIC ARTIST'S PREPARATION AREA

The preparation area is where paint is mixed for projects and stored. In many shops this area is simply called the *mixing room* or *mixing area*. Painting tools are also stored in this area. This important work area has special requirements and needs good organization and maintenance. If solvents, metallic pigments such as powdered bronze and aluminum, cyanide pigments like Prussian blue, or other materials containing Environment Protection Agency (EPA)-regulated materials are used, there must not be a floor drain here that leads to either a storm sewer or water treatment facility. Spills must be contained and waste must be picked up by a hazardous waste disposal company.

Paint Mixing

Paint mixing, testing, and sample-making needs to take place away from the scenery, in a space set up especially for it. When working in this area, scenic artists will have specific needs, and the preparation workspace should be designed for convenience and efficiency (see Figure 4.8).

> I like to compare the layout of the mixing area to a well-designed kitchen. Scenic artists should be able to move between the mixing bench or table, water source, raw color stock, and buckets with few steps, in the same manner that a kitchen is designed for efficient movement between the sink, refrigerator, stove, and countertops.

Mixing paint requires a table or bench, mixing tools, paint, water, and good light. The mixing bench should be at a height (about 36 inches) that allows scenic artists to see into buckets on the bench easily. The mixing bench should be at least 4′ × 8′, which allows two people to work at the same time and spread out as many colors as needed. If several painters work in the paint shop at the same time on

Figure 4.8
One of two paint mixing areas in the scenic studio at Scenic Art Studios, New York. This area is for mixing standard scenic colors.

multiple projects, additional mixing benches may be necessary. Mixing colors for a drop easily can require a dozen different scenic paints. The only way to work is with every can of color at hand at all times. Often the individual colors mixed for a drop have very close relationships to each other as the person mixing them tends to develop them together. In painting a foliage drop, all the green paints will be out: chrome green, emerald, dark green, green shade blue, and so on.

There are different configurations for the mixing bench. The mixing bench often is designed around the available space adjacent to the paint sink. In some cases, the mixing stock used to mix the paint is kept on a shelf adjacent to the mixing bench. Even more convenient is for the mixing stock to be stored on shelf units at the back of the mixing bench or in the center of the bench so that two scenic artists can work simultaneously (see Figure 4.9). A five-gallon bucket of white latex or acrylic paint, common to scenic painting, should be kept under or adjacent to the mixing bench with a large stainless steel ladle to make it easy to scoop out paint. To keep the paint from drying out, the lid of the five-gallon bucket can be notched out around the handle of the ladle. If the mixing bench cannot be located near the paint sink, then several

five-gallon buckets or a trash can of fresh water and a ladle should be kept at the mixing table as well.

The mixing bench should have a bucket of a dozen or so large stainless steel spoons for scooping paint out of the mixing stock. Concentrated paint is very thick; many a plastic spoon has broken off in the bucket. Metal rice spoons and ladles work very well. There also should be several rubber bowl scrapers to squeegee the thick paint off of spoons and ladles. With the bucket of spoons and scrapers, there also may be a bucket of water for dirty utensils, so the paint does not dry on them.

Stir sticks and kitchen whisks have been used to mix paint for decades, but modern paint shops rely on drills with a paint stirring attachment for mixing paint. Paint drills should be kept adjacent to the mixing table with attachments in a bucket of water to keep them clean or stored in holders connected to the edge of the mixing table with the water bucket for cleaning them directly below. The drum-style paint stirring attachments work best because they direct the paint down into the bucket and not out onto the artist's face or shoes. Some shops keep two paint drills by the mixing bench: one each for one- and five-gallon quantities. The drills relegated to the mixing bench should be of

Figure 4.9
The second mixing area at Scenic
Art Studios is for dyes and bronzing
powders.

Figure 4.10 Sculpted and painted guitars from
Showman Fabricators.

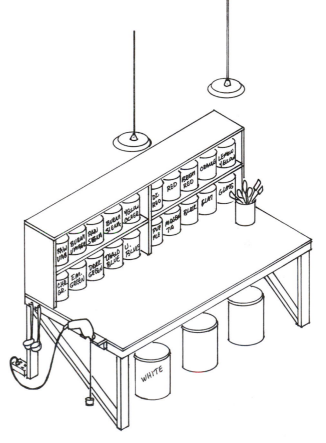

Figure 4.11 A mixing table with shelves for mixing
stock.

very good quality and powerful. A one-half horsepower variable-speed drill is needed to mix large quantities of paint and texture. A weaker drill will burn out the first time a heavily textured production comes up.

Containers for mixing paint should be located as close to the mixing bench as possible. A paint shop needs a plentiful stock of one- and five-gallon containers. Crates of one- and five-gallon lids should be stored near the buckets. There must be no mystery containers in the shop. This is not for the protection of the workers who probably know what's in the containers, but for emergency personnel, firefighters, or other responders. They need to know exactly what is in the containers—not only what it is, but the manufacturer's name and address and any hazard warnings that are required. Putting paint in a still-labeled yogurt container is also mislabeling.

All New York City and Chicago shops are now working on a variant of the OSHA system of labeling for all the paints that are transferred from their original containers. Symbols that identify each manufacturer and a wall chart of these symbols are being developed so that anyone walking into the paint department can easily identify the manufacturer. The MSDSs for each of those paints will be in a book on the counter so the hazard warnings would be right at hand.

Also at the mixing bench should be a handheld hot air dryer for drying paint samples on small pieces of primed muslin, scrim, and bristol board. A rack should be made, nine inches or so tall, that holds the dryer so that it dries the paint chip from above (see Figure 4.12) while the scenic artist moves on to mixing the next color. This way the scenic artist does not have to stop and stand at the mixing bench drying a paint chip.

Good light of the proper color temperature is absolutely critical at the mixing bench, so it may be necessary to have additional lighting in this area. It is desirable that the work area has the same light as the mixing bench, but this is not always the case. The scenic artist must be aware that the colors mixed are correct, even if they appear different in the actual painting area.

Water and the Sink Area

A supply of water is essential to a scenic artist; one could not work without it. Water makes up much of what scenic paint is, and painters use water throughout the day to wash brushes and to modify paint. Water should be available at a large sink at a comfortable working height. A supply of hot water should be

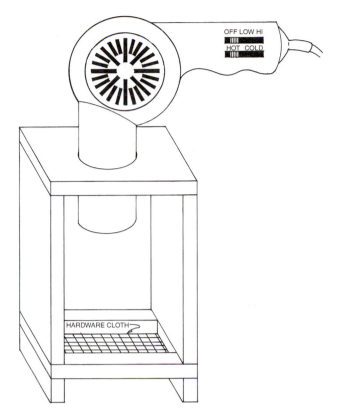

Figure 4.12   A blow-dryer rack.

available for cleaning buckets and tools. Dried paint softens considerably in hot water. Also, because scenic artists have to have their hands in and out of water all day long, hot water is essential for their comfort.

In a shop where several painters are working at the same time, a large sink should be partitioned into multiple basins with two or more faucets. Multiple basins and faucets mean that shop assistants need not be constantly interrupted by painters needing to thin paint or clean tools while cleaning buckets. Many larger shops have more than one slop sink. If only one basin is available in the shop, then water can be kept in a bucket at the bench for mixing.

Counter space on either side of the paint sink for soap, cleaning tools, a strainer, and the like is very useful. Dirty buckets often are the bane of the paint sink and should not be stored in the sink or on the counters. Theoretically, dirty buckets will be cleaned regularly so they will not stack up all over the mixing area. If they are not, however, soaking buckets should be stored under the paint sink or where they are out of the way.

The paint sink requires regular maintenance to avoid clogging. It is a very good idea to build framed wire screen inserts to fit in the bottom of the sink. These should be made of brass or aluminum screening so they do not rust. They will keep paint chips and other annoying blobs from swirling into the abyss and creating a nightmare for a plumber. These screens have to be cleaned regularly and replaced periodically. Ideally, a sink should be fitted with an industrial paint trap, installed at the base of the drainpipe. These traps contain a stainless steel box-shaped basket or screens that can be removed and cleaned. The basket or screens trap paint chips and should be cleaned regularly. All drainpipes should be fitted with removable plugs, so that the drainpipe can be cleaned out with a plumber's snake. These precautions will delay the inevitable clogging of a painter's sink.

> No trap will collect solvents or small amounts of soluble metals that are regulated in waste water. Check the MSDSs of all the paints to see whether there are substances in the paints that are regulated in waste.

Paint Storage

Two sorts of paints must be stored in the preparation area: open and unopened raw scenic colors, also called *stock colors* or *mixing stock*, and the colors mixed for shows, called *show colors*. Both need to be stored in a way that allows easy access. The opened stock color should be located adjacent to or on shelves on the mixing bench. Unopened buckets of stock colors can be stored where they can be easily retrieved when a color is used up.

In some paint shops, because of the expense of scenic paint, stock colors are stored in lockable cabinets or in a paint pantry, much like locking tools up in a tool room in the construction department. Paint always should be stored with all labels visible, so that the contents are obvious. When a paint shipment comes into the shop, the new paint should be rotated to the back of the shelves. The mixing stock color should be arranged in a predictable order, such as earth colors to warm colors to cool colors. This makes finding a color and checking stock considerably easier.

Each show color needs to be labeled immediately and clearly on the bucket, plus all the other labeling required by OSHA, not on the lid, as lids can get

Figure 4.13
The sink area at Scenic Art Studios.

mixed up. Frequently, scenic artists must be able to quickly find a color mixed the previous month. Show colors should be stored separately from stock colors. If there are multiple productions in the shop, each production needs its own storage or shelving area. Buckets of paint should not be stored or stacked on the floor of the work or mixing area because they can be a hazard to staff and scenery.

The show colors should be grouped together by scene or technique. All paint that has been mixed needs to be stored in as small a container as possible for the quantity. Five-gallon buckets with small amounts of paint in them are inefficient because the paint will evaporate more quickly. If a painter needs a larger bucket for working, the paint can be put into a working-size bucket. Often paint is mixed to a high concentration and diluted for actual use, so two buckets are required anyway.

It is crucial to store paint in a very organized manner, particularly when working on more than one production at a time. It is very irritating to lose a mixed color while working on a show. This always happens near the end of a long workday, when there is no time to go back and remix. It can be difficult and expensive in terms of wasted time to match a color that has completely disappeared.

Many other materials are used for paint, finishes, and textures in the paint shop with enough frequency that they must be kept in stock:

- Mediums like water-based finishes, urethanes, clear latex binder, and clear acrylics;
- Fabric dyes and synthetic dyes;
- Specialized powdered mediums, such as bronzing powders and powdered graphite;
- Foam coatings and heavy duty primers;
- Glues and adhesives, such as water-based contact cement, rubber latex, fabric glues, and flexible glues;
- Texture mediums such as plaster, drywall compounds, either premixed or dry, and bags of quick texture spray medium; and
- Texture fillers such as silicate sand, vermiculite, perlite, cocoa mulch, and clay.

There are some commonsense rules for storing these mediums. All of these materials should have permanent dry storage. All like material should be stored together, if possible. Easily reached areas should be used to store five-gallon quantities of stock mediums and bags of dry mediums. Heavy items such as five-gallon buckets and bags of heavy materials should not be stored where access is only by ladder. Hazardous mediums, such as bronzing powders, which are a health hazard if inhaled or ingested and an explosive hazard in the presence of a spark or open flame, should be stored in tightly sealed containers in a closed cabinet. Powdered fabric and synthetic dyes also are hazardous if inhaled or ingested and should be stored in tightly sealed containers and in a cabinet. Solvent-containing products should be stored in a nonflammable storage cabinet.

Shelves and bins in the storage areas should be thoughtfully designed to handle all the stock materials apt to be used in the paint shop. The storage areas for these materials should be designed not just for convenience and easy access, but with concern for the safety of the staff.

Storage of Brushes and Other Tools

Painters' brushes are their most important tools. (Chapter 5 describes proper maintenance of brushes). Having a storage area for brushes is part of good maintenance. Many painters own their brushes and may take them back and forth to work. Brushes stored in a shop need to be stored clean and in a rack, so the bristles dry in a usable form. Brushes should be stored where air can circulate around them. Locking away damp brushes will cause both the bristles and wood handle to mildew and rot. Because brushes are so costly, it may be best to store the more expensive brushes in a lockable cabinet. This precaution is not to protect the brushes from being stolen as much as it is to protect them from misadventure, such as a three-inch fitch (a scenic painting brush) being used to spread contact cement by mistake.

All brushes must be stored lying flat or hanging up so that the bristles do not set incorrectly. Flat-ferrule brushes can be hung from nails, since most have holes in the handles. A fitch or liner handle is too narrow to accommodate a hole but can be hung by gluing Velcro® to the handle and attaching the brush to strips of Velcro arranged in a well-ventilated cabinet or on the wall. However, when these brushes are used with extensions, the Velcro may get ripped off the end of the brush.

An ideal storage method, because nothing needs to be done to the handles, is to drill a series of three-quarter-inch holes into a piece of plywood or stock lumber, to be assembled into a shelf or storage ledge.

Cover the top of the wood with a heavy rubber pad. Staple the rubber firmly in place all around the holes, and cut one straight slit through the center of each hole. The end of the brush can be inserted through the hole and slit from underneath and the rubber pad will hold the end of the brush firmly until it is needed again (see Figure 4.14). Brushes may also be stored flat on open brass, aluminum, or galvanized mesh-covered shelves.

If you need to carry brushes back and forth from a job site, use a canvas brush bag, which allows your tools to breathe and dry out between uses. If you have a toolbox or road box, drill some holes in the compartments where the brushes are stored. If you must carry your brushes back and forth, store the flat-ferrule brushes in the cardboard cartons they came in to keep the bristles from setting in odd positions.

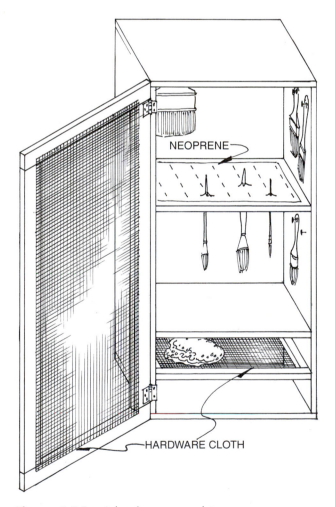

Figure 4.14 A brush storage cabinet.

For liners and fitches, you can fashion a pocketed cloth-lined roll that ties up around the outside, which, when the brushes are wrapped up inside, will protect the bristles and allow the brushes to breathe. Some painter's supply catalogues and stores sell brush bags and rolls. Always be careful about storing wet brushes in vehicles or sheds where they run the risk of freezing.

Many other tools in the paint shop must have permanent, convenient, and secure storage areas. A lockable cabinet for storing costly spray equipment, such as garden sprayers, spray guns, and airbrushes is necessary. Hooks are needed for storing reels of pneumatic hoses and extension cords, which should not be left on the floor when not in use, as they are a tripping hazard. Power cords should have ground fault interrupters built into them. Electrical cords must be used with cord protectors when placed across an area that leads to an exit.

Lining sticks pose a similar hazard and can be stored in racks or on pegs hanging on a wall so they are not left laying out in walkways. When constructing racks for line stick storage, it is important that the racks are level and the line sticks are absolutely straight when stored to prevent them from warping. Lining sticks that are too long to be stored in this fashion should be stored in a specific place in the paint shop, next to a wall where they are out of the way.

When fans are not in use, they need a storage area as well. Bamboo and dowel brush extensions should be stored upright in a bin. Large pieces of equipment, such as an airless sprayer, should be stored in specific places. If there is a concern about theft, an airless sprayer can be stored in the paint pantry or chained to a bolt in a wall. Delicate equipment, such as an overhead projector, should have a storage place out of harm's way and under a dust cover when not in use.

Cartooning tools, measuring tapes, charcoal, snap line, measuring sticks, and so forth should be stored together on a cart or in a cabinet. A cart that is dedicated to cartooning tools can be very useful, since every time cartooning needs to be done, the tools are assembled and ready to go. (We'll discuss cartooning in Chapter 8.) There should also be a cabinet for the tools essential to a paint shop, such as staplers, hammers, tack and staple-pullers, and pliers, as well as the wrenches and screwdrivers necessary for tool maintenance. Paint bridges, used to float drops (discussed in Chapter 7) should be stored on a rack or shelves.

Finally, there should be a specific place for cleaning supplies and a bucket of sawdust for soaking up paint spills. Even brooms and dustpans should have a specific storage place, if for no other reason than the convenience of always knowing where to find one when it is needed.

Storage of Flammable Products

Flammable paints, shellacs, and other solvent-containing products must be stored in a safe place. Every shop that uses flammable products should have a nonflammable storage cabinet that meets the standards of the National Fire Protection Association. These bright yellow or red metal cabinets are designed for solvent storage; they have containment trays in the bottom so a spill will not leak all over the shop.

These cabinets are required by OSHA and by local fire laws because they will delay an explosion should the room be involved in a fire. This delay provides protection for firefighters. It is also the reason the cabinets must be located far from exits or entrances to the room. Place a diagram of the location of the cabinet at entrances along with an inventory of its contents. If information on the location of hazardous chemicals is not available, firefighters have the option to "contain" the fire and let the room burn rather than enter it and risk their lives.

Contrary to common opinion, nonflammable storage cabinets are not built to contain toxic vapors. They are not airtight. They will, however, contain vapors enough to be dangerous if leaking or open solvent containers are left in the cabinet. This creates a potential "bomb" by enclosing an explosive mixture of solvent vapor and air. Be sure solvent containers are closed and dry before putting them in the cabinet.

Never store anything in the cabinet that is not labeled "flammable," "extremely flammable," or that is a "combustible liquid." Substances such as acids, corrosives, caustic, or solid materials must be stored elsewhere. In fact, some of these materials will react chemically with solvents. Storing them together also creates a potential "bomb."

In certain cases, such as when there are spigotted containers in the nonflammable storage cabinet from which solvents are dispensed, the cabinets can be vented. There are closed bungs at the top and the bottom that can be fitted with ductwork and exhaust fans. Never open these bungs unless the cabinet is vented with professionally designed ductwork and a fan.

THE TOUCH-UP KIT

Until a production has opened, none of the essential show colors should be thrown away. Always save base colors for touch-ups. If a show is going on the road, the scenic artist should make a touch-up kit (see Figure 4.15) to send out with the production. Touch-ups always are needed, no matter how carefully the load-in was handled. For very long-run productions, road shows, or scenery intended for storage and eventual rental, the scenic artist should make a swatch sheet of the important colors so that replacement color can be matched to the swatches in the future.

The touch-up kit is taken to the theatre to be used for a mini storage area and mixing bench. If the theatre is adjacent to the paint shop, it may not be necessary to have a touch-up kit. However, if the theatre and the shop are on different floors or in separate buildings, a touch-up kit is a necessity. Having to organize a touch-up kit by bringing over everything the paint department needs in cardboard boxes can be very inefficient. If the tools for a touch-up kit have to be repackaged for each show, something important will inevitably be forgotten. By having and maintaining a touch-up kit stocked with the tools and commonly used mediums and paints, artists may be more certain of having the materials they will need at the theatre. After the touch-up has been finished for a production, the kit should be returned to the paint shop so that it can be prepared for the touch-up call of the next production.

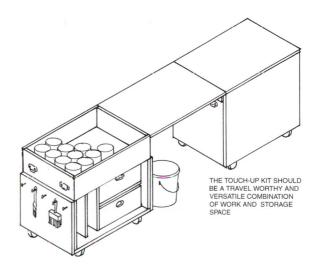

THE TOUCH-UP KIT SHOULD BE A TRAVEL WORTHY AND VERSATILE COMBINATION OF WORK AND STORAGE SPACE

Figure 4.15 A touch-up kit. (Design by Robert Elliot.)

The touch-up kit should contain an inventory list of the tools and materials that it should be stocked with. Artists should check this inventory list each time they are preparing the kit to go to the theatre. Before each touch-up, the kit is also stocked with careful selections of the paint and mediums that have been mixed for that production.

The touch-up kit should be designed so that it can be transported to the theatre by truck. It should be a self-contained road box when it is closed. All the doors and lids on the kit should have hasps that can be secured during shipping. If the side door of a touch-up kit filled with buckets of paint opens during shipping, the results could be disastrous. When creating the touch-up kits, artists should also investigate Department of Transportation rules governing labeling requirements for transporting paints and painting materials. Note that shipping any touch-up kit by air automatically eliminates the ability to ship spray paints and most solvents.

If all the areas of the kit that will have liquids in them are designed so that they are loaded from the top, there will be less chance of spillage during shipping. Also, if a bucket of paint is spilled in the crate during shipping, it will be contained inside the crate instead of seeping out underneath a side door.

The kit should sit on castors so that it can be rolled to and from the loading docks. The sides of the kit need handles so that it can be lifted on and off loading docks. Since the kit will be filled primarily with buckets of paint, it can get very heavy. For this reason, the kit should not be too large or it will be impossible to lift. By designing the touch-up kit in two sections that fit together when opened, there will be two manageable road boxes instead of one huge impractical one. Once the kit is opened, the lids should be braced so that they serve as counter spaces for color mixing.

The touch-up kit should always be stocked with the following tools and materials:

- A selection of brushes, including 1″, 2″, 3″, and 4″ flat-ferrule brushes. These should not be the shop's favorite brushes, since brushes at touch-ups receive some serious abuse. Because these brushes should stay with the kit, they will have been removed from the stock of brushes available to the shop. The selection should include small scenic liners for detail work; sash brushes ranging in size from ½″ to 3″; and foam brushes ranging in size from 1″ to 3″.

Many painters also prefer to bring some of their own brushes to the touch-up so they may be assured of having the right brush if a job comes along that requires some finesse. A selection of inexpensive chip brushes is also useful.

- Sponges, including both natural sea sponges and cellotex sponges. Nearly every touch-up requires the use of a sponge. Sponges are useful for toning down areas of scenery, particularly on stage, because use of a sprayer may be impossible due to the fact that overspray may damage other parts of the scenery or properties. Sponges will also be needed for cleaning up.
- Sprayers. This includes a couple of small one- or two-quart garden sprayers for small spray jobs and large two- or three-gallon garden sprayers for spraying the back of drops with cool water to smooth out wrinkles or to handle large touch-up notes. Small aerosol sprayers are especially useful for jobs at a touch-up requiring the control afforded by these sprayers. Note that spraying water to eliminate wrinkles may negate fire retardant products, so artists must check with the shop before spraying.
- Extensions for brushes, for painting on the deck, as well as for those jobs where artists may need to dab paint on a surface high up that they cannot reach with a ladder.
- Paint rollers and trays.
- Stir sticks.
- Can openers.
- Trash bags.
- Rags.
- Bristol board, to use for edgers or for making stencils.
- Mat and X-Acto knives.
- Markers and laundry markers.
- Pencils and a pad of paper.
- Vine charcoal.
- 25-foot measuring tapes, assorted rulers, yardsticks, and scale rulers.
- A short handheld lining stick (larger lining sticks may be brought to the theatre if there is a specific job they will be needed for).
- A framing square.
- 45° and 30° triangles.
- Visquene, rolls of long sections of brown paper, and drop cloths; the visquene should be spread out and taped down over the stage deck where the touch-up kit is located to protect the floor.

- Masking tape (a fresh roll of one-inch and two-inch for masking paint projects and taping down visquene).
- White and black gaffer's tape. These strong cloth tapes are always useful and can be used for odd projects where it is easier or necessary to tape over a surface rather than paint it.
- A fan (a small one is best to save room).
- A hair dryer.
- Clip lights and flashlights. Frequently the touch-up day is shared with the lighting department. This means that from time to time the lights will go out. If the touch-up kit is set up on stage, the paint crew will need light for working on the projects that are painted near the kit and for color mixing.
- A paint drill.
- Ground-fault-circuit interrupter (GFCI) extension cords.
- Black latex. There are almost always jobs at touch-ups that involve painting surfaces and edges black so that they will not be noticeable.
- White latex (at least one or two gallons for mixing colors, depending on the size of the production).
- Small containers of nearly all the stock mixing colors. Unexpected projects, such as decorative painting on props or a quick portrait, frequently pop up at touch-ups. Artists need a selection of mixing colors for these jobs. Some hues that can be easily mixed with other stock colors such as chrome green and golden yellow can be left off.
- Dull and gloss water-based urethanes or clear acrylics; satin sheen can be mixed with a combination of gloss and dull.
- The show colors needed at the touch-up.
- A selection of one-gallon buckets, small containers, and three or four five-gallon buckets for mixing paint in and for water storage by the touch-up kit.
- Black, gold, and silver spray paint, glass frosting for mirrors and windows, and brown wood tone sprays. These are some of the most frequently needed spray paints called for at touch-ups.
- Clear and white pigmented spray shellac and a small can of clear shellac for prime coating surfaces that do not readily accept paint.
- All crew members should bring their respirators.

- Nitrile gloves.
- Hand soap and vegetable oil soap for brushes.
- Wire or nylon brushes for cleaning paint brushes.
- Scrub pads for cleaning buckets.
- Any stencils or pounces that will be needed for specific jobs.
- The designer's elevations that are related to specific tasks anticipated at the touch-up (for instance, painting the stage deck or toning a unit of scenery).
- The charge painter or lead painter running the touch-up should have a cell phone to contact the shop or the designer as needed for questions or to request that more crew members or supplies be sent over.

Upon arriving to the theatre for a touch-up the charge painter or lead painter in charge of the touch-up should contact the head stage carpenter. This person will tell the artists where on stage they can set up the touch-up kit. Because scenery is shifted around on stage, this spot may be a different place than where the kit was set up in the last production. If scenic artists do not ask, they may find that after having unpacked the kit and set up the paint area in some corner of the stage, they have to move everything because that is where a large stage wagon is stored for the shift into the next scene.

Next, artists must locate the water source; if it is far away from the area where the kit is set up, they should bring over a couple of five-gallon buckets of water for thinning paint and for rinsing dirty brushes, stir sticks, spoons, and the paint drill. Frequently, the charge painter consults with the designer and the head stage carpenter while the rest of the crew unpacks and sets up the kit. The charge painter needs to ask the head stage carpenter what ladders the scenic artists can use. In some union theatres, scenic artists are not allowed to use ladders and lifts without a stage carpenter in attendance as the person who has gone through the training has to train and supervise the people on the lifts. If the lift is "powered"—that is, can be driven—scenic artists cannot get on it without going through a certificate course first. In this case, the charge painter must work out the schedule of the day's tasks that involves the use of a ladder or lift with the head stage carpenter.

Flying in drops is another job that scenic artists may be prohibited from doing, so a schedule for access needs to be worked out ahead of time. In any event, drops should not be flown in without first consulting the head stage carpenter, who is aware of the schedules of other departments, such as those of the stage carpentry department and the lighting department, as well as stage hazards.

If the scenic designer has not yet given the charge painter a list of the day's tasks, the charge painter needs to seek out the designer right away. The charge painter may get the crew started on some obvious touch-up notes to keep them occupied while he or she is consulting with the scenic designer. As mentioned before, it is preferable for the charge painter and the scenic designer to discuss the touch-up notes before the day the actual touch-up arrives. These notes can then be arranged in order of priority and scenery availability. Touch-up can be a very busy and hectic time for all departments. The charge painter should also consult with the properties manager to see if they have received any notes from the scenic designer that will require the assistance of the paint department. For the scenic designer, the touch-up is the last chance to adjust the set. At the beginning of the day, the list of notes may seem like an impossible amount of work, but if this list is approached systematically, it may be surprising how much can be done in one day.

SAFETY AND HEALTH REGULATIONS

Scenic shops come under regulations of the Occupational Safety and Health Administration (OSHA). Most scenic shop rules can be found in the OSHA General Industry Standards (29 CFR 1900–1910). In certain instances, however, scenic work is regulated under the Construction Industry Standards (29 CFR 1926). OSHA's definition of construction work is broad and includes any "alterations or repair, including painting and decorating." Any large construction work in shops or on stage is regulated by both standards.

A copy of both sets of rules should be kept in the shop. Call your local department of labor and find out whether you come under a federal or state OSHA agency and ask how to order a copy of the appropriate regulations.

OSHA requires a formal approach to health and safety. Examples of laws found in OSHA's part of the Code of Federal Regulations (20 CFR) that apply directly to scenic work include the following:

- Hazard communication (1926.59, 1910.1200)
- Respiratory protection (1926.103, 1910.134)
- Personal protective equipment (1926.28, 1910.132)
- Emergency plans and fire prevention (1910.38, 1926.150)
- Fire extinguisher use and training (1910.157, 1926.150)
- Ladders (1910.25–26, 1926.1053)
- Fall protection (1926.500–503)
- Scaffold regulations (1910.28 and 1926.451)
- Occupational noise exposure (1910.95 or 1926.52)
- Flammable and combustible liquids (1910.106 or 1926.152)

Figure 4.16
Drop elevation for *A Midsummer Night's Dream*, designed and painted by Xuzheng He.

- Electrical safety (1926.401–405, 1910.301–304)
- Medical services and first aid (1910.151, 1926.50)
- Bloodborne pathogens standard (1910.1030)
- Sanitation (1910.141, 1926.51)

Many of the regulations have formal written programs and training programs. The problem is that many scenic artists and their employers are not familiar with these laws. Compliance and training are rare in shops and studios. This noncompliance not only puts the artists at risk from accidents and occupational illnesses, but it puts employers at great risk of OSHA citations and fines or even lawsuits if accidents do occur.

Hazard Communication Laws

Of all the OSHA regulations, the "Right-to-Know" law is most important for scenic shops. This law mandates a formal approach to chemical health and safety. It is the cornerstone of good health and safety programs. Right-to-Know laws require employers to:

1. Develop a written hazard communication program that details how all the provisions of this rule will be met. Fill-in-the-blank programs are available.
2. Compile an inventory of all potentially hazardous products on the premises.
3. Obtain Material Safety Data Sheets (MSDSs) on all potentially hazardous materials. It is easy to obtain these if they are made a condition of payment on purchase orders. Otherwise, manufacturers usually are willing to fax or mail them.
4. Label all containers of chemicals in accordance with the hazard communication rules. Most products are already properly labeled. What scenic artists must not do is transfer materials into unlabeled containers for use of more than a single shift.
5. Train all employees who are potentially exposed to toxic chemicals. It is useless to collect MSDSs if scenic artists don't read and understand them.

MSDSs are full of technical concepts such as threshold limit values, teratogens, evaporation rates, and the like. It is not easy for busy scenic artists to take the time to study concepts or for employers to set aside time for training. Yet this training is required by OSHA.

Respiratory Protection

Employers of workers wearing masks and respirators are required by OSHA to develop a respiratory protection program. In general, the minimum acceptable program would include:

- A written program explaining how the employer will meet the requirements and how respirators will be selected. Fill-in-the-blank prototype programs are available.
- An annual check on employees' medical status to assure that they are physically able to wear a respirator and tolerate the added breathing stress safely.
- Annual formal fit testing of workers by a qualified person using one of the approved methods. Employee should be sent to a physician or clinic that can provide written medical certification of the physical fitness of each employee to wear a respirator.
- Procedures for regular cleaning, disinfecting, and maintaining of all respirators. Respirators that are shared must be disinfected after every use.
- Procedures for formal, documented training of workers.

Air-supplied respiratory protection (e.g., self-contained breathing apparatus) is needed for products that emit toxic substances for which there are no air-purifying cartridges. The most hazardous of these toxic substances are all of the two-component urethane products that outgas chemicals called isocyanates during foaming, casting, or painting. Examples include Great Stuff®, Insta Foam®, Insta Pak®, Imron® paints, and RHH Versi Foam.® These are among the most hazardous products used in scenic arts.

Protective Equipment

The use of goggles and safety glasses, face shields, hearing protection, gloves, protective clothing, steel-toed shoes, hard hats, and all types of protective equipment are regulated by OSHA. The rules also require documented training of workers. Training is necessary because it is common to see scenic artists using the wrong equipment. For example, scenic artists may mistakenly use "impact" goggles for "chemical splash" protection and vice versa, or they may use rubber gloves for protection against all products without realizing that many solvents will penetrate rubber gloves without changing their appearance.

Fall Protection

All situations in which workers could fall a significant distance to the floor (four or six feet depending on the situation) are regulated by OSHA. This includes the use of ladders. One ladder rule frequently broken is standing or sitting on the top section or the top step.

Scaffolds or paint bridges that place a person 10 feet or more above the floor come under the new OSHA scaffold rules. The scaffold must be railed and toe boarded and artists need to be tied off. Rules in effect since 1998 no longer allow belts—full harnesses must be used. No one is allowed on the scaffold unless there is a certificate-holding competent person on site who supervises and trains each worker using the scaffold.

It is important to keep up with the new rules on fall protection because theatres and shops are full of old scaffolds, paint bridges, stationary ladders, and other equipment that is noncomplying. There is no "grandfather" clause on fall protection rules. The old equipment must be modified or discarded. If there is an accident, the employer or supervisor will be found responsible for not meeting the new regulations—even if they didn't know about them.

Studio Building Hazards

Most scenic studios and shops are located in old warehouses, piers, basements, factories, and other low-rent facilities. Therefore, employers need to be certain that these locations provide minimum requirements for personal safety.

Fire Safety

If there is an overhead sprinkler system, employers must determine whether it is in working order and whether it is a dry or wet pipe system. Dry pipe systems allow a short time to turn the system off if a head is accidentally damaged during construction, thus avoiding water damage.

If there are no sprinklers, handheld ABC-type extinguishers must be located at least one every 75 feet. The tags on the extinguishers should show they have been recently inspected. OSHA requires that individuals be trained to use the extinguishers. If this is unlikely, employers must make sure their employees at least read the directions on the particular extinguishers in the facility.

Emergency Exits and Escape Routes

OSHA rules require employers to hold a formal meeting to explain workspace hazards and emergency procedures whenever new employees arrive on site. If employers do not follow these laws, employees need to protect themselves. Employees should make sure there are at least two escape routes from all areas and that exits or exit signs are visible from all locations. Fire doors and panic bolts must be in good repair and must never be chained or locked while the building is occupied.

Changes in Elevation

Any elevated platform, storage area, shaft, or hole where people could fall more than six feet must be guarded. Standard railings (either permanent or temporary) and covers over holes must be installed. Stairs having four or more risers or that rise more than 30 inches must be equipped with at least one handrail and one stairway system along each unprotected side or edge.

Electrical Safety

Outlets should be available in many areas in the painting area. If the paint shop has a large expanse of floor space, overhead reels with multiple outlets should be installed at regular intervals through the center of the shop. OSHA now requires outlets used for power tools on construction sites and outlets within 10 feet of a source of water to be ground-fault-circuit interrupted (GFCI). Extension cords must be equipped with GFCI devices.

It is an OSHA violation to break off a ground prong or to fit a two-prong plug into a three-prong outlet or vice versa. Using an adapter is not permitted. Employers should purchase good ground-wired, double-insulated tools and get rid of cheap hair dryers, drills, fans, and other equipment that is substandard.

Likewise, employers should not ignore flickering or dimming lights, frequently interrupted power, damaged wiring, service panels or conduit junctions without metal covers, or other electrical defects. Employees must always be aware of extension cords lying in areas where people walk. Such cords must be run through hard rubber covers or at least duct-taped to the floor.

Ventilation

The building's ventilation will be the deciding factor in choice of materials. If there is no spray booth, spraying should not occur except when everyone is wearing respiratory protection. If there is no good general movement of air, solvent products should be severely restricted.

Bathroom Facilities

Clean bathroom facilities must be present in sufficient numbers to accommodate the size of the workforce. If not, portable toilets must be rented until bathrooms can be installed. Portable facilities alone are not adequate. A water supply for washing hands and cleaning up must be available.

Drinking Water

In older cities and buildings, service pipes and plumbing pipes often are made of lead. Lead also may be found in solder used on potable water pipes (lead was banned for this use in 1986), faucets, and floor model water coolers. The only way to determine whether water is safe to drink is to have it tested. If the water has not been tested, or if the test shows the water is above the accepted limit, employees should drink bottled water.

Lead Paint

Buildings built before 1978 should be assumed to contain lead paint unless actual testing shows otherwise. Even well-maintained older buildings may contain painted-over or encapsulated lead paint that can be made airborne if renovation of any painted surface is planned.

The OSHA Lead in Construction standard forbids sanding, resurfacing, removal, or demolition of any painted surface unless the paint has been professionally tested and shown to be lead free. If lead is found, only trained lead abatement contractors can do the work. Scenic artists must never do this work.

Even undisturbed old paint can be hazardous. Testing of the dust in the shop should be done if there is obvious paint dust, chips, or powder near friction surfaces (e.g., places where window frames create dust when drawn over each other).

Asbestos

Employers must watch for sources of old asbestos in the shop. Common sources of asbestos include:

- Insulation around pipes and furnaces;
- Composition ceiling tiles;
- Acoustic board and tile;
- Transite® and other asbestos boards;
- Old wall board and plaster;
- Vinyl floor tiles;
- Roofing felts, tar paper, and caulks;
- Spackle plaster repair compounds;
- Wiring (e.g., fuzzy white wires on old lighting instruments); and
- Old textured scenery or papier-mâché props.

Garbage and Toxic Chemicals

Only professional waste handlers can safely remove refuse that contains animal and human waste. Only toxic waste disposal contractors can legally remove old chemical products and containers, unidentified or unlabeled substances, asbestos and lead paint waste, and other chemicals.

CONCLUSION

These are just a few of the many laws and regulations that apply to scenic work. But even if every rule is followed, accidents will not be reduced if scenic artists work without sleep, when they are faint with hunger, or when they are ill. The first and most important of all safety rules is for artists to take good care of themselves both on and off the job.

It behooves all who are working with toxic materials to educate themselves about the hazards associated with their trade. Anyone in the teaching profession has a duty to teach both through lecture and good example the proper and safe handling of toxic materials.

AN INTERVIEW WITH NANCY ORR, CHARGE PAINTER OF SHOWMAN FABRICATORS

Nancy Orr is the scenic charge painter at Showman Fabricators in the New York City region. Showman serves a wide variety of clients including Broadway, feature films, network and cable television. She and Katie (her brindled American Staffordshire dog) live in Brooklyn where Nancy remains active in her community, and in the union as a Pension and Welfare Trustee and as an instructor for the Apprenticeship program.

SC: Can you tell me what the focus of your work is here?

NO: We do an awful lot of TV here including children's shows. We have done *Sesame Street*, the regular production plus the offshoot, *Elmo's World*, which consists of dropouts, computer animation, and hand-painting. We do a lot of Food Network cable television. We do some Broadway, some off-Broadway. We have a tendency to have our fingers in a lot of things. We do a lot of museum work. We completed a Viking ship and three heroic scaled DNA sculptures for the Museum of Natural History. So it runs the gambit. We have a large production staff and salespeople who have been responsible for getting us lots of different kinds of work.

SC: What is the focus of your work as the charge artist?

NO: Basically I estimate shows in terms of costs of material and labor. I keep the shop running in terms of materials and space and I am responsible for heading off the crew of scenic artists.

SC: How many people do you have working for you?

NO: On a regular basis, I have four people in the shop. It varies from between 4 and 20 people on an off-and-on basis. Sometimes more, but that is the exception.

SC: What is the structure of your crew?

NO: I have a second, Bill Riley, who runs the floor and oversees the spray booth personnel. I also have Reynold Maher, who is a regular and does amazing work, and I have two other people, Nancy Branton and Bill Savoy, who are here in the shop most of the time. Bill Riley does a lot of charging and heads off a lot of the finishes, while Reynold leads a lot of the drop work because he is most comfortable with it. I tend to send Bill Savoy and Nancy Branton out on site a lot as we do touch-up calls, installations, and things of that nature. On site they can be doing anything from spraying to wood graining to marbleizing to painting flat color.

SC: How long have you been a scenic artist?

NO: I painted my first show in the eighth grade, but I've been a scenic artist for about 25 years. I started

Figure 4.17
A turn-of-the-century horse-drawn carriage created at Showman Fabricators.

working and getting paid for it when I was about 20. At the university I went to we ran our shop as a contract shop. We were building sets and painting drops for Dayton Ballet and Cleveland Ballet and other dance and opera troupes.

SC: Do you have a specialty as a scenic artist?

NO: I think I'm one of those scenic artists that you would say is generally an overall good scenic artist. There is nothing that I feel uncomfortable handling. There is probably nothing people will call me brilliant at, but I'm good and I have good follow-up artists, and that's a skill in itself. I think that as a scenic artist, the most valuable skill you bring to scenic painting is your ability to solve problems.

SC: Do you think that is why you are a good charge artist—because you have a good general knowledge?

NO: I think that when I am doing my best that's why. I get a lot of phone calls from places and people saying, "How do I do this? How do I do that?" and usually my answers are that I might do this or I might do that but you need to see what works best for you because circumstances might be unique. If they are painting in the desert, solutions to problems may be different than for somebody working in the Bahamas. I have gotten calls from people as far away as England about how we do certain things. It makes me valuable as a scenic artist.

SC: What kind of education have you had for scenic artistry?

NO: I have a BFA in Scenic Design and Technology from Wright State University in Fairborn, Ohio, with an emphasis in Design. I was painting all that time. I took some time off and worked for a year at a medical school in their medical illustration department. We put a textbook together and created other visual teaching aids for students. I also worked as a draftsman in an engineering corporation that built the wet ends of pulp and paper machines. I think that those kinds of visually oriented experiences are valuable. Anything that teaches you to see, to be able to observe a problem, to find a solution, that's the key. I never had a course in scene painting. It was just something I started to do and if you do something well enough that people want you to do it again, you get good at it because you are practicing. That is the only way I know to become a good scenic artist—you have to do it over and over again. It is like riding a bike or singing an opera, you have to practice.

SC: Was there anyone you had a formal or an informal apprenticeship with or who served as a mentor for you?

NO: Not really. I picked up several things from very good people who I've been fortunate to work with. I worked at Arnold Abrahmson's shop, Nolan's, and he taught me how to starch a drop properly, for instance. There were a lot of us who called ourselves "Baby Nolans" at the time because a lot of people who used to work at Nolan's were all getting close to retirement—we were the last of the young crop to come through the old place and we learned a lot there.

I think you also pick up things from designers. For instance, the first full-stage drop I ever worked on I didn't know how to approach. I painted it anyways, and it was not successful. I didn't really know until I saw it hanging in the theatre how horrible it was. I was the painter and the charge, so I went to the designer and said it was dreadful and he said he would show me how to fix it. We fixed it all right. We repainted that drop and it got worse, much worse. He finally said, "I can't teach you how to scene paint. You are just going to have to do it on your own." He left me with all the brushes and the paint and I stayed that night, all night, until the drop was painted for the third time, and although I was very tired, the drop was looking fine, and complete. So when someone asks you if you know how to do something, the answer should always be "Yes. I don't know how I am going to do that but I know I have the tools and the ability to figure it out." That's why I think the ability to solve problems is important for scenic artists. On the floor, we often have no time to do anything. How do you get wood grain that looks beautiful and precise when you only have time to do three steps on it? I need to be able to solve that problem.

SC: Can you tell me a little about women in the industry and how you see their role as having changed over the years?

NO: When I was at Nolan's, most of the charges there were men. There were some very good women there at the time, but they weren't given the opportunity to be in charge of things. It takes an awful lot of tenacity and willingness to be called names to be a female charge because people are used to men being forceful and asking for things and demanding things be done right and on time, etc. It is different when it comes from a woman—people aren't used to it and you just have to have a little faith in yourself in that you know what you're doing.

I think that women have found a niche in scenic painting now because women were always steered toward arts and humanities and men were always steered toward science and technology. So you see women coming into the field in droves because they have been encouraged to go into the arts and humanities. You see doors that have been pushed opened by people like Clair Hein who has been in business for a very long time and is much respected. A lot of women my own age—like Jane Snow, Pam Garrett, and Janet Stapleman—are taking positions as charges because it is a natural outreach for a lot of women given the way we have been educated. We are already thinking intuitively and we've been taught to depend on ourselves intuitively since we were young.

SC: Can you say a little bit more about your background in design?

NO: I actually did some design work for the Alliance Children's Theatre to tour, and for The Alliance's small black box theatre. I designed some drops and other kinds of things for other display and performance companies. But you can make a much better living at being a scenic artist than you can as a designer, unless you are one of those top-notch designers. It is very difficult as a designer to make a name for yourself and pay for your assistants. It often seems an easier path to be a scenic artist, not to say that we do it because it is easier. I make a decent income and many of the scenic artists I know are making a decent living, better than too many designers. And that's an unfortunate fact.

SC: It is unfortunate. I feel sorry for designers sometimes.

NO: It is really bad. Many young designers depend on their spouses and partners for support as they become established. They work so hard. They have unlimited hours. That is one of the reasons why I am in the union because the abuse at the regional level and at the nonunion level was so intense that it was so difficult to have a life outside of work.

SC: Have your design skills enhanced your scenic art skills and have there been other skills you've acquired?

NO: Absolutely. Design skills help because design is visual. Anything that teaches you to look at something and ask "Is it making sense? Is it working together?" is good for the scenic artist. Designers like to know that they are talking to a scenic artist or to a charge who understands the whole concept rather than someone who is just painting the 2 × 4 in the corner. I think the more well-rounded you are, the more you know about carpentry, about welding, about computers, the better off you are as a scenic artist. You have to be able to see that scenic art is

part of a process and that it is usually the last thing that happens to a unit, unless electricians are going to wire it after you. If you're dealing with a hard unit, you're at the mercy of all the others—the drafting department, the builders, the welders. You have to understand the time and work involved for everyone, which makes it easier to understand how to make the work happen in the best manner possible because there are going to be things that do not go smoothly.

SC: How did your experience as an engineering draftsman help you as a scenic artist?

NO: I learned a lot about mechanicals. I learned a lot about drafting—about being consistent and how things go together. I think it's a visual thing—you see how things work together. Some scenics only see two-dimensionally and some scenics see three-dimensionally. A lot of people come here as artists with no background at all in scenery and it's very hard for them to translate. It takes a while for them to learn that.

SC: How do you approach designers to make sure you understand where they are going with their design? What are some of the key questions you ask?

NO: Designers are as varied as the scenic artists who paint for them. Some designers come in with all their information complete, down to the little detail and the period at the end of the sentence. Some designers just pull out a number from a swatch book and say, "I need that" and we have to ask "What exact color do you want?" "What kind of finish do you want want?" "Do you want it glossy or flat?" And they can't tell you. At that point you have to steer them. You learn the gentle art of trying to steer people but you don't want to take away their job, they're the designers. It's a very careful walk.

There are some designers that you develop an instant rapport with and from then on whatever you do for them is going to be fine because you understand how they work. When you have that kind of relationship with a designer, that's a lovely, beautiful thing. It's learning how far to push, not to push too far, make sure they can do their job and that you are not walking on their toes at the same time, getting the information you need to make it work for them. It's just a question of being persistent and being consistent as much as you can, I think.

SC: Do you have any kind of philosophy that you use as a charge painter in dealing with your crew?

NO: Every artist out there is an individual. You need to know how much rope to give each of them because you need them to succeed and grow. On the other hand, you may have boring stuff to work on but it needs to be put out the door. There may be only so many good jobs to go around so you have to balance it. Give them enough that has to be done, give them enough room to grow. Some artists need constant direction, some need to take the project and run with it. You need a balance of those people. You need soldiers and crew leaders—it's identifying those strengths and skills and giving the people room to breathe, to do what they do well. The hardest thing is to step back and let them do their jobs when your fingers are itching to get into the paint yourself and say "Here's what you do." It's the hardest skill I have yet to master.

SC: What type of training do you think someone studying to be a scenic artist should obtain?

NO: What they need to do is to draw, draw, and draw—make it an extension of your arm. They need to feel comfortable with color so that it becomes intuitive. That means doing whatever they like that relates to that, whether it be taking pictures, working on Illustrator or PhotoShop on the computer, exercising that eye. I think schooling is a very good thing for everybody, the better schooled we are the better abilities we have.

One thing I've found is that I can hire somebody who can draw and may not yet know how to work on a drop, but I can't hire someone who can work on a drop but who doesn't have the faintest idea of how to draw. It just doesn't work both ways. If you can see it at the end of your hand, you can see it at the end of your handle. A lot of people get up on the ladder and they want to see the drop better. There is a part of you that intuitively should know whether it's going to look right or wrong before you get up the ladder. You should already know pretty much what you are going to see—there shouldn't be any surprises.

SC: Do you have any words of wisdom for up-and-coming scenic artists?

NO: Learn from everything you do. You asked me earlier who my mentors were and where I learned to be a scenic artist. It's too impossible to dissect it. It's like a cloth. There is a thread here, there's a thread there. I could go through and say "Oh, Arnold taught me that." But then I remember an old house painter that showed me this trick of the trade. I remember some carpenter that said, "Here's how you fold your sandpaper to make it work well." So everywhere you go you should learn from what you do.

And you may not even be taught verbally—your eyes are your best tool. Protect them too. We had

an incident recently—somebody got some lacquer splashed up in their face. They had the proper protective equipment but it got there anyway. We had an eyewash station that we just put in a few months ago and it worked and he was fine. It's a dangerous business because we are always experimenting with how to solve a problem, but you don't want to create a bomb while you do it. Find out what it is you're dealing with when you start to deal with it.

SC: Can you tell me more about safety problems you see in shops?

NO: It was a long-standing practice that people smoked in the shops, which is really not a good idea. Showman has a smoke–free policy now. There were problems associated with that. A proper written respirator program—all these things we've been talking about and giving lip-service to are finally starting to be implemented, everyone is starting to do it. The shop I used to work at had an OSHA inspection and we had to make some changes. That's when I really started to evaluate what we needed to do. When problems in other shops started happening, I went to the owners and said, "You should address these before you are forced to address them." The best

Figure 4.18 A detail of commercial scenery created at Showman Fabricators.

thing to do is to have an open dialog with the people you work for and say, "Here's a problem and I need your help in working it out." Remember that the relationship with management should not be adversarial by nature. A healthy and safe workplace is in their best interest. Most employers want to do the right thing, they want to make sure everybody is safe and to deal with it on that basis. Instead of making it adversarial, say, "What do we have to do to make this right?" Money is an issue and sometimes there is some medium ground you have to hit before you hit the high ground Just make sure nobody gets hurt while reaching your safety goals.

SC: Looking back over your career, what would you say are some of the most difficult or elusive skills you've had to learn in the area of painting and outside the area of painting?

NO: Negotiating space, negotiating time, negotiating schedules is the hardest thing to do because we're such a "fly by night" industry in the sense that things can come in today and leave tomorrow. So it's hard sometimes because we are the last ones in the process to get the time we need to do a job well. You don't want to send a job out looking bad, and sometimes we are put in that spot and it's a very hard thing not to get angry about it, because you want to send out a good product.

In the area of painting, new materials make it difficult sometimes. In can be difficult to find the time or money to do the research, or create the samples to see whether what you want to do, is actually going to work, and to make sure it's going to hold up for six months on the road. Despite your best plan, there are going to be things that don't work and usually it's a materials problem, not a personnel problem. You just don't how the materials are going to react.

SC: What do you think are some of the most common misconceptions about the profession of scenic artistry?

NO: That everybody who has their card knows how to paint. Despite the fact that you may have a union card, there are as many skill levels in the union as there are outside the union. As a charge person, you really have to recognize the strengths and weaknesses in the people who work for you. There are some people who move very, very slowly, for instance. I'm always praying that I can have somebody do something faster because I've always got somebody leaning on my shoulder saying, "It needs to go in the truck."

When people first come in as scenic artists and pass the union test or interview, whatever process they've gone through in the apprenticeship, those people are just starting on the path and they are not all the way down it and they are going to need to be taught the same way we all were. It's a learning process and as artists we never stop developing. We are evolving as scenic artists and there is always room for improvement and there is always someone who can paint better and faster than you.

SC: Would you consider scenic artistry an art or a craft?

NO: I can say that some people I know would definitely say it's an art and some people would definitely say it's a craft. At its best it's an art. Oftentimes it's a craft. When I am painting myself and I am working for a favorite designer, he depends on me to bring my own visions and abilities to the work—I'm a part of that end process. He is depending on the flair that I have, the hand that I have, to bring something to his art. The craft of it is when we have 20,000 [square feet] of wood grain to do, and it's just a process—you have to be very good craftsmen and pay attention to what is going on, but it is a craft at that point. I think it varies depending on the project, the designer, and who you are as a scenic artist. I think there are craftsmen in our union and scenic artists in our union and not one or the other is worth more or less, they are just different.

SC: Do you feel that people new to the profession are no longer being exposed to some key elements of scenic artistry?

NO: Yes, I talked about the "Baby Nolans." All of us "Baby Nolans" were exposed to brilliant artists who are no longer painting. You learn from people who are good at things. Today we depend a lot more on mechanical leads to get things where they need to be. It's not unusual to have giant Xeroxes and then correct from there because it is cheaper and faster. Sometimes we have to take as many short-cuts as we can to get the product done cheaper and faster because we have to be competitive, that's what keeps our jobs here. So giant Xerox's, templates, stencils that are cut on computers, computer technology—those are all things that debilitate the old-fashioned skills, and since those are the skills that taught us to see, you risk losing the ability to see and judge whether something is working well.

To me it's just a question of making sure that as we use these new devices, or tricks of the trade, that we don't forget that we need to bring our other skills to bear on them. If you're working at a computer, make sure you use your visual sense to make whatever you're doing work in the large scale. It's very important that someone is still making the decision, "How do you bridge the stencils properly?" You're not just leaving that to some idiot in a computer room. You can make it work well or you can make it look stupid and it is a visual task. When we used to draw those things, you would work it out as you drew, and now we're looking at it on a computer so the thinking process is different. That's why I believe knowing how to draw as a scenic artist is so important.

SC: Obviously digital prints and mechanical painting have had a huge impact on your shops. Can you discuss that a bit?

NO: We have lost a lot of work to that kind of thing. Computers only do well with what is put into them—garbage in garbage out. I am hoping that what happens is that you have a whole new generation of young designers and scenic artists who do work on the computer. There is no reason you can't be an artist working at a computer board as well as you can be an artist working on the floor, but those prints will only be as good as what is put into them. Right now, when you blow things up to a certain size and scale, they lose all definition because they don't have the necessary resolution or number of pixels in

them to be able to translate. I would assume that at some point someone is going to figure that out. Of course, the further you back away from something the clearer it becomes. One of the things that cannot be replaced by a computer is the fact that we think on the floor as we build something. So we're getting something fuzzy and hazy to deal with and we need to sharpen it. We do that well. That could be done on a computer screen but we also do it while on the floor. I think that we have to look to the future and say, "How do we make ourselves part of the process?"

SC: Can you talk a little bit more about this new profession? What resources and training do the scenic artists working on computers use and need?

NO: They actually have to go to school and learn some hard, down and dirty methods—how to work in Illustrator and PhotoShop, how to paint and change. For us it's just a question of learning the skills and embracing them and make it a part of what we do. And the computer can't do everything. There are going to be some things that need to look hand painted, that need to have that flourish and that finish. For instance, if you do a huge thing that's all hand written, it has a flourish and a spontaneity to it that will never come out of the computer, as far as I can see. We all used to laugh at electric pounce

Figure 4.19
Mechanically painted reproduction of a translucent drop. The "Oleo" stage backdrop ca. 1928, Savoy Theatre, Grand Rapids, Michigan. "The Furniture City" exhibit, Public Museum of Grand Rapids, Van Andel Museum Center. (The original backdrop was painted with dry pigments in an animal glue binder on canvas. The windows and lights were cut out and backed with silk ribbon.)

machines, but they are a great tool that just has to be used safely and used well. There was a time when people said we could never use projections, that's cheating. We are in a profession where cheating is what we do. We try to find the best way to cheat, so whatever it takes, just try to keep our work and make sure we can move into the 22nd century being able to do the work.

I don't think that anybody is going to replace scenic artists completely because there just isn't an easy way to lovingly age something or to make something look centuries old—cast a veil upon it, and do any of those romantic things that we can. There is just no way I see scenery happening without somebody's loving eye on it.

SC: Do you feel that in the future, the computers doing the mechanical painting may be getting all the best projects?

NO: No, I'm not afraid of that. I guess it could happen, but careers that are flexible and that can grow and change will remain, and the ones that aren't will lend themselves to obscurity, I think.

SC: How else do you think the scenic artist is going to evolve over the next couple of decades?

NO: I would think that we're going to have to become much more environmentally sound. I think that's one of the things we have to think about. We have a treasure to pass on to future generations and we have to make sure that the bucket loads of nails and wood and scrap paint and everything that we throw out we find a better use for. I think that's one of the major considerations. I think we're also going to have to find out how to make sure we're protecting ourselves as we work better.

I think that the other thing we will have to learn is that the materials don't change the basic skills. Even if you are sitting in front of a computer screen or standing on a drop, if there is a line that has got a bump or wiggle in it that doesn't belong, fixing it requires the same vision and sight. It is our vision that

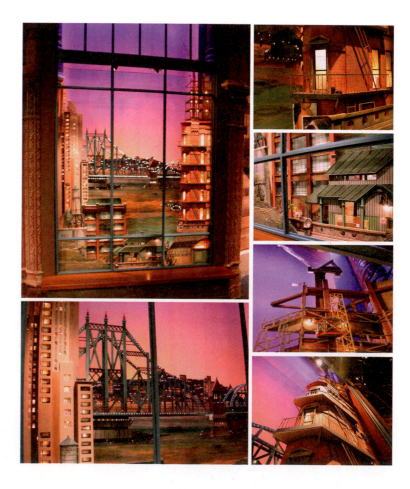

Figure 4.20
Finished set pieces for
The Late Show with David Letterman, designed
by Kathleen Ankers, Showman Fabricators.

we are training here and our hand to perform, whether it be at a keyboard or at the end of a bamboo. That's what won't change. Everything else will, probably.

SC: What do you enjoy the most about scenic artistry?

NO: I like the fact that every day I do something different—that I'm not repeating the same motion every day, that I'm solving new problems all the time, and that it's challenging. I think that artists and creative people thrive on challenge. I do, and that's what is so exciting about it. The other part of it is that we create a real product. We create something wonderful that we get to share with the world—it's got its own life. When you finish your job you have this wonderful product you're looking at that makes somebody's day a little bit more fun and interesting. That's what makes it good, when it works the best.

SC: Is there anything else you'd like to add?

NO: I think I'd just like to add that scene shops are amazing things. The idea that if you walked in on Friday you saw something on the floor that was completely different than today, and next Monday you'd walk in and there would be something else. That is what we are: an incredible machine that creates things, and at any given moment there could be something new and different happening. We don't just do this or just do that—we do so many different things. We have to carve, we have to texture, we have to marbleize, we have to paint drops, and we have to be able to work on a computer to a degree. I have

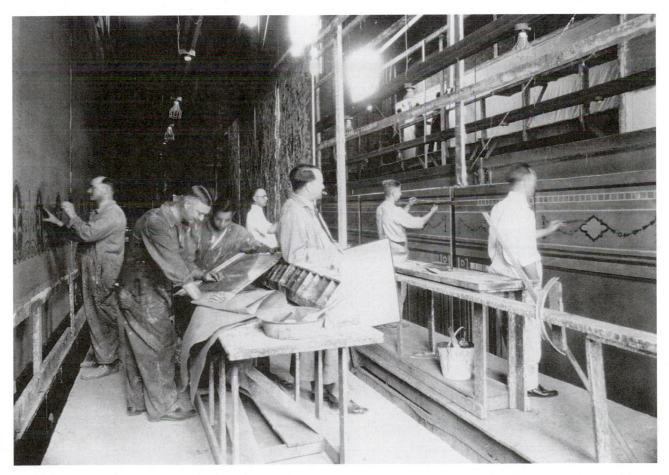

Figure 4.21   Artists, from left to right, Joe Folta, Art Rovic, Calvin Robert Brown, Frank Stengel, an unknown artist, Jack Westrom, and Bob Verne, working on the paint bridges at Twin Cities Scenic Studios, Minneapolis, Minnesota (photo courtesy of C. Lance Brockman).

to estimate numbers, I have to understand pricing systems, and I have to have an incredible inventory that I have to be physically responsible for. All those things to a certain degree we do as scenic artists.

As a charge artist you up the ante because ultimately you're responsible for every scenic artist on the floor. If something fails, it's not their fault, it's my fault. I put the wrong person on the job, I didn't do my homework in terms of knowing what that job was. I didn't have a good idea of how long it was really going to take so the responsibility sits with me. If something goes wrong it's because I didn't do something right most likely. So that's the scary part.

Part Two
The Tools of the Trade

Oleo Drop, courtesy of the Twin City Scenic's Collection, Performing Arts Archives,
University of Minnesota, St. Paul.

Chapter 5

The Painting Tools of Scenic Artistry

Fundamental scenic painting skills are gained in part by a thorough knowledge of the tools of scenic art. As in fine arts and related art fields, knowing a tool and how to use it is the first step toward mastery. Tools are the link between the scenic artist, the paint, and the surface. They are an extension of the scenic artist, and knowing which tool to use for a particular technique is something a professional scenic artist must know. Tools are to the scenic artist what language is to the writer. The wider knowledge and familiarity scenic artists have with the tools of the trade, the broader their range of skills will be.

The basic tool of the scenic artist is the paintbrush. Yet nearly anything used to spread, spray, stipple, smear, or sprinkle paint qualifies as a painting tool. Many of the tools discussed in this chapter traditionally are used in fine arts painting. Many others, though far less conventional, are highly useful in scenic painting. The creative application of tools is often what an inventive scenic painting technique is all about. Because the skills involved in scenic painting revolve primarily around painting, most of the tools discussed in this chapter are used for applying and manipulating paints and finishes. The painting techniques referred to in this chapter will be discussed in Part Three.

BRUSHES

Brushes are the age-old and obvious tool used to apply paint, and skillful handling of the paintbrush is one of the oldest crafts we know. The skill of painting is a bit like performance in that painting with a brush demands excellent control of hands and body. You may remember in the third grade when you were painting art projects, your teacher said, "Now remember, class, your brush is your friend!" Brushes are the most important part of a painter's kit of tools. A scenic artist's ability to handle them with alacrity is one of his or her primary skills.

The Anatomy of a Brush

A brush has three parts: bristles, a ferrule, and a handle (see Figure 5.1). The bristles are the working part of the brush. They absorb, hold, and spread paint. The ferrule is a band of metal, leather, or string used to hold the bristles to the handle. The handle is simply a material carved or molded into a shape that gives the user something to hold.

Within this simplicity lies a great deal of variation in the shape and style of brushes: different brushes are made for different painting applications and different paint mediums. The shape and style of a brush may depend on a traditional use for a brush or a regional preference of brush shape. For instance, a European sash brush, used for painting crisp lines and trim, has a round ferrule with tapered bristles so that the bristles at the center of the brush are the longest. A common sash brush purchased in the United States has a flat ferrule and bristles tapered toward one side of the brush. Both styles achieve the

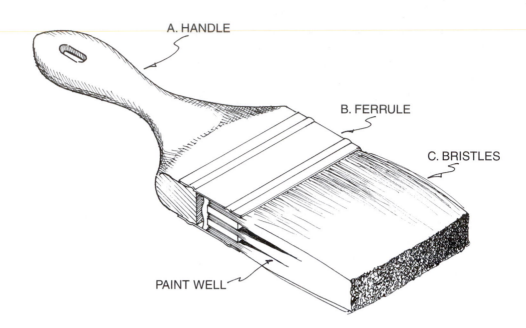

A. HANDLE

B. FERRULE

C. BRISTLES

PAINT WELL

Figure 5.1
The three parts of a
paintbrush.

same type of line but look radically different from one another.

Scenic painting for the theatre has created its own distinct class of brushes. These brushes reflect the basic shapes and styles of fine-arts brushes but are larger and more appropriate to the scale of scenic painting. For example, fitches in fine arts are oval-tipped, oval-ferrule brushes up to three-quarters of an inch wide. However, fitches may be as wide as three inches in scenic painting. The term *fitch* describes an entire group of high-quality brushes used mostly for detail work. Theatrical liners are part of this group of brushes and are particular to scenic painting and used for painting lines.

Brush Handles

The handle of a brush needs little more explanation than the handle of a coffee mug. It is designed simply to give a person something to hold on to when using a brush to spread paint. Brush handles commonly are made from wood or plastic, but they have been fashioned out of just about anything imaginable, from bamboo to ivory to precious metals. Large, heavy brushes designed to spread quantities of paint quickly have short, thick handles so the artist can get a good grip on the tool. Brushes designed for detail work that requires more finesse need to be held and controlled in the same manner as a pencil and, so,

have long, narrow handles similar to the handles found on watercolor brushes.

The Ferrule

The *ferrule* is the part of the brush that connects the bristles to the handle. The type of ferrule often dictates the name of the brush, such as a three-inch flat-ferrule or an oval-ferrule sash. The shape of the ferrule often is determined by the specific application the brush is designed for, so some brushes are also named for specific tasks, like a priming brush or a liner.

The ferrule is attached to the handle with small nails (brads) or by crimping the ferrule around the handle. The ferrule usually is made of corrosive-resistant metal, such as brass, copper, stainless steel, or nickel-plated steel. Leather ferrules were common until the early decades of the 20th century. They were flexible and a replacement could easily be cut and assembled when the old one cracked and fell apart.

Paintbrush Bristles

Animal hair and natural fur traditionally are the most common choice for good quality paintbrush bristles because they handle paint with control and ease of use. Paintbrush bristles have also been made with organic matter like pulped palm, bamboo, and yucca, but these are not common in scenic art. Modern bristles made of synthetic materials such as nylon and polyester are perhaps the most common materials used in brush fabrication. Synthetic bristles have become refined in recent years, leading to the introduction of brushes that serve a scenic artist as well as, or in some cases better than, natural bristle brushes. However, for most purposes, the finest brushes available today still are made from animal hair or natural fur, much as they have been for centuries.

China bristle is a very common bristle material found both in house and scenic painting brushes. It is valued because of the long length, useful taper, stiffness, and the snap of the bristles. Long bristles allow a brush to hold more paint as well as offer flexibility. *Taper* refers to the shape of the bristle at the tip where it meets the surface. Individual strands of hair end in a finely pointed taper in the first growth of animal hair. When many tapered bristle strands are combined into a brush, their taper naturally encourages the flow of paint to the tip of the brush. The finely tapered ends of the bristle also clump together when the brush is *charged* (loaded with paint), keeping the paint in the brush until the ends of the bristles are laid on the surface. Stiffness is self-evident, and a reasonably stiff bristle is preferable for most applications. *Snap* is a bristle's tendency to return to its original shape after it has been bent.

Common white, black, and tan china bristles are all bristles from hog. The black bristles tend to be finer than the white or tan. Until World War II, rural regions of Russia were the main producers of bristle for paintbrushes. Local farmers in the wooded areas of northern Russia raised herds of semi-wild swine that were prized for their long stiff bristle.[1] Traditionally, these bristles first came from China, which is why they are called china bristle. Hogs are raised in many regions in China; thus, each region produces hog bristles with different characteristics. Some of the softest bristles come from the regions of Tientsin and Zhengzhou. The hogs in Shanghai and Hangzhou are bred to produce a medium-stiff bristle. The province of Yunnan and the area around the city of Chongqing lead in the husbandry of stiff-bristled hogs.[2] If you ask at a paint store whether the bristles

of a particular brush are Zhengzhou or Chongqing, chances are all you will get is a quizzical look. But as you work with various types of china bristle brushes, you may begin to notice some differences in the feel and performance of the bristles.

Other less common types of bristles that a scenic artist may encounter are those from the hair of the ox, badger, squirrel, and horse. Ox and badger hair produce very soft, fine bristles, best used as lettering, sign-painting, and varnishing brushes. Ox-hair bristle is obtained from the ox's ear. Squirrel hair produces a soft, fine bristle frequently used in gilding brushes made for the application of metallic leaf and paints. Horsehair bristle is obtained from the horse's tail. This long gray bristle is used in brushes where an extra-long bristle is required, such as in some varieties of graining brushes used for faux finish work.

After bristles are harvested from animal hide, they are boiled to clean them and to satisfy health restrictions for export. This preparation also stabilizes the bristles so that when the bristles are set into a brush they will not warp. Generally, a brush is fabricated by setting the bristles into a ferrule and pouring epoxy onto the base of the bristles, bonding them to the ferrule as well as to one another. This is done before the handle is connected to the ferrule so the epoxy can be poured in from the back of the ferrule. The epoxy mixture must be carefully timed so that it sets up before running down the length of the bristles but not before saturating the base of the bristles inside the ferrule. Otherwise, the bristles will later fall out of the brush.

Brushes made from secondary bristle cuttings, other naturally coarse bristles, and some synthetic bristles may have been *flagged* or *exploded* at the bristle tip, meaning that the ends of the bristles were intentionally split into several strands so that they behave more like tapered bristles.

Bristles cut from animal hair are best placed in the ferrule in the orientation in which they grew because animal hair has a growth pattern that causes it to curve slightly in one direction when damp. If the orientation of the bristles is changed when laid into a brush, the bristles may splay in different directions. The finest brushes are built so that the bristles are aligned so that they curve inward towards the center, a consideration that is reflected in the high price these brushes demand. Yet this does not explain why some costly brushes are poorly made and unreliable.

In most brushes, only one type of bristle is used, but some brushes use a combination of bristles.

---

[1]Wagman, 1952.
[2]Ibid.

A wide-ferrule brush called a *Dutch brush* or *priming brush* is intended for use in covering large areas with paint quickly. One variety of this style brush combines black, white, and tan china bristles into the same brush. Some brushes designed for enameling and varnish work combine the softer ox hair with china bristles, whereas other varieties of brushes combine badger hair with china bristles. Some fine-art brushes combine natural squirrel and synthetic bristles for greater durability and lower cost.

Stiff bristles that do not hold their shape well are best used for larger brushes, where control and cutting an edge are not a factor. Finer bristles that "bunch" together when the brush is wet are best used for brushes intended for controlled techniques, such as lettering brushes, liners, and sash brushes.

Brush Construction

A clump of bristles may fall out of the ferrule, usually while painting a drop, giving you the opportunity to see the way they are bound. Some brushes contain something called a *paint well*, which is a plug or bar separating the rows or sections of bristles (see Figure 5.1). When the brush is dipped in the paint or charged, the paint well fills with paint. When the brush is pulled out of the bucket of paint, the bristles bunch together and hold a paint reserve in the paint well for a time. As the brush is put to a surface, the paint is pulled out from the ends of the bristles onto that surface. Sometimes the paint drops out of the well before the brush hits its mark. A painter will develop a rhythm, sometimes gently rotating the brush until it is over the target, between the bucket and the surface, skirting that moment when gravity will pull the paint out of a brush whether it is over its mark or not. This technique seems simple, so why take so long to explain it? Because as a colleague once pointed out to me, the paint comes out of the end of the bristles. This elegant observation is the first step in mastering any kind of brushwork.

Procuring Brushes

Most scenic artists collect a great variety of brushes in the course of their careers. The techniques in scenic painting are so varied that nearly every type of brush available will be put to use sooner or later. Standard house-painting brushes and flat-ferrule and sash brushes can be procured at hardware stores, lumberyards, and paint stores. Specialty brushes,

such as liners or fitches, can be purchased at theatrical supply companies and through catalogues. Lettering and sign-painting brushes can be purchased or ordered at sign-painting and art supply stores or through sign-painting supply catalogues.

Maintenance of Brushes

As with any tool, proper maintenance will increase the life of a brush. The bristles of any brush are most likely to break down first, so they should be thoroughly cleaned after each use, and paint should never be allowed to dry in the brush. If a painting technique requires the brush to be laid aside for long stretches of time between uses (more than about 10 minutes), the brush should be left in a bucket of water or rinsed well and set down so it will not dry out with paint in it. However, a brush should never be left in a bucket of water overnight because the bristles and handle will swell with water and may split the ferrule. The bristles of a brush will also become permanently curved when the brush is stored or left too long resting on the bristles.

There is a theory that if you want a brush to last as long as possible, never dip it into the paint bucket further than the ferrule. Since I am a complete failure in this regimen, I make it a rule to keep the ferrule as clean as the bristles. I always begin cleaning my brush by using a wire or stiff nylon brush to comb paint off the ferrule and the base of the bristles. Always comb the bristles in their natural direction. Never scrub across them, which forces the bristles to separate permanently. Lye-based soaps made to remove oils will dry out natural bristle brushes. It is preferable to clean and condition natural bristle brushes with a vegetable oil–based soap, like Murphy's Oil Soap®. To be sure that the brush is clean and no residual paint is hiding in the base of the bristles, wash it out with soap at least three times or until clear water seeps out from the base of the bristles when you gently bend them over.

Repairing Brushes

The ferrule of some brushes, particularly fitches and larger liners, frequently splits when the bristles first swell with water. Fitches are among the most expensive scenic painting brushes, costing up to $100 each depending on the brand. Once the ferrule has split the base, the bristles will become misshapen, which diminishes the usefulness of the brush. If this happens, you can send the brush back to the manufacturer and exchange it for a new one. However, I have found that the ferrules on the two- and three-inch scenic brushes are so prone to splitting that, after seeing how a colleague solved this problem, I also decided to fix the problem myself. To do so, braze or solder a copper wire or band around the ferrule near the base of the bristles before the ferrule splits. When soldering, wrap a cold, damp towel around the bristles to avoid singeing them. Then use a propane torch to solder the copper wire around the ferrule, using 50/50 solder and a lot of flux (see Figure 5.2). Keep a bucket of cold water nearby for emergencies and to cool the solder when you are done. Wrap the wire around the ferrule so about a three-eighths-inch band of copper reinforces the ferrule. Practice this procedure on an old brush before messing around with a new three-inch fitch.

Scenic painting brushes are large and often expensive. It is important to keep them clean, store them properly, and maintain them well. With proper care, it is not unusual for a good-quality specialty brush such as a large fitch to last for many, many years. Professional scenic artists have many hundreds of dollars invested in their brushes, so it is very important to maintain them well.

Types of Brushes

Knowledge of the various types of brushes, their uses, and applications is essential for a scenic artist. Most scenic artists gradually build up a brush kit that they bring from job to job. They may find that a particular brush works very well for a specific technique, or they may buy brushes to meet the needs of specific jobs as they arise. I find that I often buy a brush on impulse because it looks interesting. I have yet to buy a brush that did not turn out to be the find of the day on one project or another.

A great variety of brushes and variations are available. The following section presents the brushes you are most likely to encounter in a career as a scenic artist.

The Names of Paintbrushes

There are no hard and fast rules for naming brushes. Some brushes are classified by their ferrule shape, such as a flat-ferrule brush or an oval-ferrule brush. Some brushes are further described by their size, such as a four-inch flat-ferrule brush or a two-inch oval-ferrule brush. Brushes may also be described by the job they perform, such as a priming brush, foliage

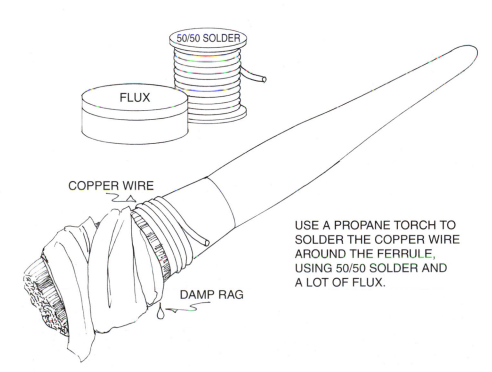

50/50 SOLDER

FLUX

COPPER WIRE

DAMP RAG

USE A PROPANE TORCH TO SOLDER THE COPPER WIRE AROUND THE FERRULE, USING 50/50 SOLDER AND A LOT OF FLUX.

Figure 5.2
Soldering copper wire into the ferrule of a brush.

brush, or a liner. A brush may even be described by what it is designed to paint, such as a truck-lettering brush or a sash brush.

Common Brushes

Scenic artists use commonly available brushes as well as those made especially for scenic painting. We will describe the common brushes first and give a description of how they are normally used. Keep in mind that all good brushes are expensive, but oddly enough, not all expensive brushes are good. Never use a high quality common or scenic brush with anything that will ruin it. Always protect your brushes while at work so that your 3″ liner does not get used for applying contact cement.

Flat-Ferrule Brushes

The *flat-ferrule* is the most common shape for brushes, and the basic flat-ferrule house-painting brush is the workhorse of the scenic artist trade. The alignment and length of the bristles facilitates both maximum coverage, using the flat of the brush, and razor-sharp lining, using the tips of the bristles. These brushes may have rows of bristles separated by a plug of wood or plastic, which forms the paint well. Some flat-ferrule brushes may have only one row of bristles with no paint well, but usually they have two, three, or four rows of bristles. The widths of commonly available flat-ferrule brushes range from one-half inch to eight inches; however, some specialty brushes may be wider. Generally speaking, the wider the brush, the more rows of bristles and paint wells it has.

> Keep in mind as you read this chapter that most brushes can be used in two ways. Generally, a brush is held so the side, or flat, of the brush gives the most coverage. The edge of the brush is best for narrow, even lines.

Lay-in Brushes, Dutch, and Priming Brushes

Lay-in brushes, Dutch, and priming brushes are all types of flat-ferrule brushes. The term *lay-in* refers to filling in basic areas of color on scenery. The size of these brushes is described by the width of the ferrule; for example, a two-and-a-half-inch lay-in brush would have a ferrule that is two-and-a-half inches wide. The thickness of these ferrules varies from three-eighths to one inch depending on the width.

Common sizes for lay-in brushes are one to four inches wide. The bristles in most flat-ferrule brushes are aligned parallel to the ferrule. These brushes are designed to be held at an angle nearly perpendicular to the surface for maximum surface contact and coverage. Flat-ferrule brushes are used for a variety of other tasks and techniques, such as base coating, wet blending, dry brushing, scumbling, spattering, and glazing. (We'll discuss these techniques at length in Chapter 9.)

A wider lay-in brush, with three or more rows of bristles, was, in earlier times, commonly called a *Dutch brush* because it was used to spread dutchman (wheat paste or scenic dope). Scenic dope, which was once used to adhere muslin to a flat or thinned for priming flats, is a mixture of whiting (a chalk-based pigment), water, and animal glue. Currently, these larger brushes, with ferrules six to nine inches wide by one-and-a-half to three inches thick, are often called *base coating* or *priming brushes* after the tasks for which they are most frequently used.

Sash Brushes

A *sash brush* has bristles trimmed at an angle from one side of the brush to the other (see Figure 5.3). This brush is used on edge, so the width of brush is parallel to the direction of the stroke. Paint is applied in a narrow, sharp line, also called a *cut line*. Sash brushes are named after the task they are used for in the house-painting industry: trimming the paint on sash windows and trim. In scenic painting, these brushes are very useful for lining with a lining stick. They hold more paint than a standard scenic liner so they pull out a longer line. They also generate a more consistent line than scenic liners.

Scenic Brushes

These are brushes especially designed for the scenic artist. These may be the most expensive brushes a scenic artist needs to have, but a set of well-made scenic brushes will last for several years with good maintenance.

Scenic Fitch or Foliage Brushes

Particular scenic brushes have developed over the centuries specifically for the scenic art and mural painting professions. The *fitch-style* is the basic form for many scenic brushes. A fitch resembles an oversized fine art brush. Fitches are the first choice for many scenic artists when developing detail, freehand, and trompe l'oeil painting. The fitch has a long, slender

Figure 5.3
1-inch, 2-inch, and 3-inch nylon bristle sash brushes.

wooden handle and a ferrule that widens into an oval opening. The bristles most commonly are white china bristles, which hold their shape and have enough spring to keep them from flattening out. The scenic fitch is a solid bristle brush and has no paint well.

Fitches are available most often in two-inch and three-inch sizes. Long bristles of one length, usually three inches, are used in these brushes. The ferrule generally is elliptical, but some have a flatter ferrule. The size of a scenic fitch is defined by the size paint stroke it generates rather than the size of the ferrule. These brushes are particularly useful for painting organic shapes such as foliage. Fitches are sold at scenic supply houses and through scenic supply catalogues.

The Scenic Liner   *Scenic liners* are a type of scenic fitch. The main difference between a liner and fitch is that the ferrule of the liner is usually gently crimped, so the ellipse of the ferrule flattens out. Some manufacturers set the bristles so that they are tapered, called *chiseling* or *cupping* the bristles, so that from the side view the bristles appear to end in a U or V shape. Bristles in scenic liners that are set this way cut a sharper line. Scenic liners range in sizes from one-eighth inch to two inches. The length of the bristles increases as the brushes increase in size. A set of liners is a standard item in the kit of every scenic artist.

You may have noticed the word *kit* used earlier in this text in reference to the touch-up kit. The term *kit* is generally used to describe a collection of tools, either a personal group of tools or an assortment of shop tools for use in off-site work. Most scenic artists assemble a kit of tools that they take with them from job to job. Even if the shop supplies a stock of brushes, many scenic artists prefer to use their own brushes for certain techniques because they know how the tool will handle and are accustomed to its idiosyncrasies. This is because every brush has its own character. This is particularly true of fitches. No two brushes perform in precisely the same way, even if they are purchased by the same manufacturer at the same time.

The term *lining* refers specifically to the technique of painting a line, either by using a lining tool as a guide to draw the brush along for straightedge work or for creating any kind of line freehand. A good liner will hold its shape when charged with paint and will not splay; in this way, the edges of the line won't become ragged or feathery.

Liners also can be used for nearly every kind of detail work: cutting in edges for base coating, base coating in tight areas, tight wet blends, foliage, and chiaroscuro work. Liners should not be used for spattering, dry-brushing, or painting on textured surfaces

Figure 5.4   Flat-ferrule brushes, clockwise from top left: four-inch and three-inch black bristle lay-in brushes; four-inch, three-inch, two-inch, and one-inch white bristle lay-in brushes; three-inch and two-inch soft black bristle brushes; an assortment of lay-in and sash brushes; priming brushes.

until the brushes are a little gray in the muzzle because these techniques are hard on brushes and will splay the bristles or wear them down. If you use a brush on a textured surface all day, you can actually see that the bristles have become shorter at the end of the day.

Various styles of liners are available to the scenic artist. Depending on the brand, some liners have ferrules that are crimped more tightly than others. Some scenic artists may develop an affinity for a certain brand of liner. Liners come in different styles of bristle as well. Some brands of liners are made with black china bristles. Some scenic artists maintain that the black bristle fitches, which have stiffer bristles, are better for painting vertically while the white bristle fitches are better for working in continental style. The *deer-foot fitch* or *angular liner* has bristles set in an angle, like a sash brush. Naturally, these brushes are very useful for straight lining with a line stick. The deer-foot fitch is also great for foliage. The *filbert fitches* have bristles set in an oval shape at the tip of the brush.

Bristles have a natural curve, which is desirable in all brushes, but the bristles in scenic liners should be laid in the ferrule so their curve turns inward towards the center of the brush. If the curve of the bristles has not been laid properly, it will be apparent as soon as the brush gets wet. Bristles swell in the ferrule when wet and might splay apart if not properly set. Sometimes, the bristles of a brush can be retrained by plastering them together with a vegetable oil–based soap or hair conditioner and then wrapping them together with string. Set the brush aside and let it sit that way for about a week. This actually sets the bristles in much the same way one sets hair. Unfortunately, this is usually a temporary solution. As the brush gets older, it will often start to splay apart as it did originally. If a new brush turns out to be unacceptable, return it to the manufacturer for a replacement. Most brush suppliers and manufacturers will stand behind the products they sell.

Liners can be purchased in sets of one-half inch up to two inches. There are usually seven brushes

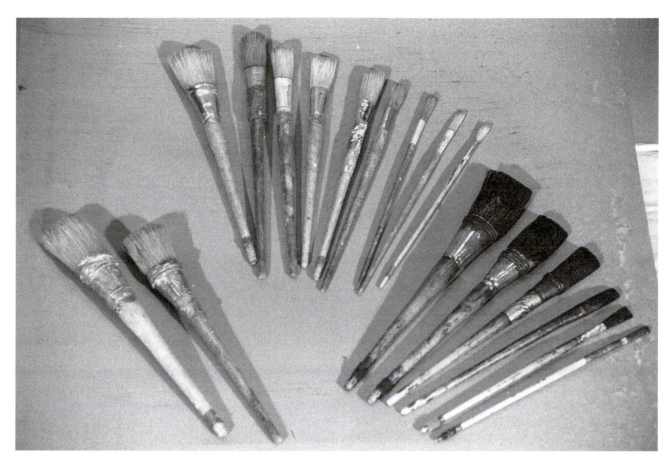

Figure 5.5 Scenic brushes, from left to right: foliage brushes or fitches and a selection of white china bristle scenic liners. (The liners on the right appear black because they are only used with aniline dyes.)

sized at intervals of one-quarter inch between these two limits. The size of a scenic liner is defined by the size of paint stroke it generates rather than the size of the ferrule. Once a scenic artist acquires a set of liners, he or she becomes familiar with the personality of each liner. A good set of liners, properly maintained, will serve for many years.

Oval-Ferrule Brushes

Oval-ferrule brushes, also called *oval sash brushes*, can sometimes be obtained at better paint stores and through scenic art supply catalogues. These brushes may be made from black or white china bristles. Their bristles may be flat across the ends or sharpen to a chisel tip, meaning that the bristles at the center of the brush are the longest and the sides are shorter. The ferrules on these brushes are usually copper or

nickel-plated steel. The brushes are generally one, two, and three inches in size (see Figure 5.6). Oval-ferrule brushes are excellent for laying in color, wet blends, and broad detail work because the bristles in these brushes maintain a tight edge.

Round-Ferrule Brushes or Ring Liners

Another variety of sash brush is the *round-ferrule brush*. This style of sash brush, also called a *ring liner*, is used most commonly in Europe and generally has white china bristles, although some brands of round-ferrule brushes have black china bristles. The ferrule of these brushes may be either copper or nickel-plated steel. To keep the bristles from splaying, the bristles are sometimes wrapped with string at their base. The bristles usually are chiseled at the ends, come in lengths ranging from one inch to

Figure 5.6 Example of foliage painting from the Lyric Opera of Chicago/Northern Illinois University Historical Scenic Collection (Courtesy of The School of Theatre and Dance, Northern Illinois University, Alexander Aducci, Curator).

two-and-a-half inches, and can be used for lining and detail work. When that rare pointillism project comes your way, these brushes will become indispensable (see Figure 5.7).

Stippling Brushes

One type of round-ferrule brush that is very specialized is the *stippling brush* (see Figure 5.8). Typically, this is an odd short-bristled, squat little brush. The bristles, ferrule, and handle all are short. However, there are some varieties of stippling brushes where the bristles are set into square-shaped wooden ferrules. These square and rectangular stippling brushes come in a variety of sizes up to one square foot. Square stippling brushes generally have handles that resemble the handle of a scrub brush more than that of a painting tool. The stippling brush may also be used to gently dry brush paint. Larger, square-shaped stippling brushes are available through supply catalogues.

Stippling brushes are not intended for brushing paint but rather for dabbing paint on a surface or texturing it once it has been applied, a technique called *stippling*. The stippling brush may also be used to gently dry-brush paint through a stencil.

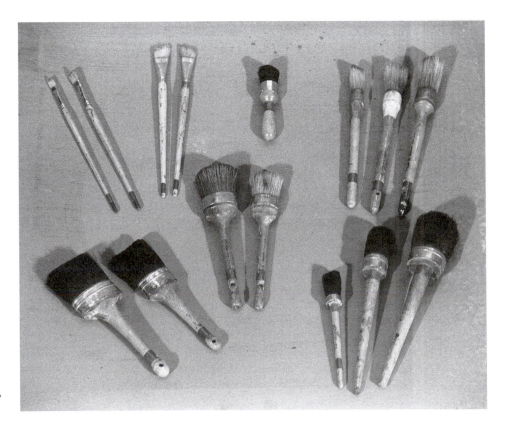

Figure 5.7
Round and oval sash brushes, clockwise from top left: fitch set for detail work, deer-foot fitches, a stencil brush, European sash brushes, ring liners, white bristle oval liners, black bristle oval liners.

Because the bristles are short and trimmed flat, the pattern this brush creates is lacy and grainy. The stippling brush is not a commonly used brush and can be tricky to master. However, once stippling techniques are learned, they can prove to be an effective method for creating controlled pattern work over a large area.

Lettering Brushes

Lettering brushes are essential for the good-quality lettering commonly called for in scenic painting. These brushes require practice, but once mastered, lettering projects will go much faster and look better when using these brushes. Very specific rules govern the appearance of lettering or signage. That is why doing signage with the right tools is an important skill for scenic artists to master. (Refer to Chapter 8 for information on lettering and signage techniques.)

Lettering brushes are sold primarily through sign-painting supply shops found in most larger cities as well as many art supply stores and theatrical brush dealers. Lettering brushes also can be purchased through supply catalogues, although they may be expensive. Lettering brushes are manufactured to be used with either water-based or oil-based paint. No one brush is intended to be used with both mediums. Lettering brushes made for water-based paint are the most common and useful for scenic painting.

Lettering brushes are available in a great many styles, sizes, and bristle types. Some of these can be extremely expensive. I once saw what I thought was a very fine-looking brush in a sign painting shop—I was right, it was a very fine brush, and it cost a week's pay. I am sure it was worth every penny, but I put it back in the rack and made another selection, knowing that theatre life would be too hard on fine sign-painting brushes. I made two selections from the more economical lines of sign-painting brushes, and they have served me very well to this day.

Lettering brushes are made with the finest quality bristles such as sable, squirrel, and badger. Their ferrules are made from brass, copper, stainless steel, or nickel-plated steel. The ferrule shape also defines the brush: *flats* have crimped ferrules, whereas *rounds*, also called *quills*, have ferrules that are not crimped. The bristles are often set into the ferrule so that the ends are squared off so the user can cut into the corner of the letter. Lettering brushes run from one-eighth inch up to two inches. As with other brushes, the size of a lettering brush is defined by the size of the paint stroke it generates rather than the size of the ferrule. It is not necessary for a scenic artist to own a lettering brush much larger than one inch wide. Lettering jobs that require a brush larger than that can easily be handled by scenic fitches. Signage brushes are useful for work on Plexiglas® or other

Figure 5.8 Stippling brushes are used to stencil. Scenic artists paint *Aladdin* at Scenic Art Studios, New York.

slick surfaces, where their softer bristles will not leave streak marks in the paint.

Because specific lettering brushes often are required for particular jobs, you might want to purchase them on an as-needed basis. I have found that one-quarter-inch and one-half-inch quills and three-quarter-inch flat-ferrule lettering brushes usually are adequate to cover most stray signage jobs that come along.

Other Specialized Brushes

Gilding Brushes Gilding brushes are divided into three categories: the gilder's tip, the mop or duster, and bronzing brushes.

The *gilder's tip brush* is not designed to get wet. Their bristles are made of badger or squirrel hair and their ferrules are made of cardboard or wood. They have no handle but are held by the ferrule. These brushes are used to pick up sheets of very delicate gold and silver leaf. The leaf clings lightly to the end of the bristles through static electricity so that it can be moved from the book of metallic leaves to the object being gilded. They are used because the leaves of gold and silver are too delicate to be touched by hand.

The gilder's tip is used in conjunction with a *gilder's block*, which is the palette used to hold and cut sheets of metallic leaf. This block is covered with chamois so that the leaf clings to the surface. The gilder's knife is a tool used to move the leaf around on the block and to cut the leaf. Burnishing tools are used to work metallic leaf into the nooks and crannies of an object being gilded and to ensure that the leaf adheres to the size medium. These tools also burnish, or polish, the surface as they adhere the material.

Another type of gilding brush is the *gilder's mop* or *duster*, used to smooth the leaf onto the surface of the object being gilded. These brushes are not designed to get wet. They are made of soft squirrel, badger, or ox hair, which will not tear or scratch the metallic leaf. The ferrules are made of brass, copper, or copper wire and the handles usually are made of wood.

Bronzing brushes are another kind of gilding brushes; however, these brushes are designed to get wet. Bronzing brushes are used to apply bronzing powder mixed with medium. These brushes are made with very soft bristles, such as squirrel, so that they leave no streak marks in the paint when it is applied. They sometimes have split quills with separate

Figure 5.9 The "Black Madonna," painted for *Polish Wedding* by Susan Crabtree.

groups of bristles set into copper wire ferrules placed side by side in a wooden handle. These brushes can be used for glazing and graining in some faux techniques because of their very soft bristles.

Generally, real gold or silver leaf is not used on stage scenery. First of all, the expense of real gold leaf is prohibitive. Second, working with genuine gold leaf requires time and an undisturbed environment, which are in short supply in a scenic studio. However, the knowledge of these tools is helpful to the scenic artist as occasionally there will be call for gilding on a specific prop or piece of scenery.

Pipers *Finger liners*, or *pipers*, are unique brushes that have several small ferrules or pipes lined up on a flat ferrule and handle that form a soldierly row. They are made of three to eight liners or pipes set into the same ferrule. These brushes are used for graining and pattern work. They do not hold a very large charge of paint, and they are expensive. These brushes are best purchased on an as-needed basis through scenic and decorative painting supply catalogues and companies.

Figure 5.10 Gilding a book spine for *Into The Woods* at Scenic Art Studios, New York.

Grainers Some brushes are marketed as *grainers*, specifically for wood-graining techniques. However, this classification can include a wide range of brushes, many of which already have been discussed, such as pipers and flat-ferrule brushes. *Overgrainers* have intervals of the bristle removed, so someone already has cut up the brush for you; however, most scenic artists prefer to pull out a pair of scissors and one of their oldest flat ferrule brushes and create their own overgrainers.

Blending and *mottling* brushes have very short bristles and are made for blending and working areas of glaze medium in faux finish work. Some graining brushes have extra-long bristles; these brushes are used for some specific overgraining techniques, such as *flogging* or a *wavering grain* stroke. A scenic artist could spend a fortune buying these specialty brushes. You should begin by acquiring basic needs brushes and collect specialty brushes when they are required. (We'll discuss the graining tools of the faux finish trade in Chapter 10.)

Other Useful Brushes

In addition to the specialized brushes just discussed, a scenic artist is likely to have a wide selection of inexpensive brushes. These are the common brushes found at paint, hardware, and discount stores. Scenic artists and scene shops always need a stock of cheap brushes on hand to handle the jobs for which one would never use fine scenic brushes, such as work with glue, shellac, alkyd paints, or textured surfaces. The surprising thing about cheap brushes is that, once in a while, they turn out to be the very brush for a particular job. For example, while once working on a scrim of the Declaration of Independence, the charge painter I was working with found that a 59-cent one-half-inch white china bristle brush, also called a *chip brush*, was the very brush for doing all the tight lettering on this project. Chip brushes come in a range of sizes from one-half inch to three inches, and every shop should always have a plentiful supply of these brushes as they never cease to be useful.

Foam brushes are very useful for sharp-edged work and detail and for tasks where a throwaway brush is needed. The marvelous thing about foam brushes is that their tips can be cut or notched in a variety of patterns. Foam brushes range in size from one inch to three inches.

Where to Buy Brushes

As mentioned throughout this chapter, some of the best sources for purchasing brushes are hardware stores and household paint suppliers. Theatrical suppliers are the most common source for the specific theatrical paintbrushes listed here. Art stores are an excellent source of brushes used for tight detail work. Lately I have discovered that white nylon-bristled flat-ferrule art brushes have been the most useful tool in my shop when generating tight trompe l'oeil work.

There are other interesting sources of brushes that you might explore. For instance, you may find that local restaurant supply stores sell pastry brushes that make terrific scenic glazing brushes. If you travel abroad, investigate the brushes available at the local hardware and art supply stores in foreign cities. Odd brushes sometimes materialize from time to time at the local hardware and paint stores and may surprise you. Buyers for these stores sometimes pick up lines of very interesting and useful brushes. For example, in a hardware store in a small Midwestern town I happened to pick up two round-ferrule horsehair brushes that are excellent for glazing. Unlike other round-ferrule brushes I have encountered, these had paint wells instead of solid bristle and hold a tremendous charge of paint that can glaze a line for many feet. Though these brushes lack finesse for tight work, I use them to lay-in long cast shadows and can usually pull a stroke out of them of 20 feet or more with one charge. These brushes were being sold as glue brushes. I am still very pleased with this find.

BROOMS, EXTENSIONS, ROLLERS, AND OTHER PAINTING ACCESSORIES

In addition to brushes, every imaginable paint tool can be found in the scenic paint shop. Anything that can be used for spraying, dripping, squirting, or smearing any kind of fluid potentially can be used with paint.

Brooms

Brooms are essential paint tools, and not just for sweeping floors. Push brooms are used in scenic art shops to smooth laundry starch, which is used as a primer on some drops. Soft plastic-bristled brooms are the best for starching drops because natural straw brooms are too coarse and horsehair brooms tend to shed. Brooms manufactured for floor scrubbing are also useful for starching and priming drops. These tools have shorter heads, usually only one foot wide, and are not as tiring to use a wide broom. They generally have soft straw bristles that are not as coarse as that of push brooms. (See Chapter 7 for a complete explanation of starching drops.) Brooms and sponge mops can also be used for broad paint techniques and blends of color.

Extensions

As we discussed in Chapter 4, the two primary ways to paint flat scenery and soft goods are in the eastern and continental styles. Painting on a paint frame, or painting up, is eastern style scenic painting. Painting scenery laying on the floor or on drops that have been stretched on a deck is continental scenic painting, or painting down.

The scenic artist actually walks on the scenery while painting in the continental style. Brushes and other paint tools are attached to extensions so the scenic artist need not bend over, kneel, or squat while working. Extensions also give the scenic artist free range of motion while working on the scenery. Some brands of scenic brushes have very long handles specifically made for working down. Some scenic artists prefer these. I find that, because my scenic work seems to be divided between painting up and painting down, the more expensive long-handled brushes are useful only half the time but a short-handled brush always can be put into an extension. Some brands of brushes have handles mounted into screw bases so that the short handle can be replaced by an extension. Telescoping extensions are sold at paint stores and through scenic suppliers for an adjustable extension.

To make a bamboo extension, cut the stalk to the desired length. If the cut is made on an angle, it will be easier to insert the brush into the extension. Split the brush-gripping end of the bamboo into quarters by tapping the end of the pole with a chisel in one direction and then again perpendicular to the first split. Only split the bamboo down to the first joint of the pole. After it has been split, lightly sand both ends of the pole, as freshly cut bamboo is full of nasty splinters. Next wrap one or two rubber bands around the splits so the bamboo will grip the handle of the brush. For larger bamboo intended to hold larger brushes, it is useful to have a rubber band placed below the inserted end of the brush handle nearer the first joint in the pole. The rubber bands will have to be replaced from time to time. Never use tape with a bamboo to grip the brush as it is messy and a hassle to deal with.

Bamboo sticks make excellent extensions and are widely used in the scenic art industry. Most scenic shops and scenic artists have a wide selection of bamboo for extensions, including bamboo sticks of varying diameters and lengths. Generally, the wider the diameter of the bamboo, the longer it will need to be. Wide-diameter bamboo accommodates larger brushes and gives the painter greater leverage.

Wooden dowel extensions are used with paint rollers, push brooms, and some styles of priming brushes that have handles that unscrew from the ferrule so that it can be fitted onto a dowel extension. Wooden dowel extensions in which screw threads simply are carved into the wood at the end of the handle wear out quickly. You may be starching a drop and the broom head will suddenly drop off. A wooden dowel extension that has a threaded metal cap on the end will last much longer. If the metal cap comes off, do not despair. Simply fill the cap with a good epoxy and tap it back on. It will not happen a second time.

Edgers

The house-painting industry has many tools to make painting faster, easier, and cleaner. A scenic artist can benefit from the use of these tools because painting some kinds of hard scenery is essentially the same as house painting. When painting a trim color, you can use edgers to guide your brush and mask unpainted areas. A piece of bristol board, or any other rigid card stock, makes a crude edger and can be custom shaped. However, after two or three uses, the edge of the bristol board will become gummed up with paint and begin to leave marks. Manufactured edgers have a steel or plastic guide that you can wipe off between uses. These edgers come in lengths from a few inches to three feet.

Another tool used as an edger is a paint pad. This is a foam rubber pad about the size of an index card with a fibrous surface. It leaves a smooth trail of paint with a crisp edge when charged with paint and drawn along a corner or the edge of a piece of trim. However, paint pads hold little paint and must be recharged frequently.

Rollers

Paint rollers are common and easily available. They are made for use with water-based paints, alkyd paints, or shellacs. Roller units consist of the roller frame, a roller cover, and a pan to hold the paint. *Roller frames* come in various widths: standard sizes are 3 inch, 4 inch, and 9 inch; industrial-size roller frames are 18 inches wide and larger.

Roller covers once were made primarily from lamb and sheep fleece because nappy fur soaks up a good charge of paint and rolls on smoothly. Fleece roller covers are still available, but they are rather expensive. Polyester roller covers paint as well as fleece at a fraction of the cost. Roller covers have a stiff core that slips over the frame. The core may be made of water-resistant cardboard or plastic. Cardboard roller covers are less expensive and fall apart faster. I prefer to use the cheaper roller covers to work with alkyd paint or shellac because the cost of solvent to clean them is not worth the price of reusing a cover. I use better-quality covers with water-based paint and clean them out after each use.

Roller trays hold the paint and allow the roller to be evenly charged, which means to ink the roller with paint. *Roller screens* fit into five-gallon paint cans and serve to squeeze off excess paint after the roller is dipped into the bucket. Standard roller trays are designed to accommodate nine-inch-wide rollers and have a grill pattern in them. This grill pattern can leave an impression on the roller cover that is transferred to the scenery. If this is a problem, cafeteria trays, condiment trays, and homemade trays fashioned out of visquene can be used to avoid imprinting the roller cover. Roller tray liners are useful when any paint other than water-based paint is used. The liner can be thrown away, saving the cost of the solvents it would require to clean the tray. Large roller trays are available to accommodate the 18-inch-wide rollers as well as industrial three-foot-wide rollers. Narrower roller trays are available to accommodate three- and four-inch rollers, although as a rule there is nothing wrong with having a roller tray that is too big for the roller.

Cleaning roller covers can be done in a few different ways. To clean the covers by hand without the benefit of some handy device takes a while. Roller covers hold paint; that is their job. Excess paint can be squeezed out of the roller cover with a cup-shaped paint scraper.

One cleaning tool available in most paint stores is a *spinner-style brush and roller cleaner*. It cleans the paint out of the cover with centrifugal force. The cover slips over the end of the spinner. When the handle of the spinner is pumped, the cover will twirl and the paint will fly off. If you hold the spinner up in the air in front of your face the first time you give it an experimental twirl, you will get covered in paint. If you spin the cover under running water or in a bucket of water, it will come clean very quickly. Spinners are marketed as roller and brush cleaners. I do not recommend using them for brush cleaning because it is very hard on the brush as it splays the bristles.

Another type of roller cleaner is a tube that the roller cover fits into, which is capped at both ends. One cap has a hole in it and the other cap has a water hose connector imbedded in it. Once the roller cover is inside, a hose is connected to the tube and the roller cover is rinsed off.

Roller cover *nap* refers to the length of the fleece, whatever its composition. Standard lengths of nap are one-quarter inch, one-half inch, three-quarters inch, and one inch. The longer the nap, the more paint the roller will hold. However, one aspect of working with rollers is that they generate spatter as the roller whips back and forth across a surface. The longer the nap, the more the roller is apt to generate this annoying spatter. The fine spatter can work itself into all sorts of surprising nooks and crannies if you are not careful. Therefore, it is best to use a shorter nap if you are doing work where spatter could be a problem. The shorter nap is also better for clear finishes. A longer nap roller cover mixes more air bubbles into varnish while it is being rolled on, which might create a milky haze in the finish when it dries.

Roller covers can be made with many products other than natural fleece or polyester fleece, such as foam or carpet loop for specific jobs like texturing and gluing. *Foam roller covers* come in a range of thickness, but one-quarter inch up to one inch are the most common. These covers do not hold a long-lasting charge of paint, so they are best used with thicker paints and mediums.

Roller covers with a solid thick foam covering can be sculpted or cut into a pattern for any variety of uses such as texturing, pointillism, and patterns. A stock of these roller covers uncut in three-inch and nine-inch sizes should be kept on hand for projects as they arise. Foam or fleece can be carved away or taped to create your own texture or pattern (see Figure 5.11). Foam rollers designed to paint rough surfaces have a three-quarter-inch foam covering with slits cut into it. These roller covers can be cut or torn up for some varieties of painted texture.

Roller covers are also available with a thick uneven sponge texture that resembles a natural sponge. These can be used with texture coats and for paint techniques that give the impression of rough

Figure 5.11   A scenic artist using a cut roller to add texture to the underpainting of a drop at the Scenic Art Studios, New York.

natural surfaces. A variety of foam rollers with patterns precut into them are available in the decorative painting departments of many hardware and paint stores. Do not discount these as tools for hobbyists—they might turn out to be the very thing to keep you from laboring late into night on some eleventh hour project.

Texture roller covers are not designed to hold any paint at all. Their surface is densely covered with short rubber loops about three-eighths of an inch long. They create a pebbled texture when rolled across a surface that has a texture coat brushed, rolled, or sprayed on it. The more viscous the texture medium, the sharper the peaks of the texture will be. If the texture is thin, the surface will settle down to a uniform pebbly surface after it has been passed over with the texture roller.

Scenic and decorative paint suppliers also market a roller cover made with crenellations of leather surrounding it. These covers are designed to create a mottled paint finish and may be used with paint or texture mediums. You may also create your own painted texture by wrapping rags, plastic, rope, or most anything around the roller cover.

Glue roller covers are covered with shallow looped carpet. These rollers are useful for spreading wood glue, laminate adhesive, foam adhesive, contact cement, and other similar substances. Fleece rollers are not very effective in pushing sticky substances around, hence the usefulness of the glue roller covers. These covers make an interesting pattern but they do not hold a charge of paint for very long. It is also difficult to control how heavily the paint is applied to the surface. These roller covers may also be used with a texture compound.

Pattern rollers are available from scenic suppliers with wallpaper-like patterns molded directly on the roller cover. These are sold as units with the carriage and cover sold together and are available in an array of patterns. They have a registration notch so that designs can be lined up. The roller is charged with thick paint and prints in much the same way a rubber stamp prints a pattern. A steady hand is needed to work with these tools and keep the repetition of the pattern flawless. These rollers are not easy to work with on units that have had three-dimensional molding applied to them.

Radiator rollers are narrow in diameter and are sold as a complete unit, cover and frame together. They are used to paint behind radiators (hence the name), refrigerators, and other appliances where the space is too tight to accommodate a full-diameter roller. A scenic artist might find them useful for reaching into tight spaces where a normal roller would not fit.

Power rollers feed paint directly to the roller cover, eliminating the need to charge the roller. Paint is poured into a reservoir connected to the roller by a hose. The reservoir provides a steady and smooth flow of paint. For large projects requiring painting with a roller, a power roller may be a consideration. The power roller will not work for jobs that need to be done on the floor because the handle has no screw base for use with an extension.

OTHER TOOLS AND ACCESSORIES FOR THE SCENIC ARTIST

Scenic artists use a huge variety of other tools to apply paint. Many of these can be made or modified for each job at hand. Keep in mind that many jobs you take on will require the fabrication of some new tool to make the work faster and better. Some of these are discussed here.

Stencils and Stamps

Stencils are used to make repetitive designs and patterns. Stencils can be more intricate than paint stamps and can be registered (that is, precisely aligned) to create very complex designs in layers. A stencil is cut from flat, durable, water-resistant materials. Paint is sprayed, rolled, or stippled across the stencil, which serves as mask for the negative areas of the design.

One important trick to creating designs for stencils is that no design can have any negative areas that are completely surrounded by positive areas or the stencil will fall apart. Negative areas in stencils must be tied together. These ties are often incorporated into the design. If the negative areas are absolutely integral to the design and ties cannot be worked into the design, there are alternatives. Cut the negative areas out with ties left in to link these negative areas together. After the scenery has been stenciled and dried, the print left by the ties can be painted out with the appropriate color. If this approach is not feasible, the stencil can be netted so the negative areas stay in place without ties.

Here is how to net a stencil. After the stencil is cut, assemble all the pieces in their proper place on something flat and rigid, like sheet stock Upson® board. Use double-faced tape or rubber cement to hold the pieces in their proper positions. The pattern should be laid out so that the finished stencil will be bobbinet side up. Stretch a piece of polyester bobbinet across the top of the stencil. Use solvent-based contact cement over the top of the stencil to firmly attach the bobbinet to the stencil pieces. Cover the top of the stencil and the bobbinet on top of it completely with the contact cement, being careful not to stick the stencil to the surface underneath. Once the contact cement is completely dry, the stencil is ready for use. This method will also work to reinforce stencils that are fragile and may fall apart through repeated use. The paint will print through the bobbinet. When using stencils reinforced in this way, make sure to clean the stencil frequently and carefully. Let the stencil dry out thoroughly if it begins to get soggy. In other words, be patient. Stenciling is a laborious process; take your time and be meticulous. Done well, the results will be very gratifying.

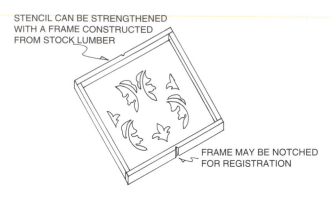

STENCIL CAN BE STRENGTHENED
WITH A FRAME CONSTRUCTED
FROM STOCK LUMBER

FRAME MAY BE NOTCHED
FOR REGISTRATION

Figure 5.12   Standard stencil construction.

Several materials are good for making stencils, such as stencil paper, Upson board, lithography or tin plate, polystyrene sheet plastic, filled fiberglass window screening, linoleum, plastic laminate, and even kraft paper. Stencil paper, the traditional choice for stencils, is paper or a hot pressed board treated with wax to make it water-resistant. Stencil paper does not hold up well to repeated use with wet techniques, such as spraying, and is not a good choice for repeated use. Upson board, or easy-curve, is commonly used in scene shops. This material comes in one-eighth-inch and one-quarter-inch thickness and is used in the same way as stencil paper. The disadvantage to using Upson board with some stenciling techniques is that it is thicker and will not leave as clean a print as stencil paper or some other products. After a stencil has been cut out of any paper product, several coats of clear shellac or oil-based enamel should be applied to both the front and back of the stencil to waterproof it, give it a washable surface, and prevent warping.

> Stencils can even be cut from kraft paper that has been sealed with several coats of shellac or laminated after a fashion on both sides with packing tape. When deciding what material to make the stencil from, consider the job that needs to be accomplished.

Lithography plate (litho plate or tin sheeting) makes a terrific stencil material. It is impervious to water, very sturdy, and easy to cut. You can purchase new litho plate at printing supply houses and obtain used litho plate directly from printers. After it has been used, it is of no further use to the print shop. Plates the print shop does not need to keep on file are thrown away. Newspaper printing departments also use litho plate for inserts. The only disadvantage in obtaining plates from this source is that they generally are only as large as the size of the newspaper inserts. Occasionally in a scenic design, there will be a call for a very large repetitive pattern.

Polystyrene sheet plastic is commonly used for thermoplastic molding. It is sold as large as 4′ × 8′ sheets and comes in a wide range of thickness, from one millimeter to one-quarter inch. Fairly thin three- or five-millimeter polystyrene is suitable for most stenciling. Like litho plate, polystyrene is very easy to cut and waterproof. Plastic laminates, or Formica®, make suitable stencils, although they are more difficult to cut. Plastic laminates can be purchased in 5′ × 10′ sheets.

Cutting stencils is labor-intensive work. You can cut out stencils made out of card stock with an

Figure 5.13   A variety of unframed stencils. Scenic Art Studios, New York.

X-Acto or mat knife blade. Change blades often to keep the job going smoothly. A *cut-awl* is a highly maneuverable power saw used to cut thin material such as Upson board, litho plate, tin sheet, and plastic sheeting. A cut-awl works like a miniature skill saw and has a rotating cuff; the blade can swivel a full 360° so it can be maneuvered around tight curves and details. It can cut through Plexiglas, stiff plastics, thin wood sheet stock, and litho plate. For cutting the materials discussed here, the best cut-awl blade to use is a #12 blade, which is a saw-tooth chisel-tip blade. Pilot holes must be predrilled when cutting plastic laminate or the laminate will shatter. When cutting other materials discussed here, a cut-awl can be set right down in the area to be cut away and the blade will puncture the material. Be sure to clamp your material firmly and work on a soft surface like Homasote. The cut-awl is a power tool, so when using it be sure to wear appropriate protective equipment.

> When preparing to cut a stencil, bear in mind that you should cut multiple copies. Repetitive applications of paint will build up on a stencil. In many techniques of paint application, the paint will drip or run under the stencil and ruin the work. Usually, only two or three applications can be done before a stencil will have to be sponged off and dried. Keeping the stencil dry on the side that comes in contact with the scenery is particularly important. With multiple copies of the stencils, the work will not be interrupted as often for cleaning. Stencils not in use can be put in front of a fan to dry.

After the stencils are cut out it may be obvious that they are too fragile to last through the job ahead. In this case, they should be attached to a frame for reinforcement. Make a frame of one-inch to two-inch wood stock, depending on the size of the stencil and the support it needs. Try to keep the frame as lightweight as possible. Always leave a border of at least six inches on every side of the design when making a stencil. This border will serve as a built-in mask and leave something to attach to a frame if needed. The stencil can be nailed or stapled to the frame from underneath. After the stencil has been attached to the frame, seal the inside edges with silicone or latex caulk so that the paint cannot seep between the layers (see Figure 5.12).

Depending on the desired appearance of the design, thick or thin paint can be used with a stencil. Thin paint is more prone to seepage under the stencil. The viscosity of the paint may determine the way paint is applied: thicker paint for stippling and rolling, thinner paint for spraying.

Stencils made for use with dyes are more effective if they are somewhat absorbent rather than waterproof. Dye is dissolved rather than suspended in water and it is very thin. The viscosity of dye can be increased by adding a gum thickener or starch. When stenciling, it may not be necessary to add thickeners if the dye is sprayed through a stencil made of unsealed Upson board. The Upson board will hang on to the thin dye so it does not drip on the project at hand. Multiple copies of the stencils will be necessary so that they can be wiped off and dried for several minutes between uses (see Figure 5.13). See the paint stamp section of this chapter for an explanation of pattern registration and color separation in multi-colored designs.

> Linoleum is a wonderful material to use for stencils. Stencils made from this material can be as large as the flooring material itself. Designs and motifs can be cut into it with a mat knife or an X-Acto knife. It is also sturdy and inexpensive. Because the linoleum is flexible, it always lays flat and will not warp, so it does not need to be framed. A technique that works very well with linoleum stencils is to cut the pattern so the soft side of the linoleum is up. Align the stencil into position on the scenery. Lightly spray the paint through the stencil pattern with an aerosol sprayer such as a Pre-valve®. Before removing the stencil, dab at the pattern with a large stencil brush to even out the paint. This method has many advantages. First, once you get a feel for the amount of spray to apply to the stencil and the stippling technique, you will never have to stop and clean the stencil off or let it dry out. Secondly because the stippling spreads the paint out so thinly, the stencil can usually be repositioned directly adjacent to the last repetition, even if it partly overlaps it, without smearing. Because of the last two points, this method of stenciling actually goes very quickly.

Texture stencils are used to create a textured pattern or design. The stencil serves as the negative area around a mass of thick texture compound. Brick-making is the perfect example of a good

Figure 5.14
These three examples of stenciling show the pattern as well as the texture techniques in use. Scenic Art Studios, New York.

application for a texture stencil. One-eighth-inch to one-quarter-inch polyethylene or three, five, or seven-mil-thick polystyrene sheets work very well for making texture stencils. The polystyrene already might be at many scene shops because it is commonly used for vacuforming. Most polystyrene sheets comes in 4′ × 8′ sizes. Once the design is cut out, the stencil is ready to use. The texture mixture can be spread over the stencil and the excess squeegeed off. When the stencil is lifted straight up, the textured pattern will remain. When preparing texture compounds for texture stencils, it is important to make sure the

compound is viscous enough that it will not settle into the negative areas after the stencil has been removed. Fine-grain vermiculite mixed into the texture compound will create body and soak up excess moisture.

Paint Stamps

Paint stamps are tools used for making repeating designs, textures, and patterns such as in wallpaper, ornamental tile, marble tiles, foliage, or terrazzo. They are made of foam rubber cut into a pattern or design and adhered to a plywood base. The stamp is charged with paint in much the same way an ink stamp is charged with ink, and the pattern or design can be stamped on the scenery repeatedly (see Figure 5.17).

The foam rubber for a paint stamp should be at least one-half to one inch thick so that the plywood backing does not make an impression when the stamp is pressed onto the scenery. The smaller the stamp, the thinner the foam rubber can be. Some foam rubber has a plastic coating on one side, so be careful that the coated side is the side glued to the backing. The foam rubber should be cut out as evenly as possible, clean through with an X-Acto knife. Change the blade often so the cutting goes smoothly.

The plywood base of the paint stamp should be cut out to approximately the same shape as the design or pattern. Attach an upright handle of one-inch stock lumber or a wooden dowel to the base before adhering the foam rubber if you are painting in the continental style. Also, a short dowel handle may be attached to the stamp for easy storage; the stamp can then be used with a bamboo extension. The handle should be firmly attached so that the stamp can be rocked back and forth ever so slightly

to ensure a good print. Large stamps can get fairly heavy, more so after the stamp is charged with paint. When constructing the base and handles for a stamp, care should be taken to keep the materials as light as possible. If it is a very large pattern, two handles may need to be attached. Use half-inch plywood instead of three-quarter inch for the base; make the handle out of two-inch stock.

Registration of the paint stamp is critical for multiple layers of color, repeating patterns, or both. Complex stamp designs should be drawn out full-scale on paper first and transferred by a pounce onto the foam rubber stamp as well as the plywood base. Pounces are large patters made by perforating paper with a pounce wheel (pounces are discussed in detail in Chapter 8). If color separations are needed, each of them should be drawn out on the pounce as well. Multicolor designs are done with multiple paint stamps. Separate each color section of the design and create a separate stamp for each color. Each stamp must be the same size and have alignment marks, called *registration marks*, so all stamps will align properly with each other. If a multicolored stamp design is made up of nonconnecting elements, the stamp may be carefully charged by hand, using

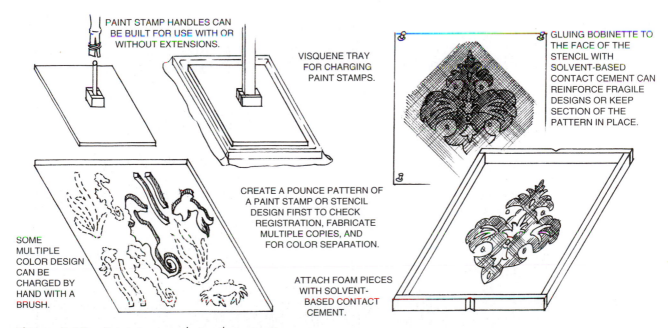

PAINT STAMP HANDLES CAN BE BUILT FOR USE WITH OR WITHOUT EXTENSIONS.

VISQUENE TRAY FOR CHARGING PAINT STAMPS.

GLUING BOBINETTE TO THE FACE OF THE STENCIL WITH SOLVENT-BASED CONTACT CEMENT CAN REINFORCE FRAGILE DESIGNS OR KEEP SECTION OF THE PATTERN IN PLACE.

SOME MULTIPLE COLOR DESIGN CAN BE CHARGED BY HAND WITH A BRUSH.

CREATE A POUNCE PATTERN OF A PAINT STAMP OR STENCIL DESIGN FIRST TO CHECK REGISTRATION, FABRICATE MULTIPLE COPIES, AND FOR COLOR SEPARATION.

ATTACH FOAM PIECES WITH SOLVENT-BASED CONTACT CEMENT.

Figure 5.15 *Paint stamp and stencil construction.*

brushes to "paint" the color onto the foam rubber. This way, only one paint stamp has to be built.

Single-color, repeating designs need registration marks as well. The registration marks must correspond to a grid or gridlines on the scenery itself. The design that must be registered should be placed on a square or rectangular base. The top side of the base should have marks at the edges that will relate to lines and marks cartooned on the scenery so that the design can be placed with accuracy. In the case of a stamp pattern registered by eye, such as with the pineapple stamping in Figures 5.16 and 5.17, the shape of the base should match the shape of the stamp pattern itself for ease of placement.

After the design has been cartooned and the foam rubber pieces have been cut out, they are ready to be adhered to plywood bases. First, draw and ink the design on the bottom of the plywood base. Cover the base and the back of the foam rubber pieces with contact cement, using solvent-based rather than water-based cement. Water-based contact cement will come apart after the stamp has been in use for a while. After the contact cement is dry, carefully place the pieces of foam on the base and press them firmly in place. Be absolutely certain of your placement of the two layers. Contact cement does not allow for shifting. Hot melt glue may also be used to adhere the foam rubber. In some cases it may be easier to cover the entire area of the design first with the foam rubber and then cut and carve the design out with an X-Acto knife.

> Safe disposal of used blades is very important when using X-Acto knife blades or any other razor-sharp blades. Often, rubbish gets stuck in the garbage pail and someone must reach in to pull it out. Always tape over the blade before it is thrown away to avoid a serious accident.

Paint used for stamps should be water-based. Shellac or alkyd paint will ruin a stamp. The paint must be fairly thick or it will drip and run to one end of the stamp. Pour the paint needed to charge the stamp onto a cafeteria tray. If the tray is not large enough to accommodate the stamp in use, drape a piece of heavy visquene plastic in the bottom of a paint cart or staple it to a wooden frame made to fit the stamp.

Figure 5.16
Upholstery foam carved into pineapple-shaped paint stamps, Scenic Arts Studios, New York.

Figure 5.17 The pineapple paint stamp in action. Applying the base coat.

Figure 5.19 The pineapple shapes are finished by hand.

Figure 5.18 The middle phase of painting pineapples with a stamp.

TEXTURE TOOLS

Texture-applying tools have been more recently used in theatrical painting and have been taken mostly from other crafts. We'll discuss the techniques of texturing in Chapter 9.

Sponges

Sponges of all varieties are essential in a scenic studio. Both natural and synthetic sponges create interesting grain patterns with paint and make soft blends. A natural sea sponge serves as a fine paint tool. These sponges grow in warm ocean climates where they are harvested by sponge divers. The softer sponges with a consistent pattern are sold for the bath, as janitorial supplies, and to paint suppliers. Coarser sponges with random patterns also are available at janitorial supply and paint stores. Cosmetic sponges, which are very small and have a very fine pattern, generally are much more expensive and not as useful for scenic painting. If you find yourself in a tropical climate where sponge diving is one of the local industries, stock up on sponges as the selection always is better close to the source.

An advantage of a natural sponge in scenic painting is that the imprint that it leaves is organic. Every natural sponge has its own unique pattern. Most paint shops and scenic artists that have a stock of tools will collect a good variety of natural sponges.

Synthetic sponges come in geometric shapes by virtue of manufacturing. In addition to everyday cleanup chores, they are useful for certain painting techniques. Synthetic sponges can be cut up or carved into shapes and patterns for creating texture on surfaces like brick or tile. Most synthetic sponges are either cellulose or foam rubber and best used for even-grained stamping. However, foam rubber sponges do not hold a charge of paint as well as cellulose ones. Cellulose sponges have reasonably good organic texture. They are very useful for distressing and smoothing out painted patinas, grime, and dirt. Cellulose sponges can be torn apart along their length. This way a grain emerges that works very well for bricks and some varieties of stone and marbles. Much like a texture stamp, sponges can be used with stencils for uneven, textured patterning, as with a stipple brush.

There should also be a good supply of synthetic sponges for cleanup around the shop. However, do not use a synthetic sponge to clean a paint spill on a drop; always use a natural sponge to clean up mishaps on scenery.

Small natural sponge pieces are available at most paint and hardware stores and are very reasonably priced. It is useful to keep such sponges close at hand in a bucket of water while painting with water-based paints so that you can deal with any stray drips immediately, without having to run to the paint sink. Spills on scenery are very difficult to clean, especially when the scenery has many complex layers of painting on it. A soft natural sponge is the best tool for carefully cleaning a paint spill. Cleaning is a skill too! Always blot or soak the spilled paint, never scrub or wipe it. Scrubbing will pull up lower layers of paint and probably work in more of the spilled color.

Rags

Rags, just scraps of cloth, have a great many functions in the scene shop. Every shop should be well stocked with rags for cleaning. Rags can be purchased by the pound at most paint supply stores, and well-stocked stores will have a choice of rags, including lint-free rags for staining. Almost every kind or grain of cloth, from flannel and linen to burlap and erosion cloth, is useful for the scenic artist. Flannel rags are very useful to have at hand when cartooning for erasing charcoal lines. (We'll discuss cartooning fully in Chapter 8.)

Rags also can be used as texture tools in a common technique called *rag rolling*. Here, the rag is crumpled up and immersed in paint, then wrung out and rolled around on any surface to be textured. This method can be done with nearly any kind of material. Different types of material create different textures. Finer weave rags sometimes are fringed on the edges to add to the texture. The coarser fabrics, such as burlap and erosion cloth used in landscaping, can be purchased through landscape material suppliers. Rags are very useful for wiping down and smoothing patinas and aging glazes on scenery. Softer, more absorbent rags will be more helpful in this application.

Floggers

The *paint flogger* is a texture tool made from strips of rag attached to the end of a stick, resembling a mop of sorts. Floggers can be used to create texture by dipping the rag end in paint, wringing it out, and striking the surface (called *flogging*) or gently twirling and dabbing (called *schlepitchka*).[3] These simple techniques produce very attractive random texture patterns. Clean muslin floggers also are used to clean dirt and charcoal off scenery after the cartoon is made. Clean floggers are a staple of every paint shop.

Feathers

Feather dusters may be used in the same manner as floggers to create texture. They are the traditional tools used for the technique of schlepitchka. They may be dragged lightly across a painted surface to create a grain. Feather dusters are sold at discount, grocery, and cleaning supply stores. At cleaning

[3]Burris-Meyer and Cole, 1938.

suppliers, a selection of different varieties of feather dusters may be found. The most common feathers to be found are chicken, pheasant, and ostrich. Of course, different varieties will create different textures or grains. Feathers by themselves sometimes are used for graining faux marbles in extremely fine detail.

Offbeat Tools

All sorts of interesting objects serve as paint tools. When you confront a new texture project or treatment, just consider what kind of object may be useful to obtain the desired effect and then give it a test. For example, for a Jackson Pollock-style painting technique, in creating long, fat strings of paint, a turkey baster was used to good effect. In another situation, a stage deck made of several plates of one-quarter-inch steel set one-eighth of an inch apart had raw wood visible in the seams. An oversized hypodermic needle obtained from a research lab was used to squirt paint into the cracks. Trying to recreate the pointillist style of Georges Seurat leads to all manner of rapid dot-painting, including clusters of ethafoam rod, foam bottle brushes, and foam orthopedic mattresses. Never rule anything out as a possible paint tool!

SPRAYERS

Sprayers are a class of tools of scenic painting so important and varied that they are second only to brushes themselves. The Viennese scenic designer Joseph Urban and his team of scenic artists introduced the practice of using paint in garden sprayers to the United States in the early 1900s. His scenic artists began one of the largest scenic studios in New York and used sprayers as a painting tool. Their innovations made the garden sprayer a standard paint tool in every scenic paint shop on this continent (see Figure 5.20).

Sprayers work in one of three ways:

1. Garden sprayers work by pressurizing the air in a reservoir tank, which forces the fluid paint out of the tank through a fluid tube into the hose, wand, and nozzle of the sprayer. Pressure pots and high-volume, low-pressure sprayers work with compressed air in this way as well.
2. Pneumatic spray guns work by sending compressed air through the spray gun, creating a vacuum that pulls the fluid paint up through a suction tube in the paint cup below the gun.
3. Airless sprayers work by pressurizing the fluid paint itself, which is sent through a pressurized hose and spray gun. The paint is sucked out of a reservoir of paint, which is kept in a bucket placed under the airless into which the supply tube is immersed.

Garden and Pump Sprayers

Garden sprayers are available in many sizes and varieties and are made to spray insecticides and weed killers. They consist of a fluid tank, a pump to pressurize the tank, a nozzle on a wand that aerates fluid as it is sprayed, and a hose connecting the wand to the tank. These tools are meant to be portable, self-contained units.

Garden sprayers are purchased at discount, hardware, and garden-supply stores. They are more easily found during the gardening season than in the dead of winter. Local greenhouses or garden suppliers can order them for you off-season, or you can order them from the manufacturer. Garden sprayers come in a wide range of quality, material, reliability, and price. Low- to mid-quality sprayers are sold most widely. If you wish to purchase a better-quality sprayer, most hardware and garden supply stores can order one for you. If you are after only top-of-the-line sprayers, place an order with the manufacturer. You may also obtain the name and telephone number of commercial dealers or manufacturers of sprayers from a large greenhouse or extermination company. This source may be out of state. Call the order department and ask for a catalogue or search for them on the web.

A garden sprayer with a tank holding one and a half gallons or more has a wand and hose between the nozzle and the tank. The tank of the sprayer is carried at your side while the spray is aimed in any direction. Three gallons is usually the maximum tank size, as that amount is about as much paint as a person comfortably can carry around.

Inexpensive plastic sprayers have all plastic parts. They are the most commonly available and break down regularly. When they start malfunctioning, they are not very easy to fix. Once clogged or unreliable, it is best to replace them. Repair kits are available for some of these sprayers, so you may replace the parts of a broken sprayer; however, the models of inexpensive sprayers usually are changed

Figure 5.20 Sprayers commonly used in scenic painting from airbrushes to hand-pumped garden equipment, Scenic Art Studios, New York.

yearly and soon repair kits are no longer available. The next step up are sprayers with galvanized steel tanks. It is easier to get repair kits for name-brand sprayers of this quality as you can order repair kits from the store where they were purchased. Stainless steel tank sprayers are the top of the line. They are expensive but very dependable. You can order repair kits for these sprayers from a commercial dealer or the manufacturer for many years beyond the purchase date.

Pump sprayers have fluid capacity of usually about one-half gallon. They have no wand or hose; instead, they have a spray nozzle attached directly to the unit. This variety of sprayer may be sold directly out of scenic art supply catalogues and designed for use as a paint tool. They are somewhat expensive but they have some metal parts and are more reliable. Pump sprayers designed to spray water and pesticides are also available in hardware and garden supply stores. There is also a variety available in some pet supply stores as a flea and tick pesticide sprayer. These sprayers are usually made entirely of plastic and the range of quality is not too vast. Replacement sprayers of this sort generally need to be purchased yearly, when they appear on the shelves in the spring, as there seems to be a percentage of failure every year. These smaller sprayers are very useful for working on smaller, tighter projects or smaller-volume jobs. They are as much a staple of the shop as their larger counterparts.

One variety of sprayers not often used in the theatre is a sprayer designed to be carried like a backpack. This type of sprayer would be more useful to a gardener or exterminator, who would not be filling the apparatus with hot starch or having to refill it six times an hour.

When using any spraying paint tool, care needs to be taken to keep the nozzle and fluid tubes from stopping up. Paint used in any sprayer needs to be fairly thin and strained through mesh or netting to keep the coarser particles of pigment from stopping up the sprayer. Polyester net strainers are sold at most household paint stores. Whenever a task is completed using a garden sprayer, the tool should be thoroughly cleaned. Empty the hose of a garden sprayer by holding it above the unpressurized tank and pouring all excess paint out. Rinse the tank with water and slosh it out several times until the water is clear. After rinsing, fill the tank with water one last time and pump up the sprayer again so the nozzle, hose, and wand can be sprayed clean.

Pumping a sprayer can be the bane of your existence, especially if you have an all-day spray project. The tank of a metal sprayer can be fitted with a bicycle tire valve so it can be pressurized from an air line. Be very cautious with this system because a tank can be quickly overpressurized and spring a leak or blow off a hose. Installing a pressure gauge on the sprayer tank will enable you to control the pressure. Many top-of-the-line garden sprayers already have pressure gauges as a standard part of the unit. However, never use a compressor to fill sprayers that have hot starch in them; just use the pump. The heat from the starch compounds the pressure, so the tank can spring a leak, the hose can pop off, or the pump of the sprayer in the tank can implode. The hot starch can scald anyone who happens to be in the way.

If disaster strikes and a sprayer begins to spray starch or paint all over a drop, do not panic. If it is hot starch, your first thoughts should be of safety and directing the fountain of starch away from people. Immediately move the sprayer away from the scenery. Turn the tank upside-down in the slop sink or a five-gallon bucket, thus stopping the flow of fluid by getting it away from the end of the supply tube. You can then turn your attention to any damage to the scenery.

You will find that each sprayer seems to have its own characteristics—its own personality, if you will. When doing a spray job, you may find a particular sprayer in the shop that performs just right. If you are in a shop that has four identical sprayers, you can lose track of your favorite. If you name and label these four sprayers John, Paul, George, and Ringo, for instance, or any other names you may be fond of, you can always be sure to find your favorite sprayer again. Also, it is a lot more interesting than naming the sprayers 1, 2, 3, and 4.

Aerosol Sprayers

Two-part aerosol sprayers that you can load with your own paint are useful for toning, props painting, tight detail jobs, and touch-up. The two parts of these aerosol sprayers are canisters, also called power units, that are fitted with the a spray nozzle and contain the compressed aerosol fluid, and the glass or plastic jar, which the paint will be loaded into. Additional power units can be purchased as replacements. This sounds rather technical, but these tools are very easy to use; you simply fill the jar with a very thin paint or dye, which can be sprayed in the same manner as a can of spray paint. Paint for these sprayers must be strained. Once the power unit is depleted, clean and save the spray tip before throwing away the unit. Later, if a tip on another sprayer becomes clogged, you will have a replacement. These sprayers are somewhat pressure sensitive, so by using a light touch you can control the amount of spray to a certain extent. The companies that manufacture these have recently changed their aerosol formulas to be ozone safe.

Pneumatic Sprayers

Pneumatic sprayers, also called *pneumatic paint guns*, work by mixing paint with compressed air. The paint to be sprayed is strained into a reservoir cup that can be attached to the base, or in some cases the top, of the spray gun. A pneumatic fitting at the back of the gun enables you to connect the sprayer directly to a compressed air hose. The spray gun is sold in two units: the spray gun and the fluid cup. Fluid cups usually are not interchangeable between brands of guns.

The one-quart gun is the most common and versatile spray gun. These guns are good for sophisticated spray work and broad airbrush techniques.

For more tricky work, the half-pint size, also called a touch-up gun, is very useful. This gun can do everything the one-quart gun can do and handle tighter detail. The disadvantage is that the fluid cup of this gun holds so little paint.

You can control the spray produced by pneumatic paint guns in three ways. First, the shape of the spray can be widened from a narrow cone shape to a fan. On the back of the gun is an airflow valve that controls the mix of air coming out of the spray tip; the spray will be flattened into a fan shape by mixing air in from the side or not to keep a cone-shaped spray. You can change the direction of the fan pattern by rotating the spray tip at the front of the gun to orient the fan vertically or horizontally. Second, you can change the proportional mix of air and fluid by adjusting the fluid valve, the knob for which usually is located on the back of the spray gun below the airflow valve.

The third way to control the spray is to regulate the psi (pounds pre square inch of air pressure) entering the tool. Most spray guns are not sold with air regulators, also called air valves, to adjust the air pressure of the spray. However, any supplier of spray guns will sell regulators for compressed air equipment. These attach at the air hose connector at the rear of the gun. I recommend getting an air valve attachment for every spray gun in your shop, as most pneumatic construction tools operate at a higher psi than pneumatic sprayers. Having a valve precludes the need for a regulated air hose or separate compressor. It also gives you greater control over the variables of your spray right at the gun.

Purchase a name-brand sprayer from a reputable dealer. Be careful of purchasing unknown brands of spray guns, as replacement parts may be hard to come by. Spray equipment is one of the more expensive investments in the painter's kit. When you invest in spray equipment, learn not only how to use it but how to service it yourself. When the gun begins to act up, you will want to know how to take it apart and fix the problem rather than stopping work in the middle of a project. When you buy your equipment, technical information should be included in the packaging, explaining how to take the sprayer apart and replace parts. Hang on to this information; put it in a file in the paint shop office or, if it is your own, keep it with your kit. It is common-sense that your equipment will break down only when you are using it, so learn how to take care of problems.

Figure 5.21 Using a paint spray gun and a large stencil to create an air-brushed appearance for a drop in *Thoroughly Modern Millie*, Scenic Art Studios, New York.

Figure 5.22 The finished drop mostly painted with a spray gun, Scenic Art Studios, New York.

Paint used in spray guns will need to be about the viscosity of whole milk and carefully strained into the spray cup. If you always strain paint thoroughly so the gun does not plug up and you clean the gun completely between uses, the gun will be more reliable. If the gun has problems you cannot resolve, look for an automotive paint supplier or call the manufacturer for the closest service center. These places will be able to service your gun or refer you to someone who can.

Spray guns are designed to be used with the solvent-based paints of the auto industry. The water-based paints commonly used in scenic painting tend to rust and corrode some parts of the gun. After cleaning, spray a little solvent alcohol through the gun and lift the gun out of the cup and spray air through it to dry out the interior parts. If, despite all your efforts, the spray tip begins to rust, you can replace it with a stainless steel tip. You may want to ask, when purchasing the spray gun, if it is possible to purchase it with a stainless steel spray tip. In the last decade, plastic parts have been appearing more and more in high-quality sprayers, making corrosion less of a problem.

Scenic painting is different than auto painting in that scenic artists often are after speedy coverage and not as concerned about sagging paint. When purchasing a paint gun, inquire if you can get it with a larger-diameter spray tip than the standard one with

which the gun is sold. This will accommodate a greater volume of fluid. Spray tips and spray needles must fit together, so a matching spray needle will be necessary as well.

As discussed earlier, be aware that some scenic shops have oiled air lines to help lubricate nail guns but, naturally, your latex or acrylic paint cannot be mixed with oil. If a shop has oiled air lines, you need to set up a clean air line that is convenient to the painters and have air hoses set aside that are used only for spray guns.

High-pressure pneumatic sprayers work by drawing paint out of a container and mixing it with high volumes of air in the gun, which atomizes the paint as it is released from the spray tip. The cup

Figure 5.23 Painting a sky with a spray gun, Scenic Art Studios, New York.

serves only as a vessel for the paint being sprayed and must draw in air to replace the volume of fluid being sucked up the fluid tube. When a high-pressure pneumatic gun is not working, first check whether the air hole in the fluid cup cap is plugged, which will make it impossible for the gun to draw fluid from the cup.

High-Volume, Low-Pressure Sprayers

High-volume, low-pressure (HVLP) sprayers became commercially available only recently. These sprayers are quickly replacing the high-pressure pneumatic sprayers in the workplace, as development of these sprayers was hastened by concerns over the environment as well as personal safety.

HVLP sprayers are designed to spray a larger amount of fluid than conventional spray guns with much lower air pressure emitted from the tip of the gun itself. The benefits of this design are a much greater control over the spray pattern and significantly reduced paint mist dispersal while spraying. Typical pneumatic sprayers and airless sprayers release considerable amounts of particulates that simply scatter in the air in normal operation. HVLP sprayers are safer to use because less atomized fluid or paint mist is being released into the work environment and directly in front of the user's face. This does not mean that HVLP sprayers can be used without the safety protection of a respirator and proper ventilation. (See Chapter 4, Safety and Health Regulations.)

The spray patterns achieved with an HVLP sprayer range from a very fine spray, similar to the controlled spray from a high-pressure half-pint touch-up spray gun, to a broad coarse pattern that resembles a fine spatter. This means an HVLP may serve many more of the needs of scenic artists, replacing currently used equipment. Because so much less air pressure is being released from the tip of the gun, usually about five psi, and because the fluid being released at the spray tip is not atomized to the same extent as with high-pressure spray guns, you have greater control over the amount and direction of fluid being released.

The HVLP sprayer works by pressurizing the fluid cup, which forces the paint up the fluid tube and into the gun. This process increases the volume of fluid that can be released at the tip and makes only as much pressure as is necessary to atomize the paint, rather than the 30 or more psi that high-pressure guns need to create the vacuum and draw fluid up through the tube.

Figure 5.24 A high-pressure low-volume (HVLP) sprayer unit.

The low pressure in the term high-volume, low-pressure refers only to the psi released at the spray tip. HVLP sprayers need to be operated with a minimum of 60 to 80 psi from the compressor. Most of these sprayers are available from the manufacturer in units with portable compressors that generate a steady psi for the operation of the sprayer. Most HVLP sprayers are already equipped with an air valve and gauge that will give you control and a reading of what psi is at the spray tip.

The other components of the HVLP sprayer—the spray tip, spray nozzle, spray needle, fluid valve, and airflow valve—work on the same principle and usually are arranged in the same manner as on high-pressure spray guns. However, most HVLP sprayers are being designed with plastic bodies, spray needles, spray nozzles, and spray tips. You can also purchase larger gauge spray needles and nozzles for these sprayers. Even the superior-quality HVLP sprayers are made with plastic parts, which are easier to clean and not subject to corrosion.

HVLP sprayers and compressor units are an expensive investment in shop equipment. However, few shops can afford to be without this very useful and versatile tool. Although the price varies among brands of sprayers, you can expect to pay between $400 and $500 for a good-quality spray gun and an additional $150 to $250 if you are buying a sprayer compressor unit. If your shop has yet to invest in pneumatic equipment of any sort, it is recommended you only consider investing in an HVLP sprayer.

Airbrushes

Airbrushes work in the same way as pneumatic sprayers but on a much smaller and finer scale. Airbrushes are useful for very tight spray work. I had gone a long time without owning one because the need had never arisen. When, at last, I needed to purchase one, I was counseled to get a top-of-the-line tool that had dual control. This good advice means that I can control the amount of fluid and the shape of the spray, from a very narrow pinpoint to a cone shape.

Airbrushes are designed to work at an air pressure of around 30 psi or less, much lower than normal shop air pressure. You can purchase valves, gauges, hoses, and fittings that connect to a regular air line so you can use the airbrush at the lower psi. You can also purchase or order special airbrush compressors from any fine-art supply store that sells airbrushes. You will want an extra-long air hose of at least 12 feet so that you are free to move around the scenery with the airbrush. Aerosol cans that give you about 30 minutes of use with an airbrush are available.

Most airbrushes are sold with small cups for holding paint, which are designed for tabletop studio work. Paint can be spilled out of them easily, and for scenic work you will need more volume anyway. You can buy spray jars that are covered and hold a larger quantity of paint. The paint you will use in the airbrush will need to be much thinner than the paint you use for spray guns. Do not store the paint in the spray jars overnight because it will settle and you will have to clean out the jar the next day.

Airbrushes are designed for use with fine-arts quality paint, usually watercolors and acrylics. Because the pigments for paints used in scenic painting are not as finely ground, they tend to clog the spray tip more often, so the paint must be carefully strained, usually through muslin or layers of cheesecloth. The spray tip and the needle that fits it should be purchased in a larger size than the standard one. The standard spray tip for an airbrush has a three-millimeter opening. A five-millimeter spray tip would be a better size for scenic painting. Always use the finest paint available for an airbrush. High-quality scenic acrylics are fine, but some lower-quality scenic paints are simply too coarse to be compatible with the fine tolerances of an airbrush system.

Pressure Pot Sprayers

Pressure pots are designed differently than spray guns. The fluid pot is not carried around with the gun. One hose, usually around 20 feet in length, carries the fluid to the spray gun, and a second hose delivers air to the pressurized paint pot. The pressure pot usually holds about two gallons of paint. True to its name, the compressed air is connected to the pressure pot so that the fluid is under pressure. The pressure pot has a gauge on top so that the painter can read the pressure.

Pressure pots can be a good solution to the problem of having to refill the spray gun every few minutes, particularly on large volume jobs. They also are an arm saver because you need not hold the paint supply out at arm's length, which can be a strain after a while. However, they take longer to clean because of the long fluid hose. Also, care must be taken not to drag the hoses through wet paint if you are working on the paint deck.

Airless Sprayers

An *airless sprayer* works without compressed air by pressurizing paint as it passes through the sprayer body. The body of an airless sprayer sits directly over a paint bucket; it has no internal reservoir. The airless sprayer is primarily good for one thing only: speed. The paint comes out at such high pressure that it will cover almost any surface with paint or starch very fast. It is an excellent tool to have if you or your shop can afford one. Backpainting and applying a base coat over many square feet of hard scenery becomes a small task for one person armed with an airless sprayer rather than an all-day chore for the entire crew. Airless sprayers use a tremendous quantity of paint very quickly and, unlike other types of sprayers, can handle almost any viscosity of paint, even very thick ones. Their ability to pump a lot of paint quickly means you may use about 50 percent more paint than normal when spraying with an airless sprayer.

The airless sprayer consists of a suction tube that is immersed in a bucket of paint, a motor that pressurizes the fluid and is contained in the airless sprayer body, and a fluid hose with a gun, generally about 20 to 25 feet long so that a fair amount of surface area can be reached without having to move the machine. The spray gun has little pressure control and only two speeds: on and off. You can control the fan of the spray and the orientation of the fan at the gun.

You can control the pressure to some extent at the motor of the airless sprayer, if there is a high to low setting. Even so, for the gun to work, it will generate at least a very powerful 100 psi at the lowest setting.

> CAUTION: Never point the nozzle of an airless sprayer at yourself or anyone else. The fluid is under enough pressure that it can pierce or be injected under the skin. This can result in an embolism or serious infection. Make sure that any injury caused by an airless spray gun is seen by a physician, no matter how slight, even if it is just water, as there is always a high probability of infection.

Airless sprayers are the most expensive of all sprayers. I recommend buying a name-brand sprayer from a nearby reputable dealer, as it will need service from time to time. It is best to have major repairs done by a professional, as a high-pressure sprayer can be dangerous if serviced improperly. Service is expensive because it is not deemed safe to use rebuilt parts, which means worn or damaged parts have to be replaced with parts from the manufacturer.

All paint or starch used in an airless sprayer first must be strained so it will not plug the spray gun. Make sure to pour all the paint or starch through a metal strainer covered with a nylon paint strainer that rests on the reservoir bucket of the sprayer, or simply wrap a nylon paint strainer around the suction tube and tie it off at the top. This will strain all paint automatically as it passes into the sprayer.

If any air is in the system of the airless sprayer, it will not build up pressure. The machine must be primed first so that all the air can be drawn off. A priming valve and drain tube usually are located at the back of most machines. Sometimes, the drain tube is positioned so that it will discharge back into the reservoir bucket. Once the suction tube is immersed in a full reservoir bucket, the machine should be turned on and allowed to run in the priming mode, located on a dial near the on/off switch, for one or two minutes or until it has completely stopped burping air out of the drain tube. Often, the machine will not spray initially because it has not been allowed to finish priming. Once primed, turn the pressure dial from prime to the desired pressure and begin spraying.

Most airless spray guns have reversible spray tips. The spray nozzle has a knob on the side of the gun so that if, while spraying, a piece of dried residue comes loose somewhere in the machine or fluid tube and blocks the spray gun, you can turn the spray tip around and blast away the offending material. Turn the spray tip back and you will be ready to spray again.

Cleaning an airless sprayer takes some time. The fluid hose alone will have a fair volume of paint in it. Many gallons of clean water will need to pass through the sprayer to flush out all the paint or starch from the body hose and spray gun. If the airless sprayer is used only occasionally throughout the day, the spray gun can be left immersed in a bucket

A

B

Figure 5.25 Drops painted with pneumatic spray techniques. **(A)** *Guys and Dolls*, designed by Anne Mundall, painted by Susan Crabtree and Ashley Smith, and **(B)** *Grease*, designed by Gregory Hill (courtesy of Kenmark, Inc., Overland Park, Kansas).

of water between uses rather than cleaning the machine between each use. After the machine is clean, squirt a little baby oil or mineral oil into the last rinse. The airless sprayer may be flushed with paint thinner if it is going into storage for many weeks or more. This will help keep the parts in the interior of the machine from sticking during long spells between uses. If there is oil or paint thinner in the airless sprayer, make sure to flush it out thoroughly with warm water before the next use.

Pattern Pistols and Hopper Guns

The *pattern pistol*, also called a *hopper gun*, is a pneumatic sprayer designed to spray extremely thick texturing pastes. The spray gun has a wheel at the spray tip with different-sized openings to accommodate different fluids and various-sized chunks of texture, rather like a multipurpose pencil sharpener. On the top of the gun is the hopper, a cone-shaped container that holds the texture and funnels it into the gun. The hopper holds about two gallons of goop, so the gun is rather heavy when full and can be tiring to work with. There is no air valve on a hopper gun; once it is hooked up to the air, it is on. The trigger pulls back the spray tip, which allows the fluid to drop down between it and the spray wheel, where it is blasted out though the selected hole in the spray wheel.

You can purchase hopper guns or rent them at contractor supply houses quite inexpensively. They are designed to be easy to take apart and maintain because all manner of goop is forced through these guns. Often, the best way to thoroughly clean them at the end of the day is to take them completely apart.

This rather simple tool is very useful for covering surfaces with all manner of water-based textures very quickly. They work well with joint compound and plaster-based textures, even those mixed with vermiculite and perlite, cellotex-based papier mâché textures, and Quick Texture mix, which is manufactured specifically for use with hopper guns.

CONCLUSION

A professional scenic artist will acquire a considerable stock of tools in his or her career. Brushes will be the backbone of that stock. By taking care of your brushes with thorough cleaning and proper storage, you'll ensure that they last many years. A scenic artist will also need to use a wide variety of other tools and

should know how to maintain them. Garden sprayers are an excellent example. Almost every job will call for a sprayer at one point or another, so it is essential to have at least one reliable and somewhat predictable unit in your tool kit. Take the time to learn how your tools work and what is needed for cleaning, safe handling, and maintaining.

AN INTERVIEW WITH MARY HEILMAN, SCENIC ARTIST AND TEACHER

Mary Heilman is a member of the design faculty at California Institute of the Arts (Cal Arts) and head of the MFA Scene Painting program there. She is one of the leading scenic artists in the United States, with extensive experience in scenic painting for feature film and network television as well as for theatre.

Susan Crabtree: What kind of program do you have at Cal Arts?

Mary Heilman: Cal Arts' Design and Production Program focuses primarily on innovative theatre development. We are interested in developing what will be the new directions of theatre. We have extensive areas of study at Cal Arts. In addition to the usual programs in design, production and performance there are also specialties in props, producing, puppetry/object theater and writing. The MFA scene-painting specialty came out of the scenic design program. There were two primary reasons for its development. First, I couldn't find enough well trained scenic artists to hire when I was the lead scenic artist at South Coast Repertory and I felt it was time to be part of a solution to that problem. The second reason had to do with the changes developing in the use of video and digital images in scene design. My curriculum balances extensive course work with production assignments. I teach from a professional viewpoint and teach what is used in the industry now. Coming to Cal Arts and teaching scene painting has been a great opportunity. Figuring out how to apply some of the concepts that I've developed in my professional work and translating them for use in the classroom has been very rewarding.

SC: What is the configuration of your shop?

MH: We have a scene shop where we both build and paint the scenery. There is a paint mixing and storage area with a large paint sink next to a large spray booth. There is a stationary paint frame and another paint area in the newly renovated prop shop. All the scenery is built and painted by students for the theatre school productions. We have faculty technical directors who teach and advise in the construction area and I teach and advise the scenic artists and the graduate prop artisans. The students have a lot of the responsibility. They schedule work-study and production students to paint the scenery and do all of the budgeting, product ordering, and management of the entire project in their discipline. Working through paint samples and conferring with the designers, technical directors and other members of the team gives them hands-on experience I feel is essential and develops their confidence levels to a degree where they can handle professional challenges.

SC: How many productions do you do a year?

MH: We do roughly 14 productions, about seven each semester, and a number of additional workshop-sized productions that require small amounts of production support. We also have a new works festival at the end of each year with up to 10 productions; those require some scenery and scene painting. It is a very busy place.

SC: So the students learn a lot about having to manage the logistics of multiple productions in your program?

MH: Yes they do; all of the students have at least one production each semester that they manage and they also work on other productions in a work-study capacity where they get to be part of a crew and experience a teamwork situation. Most of our productions are student designed. Working with their student peers is a great way to develop those supportive and negotiating skills so necessary to this profession. We have guest professionals and students from our directing program directing a number of productions each year. It gives the students quite a range of outlooks and gives them exposure to professional artists. It really stretches their inventiveness and creativity and adds to some of the professional contacts they will need upon graduation.

SC: How long have you been a scenic artist?

MH: I've been a scenic artist for 23 years. I was at South Coast Rep for a substantial part of that time, 16 years executing about 250 productions. I work as an independent contractor for Walt Disney Imagineering and have designed and painted a number of museum exhibits and dioramas and a long list of entertainment industry projects.

SC: What made you get started in scenic artistry?

MH: My education in college was in fine art. I was working on very large paintings by the time I graduated.

At my senior show, a number of theatre friends suggested that a natural transition might be working in theatre on large backdrops. I thought that was a great idea. Quite frankly when you graduate with a fine arts degree you're sort of stuck as to how to pay the rent and actually make a living. I didn't understand very much about scenic art when I first started, and I made many mistakes. I managed to fake my way through enough work until I got to the point where I met a number of helpful designers. I became an assistant to a scenic designer and painter, Noble Dinse. Working with him taught me the basic painting techniques we use in theatre. He was a wonderful mentor. I didn't go to any kind of a scene-painting program—I just learned on the job.

SC: Do you have a specialty in scenic artistry?

MH: I think that my specialty is in translating period and historic fine art into scene painting rendering techniques. I also seem to do a lot of portraiture for use on stage. A number of productions I've worked on have required some kind of a period portrait of an actor that is in that production. I also enjoy translating traditional scenic art techniques—ones that use more toxic kinds of paint materials, solvent-based etc.—into techniques using water-based products. In southern California we have a lot of restrictions on what kinds of materials we can use. Luckily a lot of the manufactures have started making wonderful products that support that. As an artist and now teacher, I have a strong interest in using the safest products available while maintaining the highest artistic product.

SC: You mentioned before that you learned about theatrical design after you got out of your fine arts program and started working in the theatre. Do you design also?

MH: Yes. After working a number of years I went back to graduate school to Otis Parsons Art Institute in Los Angeles (now the Otis College of Art and Design) and although they did not have theatrical design there, I studied in the advertising design program. For a number of years I designed sets for commercials—large products like cars and motorcycles and home theatre systems. That then translated into more theatrical design. I started teaching more workshops in scene painting and design and working throughout the different areas of the entertainment industry.

SC: Does your program in California take film work into account?

MH: Yes, quite strongly. We certainly are primarily involved in theatre production, but even our theatre productions involve quite a lot of video and some film work. Cal Arts is comprised of six schools—fine arts, theatre, film school, music, dance and critical studies—we do a lot of interdisciplinary work with the other schools. We also have a relationship with USC film school. Our students work with USC as the production designers on the thesis film projects there. As production designers they gain experience in location scouting, prop house rental, set dressing, and art direction as well as scene painting and production design for film. Whenever possible I take students with me when I work on film, theme parks, and installations.

SC: The theme park work has to be a different sort of discipline I would think; especially dealing with Disney that has certain standards.

MH: They do have certain standards. The first work I did with Disney was for the Anaheim Disneyland Park. I've been working the last couple of years with Imagineering, and their standards are very high. They have more money devoted to their projects, and most of the design for the international work goes through Walt Disney Imagineering. With WDI, I usually work on a combination of design and scene painting within a special projects department. I work directly with the production designer who can also be the entire project designer. I'm given an idea or concept, not too different from what a scenic designer would receive from a director on a theatre project, and from the research I develop the imagery and finishes, sometimes completing just the design and sometimes taking it all the way through to a finished product. I love those situations because I work through a number of different jobs all on one project. The last project I worked on was for Tokyo Disneyland, what a great job—lots of innovative design went into that park. Again I brought some students with me to work on that project.

SC: Does the institute itself have an apprenticeship or internship program where they place the students in professional jobs or do the students get this professional training through teachers and professors like yourself?

MH: They get it through teachers and professors, but luckily because we are on the north end of Los Angeles, students have lots of opportunities to work on professional projects outside of Cal Arts. I get calls from friends and colleagues in the industry asking for students who want to work on film and theatre projects. So most students get exposure to professional scenic shops and independent film projects. The new Kodak Theatre just asked for an artist

to work on a production there so I passed the job on to one of my students. She went down to Hollywood and completed the job with good pay and new professional contacts. Some students have become scenic artists on independent film projects over the summer and others work at summer stock theatres. A one-semester internship may be taken but usually the summer work serves as an internship.

SC: How do you create a dialog with designers from the various industries you've worked in? Does the dialog change depending on the type of venue that you are working in?

MH: It does change. I think that there is one key element that is the same for all of those venues. I believe that you need to establish a good relationship with all of the team on the project. I start by asking questions about the general feel of the design or the concept of the project in general before I ever get to the specifics. To me that seems key in all of those venues. You're always finding yourself in the position of making decisions when some members of the team aren't around. So it's best at the beginning to really understand the direction of the project conceptually.

Specifically, in regional theatre, you usually have some type of dialog, even if it's only on the phone with your designer, with elevations in hand, so that you can ask specific questions. I start with the elevations or any visual research the designer provides. I move on to the many questions needed to get a good grasp of the concept: "Do you want this much of the brush stroke to show?" "Do you want a softer, impressionistic look to this?" "Do you want it to look airbrushed?"

In film work, you can be working with a number of people in different creative positions, from the production designer to the art directors. It is not unusual to have a lot of interaction with the lighting designer on a film project. You usually do surface treatment samples that have to be tested on film before you go to the location or the set to shoot. Color often has to be adjusted for film. Then, of course, you'll find yourself out on location. My first film project was a movie called *Raising Arizona* by the Coen brothers. Many of the location shots for the movie were quite literally in the middle of the desert. If you hadn't brought everything with you that you could have possibly imagined needing, you were in big trouble. Don't forget the water!

Theme parks often involve working on large format parade floats and other moving pieces. I've worked mostly on large pieces in parades that are used during the day *and* night. These require another list of questions for the designer and technical production personnel. They also have to last for up to two years. If the float gets caught in a rainstorm, you can't have dye running and your colors have to be stay bright under many days in the sun. They use very nontraditional building materials for theme parks parades. I have worked extensively with huge inflatable balloons that have to be painted with special paints because the balloons are inflated and deflated usually twice a day for up to two years; you need paint that will last in those circumstances. When you work on something like a big balloon, all bets are off in terms of the traditional cartooning techniques that you use on 2-D or even 3-D architectural scenery. Sometimes the painters elevation is a two dimensional image and it is the scenic artist's job to translate it on to a sphere or other three dimensional form. It was a real challenge the first time I worked on one of these projects.

SC: How do you do something like that? What paints do you use? Do you paint it when it's inflated and then it's deflated, or how do you manage that?

MH: The company that makes the balloons, Aerostar, in Sioux Falls, South Dakota, works from a scaled maquette or model making the patterns and then sewing the vinyl balloons. They make the balloons out of a variety of solid-colored vinyls. As a contractor for Disney I was sent to Sioux Falls to work with an eight-person crew to develop the paint treatments using what at that time was the only thing that would stick: a silk-screening ink. There were some challenges with the ink. Even after it had dried it acted as its own solvent. It thinned with lacquer thinner. When you tried to layer more paint/ink over the top, it would simply wash off much like watercolor would or anything else that wasn't colorfast after it was dry.

That was a challenge, especially on a great big vinyl balloon, but we did find some great techniques, some of which I took from theatre scene painting. I used brushes cut up like you would a wood-graining brush to get some textural patterns on to the very smooth vinyl. The production designer didn't care for the smooth vinyl look so we tried all sorts of ways to get an impressionistic kind of textural look on to the vinyl. I had a wonderful crew there. They stuck it out with me as we tried all these crazy techniques on this balloon. I worked with that crew for several weeks and we painted four 35′ long × 20′ wide figures. Before painting they had to be inflated

and were rigged with pulleys and rope so that we could turn them over to paint all sides. The large spherical balloons have their own problems. It's hard to work on them as they roll around; I finally bought various sizes of children's inflatable swimming pools. Luckily I painted the spheres in Southern California where you can get those cute little pools year round. By the time I worked on the spheres I was able to paint with a great new vinyl paint call Flexart. It's available for use with either brush/roller or in a spray consistency. It has a great color palette and is thinned with water and isopropyl alcohol. It's less toxic than the silk-screening inks we used in South Dakota.

SC: What areas of emphasis do you find yourself leaning on or trying to convey to your students?

MH: I really emphasize drawing along with critical studies classes. I believe students have to read and write and develop good communication skills. There is a whole range of what I call "art-speak"—the terms we use to describe this art form—which

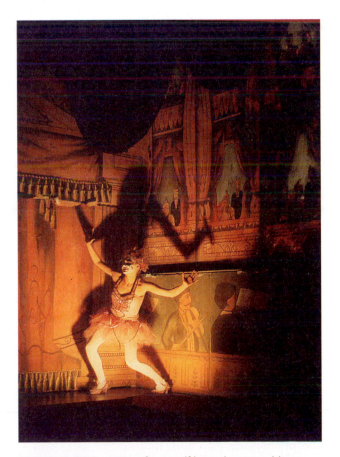

Figure 5.26 Setting for *Twelfth Night* painted by Mary Heilman.

students need to understand. I recommend they take classes in art history, studio art, and color theory. In scene painting we start with applied textures including wall textures, stucco, terra cotta tile, beaten earth floors, asphalt, cement, etc. Cartooning, layout techniques and stenciling, foliage, sky/clouds, and landscape painting come next. Trompe l'oeil, 3-D sculpting, and carving and translucent backdrop painting finish the first year. Life drawing, perspective, and figure drawing are also emphasized. We offer life drawing in the theatre school as well as many other drawing classes in other parts of the institute.

My students all take scene design and CAD. We are fortunate that we have a pretty extensive computer lab supported with a range of software. Digital imagery is so important in design these days.

Half of the program emphasizes the hands on work on production. We develop management skills and communication, budgeting, and product research and development. It gives students an opportunity to apply what they learn in the classroom to fully mounted productions. I think without the production work students would never have the autonomy to really spread their wings and find out how you react to those challenges. I believe students should learn at the outset how to problem-solve.

SC: You mentioned digital imagery. What kind of impact do you think that is having on the profession?

MH: I have to say that I love computers, what a great tool, when used well.

Not too long ago I was afraid of this technology. I didn't have a computer and didn't see any reason to have one. Then Judy Juracek's book *Surfaces* came out and designers started using that as a shorthand kind of way of applying all kinds of textures and surface treatments to their designs. I felt I had to learn how the elevations were processed in order to respond to some of the needs of the designers and their designs. I found that with digital imagery available, I was receiving a wider range of artwork and styles in the scenic designs. One of the reasons I have always loved working as a scenic artist is the constant change and variety of the designs I execute. Digitally produced images have supported that.

SC: Do you have any words of wisdom for anyone pursuing a career in scenic artistry?

MH: Paint, paint, paint! You need to get enough hands-on experience to find out if you actually like the process, the environment, and the hard work—enough so that you can find out if you can hav fun doing this kind of work. Then get yourself a good

education. I believe a graduate level college education is best as you may have the desire or opportunity to teach at some time in your career. It also gives a student the opportunity to make connections with other students that they may want to work with professionally after graduation. Never burn your bridges; you never know who will call you for a job.

SC: What do you think are some of the most common misconceptions about the profession?

MH: I think sometimes there is a misconception that with enough training or experience anyone can be a good scenic artist. I don't believe that. There is no replacement for talent and like many professions, scene painting has a number of very particular skills needed. I also think there is a lot of debate over whether you would call scenic art a craft or an art and I think it can be either or both. Some projects are purely craft with very little art involved but others require a level of input by the scenic artist that could only be possible if the scenic is also an artist. Sometimes people only look at a scenic artist job as something that seems to be fun and artistic and they rarely see the hard physical work, the stress of constant deadlines and creating on demand every day on the job. Just because you are having a bad day doesn't mean that you don't have to produce that scenery.

SC: Looking back over your career, what were some of the more elusive skills that you had to learn in the profession of scenic artistry?

MH: Understanding the designer's notes can be an elusive skill. What does it mean when asked for a color that is "warm with a cool undertone?" How about "Paint it funnier?" or "Paint it that color, you know, dark white." I don't worry that digitally produced backdrops will put scenics out of business as I don't think a computer can translate "make it more romantic."

Because we work mostly in circumstances where lighting is going to make such a huge difference, it takes a lot to understand how painted scenery will look under different kinds of lighting applications and within different environments. I feel I continue to learn about that constantly. Now that film and video are often integrated into theatre production design, it's an added element that I'm working to master and to figure out how that coordinates with traditional scenic artist skills, techniques, and applications.

Outside of painting itself, I think that the collaborative process is taken too lightly. It takes a lot of experience, negotiation, and communication to make

Figure 5.27
Landscape painted by Mary Heilman.

a strong relationship develop in this medium. As the scenic artist you are often in the very middle of difficult circumstances—the director and the designer may be at an impasse with the development of the design. This can happen when the scenery is in the shop and you're halfway through painting it. Sometimes the construction schedule is altered or labor resources are limited. Ultimately you are on the line to produce the final product. I think understanding and really listening to what these people say, to their concerns, can help you find ways to integrate solutions into the final product.

SC: Do you foresee the skills of scenic artistry changing in the future?

MH: In a certain way, not at all. I think it is more accurate to say that we will ad to what we have used in the past. I've been learning more about historical scene painting techniques so that I can translate them into something that might apply to film or to more innovative, theatrical set design. I think we will certainly be dealing with technological advancements that will inform and change some of the techniques and products we commonly use. I think that painted

scenery will remain an important design element and digitally produced design will demand a continuing expansion of the talent and skills needed by scenic artists.

SC: What are some of the highlights of your career?

MH: Working at South Coast Repertory for 16 years is certainly one of them. I have worked on over 300 theatre productions, most of them at SCR. SCR has a strong commitment to producing new plays. Working on something at the beginning of its development demands your most inventive solutions and I loved the challenge. Working with the amazing designers and directors over the years has always been a highlight for me. Ralph Funicello, Marg Kellog, Karen TenEyck, Tony Fanning, Adrienne LaBell, Ming Cho Lee, Robert Brill, Loi Arcenas and Cliff Faulkner were some of my favorites. David Chambers directed a number of productions there and always had a great appreciation for the work of the entire production team, especially the scenic artists.

I enjoyed the film work for 20th Century Fox, Warner Bros, and Disney and there was this one very interesting design project for installation at the U.S. Pentagon …

I worked with another artist executing a beautiful diorama/mural at the San Diego Natural History Museum featuring the southern California desert. The diorama required a scientifically correct representation of the desert landscape, which was not only challenging artistically but also very educational in the geology department. I had never had to paint anything scientifically correct before. I'm still proud of my representation of an alluvial fan.

SC: Is there anything you want to add about what you enjoy most about being a scenic artist?

MH: I find myself fortunate to have found an occupation so suited to my artistic background and need for constant change. I am rarely bored and find that I consistently learn more every day. Also a big plus for me is working in a community, whether it be a theater company, a scene shop or on location on a film, you work with other professionals. I'm not suited to solitary work very often and find a community atmosphere very energizing. And finally, it is no small thing that after graduating with that fine art degree I haven't been out of work in some 20 years, I definitely enjoy that.

Chapter 6

Color and Paint

Color is a key ingredient of all visual images. Colors inform, provoke, soothe, and stimulate—they elicit a myriad of responses in us. The simple presence or absence of color alters the mood of anything we look at. Many in society have come to associate the black-and-white imagery of photographs and film as serious or nostalgic. A modern movie made in black and white wordlessly communicates a certain dramatic sensibility, as does the somber palette of Rembrandt paintings and the warm pastels of Degas. A message is given through color and its context.

Colors and the pleasing color of things are also easily recognized by almost anyone who sees them. It does not take a trained geologist to appreciate a well-colored piece of marble. Nor do we need a meteorologist to know the sky is a crystal-clear blue. People recognize correct and incorrect colors based on instinct and experience. Few people can actually reproduce the color of the food they eat, but everyone knows when it is wrong. It takes an artist to create pleasing colors or manipulate them with meaning, to create a disturbing landscape, a menacing urban environment, or a perfectly tranquil sky. But as easy as a good or bad color choice is to recognize, color can be quite difficult to understand and manipulate. Knowing a color is wrong is one thing; knowing how to mix a correct color is entirely another.

Color, in painting mediums, is a raw material for scenic artists. Colors in paint, dye, metallic finishes, and other products almost always need to be carefully manipulated before being applied to scenery. Rarely does color come right out of a can onto the canvas. Paints are blended together or layered one on another to achieve the correct color. The range, or palette, of colors available to a scenic artist is surprisingly small, yet the potential colors that can be mixed from this palette are virtually limitless. It is thus important for scenic artists to understand colors so that they can combine them, through mixing or layering, into the precise color desired.

This chapter describes color and the chief medium in which it is used: paint. Color is defined by scientific theory and described through commonly accepted terminology. Paint is a combination of organic and synthetic components with a variety of behaviors, all of which scenic artists must know.

COLOR PHYSICS AND THEORY

The perception of color is a physical phenomenon, the result of correct functioning of the eyes, optic nerves, and the brain. Color is possible only because of the existence of light. Light can be of a color, like an amber sunset, or light can reveal color in an object. Through the presence of light, we see the blue sky or a green field. Color is transmitted in light waves, the visible part of the overall spectrum of electromagnetic radiation. The *color spectrum* of visible light ranges from violet to red. In 1676, Isaac Newton observed the relationship of color and white light. He discovered that white sunlight passing through a triangular piece of glass, a prism, "In the prism, the ray of white light dispersed into the spectral colors. The dispersed ray of light can be projected on a screen to display the spectrum. A continuous band of color ranges from red through orange, yellow, green, blue, to violet."[1] When this spectrum again passed through the prism, it reformed into white light. A rainbow is an excellent example of the spectrum of visible light and clearly shows the six colors of the spectrum Newton observed.

Visible light is a very narrow band of the electromagnetic spectrum, which ranges overall from relatively long radio waves to very short gamma waves. In the visible section of the band of light, each color has a specific wavelength. The red wavelength is the longest, at 650–800 microns, and violet is the shortest, at 360–430 microns. Sunlight and white light contain all the colors of the visible spectrum.

We perceive all colors through our eyes, which distinguish light waves through two types of photoreceptors in the retina: rods and cones. These rods and cones are sensitive to visible light in two different ways. The cones respond to color and daylight, and the rods are sensitive to low-intensity light. The brain combines the wavelengths sensed by the cones in our eyes into the perceived color. The cones are centrally located in the retina; the rods are on the edge. That is why we can perceive dim stars more easily out of the corner of our eye. The same stars are invisible to the cones when we look at them directly.

This also explains why color is more difficult to perceive under dim light: the cones are unable to function fully. The cone photoreceptors also are color-specific, much like the pixels of a television screen. A cone can sense only red, blue, or green. The brain combines the various levels of red and green transmitted through the cone to perceive yellow. The cones and brain ultimately combine the observable light wavelengths into the color one perceives.

The color we see is based on how objects reflect and absorb white light. An object that does not reflect light appears to have no color, or to be black. Conversely, an object that reflects all light waves appears white. If light waves pass through a material uninterrupted, or partially interrupted, that material appears to be transparent, like air, glass, or water. Objects may reflect some of the spectrum and absorb others. Simply put, a red ball absorbs most light waves and reflects only the red wavelength. The red cones in the retina distinguish this wavelength and the brain discerns the color as red. A blue-green object reflects some of both blue and green wavelengths.

The retina's cones responding to blue and those responding to green send their responses to the brain, where the two colors are mixed together into our perception of the color blue-green. This process of reflection is altered significantly if the light striking an object is not white but is instead a color. A colored light is only a small part of the overall spectrum of light. A blue object seen under primary red light appears black because there is no blue in the red light to be reflected back to the viewer.

Understanding how color results from an object's reflection and absorption of visible light is the key to understanding how colors mix with each other. Essentially, two processes are involved in mixing colors. The two processes can be confusing, and they both involve the way we perceive color. One process involves color as pigment or paint, whereas the other involves color as light. Pigment and light mix colors differently. If the six primary and secondary colors of the spectrum are mixed together in equal amounts as paint, they theoretically combine into black through the process called *subtractive color mixing*. Subtractive mixing is the process a scenic artist uses to mix paint. It is important to know that an opposite effect occurs when mixing color in light, as lighting designers do. All colors of the spectrum mixed in equal amounts as light beams will combine to make white, as Newton observed. This is called *additive color mixing*.

Bear in mind that these two processes do not operate exclusively of each other. Scenic artists work in the subtractive mode but see the effect of additive mixing on their work on stage. The reference earlier in this book to how colors appear under different light sources is an example of the additive mixing process.

The Color Wheel and Color Model

Eighteen colors are displayed on the *color wheel*, as shown in Figure 6-1. The twelve colors on the outside of the wheel divide into three groups: primary, secondary, and tertiary colors. The color wheel also shows the relationship between these colors by arranging them in a circle in the same order as they appear when refracted through a prism: red, orange, yellow, green, blue, violet (purple). Those six colors are the primaries and the secondaries. The other six colors, arranged on the outside of the color wheel, are the tertiary colors. The colors in the middle are neutrals; primary or secondary colors that have been mixed with their complementary color.

---

[1] Itten, *The Art of Color*, 1961, p.18

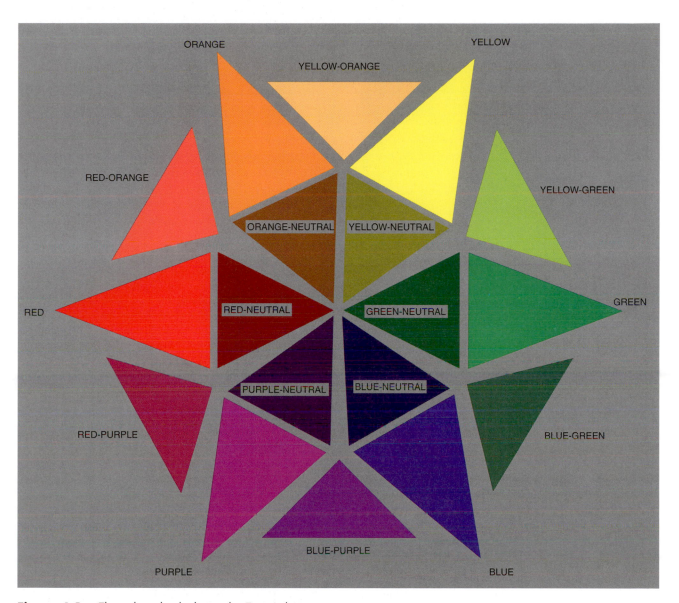

Figure 6.1 The color wheel, design by Toni Auletti.

The color model, shown in Figure 6-2, extrudes the color wheel into a third dimension and introduces amounts of black or white added to a color. In other words, the color model expresses the value and intensity and hue. Value moves vertically from black at the bottom, to white at the top of the model Hue is described along the circumference of the model, not unlike it is in a color wheel. Intensity decreases from the outside to the inside of the model.

The Munsell system of color, developed in the early 20th century, defines color based on an artistic interpretation of color rather than a scientific differentiation of hue, intensity, and value. The Inter-Society Color Council at the National Bureau of Standards (ISCC-NBS) has developed a color model based on the Munsell system of color. The ISCC-NBS color model contains 267 individual colors that were deemed to be of quantities sufficient to provide objective standardized names of color for industrial purposes. In this way, the term blue-violet or dark red-orange has a quantifiable meaning. A visit to the paint department of any hardware store proves that there are far

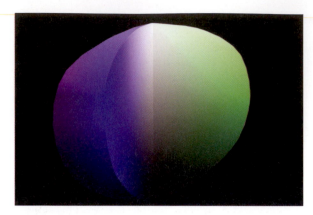

Figure 6.2 The color model.

more than 267 colors possible, and most of those are in a fairly narrow range of intensity. However, the Munsell color system is a useful and commonly accepted means of color definition. A color model like the ISCC-NBS model is an excellent means to visualize the interrelationship of colors. It is rare that a professional scenic artist would use these technical systems on a daily basis; however, a copy of a color wheel can be pretty handy to keep at hand when you are learning color mixing.

The Terminology of Color

Scenic artists must have a sound knowledge of the terms used for describing color in order to accurately discuss color. Color (as pigment) itself has three fundamental properties: *hue*, *chroma*, and *value*. These terms define what makes a color, how colors relate to each other and are classified, and how colors are perceived:

- *Hue* is the property of color itself or the perceived color of something. The hue of a clear sky is blue.
- *Chroma*, *intensity*, and *saturation* all describe the relative vividness of a hue. The three terms are synonymous. Bright red, blue, and yellow have a high intensity. If a color is mixed with white, black, or an opposing hue, its intensity will be diminished and its chroma will be lowered or neutralized.
- *Value* specifies the relative lightness (whiteness) or darkness (blackness) of a color. A value scale of 1 to 10 can be used to define the value of a color. On a gray scale, white is assigned a value

of 10 and black is assigned a value of 1. In these terms, we can more easily discuss a color's value in terms of being high or low. Primary red has low-moderate value. Adding white to red creates pink, which has a higher value. Purple is naturally a low-value color; whereas yellow is a high-value color.

- The *primary colors* of pigment are red, yellow, and blue. These are considered primary because they cannot be mixed from any other color. In theory, all other colors can be made from the primaries, with black or white added.

> There are other primary color groups: light primaries (red, green, and blue) and psychological primaries (red, yellow, green, and blue with black and white), for example. Modern printing systems operate on a system of secondary colors: cyan, magenta, yellow, and black. The primary colors of pigment are the primary colors in a subtractive mixing system.

- *Secondary colors* are the three colors made by relatively equal proportions of any two primaries: red and yellow make orange, yellow and blue make green, and blue and red make purple.
- The six *tertiary colors* are mixed from equal proportions of their adjacent primary and secondary colors. For example, the primary blue and secondary green make the tertiary blue-green or aquamarine, and yellow and orange make yellow-orange or amber.
- *Complementary colors* are located opposite each other on a color wheel. Every color has a complement. Green is the complement of red; yellow is the complement of purple. The complement of a color involves value and intensity as well as hue. The complement for a low-value, high-saturation red is a high-value, low-saturation green.
- A *neutral hue* is a color mixed with its complement. The perfect neutral would be the color that lies at the center of the color wheel, which could not be discerned as being nearer in hue to any of the primary or secondary colors. Theoretically, each pair of complementary colors mixed in the right proportion will mix to

Figure 6.3 Use of more saturated color in the flowers is an example of creating focus by manipulating chroma. Painted unit from the Lyric Opera of Chicago/Northern Illinois University Historical Scenic Collection (Courtesy of The School of Theatre and Dance, Northern Illinois University, Alexander Aducci, Curator).

the same neutrality as any other pair of complements. Neutralizing a color is an important phase of color mixing. Bright scenic paint colors often are neutralized for use on stage, such as when yellow is "grayed out" with its complement, purple, to be less brilliant. One of closest paint colors we have to the perfect neutral in pigments is raw umber.

- A *shade* is the darkened version of a color. Any color mixed with black becomes a shade of itself.
- A *tint* is the lightened version of a color. Any color mixed with white becomes a tint of itself.
- A *tone* is the relative lightness or darkness of a color. A shade of gray is also a tone.

The terms *shade* and *tint* have other important meanings, too. A shade may also be a shadow or anything shown in shadow. A tint might call for Universal Tinting Colors, a common paint product described later in this chapter.

- *Palette* describes a group of colors that are related by definition or use in a composition. *Warm palette* colors are called warm because they are the colors of the sun, fire, and the day. They are related to yellow, orange, and red. *Cool palette* colors are called cool because they are reminiscent of ice, snow, and the night. They are green, blue, and purple. *Earth colors* are those whose origins are organic minerals ground for pigment. They are the raw or burnt siennas, umbers, and ochers. Earth colors also are those associated with common rock, dirt, earthenware, mud, clay, and similar things.

Terms that Define Color Interaction

Colors normally are seen in relation to other colors. The immediate environment around a color can dramatically affect how it is perceived. Factors like lighting and adjacent colors can shift the so-called color of an object or surface into something entirely different. Green surrounded by red will look different to the viewer than the same green surrounded by raw umber. Scenic artists must train themselves to be as analytical and objective as possible when viewing color, particularly when called on to reproduce a color. The eye must be trained to understand the factors that affect perception of color.

- *Accidental color* is the phantom or ghost image of a complementary color that results from a high-chromatic color leaving an impression on the retina. One perceives a color that is not present.
- An *advancing color* is a high-intensity warm color that will appear to advance or lie in front of the picture plane.
- A *retreating color* is often a cool color but it may be any color that appears to recede from the picture plane.
- *Optical mixing* occurs when two or more adjacent colors seen at a distance are mixed by the eye to form another hue. A field of blue and yellow dots

or stripes will appear green when seen at a distance. Pointillism in the painting of Georges Seurat is an excellent example of optical mixing.

- *Push-pull* is the effect that occurs when two high-chroma complementary colors are adjacent to one another. The color fields appear to vibrate or shimmer.
- *Retina fatigue* is a condition that occurs when the retina does not see color accurately after having been exposed to high-chroma colors. Complementary colors may appear much brighter than they are and paler colors may appear even paler. If you look at a very strong color, like magenta, for a long time and then

Figure 6.4 Colors in paint for stage scenery are more saturated than one expects. Recreating this foliage from the paint elevation (**A**) for *Cinderella* to the actual drop (**B**) Scenic Art Studios, New York.

Figure 6.5 Warm highlights and cool shadows add further relief and sense of accuracy to this painted foliage. From the Lyric Opera of Chicago Northern Illinois Iniversity Historical Scenic Collection (Courtesy of The School of Theatre and Dance, Northern Illinois University, Alexander Aducci, Curator).

look at green, the green will appear extraordinarily bright. A low-chroma green may seem very bright if viewed next to a red field. So, if a scenic artist attempts to mix this same green by glancing back and forth between the bucket and the color green in the midst of a magenta field on the elevation, the green probably will be mixed at a higher chroma than the sample. Look at a swatch of pink next to that same intense magenta for a long time and then look at a swatch of pink alone and you'll see the pink will appear to be very pale or even gray even though it may be a deep pink. It is best to mix color against a white background.

THE PRACTICE OF COLOR MIXING

Mixing paint, or any painting media, to produce an accurate color match depends largely on three factors: the immediate environment of each color, the lighting in the area where the paint is mixed, and the type of paint being mixed.

The *immediate color environment* refers simply to how you actually see a color. Treat each color you mix objectively. Isolate each color to be mixed as much as possible, at least in your own mind. Mask a color with white paper if you are having trouble isolating it optically due to a high-chroma field surrounding it. Dry the paint samples on swatches of white paper or cloth so you can hold them directly adjacent to the color being matched. In a paint mixing area, it is best if the countertops and workbenches are dull colors, preferably gray, so as not to interfere with the perception of colors.

A work area's *lighting environment* further affects the way you see color. The light available for color mixing must be as near as possible to the kind of light under which the audience will view the color (see Chapter 4). Stage lighting is primarily from incandescent lamps, and most scenic designers work under incandescent light when making paint elevations. Incandescent and tungsten/halogen fixtures are the best choice in the paint shop, but bright incandescent fixtures are strongly recommended for the paint mixing area. The lighting in the paint mixing area may be different from that in the actual painting area. Ideally the light will be the same in both, but often they are not. Be aware of this when comparing the color of painted scenery to the color mixed or on a sample if they are in different lighting. A color may look correct in one and incorrect in another. The light in the mixing area must be close to stage lighting even if the paint deck area is lighted incorrectly. It may be unnerving to see "incorrect" color on the painted scenery, but if the paint is mixed correctly the scenery will look "correct" onstage.

Color mixing also is affected by the type of *paint medium* in use. Mixing color in dyes can be different from mixing color with pigments. Mixing house paint is very different from mixing scene paint. A scenic artist will encounter all these media at one time or another, but the following discussion deals with the most common stage media: scenic paint.

When mixing paint, always choose the most direct route as possible to that color. This approach will help you if that color has to be remixed at any time.

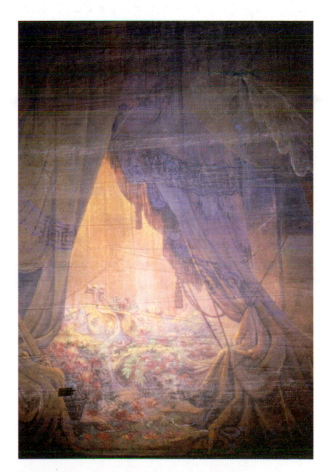

Figure 6.6 Transitions from low to high intensities also draw focus in this example of painted drapery. From the Lyric Opera of Chicago/Northern Illinois University Historical Scenic Collection (Courtesy of The School of Theatre and Dance, Northern Illinois University, Alexander Aducci, Curator).

If your method was something like, "Start with turquoise, but it will be a little too green so add some purple; now it's a little too blue so add some emerald green; the color is too dark so add some white; but now it's too light so add some black; now it's a little too bright so neutralize it with some red; now it's gone too far so add some dark green," you are in trouble. If this concoction was for your base coat and you had to remix paint in the middle of a drop, your chances of matching that color are grim.

Always try to mix the target hue with as few colors as possible. To mix a color most directly, first choose a *base mixing color* of paint from the mixing stock, the scenic paint you are working with, that is the closest match to the color you wish to mix. Every maker of scenic paint provides a color chart with paint chips so you can match from this chart. Hold the chart up to the swatch or the area on the elevation that you are trying to match and choose the most closely related color to use as your base. After some experience mixing color and working with scenic paint, choosing a base color for mixing will be automatic.

After you have established your base color, the next step is to analyze the target color for the three aspects of color itself: hue, value, and intensity. In this order, determine:

- Does this color need to be shifted in hue toward green, red, yellow, or whatever? If you need to alter the hue, do so now. Refer to the color wheel to completely understand the placement of the target color relative to the colors being used to mix it.
- Does the chroma or intensity of the color need to be neutralized by a complementary color or earth color so that it is duller or softer?
- Is the value of the color too high or low? If so, adjust it with black or white. Be aware that black often kills the chroma of many colors. Generally it is best to use black sparingly.

When mixing a color, you may combine some of these steps with careful choices. For instance, you may need to neutralize and make a yellow ocher darker. Adding raw umber to the ocher could take care of both steps. Remember, always try to mix the target hue with as few colors as possible.

A small mistake when mixing color can translate into an expensive waste of paint. Trying to fix a color that has been over-neutralized or over-tinted can result in mixing twice as much paint as needed.

In some brands of scenic paint, a mistake like this could be an enormous expense. One way to avoid this expense is to do what is called a *swatch test* first. There was a time when painters would dab and mix test colors in the palms of their hands; however, for reasons related to industrial hygiene, this is no longer done. Instead, dab the colors that you think you will mix together on a paint lid or small plates to see if you are on the right track. Such a swatch test can save time and guesswork before committing to a large quantity of paint. For example, you may find by doing a swatch test that neutralizing turquoise with burnt sienna will yield the same results as neutralizing it with orange and raw umber. Once you have decided that you are on the right track, dry test swatches of color on pieces of paper or fabric. Once the paint is dry on these swatches you can directly compare them to the hue on the paint elevation.

> If you are mixing a pastel color, always introduce the color into the white. It takes much less color to make a pastel shade than you may realize. The rule of thumb is to always add the darker color into the lighter. If a color is over-neutralized or over-tinted, add the mismixed paint into the modifying colors rather than the other way around. This approach will require less paint to fix the mistake.

THE SCENIC ART PALETTE

Theatrical paint, or scenic paint, and the scenic designer's palette are based on the traditional European artist's palette. This palette is based on the availability of pigment dating back to the time of the Roman Empire. The names of many pigments have come to us from Italian Renaissance painters. Behind nearly all of these traditional colors is a story of discovery or favor by a renowned artist.

The foundation of the fine art palette is the earth colors. Two of the most basic earth colors are named for the color of earth in the areas where they are found. Umbria is the region in Italy northwest of Rome, centered near Perugia. The soil in this area is a distinctive dull brown color. When the soil is refined and ground into a pigment, it is called *raw umber*, which is the closest color we have to a perfect neutral. When the same pigment is baked in a kiln, the heat alters its color, as heat will do to many other minerals. You may have seen examples of this if you fire a clay

Figure 6.7
A paint elevation with color swatches left by the scenic designer. *Into The Woods*, designed by Clare P. Rowe and Peter Beudert, elevation by Clare P. Rowe.

vessel in a kiln to create pottery. When raw umber is baked, the pigment deepens in color and becomes the rich warm brown color called *burnt umber*.

The city of Siena, south of Florence in Tuscany, is the source of another important earth color. This is the color of *raw sienna*, which is a rich yellow-brown color. When raw sienna is baked, the color deepens and becomes redder, as with raw umber. *Burnt sienna* is a rich, rusty brown color and one of the most important earth colors.

Iron oxide, which looks like rust, is another source of a rich red-brown color, although it tends to overwhelm other colors when it is mixed. This is why most artists prefer burnt sienna to iron oxide. *Yellow ocher*, a deep yellow mineral, is the source of yellow ocher pigment.

Through the centuries, other precious minerals for pigments had to be purchased by artists for their works at great expense. For example, the ultramarine blue backgrounds of the frescos painted by Giotto in the cathedral at Assisi were ground from lapis lazuli. This was and is such a precious pigment that, in centuries following the completion of these frescos, robbers actually scraped the pigment off of the frescos and sold it for use in lesser works of art.

Umbers and siennas form the backbone of the earth colors. They also are some of the very few colors still made from actual minerals from the source. Today, many colors are sold under the same poetic names as their organic predecessors but come from a synthetic source. *Chrome oxides* can range from a neutral green shade to a bright green and make up chrome green. *Cadmium* is a less common and expensive mineral that can range in color from a

Figure 6.8 Dry pigments, like those used for this example, were the principle choice for paints until the 20th century. From the Lyric Opera of Chicago/Northern Illinois University Historical Scenic Collection (Courtesy of The School of Theatre and Dance, Northern Illinois University, Alexander Aducci, Curator).

bright yellow to orange to red. Many of the warm colors have cadmium as their base pigments, which accounts for their expense. *Calcium carbonate* (common chalk), *zinc*, and *titanium* all are used as white pigments. These are listed more or less in the order of expense. Calcium carbonate is the most common pigment in white scenic paint.

The origin of turquoise pigment is self-explanatory, although the name now describes only the color and not the content. *Phthalocyanine* is a pigment derived from copper and used in blues and greens. In paints, it is often abbreviated to the word *phthalo*. Purple and magenta scenic paint often are augmented with dyes to help them reach the chroma that is necessary and expected. Scenic artists must familiarize themselves with what brands of paint contain added dyes, as these sometimes can stain or bleed through to the surface when painted over.

The Elements of Paint

There are three main elements in paint: *Pigment* is the material in paint that constitutes its color, and is a very fine powder suspended in a fluid. That fluid is the second element of paint, called the *medium* or *vehicle* of the paint. The third element of paint is the *binder*. Binder is the glue that adheres pigment to a surface after the vehicle has evaporated.

Pigment

Pigments that maintain their chroma through the centuries must be made of an enduring material. These are usually minerals pulverized into a very fine powder. Other pigments can be formulated from animal and vegetable matter but are less permanent. Some pigments and dyes are ultraviolet sensitive. These pigments are known as *fugitive colors* because their hue fades with time. Apprentices in the past spent arduous hours making paint for their masters by grinding color in a mortar and pestle; however, machines now do the grinding.

The cost of many traditional minerals, particularly bright colors, is prohibitively expensive for the quantities used in the theatre. Because some of these pigments are so expensive, some colors in scenic paint are augmented with dyes to improve the overall saturation of the color and to keep down the cost of the paint. In the world of theatre, the permanency of a pigment is not as important as in fine arts.

Many pigments have personalities, if you allow the allusion. Iron oxide overwhelms other colors when mixed with them. Ultramarine blue is the opposite, very shy and retiring, as the color seems to be more fragile and quickly neutralized with a very small quantity of a complement or earth color. Ultramarine blue also is a very heavy pigment and settles out of paint quickly, forming a viscous sludge in the bottom of a bucket. It must be continually mixed back into the paint or the color of the paint will change as the blue drops out. One other characteristic that ultramarine blue possesses is a slightly sulfurous smell. This smell is particularly noticeable when an entire drop is painted with this color; even if from a fresh can of paint, it may smell like rotten eggs. You will become familiar with the quirks of pigments and understand their limitations as you work with them.

The Vehicle

As noted above, the vehicle is the fluid that carries the pigment. Water is the most common vehicle of scenic paints. It has a fast drying time and is easy and economical to clean up. The vehicle is also the binder in many oil-based paints. Linseed oil is the vehicle for fine-art oil paints. Alkyd paints are suspended in a petroleum-based vehicle. Alkyd paints have been more common in other industries than theatre through the centuries because they were so much more durable than water-based paints. This is changing now with the introduction of more durable water-based paints and finishes.

The vehicle often is the *solvent* of the same paint. Solvents are used to thin the paint, so the solvent in part becomes the vehicle. Solvents serve to clean the paint off of tools and surfaces where it does not belong, like elbows and fingernails. Water is the vehicle of and the solvent used to clean up water-based paints. Denatured alcohol is the vehicle and the solvent used to clean up shellacs. Oil is the vehicle for oil-based paints and alkyds, and it can be used to clean pigment out of brushes used with these paints. A different solvent, mineral spirits or paint thinner, needs to be used to clean the oil out of the brushes as well so that it does not dry and ruin the brush during long periods of disuse. To thin alkyd paint and clean out paint residue, mineral spirits or paint thinner is used. The thinner for linseed oil–based paints is mineral spirits or turpentine. Lacquer thinner is used to thin and clean up lacquer.

The Binder

The *binder* is the substance left behind that bonds pigment to a surface once the vehicle has evaporated.

It is usually colorless so it does not interfere with the color of the pigment. Water-based paints must have water-soluble binders added to them because water itself has no adhesive properties. The binder in them classifies water-based paints. Some examples are latexes, acrylics, urethanes, and two-part epoxies. In oil paints and alkyds, the resins from the oil vehicle left on the surface after the arable content has evaporated serve as the binder.

TYPES OF SCENIC PAINT

Specific types of paint are used for the theatre because of their range of quality colors, available quantities, and ease of use. Scenic paint must be easy to prepare, broadly compatible, and somewhat extendible. To *extend paint* is to thin it down or extend the quantity. Modern scenic paint comes premixed with binder and vehicle. This type of paint has only become widely available relatively recently. For many centuries, scenic paint—in fact, all fine-art paints—had to be made from raw materials by the user.

Dry Pigment

Dry scenic pigments are a good place to start any discussion of scenic paint. Dry pigments formed the primary paint system used in theatrical work for hundreds of years. Not until premixed scenic paints were first offered in the 20th century were dry pigments phased out. Dry pigments are now used in very few theatres because premixed scenic paint is so much more convenient, generally more reliable, and safer to use. The available palette of dry pigment has correspondingly diminished over the last two decades. Many of the rich colors, such as solferino, malachite, and Naples yellow, are no longer available at all. Dry pigments can be very quirky and some colors are downright testy to mix. Thus, a large part of a scenic artist's skill in the past was the knowledge and ability to skillfully handle these pigments.

Colors still available in dry pigment include raw and burnt sienna, raw and burnt umber, yellow ocher, Van Dyke brown, vermilion red, orange, chrome yellow, chrome green, ultramarine blue, turquoise, cerulean blue, purple, and magenta, to name a few. The range of dry pigments has been narrowed down to a selection that matches modern scenic paints.

Dry pigments use water as a vehicle, although not all of them mix readily into water, particularly the saturated pigments, which have dyes in them to achieve intensity of color. Pigments that contain dye float in water. You can dump them into a bucket of water, stir them in, then stand back and watch as clumps of pigment rise to the surface perfectly dry and seemingly unaffected by the presence of water. Some aniline and fezan dyes used in dry pigments must be dissolved in alcohol before they will dissolve in water. Pigments that have been saturated with dyes must first be *pulped*—that is, mixed into a paste with denatured alcohol—before they will readily mix with water. Alcohol reduces the surface tension of the water so dry pigment will mix into it.

When I was just learning how to mix paint in a shop that used dry pigment, I was sent off on a rush job, "Quick go mix some green paint for those Venus flytraps; photo call is in one hour!" In minutes I had returned with the paint, and the Venus flytraps were laid out and painted in front of a fan. An actor costumed in white bellboy pants climbed a ladder and rigged the Venus flytraps from above while they dangled around his legs. I thought that the costume manager was very generous toward me; he honestly seemed more irritated at the actor for doing stage crew work in his costume. But I, after all, had forgotten to put the binder in the paint, which had permanently stained the white pants. The moral of the story is that dry pigments must be mixed with a binder! Everyone who has worked with dry pigment has a similar favorite disaster story of scenery that could not be touched, costumes that were ruined, or scenery that had to be washed off and painted all over again. Common binders for dry pigment are vegetable- or animal-based. These same binders have been used for centuries in the manufacture of paint. Only in the later part of the last century had plastic polymer binders been refined for common use.

One of the first uses of dry pigment was fresco painting. The paint for fresco is very unique in that it actually requires no binder. Egg white and yolk sometimes are added to help fresco paint flow onto the surface more readily. The paint was applied only in a limited area of the fresco, which had received a fresh coat of plaster for the day's work. Because the plaster, although firm, was not yet cured, the paint on it dried very slowly along with the plaster. While it cured, over the next few days, it became permeated with the lime and calcium from the plaster and became part of the plaster finish. True fresco work technically is very difficult. If the plaster is made in the wrong proportions, over the years it might develop a bloom (a pale-colored, granular surface deposit) that obscures the painting. A tragic example are Cimabue's frescos in the Duomo in Assisi. These beautiful frescos have an astringent quality that attracts moisture and is decaying the masterpieces from within.

Dry pigment suffers from a fate similar to Cimabue's frescos. Very little scenery has survived from the past due to the limitations of the pigment but mostly from the limitations of the binder. Have you ever painted a drop and expected it to last hundreds of years? Certainly nobody would. Scenery is handled roughly, stored carelessly, and rarely made to last for very long. The binder to some degree plays a role in limited longevity.

Binders for Dry Pigments and Powdered Paints

Size water is glue and water mixed into the right proportions to adhere dry pigment to a surface once the vehicle has evaporated. If there is not enough glue in the paint, it will naturally smear. Too much glue and the paint will be brittle and crack or develop dark spots that show the brushstrokes. Because dry pigments were used daily in shops of yesteryear, one shop assistant would do nothing but maintain a large bucket of size water and keep the pigment pastes moist.

Mixing dry pigments into premixed size water prepared in the correct proportions is a good way of making sure the binder is consistent. The common proportions for size water are about 10 to 15 parts water to 1 part binder. This may vary according to the shop preferences and the type of binder. In theatres where stock flattage was used on a regular basis, the stock flats painted with dry pigments, and protein-based binders would literally be washed off after the production was over and reused for subsequent productions until the muslin wore out.

Different approaches may be taken to mixing colors with dry pigments. One is to mix the color while the pigment is in its dry form. Because the vehicle will deepen the value of the color, the mixed dry pigment will be slightly lighter but closer to the color and value of the dry paint. Another method is to pulp all the color pigments beforehand with water and denatured alcohol as needed and to keep them in sealed containers that are checked every day to make sure that they still are fresh and moist. After the appropriate color is mixed from the pulped pigments, the size water is mixed in until the paint is the right consistency. Working with pulped pigments is similar to working with premixed scenic paint because most scenic paints are concentrated. Dry pigment

dust is very toxic (see Chapter 4, the section "Safety and Health Regulations").

The classic binder for dry pigment is *animal glue*. Animal glue is made of animal matter including cartilage, hooves, and parts of hide. Finer-quality glue is made specifically from the pelts and carcasses of rabbits. These parts are rendered down, similar to but not as refined as gelatin. The rendering then is strained, mixed with preservatives, and dried into sheets. The dried sheets are broken up into granules and sold by the pound. Although this process sounds a little gritty, remember that for centuries there was nothing else—it was animal glue or you did not paint your scenery. In centuries past, scenic painters (like people in many other walks of life) were closer to the source of the materials they worked with. The artist's introduction to the profession would be the responsibility of grinding the color for pigment and going to the butcher or slaughterhouse to buy the animal glue.

Animal glue granules must be rehydrated over heat to be liquefied. A *double boiler* is best for this task so that the glue does not burn while heating. Burnt animal glue has a very unpleasant and unforgettable smell. To rehydrate the glue, fill a steel bucket half full of glue granules. Then, fill it to the brim with water and let it sit overnight. The granules will swell to fill most of the bucket. In the morning, put the bucket in a double boiler and cook at medium heat for 40 minutes to an hour, stirring frequently. When the glue has a smooth caramel-like consistency, it is ready for dilution to a usable strength. If concentrated glue is left to cool, it will thicken and solidify. To soften it again, reheat it in a double boiler.

Colloid is an emulsion animal glue that will not gel. This glue remains in a liquid state and is easily rewetted. Once paint mixed with a colloid binder is applied, it can be rewetted and the binder will easily dissolve. The one advantage in using this binder is that paint can be entirely washed off of a surface after painting. Because this binder dissolves so easily, any muslin mounted on flats can be salvaged and reused later. The disadvantage in using this binder is that it is nearly impossible to put a *glaze* color or additional color over an initial layer or technique. The term *glaze* refers to a thin transparent paint treatment. Any base color or painted treatment that must be layered with paint applications, such as marble or wood, will loosen, and the paint already on the surface will dissolve into the application of glaze coats.

Flexible animal glue is sold in slabs by the pound. It has additives in it to keep it from getting brittle when it dries. It needs simply to be melted in a double boiler and mixed into size water. This glue should be stored in airtight containers. It is more expensive and usually reserved for projects where a flexible paint finish is necessary.

Dextrine glue is made from processed sugar beets and commonly has been used as a binder for bronzing powders. These pigments flow very well when suspended in a dextrine binder and they do not tarnish in this medium. The glue does not cloud when it dries, so bronzing powders maintain their brilliance. Dextrine must also be dissolved in a double boiler. Fill a steel bucket half full of dextrine glue and top it off with water. It will appear milky until it is properly cooked. Set the bucket in a double boiler and cook the glue slowly until the fluid has clarified. Watch the glue closely while it is cooking, as dextrine glue must never boil or it will foam over the top of the bucket. Burnt dextrine glue has a distinctive and unpleasant odor. Dextrine is ready to use at this stage. Thin the glue only as much as needed for the work. Then add the bronzing powder or special pigments directly to the glue. Unused dextrine glue can be stored in a sealed container for later use. It will not solidify or thicken when cool.

Casein is another common binder. It also is a protein-based binder but its origins are not as grisly as animal glue: it is made from processed cow milk or soybean husks. Some lines of premixed scenic paint use casein as the binder. Casein glue is sold in granules and flakes for use with dry pigment. It is a cold-water glue and can be mixed directly with water to make size water. A typical ratio is approximately 1 part glue to 7 to 10 parts water, depending on shop preferences. It should be mixed into lukewarm water and allowed to sit for about an hour and mixed again so that all of the granules or flakes dissolve. It then can be used straightaway. Ammonium is frequently added to premixed scene paint as a preservative because casein-based paint can rot.

The binders discussed so far are declining in use today. One of the drawbacks of many organic binders, such as the casein just discussed, is that they rot and the paint mixed from them can become putrid, especially in warm weather. Many other binders used in the past no longer are in use, such as rabbit hide glue and banana oil. Nearly all organic binders have been replaced by plastic polymers.

These new binders perform as well and have many advantages over the binders of past centuries. They are more permanent, do not rot as easily, come ready to use in liquid form, and are a great deal easier to obtain than their historic counterparts.

Modern Scenic Paint

Modern scenic paint is a relatively new arrival to the theatrical world. Halfway through the 20th century, many theatres and schools still were relying totally on dry pigments. Now, dry pigments are as common as the horse and buggy. Scenic paints are manufactured and sold in the United States by several different companies. Many manufacturers offer several lines or types of paint in very similar palettes. Economy lines, mid-range, and top-of-the-line paints are available. The differences between them are in the pigment and the binder quality as well as the price. If the paint you need is not available locally, you can order it directly from the supplier and have it shipped to you. The finest scenic paints may also serve as paints used for mural and diorama work. Some top-of-the-line paints may be available only directly from the manufacturer, as they are too costly for suppliers to keep in stock.

Premixed scenic paints generally have certain qualities in common. First, they are manufactured in the traditional European artist's palettes, as discussed earlier. Second, they are fairly affordable and available in large quantities. Third, scenic paints must dry with a flat finish, as gloss finish paints can be too reflective for general stage use and flat finishes allow the scenic designer or scenic artist to determine

Figure 6.9 Scenic paint stock at Scenic Art Studios, New York.

the finish. Fourth, scenic paint must be of a consistent hue from batch to batch. Last, scenic paint must be durable enough to stand up to the demands of traveling, folding, and shifting.

Paint Systems and Palettes

The *color spectrum*, or *palette*, of scenic paints varies somewhat from brand to brand. Although the range and selection of colors in all lines of theatrical scene paint is based on the fine-art palette, nearly every line of scenic paint boasts certain colors to be a vast improvement over other lines of scenic paint. Despite these claims, you can expect a palette to perform more or less in traditional patterns. What may vary a great deal from line to line is the quality of color. Good color is very expensive. Remember, these are minerals that are mined, ground, and refined or chemically processed. In a more economical line of paint, an orange actually may be a deep peach. If this is the best you can afford, you may be able to increase the chroma of the color with a colorant from the local paint store (we'll discuss colorants later in this chapter).

Many lines of paint use dyes to improve color saturation. Dyes lower manufacturing costs. The more dyes that are in the paint, the more problematic that paint is to use. You are either painting with paint or painting with dyes; the approaches to working with these two mediums are very different. If there is dye in paint and you attempt a gouache (the technique of putting a tinted color over a darker field), the results may not be what you anticipated. This situation is very similar to the condition of working with dry pigments earlier in the last century. Knowing and understanding the characteristics of the pigments was one of the special skills of the master painters of the 19th century. Our challenge today is that there are many different lines of paint, and these lines are often revised and changed by paint companies. Most scenic artists become comfortable with two or three lines of scenic paint and continue to work with those for many years.

Scenic paint is sold in concentrated form. A gallon may actually be extended, or thinned down, quite a lot. One general rule when working with scenic paint is to use only as much color as necessary to get the job done. Because the viewer is some distance from the subject, good coverage does not mean the same as when painting a living room. Generally, many techniques will go over the base coat, so a thin patch may well escape all but the closest scrutiny. This is not an invitation to do sloppy work. Any base coat needs to have a creamy texture to provide good coverage, but it need not be so thick that the stir stick stands up in the bucket. A lighter weight is an asset for scenery, and even thin paint increases the weight noticeably. Thinner paint is easier to apply and allows you to extend the stock of these fairly expensive paints. Also, thinner paint treatments stand up longer to repeated folding and shipping abuses when used on backdrops.

Water-Based Scenic Paint

Water-based paints are the primary type of paint used in scenic art. Many kinds of paint are available in this form, each possessing different qualities and characteristics.

Casein Paint

Premixed scenic paints with casein binders are widely available. Mostly known by the binder and often called *casein paint*, they are the dominant choice for inexpensive, quality color scenic paint. These lines of scenic paint range from economic to mid-range prices. In some cases, the quality of pigment is rather good. Many scenic artists appreciate casein because of its extremely flat finish. Some scenic artists also prefer casein binder because it may be rewetted and reworked or the paint may be completely washed off. This flexibility is also one of its disadvantages. When applying a glaze paint treatment, if overworked, the base underneath can pull up and mix into the glaze.

One aspect of casein paint that has become problematic over the past couple of decades is how it interacts with modern flame retardants. Many soft goods used in the theatre by law must be treated with flame retardants. Some flame retardants will damage the protein-based binders mixed with paint and cause them to deteriorate. When this happens, the paint becomes very fragile and flakes off the scenery. It is particularly apparent when painting on pretreated muslin used in a drop. One way around this dilemma is to use a size water made from a polymer binder to thin the paint. The size water will reinforce the casein binder and ensure the longevity of the paint job. Clear polyvinyl acrylic or vinyl latex will work as the added binder. Mix them up in a size water proportioned around 1 part binder to at least 10 or more parts water. In the case of some binders, 30 to 1 might be an adequate ratio. Too much binder in the size water will cause the paint treatments to develop a sheen. The size water should be used to thin the casein paints in much the same way it is used with pulped dry pigment.

Latex Paint

Latex, once processed from the milk of certain plants (milkweed and poppy) was one of the first water-based binders to be manufactured in the last century. Now it is synthetically produced. It was unstable at first, but in subsequent years, it was improved and eventually combined with other plastic binders to create very stable and reliable polymers. It is now used commonly in many lines of house paint, some lines of scenic paint, and in clear bases for mixing with tints or dry pigments. The polymer used in scenic paint is vinyl latex, an economical choice for smaller theatrical operations, schools, and community theatres. However, using house paints is not advised for most theatrical paint applications. Highly saturated colors are difficult to achieve when working with a line of paints designed to be used as house and interior paints.

Acrylic Paint

Acrylic binders were invented in the 19th century. These are synthetic binders derived from acrylic acid. Not until the 1950s was a system discovered whereby acrylics could be used as a binder in water-based paints. Acrylic binders are now used in many brands of theatrical and display paints. They are very reliable binders and generally used in higher-quality brands of paints. Some acrylic-based paints have a tendency to develop a little bit of sheen when applied thickly. Acrylic paints generally are of very good quality and can be thinned down so the color can be extended into a transparent glaze.

Vinyl Paint

Vinyl paint, using vinyl binder, is another synthetic binder valued for its flexibility and durability. Some lines of paint are based on straight vinyl binders, but often the binder is mixed in polymer combinations with latex and acrylic binders. When mixed with acrylics, it improves the hiding or coverage quality of the paint.

Polymers

Polymers are a mixture of two or more synthetic binders, compounding their benefits. Like acrylics, polymers were invented in the 19th century. However, they did not gain wide acceptance until the middle of the 20th century because it has taken time to perfect the technology, allowing them to be used in water-based paints.

All the binders discussed up to now are solids that are emulsified in water. When that water evaporates, the pigment that had been suspended in the water is trapped by the solids of the binder. They are forced together and bond to the surface. Common polymer combinations are vinyl latex and vinyl acrylic.

Paint Compatibility

All polymer paints can be mixed with other polymer paints. So, if you prefer to use white latex for base coating but your favorite line of scenic paint is a vinyl acrylic polymer, you can mix these paints together. It is possible to mix casein paints with polymers as well. One word of warning: If you have used casein-based white glue or wood glue to reinforce a binder and you tint this with a polymer-based paint, you may end up with a rubbery unspreadable lump.

Occasionally, despite your best efforts, strange things may happen to your mixtures. Odd blooms develop on the paint surface after it has dried, curds float to the top of the bucket even when you thought the two mediums you were mixing were harmonious. Sometimes, this may happen with theoretically compatible paints. Always try a sample first, giving the sample enough time to react. Setting it aside overnight is a good idea.

Some lines of bulk acrylic paint available actually are fine-art quality paints made available in larger quantities. These paints are very expensive and have good quality color. They are worth the price if the production budget warrants the expense. Generally, these paints are only used for very long-term or high-quality productions, murals, or display work. These fine quality colors also are handy when the design involves colors that are so intense that they cannot be made from ordinary scenic paint. Acrylic fine-art lines of paint can be thinned down to an even greater degree than scenic paint while maintaining a high chroma. For scenery that is intended for long-run productions and must hold up year after year, these high-quality paints may be the most economic choice.

Sources for Modern Scenic Paints

Rosco Laboratories dominates the scenic paint market. It manufactures and distributes Iddings Deep Colors, long a standard of casein-based scenic paint. Rosco also offers Off-Broadway paint, an inexpensive acrylic paint in a palette similar to that of the Iddings. Rosco created Supersaturated paint in the late 1970s. It is a highly concentrated acrylic paint sold in smaller quantities. Supersat, as it is called, has remarkable pigment intensity and can be thinned tremendously without losing its intensity. It is an excellent substitute for dyes and a good choice whenever truly brilliant color is desired. Supersat has a palette similar to Iddings with a few slightly different colors, including a unique green-blue shade.

There are other manufacturers of very high-quality casein and acrylic theatrical paint in the United States. Artist's Choice, Mann Brothers, Wolf, and Cal-Western all manufacture and distribute excellent paint in several levels of affordability.

Black and White Paint

In every paint shop, large amounts of black and white paints are used for color mixing. Most paint shops obtain stock black and white paints from the local paint store. The main reason for local sourcing is that the white and black paints available from scenic paint suppliers are much more expensive than house paints. Vinyl latex and vinyl acrylic are the most common varieties found at house paint distributors. As mentioned before, house paint comes in a range of mixing bases. Only straight white house paint should be used as the stock paint for mixing with scenic colors. Other mixing bases will not have the same quantity and quality of white pigment in them.

Much of the black paint that is used in theatre is used to mask out the structure of the scenery so that if by chance it is glimpsed by the audience it will be nearly invisible when seen against black masking or in the darkened backstage area. Black house paint is not the best quality, but it is perfectly acceptable for this use. Many paint shops also stock the black paint from the line of scenic paint that is used for mixing the show colors because of its superior quality.

When unmodified white or black paints are used on scenery, the white and black paints available through lines of scenic paints are often a better choice because of their superior quality.

Colorants and Universal Tinting Colors

Colorants are an essential part of the paint mixing systems used in paint stores. A colorant, also called a *tint*, is pure, highly concentrated pigment pulped into a vehicle that is compatible with most types of oil- and water-based binders. House paint is mixed by adding various amounts of these colorants to a premixed neutral base of medium and binder. The bases are gradated from white base, which is mostly white, through pastel and medium to deep base, which contains no white whatsoever. This system is an efficient cost-effective way for a paint store to offer thousands of different consistent colors in many different types of binders and finishes for its customers. Colorants, typically packaged in half- or full-pint squeeze bottles, can be purchased separately from paint stores or ordered from theatrical paint suppliers. The actual colors of the universal tints are quite similar to those of scenic paint. These colorants are very useful in a scenic studio to boost low-saturation color or adjust the hue of a paint mix.

Working with this system for stage may be useful, particularly when only a few colors are required and the paint needs to be mixed for good coverage and an exact match. When painting a set that is to be a consistent and untreated color, such as a realistic apartment interior, working with house paints may be the best approach.

Some solvent-based paints do not readily mix with colorants from the paint store. *Universal Tinting Colors* (UTC) and *Japan colors* are formulated to mix with oil-based paints, shellacs, and lacquers. Japan colors also may be used by themselves as decorative colors or they may be mixed with oil-based glazing mediums and oil- and lacquer-based finishes. Japan colors, having fallen into disuse in industry, are still available through Mann Brothers and Janovic/Plaza. UTCs and Japan colors may be mixed into shellacs, but the color in shellac finishes will be cloudy. Pulp the color in denatured alcohol to help it mix into the shellac.

Alcohol-based aniline dyes may be used to tint shellacs. Many scenic aniline dyes are waterborne dyes, so they will not mix into shellac. To determine which dyes will mix with shellac, first pulp the dye with denatured alcohol. Two-part epoxy-based paints and finishes must be tinted with colorants specifically developed for epoxy. These colorants are available from the manufacturers of epoxy paint products. Always use the proper safety precautions when using solvent-based paints and finishes (see Chapter 4, the section "Safety and Health Regulations").

DYES

Dyes are often the scenic artist's or scenic designer's choice for watercolor techniques and transparent effects. Aniline dyes are marketed by several scenic paint suppliers in a color range similar to standard scenic paint. They are the most common choice in dyes for scenic painting because the colors are so vibrant.

Aniline Dyes

Aniline dyes most often are used because brilliant transparent color is needed. Aniline is a benzene derivative created from coal tar in a chemical process. Because of hazards in manufacturing associated with benzene, aniline has been replaced by fezan in many currently available lines of aniline dye.

Aniline dyes are available through Mann Brothers, Alcone Co., Inc., Tricone Colors, Inc., and the Aljo Manufacturing Company. The dyes are sold in four-ounce, half-pound, and one-pound quantities. Most theatrical supply houses do not keep dye in stock, so it must be shipped from the manufacturer.

Some notes on mixing aniline dyes: Aniline dye is available in dry powder or crystal form. Dry dye should be premixed into a concentrate form from which the actual painting colors are mixed at the strength needed. To mix the concentrates, add three heaping teaspoons of dry dye to approximately one quart of boiling water that has just been removed from the hotplate. Mixed aniline dye is mildly corrosive to metal so the dye should not be stored or heated in metal containers. Quart-size canning jars work very well for storing concentrated dyes. Many forms of aniline dyes not used in theatre can be mixed only with oil or alcohol. Some dyes must be pulped first in alcohol and then may be mixed with water, although the manufacturers of dye are constantly reformulating the crystal or powder to make pulping unnecessary. If you are unsure of which dyes need to be pulped, try mixing a small quantity of the dye in hot water.

Mixing color with dye can be tricky. For instance, Bismark, a rich burnt sienna color, golden brown, and Van Dyke brown do not blend well with other dyes. When they are mixed with most other dye colors, they will precipitate and drop out of the solution to the bottom of the container, leaving you with dirty water. This reaction occurs because the pH of the dye solution may be too high or too low. Adding vinegar to the dye to raise the pH or baking soda to lower it may

Figure 6.10 Bavarian village painted with aniline dye, Tobins Lake Studios, Brighton, Michigan, painted and designed by Susan Crabtree.

solve the problem. However, changing the acidity of the dye may be a hit or miss unless you get very technical and use a pH meter to balance the acidity of the dyes. For this reason, many scenic artists learn early on to mix variations of brown with crystal black and orange. Orange and red dyes have their own quirks. After the concentrated red or orange dye has cooled, it sometimes congeals in the jar. To be workable again, slowly reheat the jars of dye in a double boiler.

Hazards of Aniline Dye

Do not drop dry dye into a container of boiling water when it is still on a hot plate or other heat source. Remove the container to a separate area for mixing the dye because the heat of a burner can ignite powdered dye under some situations. Also, never place alcohol or dyes pulped with alcohol close to a heat source, as alcohol is highly flammable. To reduce these hazards, use an electric teakettle rather than an open hot plate to heat the mixing water. Aniline dye is extremely hazardous if ingested or inhaled. Always wear protective gloves when handling and working with dye, and always wear a respirator when handling powdered dye or spraying the mixed dye (see Chapter 4, the section "Safety and Health Regulations").

Working with Aniline Dyes

The viscosity of mixed dye is that of the medium, which is water, so normally a painter works with dye much like actual watercolor. Occasionally, the dye is used in situations where it must have enough body to cling to a textured or vertical surface. For these applications, dye can be mixed with some water-based transparent medium, such as clear acrylic, latex, or vinyl. It also may be mixed into cooked laundry starch, wheat paste, vinyl wallpaper paste, or a solution of methocel.

Thickeners for Dyes

Methocel Gum   *Methocel* is water-soluble gum that is completely transparent when dry. It is sold by the pound by Janovic/Plaza and Mutual Hardware and in a fine granular form, which is dissolved in hot water. Mix one part methocel to four parts water for a working concentrate. Once dissolved, the methocel can be used in a fairly thick, concentrated form as a vehicle for aniline dyes that gives considerable body. The concentrate may be thinned for use as a primer for china silk, scrims, and other fabrics where bleeding or wicking of dye or transparent paint is a problem. It may also be mixed directly with the paint o dye. To use as a primer, mix one part concentrated methocel with 10 parts water. Spray it on the stretched fabric and let dry. This solution will discourage dye bleeding into the fabric as it is brushed or sprayed. A methocel primer adds some stiffness to the fabric, particularly China silk.

Irish Moss   *Irish moss* is seaweed that can be used in much the same way that methocel gum is used. It can actually be found on the beach in some areas of the northeastern United States. It is also sold as a tea and as a dietary supplement at some health-food stores. To prepare Irish moss, first soak it in a bucket of cold water until it becomes jellylike. Before cooking, you may need to add more water to the bucket so that the moss is completely covered. Cook the mixture slowly until it dissolves in the water and the solution thickens. Cooked Irish moss can be used as a vehicle for dye, or if thinned (approximately five parts water to one part cooked Irish moss), it can be used as a primer. It is best used in applications of aniline dye on China silk.

OTHER PAINTS, FINISHES, AND BINDERS

Another quality of paint is the *sheen*, *luster*, or *finish* it has when dry. All wet paint has a glossy reflective sheen. All scene paint is formulated to have a matte finish so that reflected light does not distract from the painted finishes. If a sheen is desired it can be applied as a paint application, or finish. Sheen is determined by the type of solid matter, other than pigment, in the paint. Solids used in most binders will dry to a glossy sheen.

Many binders, such as clear acrylic or latex, are also sold as finishes. *Flatteners* may be added to paint to dull the finish. Some flatteners cause the finish to cloud over chemically. Flattening oil may be added to oil-based paints and finishes to reduce the sheen. Other flatteners are solids mixed into the sealer as powder to cloud the finish. Mica dust is a common powdered flattener. Paint manufacturers or distributors may sell powdered or oil flatteners separately, if needed to create a special effect. House paints are formulated and labeled as having varying degrees of finish from flat to gloss.

The finish is usually applied over a finished paint application such as painted marble or wood finish. A typical finish product dries clear and has no color. When applied over a dried flat finish paint, most finishes deepen the color of the paint to the tone that it was when wet. The range of finishes is as follows: flat, velour, eggshell, satin, semigloss, gloss, and high gloss. Not all lines of paints and finishes are inclusive of all of these finishes, but most product lines have a selection of these.

Water-Based Finishes

Water-based finishes are a fairly recent development, and their technology is continually undergoing refinement. The advantages of water-based finishes are that they have a low toxicity, a short drying time, and a soap-and-water cleanup. The primary disadvantage is that they generally are less durable than their solvent-based counterparts. For most theatrical applications, however, the advantages clearly outweigh this disadvantage, as truly long-term durability rarely is needed.

Acrylic

Many lines of acrylic scenic paints also offer clear *acrylic sealers* to be used as both finishes and supplemental binders. They are available in gloss and flat finishes that can be mixed together to the desired luster. These sealers are milky when first applied, but as they dry, they become transparent. This is true of most water-based finishes. Care must be taken when using acrylic sealers so they do not cloud over, particularly the flat sealer. If used incorrectly, water can be trapped in the sealer, which will cause it to remain cloudy. Read all instructions carefully; these sealers are designed to be thinned. Use clear sealers only in warm environments. Do not dry sealers with a fan or use on scenery in a drafty area. Be very careful when storing scenery sealed in acrylic. Acrylic sealers have a tendency to adhere when two sealed surfaces are pressed together, particularly under warm, humid conditions.

Latex

Latex sealer may be used as a clear primer when it is necessary to maintain the natural color of a material. Latex sealer/primer is available through house-paint suppliers and manufacturers. It is available only in a gloss finish and must be thinned or mixed with flattener to cut the sheen. It is susceptible to some of the same foibles as the acrylic sealers, so take care to thin it, separate surfaces, and keep the scenery out of drafty areas.

Polyvinyl Acrylic

Polyvinyl acrylic (PVA) is used in the same manner as latex sealer/primer: as a binder in many water-based paints. This product is available through many paint suppliers and manufacturers. PVA is especially susceptible to adhering to itself when surfaces are stacked or pressed together.

Urethane

Urethane is commonly available in an oil-based medium; it has only recently become available in a water-based vehicle. Water-based urethane has the same advantages as other water-based sealers: easy cleanup, nontoxicity, and fast drying time. It is much more durable than the other water-based sealers, although it does not yet stand up well to floor traffic. Improvements are being made continually in these user-friendly, low-toxic finishes. Once cured, urethane will not adhere to itself when two surfaces are placed together.

Epoxy

Water-based *epoxy finishes* are available in pre-combined components or two-part kits. The pre-combined components are based on acrylic binders, and the kits consist of resin and hardener. Once the two are mixed together, they cure to a very hard finish. The precombined finishes are compatible with most other water-based mediums.

Available from paint suppliers, epoxies are among the most durable and costly of all water-based finishes. One disadvantage of epoxy finishes is that they are currently available only in a gloss to satin sheen. Water-based epoxy finishes are a recent development, and as research continues, paint chemists will most probably produce flat-finish versions. Proper safety precautions should be used when working with epoxy paint and finishes since they are toxic (see Chapter 4, the section "Safety and Health Regulations").

Solvent-Based Finishes

This discussion of *solvent-based finishes* focuses on traditional finishes that have been in use for centuries. The technology of finishes improved vastly in the last part of the 20th century. Until recently, finishes, like paint binders, have come from organic sources. These include vegetable oils, linseed oils, mineral oils, alkyd paints and finishes, and dissolved solids such as tree sap, lacquers, and insect excretions. Proper safety precautions must be used whenever chemical solvent–based paints and finishes are used (see Chapter 4, the section "Safety and Health Regulations").

Most solvent-based finishes can take anywhere from 6 to 12 hours to dry; however, some lacquers are formulated to dry in 30 minutes. Solvent-based finishes used on a floor can take an additional 24 to 48 hours to cure properly and before they can stand up to foot traffic. *Japan dryer* will accelerate the drying time of the finish, but it may interfere with the sheen or cause the remainder of the finish to set up in the bucket over the course of a few weeks. Too much Japan dryer can cause the surface of the paint or finish to develop a network of small cracks, called *crazing*.

Varnish

Traditional *varnishes* are cellulosic solids (tree sap and resins) dissolved in solvents. Modern varnishes are based in petroleum and lacquer mediums. The use of varnish has been widespread for so many centuries that the term has become analogous with finishes. A problem with the older varnishes was that they were unstable. In humid weather, they had the tendency to get waxy, sticky, or develop a matte white film that obscures the clear finish of the varnish (a bloom), usually caused by moisture mixing into the varnish. Solvents for varnishes usually are mineral spirits or paint thinner. Varnishes can be tinted with universal tints or Japan colors.

Shellac

Shellac is made by dissolving the excretions of the lac beetle, found on certain species of trees in India, with denatured alcohol. Its price varies from year to year because it is dependent on the harvest. Shellac is commonly available in paint supply stores. It has a tendency to crack and darken after several years but this is rarely a problem in theatrical usage. Its theatrical applications include use as a fast-drying, durable sealer for furniture and properties, as a good primer for steel, and as a vehicle for colored glazes. However, it is a rather fragile finish so it may not be very satisfactory for stage decks. Shellacs can be tinted for glazing with some aniline dyes. When shellac dries, it is resoluble in solvent alcohol.

Oils

Rubbed *oil finishes* have little use in scenic arts because they take so long to cure. For finishes on fine furniture, hand-rubbed oil is unparalleled for luster and durability. Tung oil, from the tung tree of China, and linseed oil frequently are used for such finishes. The solvent for oil finishes usually is mineral spirits, paint thinner, or turpentine, depending on the vehicle of the varnish. Oils can be tinted with universal tints and Japan colors.

Lacquers

Chinese and Japanese *lacquers*, the sort used to coat Oriental decorative and inlaid lacquerware, is a liquid tapped from varnish trees. Modern lacquers are cellulosic solids dissolved in solvent lacquer. The solvent for these is lacquer thinner or acetone. Lacquers can be tinted with universal tints and Japan colors and are excellent coatings for brass and other metals, adding luster and durability.

Epoxy

Solvent-based epoxy finishes have been used in industry for some time. These durable finishes currently come only in gloss and high-gloss sheen. When working with solvent-based epoxy finishes, take care to test the finish on the painted or stained surface. These finishes are not compatible with some combinations of mediums and have a tendency to discolor or darken some surfaces to a greater extent than other solvent-based finishes. The solvent for epoxies usually is toluene. Specific tints for these finishes must be purchased from the paint supplier or ordered from the manufacturer. Two-part solvent-based paints and finishes as well as toluene are very toxic. These mediums should be avoided unless their attributes, durability or surface compatibility are strictly necessary. Use only with extreme safety precautions (see Chapter 4, the section "Safety and Health Regulations").

Solvent-Based Paints

There is a tendency to describe all *solvent-based paints*, particularly those with gloss sheen, as enamels. High-sheen latex and acrylic paints may also be referred to as enamels. This is because the term *enamel* is analogous with the sheen and durability of porcelain enamel finishes. However, most lines of solvent-based paints are available in a variety of sheens.

Solvent-based paints are very durable. Proper preparation and priming is particularly important when working with them. The finish of paint is only as strong as its surface.

Solvent-based paints essentially are solvent-based finishes with pigment in them. The same solvents and tints applicable to a varnish work with the corresponding paint. As with solvent-based finishes, these paints can take some time to dry and cure. Japan dryer accelerates the drying time of these paints.

Alkyds

Modern petroleum-based paints are called *alkyds*. Alkyd primers also are available and work well on woods and metal. They can be thinned with mineral spirits and paint thinner.

Urethanes

Urethanes, so called because they contain urethane solids, frequently are used in porch and floor paints because they cure to a hard, scuff-resistant, waterproof finish. They can be thinned with mineral spirits and paint thinner.

Lacquers

Lacquer-based paints are excellent for applications where a rich high-gloss finish is desired. An advantage is that they are among the fastest drying of the solvent-based paints and finishes. When time does not permit lengthy drying and curing, lacquers, though costly, can be very useful. Lacquers can be thinned with lacquer thinner.

Shellac

White pigmented shellac is manufactured chiefly as a primer for wood and metal. Colorants added to shellac cause it to streak when applied. Use Japan colors or universal tinting colors when tinting shellac.

Stains

Staining products are available in either oil and water base. Stains are most commonly used on floors and furniture and may be put to use on finish carpentry in stage sets.

Solvent-Based Penetration Stains

Penetration stains are solvent-based stains formulated to soak into wood. They are available in a range of colors that can be intermixed to create a desired hue or intensity. These stains are very easy to work with. The stain is brushed or wiped on, allowed to sit for a few minutes while it soaks in, and then rubbed off. The color can be thinned down if necessary with mineral spirits or with the natural tone in that line of stain. Penetration stains dry to a flat sheen and generally need one or two coats of finish, which deepens the hue and luster of the stain.

Oil-Based Stains

Oil-based stains also penetrate the surface and can be applied in much the same way as solvent-based stains. The stain can be thinned down with untinted oil or mineral spirits. The color of these stains can be deepened with universal tints. Oil-based stains can be made by mixing universal tints into linseed or soybean oil. Oil-based stains have a dual purpose in that three or four layers can be applied to a hand-rubbed finish. However, each application of stain will be another application of color. Generally, oil-based stains take too long to dry for theatrical purposes.

Water-Based Stains

Acrylic-based stains are designed not to penetrate the surface but rather to be applied thinly and evenly over the surface, then dry to a transparent finish. Acrylic stains must be worked in and rubbed off before they have a chance to set. If the stain or the edge of the stain is allowed to dry, it will be permanent. Acrylic stains can be made by tinting clear acrylic medium with dye or universal tinting color. When working with clear acrylic medium, keep in mind that the commercial stains have drying retardants in them so there will be less working time with the acrylic medium.

Aniline dye can make an effective water-based stain. Aniline dye dissolved into water penetrates and stains clean woods and veneers. However, aniline dyes fade in time, particularly if exposed to sunlight. Unsealed aniline dye should never be used where it can come in contact with performers; it can transfer to flesh and costumes.

CONCLUSION

This chapter discusses color and the most widely available and common forms of paint. Manufacturers are continuing to make breakthroughs in the development of paint products. Keep an eye on the catalogues of paint manufacturers and take time to roam the aisles of the paint store to become aware of new products. If you encounter an unfamiliar product, or if a product has not performed as anticipated, do not hesitate to call the manufacturer. Chemists working for paint manufacturers often are easily reached and able to answer your queries or address your problems.

The composition of paint is so complex that it is becoming more difficult to determine which products are compatible. Sometimes, paint products react to one another in entirely unexpected ways. This can lead to serendipitous or, sometimes, disastrous results. Whenever you are working with an unfamiliar product or process, make samples ahead of time, being careful to work with the same materials used in the fabrication of the scenery. The time taken to create a sample will always pay off by solving problems before committing to the time and materials used on large-scale scenery.

Figure 6.11 A fragment of a drop with an arch and columns. From the Lyric Opera of Chicago/Northern Illinois University Historical Scenic Collection (Courtesy of The School of Theatre and Dance, Northern Illinois University, Alexander Aducci, Curator).

AN INTERVIEW WITH DOUGLAS LEBRECHT, HEAD OF THE SCENIC DEPARTMENT OF THE METROPOLITAN OPERA HOUSE, NEW YORK CITY

Douglas Lebrecht is the head of the scenic department of the Metropolitan Opera House in New York City. He is one of the leading scenic artists in the New York area and has contributed to many Broadway productions as well as the stage of the Metropolitan Opera during his career.

Susan Crabtree: What is your official position at the Metropolitan Opera?

Douglas Lebrecht: Officially, chargeman, but I'm usually referred to as head of the scenic department.

SC: Why is that?

DL: Because the departments are so compartmentalized here. There is the head of the stage—he is the master carpenter, but it's the stage head. There's the head of electrics who is the master electrician but whose job encompasses all the wiring in the entire building in addition to simply the stage. There's head of properties who is the prop master but whose job also includes the seats and carpeting throughout the entire building. The responsibilities tend to be bigger than traditional stage responsibilities, so head of scenic department addresses other responsibilities as well instead of just being chargeman.

SC: What other responsibilities do you have?

DL: Schmoozing. Largely anything of an artistic matter assigned to me by the technical director short of actual design work.

SC: You said that the departments are compartmentalized. How is your scenic art department compartmentalized? What would you say the different areas are?

DL: We actually have specific specialties. The costume painting department functions nearly every day while the season is in operation. Basically from September through May there is almost constantly at least one person, frequently five or six, employed, painting costumes.

SC: That is quite unusual isn't it?

DL: Very much so. Frankly I've never seen so much costume painting assigned to a unionized scenic crew. I've painted costumes in other shops but it was a rare occurrence. I've painted costumes in theatre, and in nonunion situations it happens a lot, but in union situations, the Met is the only place I know of where all of that work, all of the distressing, all of the painting work, is assigned to scenic artists. It functions that way because costumes are cleaned so rigorously here because of grueling wear with all of the singers. So sometimes within a season you'll paint the same costume more than once.

SC: What other areas are there in your scenic art department?

DL: There is certainly a heavy crafts component to it. We do all of the foliage work that you would normally find done by the prop department. All the flower arrangements are crafted here, although we collaborate. We have 17 different locals represented within the Metropolitan Opera. The jurisdictional lines are carefully drawn to allow a certain amount of overlap. Flower arrangements, it depends—if there are two of them, scenic artists will do them.

If there are 20 of them, scenic artists will do the prototypes and help supervise prop people doing the other 18. It's not that we claim the work, it's not that they claim the work, it's that we both claim the work and depending on the amount of work, the crews are utilized to make the work the least expensive and highest quality at the same time.

SC: What about painting scenery?

DL: Painting scenery is done entirely by scenic artists. The contract actually now allows for a certain flexibility that it didn't once have. Certainly we have a new scenery component because we do five new productions every year, so one of the shops uptown deals mostly with new scenery. Right now they are building a touring version of our production of *Rigaletto* because we are going to Japan in the spring with *Rosenkavalier*, *Sampson and Delilah*, and *Rigaletto*. *Rigaletto* is largely untourable, made too big and heavy, and so there is a tour version of it being built. The soft goods shop—the drop shop—does nothing but soft goods, and during the season a lot of maintenance items fly up there to be reworked. There is enough new soft goods in five new productions every year to keep John Pitts busy in his soft goods shop during the year.

Maintenance is also a critical unit of the Met and keeping the scenery looking good when it is disassembled in a heavy repertory situation is part of it. There are costumes and a heavy crafts component too because a lot of the craft work ends up here. The new construction component is different than just scene shop work too because every single production has a calculated life span of 20 years—20 years is sort of the minimum for something that is not announced beforehand to be a single season production.

SC: What percentage of your crew's time is spent on maintenance?

DL: We certainly spend as much time on maintenance as we do on new construction. So with five new productions on average we spend as much time maintaining the other 20 as we do building 5 new productions.

SC: What kind of training did you have?

DL: I worked in all areas of the business. I did a lot of Broadway scene shop work, which is how I started as a scenic artist, and during the scene shop work I largely worked as a journeyman. I did eight years of film work during which I spent most of my time running the crews. I bumped myself up to secondman but avoided being chargeman. I spent my entire career avoiding chargemen's jobs. I learned a lot

Figure 6.12 The Metropolitan Opera in New York City. Scenic backgrounds designed by Marc Chagall for *The Magic Flute* are visible at each side of the lobby.

about painting being a journeyman in the Broadway shops. I learned a lot about people being a secondman running film crews, and I learned most of what I know about designers working as a business rep in the union office filling the Broadway contracts. I handled all of the Broadway and regional design contracts when I worked as an assistant business rep. So I learned from these three components together—painting from the shops, people and crews from film work, and how to handle designers largely from dealing with them at the union level.

SC: Would you say that you have a specialty in being a chargeman?

DL: This job kicks the idea of chargeman to a level that is probably not exercised outside of the TV networks, perhaps, and some of the larger west coast entertainment companies. Probably some of the larger conglomerate entertainment companies have positions equivalent to this. But it certainly is not chargeman in its strictly traditional sense of being responsible for the painting of scenery.

SC: Did you have anybody who was a model for the type of work that you do now?

DL: I have to say not really, because as I said, it was exposure. Certainly film work came close to exposing me to the corporate level. One of the reasons I left film work was that the film business was by and large being run by corporations instead of individual entrepreneurs. The sound of the cash register ringing in the background had become louder and louder. There was more corporate interference in day-to-day painting work, something that I know is now true in the Broadway shops as well, although I have not worked there in a while. There is a lot of interference—it's much more budget and schedule driven and the artistic considerations are decidedly less than they used to be. Whereas the Met has its own artistic considerations and is not driven by profit but by long-term salability of its product.

One of the things that I like about the Met is that although decisions obviously have enormous financial impact, here an initial choice can make a big difference over the cost of something over 20 years, and a smart choice can save money, a silly choice can cost money. Those are just not cost-driven questions. Here, the question constantly asked is, "Will this work for us—is this appropriate to the Met?" which is certainly not a question you hear asked a lot in other offices. In movie and shop offices, "Is it appropriate?" has largely become an irrelevant question. "How much will it cost?" is the first question rather than the second. At least here the order is reversed. "Is it appropriate to this production?" is the first question asked, then "How much does it cost?" and then "Can we get it cheaper?"

SC: How long have you worked at the Met?

DL: I've been head of the department for nine years. This will be my ninth season, but I began working here in 1976 or 1977. I worked between the late 70s and the late 80s probably five years off and on. The longest I think I worked here was one 18-month stretch, which would have been in the early 80s. Five years more or less if you add up all the little stints in between all the other work, so 13 or 14 years total.

SC: Were you working here full-time when you were offered the chargeman position?

DL: No, I was actually working for Tony Walton on a series of Broadway shows and I had run one of the auxiliary shops in the Bronx for a short period of time for Matthew Schlacmoulder, who was the previous chargeman here. I had run one of his shops for a small period of time previously and I knew I did not want to run it again for him in the Bronx so I avoided the interview with him for two weeks when he called. I finally got cornered by him and found out that he was offering the chargeman's job because he was retiring. When I asked him, "Why me?" which was my very first question, of all the people he might have chosen including several incredibly competent people on his staff, he said, "Because you are a diplomat." Then he immediately said, "Not that you don't have the eye, but you're a diplomat first," The corporate nature of this business requires someone who can be a diplomat, who can tiptoe around enormous egos and in between the jurisdictional lines of so

many unions and still contribute to the smooth functioning of the place. The place backstage has precious little room for egos other than the talent.

SC: What would you say are some of the most difficult or elusive skills that you have learned in the profession of scenic artistry?

DL: One of the most elusive skills would be not being cautious. I have a good friend who said that once you had been out in the middle of a white velour drop with a six-inch primer and a big pot of purple dye you had pretty much achieved the apex of being a scenic artist. If you were not afraid to do that, you should not be afraid to do anything. It takes people a long time to not be cautious in the sense of not being rash. There are many people who are rash and there are an awful lot of scenic artists who would go to the center of a white velour drop with a pot of purple dye whom you wouldn't want to. The people you would are the people who are not afraid to be out there, and not being cautious about what you do is a tremendously hard thing to learn, I think. It is hard to look at a sketch that is a simple little watercolor sketch and realize that what it really needs is a big, dark cut roller pattern underneath everything or it's going to look wimpy on stage. And not being afraid to supply that whether it seems indicated by the sketch or not. It's important to paint with some nerve, to have the strength of your convictions—not that you can't be talked out of it, that you can't be told no by a designer—but to have the strength of conviction to approach all of your work with a certain amount of nerve.

Outside the area of painting one of the most elusive skills is being cautious. I think too many people reverse it and think you need to be nervy in your interactions with people and supply too much of your own opinion, and I find that something you learn if you keep your own opinion of everyone's work to yourself instead of talking about it. Be cautious about what you say. Be cautious who you refine. Be cautious with everything outside the painting but treasure the people who are not cautious when they paint.

SC: Do you have words of wisdom for someone who wants to go into the area of scenic artistry.

DL: I wish I could remember the person who said this to me. I suspect it was an older scenic artist in the shop I first worked in but I can't remember. He said, "Keep your mouth shut, keep your ears open, if you know how to do it, go do it, if you don't, for God's sake tell me so I can have someone teach you."

And it has proved to be a brilliant piece of advice and I have repeated it many times and it pretty much covers the bases for things you need to know to get along in a crew-oriented business.

I do have a card as a designer too and I did work as a designer when I first came to New York but other than the basic skills of reading a blueprint, which is something that has vanished, I'm afraid, in this business, the death of summer stock has not been a good thing for scenic artistry. People used to go out and do it. I certainly did my time in it. I did five summers worth of stock and when you're cranking out a major musical a week on $23 in budget and what you can find in the house paint cans at the back end of the garage, you learn to think on your feet. You may not learn too much in the way of professional skills but you certainly learn how to think and how to make use of what little you've got. I think it's a terrible thing that we don't have that stock system anymore, which drove so many people of my generation into the theatre and gave us our first chance to work as a scenic artist.

SC: What do you think are some of the most common misconceptions about scenic artistry?

DL: That it includes only the application of paint with a brush to canvas or wood when in reality, in the film world, it is vastly larger than that, and in the theatre world, it has changed from strictly that. Certainly, texture is as important an element in most theatrical work nowadays, at least in New York City, as the actual paint that goes on over the texture. That's a big change because when I started painting in the 70s, the master scenic artists all dismissed texture as unnecessary, they dismissed molding as unnecessary. "We can paint that" was a commonly heard sentence when I started in the shops, but I made a specialty of texture and I enjoyed it. I found I had feel for it and I didn't dismiss it as unnecessary and I saw, frankly, that a badly textured wall couldn't be well painted but that a well-textured wall could hardly be badly painted and made quite a career of it. I became a texture monger in the shops and based a large part of my theatrical career on texture, either physical texture or underpainted texture.

A cut roller to me was a revelation, it was like the light that struck down Paul the first time I saw an individually made foam roller used to apply underpainting. It was a gift from God as far as I was concerned and because that kind of work was becoming more and more in demand by the designers of the day, I got a lot of work based on that. My first job at the Met I was called in to tear up contra cloth—that fiberglass thread pressed between rollers with that obnoxious black plastic, garbage bag drooled over it. It was that nasty stuff and a tour guide at the Met once said it was manufactured as a waste product. Certainly it seemed it. I was assigned to a set of six enormous legs, 12 feet wide, 60 feet high with borders, with contra cloth torn up—not used as sheets but torn up and reassembled on netting with rollers full of glaze. No one else wanted to do it. No one else had a feel for it, everyone else wanted to cut it, everyone else was afraid to tear it up and get the fiberglass on them. I saw how it worked and I was not happy to do it because I itched for about three months afterwards, but I was thrilled to spend six weeks building those legs and borders because no one else saw it the way I saw it. And that was apparent to the chargeman at the time, obviously, because it led to more and more work, and more of that work was pieces of foam and fabric application and thick textures and potter's clay and white glue—a whole repertory of techniques that I use to this day.

SC: What are some of your favorite scenic art-related stories?

DL: Probably my favorite is about Tony Walton, who on the first film I worked with him on told me in one of his severe compliments to keep the artistry and lose the personality. Continue to care about what I was painting but essentially butt out when I reached a point in which I was intruding on the design process. It's a good piece of advice, don't assume your opinion is wanted, only your artistry. That was on a production of *Death of a Salesman* that Dustin Hoffman did, which was an amazing thing for me to be around. John Malkovich was one of the sons, Arthur Miller was sitting around a kitchen table with Dustin Hoffman while we were antiquing in the kitchen and dirtying Linda's kitchen cabinets. It was truly an amazing experience to be around that kind of talent and to be able to do that kind of work for someone who appreciated it so much and took the time, frankly, to talk that way to a scenic artist he did not know, which makes Tony Walton one of my favorites and someone who still, to this day, sees scenic artists as collaborators with him in presenting his work, as colleagues of his—major interpreters, necessary interpreters. I've never seen Tony pick up a scenic brush in my life. I've never seen him show anyone what he wanted, but he is able to communicate his desires and provide material capable of being interpreted in a sane way.

Certainly, I have great memories of working for Tony that way. He is truly my favorite designer. I adore the man, I truly do. The last time I saw him was about five or six years ago. I ran into him in a restaurant and his one question to me was "Don't you miss painting?" and I said "No, I don't get to do much of it anymore" and he said, "Waste." To be complimented that way by someone like Tony was truly wonderful.

I could give you a great story of difficulty, complete with accident, but with no names included. A designer on one of several tours through the shop separated by the span of several weeks was busy rejecting a color and a fabric that he had chosen specifically on his previous visit. After having rejected the fabric he had chosen on his previous visit and I was vaguely confrontational reminding him that he had specifically chosen this fabric and this color when he had rejected the previous and his response to it was, "What, am I on trial here? I must accept bad scenery simply because I don't remember saying 'No' to it?" That was raging ego at its absolute worst. Someone who didn't remember approving something, didn't remember specifically choosing it, and then when confronted with it had an attitude like that. It had become bad scenery simply because he didn't remember that the last time he was here it was good scenery as far as he was concerned.

Good scenery isn't dependent on whether you remember saying yes or no to it. There are a few absolutes left in the world. Certainly that should have been one of them.

SC: What do you enjoy most about your profession?

DL: What I have always enjoyed most about the profession has been the fact that you have to work with people if you are going to be good as a scenic artist. It is not something that can be practiced in this day and age in isolation. You can't withdraw into a shop, and even if you do, people are going to come find you. You have to work with designers; you have to work with people who want the scenery. You have to work with a crew sometimes. It is a people profession if ever there was one. I think of scene artists as the nurses of the entertainment world. If you don't function well in a group of people, if you're not able to be subordinate at times and authoritarian at times, you cannot function as a scenic artist. It is a place in the middle. It supports the designer; it must work with the carpenter. It has its own rewards, and some people think that sitting in the dark and watching the curtain go up and getting the round of applause is the best part of it. Certainly there is a lot of joy to being able to make people ooh and ah when the light hits something that you know is not there. But the best part of it has been working with people. If you like people and you are artistic, be a scenic artist.

Chapter 7

Preparing for Painting and Texturing Scenery

Illusion is what stage scenery is. Very little of what is seen on stage is actually made from a material anywhere close to its suggested appearance. Wood might appear to be steel and steel may masquerade as bamboo. A flat piece of canvas can be transformed into a vast panoramic vista. A humble and prosaic sheet of Masonite® can become glorious Italian marble. This ability to evoke is the heart of scenic painting. A scenic artist is expected to beautifully paint all types of materials, and the painting is expected to withstand stage use. To execute all this you must begin with a thorough knowledge of how to prepare these diverse materials for painting. This preparation is essential for successful results.

Theatre production schedules can be very compressed and the environment high-pressured. It may be tempting to try to save precious time when preparing surfaces for paint, but it is unwise to cut corners with hasty or marginal surface preparation. This is the first point where serious mistakes can be made. Regardless of the finished paint quality, an improperly prepared surface will never achieve its potential. It may never even make it to the finished stage at all. If the priming, base coat, and layout are done correctly, all the applications that follow will go more smoothly and will look better. If the preparatory work is done poorly, the problem will take more time to correct than the proper preparation would have.

WORKING WITH SOFT GOODS

Soft goods is a broad term for scenery mostly made of fabric. The backdrop is the most common form of soft goods. This term also refers to portals, roll drops, act curtains, scrims, oleos, translucent drops, floor cloths, drapery, soft masking, and soft sculpture, to name just a few. Soft goods also include scenery that is rigidly framed but mostly soft surface. For centuries, painted fabric scenery has been the principal type used in the theatre. Painted scenery, certainly, was the nearly only option of stage scenery until the 20th century. Today this sort of scenery would be made of soft goods, but in the past it might also have been made of flat wood. All of these sorts of stage decoration are two-dimensional painted scenery, which is made most easily from fabric. Very little change has taken place in the way soft goods are fabricated and prepared. However, some of the materials available for the soft goods themselves, as well as paints and primers, have changed considerably, mostly in the last 50 years.

The actual fabric of soft goods varies from application to application. The cost of goods varies widely, too, and will limit choices due to budget considerations. Drops, for example, can be made of a great variety of fabrics, mostly one of the types of muslin. Canvas, linen, burlap, scrim, silk, and velour are all alternative choices based on what the designer intends and what the budget allows. The following are the most common fabrics used in the theatre:

- *Bobbinette*—A lightweight, open hexagonal-weave cotton cloth sometimes used for invisible support in cut drops, diffusion effects, and transparent scrim-like effects. It is available in white or black. Because it has a tendency to stretch, it is not used in weight-bearing situations.
- *Burlap*—A coarse, heavy-weave fabric used primarily for the texture of the weave.
- *Canvas*—A very heavy, stiff cotton fabric most often used for ground cloths or where durability is a concern.
- *Canvas duck*—A low-thread-count canvas used to construct durable backdrops and pipe pockets.
- *Cheesecloth*—A very lightweight, extremely open-weave fabric used primarily as a covering applied over carved foam.
- *China silk*—A very lightweight glossy silk fabric that floats and moves easily on light air currents.
- *Cotton scrim*—A wash woven fabric similar to cheesecloth but smoother in finish.
- *Duvetyn*—A soft flannel-like fabric that is light-absorbent and has many practical applications for custom masking pieces. It is a common, inexpensive substitute for velour. One side of duvetyn has been brushed as it has a front and a back.
- *Erosion cloth*—A course fabric woven of heavy jute strands with a weave that is about an inch by inch square. Erosion cloth is used in landscaping to cover steep banks and reduce erosion while new growth can be established. It is used in theatre to cover scenery or to construct drops that require a very coarse-woven texture.
- *Linen*—A cloth made from plant fiber, linen is sold in tight weaves similar to muslin and in gauze-like weaves similar to cotton scrim. It is regarded as having a superior painting surface and as being a very durable and costly fabric.
- *Monk's cloth*—Frequently used in theatre because it has a coarse, raised square texture that reads very well on stage (the even square texture of the cloth is created by the warp and weft threads being grouped together). Because the material is all cotton, it is very absorbent

and takes dyes very well. It is often used for pieces that are intended to look like tapestries or have a certain coarse or handcrafted appearance. When it is used to construct soft goods, the cut edges must be well hemmed because they unravel easily.

- *Muslin*—Common 100 percent cotton sheeting available in a wide choice of widths and weights, it is the standard choice for drops and covering hard scenery. It is available in bleached (white) or unbleached (natural ecru), and is also commonly sold predyed in blue, gray, or black.
- *Opera netting*—Also called *scenery netting*, it is a cotton netting with one-inch square openings. It is constructed to hang vertically and horizontally and is used to reinforce cut openings and contours in soft goods. It is available in white or black.
- *Sharkstooth Scrim*—A lightweight, open-ladder knitted fabric very commonly used in theatre for transparent and translucent backdrops and special effects. Scrims are opaque when lit from the front and transparent when lit from behind. Available in wide widths and black, white, light blue, and neutral colors. It has a front and a back; the front side has ribs that catch the light in translucency effects. Filled scrim is a useful substitute for muslin, particularly for backdrops in touring shows, as scrim drops do not wrinkle as much as regular muslin when stored.
- *Theatrical gauze*—A lightweight, open-weave fabric, either cotton or linen and heavier than cheesecloth that can be used like scrim. It is not available in wide widths.
- *Velour*—A heavy cotton, polyester, wool, or cotton-silk fabric with a pile similar to velvet only with little on no sheen. It is used primarily for stage draperies and masking although it is also frequently used for painted drops. Velour has a front and a back and it has a directional nap. It absorbs light well and is available in a wide variety of colors and can be ordered in custom colors.

As a scenic artist you may be called on to work with many different types of fabrics and materials in soft good construction and paint applications. Soft goods constructed out of materials such as rip-stop sail fabric or bubble wrap plastic can present unusual challenges. Before constructing or painting on unusual materials, you may want to build, paint, and hang a test piece so that you can understand the idiosyncrasies of the materials before committing to purchasing yards of a problematic material.

Soft Goods Construction

Construction of backdrops is the responsibility of the scenic paint staff in some studios. In others, it is done by the carpentry staff. This varies from company to company, sometimes due to the rules of the labor organizations that represent the artisans working within the studio. In the course of a production, it may be necessary to do a great deal of additional scenic sewing for items like patterned backdrops or soft sculpture. Such pieces usually are executed by the scenic paint staff or a contracted specialist. The scenic artist, in all cases, must have a working knowledge of proper construction techniques for soft goods.

Standard Backdrop and Portal Construction

Regardless of whether staff carpenters, painters, or subcontractors build the soft goods, standards govern their design and construction. The traditional materials used for drops are linen, canvas duck, and muslin. All these natural fiber fabrics share one significant and useful property: the undyed and unbleached fabric shrinks when water is first applied to it. Linen was the standard cloth for backdrops well into the 20th century. Now, cotton muslin is the most common fabric used for painted drops because linen is considerably more expensive and difficult to find in widths useful for full-stage drops.

Muslin

Muslin is available in a wide variety of widths and weights. Rosebrand, a popular New York- and Los Angeles-based supplier of theatrical fabrics, offers no less than 17 variations of standard scenic muslin with additional choices of very wide widths for large, seamless drops. When buying muslin, order the width most applicable to your particular need. Muslin that is 120 inches wide is very common and useful for drops as well as hard scenery. Muslin that is 60 inches wide may be fine for some uses, but it would be a poor choice for a drop of any reasonable size because the drop would have far too many seams.

The weight of muslin is expressed by the number of threads per inch. The lightest weights, in the 72 threads per inch range, are best suited for covering irregular surfaces, rigid walls, and in places where muslin need not support its own weight. These lighter weights are not recommended for drops. Drops should be built of a stronger medium (128 threads per inch) or heavy weight (140 threads per inch) to endure the stress of stretching so they hang well on a batten.

Making a Drop

Some drops are made from a single, seamless piece of material and others are made by piecing together strips of muslin. The seams resulting from where the strips of material are joined run horizontally, or parallel to the floor. Horizontal seams are less likely to be visible on a finished drop once it is hung in the theatre and correctly lighted. A painted drop might be built with vertical seams if an image or pattern painted on it corresponds better to vertical seams, or if it is going to be hung on a traveler track. Translucent drops must have very carefully placed seams, for any backlighting will expose the seams instantly. A conscientious scenic designer often dictates seam placement. Other soft goods constructed out of velour, duvetyn, or other drapery materials hang most smoothly with vertical seams.

Standard horizontally seamed drop construction is a very straightforward procedure. The fabric is measured to the width of a drop, with an extra foot or so added to allow for shrinkage and for finishing the edges by trimming or turning back the excess to be either sewn or glued. Bear in mind that the side edges of a drop often are finished after the painting. Several of those horizontal panels are cut and assembled to the height of the drop. The bottom and top panels of the drop should end with the selvage of the muslin. Extra fabric may be included in the overall height of the fabric used for the drop depending on the type of *pipe pocket* the drop will have. A pipe pocket with a skirt needs only enough extra height to account for the seams between panels of fabric—two inches per seam and three-quarters inch turnback on the webbing. A hidden pipe pocket requires an additional six inches of height so it can be turned back on the backside of the drop. Figure 7-1 shows a diagram of seams, a pipe pocket, webbing, and grommets for a standard drop.

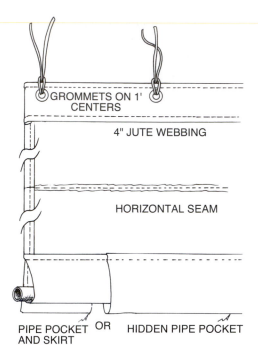

Figure 7.1 A diagram of seams, a pipe pocket, webbing, and grommets for a standard drop.

The weakest point of a drop is the thread of the seams. Heavy-duty thread should be used for sewing a drop. Industrial sewing machines handle the heavy-duty thread well with fewer breaks and snags. An industrial walking-foot sewing machine will handle the heavier fabric and jute webbing without jamming.

A pipe pocket may be sewn into the bottom panel of the drop simply by sewing a three-inch hem. However, the hem makes a poor pipe pocket because it is only as sturdy as the muslin itself. If the muslin is torn by inserting a pipe, the painted drop will be damaged. Often, a separate pipe pocket is sewn to the back of the drop or on the inside of the hem. This separate pouch of muslin or canvas is the full length of the drop. The pipe pocket is sewn about four or five inches up from the bottom of the drop so that the face of the drop masks it. If the pipe pocket is damaged, it can be replaced without damaging the front of the drop.

The *webbing* is jute or nylon, generally four inches wide, sewn to the back of the drop at the top. The edge of the muslin at the top of the webbing will need to be turned back if it does not end in a selvage; otherwise, it will fray. The webbing is sewn at the top of the drop so that grommets can be placed into the webbing-reinforced fabric. If the grommets were set directly in the muslin, the weight of the drop would pull them right out. Spacing grommets one foot apart is standard. They may be installed by hand with a grommet punch or with a foot pedal–operated grommet punch.

The side seams of the drop may be sewn before or after the drop has been painted. When a drop is stretched and primed, the sides normally become scallop shaped unless they have been strengthened. These scallops on the sides give the drop a sloppy appearance. Draw the cut and turnback lines on the unfinished sides of the drop after painting (see Figure 7-2). Then the sides can be cut and either sewn or glued back to give the drop a clean finish. Use a flexible or fabric glue to glue back two or three inches of fabric on the side of the drop.

Portals are drops containing large openings, such as doorways, archways, or windows. A portal built so that the center section is left open usually has vertical side panels, or legs. The sides need not have seams in them since they may be a width of muslin as long as the portal leg. When the drop is stretched out, the center opening should be drafted out and stapled to the deck or paint frame so that it is square.

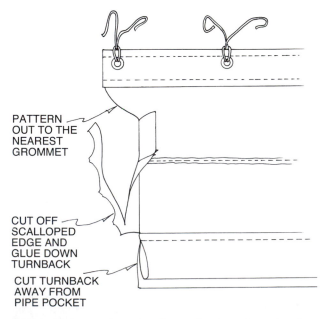

Figure 7.2 A diagram of a turnback on the side of a backdrop.

Seamless Drops

Translucent backdrops often need to be built from a single piece of seamless goods. Standard scenic muslin widths are 8, 10, or 12 feet. Wider muslin can be purchased in widths of 14, 20, 25, 30, and 40 feet. This fabric is sold by the yard through theatrical soft goods suppliers. These widths of muslin are more expensive by the square foot than standard sizes because few mills provide such widths of muslin. Obviously, seamless backdrops are used only when necessary because of the expense.

Scrim Construction

Sharkstooth scrim is the standard scrim fabric used for theatrical applications. It is available in widths up to 35 feet, in white, off-white, sky blue, and black. Scrim fabric has a grain to it and will hang cleanly if the "teeth" in the knit are vertical. Scrim also has a front side and a back side. The front has minute ribbing that catches light when the drop is lit from the front to make it appear opaque.

To cut scrim to size, measure it along the edge and carefully cut along the grain. The fabric will not rip cleanly on the grain. The fabric has so much give in it that it is impossible to lay it out and snap a straight line on it. Scrim will unravel a bit if it is not hemmed, so turn back and sew all the edges. The edges of scrim cannot be glued back, as with muslin. Glue will stiffen the scrim and cause puckers along the edges. The bottom edge of a scrim drop should have a pipe pocket sewn on the back or a separate canvas pocket sewn into the hem. Otherwise, the open knit of scrim will tear easily when a pipe is inserted at the base to weight the scrim.

Cotton and linen scrim are open-weave fabrics made of finely woven cotton or linen. Linen scrim, also called *theatrical gauze*, was the standard for scrim effects until the appearance of sharkstooth scrim. A great advantage of sharkstooth over linen scrim is its availability in wide widths. Linen scrim drops always had obvious seams, which had to be overlooked. The natural light drab color of linen scrim either may be a drawback or an asset depending on the desired appearance of the paint treatment. Cotton scrim is not as transparent as linen scrim when backlit.

Floorcloth Construction

Floorcloths are like drops but they are made for the demanding wear and tear of foot traffic. Canvas floorcloths should be measured to size and sewn in much the same way as drops, without webbing and pipe pockets of course. Their seams are less noticeable if sewn parallel to the audience (or a majority of the audience). Because canvas stretches so tightly, the floor cloth should be assembled with an extra foot of cloth on all sides, to account for shrinkage, especially if it is large. The edges of the ground cloth may be reinforced with webbing since the canvas will pull on the staples very hard when stretching. Always use pneumatic staples to hold a floorcloth when stretching it. The seams of a ground cloth are its weakest point. Only heavy-duty thread should be used. The seams should be flat felt seams, which are doubled over and sewn a second time (like the seams in blue jeans) and constructed to face away from the audience.

Working with Cut Drops and Netting

Painted soft goods include cut drops, borders, tabs, and legs. *Borders* are soft goods that do not touch the stage deck, and they may be painted pieces. They play overhead and may serve as masking as well. *Legs* and *tabs* fly all the way down to the stage deck and may be painted pieces. Legs play on the sides of the stage and may also serve as masking. When legs and borders double as masking, they should be backpainted to prevent light leaks from lighting instruments. Tabs play in the center area of the stage as scenic units; for instance, a cut tab may be painted and contoured to look like a tree. These may be irregularly shaped drops, like foliage, for example. The erratic, contoured edges generally are cut after the painting is done and sometimes are reinforced with netting. The contours are drafted and accentuated with an ink marker or paint to serve as guidelines for cutting. The opening usually should be cut out so that the marker or painted cut lines are cut off, unless the effect of the outlines is desired.

Openings or contours sometimes need to be reinforced because they receive extra stress. For this, leave about two inches of turnback. After the openings and turnbacks have been cut out, turn the drop on its face and fold and press the turnback. Then brush a diluted flexible fabric glue into the fold and press the two sides of the fabric together. Staple every few feet and at corners so that the turnback does not shrink. If the turnback needs more reinforcement, set a length of one-eighth-inch sash cord set into the inside edge of the fold with the glue. This works well around windows and door openings cut into a drop that receives a lot of contact with actors and shifting scenery.

Using Netting to Reinforce a Cut Drop

The point of *netting* a drop is to give nearly invisible support to the negative areas of a cut drop that are not self-supporting. These areas may include reinforced openings that may be inclined to sag with repeated use or contours that defy the laws of gravity. Netting is either glued across the entire opening of the drop or only those areas that need to be reinforced. Netting the drop happens after painting. In some companies, it is the responsibility of the construction department; in others, it is the responsibility of the scenic art department.

Types of Netting   Several kinds of netting are available for cut drops. *Bobbinet*, or *tulle*, is a small-weave cloth netting with octagonal openings. Bobbinet is sold with openings in assorted sizes and weaves. Bobbinet will stretch if it receives a great deal of stress or if it has to support nearly any weight. *Opera netting* is another cloth netting used in the theatre. It is made from cotton cord that has been tied in one-inch squares, giving much larger openings than those in bobbinet. Unlike fishnet, which is tied on the bias, opera netting is tied on the vertical and the horizontal so that it will hang straight.

Netting is sold by theatrical soft goods suppliers. Bobbinet is available by the yard and opera netting by the foot in 30-foot widths. Bobbinet and opera netting are available in white and black. White net can be dyed to match the background color if needed with aniline dye or a thin acrylic paint of the proper hue. Nylon garden netting recently has become common for netting drops. This black nylon extruded into one-inch squares is available at plant nurseries and garden suppliers. The netting is very strong and very inexpensive; however, it is shiny and available only in clear and black, which cannot be altered or painted over easily. The slippery nylon does not bind well with glue nor is garden netting treated with flame retardant.

Netting a Drop

As already discussed, the openings in the drop should be carefully cartooned with a marker or paint so these areas stand out. Next, the openings and contours are cut out or turned back so that the cartoon lines, if not part of the paint treatment, are no longer visible from the front of the drop. The drop then should be turned over on its face and stapled at the corners of the contour and along its edges before laying down the netting, so that it resists shrinkage, which causes puckering and shifting. The staples are placed approximately one foot apart. The turnbacks, if any, should be folded and glued.

With the drop stapled face down and the turnbacks glued, the openings and contours are ready to be netted. Stretch the netting across the opening and down to the contours needing support. Take special

Figure 7.3
Netting supporting three-dimensional leaves in a drop for *Into The Woods*, Scenic Art Studios, New York.

care to keep the opera netting vertical and horizontal to the center line. Opera netting set on an angle will bias and pucker the drop. Netting that is too taut will disfigure the drop by creating puckers. Netting that is too loose will not support the contours. To ensure that the netting will be straight and of the proper tautness, stretch and size it on netting stretchers when it is laid over the back of the drop. *Netting stretchers* are pieces of paneling, three inches wide, that have one-inch-square blocks set along one edge with a gap between them for the net. A board with tacks set one inch apart may also be used.

The stretchers can be set in position along the edge of the area to be netted and stapled in place with pieces of canvas to prevent shifting. Cut the netting to the approximate size it will need to be for each area to be netted. If the netting is being painted or dyed, dip it in the thin paint or dye. If you are not altering the color of the netting, dip it in thin size water. Allow most of the size water, paint, or dye to drip off the netting, and blot or wring out the excess. Then loop the wet netting over the stretchers and allow it to dry. Glue down the netting along the edges of openings and contours with a full-strength flexible fabric glue or hot glue, gluing down each knot to at least five rows in from the edge of the contour.

If you are using bobbinet or opera net, merely gluing it down will be sufficient. Plastic garden netting, however, will pull free of the glue because it does not actually bind to plastic. If you are using garden netting, glue muslin strips around the edges of the opening or contours over the netting to hold it in place. Hot melt glue may also be used with plastic garden netting. Keep track of the staples used to hold down the drop while gluing netting onto the back so the drop is not ripped when it is pulled up. If the netting is done on top of bogus paper or visquene, it is sometimes useful to draw small arrows with a marker around the contour of the cut piece pointing to all the staples along its edge before the netting is laid down. This will make the staples easier to find later when they have to be removed. Care also should be taken not to glue the drop to the floor or get glue on the face of the drop.

THE ROLE OF FLAME RETARDANTS WITH SOFT GOODS

Fire codes governing public buildings are strict, particularly in theatres. Tragic fires, such as the Iroquois Theatre fire in Chicago in 1903 and the more recent fire in the MGM Grand Hotel in Las Vegas, have brought great scrutiny to the safety of patrons in theatres. All materials intended for use in public entertainment and display are required to be treated with flame retardant.

The terms *flame retardant* and *flameproofing* are often confused. Every substance has a flash point, the temperature at which a given material will support a flame. Cellulosic materials, used often in the theatre, are made up chiefly of plant tissues and fibers. Their flash points are fairly low, and they quickly can catch fire if exposed to an open flame. Total flameproofing is impossible. The realistic goal is to slow down the fire by making the material flame retardant.

The scenic painting department normally applies the flame retardant to both soft and hard scenery. For hard scenery, a simple coat of water-based paint on wood will provide some protection from fire by creating a retardant barrier over the wood. Additives can be mixed with paints to make them more flame retardant, and some paints manufactured specifically as flame retardants are available from most paint suppliers. These paints are very effective in discouraging an open flame. Pretreated fire-retardant lumber is another available option, but it is expensive.

As the front of the scenery will be painted or sealed in some manner anyway, the back of the scenery needs be painted as well to make the unit flame retardant. Backpainting scenery is a standard practice in the theatre. It is best to backpaint the scenery before it has been primed or painted so any of the backpaint that finds its way onto the front of the scenery will not mar the finished work. Many shops save excess paint from past productions for backpaint. Backpainting has other good uses and is standard procedure in the profession. It masks the back of scenery, which may be glimpsed during a scene shift. For this reason, the most popular backpaint color is dark gray. Scenery that has been backpainted looks more professional and it is easier to see any identifying labels.

Drops also can be backpainted to make them flame retardant. However, this practice is not useful in many instances for a number of reasons. A translucent drop cannot be painted on the back except where it is to be opaque when backlit. If the drop is going to be repainted for another production, the extra paint on the back may shorten the use and life of the piece. If the drop is going to be shipped on a road show, the backpaint will add unnecessary weight.

Flame Retardants

To protect soft goods, clear flame retardants, available in either liquid or crystal form, are formulated for fabrics. Often these flame retardants already are licensed by the fire marshal in the state where they are marketed. They are available in liquid or ready-to-mix powder forms that can be sprayed on the fabric of the drop. Some flame retardants are concentrated and need to be diluted before being applied to fabric. These fire retardants can be loaded into a garden sprayer for application. Keep in mind that one of the main ingredients of many flame retardants is sodium, which is very corrosive to metals. Do not leave the flame retardant in the sprayer any longer than necessary. If working with flame retardant is a regular occupation in the shop, it would be a good idea to use one particular sprayer, an inexpensive or all-plastic one, for applying flame retardant.

Apply flame retardant liberally to the scenery. The material being treated should be completely saturated with the retardant. Spray hard scenery on the back before the face of the scenery is painted. Mount drops on a frame or the deck first, then completely saturate them with flame retardant. After the flame retardant has dried, prime or starch the scenery as usual. Flame retardants are manufactured by DuPont, Rosco, and Spartan.

Pretreated Flame-Retardant Fabrics

An alternative to applying the flame retardant to a drop is to construct it out of fabric that already has been treated with flame retardant. It may be more economical to buy the materials pretreated, as labor and space often are a factor in the cost of treating soft goods in-house. Pretreated muslin and other fabrics are commonly available at theatrical soft good suppliers. Bolts of muslin pretreated with flame retardant come with a certificate stating that the fabric has been treated. When ordering a drop or scrim from an outside contractor, a copy of this certificate can be requested.

Fire marshals in most major cities require a flame test be performed on the scenery to determine whether the flame retardant meets fire codes. This simple test involves exposing the material to an open flame for 10 to 15 seconds, depending on the requirements of the local fire code. The material treated with flame retardant should not catch fire; rather, the carbon buildup from the fire retardant should discourage the flame. If the material catches fire in the time allotted, it must be retreated to meet the code. To find out the code requirements for your city, call the fire marshal in your district; that office will send you literature on the local code.

When working on fabric that has been pretreated with flame retardant, it is important to remember that some flame retardants break down the binder in paint, even paints that have been designed to be used on theatrical scenery. Many manufacturers of theatrical scene paint recommend that extra binder be added to paint intended for use on pretreated fabric. The easiest way to do this is to thin all the paint out only with size water that is premixed with extra binder, such as clear acrylic or PVA. Depending on the binder, the ratios may vary; about 1 part binder to 30 parts water might be a starting point. Adjustments can be made if the paint finish begins to get too shiny (less binder needed) or there is not enough adhesion in the dried paint (more binder needed).

A common complaint with pretreated fabric is that when the flame retardant is rewetted, it dries leaving a ring of salt stains or a white bloom around each brushstroke. This bloom will go away after a number of months, which, of course, is not practical for immediate use of the scenery. One method of treating scenery with this problem is to spray it with diluted vegetable oil–based soap after it has been painted. Never spray the surface with the diluted soap until the painting is entirely finished, no matter how annoying the salt rings are. The soap may inhibit the binding properties of the paint. The bloom from flame retardant is caused by the formation of small crystals where the retardant has been re-wetted and crystallized when it dried. The soap keeps the crystal from forming while not inhibiting the fire-retardant properties. The diluted oil-based soap can be sprayed on with a garden sprayer or pneumatic sprayer. Care should be taken when spraying a drop that has been painted with dyes. The diluted oil soap may cause the dye to blur and sharp lines to run. The surface does not need to be thoroughly saturated with soap to inhibit the bloom.

All flammable scenic elements must be treated with flame retardant. Elements like scenic netting, foliage, fabric, straw, leaves, and so on can be dipped in liquid flame retardant and laid out to dry. When working with flame retardant, always read the instructions thoroughly and follow directions carefully. Flame retardant is a skin irritant. Care should be taken not to let it come in contact with the skin.

Always wear a respirator when applying it with a pneumatic sprayer or airless sprayer (see Chapter 4, the section "Safety and Health Regulations").

Synthetic fabrics need to be treated with a flame retardant manufactured specifically for these materials. If you are in doubt about what flame retardant to use on a specific material, call a flame-retardant manufacturer. Some theatrical suppliers also manufacture lines of flame retardants and may be able to answer questions that arise about a specific material or methods of application.

STRETCHING AND PRIMING SOFT GOODS

Any new drop has considerable puckers and wrinkles in it when first mounted on a frame or spread on a deck. Scenic backdrops must be primed before painting begins because unprimed fabric does not take paint evenly on the first or second coat, and a drop that has puckers in it will never hang flat in the theatre. It will not be possible to achieve even blends or solid fields of color when working on unprimed goods. The prime coat seals the fabric from the paint and sets up an even painting surface.

To prepare a drop for painting it must be shrunk into the final shape and given a surface that accepts the controlled application of paint. This sizing usually is done with a primer coat that also prepares the surface for painting. The process is similar to preparing a canvas for painting with gesso.

No priming is necessary with a drop constructed out of velour or duvetyn. However, these fabrics must be squared and stapled down as they will shrink. Once mounted on a frame or a deck, the fabric is ready to paint. Velour and duvetyn are somewhat resistant to dye, paint, and other water-based products in general. Adding a wetting solution to the paint or dye will help it penetrate the fibers. Leather stores sell wetting solutions as a preparation for dying leather evenly. Add a small amount, about one ounce per gallon, to all of the paint or dye to be used in the paint treatments. Wetting solutions are particularly useful with dyes, as they will not interfere with the color. If the fabric still resists paint, add laundry detergent to the paint to help it penetrate the fiber. If suds are a problem, add a defoamer (from the carpet cleaning section of the grocery) to the detergent.

A drop constructed of predyed or bleached muslin should be mounted tightly before it is primed because it will have less shrinkage left in the fabric after the dyeing or bleaching process. The starch or paint used to shrink predyed or bleached muslin should be heavier than usual, as the fabric tends to be more absorbent than unbleached muslin. Unbleached muslin will shrink considerably during the first prime coat so it should be mounted on the paint deck or frame so the fabric is a little loose.

Figure 7.4
Foliage paints beautifully onto velour. Scenic Art Studios, New York.

Mounting Soft Goods for Sizing and Priming

Soft goods must be firmly secured to a frame or deck before sizing and priming. It is important to use long staples when stretching a drop. Three-eighth-inch staples are the minimum length that will hold, but one-half-inch staples commonly are used, either in handheld or pneumatic staplers. It may be necessary to use pneumatic staples in the webbing of the drop because the handheld staplers may not get enough of a bite into the wood or sheet stock of the paint deck or frame through the thick jute webbing. If a pneumatic stapler is tilted slightly to one side so one corner of the staples do not bite all the way into the wood, they will be easier to pull out when the time comes. Load handheld staplers with chisel-tipped staples for use with wood and Masonite. Always set the staples about four inches apart around the entire piece of soft goods for a secure hold.

The most important aspect to *stretching*, or *laying*, a drop on a frame or deck is to keep the bottom and the top edges parallel. Unfinished sides of a drop may not be completely square (that is, perpendicular to the top of the drop and parallel to each other). These can be squared and finished later. If the sides of the drop are finished, they should be mounted as straight and square as possible; although there may be wrinkles and puckers, these will stretch out when the drop is primed. It is important to make sure that the drop is not torqued to one side or pulled at an angle, as this will cause any verticals on the drop to warp out of square.

Working on a Deck

Follow this sequence when stretching a drop with an unfinished side on a paint deck for best results.

First snap a chalk line the full width of the goods to align the top edge of the drop. Use this line as a guide for the layout of goods and a reference line for the height measurements. Attach the top edge of the drop with staples, working from the center out and smoothing the drop as you go. Then pull the entire drop out until it is relaxed and flat on the floor, smoothing out as many wrinkles as possible. Stretch out and measure the height of the drop at what looks to be the drop's shortest point. Snap a line parallel to the top to guide the stapling of the bottom of the drop. The top and bottom of a drop must always be parallel.

Staple the bottom of the drop in the center first and then work out toward the sides. Staple the sides down, once again starting in the middle and working out toward either end, leaving a section open for the paint bridge (see Figure 7.5). Keep the staples parallel to the edge. If the edge of the muslin being stapled is unfinished, turn back a half-inch or so of fabric so that each staple goes through two layers. This will lessen the chance of the fabric pulling through the staple. The turnbacks on the sides of the drop will be cartooned and trimmed when painting is completed.

If the sides of a drop have been sewn and are finished, they will have to be stapled so they are perpendicular to the top and bottom of the drop. If the drop is to be a specific size—for instance, 20 feet by 40 feet—the drop should be stapled into a rectangle cartooned on the paint deck or bogus paper to those dimensions. However, first measure the drop itself to make sure it is not too narrow or too short. You may need to alter the size of the cartoon slightly to fit the actual size of the soft goods. It is important that the width of the cartoon is the same as the webbing at the top of the drop. (We'll discuss methods for drafting a perpendicular line so the drop can be squared

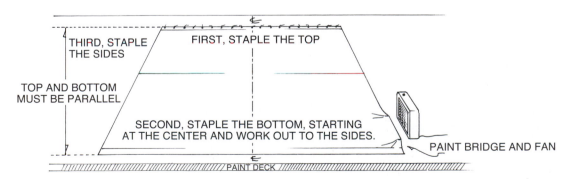

Figure 7.5 Laying out a drop with unfinished sides on a deck for stretching and priming.

Whenever you are laying a drop to be primed for the first time, stretch out the fabric so it lays completely flat and is somewhat taut once it has been stapled down. Once primed it will become drum tight. Do not stretch out the fabric so that it is as tight as a drum initially or it may pull out of its staples. Muslin that been treated with flame retardant may not shrink as much as untreated muslin. Stretch drops that are being repainted more tautly than those that are not. You may encounter some differences from time to time in the amount certain muslin is apt to stretch. I worked for years in a rental drop house that bought muslin in thousand-yard orders, and I painted one drop after another. I would sometimes encounter a batch of muslin that was noticeably different in the way it shrank—sometimes so forcefully that it warped the paint frame, sometimes so little that I had to stretch it out for priming with all my strength.

in Chapter 8.) To double-check that the square of a cartoon is accurate before the drop is stapled down, measure the cartoon diagonally from corner to corner and then again in the other direction. These measurements should be the same; if they are not the same, the cartoon is not square. Staple the corners of the drop first. If there seems to be a little extra fabric, carefully divide the extra up between several staples. When stapling the drop into a cartoon, there may be sections that are a little baggy, but once the drop is sized or primed it will shrink into shape.

Working on a Paint Frame

When securing a drop to a paint frame, first staple or hang the drop along the top of the frame. Line up one side of the drop with a vertical frame member to staple to. You may need to nail additional *battens*, or wooden supports, to the frame where the other side of the drop falls to provide a firm support for stapling. Staple the drop to the frame along the bottom as well, starting in the center and working out, adding battens as needed. Lastly, staple the sides (see Figure 7.6).

As with laying a drop on the paint deck, the top and bottom of the drop must be parallel to one another, and if the sides of the drop are finished, they will have to be squared to the top and bottom. An advantage of working on a frame is that gravity helps you to find true vertical. As you staple the top edge, measure in and find the center of the drop, then mark it for future reference. You will be able to drop a plumb line down from a nail or safety pin at the

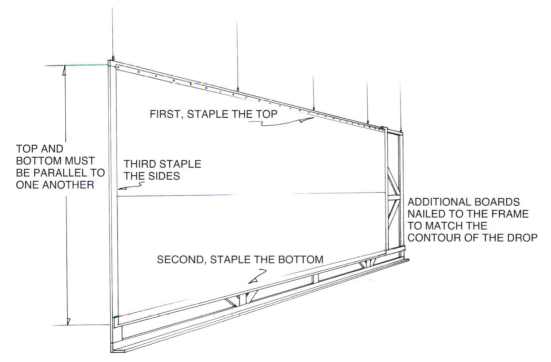

Figure 7.6
Mounting a drop on a paint frame for stretching and priming.

center to find the center bottom of the drop. You can use this method to establish any vertical on the drop. You also can drop a tape measure from a nail on either side of the drop for measuring heights.

Sizing and Priming Soft Goods

Soft goods are painted in either the eastern or the continental style, and each technique has some particular requirements for preparing the goods for painting, which we discuss here. (Refer to Chapter 4 for a comparison of these two painting techniques.)

Floating Soft Goods on a Deck

Gravity will cause a drop to hang slightly out on a vertical paint frame so that it does not stick to the frame itself. However, sizing and priming a drop on the deck is somewhat more problematic than working on a frame. If the drop is allowed to dry while resting on the floor, it will stick to it or whatever is covering the floor, such as the bogus paper under it. One alternative is to cover the deck with a visquene sheet. The drawback of priming a drop on visquene is that the primer will go all the way through the fabric and collect in the folds of the plastic. The drop will always have the pattern of the visquene when the primer dries. This pattern will show through all subsequent layers of paint. The way to defeat these problems is to *float* the drop, which means to force

air between the drop and the deck so that the drop rises off of the floor while drying. Floating the drop will result in a very clean prime coat and an excellent base for all layers of paint to follow.

To float a drop while it is being sized or primed, begin by putting a paint bridge under one edge of it (see Figure 7.7). A *paint bridge* is a structure that holds the edge of a drop about three to six inches off the floor over a span of about four feet. Air will force the drop up off the floor when a running fan is placed at the gap made by the bridge. A funnel built out of plywood can be set between the fan and the paint bridge to channel more air under the drop.

Box fans designed for drying carpets move a great deal of air under the drop. They are terrific for getting large drops off the ground, but sometimes these fans move too much air and distort the fabric. A second paint bridge can act as a safety valve to let air escape quickly, but most often, one paint bridge is adequate. If the drop is an irregular shape—a portal arch, for instance—it might be necessary to put a bridge and fan in each leg of the portal to let air pass up and around the arch. When priming a drop that is being floated, start priming on the side that has the paint bridge on it so that the drop starts floating as soon as possible.

The drop should be left floating until it is completely dry. A drop is best sized or primed and floated first thing in the morning, so that it can be watched during the course of the day. If this is not

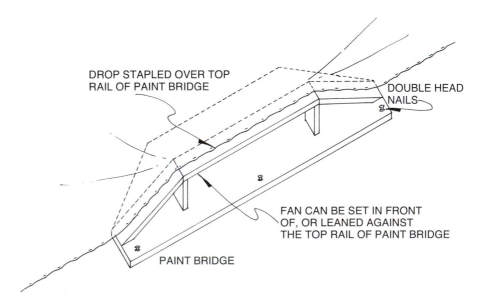

Figure 7.7
A paint bridge used to float
a drop.

DROP STAPLED OVER TOP
RAIL OF PAINT BRIDGE

DOUBLE HEAD
NAILS

FAN CAN BE SET IN FRONT
OF, OR LEANED AGAINST
THE TOP RAIL OF PAINT BRIDGE

PAINT BRIDGE

possible then it should be left floating overnight, with the fan on the lowest speed necessary to keep the drop in the air. A drop will stick where it is still wet if lowered to the deck before the back of it is completely dry. If left floating overnight, it may be stretched slightly out of shape. It can be sprayed down with warm water to tighten it up again.

Sizes and Primers

Soft goods must be primed or sized with something lightweight and fairly flexible. Generally, the term *size* refers to the coat of thickened starch or thinned animal glue applied to the drop, as this will shrink or "size" the muslin to the shape it has been mounted in, usually a rectangle on the paint deck or frame. The term *primer* usually refers to the first coat of paint applied to the surface to prepare the drop for the base coats and the ensuing layers of paint. In many instances, the primer is skipped and the base coats are applied directly to the size; less frequently, the prime coat is used to size the drop. Traditionally, canvases are stretched when the prime coat of gesso (a thick mixture of glue and gypsum or plaster of Paris) is applied to the fabric. For theatrical backdrops, different methods have been developed.

Paint adds weight and inflexibility to a drop. Using a lighter, more supple prime coat will add to the life of the drop. Some fabrics, such as velour, do not need size or primer. Scrim may or may not need to be sized according to the scenic artist's preference.

Thickened *laundry starch* is the standard size for soft goods. Often the term *starch* is used as the term for the prime coat and as a verb, "Time to starch the drop!" Laundry starch makes an excellent prime coat because it is inexpensive and very lightweight. It gives the drop an excellent finish that is conducive to painting. The starch basically is regular cornstarch with bluing added, so that white garments treated with laundry starch appear brighter. Laundry starch is also sold without the bluing. Regular cornstarch sold for cooking seems to have an astringent quality. Drops primed with straight cornstarch rather than laundry starch tend to become damp in muggy climates.

After the starch has been cooked and thinned, it is ready to apply. Starch may be lightly tinted with scenic paint or a small amount of colorant to make it easier to see while being applied to a drop and, as a result, it will be easier to see that is applied more evenly. The tint should relate to the local color of the

Starch comes in one-pound boxes, so the following proportions are for mixing a full box of starch. Bring a gallon and a half of water to a boil—it must be boiling—in a large steel bucket or two one-gallon buckets. If the buckets are covered, they will come to a boil faster. Meanwhile, mix the powdered starch into a half-gallon of cold water. (Mixing the powdered starch directly into hot water will cause clumping.) Blend the cold water solution with a paint drill to make sure that the solution is smooth. Briskly stir or drill the boiling water while slowly pouring in the cold water solution. Because hot starch can sometime splash up from the paint drill, you should always wear eye protection while doing this. If it is too precarious to use the paint drill above the hot plate safely, pour the boiling water into a five-gallon bucket on the floor to mix in the cold solution. As long as the boiling water has just come off the hot plate, the starch should thicken and the milky appearance of the cold water solution will disappear. If it does not thicken and clear, the water was not hot enough. Once the starch has been thickened, take it off the hot plate immediately and transfer it to a larger bucket. If several drops are being starched at once, a clean plastic trash can can be a convenient receptacle for the prepared starch. Next thin the starch with hot water, about one to one and a half gallons of hot water per box of cooked starch. The point is to have the starch thick enough to seal the fabric but not so thick that it cracks or leaves brush or spray marks as it dries. Each box of powdered starch will yield about three to four gallons of cooked starch. This will be enough starch for approximately 350 to 450 square feet.

drop to be painted; for example, use turquoise or ultramarine blue if it is a blue sky drop. The starch must not be tinted if the drop is to be used as a translucency or it will affect all the colors used on top of it.

If the starch is used on muslin or material that has been pretreated with flame retardant, the retardant may break down the starch and subsequent layers of paint. However, starch can be reinforced with a binder such as PVA or latex so that it will stand up to the corrosive nature of the flameproofing. Approximately two cups of liquid binder per box of starch is adequate to strengthen the starch. Binder should be added after the starch is fairly cool or it might curdle.

Old-fashioned laundry starch is getting difficult to find, as there is little demand for it anymore.

Starched collars have passed out of fashion. Some markets in old-fashioned neighborhoods may still carry boxes of laundry starch, but this is becoming rare. Argo Gloss Starch is the most commonly found brand in America. Most grocery stores stock Argo cornstarch for cooking, so they will be able to special order the laundry starch by the case from their suppliers. The cost of laundry starch is not much over a dollar a box, so ordering it by the case is not too costly. It also is available by the case from the Mann Brothers and Rose Brand catalogues.

Instant starch is an alternative to corn-based laundry starch, and it can be obtained from commercial laundry suppliers. Instant starch need not be cooked, as it mixes in cold water. Instead, it is mixed in much the same way that wheat paste is mixed, by sifting it into cold water while blending it until it begins to thicken. If blended with a paint drill, the starch will be smoother. After the starch is blended, it should sit for about 30 minutes to finish thickening. After sitting, it should be blended with a drill again until it is smooth; this will thin it if it has thickened while standing. It should then be thinned to the desired consistency for sizing.

Some theatrical suppliers sell muslin prime coat. These products are formulated to be used on either hard or soft scenery. They are flexible, fairly light-weight when dry, can be thinned to a great extent, and they seal the fabric so that if used to size a drop it will float. Once thinned (usually one part muslin prime coat to two parts water), it can be applied in the same manner as starch to size a drop.

Some shops size drops with animal glue. Animal glue is a flexible and effective size and was the standard size as well as paint binder in the years before premixed casein paints became available. The results are excellent. Cooked animal glue is mixed 1 part glue to 14 parts water for a sizing solution. It is applied in the same fashion as the starch sizes. (See Chapter 6 on how to prepare animal glue.)

Soft goods also may be sized and primed with latex paint, but a polymer paint finish does not take paint as smoothly as starch and animal glue primers. Paint used as a primer also makes the drop heavier, and creases will be more persistent when folded. It also retards any shrinkage later on. Drops primed with starch or glue, however, are resilient and usually can be unwrinkled after storage with a spray of warm water. Paint used to size and prime should be thinned at least four parts water to one part paint.

Applying Size or Primer

Methods of applying prime coats to soft goods may vary, depending on how the goods have been stretched, but one rule never varies: *When priming or sizing a drop, the job must not be left until it is finished.* If the drop is partially primed at break or quitting time, a seam will be evident where the primer was allowed to dry between the first and second attempts. Have enough crew members available to ensure the sizing or priming is applied quickly and evenly. A drop that is mounted on a paint deck or framed out on the floor should be floated as soon as possible to keep the surface of the fabric from acquiring the pattern of the floor. Drops stretched on the floor can be sized very efficiently with a push broom and sprayer.

When sizing a drop on the paint deck with starch, spray the starch on with a garden sprayer in a large swath about three feet wide. Then, smooth out the starch with a clean, soft-bristle push broom. At the end of each swath, before the next swath is begun, the broom should be pulled across the whole length of the drop so the broom marks are smoothed out. I found, after having a bad time with garden sprayers one day, that the primer can be just as easily spattered on the drop as sprayed. This method actually goes a little faster. The difference between spattering and spraying is that the spatter marks may continue to show through the finish as successive layers of paint or dye are applied, more so than if the primer was sprayed. Since it was for the sewer scene for *Guys and Dolls,* this blotchy size coat was actually a plus.

An airless sprayer also may be used to prime a drop stretched on the floor. A pitfall of priming with an airless sprayer is that it is very easy to put too much starch in one spot. Constant movement, an even speed, a repetitive pattern side to side, and an overlap on each pass by half will help ensure the even application of starch or primer. When priming a drop on the floor with an airless sprayer, it is necessary for two people to work together because the hose of the sprayer needs to be reeled in so that it does not drag through wet starch.

When working on the paint frame, it is possible to apply the starch with a brush, but there will be drips and brush marks, which may not result in a clean finish. Size sprayed on with an airless sprayer results in the cleanest finish on framed drops. When priming a drop on a frame with an airless sprayer, each pass made should overlap half of the previous pass, just as on a deck. Each pass made with the airless should be as long and even as possible. The sprayer should be in constant movement so that starch does not pile up in one spot.

If a drop is sized and primed with paint on a paint deck, the same care must be taken to ensure that it does not stick to the deck when it dries. The paint should be applied in swaths starting at the paint bridge, working outward. Paint can be applied as a primer and size to a drop on the paint frame with an airless sprayer or large brushes. The paint should be no thicker than necessary to seal the fabric. White latex commonly is used because it is cost effective and can be tinted to a color close to the primary local color of the drop for even application. As mentioned before, many scenic paint manufacturers sell a brand of primer in their scenic paint line. Often these primers are formulated for hard scenery more than soft goods. A quick phone call to the district office of the manufacturer will clear up any questions you might have about the firm's products and their intended uses.

Once the size or primer is dry, the drop will be ready to cartoon and paint. If the drop has a paint bridge in the edge, the bridge should be removed and that edge stapled down dividing the stretched fabric up between the staples. Some puckers and wrinkles will be left from where the bridge was placed, which should shrink out when sprayed with hot water.

Problem Solving

If the fabric used for the backdrop is behaving oddly, not shrinking to size when it dries for some unknown reason, the problem may be reconcilable. Astringent *alum*, which can be purchased at a local pharmacy or grocery store, increases the shrinkage of natural fiber fabrics such as muslin, canvas, and linen. The alum should be dissolved in hot water at the ratio of about one tablespoon per gallon of water. It should then be loaded in a garden sprayer and sprayed on the trouble spots. Alum should not be used on dyed drops, particularly in humid climates. Because it is an astringent, it will absorb and hold humidity. This can cause the dyes to get fuzzy edges or, if it is humid enough, even imprint a pattern from one section of the drop onto another while it is folded.

While a drop is drying from its size or primer coat, it should be watched closely for the first hour or two. This is the time when it is most apt to pop its staples on one side or another. If an edge begins to pull out, it will be easy enough to reinforce the staples if you catch it early. Pull the edges that have popped back into shape with canvas clamps, pliers, or vise grips, and staple them down again. *Canvas clamps* are pliers with a set of textured paddles designed to grip and hold canvas or muslin. Once the drop has been primed and is dry, the risk of it popping any staples is very low.

If you are priming a drop on a paint frame that drops down into a well, keep an eye on the seams as the drop is raised up. If you notice a seam bowing up, the bottom of the drop has pulled loose. Don't panic if disaster strikes and the drop pops the staples along several feet or an entire side. First, reinforce the staples that have not popped on either side of the gap. Add staples along the edge of the gap, about every foot, to keep the drop from stretching further out of shape. Then begin working in from either end of the gap, pulling the edge of the drop back into shape. One or two people should pull the drop with the canvas clamps while another person staples the edge as it is stretched back into shape. Pulling a wet drop and stapling at the same time is much too difficult.

If the drop resists all human efforts to be stretched back into shape, or if you are alone when you discover the mishap and can only hope to localize the damage on your own rather than repair it, do not despair. Later, when the drop is completely dry, it can be blocked back into shape with the help of one or two crew people armed with staplers, canvas clamps, and a large garden sprayer full of cold water. First, remove the staples from the edges that pulled loose. Next, dampen the drop along the bad edge and 10 feet or so in from that edge. Do not soak the drop or it will begin to shrink in again; if the fabric is just dampened, it will become more elastic. Methodically pull the drop back into shape from the sides of the gap to the center and staple along the line that is its intended shape. Once stretched back into shape and dried, the drop will be ready to cartoon and paint. If the starch on the drop was particularly heavy, there may be a network of stretch marks on the drop that will show with dye or transparent paint. These marks will not show under opaque paint.

Sizing Translucent Drops

A *translucency* is a drop or an area of a drop intended to allow light through the muslin for a special effect, such as a sunrise or a lighted window at night.

To prime a translucency, the drop may be laid down and primed on the back with clear starch only, no tints. While sizing the back of a translucency with seams, be careful not to glue these seams down with the starch as they will develop puckers or welts when they dry that will be viable on the front of the drop.

After the starch is dry and the bridge has been removed, the back of the translucency should be cartooned using a reversed line drawing to lay out the translucent areas. The designer will have provided an elevation and possibly a line drawing that will very clearly show where the translucent areas are. This cartoon must be accurate because the masking process is irreversible. The lines of the cartoon should be made with a heavy ink marker so they are visible from the front when the drop is flipped over. When cartooning clouds or color shifts in the sky of a translucency, one must be very careful about imposing the hard-edged lines of charcoal or an ink marker on the design. These lines will become visible when the drop is lighted from behind.

The opaque areas of the drop should be painted over, after the cartoon is completed. This creates a light-proof mask. Use a color similar to the local color used on the front of the drop. If backpaint showing through to the front is a concern, these areas can be primed first with white muslin–colored paint.

The front of the drop also must be sized after the drop has been flipped onto its back and stapled down again. If not, the painting will be arduous, due to the absorbency of the muslin; the paint job, as a result, will be splotchy. The starch used on the front of the drop can be very thin, as the drop already has been sealed from the back. It will not be necessary to put in a paint bridge to float the drop if it has been sealed on the back. The cartoon then should be restored on the front of the drop and completed, if parts were left undone. This process may be abbreviated to one step. The process of opaquing a drop from the back may be difficult with very complex images. It is possible to do all the work on the front surface. Two coats of heavy front paint will opaque it fairly well, if not as flawlessly as opaque paint on the back and the front.

The translucent areas of the drop first should be painted using dye or very thin, high-quality paint. Poor-quality paint contains fillers that impair the translucency of the muslin. Aniline dye is completely transparent, but if paint is used, thin it as much as possible and avoid using white paint as it will interfere with the translucency.

If the front of the drop is to be painted in a watercolor style, requiring a relatively thin translucent paint technique that relies on applying paint glazes directly to a starched surface, then it may be cartooned and entirely opaqued from the back. First cover the opaque areas on the back of the drop with a muslin-colored back paint so if it bleeds to the front it will not be noticeable. Then, apply a second coat of gray paint to the opaque areas, being careful not to go over the edge of the first coat of back paint, to make these areas impenetrable to light.

If the opaque area on the back of the drop is different than the design on the front (for instance, storm clouds that are revealed in a clear sky), the back must be primed and cartooned first. Use white or pastel chalk for the cartooning if visible dark cartoon lines are a problem when the drop is lighted from behind. The opaque areas must be given a base coat in a white, muslin, or local-color-tinted paint, depending on the design of the front of the drop, and then may need to be recoated in gray to ensure opacity. If the areas of opaque color need to be very soft along the edges, apply the opaque paint with a spray gun.

Figure 7.8
Translucency is evident in the backlighted windows of the drop for *A Christmas Carol*, Scenic Art Studios, New York.

Figure 7.9   A translucent drop for *State Fair*, seen in its daytime appearance. Designed by James Joy and painted at Cobalt Studios.

Figure 7.10   A translucent drop for *State Fair* at night. Designed by James Joy and painted at Cobalt Studios.

Priming Scrims

The magic of *scrim* is that any image painted on it appears opaque until the objects or scene behind it is lit and the lights on the front of the scrim are dimmed. Then, it becomes transparent, revealing what is behind the scrim, be it a three-dimensional version of the scene on the scrim itself, another scene entirely, or the ghosts in the walls. The open weave of the scrim allows this to happen. The point simply is not to fill in the weave of the scrim or it cannot work its magic when backlighted. Dye and high-quality scenic paints work best on scrim, delivering good-quality color without having to be overly thick.

Scrims may or may not be treated with a primer. The fabric cannot be completely soaked down if it is primed or it will stick to the surface below and become very stiff. This is because scrim fabric is very absorbent. Scrim may wick paint as it is applied, making the lines blurry. A measure some scenic artists take to gain a little more control over the fabric is to spray the scrim with thin starch or animal-glue size water after it has been stapled in place on the paint deck or frame. After working with scrim for a time, most painters develop a habit of blotting the brush on a rag after it has been charged so that lines are crisper. The viscosity of the paint will affect control when painting a scrim. Very thin paint or glazes will tend to blot or wick into the scrim more than heavy-bodied paints.

Before a scrim is painted, a full-size cartoon of the elevation is made on another surface as a reference. The gauzy and stretchy nature of scrim makes it difficult to cartoon on. It is simpler to follow a cartoon that is drawn out on the deck or on paper underneath the scrim. This cartoon is visible through the weave of the scrim. If you are drawing directly on the paint deck, you must first paint the area white so that the cartoon will be discernible; paint decks can be very splotchy due to previous paint applications. *Bogus paper* is often used under scrims because it absorbs some of the moisture from the scrim, which helps somewhat with the problem of blurry lines. (As noted in earlier chapters, bogus paper is an absorbent, heavy paper made out of recycled paper products that may be obtained through theatrical paint and fabric suppliers.) *Kraft paper* is a heavy brown paper similar to the paper that grocery bags are made of. You can purchase rolls of brown paper from local industrial paper goods supply houses. Kraft paper does get very ripply when it gets wet and can be a problem when it is used under a scrim.

To create a surface for a cartoon, lay lengths of paper across the entire area of the paint deck that the scrim is to be stretched out on. Tape the sides of the paper together, edge to edge. Once you have taped the sides together, you can flip the entire drop-size piece of paper over so that the lines of the lighter-colored masking tape are hidden underneath.

A starched backdrop is a wonderful surface to use as a cartoon and to lay a scrim over. The muslin always lays flat under the scrim no matter how wet it gets and it easily pulls away from the back of the scrim when it is finished. Granted, this solution may be rather costly, but if the scrim is being painted in a shop that also fabricates soft goods, you can sew end pieces of muslin together for the scrim backing.

Though a rare occurrence, multiple copies of a scrim sometimes need to be painted; a muslin scrim backing can be used several times over without having to redo the cartoon. In either case, working on paper, a drop, or directly on the deck, you can stretch the scrim over the cartoon once it has been completed and the line work has been set with ink or paint.

Figure 7.11 Airbrushing a portrait onto scrim. *42nd Street* being painted at Scenic Art Studios, New York.

> When painting a scrim on the deck, it may be difficult to avoid blotches of paint that fill in the holes or paint that dries to the backing. A simple device called a *scrim pick* can be used to hook the scrim and gently pull it up and then let it snap back down so the paint drops out of the holes. To make a scrim pick, tape an open safety pin to a yardstick or drive a long finish nail through the end of a stick.

Figure 7.12
The finished scrim for *42nd Street*, Scenic Art Studios, New York.

If the scrim is to be painted on the frame, it is necessary to first hang and size a full-size backing drop for the cartoon. After completing the cartoon on the backing drop, you can stretch the scrim in front of it. The backing drop also serves as a solid surface behind the scrim, which helps the scenic artist focus on the scrim itself rather than on the paint frame and the wall behind it. The backing drop can be made out of nearly any kind of light-colored fabric or even scrap fabric, since once it has served its purpose as a scrim backer, it will not be good for much else. Scrims can be painted with either dye or paint.

Priming Groundcloths

Groundcloths usually are constructed of the heaviest material available, which is frequently canvas duck. Care should be taken to secure groundcloths extremely well when stretching them. Canvas can generate tremendous force as it shrinks. Pneumatic staplers are preferred over handheld staple guns for mounting groundcloth because of the strength of the staple itself as well as the reliable force of a pneumatic gun. If the ground cloth is mounted to a frame rather than a paint deck, the frame must be very sturdy. Canvas stretches so tautly that it easily can warp or break a paint frame.

If the canvas groundcloth is painted on a deck, it can be stretched and primed in a manner similar to priming a drop. The groundcloth will not need to be floated because not enough paint will seep through the heavier fabric to create problems. The cloth should be primed and painted with acrylic, vinyl, or latex-based paints because of the heavy use it will receive. Protein-based paints and primers, like caseins, do not hold up to foot traffic as well and break down if liquid is spilled on them. For this reason, and because the groundcloth will come in direct contact with performers, aniline dye should never be used.

After the groundcloth is painted, seal it with a spray coat of clear acrylic or water-based urethane to increase its durability. Do not use a brush to apply the sealer on canvas groundcloths because brushing will trap air bubbles that will ruin the paint job because the finish will have a white or milky appearance in places when dry. Also, never put a fan on clear water-based finishes while they are drying, as cool air blowing across the finish may cause it to cloud.

Preparing China Silk

China silk has a tendency to bleed paint, so details and line work become blotchy. One way to inhibit this is to give the silk a light spray of gum thickener, also called methocel, or Irish moss mixed into a solution of size water. Either one of these must be applied in moderation. If applied too heavily, they will stiffen the silk, compromising the quality of flow and grace. (Methocel and Irish moss are discussed in Chapter 6.)

Only aniline or batik dyes should be used to paint China silk. Any paint, no matter how thin, will stiffen and flatten the finish of the silk. The dyes may be mixed into a vehicle of methocel or Irish moss to thicken them. This will reduce the problem of blotting and wicking somewhat. It may be best to dye an entire panel in a vat before it is stretched if the background color of the silk must be altered. Dye applied to China silk pretreated with flame retardant tends to bleed far less than on untreated silk.

Monk's Cloth

Monk's cloth can be painted just as it is or after spraying a light coat of starch on it to help reduce wicking. However, the surface of monk's cloth can never be truly sealed.

PREPARING HARD SCENERY

If a scenic unit is not a piece of soft goods then it is *hard scenery*. Typical flattage, platforms, sculptural items, metallic frames, and plastics fall under this umbrella. Hard scenery, like soft goods, requires considerable preparation, and a primer coat is absolutely essential for most items. It is very rare that any material is seen on stage in its raw form without at least a sealant and flame retardant. The materials that constitute hard scenery are as various as can be imagined. However, milled lumber, plywood, composite boards, plastics, plastic foams, aluminum, and steel probably make up 95 percent of hard scenery today.

Working with Flattage

Flattage, or walls, represents the vast majority of hard scenery. Flats may be hard- or soft-covered. Hard-covered flats have a thin, rigid skin over the frame. This skin is generally one-quarter- or one-eighth-inch thick lauan, an inexpensive three-ply mahogany. Other common skinning products include heavier plywood, wall paneling, composition board, and even rigid cardboard. It usually is preferable to cover any sheet stock with a layer of muslin to hide the texture and the seams of whatever material is used. The seams of lauan are difficult to hide, and they often crack and show through any paint application no matter how well patched they are. Soft-covered flats are just empty frames covered with muslin, duvetyn, velour, or other fabric. Muslin is the most common fabric for soft-covered flattage as it is with backdrops.

Flat frames usually are made of wood, aluminum, or steel. The construction styles vary with the material. *Standard* or *Hollywood construction* are the primary options for wood- and metal-frame flats. Standard flat construction uses milled lumber laying flat and joined together with plates of plywood on the back over the joints. This makes a frame about one inch thick. Because these flats are so thin, they can torque easily under the stress of fabric shrinkage. However, they take up very little space in storage and during transport. Hollywood flat construction places the same milled lumber on edge for a much more rigid but thicker frame.

Flats should be laid out on the shop floor or secured to the paint frame for painting in the order that they will be joined, from stage right to stage left. Flats for different scenes should be stored together and painted as a group to avoid redundancy of time and effort. The bottom of the flats should be set in a parallel line if they play together on the same level, or adjusted so that the bottom of the flat is the correct distance above the baseline of the rest of the flats, as it would be on stage if set up on a platform. This is so measurements that need to be carried across all the flats can be marked without having to stop and recall the relationship of the flats to one another.

A foot of space or more should be left between the units for walkways if the units are being laid out on a floor or paint deck. If a unit is wider than four feet, it may be necessary to walk on it to paint and do detail work. "Walk on the wood not on the goods" is an old and practical adage in scenic painting when working on hard scenery. A scenic artist must have an ear for and sense of the stress on flattage when working on it. Special care must be taken when working on Hollywood flats. These flats are framed with one-inch by three-inch stock lumber used on the edges. A foot in the wrong place can put a hole in the flat. If you must work out into the middle of a Hollywood flat, lay an eight-inch plank across the flat to give yourself a surface to walk on. If a unit is particularly bulky, a bridge or scaffolding may need to be constructed so scenic artists can access the areas that need to be painted. Naturally, one of the missions of the scenic artist is to return the scenery to the construction department undamaged, especially if he or she wants to encourage the same consideration.

Preparing Hard-Covered Flats

Lauan is the most common sheet stock used to cover hard scenic flats. A lauan surface has to be primed with a solvent-based primer such as an alkyd primer or white-pigmented shellac. Like any other wood product, lauan tends to stain through water-based paint in varying degrees from one sheet to another. Lauan also has a very distinct texture and hard edges. A yellow rectangle of lauan may begin to stain through painted baroque drawing room wallpaper if improperly primed. Yet, if the set is a location on the seamy side of life, a dockside tavern for instance, unprimed lauan may add a beneficial aspect to the paint job. If lauan is to be stained for a wood deck or paneled walls, it should not be primed. A cover of muslin will also eliminate the staining problem; this is called *skinning* a flat with muslin. If a hard-covered flat has a skin of muslin on it, it can be primed with a regular water-based paint, latex, or acrylic house paint. The muslin will provide the barrier between the lauan and the painted finish so there will be no staining through to the top coat. Solvent-based or heavy-duty primers are not necessary.

One way to hide the lauan finish without a muslin cover is to put a fine silicate sand in the base coat. This kind of sand is sold at brickyards for pennies a pound, in 40- or 80-pound bags, as a mortar additive. The paint with sand in it must not be too thin and should be stirred every few minutes while in use. The proportions should be about two cups of sand to every gallon of paint. It should be brushed out with an omnidirectional paint stroke when applied so as not to develop a grain. The sand will leave behind a fine, consistent finish once dry (very much like fine sandpaper) that helps defeat the grain of the lauan. This treated sand paint also helps hide the grain of other sheet stocks such as plywood.

A problem with muslin-covered hard flats is the need to use glue to adhere the muslin cover. Dried glue resists paint and shows up as glossy spots once painted over. A little glue overstepping its bounds is hard to avoid while covering a flat. The flat will take paint better if the glue spots are pounced with whiting (dry white pigment) before they dry.

White pigment commonly is made from calcium carbonate or chalk. This breaks the surface of the glue and makes it much more accepting of paint. If the scenic artists are not covering the flats, it would be in their best interests to mention this technique to the carpenters and provide them with pounce bags of whiting. Use a pounce bag filled with whiting while the glue is still tacky. (See Chapter 8 for more on pouncing.)

Preparing Soft-Covered Flats

Some soft-covered flats are covered by gluing the fabric to the face of the flat frame with casein-based glue (wood glue, white glue, or fabric glue) or scenic dope. Casein-based glues must be thinned down for gluing muslin. Recently, many water-based glues have become available from theatrical suppliers that are not water-soluble once they are dry. Many shops prefer to use these because they more reliably adhere the fabric to the frame or the sheet stock when skinning a flat, and they are less likely to redissolve when the flattage is being painted. When the glue is dry, trim the excess fabric off the edges. When covered in this fashion, glue that may be on the surface of the flat can be fixed with a pounce of whiting. Scenic dope is animal glue mixed with a paste made from whiting and water. Scenic dope accepts paint very well and does not need to be pounced with whiting. Soft-covered flats also may be covered by stretching the fabric around to the back of the flat and stapling it to the frame, but this may cause the seams between flats to be wider than desired.

All soft-covered flats may be primed with any water-based paint. Always consider whether the primer should be tinted to a hue related to the local color of the base coat. A tinted prime coat helps in achieving even coverage of the base coat, particularly if the base coat is a deep or saturated color. A tinted prime coat may even serve as the base of the paint treatments to follow. The flats also may be primed with starch. The starch will take differently to those areas where the muslin covers the frame and those where the muslin was glued to the frame. The primary reason to use starch instead of paint to prime a flat is for translucencies. If this is the case, the flats should be treated like a translucent drop, as described earlier in this chapter.

Dutchmen

Hiding the seams between adjoining flats is part of the preparation. This can be done by gluing on a strip of cloth, known as a *dutchman*, made out of the same material as the flat covering, which is usually muslin. The strip of cloth should be as long as the seam that it is intended to hide and about four inches wide. The edges of the dutchman strip should be frayed a quarter of an inch or more along the edges so that they blend into the surface. Then brush the back of the dutchman with glue, scenic dope, or wallpaper paste, being careful all the while to keep the glue off the front of the dutchman. Lay the dutchman in position on the seam, glue side down. Smooth the dutchman over the seam with a damp sponge from the center out to the edges and sponge up all excess glue that seeps out from under the dutchman. Then, smooth the frayed edges of the dutchman to blend into the surface of the flat. If glue is used to attach the dutchman rather than wallpaper paste or scenic dope, the entire dutchman should be pounced over with a bag of whiting while it is still tacky. Allow the dutchman to dry thoroughly before the flat is primed or it may shrink and leave gaps in the prime coat.

Preparing Floor Coverings

Painted stage floors are common, but rarely are they painted directly on the stage itself. A temporary cover can be prepainted and easily installed. The most common materials used for a painted deck are groundcloths, sheet stock, and covered platforming.

Floor Sheet Stock Masonite and MDF are common choices for painted stage decking because they are thin, smooth, sturdy, and relatively inexpensive. The two materials are virtually the same from a painter's point of view. If a paint treatment is one color or a color and a finish, then painting a full stage deck of Masonite is a simple issue. It can be painted several sheets at a time in a corner of the shop and the process can stay more or less out of the way.

More complex patterns or treatments require that the Masonite be laid out and treated as a whole either in the shop or in the theatre during load-in if the schedule allows. The Masonite deck may be loaded in early and left for a few days to be painted before the rest of the load-in proceeds. If any deck is painted on stage, the entire stage deck needs to be covered with visqueen before the painting surface is installed. Otherwise, the paint will seep through the seams of the Masonite and ruin the floor underneath. Later, the visqueen can be trimmed away from the edges of the painted deck so that it does not present a hazard during the run of the show.

Normally, a deck is painted on Masonite before the load-in. A fully painted deck then can be installed in a matter of a few hours. A Masonite deck painted at an earlier point in the schedule, either in the shop or on stage, will be pulled up and stored until load-in. Each sheet of Masonite must be numbered and referenced to a deck plan. That way, when the stack of Masonite is brought in during load-in, the stage carpenters have a clear guide for assembly.

Priming Sheet Stock for Floors Raw Masonite has two finishes that require some preparation before they will accept paint evenly. Masonite is made by heating and compacting wood chips with graphite. The result is a product that is very slick on one side and rough on the other. The rough surface takes paint so poorly that only rarely is it used on a stage deck. Because the smooth surface of the Masonite is slick and slightly oily, many water-based primers will not bond well to its surface. Prepare the smooth surface for painting with an alkyd-based primer. Shellac-based primers are very brittle and may chip off the Masonite when it is flexed or under compression from casters on heavy stage wagons.

MDF is smooth on both sides and should be prepared like Masonite. Recently, very tough water-based primers have become available. Some of these are formulated with epoxy binders. I have had a great deal of success with water-based primers that were formulated for priming metals. Stain blocking is not an issue with Masonite. These primers are fairly expensive, but since Masonite decks tend to be used over and over again but only have to be primed once, the trade-off in terms of the health and safety of the people working in the shop may well be worth the price.

For the best coverage, use a roller to paint Masonite. It has such a smooth finish that it is difficult to get good coverage with a brush without leaving streak marks. When applying a base or primer coat with a roller, take care to work the roller in many different directions so that the paint finish does not develop a directional grain.

Lauan is generally used for stage decks when a stained wood floor is called for. When the lauan is to be stained, no primer is necessary, although the finish may be very important to create the appropriate sheen. Sometimes lauan must be primed for a paint treatment; in these cases, the same considerations and products are used as would be for priming lauan on flattage. Frequently lauan used for stage decks is cut into board widths so that the strips of lauan can be stained or painted with slight variations from board to board. In this case, one of the scenic artist's primary concerns should be to ensure that all the edges of the lauan boards have received the stain or paint treatment as well. That way, when the deck is installed, the artist is not confronted with a plethora of lauan edges to touch up.

Priming Wood

When dealing with any wood or wood-based product, the primer must serve as a barrier between the natural stains in the wood and the paint. Tree resins and natural color in lumber and plywood will show through any water-based primer. If a primer coat has a different solvent base than the scenic paint (something other than water-based), the stain will not be able to travel between the two layers but will stop at the primer coat. White-pigmented shellac and alkyd primers are excellent sealers and are available through commercial paint suppliers. Water-based primers now on the market are reputed to stop the natural stains in wood from penetrating through to the finish color, but these are relatively new and I have observed that stains from knot holes and darker woods still can come through these primers.

PREPARING AND PRIMING OTHER SCENIC MATERIALS

A wide variety of materials are used for scenic construction and, therefore, a wide variety of methods are used to prepare materials for painting. The common thread to this preparation is that most materials need a primer just as fabrics and wood do. Some of these materials will not accept standard scenic paints at all and must be coated in advance with another adhesive or sealant. Many sculpted surfaces must be primed or skinned first before applying paint. Other surfaces need to be smoothed, and still others need to be reinforced so that they can stand up to trucking, loading, or hard use.

Preparing Noncellulosic Materials

Noncellulosic materials, such as plaster, metals, plastic, and foams, are common in set construction, and

their use is increasing. This section discusses how to prepare these materials for painting. One aspect of using many modern materials in the theatrical industry is that designers and construction crews are always coming up with different applications and expectations for these materials. When confronted with a new challenge or problem, the scenic artist may have to do some research and experimentation with as-yet-untried methods and materials to get the desired effect. If you are unsure about how to approach a material, ask other scenic artists what they have tried, call the manufacturer, and make samples. (Additional treatments of these materials may be found with the techniques discussed in Chapter 10.)

Plaster

Plaster must be primed before it is painted because the surface is too absorbent to take paint evenly. Plaster can be primed well with a water-based primer. If the finish of the plaster still needs smoothing, joint compound mixed with clear latex or acrylic binder can be added into the primer to give it more body. When they are dry, vinyl, latex, or acrylic primers serve as a barrier to the water-leaching tendencies of plaster, smoothing the way for the paint techniques to follow. Casein-based paint does not form this barrier but behaves like a fresco by penetrating and absorbing the minerals from the plaster. In European countries, casein-based fresco paint is still used to paint the stucco finish on the exteriors of buildings.

Several options are available for reinforcing the brittle finish of plaster. Fiberglass and two-part resin is a time-consuming but long-lasting process, but it presents health hazards. More simply, plaster can be primed first with undiluted flexible glue. Do not use regular white glue or a wood glue because both are very brittle and do not accept paint. After the glue coating is dry, coat the plaster entirely with a vinyl, latex, or acrylic-based paint. After the base coat is dry, the plaster can be painted in any fashion with any common binder or medium.

Priming and Sealing Metals

Steel straight from the distributor has an oil coating to inhibit rust or corrosion. The first step in painting it is to clean off the residual oil. Solvents such as mineral spirits and lacquer thinners will clean off most of the oil, although they will leave a little residue of their own and present health hazards. The metal may be cleaned off with a concentrated cleaner/degreaser.

If the metal has been further fabricated into a unit by welding, the welds must be cleaned before priming or painting by scrubbing them with a wire brush. To prime coat steel, use a solvent-based primer that can cut through the residual oil still on the metal. A shellac- or alkyd-based primer works well. After the primer has completely dried, the unit can be painted with any standard water-based scene paint (see Chapter 4, the section "Safety and Health Regulations"). Water-based epoxy metal primers work well and do not present health risks. However, care should be taken to ensure that the metal is clean of any residual oils before using these.

If the natural sheen of steel is desirable, use a clear shellac, lacquer, or solvent-based urethane to seal the steel and keep it from rusting.

Preparing Plastics and Foam Plastics

Plastic, Plexiglas, and PVC by themselves resist most water-based paints. Shellac or alkyd primers adhere to most plastic surfaces, but if the surface is very smooth and even slightly flexible, they can easily be scratched or flake off. Water-based contact cement adheres very well to most plastic surfaces (see Chapter 4, the section "Safety and Health Regulations"). If a Plexiglas surface must be paintable but remain clear, water-based urethane will not cloud up when it dries and will adhere beautifully to Plexiglas. The urethane also may be tinted with aniline dyes and thinned with acrylic floor wax.

The many kinds of foam plastics used in scenic construction fall into two broad categories: rigid and soft. Rigid foams include styrene foams, such as bead boards and blue foam, and urethane foams, like florist foam and two-part (or A-B) foam. Soft foams include ethafoam rod and foam rubber used in upholstery and weather stripping.

Rigid Foam *Styrene* and two-part *urethane foams* are used for fabrication of sculptural elements and three-dimensional scenery because they are lightweight, rigid, and cut and carve easily. These qualities become liabilities when used on stage, where they may receive a fair amount of abuse. Hence, when preparing foams, it is necessary to create a surface that is both paintable and durable.

Usually, a scenic artist is apt to deal with two types of polystyrene foam. One is *beadboard*, also called *Styrofoam*® after its trade name, so called because it is made of compressed polystyrene beads. Large beadboard blocks, up to 128 cubic feet, commonly are used for carving sculptural pieces, such as stone detail, rocks, and stone blocks. The texture of hand-carved beadboard is very pebbly and appropriate for simulating the texture of rough or carved stone. The surface of beadboard is very weak and must be sealed. If a smooth texture is sought for simulating wood or plaster, the foam can be skinned with a texture compound or fabric. Lengths of large profile molding often are cut from beadboard because it is lightweight and inexpensive. These lengths of molding are normally eight feet long, so it may be necessary to spackle the seams or skin the entire molding with fabric. An explanation of texture compounds and fabric skin occurs later in this chapter.

Polystyrene foams are manufactured in solid, even-density sheets sold as insulation in the construction industry. Many scenic shops use this blue or pink sheet foam, sometimes simply referred to as blue board, for deep profile lines on scenic units. Foams are easily built up and carved for bas-relief. Because of the density of these foams, they can be sanded down to a smooth finish. Furthermore, these foams are so dense they are not as fragile as beadboard. They can be coated with a texture compound or sculpture coating.

Urethane foam is a two-part foam that sets up with a crisp density that can be carved. It can be purchased in sheets and blocks. It is also known as A-B foam for the two components of it that get mixed together. The two-part resins also may be purchased, mixed at will, and poured into your own molds. The premade blocks and sheets and the two-part resins of this foam are available in a range of densities from very firm to the soft foam that florists use as the foundation for arrangements. The two-part resins you mix yourself may be less evenly dense and show a honeycomb of large air bubbles due to inconsistencies in the mixing process. All of the urethane foams tend to be somewhat brittle and fragile. Once carved and sanded, they will have to be skinned with either texture compound or fabric. Always use proper safety precautions and protection when carving Styrofoam, beadboard, or urethane foam and when mixing two-part urethane foam (see Chapter 4, the section "Safety and Health Regulations").

Vacuformed and Premolded Plastics

Vacuforming is the process of heating sheets of either polystyrene or PVC until they become malleable. The softened sheets are then dropped over a positive mold made out of a dense heat-resistant material such as particle board, thoroughly cured molding plaster, hydrocal cement. The mold is prepared for vacuforming by drilling small holes through all the areas of low relief. The mold sits on a sealed vacuum bed connected to a vacuum chamber. The vacuum action quickly pulls the softened plastic onto the mold. Once the plastic has cooled in its new form it can be lifted off the mold and the process can be repeated. In this way, hundreds of copies can be made of an intricate architectural detail from a single mold. Commercial vacuform machines can handle objects approaching 4′ × 8′ in size.

Polystyrene and PVC plastic used in vacuforming can be primed with a shellac-based primer. Alkyd-based primers should be avoided, as they may soak into the plastic and soften the impression (see Chapter 4, the section "Safety and Health Regulations"). Vacuform pieces have a matte finish and can be prime-coated with water-based primers. Acrylic-based stain blockers are sold by house-paint suppliers. These primers have a high binder content and are very tough. They adhere very nicely to polystyrene or PVC vacuform.

After vacuform pieces have been primed, they can be painted with any water-based paint or medium. The plastic sheets used for vacuform may also be pre-painted with acrylic-based paints. The advantage of prepainting the plastic sheets is that a wood grain, for instance, can be painted on a flat surface very easily. Once the plastic sheet has been molded, executing the wood grain technique becomes more problematic. Prepainting works best on forms that will have a low relief. If the prepainted plastic is stretched too far, gaps will appear in the paint treatment.

Premolded elements may be purchased from theatrical and architectural supply houses. Some elements are vacuformed and may be painted in the same manner already discussed. Molded elements from architectural supply houses are frequently cast with PVC, plaster, or urethanes. These elements are marketed to be paintable, and in some cases they are cast out of polyresin material and tinted to a wood grain color that can be stained.

Flexible Foam

Ethafoam rod is a flexible foam rod used in building construction as a temporary expansion joint in concrete work. These long, round, flexible foam cords come in a variety of diameters from one-quarter inch to three inches. They are ideal for many three-dimensional applications in set construction.

Ethafoam has a slick flexible finish that resists almost all efforts to paint it. PVA and vinyl-based binders do not adhere to ethafoam: they easily can be peeled away when dry, as the ethafoam is handled or scraped. Shellac and alkyd primers will adhere to it, but they will crack when the ethafoam is compressed. The best choice is water-based contact cement, which adheres to the surface and flexes when the foam is handled or compressed. Once it is dry, the ethafoam can be painted with standard scene paint.

Some theatrical paint manufacturers have developed a primer specially formulated to adhere to foams of all descriptions. These primers adhere well even to ethafoam and have the added benefit of being tintable. To be made even more durable, ethafoam can be skinned with cheesecloth or cotton scrim after priming. If a smooth finish is not necessary, ethafoam rod can be sanded to break down the skin and open the bubbles beneath it so the paint can penetrate and adhere.

Foam rubber, being very absorbent, first must be primed with something that will seal it. Often one coat of primer is not enough to provide a paintable surface; two coats of primer generally are necessary. Water-based paints of all descriptions will adhere to foam rubber, but if the foam is bent or dented after it has been painted, the surface may crack or the dent may remain evident. A flexible primer, like water-based contact cement or a theatrical paint manufacturer's durable primer coat, will work best for application on foam rubber. Several scenic manufacturers supply durable primers. Foam rubber may also be dyed with aniline dye so that the priming step can be avoided.

Sealing Plastic and Plastic Foams

Rigid foams can be painted with water-based paints. Vinyl, latex, and acrylic binders adhere best to these foams. However, paint alone will not strengthen the surface and smooth the finish. Primers are sold by theatrical paint manufacturers specifically for priming and sealing foams. Joint compound can be added to a water-based primer to give it more body, which will help smooth the finish of the foam. Joint compound works best when added to vinyl-, latex-, or acrylic-based paint.

A prime coat with a lot of body can be made by mixing clear latex-, acrylic-, or water-based glue and joint compound. This will make the joint compound less brittle and more resilient. Water-based roof patching is another good viscous coating for foam. If the finish of the foam needs to be smoother than a heavy brush coat will accomplish, the foam can be coated with straight joint compound on top of a primer coat. After the joint compound has dried, it can be sanded to a very smooth finish and then another primer coat applied before painting. Water-based contact cement gives the foam a more resilient surface and serves as a good base for all water-based paints. Once the surface is covered with contact cement, it no longer can be sanded, nor will contact cement fill in and smooth the surface of the foam.

Fabric Skins, Sculpture Coatings, and Other Preparations

Fabric skins are applied to reinforce fragile surfaces and conceal porous or very distinctive textures. Almost all sculpted items are skinned after the carving process. This skinning can be done with fabric and adhesive or just an adhesive. When covering sculpture, a looser-weave fabric must be used so it will stretch on the bias and mold to the contours of the piece. Loose-weave fabrics are less apt to pull away from recesses of the form as they dry. Cheesecloth, gauze, and cotton scrim frequently are used for fabric skins. For small pieces, plaster or fiberglass bandages, purchased through medical suppliers, make an excellent skinning material. These must be soaked in water for a minute or two and then applied and smoothed over the form; they require no additional binder. Cheesecloth is one of the most commonly used and inexpensive skinning fabrics. It is sold by the yard or by the 50-yard box at most fabric stores. Cotton scrim is a woven, gauze-like scrim and should not be confused with the more expensive sharkstooth scrim. This scrim is available from theatrical suppliers by the yard or bolt. Muslin produces a very durable coat, but it is not well suited for intricate detail because it is relatively thick and pulls away from low-relief areas as it shrinks.

Rigid foams may be covered with other materials to give them a more durable and paintable finish. Materials can be adhered to the foam with thinned flexible glue, vinyl wallpaper paste, or clear polymer binders. A papier-mâché can be made using newspaper, cellotex insulation, or even paper towels.

In some cases, a crinkled texture may be desired and paper towels or even toilet paper will do this nicely.

Smooth Sculpture Coatings

Some foam carvings are finished to a smooth surface by sanding. Foam details that are cut, such as hot-wired foam moldings, also have a very smooth surface. If these scenic elements are to be loaded in and used on stage in such a fashion that they will not receive much wear and tear, then simply coating these elements with a heavy primer coat, such as sculpture coating, flexible glue, or reinforced joint compound, may suffice.

Foam-Coating Materials

Commercial foam coatings are available through theatrical paint suppliers, either Foam Coat from Rosco, or Sculpt or Coat from Artist's Choice in North Carolina. Foam Coat is more rigid when it dries and has fibers in it for reinforcement. Sculpt or Coat is a more flexible surface. These highly viscous coatings are formulated to fill in the pores of foam and dry to a smooth, paintable finish. Foam-coating products are formulated with water-based polymer binders. They can be applied straight or thinned as needed. Most water-based foam coatings can be tinted with paint or colorants. A homemade sculpt coat may be mixed with a drywall compound and a flexible polymer glue, which will give the coating a matte, opaque finish. Always try a small test sample before mixing large quantities of these coatings with other mediums, in case they are incompatible with each other.

Roof Patching

Latex-based roof patching and roof coatings are sold at lumberyards and home-remodeling stores. Roof patching is more viscous than roof coating. These products can be tinted with colorants. Do not use asphaltium-based roof sealers as bases for texture. These tar-based products do not dry completely and will stain through any top coat as well as soften under the heat of stage light.

Two-Part Resins

Two-part resin systems consist of a resin and hardener. Until mixed together, these elements will not dry or set up properly. When mixed together in the correct proportions, these resins do not air dry but rather cure through strong chemical reaction. Two-part systems are used in adhesive, paints, and hard-shell coating processes.

Present-day two-part resins are much easier to use than their earlier counterparts. The resin and hardeners can be purchased in kits that range in volume from one pint to five gallons. Recently, the Aqua-Resin® system has become available. One part of this system is liquid, while the other is powder. Aqua-Resin is nontoxic and does not present the same health risks of other two-part systems. It is also compatible with most surfaces. Because of the powder component, the viscosity and setup time can be controlled by adding more or less powder to the liquid component.

Most two-part resins must be carefully proportioned, and you cannot add universal tinting colors to the resin or it will not harden properly. Some manufacturers of resin have tints available for their products. Also, if a resin is too thin for the desired texture, most manufacturers sell fillers for mixing into their systems. Inert materials and fillers also can be mixed or coated with the resin, such as vermiculite, natural fiber fabrics, or chopped polyester fibers. Mix the resin and hardener thoroughly before adding the filler. If you are unsure whether a filler is compatible with the two-part system you are using, do a sample beforehand.

Once cured, resin finishes are very hard and durable. When reinforced with fiber, they stand up well to the most punishing moving and trucking schedules. These systems are excellent for coating scenic sculpture that otherwise might be damaged easily. Be aware that some two-part systems heat up as they cure and may actually melt or dissolve some materials, such as polystyrene foams. Use proper safety precautions and protection when using these products (see Chapter 4, the section "Safety and Health Regulations").

THE TOOLS AND MATERIALS OF TEXTURING

Creating a layer of texture on scenery is the work of the scenic artist. A texture coat transforms the construction materials underneath into a unified surface resembling stone, plaster, wood, or simply a unified mass. A texture coat may fully conceal the materials underneath or enhance and unify the natural texture of the surface at hand.

When a texture is part of an overall paint technique, it needs to be handled before the painting is done. The texturing should be executed separately from painting and allowed to dry before paint is applied. Occasionally, paint is applied directly to wet texture by spraying or spattering. The paint then mixes into the texture to some extent, which works particularly well with stone or rustic textures.

Texture Tools

Textures can be applied with all manner of tools. As in applying paint, tools can be either traditional or handmade, and each tool used to apply texture has its own signature of patterns it creates.

One of the simplest and most effective tools used to spread and create texture is one-inch stock board. Cut to short lengths, the board can be used like a paddle for scooping and spreading a texture medium or to stipple small peaks into the surface of the texture once the mix is spread. *Blocking*, the technique of lightly pulling the board across the surface, may be used over texture after it has been stippled or to spatter with, creating a stucco effect.

Drywall knives are useful for paddling out and spreading texture medium. These knives are used to create a smoother fresco texture or a fan pattern stucco. Tiling adhesive knifes are made in various sizes and configurations of teeth, ranging up to one-quarter-inch deep. These knives are used to create more elaborate patterns and textures.

Graining tools are used to create texture grains in the same manner as with paint (see Chapter 10). After the texture compound has been applied to the surface, a rough wood texture can be developed by graining it with graining combs or rubber grainers. The stiffer the texture compound, the more pronounced the grain will be. Other types of rough wood textures may be developed by graining or dry brushing a texture compound with straw brooms, stiff brushes, or wads of newspaper. A technique called *roping* is traditionally done by dragging a loop of hemp rope through texture compound; a brush may be used for roping as well. The result of roping is a texture that looks like a heavy paint build-up such as you would see on surfaces that have been painted many times over.

Sponges can be used to apply texture or pattern a textured surface. Like the paint techniques, texturing done with a natural sponge will have an organic appearance. This texture works well for stone or rough concrete. Stippling the surface of a texture with square cellulose sponges creates a pattern that looks more humanmade and regular, like brick or block.

Fleece rollers can be used to apply texture medium as well as to stipple the surface of texture. Most texture rollers are made not to apply the texture but to stipple the texture medium once it has been brushed or sprayed on the surface.

Some pneumatic spray guns called hopper guns (discussed in Chapter 5) are specifically for spraying textures. No spray gun should be used for the application of texture other than those made specifically for it. Caution must be taken in the choice of material put through the gun, as some substances described next cannot be used with a gun or they will clog it.

Texture Mediums

Texture frequently is the key to creating a surface with a realistic appearance. If texture is involved in the overall paint treatment, it should be the first consideration of the scenic artist's process. The scenic artist must plan a texture thoroughly from a standpoint of function as well as visual effect. Textured scenery still must be handled and installed in a theatre. A flown unit covered with texture, for example, cannot exceed the weight limit of a batten, and often a large unit will rapidly increase in weight as texture is applied. The unit must still be gripped, and the weight of the texture cannot outstrip the strength of the structure. The texture must stay on the unit and pose no health threats to the stagehands or performers through dust or overly abrasive surfaces. Of course, the texture must take paint well and dry thoroughly in the amount of time available for the painting. For all these reasons and more, samples must always be done for texture.

A medium should be mixed with enough body to hold the texture pattern. Many texture mediums are mixed from a spackle or drywall compound reinforced with water-based adhesive. Texture mediums should be applied to a clean, primed surface for a good bond between the medium and the surface. Texture mediums can be tinted to a hue that approaches the base-coat local color of the intended finish. Then, if the scenery is scraped in moving and trucking, the texture coat revealed will not be too different from the local color. Once the texture medium is dry, the surface can be painted, glazed, and given a finish.

Viscosity in texture mediums is very important. If the texture medium is stiff, the resulting texture will be very pronounced. If the texture compound is thinned, the texture will settle out and have a softer appearance.

Note that some compounds discussed here, like paint, harden through evaporation, and others cure through chemical processes. It is critical that no additives, other than those sold by the manufacturer, be added to a curing compound or it will not set up properly.

Line Thickener

Line thickener is a medium used to thicken polymer-based paints. A very small quantity of line thickener will thicken a full gallon of paint. Paint may be thickened to the consistency of paste. One drawback to using line thickener and paint for texture is that thickened paint is a very expensive texture medium. Paint thickened with line thickener loses a lot of its volume when it dries. However, texture done with line thickener is a very durable and can be mixed to the color desired.

Drywall Treatments

The construction industry is a source for many of the tools and materials used in texture application in the theatrical industry. Spending time in the isles of a home-improvement store can lead to all sorts of useful discoveries of implements and mediums that can have theatrical applications.

Drywall Compound Drywall compound is available at paint supply stores, lumber yards, and home-improvement stores. It is sold premixed and dry. Normally used in the construction industry, drywall compound is a very useful texturing medium for theatre and display work.

Premixed drywall compound is available in regular weight and lightweight. The lightweight mixture is made with air mixed in, so when mixed into paint it loses its volume. Regular-weight drywall compound should be used for texture mediums. Drywall compound in dry or powdered form can be mixed with water or paint to the desired consistency. All drywall compounds are water-based, porous, and sandable when dry. They are intended to be used on permanently installed surfaces and not formulated for surfaces that are frequently handled or that flex in any way. Drywall texture compounds must be reinforced with flexible adhesives or polymer binders or they will crack or chip off the surface.

A

B

Figure 7.13 Three examples of texture treatments used for the production of *Hansel und Gretel* at the University of Michigan, designed by Francesca Callow.

C

Figure 7.13 Continued.

Flexible polymer glue, latex binder, and PVA all work well in this respect.

If straight, undiluted drywall compound is applied too thickly, it will crack when it dries. For thick applications of drywall compound, additives can be mixed in. Drywall compound should never be mixed in with concrete, plaster, or any other compounds that cure.

A term frequently used in the theatrical industry is "Goop and Glaze." By referring to texture treatments as "goop" it helps to distinguish the medium and the techniques associated with it from two-dimensional texture techniques. (Two-dimensional texture treatments are discussed in Chapter 9.) Hence, any texture compound may be referred to as *goop*. The term *glaze* refers to a thin watery paint that is translucent when it is dry. When applying glaze either in a spray or a spatter to the texture compound before it has dried, the glaze will mix with the color of the goop and settle in the low areas, emphasizing the texture.

Latex Spackle   Latex and vinyl spackle are used to patch drywall. They are premixed with binders to be durable. Because this spackle is polymer-based,

it is more expensive than drywall compound. And because it has a very durable texture, latex spackle is useful for treatments on sets and displays that will have to undergo a fair amount of moving and trucking. Polymer-based spackle can be purchased at lumberyards and paint supply stores. The spackle can be tinted to an appropriate base color with colorants or scenic paint.

For some techniques where specific placement is necessary, such as filling in the mortar between faux bricks, you can fill a pastry bag with either drywall compound or latex spackle–based texture. (You can purchase professional-quality pastry bags and tips from restaurant suppliers.) By choosing the appropriate tip, you can apply the compound in a very controlled fashion. You can even decorate a prop birthday cake. Squeeze bags designed specifically for application of mortar in between faux bricks can be purchased from faux brick suppliers.

Quick Textures   Quick textures, or QT mixes, are available through contracting suppliers. These mixes are available in different grades of texture: fine, medium, and coarse. These textures produce a pebbly texture that covers most imperfections and seams. Quick textures are designed to be sprayed through a hopper gun. The spray tip of the gun can

Figure 7.14
Lindberg Gun Shop,
Public Museum of
Grand Rapids,
Michigan. Painted by
Crabtree Scenic,
signage painted by
Grand Rapids
Museum staff.

be adjusted to accommodate the grain of the QT mix to be sprayed through it. Most commonly, QT mix is sprayed on ceilings. The QT mix comes in 40-pound bags and should be prepared according to the instructions on the bag.

QT mix is not designed to endure much wear and tear. It may not hold up well through the rough handling that the scenery receives from trucking and load-in. A main component in QT mix is polystyrene beads. When the surface covered with this texture is scraped, these granules break up and leave a white mark on the finish. The QT mix can be tinted with colorants and the texture can be reinforced with flexible white glue, which will make it more durable and less likely to show the inevitable scrapes and scratches.

Plaster   Plaster of Paris is gypsum baked to reduce its natural water content. When remixed with water, it regains the lost water content and hardens to a solid mass. Plaster warms as the gypsum rehydrates. Plaster sets quickly, so there is no shrinkage, making plaster very useful for molding. After plaster has set, any extra water trapped in the plaster will evaporate slowly. While evaporating, the plaster will remain cool. Once the plaster has completely cured, the surface of the plaster will feel the same as the ambient temperature in the shop to the touch.

Hydrocal cement is made of thoroughly burnt gypsum mixed into a compound with salts. It has a smooth texture that looks and handles like plaster but is much more durable. It will cure to a very hard mass that can be used for coating surfaces and building up layers on three-dimensional elements. Both hydrocal cement and plaster can be reinforced by mixing them with polyester fibers or by layering them with webbing or screen.

Neither plaster nor cement can be tinted with universal tinting colors or mixed with additional binder, as these interfere with the ability of the compounds to set up or cure. Dry tinting colors can be purchased from construction suppliers for use with plaster or hydrocal cement. Plaster can be carved, but the hydrocal cement is more rigid and can be used as surface treatment only.

Adhesives for Texture Mediums   Some adhesives can be used as textures themselves or added to other compounds for elasticity. Most texture compounds are not formulated to be used on anything other than stable, rigid surfaces. Scenery has a tendency to flex because it is made of lighter materials and undergoes considerable handling after painting, which makes the addition of flexible adhesives necessary.

Polymer Glues and Theatrical Coatings

Some polymer adhesives, such as Sculpt or Coat, are formulated to a thick paste-like consistency. These adhesives are useful as coatings for polystyrene foam, foam rubber, or texture coats that need to be protected. They may be used to reinforce drywall compound or QT mix. The thickened adhesive itself can be used as a texture but is somewhat costly. Theatrical coatings can be tinted easily.

White polymer glue can be used to strengthen the bond and durability of texture compounds. Because the glue is liquid, be careful not to thin a texture compound too much before adding the glue itself, as the liquid glue also will thin the compound. When using glue to strengthen a texture medium, it is important to use only glues that remain flexible after they are dry. Glues that dry to a brittle finish result in a rigid texture could pop off hard-covered scenic units or crack on soft-covered units when they are handled.

Contact Cement

A great variety of industrial adhesives are available through contracting suppliers and adhesive manufacturers. One adhesive commonly used in theatre and display is *contact cement*. The primary use of contact cement is to permanently bond together two surfaces. Both surfaces are coated with the cement and allowed to dry thoroughly before the surfaces are pressed together. Contact cement works well for bonding wood, plastics, foams, and plastic laminate. There are many varieties of contact cement, and some work best for certain applications. If you have any questions about what type of contact cement to use for a given application, call the manufacturer for information about its line of adhesives.

Contact cements are either solvent- or water-based. Solvent-based cements are used primarily to bond materials and cannot be mixed into any sort of texture medium. Water-based contact cements can be mixed with almost any water-based compound, such as drywall compound. Not all water-based cements are compatible with other binders, such as acrylic or vinyl. If you are going to try to tint or mix the contact cement with any paint that has a binder, do a test first to make sure the mixture will not clot. Water-based contact cement can be tinted with colorants.

A texture medium reinforced with water-based contact cement is useful for texture that must be particularly durable, such as texture for groundcloths and decks. It also is useful for texture applied to flexible surfaces like soft sculpture.

Rubber Latex

Rubber latex dries to a flexible rubbery surface and is excellent for mixing with particulate mediums, such as clay or vermiculite. A texture medium made with rubber latex as the sole binder dries to a very soft, durable surface. Rubber latex-based textures are particularly useful where a texture may come in contact with human skin, such as bare feet on a groundcloth. You can make a useful texture compound for this application by mixing rubber latex with vermiculite. The rubber latex will hold up to dancing, stage combat, or similar activities. Many particulate additives soak up a fair amount of water from rubber latex, making the medium thick and difficult to spread. Thin it with water to keep the mixture pliable. Bear in mind that, if a rubber latex surface is folded face to face, it must be sealed with a thin coat of paint or flat sealer to prevent the folds from bonding. Note that, although most texture compounds can be sprayed through a hopper gun, absolutely no mixtures containing rubber latex or contact cement can be, as they will bind up the gun and ruin it (see Chapter 4, the section "Safety and Health Regulations").

Tile Adhesive

Tile adhesives are sold through tile-supply stores and lumberyards, with a fair range in the type of tile adhesive available. Adhesives used for installing asphalt floor tiles set up to a malleable, tacky finish that works well for laminating surfaces. Asphalt tile adhesive should not be used to reinforce texture mediums because it remains in a tacky and malleable state.

Adhesives designed to adhere ceramic tile to drywall dry to a tough, rigid finish. This adhesive works very well for texture that must stand up to a lot of wear and tear, such as on stage decks and platforms. This texture is very rigid and it should not be used to create a rough texture for a deck where performers will have bare feet. The adhesive may be used by itself as a texture, added to drywall compound, or mixed with nearly any dry particulate. Water-based adhesives are easily thinned and tinted with universal tinting colorants to the desired color.

The adhesives used for adhering marble tiles to concrete or durarock sheets are silicate-based and

Figure 7.15
Textures: drywall compound with trowel, cellulose insulation, drywall compound and sand, drywall compound and vermiculite, joint compound and cocoa mulch.

have latex or acrylic binders premixed in them. These compounds are sold in dry form and should be mixed according to the manufacturer's directions. Some marble tile adhesives are designed to be mixed with a separate liquid binder for even greater strength and durability. Some marble tile adhesives cure rather than simply dry. Any additives mixed into the compound such as colorants or extra binders may interfere with the curing.

Texturing Additives

Many texture compounds discussed have a paste-like texture. Adding dry materials or particulates can change the substance or character of these compounds. Depending on the material added, the texture can resemble brick, stone, mortar, tree bark, or other textures that a scenic artist may need to emulate. Remember that concrete, marble adhesives, plasters, and other materials that need to cure cannot be mixed with additives (see Figure 7.15).

Clay

Dry clay can be purchased in bulk form through pottery suppliers and can be added to other texture compounds, such as drywall compound or QT mix. Because clay, when dry, has no binders, these compounds must be strengthened with binder or adhesive. Clay may be mixed with water and binder for use as a texture compound on its own. An advantage of using clay is that it is earth and therefore keeps its natural hue. Also, when a texture compound based on clay dries, it will develop cracks and cupped plates just like clay earth does in nature.

Sand

Sand is an additive that gives an assortment of finishes depending on the variety of sand used. Sandbox sand is readily available and renders a coarse, pebbly texture. Coastal sand, which is available in some areas, is finer and must be sifted through a screen to remove debris. An even finer grade of sand is white silicate sand, which is sold at brick dealers and hardware stores and is made to mix into brick mortar. Clean sand can be purchased from sandblasting suppliers. This sand is strained carefully according to its coarseness and is much more expensive than other kinds.

Straight sand can be used to simulate soil. Real soil will dry out in the theatre and may create a distracting and hazardous dust cloud. Sand is a reasonable alternative because it is not as dusty as soil. Most readily available sand is either a yellowish-brown or off-white. Sand can be painted as needed with water-based paint. To paint small amounts of sand, spread it out thinly on visquene and spray it. Mix and spread the sand out to dry several times until it approaches the right hue. You can also put small amounts of sand in a gallon bucket and use a paint drill to coat it with paint. In either case, be careful to not overly moisten the sand so that it clumps together.

If you need to paint a large amount of sand, doing it by hand is too tedious and strenuous.

A rented mortar mixer will do the job. Small mortar mixers with a 30-gallon barrel are easy enough for one person to move around and operate. The difference between a mortar mixer and a concrete mixer is that, even though both have barrels that rotate, the mortar mixer also has arms that rotate in the opposite direction to thoroughly mix the mortar. This tool works very well for coating sand with paint. After the sand has been blended with the thinned paint in the mortar mixer for several minutes, pour it over some visquene and spread it out to dry. When the sand comes out of the mixer it should not be so damp with paint that it clumps together when a handful of it is squeezed. If this is the case, increase the ratio of sand to paint. Over the several days it will take the sand to dry, stir it frequently to ensure that it doesn't dry in clumps. Use proper safety precautions and protection when working with silicates (see Chapter 4, the section "Safety and Health Regulations").

Perlite

Perlite is a very lightweight white synthetic grain particle that can be mixed easily into many texture mediums. It is available in a variety of pellet sizes, from a grain about the size of coarse sand to a pellet the size of large-curd cottage cheese. Fine-grain perlite is sold through paint and theatrical suppliers specifically for use as a texture additive. It is mixed directly into the paint. As light as it is, perlite will float to the top of thin paint mixtures so it must be stirred frequently. Perlite also is available through landscape suppliers, where it is used as a soil additive. It is available in large quantities, four square feet to the bag. Bulk perlite is categorized by the size of the pellets: 1 is a fine grain, 5 is the coarsest. A disadvantage to using perlite in a texture compound is that the white pellets leave a noticeable white mark when the scenery is scraped. For this reason, perlite works best for texture applications with naturally light colors, like stucco, rock, and mortar.

Vermiculite

Vermiculite is another useful texturing product available from landscaping suppliers, where it is used as a soil additive. The pellets of vermiculite are angular and light bronze to gray in color. Vermiculite is available in different size pellets from fine to coarse, like perlite. It also is an excellent soil substitute for the theatre. The surface of the pellets are somewhat reflective, like the surface of mica, so for simulated soil the vermiculite may need to be sprayed or given a spin in the mortar mixer with thinned paint or a flat acrylic finish.

Vermiculite is an excellent texture compound. Its extremely light weight makes it ideally suited for extensive use in the theatre. The overall weight of even the largest scenic units will remain manageable when textured with vermiculite. Even when the scenery is scraped during load-in, the color of vermiculite will be far less pronounced.

Cocoa Mulch

Cocoa mulch is a landscaping product sold through landscape supply stores and garden nurseries for mulching gardens. It is packaged in bags of four square feet, like perlite and vermiculite. Cocoa mulch mixed with drywall compound renders a very distinctive, coarse organic texture that is excellent for simulating the appearance of tree bark and stone. The cocoa mulch will stain unevenly through the drywall compound and any paint applied over it. So this compound must be used only for textures that will be enhanced by the brown dappled stain.

Paper and Fabric Textures

Papier-mâché is made by saturating paper with glue or any binder and then layering it onto a surface. Papier-mâché can be used as a texture itself or it can be used to strengthen a textured surface or sculpture. Most any paper can be used in papier-mâché. A paper used for this process should be rather absorbent, so that it completely soaks up the glue or binder. Newsprint is the standard choice for papier-mâché, being absorbent and abundant. White or brown commercial paper towel, available in quantity from janitorial services, makes an excellent paper texturing product. Brown paper towel is excellent for emulating tree bark, particularly that of palm trees. The color of the brown paper towel functions as a base coat for the paint treatment. White paper towel works equally well as a base for birch tree bark. Stucco texture can be made in a papier-mâché process by using toilet paper. Because toilet paper is so thin and fragile, the binder should be sprayed or brushed first on the surface, the dry toilet paper applied to that, then a final spray of binder applied.

Cellulose

A papier-mâché paste made from pulped paper can be used as a texture or skinning product. Some art supply stores sell pulped papier-mâché that has a binder mixed into it; just add water. This product is not packaged in the volumes often needed for theatrical applications. A good substitute is cellulose insulation. It usually is available from lumberyards or a construction materials supplier in bags of three square feet. When working with cellulose, be very careful to contain it well and always wear a respirator with dust cartridges while handling it when in its dry form.

Fabric

Erosion cloth, burlap, cotton scrim, cheesecloth, and nearly any fabric can be dipped in thin glue, vinyl wallpaper paste, or wheat paste, then applied or sculpted to some degree directly on scenery. Once dry, it can be painted as needed. The same process used for paper can be used with fabric to create texture. Highly absorbent fabrics are the easiest to handle. Fabrics like cheesecloth, felt, and gauze should be cut into easily manipulated pieces and treated like the paper just described. Textures like bark, shingles, and even bas-relief architectural details can be created in this way.

Binders

Wheat paste has been the traditional binder for papier-mâché. Note that you should never use glue in combination with shellac-based mediums. This combination may cause the papier-mâché to peel away from the surface. Applying shellac-based mediums over a wheat paste finish is an age-old recipe for a crackle or peeled paint finish.

For the most part, contemporary vinyl paste products have replaced wheat paste. Other binders for papier-mâché and fabric can be made with joint compound reinforced with glue. Thinned water-based glue may be used as well.

Cellulose can be used as a papier-mâché by mixing it with wheat paste or vinyl binders. Paint also can serve as the binder with cellulose so that when the texture is applied, it is the desired color. The binder in the paint will be sufficient to hold cellulose to most surfaces. Before using a texture compound mixed with cellulose, let it sit for about 30 minutes. Cellulose will soak up a fair amount of water from the binder, and it may need to be further thinned out.

Texture Stencils

Textures can be applied through stencils to create specific, repeating patterns like bricks and cinder blocks. The stencil itself must be cut out of a flexible, durable material. Polysytrene, the same material used in vacuforming, is an excellent choice for the heavy-duty demands of a texture stencil. Polystyrene is sold in 4′ × 8′ sheets through wholesale plastics suppliers. Polystyrene is made in a wide range of thicknesses, from a few millimeters to one-half inch. Select a thickness based on the depth of the impression needed. Polyethylene is available in the same sizes and is equally flexible and washable.

Prepare a texture stencil in the same manner as paint stencils described in Chapter 5. Cut texture stencils so that they register right up to the edge of the last repeat. The reason for this is that most heavy textures take somewhere around 24 hours to dry, so it would be inconvenient to have to wait that long to do the adjacent repeats. The stencil should be hosed off and scrubbed well after the application is finished for the day. Any texture allowed to dry on the stencil will be very difficult to clean off.

A texture compound for bricks can be made with drywall compound reinforced with glue. Sand, perlite, or vermiculite can be added to give the compound body and texture. The compound can be sprayed on with a hopper gun or dropped directly onto the stencil then smoothed out so it is more or less even with the top of the stencil. The compound can be smoothed with the edge of a board, a trowel, a drywall knife, a silk-screen squeegee, or a tar squeegee.

The following is a recipe for brick texture to be used with a texture stencil:
- Five gallons regular weight drywall compound
- Two gallons vermiculite
- One gallon PVA binder
- Tint with scene paint

Mix in a mortar mixer until smooth. Ten gallons will cover approximately 100 square feet using a quarter-inch-thick brick or cinderblock stencil.

The texture stenciling process for large surface areas must be planned to maximize time and effort. Normally, stencils are made in a size that one person can handle. When faced with hundreds of square feet of surface area, however, the stencil should be cut out of a full 4′ × 8′ sheet of polystyrene or polyethylene. Two people are needed to work with this large a stencil. The ratio of texture compound to surface area may be as much as five gallons for every 100 square feet covered, based on a coverage depth of one-quarter inch. This ratio could result in hundreds of gallons of compound being mixed for a reasonably large production. A mortar mixer should be used to mix large volumes of texture compound, which can be stored in plastic garbage cans for convenience.

CONCLUSION

It is important for scenic artists to understand the preparation of materials as thoroughly as possible. Sound preparation is essential for the painting that will follow. The paint's adhesion, flexibility, durability, and the strength of its surface are crucial for the scenery to survive handling in the shop and on stage. The natural quality of a material, such as the transparency of scrim, can be ruined by poor or uninformed preparation.

A myriad of new products are available to scenic artists for making scenery and props. Many of these products are synthetic or extensively processed natural materials. Some may contain dyes or binders that could react with common theatrical paint products. When using a new product or material, take the time to investigate how best to approach preparing the surface of that material for paint while preserving its desirable qualities. If you and your colleagues are stumped, call the manufacturer of the material in question or a paint manufacturer for advice. Keep in mind that actors will be using your product (the scenery), and their safety and comfort is a serious consideration. Exercise caution and use common sense when handling unfamiliar products.

INTERVIEW WITH KAT SHARP, PROFESSIONAL SCENIC ARTIST

Kat Sharp is a leading professional scenic artist and was an instructor at Cobalt Studios at the time of this interview.

Susan Crabtree: What is your position at Cobalt Studios?

Kat Sharp: I don't have an official title. I paint, I charge shows, I bid shows, I talk to designers,

I teach students. Primarily we're a school so there is a lot of teaching as well as all the other things that have to do with running the business.

SC: Can you tell me about the focus at Cobalt Studios and how you balance that with the professional work that comes in?

KS: It's all about the students here. It's a professional scene painting shop, but it's all about the students, and during the usual year we accept up to eight of them. It's a very small school with just two full-time teachers. The students' time is divided half and half: half is commission work and half is projects and lectures and more academic work or projects that they do on their own. The work that they do on commission is similar to what an apprentice would do. They work alongside a professional scenic artist, either me or Rachel or someone we've hired to work on a specific job. Often the jobs happen to somehow have to do with what we are teaching at that moment. If we are doing drapery, oftentimes it happens that we'll have a show or a bit of a show that has to do with what we are doing in class. A lot of the choices we make, the work we accept, or what work we encourage to come here, is based on what we want to teach the students. We work exclusively on painting and drops. We don't do any carpentry and we don't do any scenic design.

SC: How many schools like this are there in the country?

KS: I think there are some graduate programs that are starting to develop a scenic painting program, but we're it as far as conservatory atmosphere—students come here as if they are coming to work.

SC: Can you tell me a bit more about your curriculum?

KS: It's a two-year program, and each month we have certain lectures or things that we want to get to during that month in addition to their commission work. There is some structure to their schedule and some progression of starting with intro to drawing, color theory, brush lecture, tools and techniques, health and safety, just learning your way around the paint shop. It progresses from there to wood graining and marbling and clouds and foliage—lots and lots of drawing.

SC: Why so much drawing?

KS: It's good for them because you don't have to come to school here to be a scenic artist. Anybody can go and be a scenic artist, but when you start out that way you're going to be the kind of scenic artist who is doing a lot of base-coating. When you walk into a shop, they're going to give you work that's at whatever level you're in. If you walk into a shop and they ask you if you can draw and you say "Yes" with confidence and you know that you can, you are going to be in a better position to get more interesting work, so that's why people study here.

SC: What kind of professional do you envision your students being when they finish your program? What is your goal for your students?

KS: They should have very good work habits, know how to work on a crew. They are starting to know how to charge other people, how to budget time, budget money. They have very strong drawing skills, color matching—those kinds of basics. They really have a good handle on all the classic scenic art techniques, but they also have a really strong problem-solving ability for whatever comes their way. Maybe they haven't done it before but they can figure out a way to do it and it doesn't stump them too much. They'll try it, they'll test it out, they'll call someone, and they'll experiment until they find a way to do it. Problem solving is a big thing.

SC: How long have you been a scenic artist?

KS: I started off pretty early, in high school, and I'm 38 years old now, so about 20 years. While I was in high school, my sister-in-law had work with a marionette troupe in town and she got me interested in it. I kept with it and I studied set design in college and then I went to New York City after college. During the summers of college, I went to various summer theatres and people who were from New York would say, "You ought to come up and try it and see how you like it." So I went up to try it and I stayed for 10 years and I decided I didn't want to set design at all. I did a lot of assisting, which I really liked. I liked drafting and I liked doing research. I found out that I don't like being the person that comes up with the ideas. I don't like doing the abstract thinking about it. I really like scene painting; I like the craft of it, I like holding the brush, I like moving paint around on a canvas. So when I was in New York I started working with designers, I would be their assistant, I would be doing a small show off-Broadway and I would work with them painting their show and assisting them. That's how I started really getting into painting.

SC: Do you think of yourself as having a specialty in the area of scenic art?

KS: Not really. I thrive on the variety of it. I love doing figure drawing and I like when that comes my way, but I really don't have a specialty.

SC: Did you start out by studying scene design?

KS: Yes. I was at Virginia Commonwealth University in Richmond, Virginia, my hometown. They had a good art school, a strong theatre program, and a good scenic art class, and the design professors were really into it. It was a good basic start for me.

SC: Was that rare for there to actually be a scenic painting/scenic art class 20 years ago?

KS: I think so. It just happened that my teacher, Rick Pike, was a very good scenic artist and really wanted us to learn that so that's where I started. I think at that time that if people really wanted to attend a scenic painting class they would go to New York City. It was unusual to have a scenic painting class in the colleges or the universities.

SC: Do you think your education was instrumental in developing your skills as a scenic artist because you studied fine arts, not just scene design?

KS: Definitely. It helps a lot to just move your pencil around and look. It helps you to see, it helps you to study art history, look at the work of other artists and think about things that artists think about— think about composition, think about lighting, think about other things.

SC: Were there any scenic artists who were instrumental in helping you develop your skills as a scenic artist?

KS: A lot of the work I did when I first started out was directly with designers. I did a lot of work for Chris Barecca for instance. After two years in New York I charged at Yale Repertory Theatre for several seasons, so I've brushed shoulders with Katie Dilkes and Steve Purtee there. Of course, Ming Cho Lee and Jennifer Tipton and Michael Yeargan—the whole crew—I learned a lot there and I was really challenged by the students. It's a school but it's a regional theatre situation. One of the first shows was a show called *Little Eyolf* and we were to recreate Delacroix paintings as if they were enormous tapestries. We turned the stage into sand dunes with real sand, we sculpted a larger-than-life-size horse that would fly, be climbed on, bleed, and hold small children in a trap door in it's belly—really over-the-top kind of painting and sculpting, everything that would really challenge a scenic artist. In my years there, I had to open my mind to all kinds of experimentation to keep up with the visions of the students and professors. When I was there I got into the union and started working with union painters in union shops. I worked at Nolan's in New York alongside all the old-timers there.

SC: What are some of the most important lessons you learned while your skills were developing at Yale and while you were working for and with these other scenic artists and designers. What are you trying to pass on to your students?

KS: One is simply to have a critical, discerning eye for your work and what goes on stage—really working with the whole picture and being able to tweak things until they are right. I think the designers really appreciate that. I think the other thing is to take new things on as a challenge. If you see a design that looks like nothing you've ever seen before, there is probably something in it that is sort of like something you've done before. You can start there, start with what you know, and experiment and make it happen. Don't do the same thing that you've done before. Be willing to experiment with techniques and looks and styles and everything.

SC: How do you think your education in design and your work with designers has enhanced your scenic art skills?

KS: If you have assisted or designed yourself, I think it helps you communicate with designers more easily. I am a second set of eyes, I can put my head into what the designer is going to look for and see it before they do. I love working with designers. One of my favorite and most horrible experiences was working with a designer on my first show at Yale. She was designing the sculpture of the horse, and the words she was using to describe what she wanted were so different from the pictures she gave me. I said that something was not working—the pictures weren't telling me what she was telling me. We sat down and sketched together and we really started to figure out what she wanted and developed the look of the horse for the show together. Those kinds of experiences are what are really cool. You don't often have that kind of experience in a scenic shop; you have it in regional theatre where you're working more with designers. I love being able to use a real visual language— "is it soft or is it fuzzy?"—trying to get around to what it is.

SC: Do you have a methodology for developing a dialog with designers as a scenic artist?

KS: It really depends on the situation and on the person. It depends on if it's someone I've worked with before and we already have a secret language we share together. Oftentimes I want to see a picture and I'll ask them what it is that they like about this elevation or rendering of a show. Usually I won't frame a question like, "Why did you make this not like the other part of the rendering?" but instead more like, "Can you point to the part that you like the most and tell me why you like it?" Very often when you start asking questions of the designer you'll find out that they really don't want it to look exactly like the elevation.

SC: What kind of training do you think someone wanting to be a scenic artist should obtain?

KS: It depends on what kinds of scenic art you want to do. Some people are scenic artists but they work in amusement parks and they paint the walls flat colors. The kind of training you need to do that is different than what you would need if you wanted to paint at the Met. Certainly if you want to do the most interesting kind of work, drawing is an important skill as is real knowledge of art history. Not just by looking at it or by going to an art history class and memorizing slides but really experiencing it, somehow making it real for yourself and understanding periods of art and architectural styles and all that stuff. Whether you go to school or work on the job, it is important to find someone who is a good teacher— it might be a boss or it might be an academic kind of teacher. Find someone who is really good and who wants to teach you.

SC: Do you have any words of wisdom that you would like to offer someone who is planning a career in scenic artistry?

KS: I think you have to like painting or you're not going to like the job. It comes down to that. You can't think of it as a glamorous career, you're not going to like it as a lifetime career if you simply like theatre and like being in the audience. If you're thinking about being a scenic artist, consider whether you like being messy, or being in an atmosphere that may be loud, where different things are happening all the time. Simply put, do you love the pure sensual feel of a brush loaded with paint moving across a canvas? If you really like that, then you will love being a scenic artist. If you don't like that you're going to be miserable.

SC: What are some of the most difficult or elusive skills you have had to learn in the profession of scenic artistry?

KS: People skills perhaps, getting along, finding your way when you're the new guy in the shop. I think maybe what people don't know about scenic painting is how physically demanding it is. Simply standing on your feet all day looking at your toes, stooping, crawling around on your hands and knees—it is hard, physical work. I don't think people expect that.

SC: What do you think might be some of the most common misconceptions about the profession of scenic artistry?

KS: I think a lot of people just don't know what the profession is. You tell a person you just met on the street that you're a scenic artist and sometimes they think you paint watercolors of landscapes. I think a misconception that young scenic artists have is that every day is going to be fun painting, but it's not always fun. A lot of it is boring. A lot of it is monotonous. You work out how to do a stencil wallpaper—that's the exciting part. Then come the hours and hours on your hands and knees repeating the stencil—that's the tedious part. It's not a glamorous career.

SC: We've seen a lot of digital painting come into the world of scenic artistry. Do you think that is going to have an impact on scenic artistry?

KS: Yes, it is now. A lot of the renderings we get from designers are computer generated. Elevations get sent to us as attachments through e-mails. I'm sure that will expand even more. I don't think the computers will take over, though. I think it will be different, but I think there will always be a need for human touch or a human eye to look at something that goes on a stage. There are lots of great applications for the computer on displays, industrial things, trade shows. Anything that looks very slick, the computer is probably going to do better than a paintbrush. I think it's wise for scenic artists to get savvy with computers. I think people are doing that. I hear more and more of scenic artists and designers who use computers in their work. To have that skill is wise. I don't think you should turn your back on it.

SC: Do you have any favorite scenic art–related stories you would like to share about productions you have worked on in the past?

KS: As time goes by, the things that seemed the most difficult at the time are not such a big deal anymore. They become your interesting stories and you're glad for the experience. For instance, I was working on a set for an AT&T commercial whose plotline was a construction crew on Wall Street digging the foundation for a new building coming upon what they think might be part of an old ship. There are a lot of phone calls back and forth and they discover that it's an old, very important artifact and they dramatically pull out the figurehead of the ship and shards of pottery. In the shop, we sculpted a beautiful figurehead then smashed and distressed crockery. We actually went down to a vacant lot on Wall Street and the crew excavated a huge hole and we sculpted the ribs of the ship into the hole and rented this cement mixer for making large quantities of goop and filled in the sides and made it look like dirt—just the right color of dirt, of course It was quite fun to be in downtown Manhattan really doing this in this hole up to my mid-thighs in mud. At the time it was a big pain in the neck, but looking back it was kind of fun.

SC: What is it that you enjoy most about the scenic art profession?

KS: It's changed throughout the years. When I first started out doing theatre, I liked that it was kind of like a family and we had a lot of fun together and had a lot of laughs. Later on I liked that I had some freedom and a variety of work to choose from in New York City. Lots and lots of work was available and I could be very choosy about what I wanted to do, who I wanted to work with or for. The variety was great; being able to travel was great. I guess the thing that continues is working with a small group of people. I like that it's one part "professional" and one part "blue collar."

Part Three
The Techniques of Scenic Painting

Forest Drop, Monument Valley Drop. Drops are property of Kenmark Studios, Inc., Las Vegas, Nevada (painted by Crabtree Scenic at the Power Center Scene Shop, University of Michigan, Ann Arbor).

Chapter 8

Cartooning, Layout, and Lettering

Drawing the cartoon is the next step in scenic painting after priming. A *cartoon* is the line drawing of an image representing the visible edges or intersecting planes of objects, sometimes known as a *contour drawing*. Cartooning is a significant interpretive and artistic part of the scenic artist's work. This is because as the image is being enlarged, many decisions have to be made about detail and motif. The cartoon serves as a guide for placement of shade, shadow, and color. Cartooning precedes painting, in most cases, and gives the scenic artist a reference for the painting on the surface of scenery. Cartooning usually is done after the scenery is stretched and primed and may be drawn freehand or mechanically drafted. Cartoons also may be drawn onto paper and then transferred to the scenery in a process called *pouncing*.

An accurate cartoon is an essential guide to accurate painting. A poor cartoon usually cannot be corrected by subsequent painting because of the physical size of the scenery. The scenic artist paints at arm's length from the scenery, and it is awkward to step back to check the painting continually. The scenic artist should be able to paint with confidence using an accurate cartoon as the guide to the placement of color. If good preparation of the scenery is the first step toward high quality, then cartooning is the next, equally important step. Even a relatively simple painting, such as a gradient blend or wash of color, can need a guide. Reference points are placed where color values shift and guidelines are drawn to establish the direction of washes.

To paint well you must also learn to draw well. Cartooning is not something to be rushed through so the "real work" of painting can begin. This is the first point at which the scenic artist begins to interpret the scenic designer's intent onto the scenery. The cartoon forms the foundation for all work to follow. There are many instances in scenic art when the cartooning process takes as much time and effort as painting. For example, a scenic element might depict a complex line drawing of an Italian Renaissance street scene that is painted with thin color washes. In this case, the cartooning may constitute the majority of the work. Effort taken to do an accurate cartoon is never wasted in terms of creating beautiful and more professional looking scenery.

Cartooning is only done after the scenery has been properly primed because the priming (discussed in Chapter 7) not only prepares the unit for painting but also prepares it for smooth cartooning. Drops should never be cartooned before they are stretched and primed or lines will warp and distort as the fabric shrinks. Hard scenery could be cartooned before a primer coat, but the primer would obscure a cartoon. Unprimed scenery is difficult to cartoon due to the uneven and inconsistent texture, so with hard scenery as well as soft, the cartooning is done immediately after the prime coat.

Figure 8.1
Starting the cartooning in charcoal. These drawings
were transferred with a pounce. *The Producers*, Scenic
Art Studios, New York.

Figure 8.2
Inking the cartoon. *The Producers*, Scenic Art Studios,
New York.

Figure 8.3
These fabulous renderings start with an
excellent cartoon. *The Producers*, Scenic Art
Studios, New York.

THE TOOLS OF CARTOONING

The tools for cartooning fall into three categories: measuring, drawing, and transferring. These tools, like the tools of painting, are somewhat specialized for scenic art, mural, and display painting. But they are different from the painting tools. A scenic artist usually keeps cartooning tools in a cabinet or storage locker separate from the painting tools. In some shops where it is convenient to do so, the cartooning tools are always kept on a cart that can be rolled to the project being cartooned at the time so they are always together and accessible (see Figure 8.4).

Measuring Tools

Scale Rule

Scenic designers work in scale (that is, proportionally reduced) so the work can fit into a studio or on a drafting table, can be transferred as a design package from the designer to the departments, and so the design can be examined in a relatively comprehensible format. One job of a scenic artist is to "read" this scale drawing and recreate that image in full scale, or its actual dimensions.

The *scale ruler* is the measuring device used to transfer measurements from the drafted scale of a paint elevation to full scale. A scale ruler may be in feet and inches or in metric scale, depending on the country where you or the designer work. Theatres in the United States still use feet and inches, although most of the rest of the world, including Canada and Mexico, use the metric scale. A scale ruler generally has two scales on each edge of the ruler that are compatible, such as one-inch and one-half-inch scale or three-quarter-inch and three-eighth-inch scale. A scale rule may have two or three sides with two scales noted on each edge and up to 12 different scales on it. Although many different scales are used in theatrical scenic design, the two most common scales used by scenic designers for paint elevations are one-half inch to one foot and one inch to one foot. Half-inch scale is roughly equal to 1:25 metric scale. Other scales may be used to delineate detail

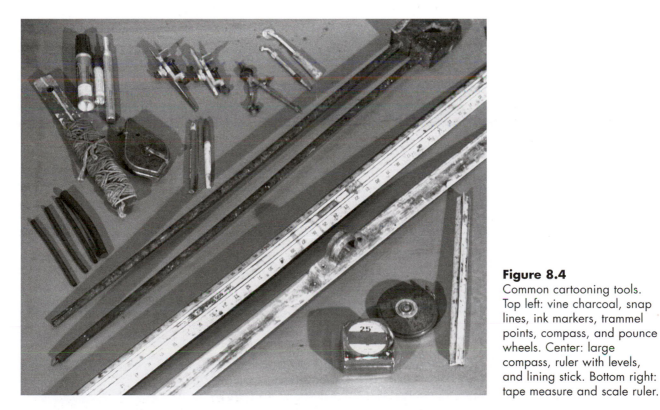

Figure 8.4
Common cartooning tools. Top left: vine charcoal, snap lines, ink markers, trammel points, compass, and pounce wheels. Center: large compass, ruler with levels, and lining stick. Bottom right: tape measure and scale ruler.

drawing, simpler forms, large formats, or by preference of the scenic designer or technical director.

Paint elevations often need to be adapted to a new shape or size. A drop may get built shorter and wider than designed. A scenic designer might solve special problems by telling the scenic artist to move the height of a skyline to 8 feet instead of 11 feet and ask for some clouds to fill in on the top, where three feet of additional muslin is exposed. Sometimes, the proportions of the scenery do not change but the actual size is different. Imagine a drop becomes 10 percent larger. What the scenic artist needs is a scale to fit the new dimensions. A simple solution is to take a scale ruler to a copy machine, enlarge the scale 10 percent and print it out. That copy of the scale can be used to read the measurements throughout the elevation, and the elevation will stay in proportion. Another solution is to make an enlarged or reduced copy of the elevation that corresponds to a specific scale suited to the true size of the goods.

> Never assume you know the scale of an elevation. If the scale is not noted on the elevation, check it before you begin. Often you can verify the scale by measuring the scenery and the elevation to see which scale fits. It would be unfortunate to have assumed the scale when ordering materials and supplies and come up short when it is time for work to commence.

Tape Measures

Flexible tape measures are a commonly used measuring tool for a scenic artist. Most paint shops need several 25-foot, two 50-foot, and one or two 100-foot tape measures. Smaller tape measures are great for small projects but are exasperatingly useless for most needs. The longer tape measures are needed for large backdrop cartooning. Equip yourself with a good-quality tape measure, as it will need to hold up for a while. A good tape measure should have a replaceable tape or blade. Be certain to get 25-foot tape measures with a one-inch-wide blade as any narrower blade is too flexible for the kind of work a scenic artist does.

Rulers and Square

Rulers come in several varieties and lengths, from the common wooden yardstick to six-foot-long steel rulers.

For small projects, they are indispensable. Rulers can be used in place of a tape measure for measuring long lengths but are less accurate. Over the course of long measurements, in addition to wasting time, small errors add up; these are made each time the ruler is picked up and laid down. A tape measure is more accurate and far more efficient with long lengths, especially when working on the floor.

When cartooning on a paint frame, however, tape measures are not as useful as yardsticks. A four-foot-long plastic ruler with vertical and horizontal levels is very useful when working on a paint frame and easier to handle. You can establish true vertical and true horizontal any place on a drop by using the levels in the ruler. You can avoid having to take two sets of measurements, over from center and up from the bottom, to find a single point. Care should be taken when using the shorter rulers to not distort a long measurement while moving the ruler end to end.

Steel rulers come in a variety of lengths, from one to six feet. The paint shop should have various size steel rulers for small cartooning and layout tasks. Steel-edged rulers have other uses, particularly as a guide for cutting cardboard stock. Steel framing squares also are used for cartooning. When working on small projects, it is frequently necessary to find the perpendicular of a line, so framing squares should always be near at hand.

Flexible steel and plastic rulers are available from sign painting supply stores. These are useful for patterning, because they bend evenly. They are used as a guide for drawing curves, called *splining*, on smaller cartooning and layout projects.

Drawing Tools for Cartooning

Drawing on a large scale requires some specialized tools and art materials. Pencils are used only in certain situations (see the comments on graphite in the following section) whereas charcoal and chalk are the most common medium.

Vine Charcoal

Medium-density vine charcoal is the standard cartooning medium for scenic painting. The advantage to using vine charcoal is that when it is flogged or blown off the surface of the scenery or paper, it comes away fairly cleanly. Vine charcoal is made from fired sticks of softwood. Real vine charcoal is made from lengths of fired grapevine and is not as consistent in density as charcoal made from softer woods. Avoid using compressed charcoal, which is made from finely ground charcoal formed into sticks. Compressed charcoal is sooty and will not come off the surface cleanly. Light oil is added to compressed charcoal to help bind it, which explains why it does not erase.

Vine charcoal is sold by some theatrical suppliers and art supply stores. It is usually available in small, medium, and large (sometimes called *jumbo*) sticks. Most scenic shops stock at least two if not all three sizes of charcoal. The size of charcoal most commonly used in the shop may depend on the scale of the work the shop most often generates. The size of charcoal also may be a personal choice: one artist may prefer to work with medium and another jumbo. Because of differing applications, it is sold in soft, medium, and hard densities. For application in scenic art, medium-density charcoal works best. The hard-density charcoal etches the surface and does not clean off well, while the soft-density charcoal wears down too fast and smudges easily.

Chalk

Some materials cannot be cartooned with vine charcoal. Black charcoal lines can get lost on a dark-colored surface, such as velour. Even a faint charcoal line might be distracting if used to cartoon clouds in a translucent sky drop. White blackboard chalk is an excellent cartooning medium for these applications. In other situations, the cartoon is best rendered in a contrasting, or less distracting, color. Multicolored chalk is useful for these applications.

Charcoal Holders

In cartooning, just as with brushwork, extensions are used when working on the floor (see Chapter 5). Although charcoal and chalk can be used with bamboo extensions, they break off easily in bamboo during use. The solution is a charcoal holder, which is manufactured to hold pastels, pencils, and charcoal. Charcoal holders are made from brass or nickel-plated steel and have two prongs to hold the charcoal with a ring that slides over the prongs to grip the charcoal. They are used by artists to hold charcoal or pencils down to the nub while providing a handle for leverage. In scenic art, they are used in the same way. By inserting the holder into a bamboo or attaching one to the end of a wooden dowel, they make using

charcoal very convenient and enable the scenic artist to use every stick of charcoal down to last half an inch so there is little waste. Charcoal holders can be purchased or ordered at art supply stores.

Floggers and Air Nozzles

A *flogger* is a simple tool used to clean charcoal lines off scenery. It is made of a short handle, between two and three feet long, with strips of fabric, either muslin or canvas, about 18 inches long, secured to one end. It resembles a short-handled mop. Floggers are used not just to clean off charcoal but to clean off dust, footprints, and assorted grime that would otherwise mar the finish of the paint. Flogging means to beat or whip, and that is how you use a flogger: you beat the charcoal or dirt off the scenery. It is best to start flogging from one end of the scenery and work in a single direction so that you are not just spreading the dirt and charcoal dust around. Floggers cover a fairly large area in one swipe, so if you want to clean up only a little of the drawing or carefully wipe away specific lines, a dry flannel rag works well.

Compressed air is great for blowing charcoal thoroughly off a drop. Some air nozzles are equipped with a short tube used to roughly aim the pressurized air, but with these you may end up blowing away more charcoal than you intended. Automotive paint stores carry pinpoint air nozzles with cone-shaped tips. These nozzles, manufactured to blow dirt out of crevices and small opening in car parts, work beautifully to selectively blow away charcoal lines. When using air nozzles you can control the strength of the airflow more or less by feel, so you can carefully delete a line or blast away everything in your path. Most paint studios will use both floggers and air nozzles for cleaning off charcoal and dusting off scenery.

Ink Markers

After the cartoon is drawn in charcoal, it needs to be set. The term *set* means to clean up the cartoon so the correct lines can be distinguished from the mistakes. It also means to make the lines permanent or to trace over them in a permanent medium. Charcoal lines that have not been set may mix into the paint or be inadvertently wiped off. If the lines of a cartoon are set in ink and the charcoal is flogged or blown off the surface, then the cartoon will be crisper for the painting that follows. Also, charcoal lines by themselves may disappear under layers of paint. A cartoon set in ink usually will be retrievable under several layers of paint.

Felt-tip ink markers are perfect for inking and are widely available. As ink markers are made with a variety of inks, the best markers for scenic art use solvent-based ink. The solvent usually is naphtha or alcohol, easily identified by a chemical solvent smell. Most art markers are solvent based. The advantage in using a solvent-based ink marker is that lines drawn with it will lightly "ghost up"—that is, reappear faintly—through layers of paint, even after application of an opaque color. Any line set with a water-based marker will mix into paint applied over it.

All the lines of the cartoon should be traced over with ink markers. Any line work around organic shapes that does not have a solid contour, such as clouds and clumps of foliage, needs to be traced with a dashed line. This is so the ink does not reappear through the paint as a solid line to distract from the brushwork or spray work that defines the leaves. The contour of the leaves then can be rendered more realistically with paint. Other types of foliage, such as palm and fern leaves, should not be cartooned in solid outlines either. These leaves can be drawn in the cartoon with a single line defining the spine of the frond or leaf. The shape of the leaf can be filled out later with brushstrokes when the base colors are painted.

After several applications of water-based paint, even an inked cartoon may become invisible. To retrieve a cartoon, spray the surface lightly with denatured alcohol where you expect the lines of the cartoon to be. Always wear a respirator when doing this. After a few minutes, the lines will soak up through the paint in those areas treated with alcohol. Many different solvents will bring the lines to the surface; however, denatured alcohol is preferable because it is one of the least toxic solvents. Nor does denatured alcohol melt or change the surface of water-based paint or leave behind a residue as it evaporates.

A cartoon set in solvent-based ink will reappear, whether you want it to or not, with any solvent-based paint treatment over it. Water-based markers can be used under solvent-based paint if you do not want the cartoon to be seen. However, water-based inks dissolve in the first application of water-based paint, and the lines will disappear as you paint. Water-based ink lines are not retrievable, like the solvent-based ones are, after they have been painted over with opaque mediums.

Most shops keep a good supply of black markers specifically for cartooning. Different color markers can be used to set cartoons, too, just like different colored chalk. A black marker ghosting through a transparent or very light paint application could be distracting, depending on how close the audience is to the scenery, so a colored marker might be preferred. Various colors of markers are used for some kinds of detail painting, such as making the seam lines in a plank floor or for graphic line drawing. Art markers are available in a wide range of colors, including earth tones, warm and cools grays, and subtle tints and shades to meet most needs.

Markers also come in many sizes and with a variety of tip sizes, depending on the brand. Standard chisel-tipped felt markers are frequently stocked in scenic paint shops. Felt-tip markers have a case filled with felt that is saturated with ink. The tip is an extension of that filling. This means that, as well as a waste of volume in the case that could be filled with ink, when the tip of the marker is worn down to the metal collar, the marker must be discarded whether it still has ink or not. Other ink markers are made to be recharged. Rechargeable markers have a case filled with liquid ink. The marker has a cone- or chisel-shaped tip that can be can be replaced when it has worn down. In the metal collar of the marker is a valve that controls the ink flow to the tip.

Jumbo-size ink markers have a large chisel tip, about three-quarter-inch square. Jumbo markers currently are available only in bright colors and black. These markers come in handy for the occasional odd job where the line work must be exceptionally wide or pronounced and generally are not used for cartooning. Permanent laundry markers have a finer, cone-shaped tip, useful for any fine-line cartoons and scenic applications. They may also be used for writing notes on the clear protective covers of scenic elevations. It is useful to keep a few of these in stock in the shop.

Dye

Most cartoons need to ghost through the paint to some degree to be useful. Aniline dye was the standard medium used to achieve this before ink markers became available. Once the cartoon was drawn in vine charcoal, it was set with aniline dye, painted on with a small lining brush. For each job, the aniline dye was mixed to an appropriate color, depending on the local color of the final image. Today, aniline dye is still very useful for some cartooning, particularly in situations where a color other than black is desired to set the lines. Aniline dye can be thinned down to make a much fainter line, something you cannot do with a marker. Drops entirely painted in dye should have the cartoon set in an appropriate color of dye, as the solvent-based ink cartooning would show completely through a dye drop. A cartoon can be set with dye in the same manner as with markers. Do not use crystal black aniline dye to set a cartoon because it is very soluble in water and will mix into subsequent layers of paint.

Graphite

Most theatrical painting is done knowing that the audience will see it only from a distance and that the scenery is not intended to last forever. Most scenery is not needed beyond the run of a given production. If made to last any longer, it rarely is expected to be used for too many years. Ten years is a fairly long life for a piece of scenery; and even at that, it will need to be touched up and refreshed from time to time. But a scenic artist also might work in areas of the arts where longevity is an important consideration. Many techniques and materials in scenic art cross over to other areas of the visual arts, but setting a cartoon in ink or dye does not. Neither of these is suitable for long-term display, exhibition, or mural work. Dye will quickly discolor subsequent layers of paint. Ink, even if completely obscured by layers of paint, will slowly and inevitably ghost up through the top layer of paint. For these reasons, all cartooning for murals or exhibits that are to be permanently installed should be executed or set with graphite. The cartoon may be worked out in charcoal first and the lines can be set with graphite, just as they are set with ink or dye in other circumstances. A graphite block or soft pencil, 4B or even softer, can be used depending on the size of the line desired.

It is possible to seal dye or ink cartooning from showing through by covering the cartoon with a coat of shellac or solvent-based sealer in situations where an unwanted cartoon could ghost through after a long period of time. This method also is useful for covering a cartooning mistake on hard scenery. This should never be done on soft goods of any kind.

Fixative

The issue of the cartoon ghosting through paint is irrelevant when a transparent, or nearly transparent, medium is to be used to paint a piece. It would be a waste of time to set a cartoon in ink when charcoal would be perfectly visible throughout the medium. It is necessary only to fix the charcoal lines so that they do not smudge. In these cases, the charcoal is set with a *fixative*. Smaller pieces may be sprayed simply with workable fixative purchased at an art supply store. Always wear a respirator when doing this (see Chapter 4, the section "Safety and Health Regulations"). As the name implies, a fixative will fix the charcoal to the surface and will dry in a finish that does not alter the workable surface of the piece.

Large cartoons drawn on scenery that has been primed with paint may be set by spraying the cartoon with a very thin solution of either the primer, the base coat, or clear flat acrylic sealer. Cartoons drawn on drops sized with either starch or animal glue can be set by simply spraying them with water. The water melts starch or glue size, which is absorbed by the charcoal lines. When the drop is dry, the line will be permanently set in the size. If the drop is to be painted with aniline dye, the first few sprays of local color will accomplish the same thing. If the cartoon has been set into the size with water or dye, the line may still be inadvertently scrubbed off if overworked with wet brush techniques.

Before setting the charcoal lines, either with ink or fixative, always check the cartoon carefully to make sure the lines are correct. Inking over the lines to set them also is a way to check each line individually for accuracy. Mistakes are easy to miss when the whole cartoon is sprayed over. Also, when fixing the lines with hot water or a fixative, clean up the charcoal lines so that the correct lines are very clear and any incorrect lines are flogged or blown off as cleanly as possible.

Mechanical Drawing Tools

Most scenic artists have been trained to draft either traditionally by hand or using Computer-Aided Design software (CAD). Scenic designers draft set designs either on the drafting board or on a CAD program, or both. When the line work design is transferred to the scenery in the shop, or when patterns for profiles of the scenery are created, the process is very similar to that of the designer but on a larger scale. Where the designer created the line work with a T-square, pencil, and templates in scale, the scenic artist will produce the full-size line work with snap lines, charcoal, and line sticks. Both processes involve drafting skills; scenic artists just get to work with bigger tools.

Snap Lines

When cartooning a large area, the first lines that need to be drawn are the base, or reference, lines. A *snap line* is used to make these long straight lines from point to point. A snap line is a length of string coated with powdered charcoal, chalk, or pounce powder. It is held firmly at the two points at either end of the line to be drawn and pulled taut. When the line is pulled up and released, it snaps back into place leaving a perfectly straight line.

Snap lines may be as simple as a piece of cotton string coated along its length with a stick of charcoal or chalk to "chalk" it. The string is stored wrapped around a stick when not in use to keep it from getting tangled. Commercial snap lines spool the line up into a case filled with powder. These are convenient to use because they recharge the chalk line every time they are wound or unwound. Doubled-geared snap lines that reel in twice as fast are very handy. The lines in commercial snap lines can be replaced if they get frayed, knotted, or if the color of chalk needs to be changed.

Snap lines commonly are called *chalk lines* because carpenters load them with various colors of powdered chalk. This chalk is not used in scenic painting because it leaves a permanent mark. Often, snapped lines on drops or scenery are used as guides for locating the cartoon lines on a drop; these guidelines will need to be cleaned off later. So the snap lines in a paint shop are filled with either pounce powder or powdered charcoal. Talcum powder or white pounce powder works well for snapping lines on dark surfaces. Pounce powder can be purchased from sign painting supply stores or ordered through sign painting supply catalogues. Available in black or white, they are very economical and clean off surfaces easily. Powdered charcoal was the standard filler for snap lines until the advent of pounce powder. The main drawback to powdered charcoal is its expense. Store pounce powder or powdered charcoal in a plastic squeeze condiment bottle for refilling the snap line case.

It may not be possible for one person to hold each end of the snap line when laying in vertical lines while working on a frame. Tie the head of a safety pin to the end of the snap line so the pin can be inserted at the top of the drop, then raise the drop or lower the bridge to snap the line from the bottom. The snap line case doubles as a plumb bob (it will hang from the string at a perfect vertical) so it will be necessary to place the verticals only at the top of the drop. Gravity will accurately extend the line to the bottom. One person, using several snap lines, can set several verticals each time the drop or bridge is raised and lowered. Safety pins on the end of a snap line make it possible for one person to snap lines alone while working down.

> One drawback to commercial snap lines is that they generate a lot of unwanted powder as they unreel. The powder can make a mess of a drop stapled to a deck. Snap lines should be unreeled away from the edge of the drop and carried to where they are needed.

A *snap bow* is made for one person to snap lines alone (see Figure 8.5). It is a length of lumber, square aluminum, or conduit with a large corner block at each end. The snap line is stretched between them. The snap bow can be as lengthy as can be handled comfortably. Because they are easy to make, a snap bow can be assembled for a specific project. The line of the snap bow can be chalked by rubbing it with charcoal of chalk.

Lining Sticks and Straight Edges

Lining sticks are guides for drawing or painting straight lines (see Figure 8.6). Lining sticks can be short or very long, used in painting up or down. They are made of wood that has been beveled on the bottom edges. This bevel keeps the bottom edge of the lining stick from coming in contact with a paintbrush. This way, paint will not be drawn under the lining stick and blemish the surface. Lining sticks for use on a vertical surface should be made out of lightweight materials. Oak, poplar, and birch trim molding works very well because some profiles already have a bevel and these trims tend not to be warped as often as one-inch stock lumber. Finding straight

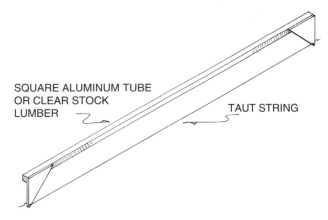

SQUARE ALUMINUM TUBE
OR CLEAR STOCK
LUMBER

TAUT STRING

Figure 8.5   A snap bow.

Often lining sticks can be made for specific projects as needed.

Lining sticks used on the deck or horizontal surfaces must have handles that extend up to the standing painter's grasp. The handle, placed in the center for balance, is just a block of wood or a drawer handle placed away from the edge so as not to be in the way. The base of the handle needs to be reinforced with angle braces where it is attached to the lining stick. Some scenic artists prefer the handle to be bolted to a joint in the base so it can fold up for easy transport. These extended lining sticks should be able to stand up on their own because they are a real nuisance if they are forever falling over. Lining sticks for floor use can be quite long because the painter need not have a hold of the handle while drawing the tool along the edge.

lumber for lining sticks out of one-inch stock can be a challenge. Buying a better grade of lumber for building lining sticks will help.

The shop should be equipped with lining sticks for use on the deck and the frame. A lining stick for use on the frame or vertical surfaces can be a maximum of six feet long; if it were longer, it would be beyond the painter's reach. Shorter lining sticks are useful to have on hand for tighter work. Most shops have lining sticks in a variety of lengths, from six-foot sticks for tight work on up to 16-foot sticks. Eight to 10-foot-long lining sticks are very useful, and many shops have a fair amount of these.

Lining sticks should be constructed out of the lightest weight materials as possible. A full day's work with a lining stick can become arduous if the tool is several pounds heavier than it needs to be. Lining sticks should be stored in a manner that will not cause them to warp, usually flat on the floor or hanging in racks carefully constructed to be absolutely level and to support their weight every few feet or so. Never store lining sticks by leaning one end against the wall.

The top of lining sticks can be notched with inch and foot increments so that they can double as measuring devices. It is very convenient when working up

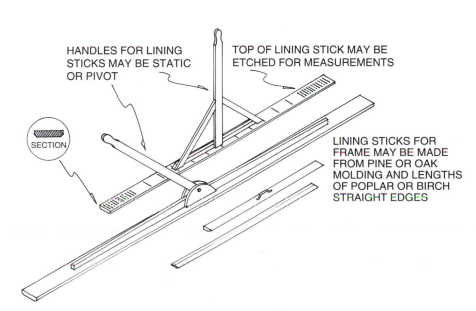

HANDLES FOR LINING
STICKS MAY BE STATIC
OR PIVOT

TOP OF LINING STICK MAY BE
ETCHED FOR MEASUREMENTS

SECTION

LINING STICKS FOR
FRAME MAY BE MADE
FROM PINE OR OAK
MOLDING AND LENGTHS
OF POPLAR OR BIRCH
STRAIGHT EDGES

Figure 8.6
Lining sticks for the floor and
the frame.

not to have to bend over and reposition the tape measure for every adjustment. Some shops have a lining stick that has been fitted with very small castors on one edge so when the tool is tilted back on its wheels, it can be rolled to the next position. This tool is very useful for jobs involving hundreds of parallel lines, such as drawing or painting the seams between boards to create the appearance of a hardwood or wood-slat floor.

Splines

Splines are guides for drawing or painting curved lines. A spline is a piece of flexible thin wood or plastic bent to meet points of a curve. Splines bend smoothly and conform to almost any shape. With a few points plotted and the help of two people, long irregular curves can be drawn quite easily. The spline also may be used as a guide for inking or painting a circle that has been drafted with a compass.

A shop usually will have splines of various lengths and flexibility. A 10- to 20-foot-long spline is handy to have around. Good wood splines must be free of knots to bend evenly. Once found or made, these splines should be stored carefully, like any good tool. Shorter, more flexible splines can be made from one-eighth-inch-thick Masonite® or Upson® board. Metal rulers and curves for very tight work are sold at sign painting, drafting, and art supply stores and come in very handy as well. Other materials work well for splining. Long sections of plastic molding and rubber hose may all be used to draw curves. On the paint frame, the lines that curve downward, such as the curve of a window valence, can be drawn by using a chain or a rope secured at either end of the curve with safety pins. A small-link chain works very well because it hangs in a smooth curve; rope often tends to have kinks in it. A chain can be used if working on the floor to lay out and adjust any variety of curved line. When the scenic artist is satisfied with the positioning of the chain, a line can be gently traced along it.

It may take some practice to learn how to hold a spline so the curve it describes is natural looking. By holding the spline only at the ends and adjusting the pressure, the spline will shift into a curve that will intersect the points that have been drafted for the curve. When several points have been drafted to delineate a curve, some of them will be slightly off. Adjust the spline so that it hits as many of these points as possible. Forcing the spline to hit every point will warp the curved line.

Compasses

A scenic artist needs a drafting *compass* for drawing and geometric analysis of an elevation. For actually cartooning circles or arcs on scenery, the painter will need an oversized compass. Some sign painting and art supply stores may carry oversized wooden compasses made for blackboards. These are useful but usually too small for scenic painting. Homemade wooden compasses are a good solution. A compass can be made easily with two pieces of one-inch by two-inch stock lumber and a wing bolt. Leave a round profile at the top of the lumber so there is enough surface area for tightening the wing bolt. The compass can be as tall as is comfortable to work with; two to three feet tall is a useful height. One leg of the compass should end in a nail, the other leg should be cut off one foot shorter and have a short length of narrow bamboo inserted into a hole drilled in the end. The end of the bamboo will be split and have a rubber band grip for charcoal, a pencil, a brush, or a laundry marker for different applications. Alternatively, the end of a scenic lining brush can be inserted into the hole of the short leg of the compass.

String

To draft any size circle, all you need is string, a nail, and something to mark with. Pound the nail into the compass point of a circle and pull a string taut to the length of the radius. Tie a slipknot in the string to mark the radius in case the line slips. You also may tighten the slip knot over your marking tool and extension so you can stand while drafting the circle. The problem with using string is that it tends to stretch as it is pulled, so as the circle is completed, the lines might not meet up. If your circle is 20 feet in diameter and you have a discrepancy of two inches in the length of the radius, this may not be enough to be perceived on stage once the lines where the difference has occurred have been smoothed over. Some cords and string stretch more than others. Nylon stretches less than cotton string or cord.

String also is used as a guide for plotting points when working with linear perspective. By putting a nail in the center of a geometric form or on the vanishing point of a perspective cartoon, the string can be used as a guide for extending a line from one point through another.

Walking a line is a technique of cartooning a straight line using a string. Walking a line is not a very efficient way to draw a straight line, but it can be useful in some situations or when working alone. To walk a line, attach one end of a clean string at the endpoint with a nail or hook it with a safety pin and pull the other end of the string past the far point. Holding the excess string behind you, line it up on the point and pull it tight. Put your foot on the string to hold it in place. Begin marking a line lightly on the side of the string, being careful not to move it. Work on the same side of the string so the marked line does not jump side to side. Slowly walk forward as if on a tight rope, being careful not to disturb the position of the string and keeping it tight while marking the line in front of you.

Trammel Points and Bar Compasses

Trammel points are used for drafting large circles accurately. Trammel points are a pair of small clamps mounted to any rigid bar, the trammel bar. If the trammel bar needs to be very long, then two pieces of wood can be clamped or screwed together. The clamps hold pencil-thin rods of steel that end in sharp points; these are the trammel points. The point can be taken out of one of the clamps and replaced with a pencil. The trammel point can be set and actually hammered into the compass point. As the trammel pivots, the pencil marks the circumference. If the circle is very large, it usually is necessary for one person to hold down the compass point while another person walks the pencil around the circumference. If the trammel points are clamped to a lining stick with an extended handle, then, after a little getting use to, one person can draft circles on his or her own.

Bar compasses work in the same way as trammel points only on a smaller scale. Bar compasses are used primarily for drafting.

Triangles and Templates

Any paint shop should have a selection of drafting templates for intricate projects, such as patterning and signage. During cartooning and layout, there will be call for larger triangles. The shop also needs assorted sizes of standard 45° and 30° drafting triangles at least 18 inches long. Large circle and oval templates with assorted sizes on them and a variety of sizes and styles of lettering templates also are useful in the paint shop. Large 45° and 30° triangles and circle templates, suited to the scale of scenic painting, can be drafted out of Masonite or lauan. Very large triangles can be framed out of lumber or steel.

TRANSFERRING A CARTOON OR REPEATING PATTERN

Often, scenic artists choose not to cartoon directly onto the scenery first but to cartoon a pounce and transfer the image. There are a whole host of valid reasons for transferring the cartoon to the scenery from a prepared pounce, template, or stencil, but these almost always involve saving time and increasing accuracy. In many circumstances, the most straightforward approach to cartooning may involve patterning. It would be foolhardy to accurately cartoon dozens of identical copies of an intricate wall sconce design without a pattern to trace. In situations where the time available to actually paint a drop is limited because of availability of space, the entire cartoon may be completed on a pounce so that more time can be dedicated to painting.

In some instances, there is an expectation that additional copies of a drop may be needed for the touring company of a production or for a backdrop rental inventory, so the cartoon is done on a pounce to save time on the next copy. Many designs are symmetrical. A perfectly symmetrical design can be made by drawing half the design on a pounce or transfer screen. Then the mirror image can be traced or pounced. Entire drops can be cartooned in this manner. This is called *reverse and repeat*. The layout of almost all lettering is best prepared on a drafting table, off the scenery, where the scenic artist can work in more controlled conditions with a T-square and triangles.

No matter how simple it is to draw on muslin, it is far easier to work complex images on paper with pencils or charcoal. Almost any cartoon can be transferred, and several simple ways to do this are described here. The cartoon transfer, usually using a pounce, also guarantees the scenic artist more control over the cartooning. A pounce, stencils, and templates are normally generated away from concerns of priming and stretching the soft goods.

Using a Pounce

The pounce is a centuries-old means of transferring an image and is still one of the most common methods. Fresco painters in the past worked by cartooning an entire fresco on paper first. Because a fresco must be painted onto a wet plaster base, there is a limited amount of time to work on it. The overall painting would be divided into small sections that could be painted completely in a day's work. A paper pounce covered with that segment of the cartoon was hung in front of the section of freshly applied plaster. The image was transferred either by rubbing over perforations in the lines drawn on the paper with a bag of powdered charcoal or by tapping indentations through the paper into the plaster along the lines. When the pounce was taken down, an impression of the lines remained on the plaster as dotted lines or as indentations. Then, the day's painting would commence.

Today, in the theatre, a very similar approach is used. A paper pounce is not jabbed with sticks, but it is perforated with a spiked wheel so that all the lines are traced by a series of little holes. A powdered medium is dusted across and through the perforations, leaving behind a fine dotted line pattern of the cartoon on the surface to be painted (see Figure 8.7).

Then these dotted lines are usually traced over with charcoal or set in ink.

The cartoon for a pounce usually is drawn on butcher or kraft paper. The cartoon is marked with ink and given registration marks for positioning the pounce on the scenery. The perforations are done with a tool called a *pounce wheel*. This is a little wheel manufactured with various length spikes held in a metal or wooden handle. Several types of pounce wheels are available. The larger wheels, one-half-inch diameter and up, work the best for scenic painting. Select a pounce wheel that has sharp long spikes, as smaller spikes will over-perforate and tear kraft or butcher paper. Small pounce wheels are designed for much finer patterning work. The cartooned paper needs to be pounced on a surface that gives a little bit, such as a piece of velour or Homasote®.

Figure 8.7 Paper pounce, pounce wheel, and pounce bag.

This allows the spikes of the pounce wheel to sink through the paper. After the paper has been perforated, the back of it should be lightly sanded with medium-fine sandpaper to open the perforations on the back of the pounce.

Once positioned on the scenery, the pounce may need to be taped, tacked, or pinned at the corners so that it does not shift while being dusted. The powdered medium used to dust a pounce can be anything that is fine enough to drop though the perforations. Pounce powder, the very thing recommended earlier to use in snap lines, works very well. Powdered charcoal works very well also, but it is expensive. To pounce on dark backgrounds, white pounce powder is available, or you can use talcum powder. The blue chalk in chalk lines is usable for pouncing, as is powdered pigment, but both leave permanent marks.

Pounce powder is put in what is called a *pounce bag*. This is a bag made from several layers of cheesecloth, gauze, muslin, or flannel, holding the pounce powder, charcoal, or chalk. The pounce bag may also be filled with cotton balls to help the powdered medium come through the mesh of the bag evenly. The powder evenly sifts through the layers of gauze as the bag is lightly pounced and rubbed across the perforations.

Pouncing works somewhat better when done flat rather than up, because gravity works for you. In either case, before the pounce is removed, a corner of it should be lifted, keeping the rest in place, to make certain that the cartoon can be seen easily. If not, replace the corner and go over the cartoon again with the pounce bag.

If the pounce is being used for a reverse and repeat, it should be moved away from the scenery and thoroughly swept and flogged off before flipping it over to pounce the reverse image. It may be useful to keep a dust mop in the shop that is only used for the final sweep across reverse and repeat pounces.

When doing a fair amount of work with large pounces, wear a dust mask as pounce powder and charcoal are very fine and can take a while to settle out of the air. When finished with a pounce of a particular cartoon, roll it up, label it, and store it away at least until the show is out of the shop. Pounces are easy to store, and once in a while, there is cause to need that cartoon again because of an added piece of scenery or paint treatment, loss of the cartoon lines, or damage to the scenic unit. Generally it is a good idea to save all pounce patterns as long as there is space to store them. Years later that egg and dart or arabesque pattern may prove to be useful again. Shops that work on Broadway productions never throw any pounce away so if an addition copy of a drop is needed or a damaged drop must be replaced, the pounces can be pulled back out.

Pounces also can be made out of visquene or clear vinyl plastic sheet. These pounces are more difficult to make and work with, but they are useful for some applications because they are transparent and waterproof.

Positioning a pounce can be a problem sometimes, particularly if the image must work together with other elements. At times, it would be a great benefit if you could see through the pounce to position it or to trace an image already there. Another occasion when plastic pounces are useful is when working up on the frame. Because the fabric of a drop gives in places where no framework is behind it, getting the pounce powder or charcoal to penetrate the perforations can be difficult.

The image from a plastic pounce using pounce powder is not as crisp as that from a paper pounce. A visquene or clear vinyl pounce can be lightly sponged over with a thin solution of dye, however. Thin black aniline dye works well, and it is one of the most forgiving colors of dye. Black aniline dye is water-soluble so it will not stop up the holes in the pounce. It can also be washed off more easily than other colors of dye if a mistake is made. The dye should be only as dark as is necessary to see it. Do not use paint for this, because if the pounce needs to be reused in the future, the paint will have dried up and blocked the perforations. Use a cellulose sponge to apply the dye. Wring most of the dye out of the sponge, then press it along the perforations. It may take a while to get the knack of this technique.

To make a plastic pounce, draw the image on paper, set it with ink, and label it with the necessary registration marks, as usual. Then smooth out and tape the plastic over the drawing and trace the cartoon with an ink marker. Just as with a paper pounce, the plastic will need to be perforated on a surface that gives a little. Because the plastic tends to stretch rather than puncture, a firmer backing surface such as Homasote works best. The back of the plastic pounce also must be sanded carefully to smooth the perforations.

The Transfer Screen

Another method of repeating a pattern is with a *transfer screen*. This is a screen made from linen scrim stretched tightly over a frame that has no interior braces. Once the repeating image is drawn on the scenery, the screen is laid over it and the cartoon is traced onto the screen with vine charcoal. Then the screen is laid down in its new position and the cartoon is traced once again with vine charcoal applied with a heavy hand. When the screen is taken away, a charcoal impression will be left on the scenery. The transfer screen works well enough for repeating an image maybe half a dozen times, by which time the original image has become obscured and the screen very messy. This is not a highly accurate tool. If the design needing to be transferred is very intricate, use a pounce. The screen will need to be blown off with an air nozzle for its next use. The expression "quick and dirty" is apropos for the transfer screen, but it is useful for some situations, particularly when working on a paint frame where paper pounces can be problematic.

Templates, Stencils, and Stamps

A *template* works well for a simple repetitious pattern or outlines such as finials or balusters. Templates can be cut out of any stiff board such as bristol board or Upson board, or they can be cut from sheet stock. Also, the same stencils and stamps used in painting may serve as a cartooning tool. These might be helpful in quickly applying a cartoon of a pattern in a contrasting or altered color of the base.

Early in the building of a production, the technical director should confer with the charge painter about pieces of scenery that have profiles so that the scenic artist can have the final decision on the shape of any contours. Often, the scenic artist is responsible for drawing all contours because, ultimately, the scenic artist will have to match the paint treatment to the constructed contour. Often, the paint elevation contains information crucial for the contour. What appears as a simple curve in the construction drawing may be a critical shape within the painted image as well. The scenic artist should inspect the paint elevations as well as the construction drawings to locate areas where discrepancies may occur. The scenic artist also may need to generate pounces and templates for the carpenters.

PREPARING SCENERY FOR CARTOONING

Preparation for cartooning starts with a thorough reading of the information supplied by the scenic designer. A scenic artist can expect a complete set of draftings for the production to supplement the paint elevations. Once you have assembled the information needed to execute a cartoon, layout the scenery so it is in a logical order to itself and establish that it is properly aligned. With these steps completed, the actual work of cartooning can begin.

Preparing the Design Information

The scenic designer supplies the scenic artist with a full set of ground plans and drafted front elevations of the entire design to complement the set of paint elevations. The ground plans tell the scenic artist how all the units relate to one another on stage. It is certainly worth knowing that intricate marble paneling is downstage in full view, as opposed to half-hidden behind a window. From this information, the scenic artist can set priorities in the painting schedule.

A scenic designer usually provides three types of information or some combination of these three that are specific to the painting and cartooning information: the paint elevation, a cartoon, and a model (refer to Chapter 2 for a full description of the scenic designer's information and how to interpret it). These are in addition to the drafted front elevations, which may hint at paint information or even function as the guide for the cartoon. The drafted front elevations essentially are construction drawings and may not contain all the information required for cartooning. The front elevation of a typical drop can be as simple as an empty rectangle or contain a line drawing of the painted image in scale. Many scenic designers like to do a separate cartoon for the line work of the drop.

Make certain that you have an elevation of all the scenery to be painted. Look carefully at the ground plan and count the units and cross-reference them to the elevations.

Paint Elevations

The color elevations should match, in dimension, the scenic designer's front elevations. In fact, in some instances, the designer will cut the front elevations right from a set of bluelines and laminate them to an

Figure 8.8   A cartoon for *Guys and Dolls*, designed by Peter Beudert, University of Arizona.

illustration board for painting color elevations. The paint elevations are the most important guide to painting and cartooning the scenery. Often, copies of the color elevation—and cartoons, if provided—are made so that several people can work with them simultaneously. Color copies frequently differ in color from the original. For this reason, color always should be mixed only from the original paint elevation.

As soon as the paint elevations arrive at the shop and the copies have been made, they should all be given a protective cover of clear vinyl or acetate. This protective cover should be sealed on all edges to prevent spilled paint from seeping under the edge of the protective covering and damaging the paint elevation. The elevation, in spite of being a working guide, is an original work of art and should be returned to the designer in good condition. If notes

Figure 8.9   The paint elevation based on the cartoon in Figure 8.8 for *Guys and Dolls*, designed by Peter Beudert, University of Arizona.

need to be made on the elevation, they should be written on the protective covering or on tape or notepaper taped to the cover.

Additional drawing may need to be done on the protective cover of the elevation for cartooning. A centerline or a grid may have to be applied for reference during cartooning. China markers, laundry markers, acetate markers, and ballpoint pens all work well for making notations on vinyl or acetate. If a lot of reference line work needs to be laid out on the paint elevation, a separate black- and -white copy should be made to work off of during cartooning. If you are superimposing a grid, centerline, or layout of any kind over an elevation on a black-and -white copy, use a pen or marker of a color that will stand out to avoid confusion. Make sure that all copies of the elevation used by painters involved in the project have identical notations and layout on them.

The Scenic Model

Instead of paint elevations, the scenic designer may provide a color model. Each piece of the model is used as a guide for the scenic painting on specific units of scenery. This means that the scenic artists may need to disassemble the model. Ideally, the designer has engineered his or her model with this practicality in mind. These model pieces still need to be treated as works of art and carefully wrapped with a protective layer of cellophane or kept in a vinyl pocket or freezer bag. If possible, make color copies of separate model pieces. Models are often rather delicate, and in spite of the care given them, constant handling may damage them. After the production, the charge painter should see to it that the model is repaired as necessary and returned to the designer.

> One other aspect of the scenic staff relying on a model as the color elevation is that, as mentioned before, the model is very useful to the director and performers. When the set is being painted, the scenic art staff must have primary possession of the model to do its work. Before removing the model from the paint shop for any period of time, the stage management staff must clear it with the charge painter.

Preparing Hard Scenery for Cartooning

Hard scenery should be laid out so that similar paint processes are done at the same time. All flats and pieces that relate to one another in any given scene should be laid down together, all the backing flats for one off-stage room together, and so on. This helps speed up cartooning and painting and maintains stylistic continuity. A paint technique done by one person on a flat on a Monday may look very different from the flat it plays next to if that flat was painted by someone working on the other side of the shop on the following Friday.

When the flats or units of hard scenery are laid out, the charge painter or lead painter should check through the front elevations and the floor plan carefully to make sure he or she has a clear understanding of how the units are assembled. The scenery should have all hardware, reveals, and trim either installed or easily accessible so they do not need further painting later and so the separate elements of a single unit are painted together. Most carpenters are not painters; most painters are not carpenters; both may have needs and limitations that must be discussed. The more complex the set, the more crucial is this communication. Issues may need to be addressed when the scenery goes from the construction shop to the paint shop. Scenery may need to be made more accessible, stiffeners removed, a paint scaffold assembled, and so forth. If a hard scenic unit is large, an important question will be, "Where is it safe to walk and stand?" This question should be asked before the cartooning commences.

In terms of cartooning hard scenery, the contour of the scenery itself serves as a frame of reference for the cartooning. The top, bottom, and sides can be used as baseline references in the cartoon. Often, horizontal lines of painted molding extend across a group of walls or an entire box set. The alignment of those lines is crucial. Care must be taken to assure that the lines correlate from one flat to the next. One way to assure continuity in cartooning is always to measure up from the bottom of the flat. That way, any discrepancy in the height of the flat will not affect the cartooning.

If the measurements of the horizontals are complex, draw the lines on one flat, double-check measurements for accuracy, then lay a piece of lumber along that edge and transfer all the measurements to it. Use this piece of wood as a measurement template for all the other flats sharing those lines (see Figure 8.10).

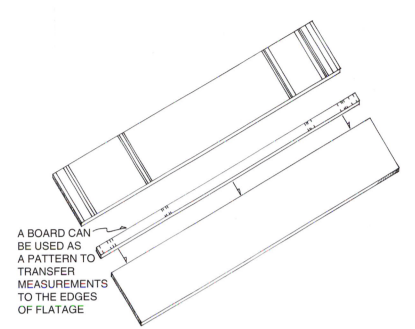

A BOARD CAN
BE USED AS
A PATTERN TO
TRANSFER
MEASUREMENTS
TO THE EDGES
OF FLATAGE

Figure 8.10
Transferring a continuing horizontal wall pattern.

If there is not enough room to lay out all the flattage that has these measurements in common, save the measurement template for later use. Be aware of any flats that are placed on platforms but that have horizontal measurements in common with flats that sit directly on the stage deck. If complex verticals progress across a series of flats, such as wallpaper stripes, butt the flats together to make measurements for these verticals, then pull them apart to make room to walk between them.

Frequently, the painting area available is not large enough to accommodate all the related units. The technical director and the charge painter must then decide what is to be laid out in what order. A box set may have to be painted in two groups, stage right and stage left, depending on the constraints of the shop space. After the first group of units is done, a unit adjacent to the next related group of flats should be retained for reference while the next group is being cartooned and painted.

Imposing a ruled design on irregular three-dimensional scenery can be a challenge. Making a pounce that covers the surface area of a curved plane or a section of that surface area to be cartooned with a repeating design can be an approach to any plane that is curved in one direction only. The pounce can be cartooned, inked, and perforated while flat, then laid on the contour of the surface so the line work can be transferred to the scenery.

If the scenery is contoured in two directions and there is a fair amount or cartooning on it, it can be approached in a couple of ways. First, if it is possible by using flexible rules and tape measures, the cartoon can be gridded out and cartooned directly on the scenery. Or, it may be feasible to project the image to be cartooned on the scenery and transfer the image if the scenery can be moved into a position where it is convenient to work with a projection. We'll discuss using a projector to cartoon scenery later in this chapter.

Preparing Soft Goods for Cartooning

Cartooning soft goods requires first that specific and accurate reference lines are drawn onto them. No point can be accurately placed without horizontal and vertical baselines to guide the cartooning. All lines cartooned on the drop in one way or another will have been plotted from these two baselines. The two most common baselines that are used as a frame of reference for cartooning are the vertical centerline and the horizontal bottom edge of the drop. These baselines correspond to the centerline and bottom edge of the image on the paint elevation. Once the baselines have been established, be very careful about using any other vertical or horizontal lines, such as the top or sides of the drop, to locate points.

It is not uncommon for soft goods to be built taller or wider than the designer had specified. Sometimes a technical director will decide that a drop will be built a foot or so taller than indicated to avoid a masking problem. Frequently the sizes of the constructed soft goods are just off by a few inches or so because of the properties of unsized muslin. This is why it is important to use the centerline and the bottom of the drop as the baselines for cartooning. Regardless of any discrepancies between the size of the actual soft goods and the size of the image, by using these two baselines, the scenic artist will ensure that the image will relate to the centerline of the stage and the stage deck as the designer intended.

Figure 8.12   Flip drop being taped after cartooning for *Hairspray*. Scenic Art Studios, New York.

A difference of even half an inch can skew a grid or cause mistakes in measurements. In other words, when establishing reference lines or locating major verticals and horizontals, always measure up from the bottom and out from the center.

When a piece of soft goods is properly stretched and primed (see Chapter 7), the top of the drop will be stapled in a straight line. If the bottom of the drop is a finished edge, it will be stapled in a straight line parallel to the top. If the sides are finished edges, they will be stapled to straight lines perpendicular to the top and bottom. Not all soft good pieces are conveniently rectangular. The sides and the bottom of a piece of soft goods may not be straight, parallel, perpendicular, or correspond to the baselines of the paint elevation because the piece has unfinished sides

Figure 8.13   A scenic artist spraying the flip drop for *Hairspray*. Scenic Art Studios, New York.

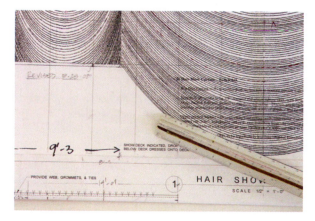

Figure 8.11   A section of the cartoon drawn by the scenic designer for *Hairspray*. Scenic Art Studios, New York.

Figure 8.14   The hair drop for *Hairspray* with highlight and shadow. Scenic Art Studios, New York.

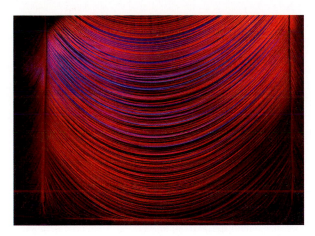

Figure 8.15 The hair drop for *Hairspray* under stage light. Scenic Art Studios, New York.

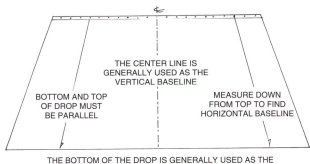

THE CENTER LINE IS GENERALLY USED AS THE VERTICAL BASELINE

BOTTOM AND TOP OF DROP MUST BE PARALLEL

MEASURE DOWN FROM TOP TO FIND HORIZONTAL BASELINE

THE BOTTOM OF THE DROP IS GENERALLY USED AS THE HORIZONTAL BASELINE

Figure 8.16 Finding a horizontal baseline on a drop.

and bottom. Drops often are finished after they have been painted. Also, pieces of soft goods may not fly in to the stage floor or may not span the centerline of the stage, yet vertical and horizontal baselines still need to be established for cartooning. These horizontal and vertical baselines must be parallel to the deck and the centerline of the stage. All you need to locate the baseline of a piece of soft goods is one straight line. The baselines usually are measured or found with a geometric equation (described in the next section) from the top edge of the drop.

When cartooning a drop, the horizontal baseline is usually the bottom of the drop, which, when it plays on stage, rests on the stage floor. If the bottom of the drop is stapled in a straight line parallel to the top, you have already found the horizontal baseline. If the bottom of the drop is uneven or unfinished, you will need to find the baseline by measuring down from the top of the drop to establish the actual height of the finished goods (see Figure 8.16). Scale the height of the drop off the elevation. If the height of an unfinished drop exceeds that which is specified on the elevation by several feet or so, put in a call to the technical director to ask if the height of the drop has been changed. If the bottom of the soft goods is an uneven contour—for example, a foliage border—the top of the drop may be used as a horizontal baseline.

The vertical baseline may be the centerline of the drop—the centerline of the image on a tab, for instance, or the offstage edge of the soft goods as

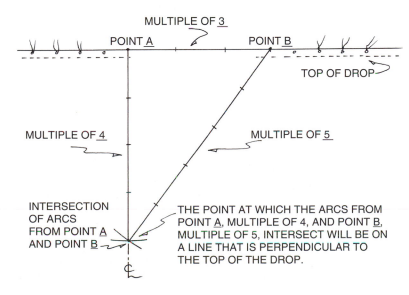

MULTIPLE OF 3

POINT A   POINT B

TOP OF DROP

MULTIPLE OF 4   MULTIPLE OF 5

INTERSECTION OF ARCS FROM POINT A AND POINT B

THE POINT AT WHICH THE ARCS FROM POINT A, MULTIPLE OF 4, AND POINT B, MULTIPLE OF 5, INTERSECT WILL BE ON A LINE THAT IS PERPENDICULAR TO THE TOP OF THE DROP.

Figure 8.17
Pythagorean Theorem.
Three steps to creating a vertical baseline perpendicular to the horizontal: (1) strike an arc from A to find points B and C; (2) strike arcs that intersect from B and C; (3) connect the intersection of these arcs to point A to find the perpendicular.

may be the case when cartooning legs. To find a line perpendicular to the horizontal baseline, first locate the intersection of the vertical and horizontal baselines, often this is the center of the drop. If the piece is very small, a framing square or triangle can be used to find a perpendicular line. If working on a paint frame, just use the snap line as a plumb bob for finding a perpendicular centerline.

Two Methods for Finding a Perpendicular Line

If working on the floor, use trammel points and a piece of stock lumber as a trammel bar (you may also use a measuring tape if someone will hold the end of it for you), to do the following (see Figure 8.17):

1. Measure the width of the drop at either the top or the bottom to find the center. This will be point A.
2. Strike an arc from point A equal distance on either side of the center point.
3. Strike a larger arc from each of the new points B and C. These arcs must cross at a perpendicular point below point A.
4. Snap a line between the intersection of the arcs and point A extending as far as needed. This is the vertical baseline.

The *Pythagorean Theorem* also is very useful in establishing either baseline perpendicular to the other, and may be used to square a large area.

The theorem states that the sum of the squares of the lengths of the two sides of a right triangle are equal to the square of the length of the hypotenuse. If you can measure the length of the horizontal baseline of a drop (either top or bottom) and the length of the vertical base line (the center line), this formula can be applied to determine whether they are perpendicular to one another. Measure the length of the vertical baseline (AB) and one-half the horizontal baseline (BC). If they are perpendicular, the length of (AC) squared will equal the sum of the squares of AB and BC: $(AB)^2 + (BC)^2 = (AC)^2$.

An even simpler means of expressing the Pythagorean Theorem is the three, four, five method. That is, A3, B4, C5 also will plot a right triangle. To use this method to find the centerline on a drop, find the center point at the top of the drop. Measure down 18 feet (3-foot × 6-foot) from the center point and draw an arc that crosses the area where you think the centerline will be. Measure 24 feet (4-foot × 6-foot) over from the same center point. From the point on the drop that is 24 feet over from the center, measure 30 feet (5-foot × 6-foot) over to the center of the drop and strike a second arc that intersects the first. Snap a line from the center point at the top of the drop through the intersection of the two arcs. This is your centerline. Someone may assist you with this or you can use nails driven into your points at the top of the drop to strike the arcs. For smaller drops, multiply the numbers 3, 4, and 5 by a smaller factor. If you used a factor of 4 feet, your measurements would be 12 feet, 15 feet, and 20 feet.

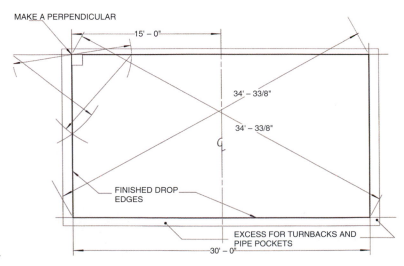

Figure 8.18
Using diagonals to verify that a drop is square.

If you are working in a shop that has a square paint deck and the drop is laid out square to the deck, the baselines can be located by measuring in from the edge of the deck. Make absolutely certain that the deck is square. Do not assume this is the case if you are working in an unfamiliar shop.

Measuring the Drop

Now that you have horizontal and vertical baselines, you can find the dimensions on the sides of the drop, if needed. The finished dimensions of the drop need to be marked on the back of the webbing when the drop is pulled up. The change in the size of the drop should not change how the elevation is scaled out unless the scenic designer specifies a change. It may be that there is simply a few extra inches of sky at the top of the drop, or a few less. It may mean that the scenic artist will need to improvise some tree limbs or architectural detail if the drop is too wide. If there are major discrepancies between the size of the drop and the elevation, the technical director and the scenic designer should be consulted.

The side edges of the drop are found by measuring half the width of the finished dimensions of the drop from either side of the centerline, at the top, and at the bottom of the drop. If the bottom edge is unfinished, measure these points on the horizontal baseline. Make sure to leave enough extra fabric for a turnback or pipe pocket, if needed. To make certain that the drop contour is square, measure the inside dimensions diagonally from corner to corner. If these measurements are the same, the drop is square. Once the outside dimensions are done, you are ready to cartoon the drop.

DRAWING THE CARTOON

Artists and writers often say that the blank canvas, or page, is the greatest challenge. Where do I start? For the scenic artist that same challenge comes in a very large form. A cartoon on a paint elevation is the line work that is used as a guide for painting it. A cartoon on a drop is the full-scale version of the same image. When a scenic artist is transferring a cartoon to a drop, he or she is also enlarging that image. The scenic artist has many avenues of approach to the cartoon,

and with experience he or she will become more confident in selecting the most appropriate method.

An architectural layout is much like large-scale drafting and will render a crisp, highly accurate copy of almost any image, but this clearly is best suited for structural designs. Linear perspective used in combination with architectural layout generates the two-dimensional image of the contours of planes projecting into three-dimensional space. A grid transfer may be better for organic forms. Mechanical devices like an overhead, slide, power point, or opaque projector are useful for certain types of cartoon layout. The knowledge of geometry will aid you in any type of layout.

Do not forget to keep a thorough record of all reference lines on the elevation. In cartooning, this means recording all superimposed reference lines or marks on the protective covering of the paint elevation. When using a grid, the grid must become part of the elevation the scenic artist uses.

Architectural Layout

An *architectural layout* is a very direct approach to cartooning an image. This works best with images having a lot of straight structural and geometric line work that can be plotted off the horizontal and

Figure 8.19 An example of a drop with architectural complexity. Twin City Scenic Collection (courtesy of the Performing Arts Archives, University of Minnesota Libraries, St. Paul, Minnesota).

Figure 8.20
A sliding scenic unit for *Oliver!* that relies considerably on an accurate architectural layout. Scenic Art Studios, New York.

vertical baselines. Essentially, it is the same process as drafting the image on paper, only in a larger scale. Instead of a T-square and triangle, your tools are a measuring tape and snap line. Horizontal and vertical lines can be scaled off and referenced to the baselines on the elevation and transferred full scale to the scenery. An angled baseline also can be drawn to serve as a major reference point if the drawing is at an angle.

The horizontal baseline should correspond to the bottom of the elevation. If working on a paneled wall, for example, plot all major horizontals, such as chair rails and cornices, from the baseline. The same is true for plotting vertical lines, such as doorframes and the sides of buildings, working from the vertical baseline. Once these primary vertical and horizontal lines have been marked on the drop with a snap line, the drop is effectively sectioned into smaller areas in which details can be refined. Odd-shaped elements, such as wall sconces, arabesques, or picture frames, can be placed and drawn in relationship to these major vertical and horizontal lines.

Using a Grid for Cartooning

Cartooning with a grid involves creating a frame a reference over an image as an alternative to the architectural layout. This method of cartooning is very useful for organic shapes and sketchy or abstract images that are more easily approached when broken down into small units.

A grid is a network of squares evenly laid over the elevation that corresponds to a full-scale grid on the drop. There is no standard grid size; it is based on personal preference and the complexity of the image. When first working with a grid, one is inclined to use a grid small enough to ensure absolute accuracy, like one foot square. Rarely is a one-foot grid necessary; a four-foot grid usually is adequate. If you have to keep track of your place and fill in all the grid

Figure 8.21 Example of architectural layout.

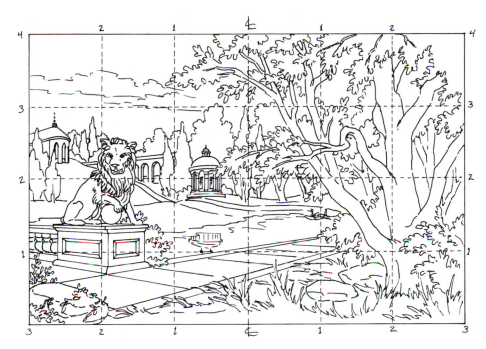

Figure 8.22
Grid layout.

squares of a one-foot grid, it will take you much longer to transfer a design than with a four-foot grid.

A four-foot grid is an excellent size. Most forms easily can be proportioned and transferred in this grid. If a section of the image is more complex, the grid can be subdivided, so tighter detail can be transferred easily. A small piece of clear vinyl subdivided into a scaled two-foot grid can be taped to the edge of the paint elevation and, when needed, placed in position over the scaled four-foot grid to serve as a guide for more precise detail. If you generally use grids of either four feet or two feet, you will develop a pattern of eye-hand coordination that naturally fits into that size. You can adjust easily enough into a three-foot or five-foot grid, but there may be fits and starts where you just cannot seem to get the proportions right.

The grid lines should be labeled. It is easy to lose track of your place when working on a full-stage drop. Avoid labeling the grid line with some fancy Able-One, Baker-Two labeling system. It is better to label the grid lines with their actual dimensions; 4 foot, 8 foot, 12 foot, and so on. These numbered dimensions should correspond to the dimensions labeled on the grid laid over the paint elevation. This also will help you keep track of where you are in distances. The centerline is labeled CL just as it is on the elevation, which makes it reference dimension zero. The vertical grid lines are labeled out from the centerline, according to distance. The horizontal baseline also is zero. Adjust dimensions accordingly for whatever grid size is used. Label the grid dimensions clearly all the way around the drop and up the centerline. Do the same on the elevation.

Once corresponding grids are marked on the drop and the elevation, the image can be transferred. If you are unaccustomed to working with a grid, it may take a little time to get the hang of it. It may be wise to begin with the sections on the side of the drop until you are comfortable. Begin by analyzing each grid square separately from the one adjacent to it. To train yourself to do this, cut a hole in a small piece of bristol board the same size as a grid square on the elevation and tape it over one grid square at a time. Be careful with this first square; make sure that you are beginning with the correct corresponding square on the drop. Even seasoned scenic artists sometimes carelessly start drawing on the wrong square and have to start over when they realize that the drawing is off by a square.

Start by making marks along the edge of the grid square of the drop where the lines of the image intersect with the grid lines. Look for proportions. Does this image line intersect with the grid line about one half of the way up from the bottom? Two-thirds? Then lightly fill in the lines of the grid, always being mindful of these proportions. Move to the next

Figure 8.23
Atmospheric perspective.

square and repeat the process. Once the image begins to take shape across several grid squares, analyze it for nuances and accuracy. Once you are satisfied that the image is accurate, you may want to darken the lines that are most correct and erase the lines that are inaccurate. It will not be long before you are doing this process automatically and are barely aware of the grid because you are more focused on the image.

Perspective

Scenic designers rely on perspective to create depth in two-dimensional and three-dimensional scenic compositions. Scenic artists need to understand the rules of perspective to fully translate the designer's work.

Atmospheric Perspective

Atmospheric perspective is based on the observation that objects seen at a distance are affected by the atmospheric haze and the eye's reduced ability to perceive detail. Far-away objects usually appear lighter, less colorful, and less detailed. Scenic designers manipulate atmospheric perspective in backdrops, and it is not uncommon to be asked to make some part of a drop look "farther away." This normally is done in the painting process, but it can be important in the cartooning. The amount of detail of the cartoon should be adjusted so that far away forms are less detailed. However, resist the impulse to discount

images in the background. Just because these images are hazy and the paint strokes that were used to create them are more gestural than precise does not mean that the scenic artist does not need to have a firm concept of what that dollop of paint is meant to depict. Is it a house or a tree? Remember that quarter-inch tall smudge of paint on the elevation will be six inches tall on the drop. The paint strokes that are used to create these images may still be gestural, but a gesture of what?

Figure 8.24   Example of atmospheric perspective. Twin City Scenic Collection, sketch by John Z. Woods (courtesy of the Performing Arts Archives, University of Minnesota Libraries, St. Paul, Minnesota).

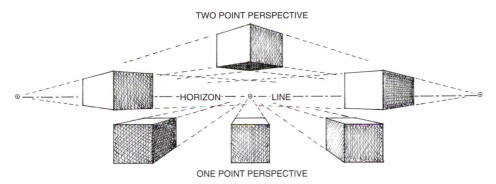

TWO POINT PERSPECTIVE

HORIZON — LINE

ONE POINT PERSPECTIVE

Figure 8.25
Linear perspective.

Linear Perspective

The concept of atmospheric perspective and the observance that, in comparison to nearer forms, the size of objects and forms diminish at a distance was not lost on the medieval artist. What was missing, until Renaissance Italy, was a convincing method of methodically plotting in a drawing the effect of objects and shapes receding, both in distance and size. This method, called *linear perspective*, has been refined and used to great effect by artists throughout the world. Linear perspective has been an integral part of scenic design and scenic painting since the Renaissance changed the expectations of form and content in the visual arts.

In cartooning scenery, linear perspective, along with the grid method and architectural layout, provides a useful way to reproduce and enlarge a line drawing. In many ways, linear perspective is the most accurate method of plotting lines because it replicates the manner in which a perspective drawing is created.

The Principles of Linear Perspective

Linear perspective creates an illusion of depth in cases where the image represented spans about 60° or less of the field of the viewer's vision, which corresponds approximately to the field of clear sight of the human eye. Beyond this, one has to rotate one's head to view a larger expanse, which changes the point of view. Believable perspective depends on a stationary point of view.

Linear perspective is predicated on the perception that straight lines of vertical and horizontal planes converge to a single point on the horizon. If you continued the lines of the side of a square plane from the forward edge to the distant edge and beyond, these lines would meet at the vanishing point.

This vanishing point is the place in the distance where objects have receded to a size so infinitesimal the human eye is no longer able to distinguish forms.

Linear perspective does not take into account the curvature of the earth. A nuance of the vistas we see in reality is that planes in the distance subtly curve away from us, like the observation that Columbus reportedly made of ships on the ocean. Only very rarely are we aware of this slight curve, as forms in the foreground, the atmosphere, or the terrain occlude this subtle occurrence from us.

The Method of Perspective

Gaining a working knowledge of the application of linear perspective is a skill that every scenic artist must have. You can interpret and reproduce a linear perspective drawing only if you understand it. Once you have a working knowledge of linear perspective you will find that it all fits together and has a logic governing it.

The *picture plane* represents a stationary point of view, which generally relates to a human viewer based on an average height of 5'6" and a 60° range of human sight. From this stationary point of view, there is a fixed horizon, which is a straight line across the picture plane at the height of the viewer's line of sight. This line is always referred to as the *horizon line*. In theatre, the scenic device of linear perspective is most frequently used in a proscenium theatre and the picture plane is usually the scenic vista we see as framed by the proscenium. All objects appear to recede uniformly in size until they disappear into the distance at this horizon line. As objects recede into the distance, the distance between these objects

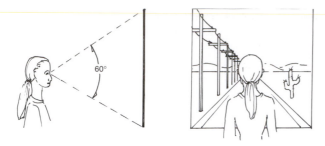

Figure 8.26 The picture plane.

appears to recede as well. In a theatre, the height of a person's line of sight may depend of the viewpoint of the average audience member as well as the rake of the auditorium seats and the height and rake of the stage. The illusion of perspective may not work as well for a person seated in the balcony as it does for the person seated in the center of the orchestra.

The Vanishing Point The edges of planes parallel to the picture plane do not converge to a point, but remain parallel to the picture plane. All lines

perpendicular to the picture plane appear to converge on the same point on the horizon line at the centerline of the picture plane. This is called the *vanishing point*. If these converging lines are the top and bottom edges of square planes that are perpendicular to the picture plane, then the lines on the front and back edges of the square planes will remain parallel to each other and the picture plane. So, two of the edges of all square planes that are perpendicular to the picture plane will appear to converge on the same point on the horizon line. This is called *one-point perspective*.

All square horizontal or vertical planes not parallel or perpendicular to the picture plane have two edges whose lines converge on the horizon line, while the other two edges remain parallel to each other. This may result in two-point perspective or multiple vanishing points.

All parallel lines that are not vertical, horizontal, perpendicular, or parallel to the picture plane converge at some distant point, called an *oblique perspective point*, or sometimes called the *uphill* or *downhill perspective point*. If the top and bottom edges of a square oblique plane are horizontal, they converge on a point on the horizon line. These oblique

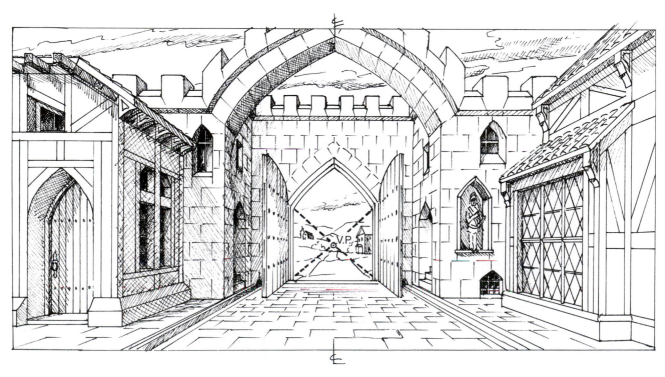

Figure 8.27 One-point perspective.

Figure 8.28 One-point perspective is evident in this street scene. Twin City Scenic Collection (courtesy of the Performing Arts Archives, University of Minnesota Libraries, St. Paul, Minnesota).

plane appear as perfect ellipses, unless seen on edge, in which case they are appear as straight lines. All sections of a sphere not parallel to the picture plane also appear as perfect ellipses. All perpendicular sections of a perfectly round cylinder appear as perfect ellipses. The spatial relationship of ellipses foreshortens, but the perfect shape of the ellipse remains. An ellipse can be plotted into a square plane that is drawn in perspective. By doing this you can determine how much you should foreshorten the ellipse.

Drawing the bottom of a round column sitting on a square base is a circumstance where you might need to do this. If you are drawing a tall urn with several segments, you may need to plot an ellipse into a square plane for each segment—at the top, the bottom, and in between. These plotted ellipses should be drawn on a central axis.

vanishing points can be used directly for oblique planes such as roofs or as guides for inclined planes such as steps and staircases.

Spheres and Circles All spheres in perspective appear as perfect circles that diminish in size as they recede in space. All circles not parallel to the picture

Foreshortening An object or form drawn as compressed in length because it tilts away from the viewer is called a *foreshortened form*. To plot foreshortening, first draw the form straight on with no attempt to fit it into perspective. Next, impose a grid over the form or draw in lines of reference.

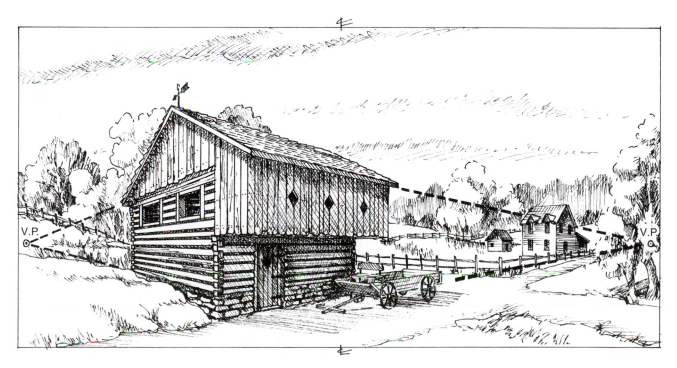

Figure 8.29 Two-point perspective.

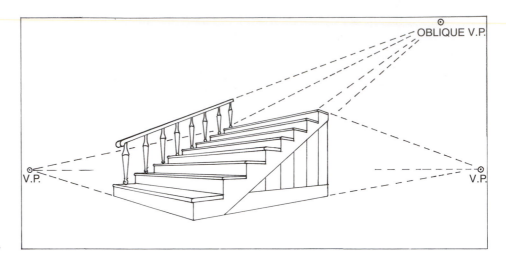

Figure 8.30
Oblique perspective.

Then, plot the grid into the linear perspective drawing, boxing it out for the depth of the form, and redraw the form in this shape.

Drop-Point Perspective   As a guide to working out more complex forms, an elevation or ground plan view of that form, in full scale, can be set on the side or the bottom of the picture plane. Then, the lines of the form are carried straight up or over to the edge of the picture plane. This drop-point perspective also can be used to plot the height and proportions of a form through varying depths in the picture plane. From the bottom or the side, the proportions of the form can be projected back to the vanishing point, and at the point where guidelines reach the position

of the object or form in the depth of field, its proper proportions will be established in the picture plane.

Finding Depth   To find depths for any series of equidistant forms made up of squared planes, section the plane that has been drawn in perspective corner to corner with diagonals. The center of the square plane as it appears in perspective will be where the diagonals cross. Draw a vertical or horizontal at that point. Draw diagonals again in these subdivided planes to find their centers.

Another method of achieving the same end, which gives you control over the width of the receding depths, is to project a center line through the plane, drawn in perspective, back to the vanishing point. Place the first two verticals at the distance that looks

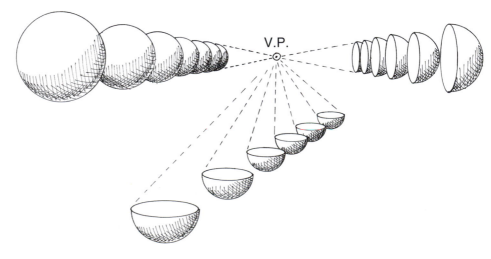

Figure 8.31
Circles in perspective.

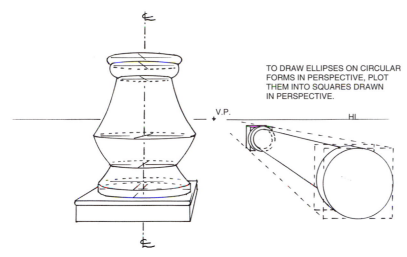

TO DRAW ELLIPSES ON CIRCULAR
FORMS IN PERSPECTIVE, PLOT
THEM INTO SQUARES DRAWN
IN PERSPECTIVE.

Figure 8.32
Segmented column and cartoon of
an urn plotted on a central axis.

proportionally correct, then draw a diagonal from the top corner of the first vertical through the center of the next vertical and on down to the bottom of the plane. At that point on the bottom of the plane, draw in the third vertical. From the top of second vertical repeat the process. The verticals will then become evenly spaced posts, columns, or evenly divided squared planes that appear to recede into the distance.

The distance between forms that are receding in two-point perspective may be drawn by dropping points down to the baseline. First plot the points of

the front edges of the columns if they were sitting on the baseline. Then project lines from these points to the vanishing point. This is the same principle as that used in drop-point perspective. Next, across these guidelines, plot a guideline at the base of the columns to the second vanishing point. Where these guidelines intersect will establish the position of the front vertical edges of the columns in the picture plane.

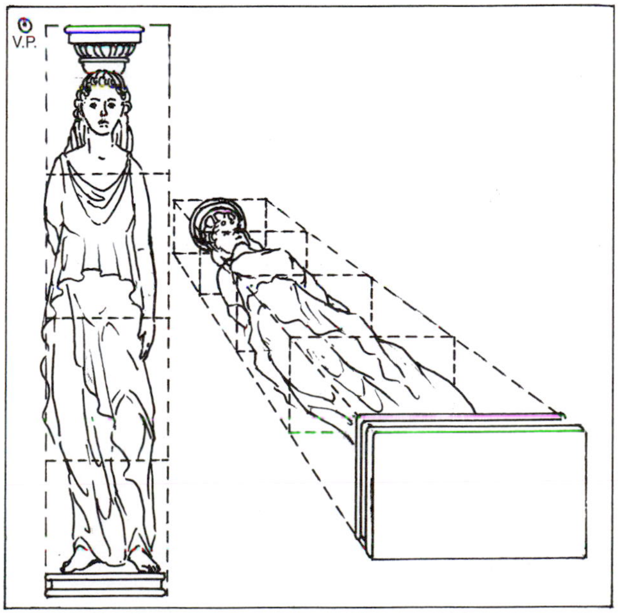

Perspective for Artists by Rex Vicat Cole is a text that every scenic artist who works with linear perspective should have in their possession, or better yet in their kit. When a question arises, you can check Rex.

Figure 8.33   Foreshortening.

Perspective for the Stage

Linear perspective works very well in a flat picture. However, if you enlarge this picture, put it in a box, and have people walk back and forth in front of it, the illusion could fall flat when the people wander into areas of the picture plane where the receding forms make them look like giants. Part of the challenge of manipulating perspective on stage belongs to the director, who may have to avoid blocking performers in areas where they appear out of proportion to the scenery. But the designer, along with the skill of the scenic artist, must create an illusion on stage by subtly manipulating design and painting so that the vista and the performers merge gracefully.

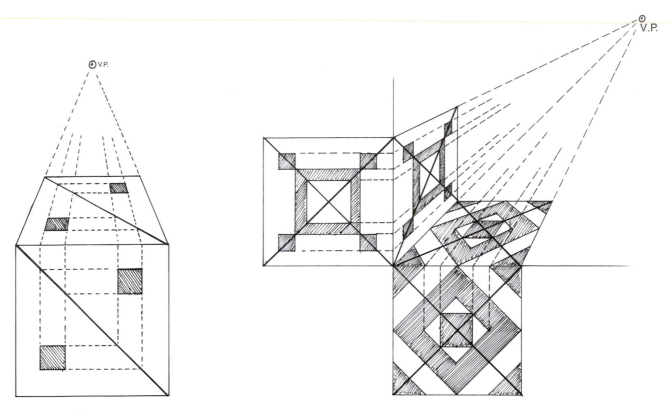

Figure 8.34 Drop-point perspective.

One of the realities of the stage is that any two-dimensional image is in a three-dimensional volume, not a flat picture plane. The lines of an image as it comes into the foreground may be cut off by the floor. All lines and planes can be related to the perspective point, save the stage floor and platforms, which may need to remain level for safety and believability. Generally in stage design, the most obvious perspective technique is reserved for the background, and these images of depth are merged carefully with the elements in the foreground. All elements in the acting area of a stage need to be carefully designed in regards to human proportion.

When creating an interior using perspective, one method of keeping the image believable in relationship to human scale is to keep all elements that are close to the ground, such as baseboards, wainscoting, and pillar bases, at a constant height and begin the linear perspective at about four feet above the deck. This also avoids the quandary of painting a section of floor, which suddenly appears to tilt up onto a vertical plane. That way, whatever piece of scenery the performer approaches will appear natural. The design of the stage scenery cannot be disassociated from the performers unless the point of the design is to place the performers in a meta-theatrical environment.

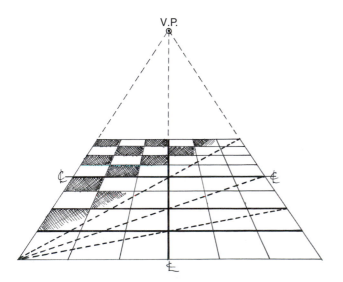

Figure 8.35 Finding depth, first method.

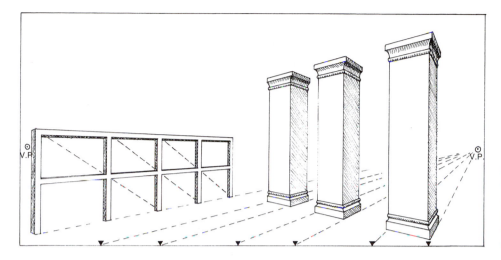

Figure 8.36
Finding depths by drafting diagonals through the center points of receding parallels and by dropping points down to the baseline.

The Raked Stage and Traditional Wing and Drop Perspective

The traditional use of perspective on stage is an arrangement of wings, drops, and borders on a raked stage, creating a perspective box. This approach to the stage picture now is antique, but for a span of two centuries, it was the most constant of approaches to stage design and occasionally is revived. (Refer to Chapter 12 for a discussion of perspective stage design.) In this genre, the methods of perspective are used to their utmost potential, no longer relegated to the backdrop and singular elements. Every component on stage relates to the horizon line and the vanishing point. In this case, the raked stage deck—in addition to all the vertical elements—becomes a consideration in the application of linear perspective.

The basic format of the design remains standard from production to production, although additional elements may be added. The stage picture is set with a vanishing point that, in some theatre houses,

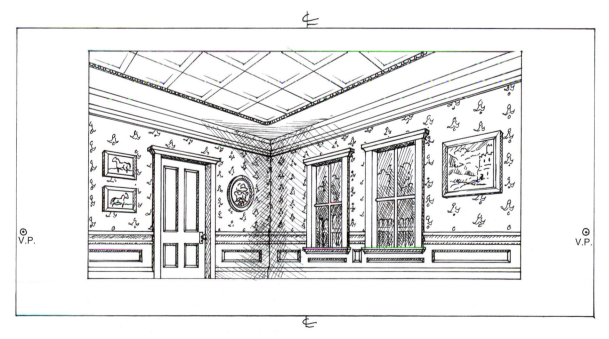

Figure 8.37   Perspective for the stage, demonstrating the use of parallel lines below the horizon line.

related directly to the center balcony box, where the most prestigious members of the audience would sit. The rake of the stage and the position of the wings lined up with this vanishing point. When these set pieces were cartooned and painted by being plotted off of this vanishing point and horizon line, the illusion was very convincing. Staging performers on these designs was necessarily shallow, for as soon as someone moved too far upstage, the effect unraveled.

Contemporary scenic artists may encounter projects designed in this way, where every piece of scenery on stage must relate back to a very specific vanishing point and horizon line. In a project like this, although the scale of the image should relate to human scale, there is less concern about manipulating the image so that it works with the human performers because the designer has the additional agenda of creating a seamless illusion of depth.

Methods of Doing Linear Perspective in the Shop

The tools and approach to doing linear perspective full scale on theatre sets are the same as the tools for cartooning. Straight edges are needed for plotting out the vanishing points and the horizon line. Once again, the same lines of reference will need to be marked out on the scenery. It helps to mark the vanishing points with nails so that a string can be attached to them or they can be used as a swivel point with the edge of a line stick. Mark the nail with ribbon or construction tape so it is easy to find and avoid stepping on. When plotting lines back to their vanishing points, it is practical to use straight edges, but there are limits. When the lines are beyond the 16-foot length of the longest lining stick or when two or three people are trying to plot lines on a drop, a lining stick will get in the way.

A length of clean string or cord attached to the nails at the vanishing points can be used to plot lines from point to point. A design may have several vanishing points. The strings should have a loop on the end so they can be moved from point to point easily or removed so that you do not end up with a web of strings on the scenery. If you are working on hard scenery and the vanishing point is off the scenery, the nail may need to be driven into a section of 2″ × 4″ that is weighted down so that it will not slide around. This way, the string or cord will not snag as easily on the edge of the scenery.

Be careful not to let hard scenery shift once you have established a vanishing point. Do not overdo using the string or cord as a guide to walk the lines. The string is flexible, no matter how tightly it is pulled, and lines using the string as a guide are apt to be warped. Use the string to plot the points of the line that extend to the vanishing point; then use a lining stick or snap line to actually draw these lines.

Perspective itself works as a method of enlarging an image to full scale by plotting the point where lines originate and extending them to their terminus. You need to know only at what measurement the line stops; relating it to the vanishing point will plot it in the right place. As in an architectural layout, start with the major lines and define the primary planes, then locate and define the elements and keep working into ever-tighter detail. If, at first, the primary parallel lines are laid in—these are frequently verticals—it will be easy to locate the points on these lines from which perspective lines need to be plotted and to know just where they must end. Cartooning a full-stage drop completely in perspective can be rather intimidating at first, but if it is broken down into specific elements, it can be approached step by step. Frequently, elements drawn in perspective are combined with compositions that primarily are in an architectural or grid layout.

> Remember that, in perspective, many of the lines are interdependent. A line that is out of place may throw off many other lines throughout that section of the drawing. Be aware that if lines are not meeting as they should, it might be time to take an objective look at the image and search for an oversight.

It is not always simple to plot large-perspective drawings in a scene shop. One of the first things an art teacher will tell you about drawing in perspective is that you should have plenty of room around the page for plotting out the horizon line and vanishing points. In the scene shop, it is not uncommon for a drop to be wedged between a post and the wall. There may be no room to plot vanishing points unless they were placed in the parking lot next door. Many designers, when they choose to use perspective in their designs, bear in mind the limitations of the shop space. If the shop has an expansive 150-foot-long paint deck, the designer will take advantage of it;

but if the shop has barely enough room to accommodate the drop itself, the designer may keep the vanishing points within the confines of the drop.

When arranging scenery or stretching a drop that has an image on it in perspective, the charge painter should plot out the vanishing points beforehand on paper. Depending on the placement of the horizon line and vanishing points, it might be necessary to arrange the scenery so enough space is left in one direction or another to plot vanishing points. Obviously, this should be considered before and not after the scenery is in position.

In spite of thoughtful shop arrangement, a scenic artist may need to plot perspective where there is not enough room to do so. In some cases, a vanishing point cannot be plotted out because there was no way to avoid a post or wall. In other cases, the design was not plotted out with linear perspective, but an agreement with the designer has decided that the application of perspective will clean up the lines of the design. The dilemma is how to do the perspective when there is not enough room. Often, there will be room enough for some vanishing points but not all. First, try to get around the problem. If plotting a point is only a matter of moving it in on the horizon a foot or two, get the scenic designer's approval. That would be the easiest solution. You cannot move the point above or below the horizon line because that would distort the design.

Another way to get around the problem is a pounce. Cartoon the drop or part of the drop in a space where there is enough room to plot the points. After the cartoon is done on paper, it can be transferred to the scenery. A full-stage drop-size pounce may be the best solution for this logistical problem, or you may need the pounce to do only part of the image. If only one side of an image is dependent on a vanishing point you cannot reach, the major lines and forms on that side can be cartooned on a pounce. After it has been transferred to the drop, the other side can be cartooned to merge into it.

Also, in many cases, one-point perspective is used for a symmetrical image, which can be done as a reverse and repeat. The pounce should be used as a time saver because exactly half of the image can be cartooned, then the pounce can be flipped over to do the other half.

Frequently, scenic artists encounter designs that look like they have been drawn in perspective, but actually they are not. Sometimes the designer is purposely "breaking the rules" for aesthetic reasons.

In these circumstances it is very important for the scenic artist to understand the rules of linear perspective even if the mechanics of perspective are not being applied to that design. Understanding how structural elements relate to one another and are perceived in three-dimensional space will result in better drawing technique, even if that means knowing how best to break the rules.

Perspective Problem Solving

If all else fails, you may have to rely on your educated knowledge of how these forms will behave in spatial depth. First, work on the copy or line drawing of the elevation to make sure the line work is very clear and easy to measure. The line drawing also should be examined to eliminate any mistakes that, once blown up to full scale, will look odd. When drawing perspective on a drop, the points are scaled out off lines of reference and then plotted back to the vanishing point. As lines are drawn in this manner, they must be double-checked against the elevation to make sure they end about where they were expected to.

Frequently, there will be some differences that are subtle on the elevation but amount to several inches in full scale. Also proportions of some elements, such as doors, windows, and other architectural details, can appear to be perfectly natural when on the scale of the elevation but at odds with other

---

Rectangular planes plotted in perspective are always trapezoid shaped. When you cannot use a vanishing point, there is a very simple trick for plotting horizontals that appear to recede proportionally within a plane. First draw the contour of the trapezoid plane in place on the drop. Next plot the points for these horizontals on the front edge of the plane (the longer side of the trapezoid). Transfer these measurements to a board including the measurements for the top and bottom line of the trapezoid. Finally, place the board angling into the plane on the small side of the trapezoid so the top point meets the corner and the bottom point meets the bottom line. Transfer all the measurements to the drop. When you draw the horizontal lines from the measurements at the front edge of the trapezoid through the points that angle through the interior of the plane to its far edge, they will recede in depth proportionally.

elements when transferred to full scale. These are the kinds of incongruities that scenic artists will encounter and work out in linear perspective. So, when you are denied working the image out in perceptive in full scale, make sure to go over the elevation or line drawing carefully. Draw in lines of reference that you can transfer to the drop. These lines of reference may be the top, lower, and middle lines of the plane that you cannot plot off the vanishing point. You may impose a vertical scale on the side of the drop, from which your lines—should they continue past this scale—would meet up more or less at the vanishing point. You can sight along the length of your line stick using this scale as a guide. A grid may be very useful, as long as the elevation that you are working from is correct.

The final tool you will have to rely on if working without access to a vanishing point is your own innate sense of what looks natural. This is a sense that will develop over the years you spend drawing and observing.

Using Projectors for Cartooning

Projectors are useful for the direct transfer and enlarging of almost any image in cartooning. In fact, cartooning complicated images can proceed very quickly by using a projector. However, projecting an image does not mean that you can dispense with the straight edge and compass. Neither should you dispense with your own eyes or brain. The projected image is just a guide to show you where the lines should be. If the form is a drafted pattern or lettering, the projected cartoon usually needs to be carefully cleaned up with a straight edge. In some cases, the cartoon will be broad and sketchy enough that you can trace the lines straight away with a marker as you are projecting the image. In rare cases, a scenic artist can use the projection itself as a cartoon and paint directly onto canvas with only the projection as a guide.

Four projectors are commonly used in cartooning: opaque, slide, video, and transparency. Only opaque projectors are capable of projecting directly from a traditional elevation or drawing. These are versatile and convenient, as any source, even books, can be projected from an opaque projector. The slide, video, and transparency projectors require that the elevation or image be scanned or copied to film or to an acetate transparency first.

The opaque projector is the bulkiest and least bright of the three types. It also generates heat, which could endanger the elevation. Slide projectors have many advantages. They are quite bright, a broad selection of lenses is available, they have superior optics, and they are very compact. Slide projectors require that any projected material be photographed in advance and made into a slide. Theatrical slide projectors, which often use large 4″ × 5″ transparencies, are even brighter and better than the typical 35-mm carousel projector. These large-format slides are expensive to produce.

Transparency projectors, or overheads, offer a happy medium. They are uncomplicated machines that can produce fairly large images. They require that the image be copied onto a transparent acetate sheet as close to elevation size as possible. That sort of copying is easily done with a copier onto xerographic acetate. 35-mm slides are too small for the overhead projectors. Overhead projectors work particularly well for projecting simple line drawings, where shade and color are not present.

Video projection units provide good optics and excellent image quality. Some video projectors can also correct for keystoning (see following paragraph), saving the scenic artist a lot of trouble. Video projectors are much more expensive and fragile than slide projectors and overhead projectors which may make then inappropriate for scenic studio use. Most video projection units will require a computer or DVD player in conjunction with them to play back the image, adding more expense to the projection system.

When finally set up, projectors make cartooning easier. The preparation is considerable, however. First, almost all projectors function best in very low-light situations. Other workers may balk at having the lights out. An alternative space may be necessary. Projectors need to be isolated from vibration. Even foot traffic on some shop floors can cause a projected image to gyrate wildly. Projectors also need to be focused dead center on the drop or flat. This sometimes means that the projector must be 12 feet or more off the ground, depending on the scenery. If the projector aims up from floor level, the projected image will keystone (that is, distort abnormally as it projects away from center). What appears to be in proportion at ground level will be oversized and distended at the upper edges. Projectors must not be moved once set. It is very difficult to perfectly realign a projected image. Finally, the beam itself must be unobstructed. Even when the projector is on and aligned and the lights are out, a scenic artist standing in front of the drop to draw will discover that his or her own body blocks the light. One needs to develop a sidearm drawing technique and a good short-term memory.

Projected images will distort toward the edge of the image unless the optics of the projector and lens are of top quality. For very large images, a scenic artist may choose to work in segments of the drawing and slightly overlap one portion to the next as the work progresses. It is helpful to grid the projected elevation and the surface onto which it is projected as well. The grid helps maintain alignment and scale as the artist works.

Remember when using the projector that you are still the artist and the interpreter. Do not draw every single little line, only the ones that mean something and are applicable to the form. It is very important not to use the projector as a crutch, as more often than not, the scenery will have to be cartooned by the other methods discussed here. When studying scenic artistry, become adept at all methods of cartooning if you want to be a viable professional. A projector is a time saver, but your value as a professional will depend on your alacrity in all methods and techniques.

Using Geometry for Cartooning

The ability to draw shapes accurately using geometry is a powerful tool for a scenic artist. Large arcs, ovals, polygons, and architectural shapes frequently must be reproduced on a very large scale, and only with geometry can these things be drawn absolutely accurately. Geometric analysis of a shape may render seemingly complicated forms into a series of simple arcs and polygons, easily replicated. Very large geometric shapes can be drawn with ease with the simplest tools, a string and a straight edge, provided the proper points are located. The following are some useful formulas for creating shapes using geometry.

Constructing a Perpendicular Line

Finding a Perpendicular from a Given Point
From point C as center on a line, strike an arc of any convenient radius R1, finding points A and B. With any convenient radius R2, longer than R1, strike arcs from A and B equidistant from C, describing D. Connect C to the intersection of those arcs D. CD is perpendicular to the base AB.

The Perpendicular Bisector Start from any point on a line. Figure 8.39 shows a baseline and

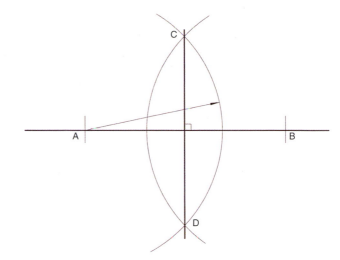

Figure 8.38 Constructing a perpendicular.

a presumed center point B. Strike two equal arcs from B to points labeled A and A'. From there, strike two more arcs longer than AB, A'B which are AC', A'C. These second arcs will intersect at a point (D), which will fall on a line perpendicular to point B.

Finding the Center of a Circle Draw any straight line across a circle, finding points A and B. Erect two perpendicular lines from A and B. The intersection of these perpendicular lines with the circle finds points C and D. Connect AD and BC with diagonals to locate E, the center of that circle.

Describing a Circle Through Any Three Points Given points A, B, and C, draw lines AB

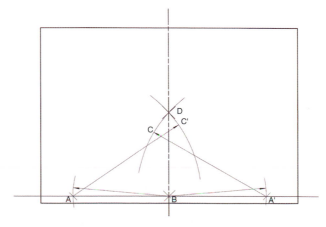

Figure 8.39 The perpendicular bisector.

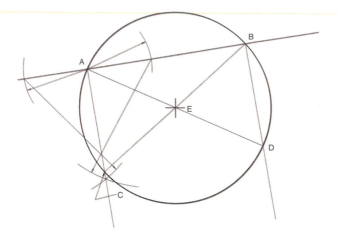

Figure 8.40   Finding the center of a circle.

and AC. Draw the perpendicular bisector for both lines at the same distance from point B. Their intersection at P is the center of the required circle.

Constructing a Hexagon: The Compass Method   Given line AB, find its center, E. Draw a circle with AE as the radius. From A and B, strike arcs through E, finding C, D, F, and G. Connect the six points around the edge of the circle to describe the hexagon.

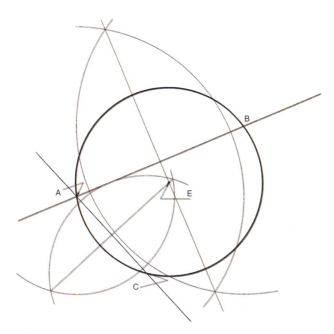

Figure 8.41   Describing a circle through any three points.

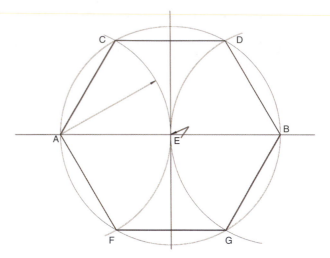

Figure 8.42   Constructing a hexagon: The compass method.

Constructing a Pentagon and Pentastar in a Circle   Draw line AC. Mark the center of AC as E and describe a circle using AE as a radius distance. Describe the perpendicular bisector of EC to find point X. Use X as the radius point of an arc from point B (arc XB) and extend that arc to the baseline AC. This finds point Y. Draw an arc from B, BY, to the edge of the circle to find point Z. This will determine length BZ, which is one leg of the pentagon. Walk line BZ around the circle to describe the pentagon fully. Use the pentagon to make a pentastar by drawing one straight line between each of the five points of the pentagon.

Drawing Accurate Architectural Shapes

Most architectural forms are based on geometric construction. The following is a guide to the creation of some of the most common architectural shapes.

Drawing an Ellipse   An ellipse, or oval, is a shape generated by a point moving around two fixed points, always maintaining a distance equal to the added distances to both points. A simple construction method illustrates this easily. This is the pin and string method. Describe line BC and the perpendicular bisector AE, note their intersection at E. Strike an arc to set the two center points of the ellipse labeled BC in the illustration. The placement of these two points must be equidistant from E. Their distance from center may be adjusted to increase of decrease

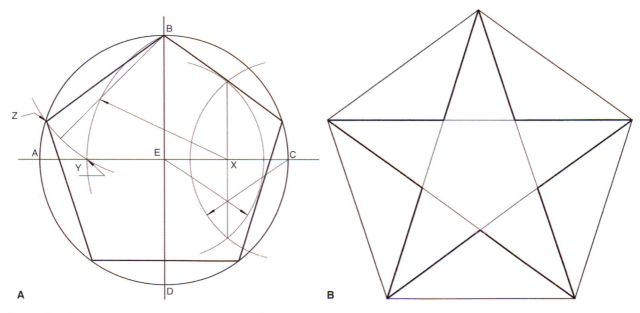

Figure 8.43 Constructing (A) a pentagon and (B) a pentastar.

the width of the oval as desired. Tie a piece of string in a loop to fit snugly around pins set in points AB and C. Carefully draw the ellipse by keeping even pressure on the string as you walk it around the circumference of the ellipse.

Plotting an Ellipse To plot an ellipse, draw the horizontal and vertical axes and mark their intersection as E. Strike an arc from E to find the radius points A and B. The length of EA is one-quarter of the major axis of the ellipse, or the center of line AE, and is found using a perpendicular bisector.

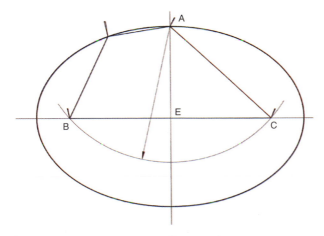

Figure 8.44 Drawing an ellipse with string.

This defines points C and C'. From them, draw an equilateral triangle downward to find point D.

The Roman Arch Draw the baseline, or spring line, through center point E. Mark AB equidistant from E. Strike a semicircle from E connecting A and B.

The Gothic or Ogive Arch Draw the baseline, or spring line, through center point E. Draw a perpendicular vertical through E to the assumed height of the arch. Mark AB equidistant from E. Strike arc AB up to the center line and repeat for BA.

The Tudor Arch Draw horizontal and vertical baselines and label the intersection. Draw a half-circle below the horizontal baseline from E, the width corresponding to the desired arch width and mark the endpoints A and B. Draw a circle from E to find points C and D. The radius is one-half AE, which can be found with a bisector. Draw an equilateral triangle from CD down and extend the legs until they intersect with the half-circle, finding points F and G. Also extend the legs upward to intersect with circles lightly drawn from C and D. This finds points H and I. Strike arcs CH and GH and repeat for the other side.

The Moorish or Horseshoe Arch Describe the horizontal and vertical baselines, label the center

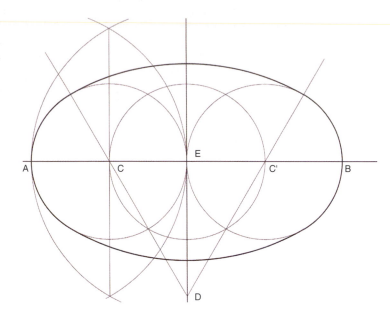

Figure 8.45
Plotting an ellipse.

point R1. Lightly draw a semicircle from the center point as a guide for finding A and B, and lightly draw vertical sidelines through them. Draw 45° guidelines upwards and out from R1 to find R2 on the vertical guidelines. Strike arcs from R1 and R2 meeting at

C and D. Draw guidelines 30° from vertical down from R2 until they touch a horizontal line that connects C and D; label those points E and F. Draw an equilateral triangle from EF and draw a horizontal guideline connecting R2. At the intersection of the triangle and line R2 are points R3. Strike an arc from them to complete the arch.

The Russian Reverse-Ogee Arch Draw horizontal and vertical baselines and label the intersection R1. Draw 45° guidelines from R1 up and strike arcs from R1 to A and B (the width of the desired arch) to meet the 45° guidelines. Label those points C and D and construct an equilateral triangle up from there. From the center of CD, draw guidelines 60° from vertical upward a good distance. Label the intersection of the triangle and the guidelines as R2. Draw arcs from there as shown in Figure 8.50, stopping at the guidelines. Transfer length CD further out on the 30° guidelines to find G, and strike the final arcs from G. Repeat on the other side.

SIGNS AND LETTERING

Lettering and proper sign painting is an art in itself. Many extremely skilled painters are lettering specialists. The craft relies on tools similar to those of the scenic artist, but the investment in good lettering brushes can be considerable. A theatrical scenic artist

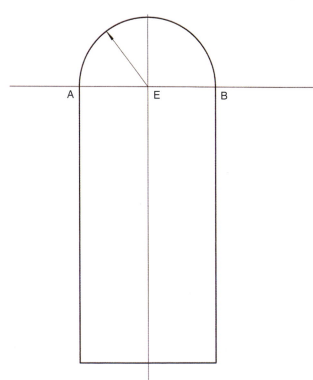

Figure 8.46   Drawing a Roman arch.

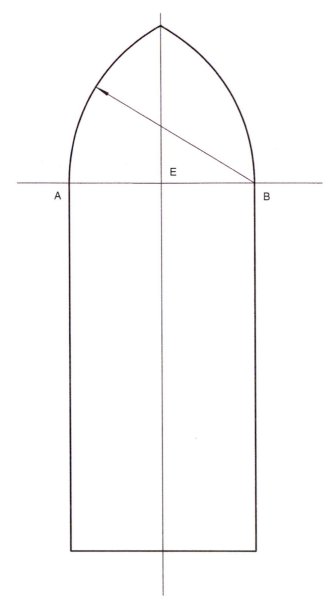

style to work with at first. The object is to learn one style completely before moving on. I encourage students to do the same thing. Once you are thoroughly acquainted with one lettering style and can do it without referring to a guide, other styles and variations will come easily.

Lettering styles for scenery are chosen by the scenic designer. Many designers include copies of the fonts they have chosen for the signage in the research pack they present to the scenic artist. Unless the signage is very large, it is much too difficult to render lettering accurately in half-inch scale. If signage on the elevation comes through to the shop with no research and its style is not evident, the charge painter should ask the designer to choose a font. Most shops keep several books on hand of lettering and font styles from which the designer can make a selection then and there. If the designer has some of the same books, this decision can be made over the phone.

Tools of Sign Painting

In the scenic arts, there are two types of painters: those who can do sign painting and those who cannot. As most scenic artists can spend a lifetime of education and study on the skills of painting alone, a great many scenic artists would not venture to say that they are sign painters as well. Also, in this day and age, a good hands-on sign painter is hard to find. Most sign work is generated on computers. The best way to learn signage is to do it. Embrace the opportunity to work on several sign painting projects until you feel comfortable with your skills.

Layout Tools

For the most part, the tools used for the layout and cartooning of signage are the same as the tools discussed earlier in this chapter: scale rulers, measuring sticks, straight edges, and triangles. At sign painting supply stores, you may be able to pick up clear plastic straight edges that have a grid printed on them. These sign painters' rulers are very useful in three ways. First, they come in a variety of widths so that they can be used for drawing the widths of the downstrokes and crossbars of larger letters. Second, their width and the grid can be used for figuring out spacing between letters and words. Third, they are very flexible and can be used for splining the tight curves of letters being cartooned.

Figure 8.47 Drawing a Gothic arch.

will be called on to do signage often so should know some basic rules of the craft.

We see signs every day in shops, on the road, in advertising—everywhere. We know no set of symbols better than the alphabet. Therefore, it is obvious when these symbols are laid out incorrectly, although we may not know why. When learning to draw and cartoon, signage should be given a lot of attention. Once the rules of signage are clear, they will make logical sense. When apprenticing sign painting, most students are encouraged to learn one font or lettering

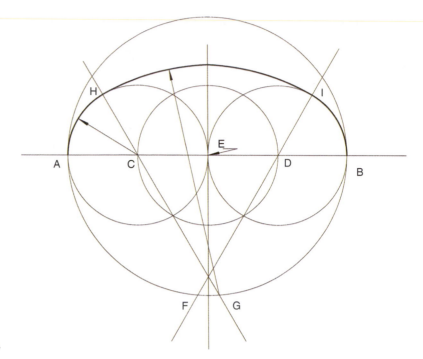

Figure 8.48
Plotting a Tudor arch.

Frequently, signage work involves drafting the cartoon of the sign first on paper. A drawing bench should be set up in the shop for complex cartooning projects like signage. A simple drawing bench can be just a 4′ × 8′ piece of AB plywood. The drawing bench should be tilted up steeply at a 60° angle or better to relieve back strain. The bottom of the bench should be about two and a half feet off the floor. This way you can work more comfortably and look at your work objectively from a distance. If space is a problem in the shop, the drawing bench can be designed to fold up against the wall. If built carefully and thoughtfully, it can be used like a drafting board. Horizontals and verticals can be set using T-squares and triangles.

If a great many signs need to be done for a given production, shop skids can be used to prop up the signs against the wall at a good working height. The shop skid is simply a five- to eight-foot piece of 2″ × 4″ stock with bolt holes drilled in it at regular intervals. The 2″ × 4″ needs a foot to stabilize the skid against a wall and keep it from falling sideways. A pair of shop skids with bolts inserted at the same height can hold a sign at a comfortable working height.

Sign Painting Brushes

When buying lettering brushes, remember what trade you are in. Chances are that any lettering you will be doing will not be seen from closer than 20 feet. Also keep in mind your own skills. The best brush in the world will not make you a terrific sign painter, it will help, but it has no brain.

When you are buying brushes, ask for brushes that are made for use in water-based mediums (refer to Chapter 5 for a full discussion of lettering brushes). If you have cause to use your lettering bushes in oil-based medium at some point, do not bother trying to revive them for use in water-based mediums again. The bristles will start to get frizzy and loose their snap. Store brushes that are used with oil-based mediums in lard oil or olive oil. Lard oil does not dry out, so it is very good for storing and conditioning oil-medium brushes. Lard oil can be purchased through sign supply catalogues and stores.

Basic Fonts of Lettering

There are hundreds of styles of letters, called *fonts*. Most of these fonts have their own drawing conventions. The primary divisions between the common styles of fonts is the distinction between block letters and script or sans serif and serif. A *serif* is a small foot placed on the ends of downstrokes and crossbars. These flourishes give the letters a more elegant appearance. Beyond these there is a huge range of specialty and trick lettering. Some fonts have been

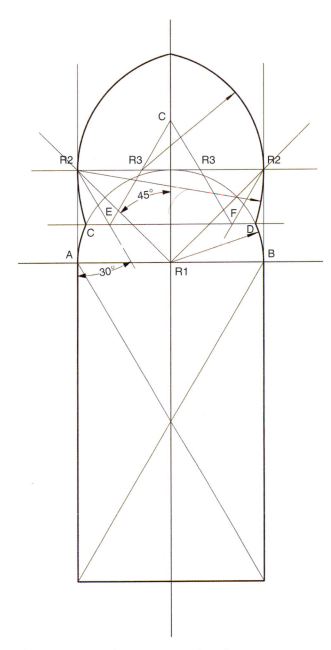

Figure 8.49   Plotting a Moorish arch.

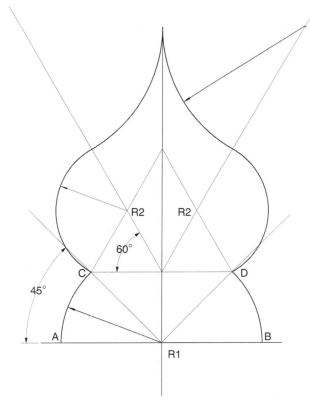

Figure 8.50   Plotting a Russian reverse-ogee arch.

designed for uppercase (capitals) and lowercase letters; some have been designed for only one or the other. The following are some simple guidelines to font styles.

Gothic Fonts

The one-stroke gothic alphabet is one of the most commonly used, straightforward lettering styles. It is a block or sans serif style. The uppercase and lowercase letters are made up of lines of equal width. Once this font is mastered it can serve as a jumping off point for all other block-style letters.

Certain practice strokes will aid you in developing prowess as a sign painter (see Figure 8.53). These are the stokes that are repeated in different combinations to create the alphabet. Do not indulge in personal variations. The purpose of learning a font is to master a style that is inseparable from professional signage work.

Roman Fonts

Building on the gothic fonts, one can move to roman fonts. In these fonts, the letters are composed of thick and thin strokes. The basis here is that, if the letters were being generated with a lettering pen, the downstrokes would create thicker lines. What started perhaps as function of the tool or brush years ago has become a convention.

Either gothic or roman fonts can be built on further by adding serifs, playing with the widths of

Figure 8-51 A drop for *Into The Woods* where good lettering is crucial. Scenic Art Studios, New York.

the letters, putting in drop shadows, or italicizing them by placing all the letters on a slant toward the right. This slant must be kept consistent throughout the italicized letters in the layout.

Script

Script lettering is as much about the way the letters connect to one another as it is about the shape of the letter itself. A fair amount of variation is allowed from one script to another. When working with a script, maintain any conventions of letter shape or connection throughout the font on that piece of signage so that the script has an overall uniform appearance. The emphasis in a script is that it have a grace throughout the sign; the letters should appear to flow together smoothly.

Rules and Techniques of Signage Layout

In signage, the lines you do not see are as important as the lines you do see. The negative space around the letters and between the words are as essential as the letters themselves. The following are some general rules of lettering that, if followed, will add a professional polish. These rules are applicable to most fonts but may vary in some styles of lettering.

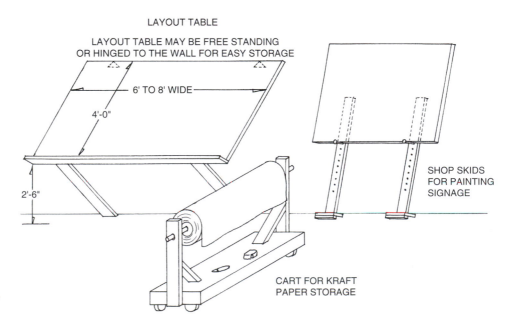

LAYOUT TABLE

LAYOUT TABLE MAY BE FREE STANDING OR HINGED TO THE WALL FOR EASY STORAGE

6' TO 8' WIDE

4'-0"

2'-6"

SHOP SKIDS FOR PAINTING SIGNAGE

CART FOR KRAFT PAPER STORAGE

Figure 8.52 A drawing bench, shop skids.

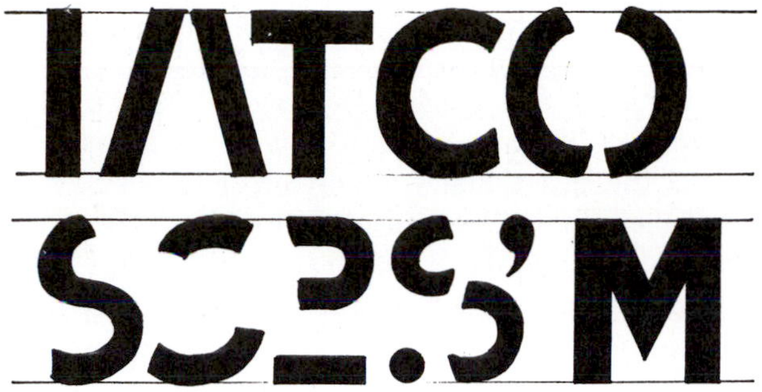

Figure 8.53 Fundamental painting strokes for lettering.

1. All letters based on circles or ovals should use the same shape circle or oval. So, if you laid a template of the letter O over a C, the contours would be nearly identical except where the C is broken.
2. All round uppercase letters O, C, Q, G, and S and lowercase letters o, a, e, c, d, b, p, q, and g should go slightly above and below the top and bottom layout lines. If these letters are taken right to the guidelines, optically they or parts of them will look smaller than the other letters. This is an optical correction and should not be exaggerated to the point where it is perceptible without applying a straightedge to bottom or top lines.
3. The bottom of the B, R, and the S should be slightly larger or wider then the top so that the letters look grounded. Once again, this should not be exaggerated to the point where it is noticeable; it is an optical correction.
4. The crossbar on the uppercase A should be lower than the center layout or middle bar lines of the other letters. If the crossbar of the A is too high, the letter will appear to be top heavy. The crossbar should not be dropped down too far, or the letter will appear to droop.
5. All letters, and in particular the square letters H, N, M, Z, and X, should be boxed in when laid out so that the letters do not lean.
6. The letters W and the M need about one and a half times the width of other letters. Round letters such as O, C, Q, and G need about one and a quarter times the width, or they will appear to be crowded and narrower than the other letters.
7. If spacing is a problem E, F, and T can be somewhat diminished from a full width without appearing too narrow.
8. Embellishments in a font such as serifs, the little tails sometimes added at the top and bottom of letters, should be done consistently or not at all. Doing these embellishments half and half will make the lettering look amateurish.
9. Any variation done in a given font on a given piece of signage should be consistent

a b c d e f g h i j
k l m n o p q r s
t u v w x y z
A B C D E F G H
I J K L M N O P
Q R S T U V W X
Y Z
1 2 3 4 5 6 7 8
9 0

a b c d e f g h i j k l
m n o p q r s t u v w
x y z
A B C D E F G H I
J K L M N O P Q R
S T U V W X Y Z
1 2 3 4 5 6 7 8 9 0

a b c d e f g h i j k
l m n o p q r s t u
v w x y z
A B C D E F G
H I J K L M N
O P Q R S T U
V W X Y Z
1 2 3 4 5 6 7 8 9
0

Figure 8.54 Gothic, roman serif and script lettering.

throughout the signage. So, for instance, if there is a G of a certain style, then that G should be used throughout the font.

General Layout

As in any kind of complex layout and cartoon, take the time to learn the skill of signage. Work it out on brown paper first and then make a pounce of it. This also is a convenience because once the signage is pounced in position, it is not uncommon for it to have to be moved or shifted. It is easy enough to blow off the charcoal and repounce a sign moved up two inches, a different matter entirely if the sign was drawn in place. Also, the whole sequence of letters may need to be erased and reworked. If this is done on the scenery, that area will get smudged and dirty from being overworked. Another reason to pounce signage is that it can be done on a workbench or in a clear space rather than hunched over a piece of scenery.

As your skills increase in sign painting you will be able to discern which signs you need to carefully pattern out and which ones can be drawn in place. A useful trick is to break a piece of charcoal to the width of the stroke and sketch the letter using the side of the charcoal. Eventually you will have to paint a drop that has dozens of signs on it and get all the practice you could hope for.

Often lettering is placed on the back of a sheet of Plexiglas. Do not try to lay out signage backward. You will be unaware of several mistakes until you view the piece from the front. Do a cartoon on frisket paper, or make a pounce, then simply flip it over to use it.

Spacing

Letter spacing is done in two ways. In mechanical spacing, the boxes around each letter are exactly the same distance apart from each other. This spacing works well for an H that is next to an E, but when an A is next to a Y, the letters will look like they are too far apart. This can be corrected with optical spacing. In optical spacing, the A and the Y are moved closer together so that they look like they are the same distance apart as the H and the E.

Before inking the lines or applying paint to the layout, take a moment to actually read what has been written. First, see whether the sign flows together optically. Also check your spelling or, better yet, have someone else check it for you. In sign painting, it is easy to become so involved with the layout and style of the letters that you may be oblivious to having spelled Taylor instead of Tailor. Yes it is a true story, and we discovered it on opening night.

Margins

Margins are very important to the flow of a sign. To make a sign clearer and easier to read, it may be more useful to actually sacrifice a little on the height and the width of the letters so that there is adequate space around the letters and words. Crowded, unplanned layouts are more difficult to make sense of regardless of the size of the letters.

Layout on Transparent Surfaces

Frequently a designer will call for signage on a window. In theatre, Plexiglas is almost always used instead of real glass for safety reasons. The advantage here is that you can ask the construction department to leave the paper protective cover on the Plexiglas and do your cartoon directly on that paper. Later, the letters can be cut out with an X-Acto knife. The paper cover will serve as a spray mask, also called a frisket. Frisket paper is available for this sort of work anywhere airbrush supplies are sold. Shelf and contact paper can also be used as friskets, just make sure they are well adhered to the surface and beware of paint leaking under the edges. The letters can be drafted out on the contact paper before it is adhered and cut out. Contact paper also works well on painted scenery or as a stencil for letters that need to be painted in reverse.

CONCLUSION

Good cartooning technique involves putting lines in the right places to begin with rather than probing around for the form by drawing one line after another until one happens to fall in the right place. It is important to select the most efficient approach to the cartooning based on the form. This may involve combining methods of cartooning. For instance, a park drop may have a structural element such as a gazebo on one side and a vista of the park on the other. In this case, it would be best to grid only the section of the drop that is composed of trees and park paths. On the gazebo section of the drop, the grid lines would be confusing because of the linear nature of the grid, so that area should stay free of the grid.

Considering the order that forms are cartooned in is also important. For instance, on a simple drop with palm trees and a horizon line between the sky and the ocean, it does not matter whether the foreground or the background is cartooned first. However, if there is a complex image on the drop, the order in which images are cartooned can be important. A complicated view of a street in linear perspective can be difficult to manage, particularly if all the line work that projects from the vanishing point is snapped through other planes. It is generally useful to define planes and structures in the foreground first. By working front to back, you can keep the images in the front clean of extraneous line work. Once you have cartooned images in the front of the picture plane, lay sheets of kraft paper over them so that the line work is not smudged due to foot traffic or the perspective line.

Cartooning a complex drop—such as the layout of the interior of a rococo cathedral—can be overwhelming. Compartmentalization is a valuable ability on projects of such intricacy. First identify the overarching structure of the image. Next separate out the different elements of each section of the structure. Work the detail of each section of the structure, such as column capitals, brackets, and trim, front to back so that the perspective can be projected back through the depth of the picture field. When working through the depth of field in an image, it is easier to measure dimensions accurately in the foreground.

The cartooning of scenery is as important—and as enjoyable—as painting itself. It allows the scenic artist to become completely immersed in the design. This is the time to explore and understand the work of the scenic designer before committing to the more permanent painting ahead. Cartooning is a satisfying job as the scenery begins to take on the form it is intended to have.

Cartooning calls on the skill of drawing, a skill that good scenic artists need. In this step, the scenic artist transforms the often tiny squiggles and gestures in the paint elevation through his or her understanding of art and a sense of the scenic designer's style.

Only after the cartooning is done can the work of applying color begin.

AN INTERVIEW WITH HOWARD JONES, RESIDENT SCENIC ARTIST AT THE NORTH CAROLINA SCHOOL OF THE ARTS

Howard Jones is the resident scenic artist at the North Carolina School of the Arts. He cofounded Cobalt Studios with Rachel Keebler in the late 1980s.
Susan Crabtree: Tell us about your position at North Carolina

Howard Jones: The focus of my work is to teach a curriculum of scene painting and drafting for both the graduate and undergraduate students. The main focus is the scene painting and the three levels of painting that I teach over a period of years with my students. It's a lovely place for me to be because I have a great shop that is probably the envy of many professional shops. It is really set up to be focused toward large classes more than producing large amounts of scenery, although we do produce a great deal of scenery for the productions we produce at the school. Last year we did a whole *Sleeping Beauty* in wing and drop style. A very nice thing to do. That is the shop situation.

SC: How long have you been a scenic artist and how did you get your start?

HJ: I've been a scenic artist for 27 years, the year my son was born. In terms of getting started in scenic art, I think it was just a progression because I loved theatre and my family is a group of artists and talked art. It just gradually became clear to me that that was what I wanted to do. I got out of grad school and started working for a company and I began painting more and more. That became the attraction. I'm a designer/painter and my career has been going more toward design and less toward painting. I'm a design/scene painting teacher instead of a designer/painter. That is an interesting combination and I guess there are not a lot of people who would do that.

I think it is interesting that people assume my design work is very painterly, and yes it can be. I think when I need to design a painted piece like a *Nutcracker* or a ballet backdrop that I actually design it for the painters as much as I design it for the piece. Barring some of their strengths and skills,

I know what kind of labor or spirit that they can bring to it because I like energy in the painting that I see onstage.

SC: Do you have a specialty in scenic art?

HJ: I don't think I really have a specialty in scenic art, although I do teach a lot of drop painting and I think that is one of my strengths—drops and moldings and architecture—those kinds of elements are a few things that I seem to be strong at.

SC: In one sense wouldn't you say that your specialty is teaching?

HJ: You are very accurate in regards to the scene painting. I have really tried to focus on teaching that both as an art and as a craft because a great deal of it, I must admit, is simple skills. You need to learn how to stand up straight and draw a straight line with a bamboo and a lining stick. Anybody can do that, it's just learning the technique—it's a process, a craft. It is your eyes that are the art. It's what you can see and how you can develop a painting beyond the simple replication of the grid.

SC: Who are some of the scenic artists that were influential in your development as a scenic artist?

HJ: I was working at Missouri Rep with Jim Cole Gohl, who was a designer and an interior designer originally from Kansas City—I believe taught at Columbia University and worked in theatre in New York for years. He was insistent on beautiful, accurate drawings and absolutely loose fluid paint over the top of the drawing. As long as you have a beautiful drawing it doesn't matter whether you get everything in the right place when you paint it. That is probably where I was exposed to that kind of energy on stage—and that's beautiful.

In addition to Jim Cole Gohl, there was Bob Benstead, who I never really got to work with for any length of time but he painted with Starlight in Kansas City and that's where I grew up. So I saw his work for years and years and years at Starlight and I can remember thinking, "I would love to paint some of that stuff." Just looking at his body of work, it was all very fluid, very fast, but the dimension was all there. So I think I was influenced by the Kansas City Starlight style—a fast summer stock, loose, high color kind of painting.

SC: Big emphasis on the fast there, right?

HJ: Very big emphasis on the fast. You do have to have some speed and it depends on how much money you really want to earn. You have to look at your students in class and say, "OK, that was a nice simple item, you took four hours to draw that, how much do you think that is really worth and how much do you want to get paid? Now that tells you how much faster you guys need to get." You can actually make a living at this. It is just part of the process that there is always going be a deadline and scenery must be finished by a certain date in our particular business. That is a given.

SC: How do you think your design career has advanced your career as a scenic artist in terms of the skills or in terms of what you put an emphasis on in scenic artistry?

HJ: It is interesting how my design complements my scene painting and my scene painting complements my design. I know I do things in my design package that frequently help a scenic artist. Sometimes I may grid a drop around 0 so that it's easy to work within the shop, little things like that, which a scenic artist would do to prepare for a project. Sometimes when you are at the drafting board it is just as simple to knock down a couple of lines that will make all the difference in the shop.

I think that I design for a paint shop so that they can do it quickly so that I can afford more bang for my buck. I will focus where the painting goes as opposed to painting all the way to the edge past the sight lines where you don't see it—if you don't see it, don't paint a lot of detail out there. I'm very careful about that because I've gotten stung so many times painting full drops that you see a sliver of, and that hurt. Weeks of my life went into those beautiful little vases that are now behind those lovely pieces of black masking. I really avoid that.

I think it has helped me as a scenic artist in that I have the questions to try and understand what the designer's intent is, which then allows me to make certain paint choices. If you understand their intent, what kind of world they want to create, then you can make some of the simple decisions in texture and quality and translucency that may not be evident in a rendering. It is very difficult at times to render what will become full-scale—fully textural with gold-leaf and built-up—it's the difference between looking at a photograph with an absolutely stunning surface and being able to see the stunning surface. You can get a photograph but it's still not going to have the same impact. You have to develop that as a scenic artist for the scenery, you go beyond the photograph. You have to understand the intent behind the color choices on the designer's elevations; they weren't just selected from a color chart. They were developed together for a reason.

SC: Do you think that being a designer has informed the way you speak with designers when you are trying to understand their intent?

HJ: No, because I talk to them like artists and I think that scene painters talk to each other like artists. When we are in the shop talking about the scenery we all talk about it like a piece of artwork, then that will make the connections that we need to make.

SC: So do you have a pat method that you use when you begin a dialog with a designer or is it different every time?

HJ: I would have to say that I probably have a tendency to be different every time because it's whatever I'm presented with that will lead me to the questions. It's the classic "How much does a drop cost?" Well is it a sky, is it a fort, is it a palace—what the devil is it? And I might be able to give you a ballpark if we can narrow it down. The same thing is true with painting scenery for a designer; what is he presenting me, what do I know, what are the materials—you have to look at the whole that you are presented. I think every time it is different and that is one of the things that I love about theatre—looking at a different period, looking at the colors, maybe some new materials—it's like going to school for your life and I like that.

SC: In terms of school, what kind of background and formal education do you think students should have?

HJ: I would like them to have a liberal arts education because I think that part of learning to talk art speak (if you can call it that) is to have a cultural background that you can draw on. Which means that you know a little about art history, theatre history, world history, literature, because all of those are references that give meaning, that allow us to make connections when talking to one another about what we see. And of course a good foundation in drawing. It doesn't matter where that comes from but that is the primary language of an artist when you are painting. That's the foundation of everything that we do even if it's just throwing paint on a surface, there is still some drawing in there and so the drawing is very important.

SC: What types of drawing do you think are important?

HJ: All kinds of drawing, I like perspective drawing, I think figure is very important. I think every artist should keep a journal so that when you are in a bus station you put down what you see. Sometimes you do that in a very careful, analytical style and sometimes you're allowed to put that down as an expression. I think both of those have validity in terms of learning how to express yourself with the line.

SC: Do you have words of wisdom for people who are interested in a career in scenic artistry?

HJ: One of the most difficult things to understand is that everyone does it differently, and part of that is the fact that they are artists and they will see a scene put together differently. Different doesn't mean wrong or bad, it's just different. There are many different techniques and approaches and ways to do things. It's very difficult for them to wrap their heads

Figure 8.55
Howard Jones in the scenic painting area at North Carolina School for the Arts.

around it. I know that I teach a very strict regimen. Part of that is survival in keeping my own shop organized. It really has taught me good painting technique, Some things are going to be different when they go to another shop. They are always quite shocked about that.

SC: But organization is very important and I think that sometimes gets left out. How do you feel about that?

HJ: I think organization in the shop can either make or break a shop in terms of productivity. Having a good shop person who makes sure that all the stock is there and you've always got the right number of brushes is important. That way, as a scenic artist, you don't have to pay attention to those kind of issues. You cannot afford to wait for somebody to go to the store to buy staples and have your scenic artists standing around waiting for them; that's wasting money. It's the efficiency of being able to always move through a project, to walk in the door with confidence that you are going to make some progress.

SC: What are some of the more elusive skills that you have had to learn in terms of scenic artistry?

HJ: I didn't know always how to clean up or be prepared for a project. Probably the most elusive thing for me is trying to sit down and get it tight enough. I have a tendency to be a little too loose, and don't always take the time-to-draw carefully. I am eager skip to painting, I would be too eager to get to painting and I would not do all the preparation appropriately. It's like holidays in the paint of a basecoat, they will come back and curse you and cost you hours and you just have to mess that up a couple of times and then you'll learn it. And you have to forgive yourself for that. I remember when I was in high school, I painted a backdrop for *Harvey* and it was all books and we had dry pigment. Well I thought dry pigment was like tempra paint where you just mix it up in water, it sure looked and handled like paint when you mixed it up and put it on the surface. So we hung the drop up and for the next two weeks swept the floor everyday of all the pigment that I had put on flaked off. But I had no idea what I was doing and that was high school. So you have to forgive yourself for those things.

SC: What do you think are some of the most important misconceptions about the profession of scenic artistry?

HJ: How we fit into the overall product. Sometimes I think it's curious who we work for because we work for so many different people. If you're in a Rep setting you're working with and for the technical director, but you also have primary responsibilities to get the designer's vision on stage. We have to work with the scenery that they build but we probably have something to say about the surface of what we paint on so that we can make it look right with all of the specifications. We have to work with the production manager in terms of our scheduling and being able to do the touch-ups late at night. There are so many different ways that we interact in a theatrical organization. I sometimes think that it is difficult for people in other disciplines to wrap their head around the whole job that we do, even though they may be working next to us in a shop. That we work for the TD is the big misconception. I also think that people have no idea how much time it really takes or think it is light work. Five gallons of paint weighs 35 to 40 pounds and that's a lot of stuff to heave across a room. It is work, don't think we just swing a brush.

SC: People outside the profession look at us painting and we always look so calm, well, not always, but frequently.

HJ: Indeed the appearance is different than the reality. Standing in the middle of a room with a bamboo and a lining stick all day, you don't move quickly, you're in a nice posture, possibly. It looks very relaxed and casual. However, they haven't had the six-inch brush on the end of that bamboo for three hours pushing it—that's pushing five pounds at the end of a stick. That makes your back hurt by the end of the day if you don't stand up straight. It is physical labor. Simply think of the acreage that the scenic artist covers and you begin to understand. If you put it into terms of mopping a floor that large everyday, I think people would understand, and that's really what we are doing. We are mopping the floor everyday. That might help people understand what we do, that it is physical in terms of actual work, not everyday but certainly many of them.

SC: The last century [1800s] was witness to many significant changes and innovations. Are there painting techniques and skills that people new to the profession are no longer being exposed to?

HJ: I definitely think so. I think floor painting and painting backdrops is probably not common among a lot of scenic artists because they are dealing instead with dimensional work and doing build-ups with joint compound or goop or something that has a real build-up texturally with different glazes. Those are all new things. It used to be all flat painted scenery.

I think too that most people don't know how to properly use scenic ink instead of magic marker, it's not common. I think it's nice to know those things. You don't always have to use them but to know them allows you another choice. How many people actually paint with dry pigment? Nobody actually in a shop that I know of. Is it good to know how to do that? Yes, because it opens up the possibilities and you understand how paint is really made. I think that is good for a painter.

I think that computers are also having an enormous impact. If nothing else, the renderings we get in the paint shop now frequently are digital. I'm part of that wave. As a designer, I use a lot of work that I have done on my computer. I've got some PhotoShop® work with pasted up photographs and presented that as a painter's elevation to be interpreted. Therefore our visual memory of what wood grains look like is very important. Don't think you are going to get a beautifully painted sample from a designer. He's going to simply ask you for a lovely Oak woodgrain. So the interpretation factor of digital media, I think, is difficult. It's not like a gouache rendering from a designer. That usually transforms well into scene paint because it's the same kind of material. The printout is completely different than paint. I do think it's a great time-saver to use digital media in the paint shop to eliminate drawing time for lettering layout and even certain kinds of large-scale blow-ups or patterns. It is a tool that we should continue to exploit as it develops.

SC: Do you worry that this tool is going to take over large parts of our skills in our profession?

HJ: No because a printout doesn't look like a painted set. A printout will never look like scenic art, it's not going to have layers and washes and be able to mutate under light the same way. It may look like the same from a long distance in terms of black-and -white photos and that's great. Sure, let's use it there, but I still think that it will be called painting. You're never going to find a machine that is going to be able to do marble over a three-dimensional set. I just can't imagine that. It could simply be my limited imagination but I can't imagine that we could have a spray gun or a portable printer that will wrap around three-dimensional scenery. I also think people enjoy painting. There is a real renaissance in the last 10 to 15 years of murals and mural work from scenic artists. You see so many more murals, large-scale in arts districts and those kinds of places and that's wonderful. People love their paintings.

I think people are attracted to them. I'm not really worried about it.

SC: Do you foresee the skills of the scenic artist changing in the century [2000] to come?

HJ: I think they will have to be more computer literate so that they have that as part of their tools in their paint bag, but I think that the same basic skills of drawing, color mixing, and the ability to assess and develop a texture with different tools are going to remain the same.

SC: Do you have any interesting stories in your career?

HJ: You know what has always fascinated me, and that's toys. I am a big one for toys. You don't have to paint everything with a brush. I love it when the brooms come out and the hoses start spraying across the ground. It's really kind of chaotic, working with Alice Carol, she and I did a drop that was supposed to be a beautiful rusted/galvanized metal and Alice and I used a super-soaker and balloons full of paint to throw and splash color on the drop. We proceeded to develop something on top of that. I love that kind of chaotic impulse to throw paint and make something really beautiful. I love those experiences. You should try Swiss cheese; it's one of my favorites. You take a piece of velour and you cut all these holes until you get Swiss cheese. Then you dip it in paint like you would rag roll and squeeze it out, let it drip off your hand and then throw it (spin it like a pizza) and it will land and it gives you these beautiful organic spaces. It's terrific for marble and I've had people use it for foliage.

SC: What are some of the highlights of your career as a teacher and as a scenic artist?

HJ: When Rachel [Keebler] and I went to set up Cobalt. That was a great experience and I treasure that and being here at the North Carolina School of the Arts. That has also been really inspiring. I have a whole group of wonderful, energetic people who all love painted scenery. Usually it is about the people in the room painting, being part of the group and doing something really beautiful. I remember the summer at Starlight that we worked together. That was a magical group of people and so was the work.

SC: What have been some of the most difficult aspects of your career?

HJ: Some days you do have to paint a lot of just green walls. There are days when our job is boring and that also is the variety that is presented. Sometimes we get a realistic box set and they say "We'd like it this black color." Those can be the most difficult because there is not much to contribute there. I think anybody who loves to paint feels the same way there. Also balancing family and the work hours presents some difficulties because we do have deadlines; shows have to be finished by a certain time and date. You work through them but that doesn't make it easy and I think we all understand that.

SC: Do you think that the scope of the profession will narrow? I'm concerned with the future of drop painting partly because it's so near and dear to me.

HJ: I still think that ballet, opera, and to a degree theatre will still maintain it—even the movies. We are in an amazing digital age in cinematography but when they want the quality of a painting they still paint it, and there have been movies in the last year that have painted backdrops. It may not continue to exist in the same amount but I think it will still be there. In some ways I see our profession opening up more than closing down because there are more ways that you can earn a living as a large-scale painter such as painting murals and doing interior decorating as well as drops. If you can do the drops, you can make the switch to any of the other projects, and still make a living.

Chapter 9

Two-Dimensional Scenic Painting Techniques

Here you are at last. The scenery is primed and cartooned, the colors are mixed, and you are ready to paint. The first piece of advice is simple: just put the color where the color goes. The second piece of advice is also simple: make every brushstroke count. Proper application of paint is not about smearing color around until it ends up in the right place by chance, nor is it about drowning the scenery in glaze coats all day long. It is the careful, thoughtful application of color in the proper sequence with the right tools. This chapter illustrates methods for many traditional painting techniques. Learning and practicing sound methodology will help you realize the two simple rules just stated.

The basic two-dimensional paint techniques discussed and illustrated in this chapter are the fundamental building blocks for how to paint almost anything on scenery. Two-dimensional painting technique is one-third of a triad that forms an image, with color and line being the other two. These techniques also form a vocabulary of scenic art and are a means of communication between artists. All scenic artists should be proficient in these techniques and understand the full meaning of them. Because they speak the same language, a scenic artist in New York can talk to a scenic designer on the phone from Los Angeles, describe the color and opacity of cast shadows for a drop, and execute the work at hand without needing the designer to be there.

The techniques described here are fairly simple on an individual basis. A good scenic artist knows how to use them repeatedly, consistently, and with appropriate adaptation to whatever medium is used. These techniques are part of the trade of a scenic artist, the artist's skills. Two-dimensional painting techniques range from simply covering a surface with a color to creating the illusion of three dimensions on a flat surface. Specific textures and patterns also are created with two-dimensional painting techniques.

You may encounter some regional differences in terminology, descriptions, and even pronunciations of paint techniques. If you work outside the United States, you will encounter many striking differences in terminology, even in other English-speaking countries. While it is important to understand which technique is being described, the essential issue is to understand how to do the technique well.

PUTTING A PRODUCTION TOGETHER: THE PAINTING

We'll start the chapter by discussing the organization and planning of large-scale scenic painting before describing the details of how to paint hard and soft scenery. Up to this point we have dealt with the organizational elements and techniques of scenic artistry in a compartmentalized fashion. But ultimately the point of this text is to explain how to put all of these fundamentals of the profession together to paint beautiful scenery efficiently. This process can be further complicated by the fact that the scenic artist may have to work on several productions simultaneously. While seeing one production through the shop, there may be another production in the planning stages and yet another in touch-up in the theatre. A sophisticated sense of artistry must be combined with superior organizational skills.

Starting the Painting

The reason for all of the organization and careful planning is, of course, to paint scenery. The scenery itself must be cartooned (refer to Chapter 8) and painted in a systematic fashion and, the organization of the approach to the scenery is indeed very important. However, there is a point when the focus of painting the scenery has to change from organization to artistry.

The Prime Coat

Before priming, consider the overall paint treatment for the scenery. For instance, if the base color is a deep blue, you may want to tint the prime coat or starch with a fair amount of blue. This improves the coverage of the base coat. Any painted scenery intended to function as a translucency should be painted on a clear starch prime coat. Some paint treatments based on watercolor technique work best when applied directly to a clear rather than a tinted size coat. In the case of hard scenery, the surface is be too smooth for the intended paint treatments, in which case the prime coat may need to have some drywall compound or fine sand mixed in to give the surface some tooth. A full discussion of priming and other surface preparation techniques is in Chapter 7. Because of these considerations the overall painting techniques of a scenic unit must be conceived of before the size and prime coats are applied.

Planning the Painting Process

As the drop is being cartooned ideas should already be formulating in the scenic artist's mind about how the painting will be approached. This is the time when the job ahead will begin to take shape. The order in which paint treatments will be done can be planned as the forms emerge in charcoal.

Details and Hard Scenery

The elements that comprise hard scenery include flattage, the stage deck, platforms, staircases, ground rows, and a wide variety of scenic pieces. The term *structural pieces* can mean anything: scaffolding, sculptural pieces, architectural elements, rocks, trees, even dirt. There are a lot of details that the paint elevations do not cover, including seams, bolt heads, edges, hardware—the list goes on and on. The scenic designer depends on the scenic artist to catch these details and resolve them. Sometimes the resolution of these details may entail a call to the designer to ask for instruction, other times the solutions will be obvious. The more details that can be dealt within the shop, the less will have to be handled at touch-up.

Figure 9.1
Laying out a precise cartoon and masked areas for preliminary painting of the "Money" drop for *42nd Street*. Scenic Art Studios, New York.

Soft Goods

It would seem that painting soft goods would be simpler than painting hard scenery because there are no edges to deal with and because fairly substantial areas of square footage can be dealt with at the same time. But the fact is that frequently, the converse is true because when designing soft goods, the scenic designer has been liberated from adherence to structural reality and can create the illusion of very complex structural arrangements. The most complex imagery is frequently painted on soft goods. Also, because of computer imaging and collage, the designer can create visual images of exceeding complexity that require a masterful array of skills to reproduce. It is sometimes necessary to put as much thought into the selection and arrangements of techniques for a backdrop as for a full stage of hard scenery. In this statement is one of the keys to approaching backdrops: If the image is complex, divide it up into applications or groups of applications. Plot out these applications in an order that has a logical progression and involves as little backtracking as possible.

Compartmentalization is also valuable in working out the order and processes of paint techniques. Where as in cartooning you should work front to back, when painting you should work back to front, isolating and toning areas of depth as you move forward in the composition. On a cityscape you would never paint the buildings first and then attempt to spray the sky afterward. So too if painting that same

complex layout of a rococo cathedral, referred to at the end of Chapter 8. Start the images of greatest depth in the picture plane. Deal with the color and value correction on these areas first before basing in the next layer of columns and arches. This is easier then basing everything out at once and then having to carefully cut around profiles with corrective glaze colors, or masking those profiles out for color corrective sprays.

BASE PAINTING TECHNIQUES

Every paint job starts with the *base coat*, which is the foundation of color and texture. Choosing which style of base coat to use depends largely on what materials are being painted as well as the result desired. In a few cases, no base coat will be needed, as the sizing or primer serve as the base in certain techniques used on backdrops, such as working with aniline dye or painting a translucent area. However, there is almost always a base coat, and it does two important things. It is the base of color for the techniques to follow, which might be a single color or several blended colors. It also creates a pattern of grain or texture. Every brushstroke has direction and creates a texture signature. Creating wood in paint is the most obvious example of this, as it is natural to pull the brush with the direction of the wood grain. Many other grain patterns can be made in base

Figure 9.2
The finished "Money" drop. Scenic Art Studios, New York.

Figure 9.3 A backdrop for *42nd Street* nearing completion. It is painted mostly in large blocks of flat colors. Scenic Art Studios, New York.

coating as well as random patterns of texture. Smooth, grainless bases can be painted as well, using the proper technique.

A base coat of paint can be mixed out of any water-based painting medium, such as dry pigment, casein, latex, or acrylic. Always be certain the paint has sufficient binder when working with dry pigment so the base coat is firm enough to sustain further work on top of it. With lighter colors, the base may be mixed from a less-expensive paint, such as household latex or acrylic, because so much of it is needed. Large painting suppliers offer very inexpensive off-white contractor's paint, which can be ideal as a base coat for hard scenery.

Brushed Base Coat Techniques

When choosing the colors and technique of the base coat, you are taking the first step toward completion of the application of color and painting style. It is tempting to just put color on the scenery for the sake of the satisfaction that comes of getting rid of the bare primed or sized scenery. But before you paint your base coat, consider your strategy of color and technique, even if the scenery is only going to be toned down with a spray. Will the base coat be a warm color that is sprayed down with its complementary color so that the final finish will have a more dynamic color content? Should the base coat be a blend of two subtly different hues so that there will be more variation in the nuance of texture in the final product? Should the brushstrokes that are used to apply the base coat be oriented in one direction to

Figure 9.4
The same *42nd Street* drop on the floor. Scenic Art Studios, New York.

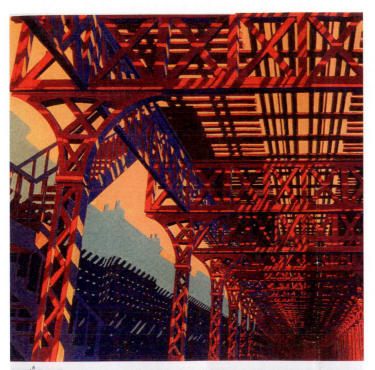

SION" DROP

SS MUSLIN (PART. TRANSL.)

Figure 9.5
A fragment of the paint elevation for the *42nd Street* drop. Scenic Art Studios, New York.

augment that application of paint in subsequent techniques? Try to envision the entire process so that the base coat step can make as much of a contribution to the final creation as possible.

Base Painting Large Areas without Leaving a Grain

The brush used to paint the base coat should be the largest brush you can handle with control in the area to be painted. It should hold a large charge of paint, particularly when base painting a large piece of scenery. Covering a large area each time you charge the brush means a more efficient base painting technique.

A typical brush for large jobs is a Dutch brush, a six-inch- to eight-inch-wide flat-ferrule brush with two or three paint wells. A brush such as this covers about 10 to 12 square feet with each charge. The direction the brush is moved is important, as most paints develop a grain when applied in one direction. A simple figure-eight stroke or a sort of omnidirectional paint stroke leaves virtually no grain when the paint is dry (see Figure 9.6). Changing the brush direction,

as with the figure-eight stroke, provides better penetration of the paint, particularly on rough surfaces. The viscosity of the paint is important as well. It should be thin enough to spread easily but thick enough to cover. Paint that is the viscosity of heavy cream usually works well for a base coat.

Unlike house painters, scenic artists are not as concerned about durability of paint surfaces. Base coats need only be as thick as necessary to obtain a smooth flat coverage. In fact, a base coat that is too thick on muslin may hinder the scenic artist in the refined execution of subsequent paint techniques. Like the artist working on canvas, the scenic artist is attune to the subtle texture of the muslin grabbing onto the paint and holding it in place. Anytime you have to execute a thin wash on the slick surface of Masonite®, the difference between that surface and the muslin will become apparent. A base coat that is too heavy, besides wasting pigment and adding weight, will smooth over that wonderful muslin texture.

Figure 9.6 Omnidirectional stroke and brush.

Figure 9.7 Creating grain with the base coat.

Creating a Grain Pattern in the Base Coat

Some materials emulated in scene painting have a distinct grain, such as wood or marble. Creating a grain in the base coat is an advantage in convincingly simulating these materials. Loosely follow the direction of the grain intended for that surface, even when working with only one color, so the grain of the base coat does not interfere with subsequent paint techniques, such as dry brush or glaze treatments (see Figure 9.7).

Cutting a Hard Line in a Base Coat

Landscapes or architectural details may have several different colors of base coat for different areas of the scenery. A light single-color base coat may have areas of different colors painted over it later. Base painting the scenery area by area with different colors is called *cutting in* a base. In either case, cutting in calls for careful painting up to the cartoon line, where the color shift takes place.

The natural inclination when cutting in is to do the edges first, then fill in the rest with a large brush.

The problem with this is that the initial cut-in lines dry quickly. The overlapping larger brushstrokes used to fill in leave a different texture, which may show through subsequent techniques. Avoid this by cutting in the line for a few feet and filling in with a bigger brush while the paint still is wet. Another solution is to cut in all around the cartoon first, but break up the cut-in strokes as you go so that a sharp dry edge does not form.

When cutting in an edge, always use the largest brush possible that still gives control. As noted earlier, larger brushes hold more paint, have to be charged less often, and get the job done faster. Long edges can sometimes be cut in with a four-inch flat-ferrule or even a priming brush (see Figure 9.8).

Base Coating with a Sprayer

Base coats may also be applied with pneumatic or airless sprayers (these tools are discussed in Chapter 5). This is commonly done on dimensional or sculptural

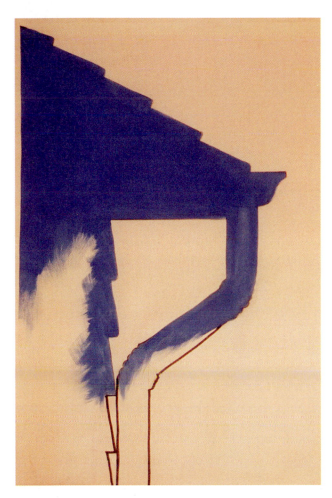

Figure 9.8   Cutting in the edges while applying a base coat.

units of hard scenery that would be too laborious or even impossible to paint with a brush. One important tip to keep in mind is if the reason you are spraying the base coat is because the nooks and crannies are nearly impossible to reach with a brush, they will also be nearly impossible to reach with most other painting techniques as well. In this situation, it would be wise to mix the base coat to the darkest or near darkest value of local color on the paint elevation. The lighter and more chromatic colors will probably be on the surfaces easier reached anyway, while the nooks and crannies will have the deeper valued colors to contrast and emphasize the sculptural dimension of the piece.

Texture Base Painting Techniques

Another texturing step often is called for in combination with the base coat. The texturing can be done with a variety of tools, including brushes, sponges, rollers, rags, feathers, and other tools you can create for your own projects. Many of these are addressed in the section later on in the chapter on overpainting techniques, but they can be done in combination with the base coat.

Wet Blending

Wet blending is the technique of blending together two or more colors while they are wet (see Figure 9.9). The blend can be done with any consistency of paint, from glazes to opaque. A wet blend often serves as the base coat. If a very large area needs to be wet blended, then the leading edge of the blend can be kept moist by spraying it lightly with water from a garden sprayer. Generally, the blend is done by laying in all the colors save one in the right proportion and pattern. The last color is used to blend together the other colors. This last color is the dominant color of the blend. In some wet blends, the object may be to keep the colors as pure as possible by having a separate brush at the ready for each one. In other blends, the subtler merging of colors that occurs when the same brush is used to apply all the colors may be the best approach.

Smoothing or Feathering a Wet Blend   A wet blend can be patchy or quite smooth. If the blend is to be smoothed, then a large dry brush that is never actually dipped in the paint should be used to do the final smoothing, to give the surface a feathery finish (see Figure 9.10). Wet blends also may be done on surfaces that have been moistened with water first, so that the colors melt into one another more readily.

Wet Blending for a Grain Pattern   If the wet blend is part of a treatment that emulates a grained material, such as wood or marble, the blend should be done in the same direction as the grain (see Figure 9.11). When painting grained materials such as wood or marble, this wet blend is really half the battle of the paint job. When doing a wet blend for specific effect, always try to capture the characteristic of that material.

Graded Wet Blending or Ombré   Graded wet blending, or an *ombré blend*, is a smooth even transition from one hue or value to another. In a wet blend you can do this by laying the separate colors or values in stripes across the width of the blend and systematically brushing one color into the

Figure 9.9
A typical wet blend.

other (see Figure 9.12). Then, brush horizontally across the blend with a clean dry brush working from the first color field to the last. Usually, this final blend begins in the lightest value color and works toward the darkest. If the area being blended is too large to manage the technique ahead of the drying time, the paint can be kept moist by lightly spraying it with water. Do not use too much water when keeping an area moist, as this will cause control problems.

If you need to cover a very large area with an ombré blend, use a garden or pneumatic sprayer rather than a brush. To spray an ombré blend, mix the range of colors in the blend at what appear to be even incremental steps in the shift from one color and

value to the other. For instance a blend from a pastel yellow to a dark red might require five steps. Begin by spraying the darkest color, fading it out about one quarter of the way through the blend. The next color will be an orange-red that is lighter in value. Overlap the dark red area by about one half, spraying very lightly at first and then increasing the coverage of the spray until it is solid. Then fade it out as you reach the halfway point of the blend. The next color will be an orange of a hue and value that is halfway between the red and yellow. Repeating the process with this color and the two to follow will result in an ombré blend that shifts evenly from one color and value to the next. Make sure to let each coat dry completely before applying the next.

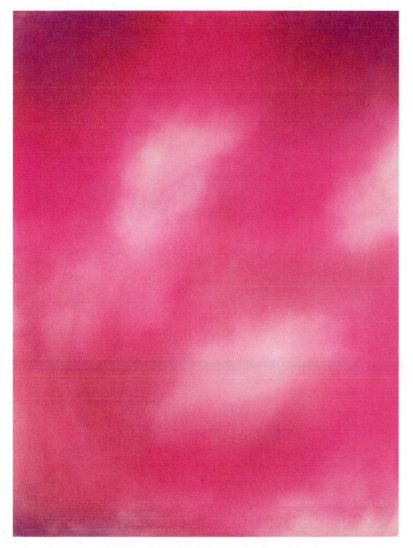

Figure 9.10
A smooth wet blend.

Scumbling

The terms *scumbling* and *wet blending* often are confused. In scenic art, the term *scumble* typically means covering a surface by laying two or more colors next to one another using paint strokes in X-like patterns (see Figure 9-13). A typical mottle photographic backdrop is frequently executed with a scumbling technique. The surface of a scumble may then be further refined by wet blending the colors together.

Generally, the object of scumbling is to let the colors mingle together without necessarily making an effort to blend them. Sometimes the paint strokes in a scumble merge into one another with very dry paint strokes. They may have the quality of being drawn or sketched, so that one layer of paint shows through the gaps of another layer. A scumble is done on a dry surface or a moist surface that will melt the edges of the paint strokes. A scumble may be done over a large area for color shift and modeling or it can be done in a tight and specific application for detail work (see Figure 9.14). Areas of one color may even dry before another color is scumbled into them.

A scumble can be done with any size or style brush and with any consistency of paint. Whether the treatment is to be done with a glaze, a thin wash of color, or opaque paint will depend on the needs of the project and the elevation.

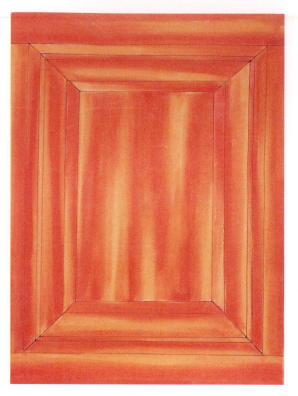

Figure 9.11   Wet blend for wood.

Base Coat Painting with a Roller

The most common purpose for a roller is to quickly cover a lot of square footage with paint or finish. Like brushes, rollers can leave a grain if worked in the same direction. So, as in base coat painting with a brush, the roller should be worked in different directions and the strokes should be overlapped to spread the paint evenly (see Figures 9.15 and 9.16).

A roller is a very efficient tool for covering a large flat area with paint. Beyond this, rollers can be used for a variety of paint techniques, such as lining work and painting texture, as they have characteristics that are very different from brushwork. Rollers have their own signature and can be used in instances when a more organic quality is desired. (Rollers are fully described in Chapter 5.)

When working with finishes, the opposite sometimes is true. Overworking a finish can trap air bubbles in the finish, which will dry cloudy. This can be particularly noticeable if the finish is tinted to perform as a dark paint treatment as well. In the case of finishes, particularly fast-drying ones, it is sometimes best to apply the finish with even, minimal

A

Figure 9.12   The steps of an ombré blend. (**A**) Lay the colors in next to each other.

strokes, with the grain if there is one. Two layers applied in this manner should result in a polished finish.

Texturing with a Roller

Frequently, a base coat is worked over with regular or texture rollers charged with other colors while it is still wet. This way the colors can melt or be blended together. Rollers also are used for overpainting two-dimensional texture. After charging the roller, wring out the excess paint on a flat tray or flat scrap of wood; screens and roller trays may leave an imprint in the fleece of the roller cover. A mostly dry roller will leave a grainy pattern of paint that will be more pronounced if you do not comb out the fleece before

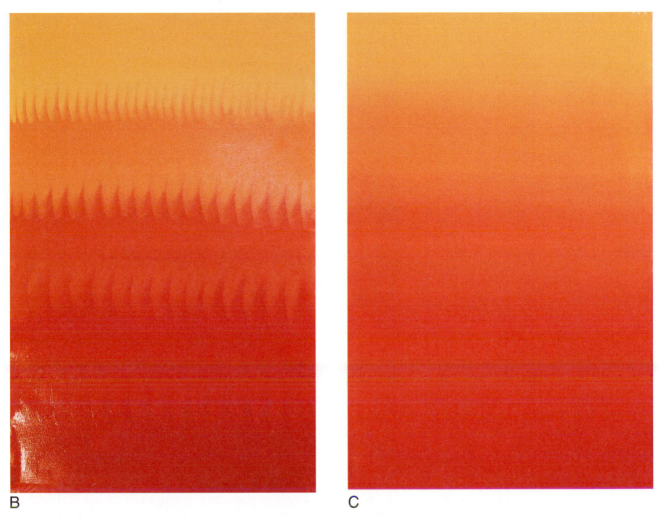

B

C

Figure 9.12 The steps of an ombré blend. **(B)** Blend the bands of color. **(C)** Smooth the blend between colors with a clean brush starting with the lightest color and working toward the darkest.

using it. The roller is worked from several directions so a direction in the grain does not develop. A dry roller can be used with a stencil or by itself.

A fleece roller can be segmented with strips of any waterproof tape wrapped tightly around the nap. If evenly segmented, the roller will leave a stripe pattern that works well for an ink block or cross-hatched effect. A roller segmented so the tape crisscrosses it leaves a broken pattern not unlike tree bark or other organic textures.

Some techniques relate to specific types and styles of roller covers. For example, foam covers come in a variety of naps, from one-quarter inch to one inch. Foam roller covers hold less paint than fleece covers, but foam rollers can be carved into an

imprint or a specific design. One very useful variety of foam roller is manufactured for painting over rough surfaces. This roller is covered with a three-quarter inch layer of foam with slits in it for working into the nooks and crannies of a textured surface.

Other types of rollers not made specifically for paint can be very useful in creating textures. So-called *texture roller covers* have a looped nap and render a texture coat with very uniform grain. These make an even texture in the thick wall-surfacing compounds used in homes. The texture compound is applied first with a brush or a fleece roller, then is reworked with the texture roller before it sets up. If the texture roller is used with plaster, it must be washed out immediately after use. Glue roller covers are surfaced with

Figure 9.13
Tight scumble technique.

What paint should be used with a roller? Any standard water-based scenic or house paint can be used with rollers. The paint used with rollers should be fairly viscous. If paint used with rollers is too thin, it tends to settle on one side of the roller cover. If a translucent color application is desired in combination with a roller technique, color can be added to a clear acrylic medium. All standard solvent-based paints may be used as well, just remember to get extra roller covers when purchasing these paints. It is not worth the expense to clean these.

looped carpet. These rollers work well with highly viscous materials. Scenic supply houses sell mottled leather roller covers that leave their own particular imprint when used with paint or texture. Roller covers with a sponge texture very similar to a natural sponge are sold for decorative paint techniques.

OVERPAINTING TECHNIQUES

Once the scenery has its base coat, it is very rare that the painting is considered complete. Action and character in theatre are often enhanced and exaggerated. This is reflected in the scenic elements. The motifs and patterns of an elegant interior or the shabbiness

Figure 9.14
Broad scumble.

of a lonely country inn may be exaggerated. Colors may be more intense than what you would expect to find in reality. Shadows may be tinged with purple, highlights with yellow. This is because the world of the stage is often presented as a place that is larger-than-life, embellished, and more intense than that of the real world.

There is also a very pragmatic reason for this: The stage picture should read well to audience members at a distance from the stage as well as to those up close. For the scenic artist who is creating the painted surfaces of the scenery, there is another practical consideration as well. Stage lighting is also exaggerated over the quality of light found in the real world. Scenery standing under stage light painted with nothing but base coats and opaque color will look washed out under stage light. While the shifts of

focus and colors of the scenery are the responsibility of the scenic designer, the way in which the scenic artist accomplishes these variations is geared to what reads well under stage light. Over the centuries, scenic artists have learned what techniques and combinations of color give the most intensity and vitality to the painted surface under stage light.

Some overpainting techniques are intended to change or create shifts in the overall color and value of a surface. Other techniques create the two-dimensional appearance of texture. Some techniques serve to emphasize the actual texture that is already there. Usually this texture, whether actual or painted, is intended to give the surface the appearance of some other material such as stucco, wood, or stone. Many of these techniques are used in combination with one another. For instance, a painted wood paneling may

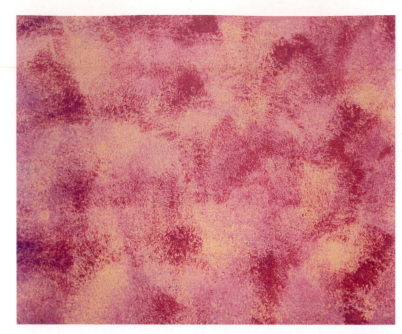

Figure 9.15
Dry roller technique: base coat.

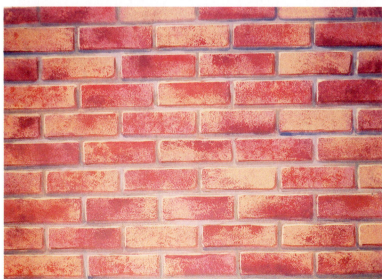

Figure 9.16
Detailing bricks with dry roller technique.

Figure 9.17
Variations of roller types.

Figure 9.18   Rollers used on edge.

Figure 9.19   Taped rollers.

be based with two colors, and then the overpainting may involve graining, combing, then trompe l'oeil detail and toning with a spray around edges.

Washes and Glazes

A *wash* or *glaze* is a thin coat of translucent paint used to tone down a harsh color with a shade, to make an image soften or recede, or to faintly color an area like the panes of glass in a window. Generally, a wash refers to a large area of translucent color, whereas a glaze is more localized. Washes and glazes are made by working with very thin paint or by using normal-strength paint and dipping the brush into water to thin it. For exmple, washes and glazes can be put on over wet or dry surfaces, a wet wash onto wet wash or glaze yields a smoother result, like watercolor.

The scenic arts share many techniques with the interior decoration arts. Sometimes the names for these techniques have somewhat different meanings. In decorative painting, the term *glaze* generally refers to paint or colorant being used to tint a *glazing medium*. This medium is used because when painting on smooth surfaces or vertically, the glaze must have body to it so it will stay where it is applied rather then dripping down or pooling. The glazing medium also gives the painter more control over the amount of color that is applied. A glaze medium can be spread out very thin or put down in heavy layers. Glaze mediums also stay workable for several minutes so more refined techniques are possible. The scenic artist will have use for glaze mediums from time to time, for smooth vertical surfaces that must be toned or textured or faux or decorative paint techniques.

Figure 9.20   Examples of taped roller technique used to create the appearance of tapestry.

Figure 9.21   A variety of rollers cut for unique textures from Scenic Art Studios, New York.

Many techniques rely on wash work, such as wood graining, perspective effects, and stone and marble. Washes of color also can be built up in layers to give flat color fields greater depth.

Any water-based paint can be used as a wash or a glaze. Aniline dye, which is completely transparent when dry, may also be used. The wash can be applied with a large brush, sprayed on and brushed in, or even rolled on.

Combing (Dry Brushing)

Combing is also known as *dry brushing* in some regions. When discussing the techniques explained in this section, be sure to be clear on the terminology. (Dry brushing is discussed later in the chapter.) Combing is done by separating the bristles of a charged brush and dragging them across a wet or dry

Figure 9.22 Combing technique.

surface to leave a very streaky, linear paint stroke. A brush for combing should be fairly well charged, so that you can pull out as long a stroke of paint as possible (see Figure 9.22).

The Tools and Paint for Combing

Usually, flat-ferrule brushes are used for combing. Because the bristles need to be separated, this technique is very hard on liners and nicer brushes. If you are using a good-quality flat-ferrule brush to comb, the bristles will tend to clump together, just as they have been designed to. Gently separate the bristles across the lip of the paint bucket. The bristles of some older, much used brushes usually separate on their own, and these could be the best choice for combing. Any brush can be cut up to give the bristles a specific pattern.

Combing Techniques

Scenic artists use combing to represent a variety of materials, like wood grains, tapestry and other

Quality brushes tend to pass though stages of life just as we do. At first when they are new and still have their snap, they are used to their utmost potential for cutting in lines, base coating, and glaze work. As their bristles get a little shabby and begin to splay, the brushes may be used for texture projects, hard work that ages a brush fast as the bristles get worn down. Finally they have a little cosmetic surgery. Their bristles are cut into "fingers" so they can be used for combing techniques.

woven materials, grasses, and conifer trees. An important aspect to good combing is paying attention to where it starts and stops. If you lay the width of the brush down and start a stroke in the middle of what is intended to be a heavy wooden plank, this will remind the viewers that they are looking at a poor paint job and not a wooden plank. Generally, begin a comb brushstroke at the end of the plank or a natural division in the material.

Finesse also comes into play (see Figure 9.23). You might do nothing but comb brushstrokes using the full width of the brush from the beginning to the end of a stroke. In some instances, that is what is called for. However, often, some variation in the technique will enhance the treatment. Learn to begin the comb brushstroke with the corner of the brush, then ease the rest of the brush down while pulling through on the stoke. You also can end a stoke in this manner by rolling one corner of the brush up and trailing off the stroke. By pulling the brush with a slow, even hand, you will get the most out of every charge of the brush. Remember, the paint comes out of the ends of the bristle, so use a light touch.

What paint should be used when combing? The paint used in dry brushing should be thin enough to flow smoothly. If you use a paint that is too thick, you will not be able to get a very long paint stoke out of your charged brush. The paint can be either opaque or a glaze, depending on the technique at hand.

Strié

Strié is a French word meaning striated or scratched. In theatrical application, a strié is a straight comb

Figure 9.23
Combing in an area moistened with water.

Figure 9.24
Standard combing technique:
crosshatch and basket weave.

brushstroke, evenly applied, beginning to end, with no variation or tilt of the brush, creating stripes of color. A finger, piper or cut bristle, or foam brush can be used for this.

In decorative painting, this term is more frequently applied to the process of combing through a glaze medium in straight even strokes with a brush, a cut squeegee, or even the cut edge of a piece of cardboard to reveal the base color beneath. This technique works best on a base coat surface that has sheen so the glaze can be combed off.

Dry Brushing

Dry brushing is the technique of using the flat of the brush to accentuate the texture of the surface with paint. The term *dry* is somewhat misleading because the brush used in dry brushing technique is not dry, nor is the paint necessarily thick. A very thin glaze may be used in the technique of dry brush. This technique may be used in cross-hatching or in straight linear brushstrokes. It may be done with the tips or the flat of the bristles. Dry brushing is frequently done on textured surfaces either to create a course surface with the texture compound or to manipulate its surface before it is dry. Once the texture compound is dry, several different colors of paint may be applied by dry brushing it to emphasize contrast at some point in the paint treatment.

Graining

Wood and stone, particularly marble, have very distinctive grain patterns (see Figure 9.25). The patterns evolve in the actual material through normal growth or formation. When wood or marble is cut for use, it reveals a variety of grain patterns. A tricky aspect to painting the grain of naturally formed materials is that the grain follows no set pattern yet is repetitive in form. It is completely human to paint a grain with a repetitive motion, producing a pronounced recurring pattern. When the same pattern repeats itself over and over in an image, it reminds the viewer that this is just paint. With either of these materials, or any naturally formed material, the scenic artist needs to understand the logic behind the pattern. These grains may appear completely random, but they are not. The structure of marble and wood reflect the means of their development, which are clear and distinct, all of which the scenic artist should understand.

Figure 9.25
Example of wood graining with a brush.

Graining Techniques and Tools

A variety of tools are used for creating grain. Brushes are a good choice for many graining projects because they create a natural pattern when handled correctly. A brush is handled differently for graining than for other techniques. Whereas normally you would have a firm hold on the brush, in graining you hold the brush loosely and roll it around in your hand to alternate between painting with the edge and the width of the brush. This works particularly well when graining marble.

The type of brush used for graining will vary; sometimes a liner will do, for other applications a small flat-ferrule brush is preferable. As with other techniques, always use the largest brush you can, for theatricality and efficiency. A large brush can actually create a very thin line when applied with a light touch, and a larger brush will also give you more control over the variety of thin and thick lines.

When grain is first done with a brush, it can end up looking a little hard-edged. To soften the wood or marble, drag another brush through the grain in the direction of the grain while the paint is wet. You can also apply the paint to a moist or wet surface so the edges of the paint stroke melt into the adjacent colors.

Wood

We all know that wood develops a ring pattern during normal growth. Dozens of different grains are revealed in wood when the tree is cut for use. Trees are cut into lumber lengthwise, widthwise, or for veneers, which means they are shaved while being rotated. Each type of cut produces a distinctive grain, which varies depending on the type of wood and the part of the tree from which the wood is milled. Painted wood grain can be a long, stringy grain, semicircular arcs, or a small bull's eye pattern, to name just a few. Crosscut wood has rings that give the grain a V-, U-, or oval-shaped pattern. A scenic artist may be tempted to return to these patterns frequently when graining wood. However, when these patterns are overdone, they may appear ridiculous and the graining will become a parody of wood.

There are many ways to make wood grain with paint. A variety of faux finish tools are used for graining wood. Some of these tools work well for the larger scale of theatrical painting, and many are available at paint and decorator supply stores and through theatrical supply houses. The *grainer* is a tool that makes wood grain with paint. A grainer may be either a rubber pad adhered to a curved block, sometimes called a *rocker*, a hollow rubber tube, or a rubber pad that has been molded into a grain pattern in relief. Such tools are available in different variations of grains. These tools selectively squeegee a pattern off the surface, leaving a pattern reminiscent of a crosscut wood grain. The grainer is dragged through the paint or tinted transparent glaze medium while it is wet. The tool works best if the base paint has a satin finish or a satin finish is applied over it that the glaze medium can squeegee off easily. While working with this tool, occasionally rotate it in relation to the direction of your stroke for more variety. The finesse in using this tool comes in not overdoing it. Because it leaves such a distinctive pattern, a little goes a very long way.

Graining combs are made out of rubber or stainless steel and may be used in conjunction with grainers or by themselves to squeegee or scrape wet paint off a surface in a linear grain pattern. Combs retailed as faux finish tools have been cut into uniform widths so there is no sense of natural variation. Rotate the comb in relation to the direction of your stroke to add variation. Also, the teeth of these combs tend to be spaced too tight to read well for broad theatrical style. One solution may be to cut gaps in the teeth. However, it goes against the grain, so to speak, to cut up a set of costly stainless steel combs. You can easily fashion your own combs out of rubber or plastic sheets to fit the type and scale of wood grain needed. Wadded newspaper also works well as a comb of sorts. Because every wad of paper will leave a different grain, there will be no repetitive patterns.

A *checker grainer* is an odd tool made up of several stainless steel rings that swivel on a small roller carriage. These rings have indentations cut into the edges so that, when charged with paint and rolled across the surface, they leave a series of choppy lines, much the same as you would find in an oak grain. A similar pattern can be created by lightly spattering the surface with paint and dragging a dry brush through the paint to create a series of small choppy lines. This technique is called *spatter and drag*.

Marble

Stone and marble have extremely wide variation in grain pattern. Understanding marble's structure will give the scenic artist an insight into how it may be recreated with paint. Serpentine marbles are a mixture of stone pieces and liquid bands of minerals, formed by centuries of heat and compression. Drift marbles tend to be formed by layers of sediment that have solidified into a solid mass.

The original fluid state of marble lends itself to endless variations of pattern. Marble, like wood, might be cut in different ways that profoundly affect the grain pattern. Sheets of marble are the most common architectural format for large panels of marble, whereas a large carved block is the basis for sculptural and ornamental pieces. In graining marble, the most common mistakes are to keep forking off the grain until it looks like tree branches or to interconnect the grain until it has a cellular pattern. Make comparisons frequently between your work and the research. Avoid mechanical repetition when graining and always think of how the material actually was formed. Remember that less is more; sometimes, a suggestion of grain will be more convincing than a densely grained surface (see Figure 9.26). It is like

Figure 9.26
Example of marble graining with a brush.

an actor finding a motivation for any action. Method painting—imagine that!

There are a variety of painting tools commonly used to create the effect of naturally occurring grains in marble. Using a tool other than a brush may help you avoid repetitive patterns. Feathers have been used to grain marble for centuries (see Figure 9.27). A large bird feather is used by dragging it through a fresh wet blend or by dipping it in grain-colored paint and dragging it across the surface. As you turn the feather over while dragging it, the grain will abruptly change direction, as it would the marble.

This technique works well enough for small-scale faux finishes. The problem with using this technique on a scale common to theater is that a bird feather does not hold a lot of paint. Having to recharge the feather every few seconds really can slow down a process, especially with an entire deck to paint. One solution is to use a feather duster of pheasant or ostrich feathers. Several feathers will hold a great deal more paint then one scrawny feather.

A muslin flogger or a rag may also be used in this manner. The grain lines from these will be somewhat softer and denser than the graining done by a brush. Three-inch-wide rollers are also very useful for marble grains. The roller line can be used alternately on edge or flat. This is very useful for large areas of marble. A dry roller can also be used to soften or finesse the marble grain and has the advantage of inadvertently creating softer random traces of grain. Serpentine marble can be created using paint stamps cut in different patterns to simulate the natural mix of solid minerals in liquid. Use different colors of paint for a convincing serpentine paint treatment (see Figure 9.28).

What paint should be used when graining? The paint used for brush-applied grain in a marble or wood can be standard scene paint. The paint can be thinned down to whatever consistency is most workable. A glaze medium is necessary for working with faux wood graining tools. The glaze medium may be a clear finish such as water-based urethane, PVA, or clear latex. Add tints to the glaze medium to create the desired hue and saturation.

Lining

Lining simply means painting lines. They can be straight or curved, done freehand or guided with a lining stick. Lining is useful for creating emphatic shadows, architectural moldings, linear patterns, or any image that looks "drawn." Being able to use any size brush and a lining stick, either vertically or on the floor, is a key skill for scenic artists.

Figure 9.27
Marble graining with a roller on edge (top)
and feather duster (bottom).

Lining sticks are used to help scenic artists make perfectly straight brushstrokes. They come in a wide variety of lengths (as described in Chapter 5) and are made for use on a paint frame or on a deck with extension handles. A lining stick can be almost anything, from a 2″ × 4″ to a stir stick, but the better ones have three important characteristics: they are lightweight, easy to hold and move, and are beveled underneath to prevent paint from wicking under their edge onto the scenery. Straight lines are both cartooned and painted with these tools.

The spline and a compass are useful lining guides for curves and arcs. A spline of any reasonable length takes at least two people to set down and hold for the painter. Splines (as described in Chapter 8) are often homemade tools and will not behave as well as conventional lining sticks in preventing paint from running underneath them. Use splines very carefully for lining curved lines (see Figure 9.29).

It is useful if the people who are holding the spline keep dry rags in their pocket. Each time a painted line is completed, the spline should be lifted straight up and the bottom of the spline should be wiped off so that it is clean before it is set into the next position. A shop compass can be fitted with a brush on one leg. Smaller circles can be painted evenly in this manner. A lining brush may work better than a flat-ferrule brush to paint curves with a compass (see Figure 9.30). When painting any kind of tightly curved line, a flat-ferrule brush may not be able to track the curve while maintaining the width of the line.

Figure 9.28 Drift (above) and serpentine (below) marble.

Lining Brushes

Brushes used for lining can be of nearly any sort to suit the demands of the particular task. A four-inch-wide transparent cast shadow and intricate crosshatching both are lining tasks, but each of these jobs calls for a very different brush.

A brush used for lining must have bristles that are tight and do not splay out. Errant bristles will cause line work to look sketchy. Always use a brush that gives the desired line width and holds as much paint as possible. Oddly enough, fitch brushes sold by theatrical supply companies as liners are not always the best choice for doing line work because they do not hold a large charge of paint like other styles of brushes. Flat-ferrule brushes, particularly sash brushes, are often an excellent choice for lining. These brushes hold a good charge of paint so they can go for a long distance between chargings. A one-inch sash or flat-ferrule brush used on edge can deliver a good one-quarter-inch or one-half-inch line (see Figure 9.31).

Lining is easy to practice, and any scenic artist not comfortable with the skill of lining should become comfortable through practice. Lining is one of the basic components of trompe l'oeil (described later in this chapter). It is relatively easy to pull the brush along the edge of a lining stick. Always use the

Figure 9.29
Lining with a spline.

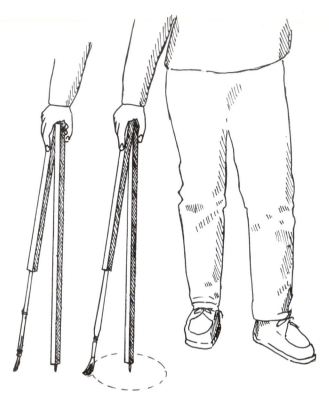

COMPASS MAY BE USED WITH EITHER BRUSH OR
EXTENSION

Figure 9.30   Lining with a compass.

Figure 9.31   Painter working with a lining stick. Drop for *Carmina Burana* designed by John Schak, University of Michigan paint shop.

thinner side of the brush if possible to get as much out of each charge of the brush. For example, a four-inch sash brush held sideways should generate a one-inch-wide line that is several feet long, but a one-inch wide brush will give up the ghost pretty quickly.

Remember to keep the brush as vertical as possible, keeping the bristles from running under the lining stick. Keep your eyes slightly ahead of the brush at the path ahead. This method avoids mistakes and improves control. Keep an even pressure on the brush so the line stays the same width. Do not tilt the brush toward or away from the lining stick while drawing the line. Doing so will cause the line to waver. If you are merging one painted line into the end of another, begin moving the brush along the edge of the lining stick before the tip of the bristles come in contact with the surface. In this way the separate paint strokes will merge into one another.

What paint should be used when lining? Any scene paint can be used for lining. Keep in mind that the paint should be as thin as possible but still keep the quality of color desired. If paint is too thick, the line will not pull out well. The stroke will get sketchy and quickly start to skip. If you must do line work with an oil-based paint, thin the paint with the appropriate solvent. Use proper safety precautions (see Chapter 4, the section "Safety and Health Regulations").

Sponging

Sponging simply means applying paint or texture with a sponge. Sponges can be used to create a very convincing organic texture. They may also be used for blending fields of color and chiaroscuro shading. Various types and styles of sponges should be stocked in the shop and the scenic artist's kit.

Since every natural sponge has its own pattern, a scenic artist may want to collect a variety of sponges in different sizes and grains. As noted in Chapter 5, if you ever have the opportunity to vacation on an ocean coast, keep your eye out for sponges you may want to add to your kit. Damp sponges can be compressed and rolled tightly in plastic bags so that they fit into luggage and then cleaned with mild detergent as soon as you get home. Sponges should always be stored where they can dry out, otherwise they may mildew.

Sponge Technique

A natural ocean sponge often is used to create the illusion of texture on two-dimensional surfaces because of its organic quality. Sponging can be used to create the appearance of a variety of materials such as rock, tree bark, distant tree foliage, coral reefs, and so on. A lightly charged sponge can be used for applying color through a stencil. Natural sponges frequently are used to soften edges and blends in painting. The natural sponge works well putting paint on a texture compound or for applying or finessing the surface of the compound itself. A sponge dabbed over a surface after texture compound has been applied gives it a more natural or organic appearance (see Figure 9.32). In any technique

employing a natural sponge, it is important to remember to rotate the sponge between dabs so that a pattern does not develop (see Figures 9.33 and 9.34).

> Sponges are an important cleaning tool. Scenic artists should keep a bucket of water and a natural sponge nearby for cleaning up drips while working. When a bucket of paint gets spilled on a drop, a soft natural sponge is the first tool to reach for. Be sure not to rub a spill. Dab up the spilled paint and clean out the sponge thoroughly each time it is wrung. If necessary, spray the edges of the spill with water to keep them from drying before they can be cleaned up. It is important to remember that a sea sponge should never be used with bleach. The organic composition of the sponge will dissolve in bleach.

Synthetic sponges are manufactured out of cellotex or foam rubber. They can be torn up so they have a more natural texture. Both the cellotex and the foam rubber sponges give a specific texture when torn that may be applicable for particular surfaces. They also can be cut up or used in block shape to print or texture repetitive shapes like bricks and tiles. They may be carved into a pattern to be printed on scenery. Because of the limited size of foam rubber and cellotex sponges, it may be necessary to use sheets of foam rubber and make paint stamps for larger pattern work.

Figure 9.32
Sponge roller and ocean sponge texture.

Figure 9.33
Coarse ocean sponge texture.

What paint should be used with sponges? Any kind of water-based paint can be used with sponges. This paint can be of any consistency, from very thick and opaque to a glaze. Sponging also may be done with any water-based clear medium. Joint compound can be sponged to make a three-dimensional texture. Do not use a sponge with plaster or solvent-based paint unless you are prepared to throw it away afterwards.

Rag Rolling

Rag rolling is exactly that: a paint-soaked rag loosely twisted or wadded up and rolled around on a surface. This creates a broken texture that is even but not repetitive (see Figure 9.37). A wadded up rag may also be used in a manner similar to a natural sponge by blotting the paint on and rotating the rag to avoid repetitive patterns. Nearly any kind of fabric can be used for rag rolling. To soften a texture, the edges of the rag can be frayed. Burlap and muslin are terrific for rag rolling and are almost always found somewhere in a scene shop. Another rag rolling technique involves wrapping and tying rags around a roller cover. Use this in a multidirectional fashion or in a single direction to create a grain on the scenery.

Flogging and Schlepitchka

Flogging as a paint technique is similar to flogging done in cartooning except that paint is being applied

Figure 9.34 Field stones painted with an ocean sponge.

What paint should be used when rag rolling? Any kind of paint can be used for rag rolling, from thin glazes to fully opaque paints, depending on the desired effect. Rags also are used to spread and work in stains and finishes on wood and in some faux finish techniques.

CAUTION: A note about using rags with solvent-based paints. Rags soaked in solvents and oils, particularly cotton rags, can and will combust spontaneously. Many fires have been started by solvent-based rags left in a pile. Once, when working with a cotton rag and linseed oil, the rag began to heat up in my hand while I was working on a scaffolding. I tossed the rag to someone on the deck who got it to the sink just as it caught fire. Solvent-soaked rags should be disposed of in buckets of water or spread flat and allowed to dry outside. They should be labeled as toxic waste and disposed of through an OSHA-approved agency. Always use proper safety precautions.

rather than charcoal being cleaned off. Flogging is an excellent approach as a base coat for foliage and grass. *Schlepitchka* is a texturing trick done by twirling a feather duster or flogger around gently and dabbing it on the surface of the scenery between each twirl of the tool so that the splayed pattern prints on the scenery. This technique is frequently done as a background for foliage or wallpaper. Schlepitchka is more difficult to

Figure 9.35
Underpainted texture is essential for convincing trompe l'oeil as evident in this photo of a portal used in *42nd Street*. This is a close-up detailing the painting technique. Scenic Art Studios, New York.

Figure 9-36
Underpainted texture is essential for convincing trompe l'oeil as evident in this detail of a portal used in *42nd Street*. This is a large section of the portal. Note the very long lining stick at the top of the photo. Scenic Art Studios, New York.

Figure 9.37   Rag rolling technique.

do on a paint frame. If working vertically with a rag flogger, the handle length should be short so that the tool is easier to manage (see Figure 9.38).

Tools and Paint of Schlepitchka and Flogging

Flogging and schlepitchka can be done with a flogger made of any material you can think of, such as burlap, netting, fishing line, muslin, or sash cord. Feather dusters commonly are used as tools for flogging and schlepitchka. The types of feathers used are chicken, ostrich, and pheasant. Feather dusters can be found in most discount and grocery stores, but the longer and more elegant feather dusters of ostrich and pheasant can be found primarily at janitorial supply stores. The type of texture created in flogging depends on the type of feathers or material it is made from.

Which paint should be used with floggers?
The paint used for these techniques can be any consistency necessary, from thoroughly opaque to thin glazes. Floggers drip a lot when working with glazes. It will be necessary to wring a fair amount of paint from the tool after charging it. If a flogger or feather duster is sopping wet, the feathers or rags cling together in a bundle rather then separate.

Figure 9.38
Examples of schlepitchka with various feather dusters.

Spattering

Spattering involves flinging paint on the scenery so that the paint lands on it in blobs. It may sound reckless but it is quite controllable as well as a lot of fun. A scenic artist with a good spattering brush can make spattered patterns from extremely coarse to extremely fine textures or can toss the paint in a linear pattern quite a distance. Spattering is used both up and down and in almost every imaginable circumstance. Spattering is one of the most commonly used techniques in scenic painting. Many painted surfaces

Figure 9.39
A grass field painted by using a flogging technique with a feather duster.

and scenery involve spattering in at least one, if not several, stages of painted development. A spatter may be used in combination with the base coat, wet on wet, applied after the base coat has dried, or onto an area that has been wetted down first with a spray or spatter of water, glaze, or paint so the color of the spatter melts into the surrounding area. The paint used for spatter may be either opaque or a glaze. Some techniques such as graining or scumbles may also be spattered with straight water or a thin glaze while the paint is still wet to soften some edges of the applied colors.

A finished piece or scenery frequently is given a *dirty-water spatter* as the final paint application to break up the crispness of the paint job. The term *dirty water* refers to the bucket of water the painter would keep nearby for rinsing out brushes. This very lightly tinted water spattered on the scenery as a finishing touch softens the edginess of the painted detail because objects in reality usually do not have perfectly sharp edges or surfaces that reflect light seamlessly. The dappled grain of a dirty water spatter adds to the realism of the piece.

Spattering Technique and Tools

Basically, there are three techniques of spattering. One is to gently shake or rock a charged brush over an area and let the drops of paint fall in an evenly dispersed pattern. The second is to pitch or fling the

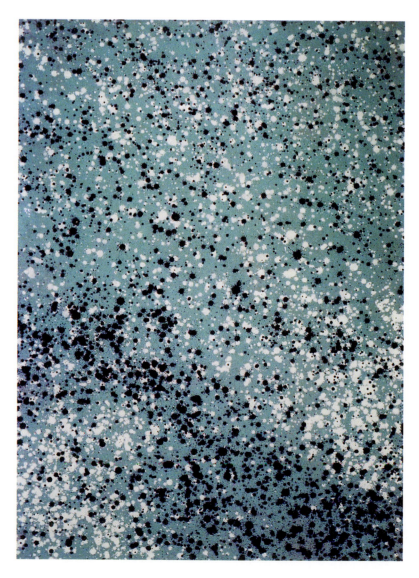

Figure 9.40
Example of course spatter.

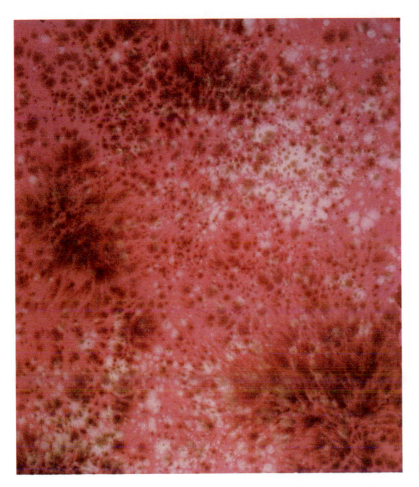

Figure 9.41
Example of spattering onto a wet surface.

paint from a charged brush so that it falls in a line or an arc. The third is to slap the ferrule of a charged brush against your hand or a piece of wood so the bristles snap and paint flies onto a surface. Each of these methods result in a different texture (see Figures 9.40 and 9.41). The first two techniques are primarily for work on a horizontal surface. Coarse spatter will run if attempted on vertical scenery. The viscosity of the paint will also have an effect on how coarse or fine the spatter is, and with practice you will become attuned to how much the paint should be thinned to get the spatter pattern you desire.

The technique of spatter and drag, discussed as a graining technique, involves spattering the surface and dragging a dry brush through the spatter to elongate its pattern before the spatter has dried (see Figure 9.42). This technique can be done more heavily with coarse spatter for other texture applications.

Larger brushes, four inches wide and up, should be used for spattering. It is difficult to get a well-dispersed spatter pattern with smaller brushes. Brushes with longer bristles have more snap, making it easier to throw and disperse the paint. A garden sprayer can be used for fine and even spatter. The sprayer can be pumped to a very low pressure to spray fairly large droplets. Point the nozzle up while spraying to

Which paint should be used when spattering? Paint used for spattering should be thin enough to drop off the brush with ease when working down. If the paint is too thick, it will be particularly difficult to get an evenly dispersed spatter. Working up, the opposite is true. If the paint is too thin, then it is likely to run once it hits the surface. If a glaze or transparent spatter effect is necessary on vertical scenery, try adding a flat acrylic, methocel gum thickener, thickened starch, or wheat paste to the paint to give it body without adding to its opacity.

Figure 9.42
An example of spatter and drag.

diffuse the paint over a wider area. It may take some getting used to, but this method will cover a large area with a fine spatter quickly.

Blocking

Blocking (also called *boarding)* is a technique used in conjunction with other techniques, such as spattering or scumbling, or can be used on its own to create a new texture (see Figure 9.43). Blocking involves using the edge or flat of a board to smear wet paint across a surface, creating a texture or adding dimension to what is already there. Paint also can be applied to a board and smeared straight off it onto the surface of the scenery. Any flat-sided board will

work for this technique. If a great deal of boarding is to be done, you can improvise a tool by fastening a handle or extension to a board for convenience. Spattering and boarding are excellent ways to create a linoleum pattern or the appearance of peeling and distressed paint.

> What paint should be used when blocking or boarding? Paint of any consistency can be boarded. The thinner the paint, the farther it spreads. More viscous paint is preferred with boarding. It has more impact than glazes, which tend to spread too thin.

Figure 9.43 Examples of blocking or boarding.

Stippling

Stippling is applying paint by dabbing or lightly dry-brushing a surface with only the tips of a brush's bristles held perpendicular to the surface. Theatrical and decorating supply houses sell stippling brushes made expressly for this purpose. The bristles in these brushes are very short and set in a wide ferrule. They are trimmed to the same length so all of them can hit the surface at the same time. Until the advent of sprayers and rollers, stippling was the primary technique used to stencil. Stippling can also be used to create very fine texture. The stippling brushes sold for use in decorating tend to be small, so they are not as useful for broad theatrical applications. Some theatrical supply houses carry large stippling brushes useful for theatrical techniques.

Pointillist painting techniques rely heavily on stippling (see Figure 9.44). Smaller brushes, such as a small theatrical liner, can be used to apply color dot by dot for detail work. There is a wide array of methods for providing a broad coverage of paint in pointillist dots. Foam bottle brushes, foam orthopedic mattresses, and bundles of ethafoam rod all can be used for stippling the general areas of color.

A bunched-up rag or newspaper also can be used to stipple. The technique is very similar to sponging, but the different materials create different textures. With this application, it is important to rotate the wad of cloth or paper between each dab so that a pattern does not develop.

> What paint should be used when stippling? Paint used for stippling techniques should be rather thick. If the paint is too thin, it will be difficult to keep the texture consistent and even. If the paint needs to be transparent, the color can be mixed into a flat acrylic medium so that the paint will have body. Stippling must be done with a rather dry tool. If the tool is fully charged, there will be no stipple patterns, only blobs (see Figure 9.45).

Garden Sprayers

Garden sprayers are indispensable scenic art tools and can be used for smoothing and blending color over large areas. Seen from a distance, the pattern of the spray blends together smoothly into a solid color or even gradation. Sprayers are much easier to use on scenery painted on the floor; however, with practice, they can be used on vertical scenery or drops on a paint frame. Note that pneumatic sprayers may be more useful for vertical work.

Sprayers are available in many different varieties as described in Chapter 5. A paint shop should stock the large two-and-a-half-gallon and three-and-a-half-gallon sprayers as well as smaller one-half-gallon sprayers. Small sprayers are convenient for smaller jobs because they take less paint and are lighter and easy to clean. They spray a lighter pattern suited to detail work and toning smaller areas. Larger sprayers are essential for large-scale work, such as toning an entire drop.

Figure 9.44
Stippling pointillism.

Garden Spraying Techniques and Tools

Smoothing the texture of brushstrokes in a base coat or wet blend can be done by spraying over the brushwork with the same base colors. If two or more related colors are sprayed on the base coat, such as cooler and warmer variants of the base colors, the resulting colors are more brilliant under stage light. This is standard practice when painting flat color fields, so that the color fields are smoothed and respond well to stage light. Altering the value or hue of the base coat also can be done by spraying.

To spray evenly over a large surface, use a large sprayer with a wand. The pressure and the spray nozzle should be set so that the spray does not come out too fine. A heavier spray will go where it is aimed,

whereas a too-fine spray will be turned into wispy patterns because the spray is affected by air drafts. For an even spray, the person spraying should traverse the drop or scenery in a very methodical pattern, walking slowly in straight lines while taking care always to keep the spray nozzle high and the same distance from the scenery. The wand should be rotated in a small circle while keeping the nozzle perpendicular to the surface or object being painted. This rotation helps avoid uneven spray buildup and keeps the pattern of the spray much smoother. Overlap every pass of spray pattern over one-half of the preceding pass.

Work methodically and take time when blending different hues or values by multiple applications

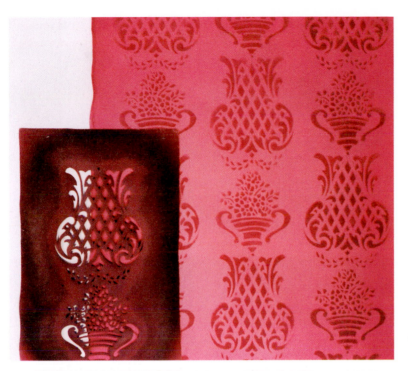

Figure 9.45
Stippling through a stencil.

of spray. Always let spray applications dry before applying the next one. Widen the revolutions of the wand and walk more quickly to lighten the density of the spray while progressing through the blend. When doing a blend with a sprayer, it helps to have the paint hues or values shift in several stages for a smoother blend. For example, a shift from blue-violet to emerald may take four or five steps in color shifts.

Small garden sprayers are ideal for detailed spraying jobs, such as contouring clouds or spraying into foliage. The small capacity can run out quite quickly, so do not attempt to spray a large surface with a small sprayer. Small sprayers produce a smaller pattern and hold less pressure as well, so your range is limited. They may also be used in places where space is limited or when painting small areas, as with working inside fully assembled scenic units.

A common problem with garden sprayers occurs each time the spray is started. The initial spray forces out the entire contents of the spray nozzle, resulting in a splattering of paint drops. Always start the sprayer aimed away from the scenery, if possible. If you are working in the middle of a drop and have nowhere to aim but on the drop itself, carry a sponge to catch the drips or start the spray in a bucket.

A mask or template can be used in conjunction with a sprayer to paint along a contour or pattern

(see Figure 9.46). Evenly placed strips of a masking can form the basis for a wallpaper pattern. If there is an object such as the mountains in the distance, and the spray must not go into the adjacent sky, the area around the mountains can be masked out with paper, cloth, or plastic. Masking along a straightedge can be done with strips of lauan or Upson board, which can be shifted and reused repeatedly. If using a visquene or any plastic mask on a deck, the edges should be taped down to keep the lightweight mask from moving or floating while spraying. Safety pins can be used to hold a mask in position on a paint frame. Be careful that the edges of masking do not get too wet. Visquene masking takes longer to dry than the surface of the scenery. Excessive paint built up on the masking will bleed onto the scenery.

Normally, solvent-based paints should not be used with garden sprayers because they will shorten the life of the tool considerably and require a large amount of solvent to clean the sprayer. If the need arises, take care not to use one of the shop's favorite sprayers. French enamel varnishes (FEVs) made with denatured alcohol, shellac, and dye are the most common solvent-based mediums used in garden sprayers. This can be cleaned out fairly well with the denatured alcohol (see Chapter 4, the section "Health and Safety Regulations").

Figure 9.46
Example of masked spray with a template.

What paint should be used in a garden sprayer? The paint used with garden sprayers should be water-based scenic or house paint. It must be fairly thin for the tool to work properly and it must be strained through a nylon strainer or particulates in the paint will clog the nozzle. Dye also can be used with garden sprayers. After spraying with dye, it may be necessary to clean the sprayer with a 25 percent solution of bleach before using it again with paint. If the sprayer has metal parts, rinse it out with a 25 percent solution of vinegar to prevent the bleach from corroding the metal parts. Do not use bleach to clean a sprayer before using it with another color dye. The residual bleach will ruin subsequent dye colors.

Pneumatic Sprayers

There are three basic reasons for painting scenery with a pneumatic sprayer. First, some three-dimensional forms are too complex or lacy to be painted with a brush and are covered more easily with a sprayer (see Figure 9.47). Second, an airbrush style demands the smooth coverage and even blend of a sprayer. Third, smooth application of a medium such as dye is accomplished more easily with a pneumatic sprayer. Pneumatic sprayers are capable of delivering a much thicker paint than garden sprayers. In general, these two types of sprayers are used for very different applications.

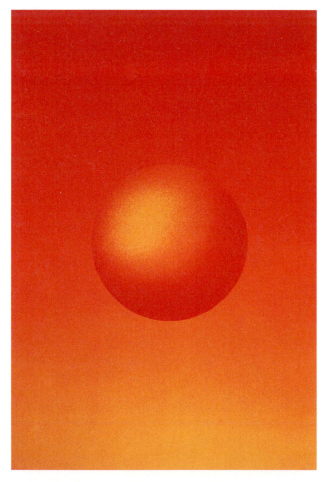

Figure 9.47   Example of pneumatic spray gun technique.

Pneumatic Spraying Techniques and Tools

For base coats, pneumatic sprayer is passed slowly back and forth across a surface to evenly coat it with paint. Each stroke should overlap by about one-quarter to one-half of the preceding pass to ensure good coverage. When spraying a three-dimensional form, the recesses should be sprayed first, then the raised areas of the form to avoid excessive paint buildup.

An airbrush technique can be done on a large scale using pneumatic sprayers. Separate areas of colors can be filled in and blended using masks. The masking used with garden sprayers, visquene and lauan, also works well in pneumatic sprayers. Kraft or butcher paper masks tend to curl when the paper gets wet, so use them only on a limited basis. Do not rush the painting when working with a mask, particularly if the area being sprayed is highly saturated or a blend of several applications of color. If too much paint is sprayed on the mask at a time, paint will seep under the edges of the mask. To avoid this, take the time to spray two coats of saturated colors. Areas of large color fields are difficult to lay on evenly, particularly with dyes; spraying the color on in two applications of lighter dye results in a smoother fill. Do not apply the second coat until the first coat is completely dry or the result will be a patchy surface. If you are working with any mask, be careful not to spray at an angle that forces the paint or dye under the edge of the masking. Conventional artists' airbrushes can be used in scenic painting when the demand is for extremely fine or detailed work.

Photo-realism is a style where the exacting control of an airbrush is particularly useful.

Using pneumatic sprayers as tools is discussed in Chapter 5. Quart- and pint-size sprayers are the primary types used for these applications. They offer great control and are easy to hold. Airless sprayers should be confined to covering large areas with paint. They should not be used for work where finesse is called for because they are highly pressurized, high-volume sprayers. All pneumatic sprayers should have regulated airlines or air valves attached to the sprayer for more control. When working in a masked spray technique, set the spray pressure at the lowest setting possible so the masking is not blown around.

Paint Stamps

A *paint stamp* is a tool similar to a giant rubber stamp and inkpad that makes repeating patterns (see Figure 9.48). These are custom made and assembled in the scene shop by the scenic artists, who use foam rubber glued to a piece of rigid sheet stock. Paint stamps can be used on both vertical and horizontal flat surfaces. They may have an irregular, broken texture, such as foliage, as well as a specific pattern, such as wallpaper. Stamps are charged by setting them into a shallow tray of paint. Because paint stamps can be large, it is frequently necessary to create a tray to fit each stamp. A paint tray can be made of visquene draped in a one-inch stock lumber form.

Stamp Registration

Registration in printmaking means aligning one print plate to another so the different colors of the image merge accurately. Registration of a paint stamp guides the scenic artist in repeated and accurate placement of colors in a pattern. Although in terms of theatrical scale, the registration need not be as perfect as in printmaking, it does need to be thoughtfully worked out and tested before applying the stamp to the scenery.

The pattern for a paint stamp is drawn and pounced first on a piece of kraft paper. If the pattern is a repeating wallpaper design, use the pounce to check the alignment and registration of the pattern top, bottom, and sides. Once you have checked the registration, use the same pounce as the guide for patterning the different color patterns for each stamp.

What paint should be used with pneumatic sprayers? Paint used in a sprayer must be thin enough to allow it to flow through the sprayer evenly. Paint that is too thick will not atomize evenly. If the paint is too thick, it will come out in droplets rather than a spray or the volume of the spray may change rhythmically, which generates a pattern on the scenery. All paint and mediums used in a sprayer should be strained through a nylon strainer. This is very important with scenic paint, as the paint is mixed in buckets that have been used several times before. Some remnant of old paint in the bucket can stop up a sprayer if the new paint is not strained thoroughly.

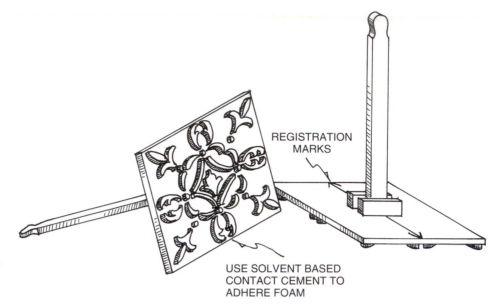

Figure 9.48
Patterned paint stamps.
(See Chapter 5 for more
information about paint
stamp construction.)

REGISTRATION
MARKS

USE SOLVENT BASED
CONTACT CEMENT TO
ADHERE FOAM

Because you look at the back of the stamp base as you work with the stamp, the registration will have to relate to the outside edges of the stamp base. Reference lines are normally snapped on the scenery and the registration marks are made on the snapped lines relating to the top and bottom registration marks on the back of the paint stamp (see Figures 9.49 and 9.50). You can use a detail of the actual stamped pattern near its edge as a registration mark. It may be possible to cut part of the stamp base away around this detail. You should shape and register multiple paint stamps for color separations in exactly the same way. It is always a good idea to label the back of a paint stamp top and bottom (as the pattern relates to the scenery), indicate what color of the pattern it is, and even partially draw the pattern on

MASTER PATTERN

COLOR SEPARATION

GOLD

GREEN

WHITE

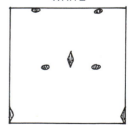

Figure 9.49
Stencil and stamp color
separation.

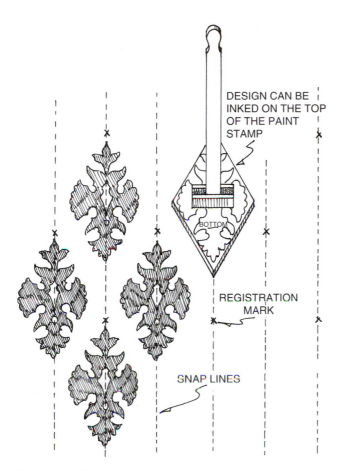

DESIGN CAN BE INKED ON THE TOP OF THE PAINT STAMP

BOTTOM

REGISTRATION MARK

SNAP LINES

Figure 9.50 Paint stamp registration.

What paint should be used with paint stamps? The paint for paint stamps should be fairly thick. Paint that is too thin will seep to one side of the stamp and leave an uneven print. If the paint is to be translucent, the color can be mixed in flat transparent medium for body. The paint also must be water based, as any solvent-based paint will melt the foam rubber of the stamp. It may take a few applications of paint for the paint stamp to get evenly charged. Always wash the paint out of a stamp immediately after it has been used; once the paint has dried on a stamp, it ceases to be useable. Be particularly careful to thoroughly clean bronzing powders suspended in binders out of a paint stamp. These paints tend to dry very quickly and are intractable once they have dried. Because the paint used with a paint stamp is so thick, stamping is not a good technique to use with materials that need to stay soft, such as silk or scrim. A stencil might do a better job.

and checked first, just as with paint stamps (see Figures 9.48 and 9.50).

What Tools to Use with Stencils

One of the most common paint tools used with a stencil is a pneumatic sprayer. In this case, the paint should be just thin enough to go through the sprayer but as thick as possible for coverage and to deter it from seeping under the edge of the stencil. A stencil to be used with a sprayer should be adequately masked on the sides so the scenery is protected from overspray. It is best to cut the pattern in an oversized stencil so that the stencil itself masks the overspray. It may be necessary to stencil every other repeat so that adjacent patterns have a chance to dry. When spraying a stencil, you may need to experiment with the color and consistency of paint so that the least amount of paint can be sprayed on the surface and on the stencil and still do the job. The airflow of the sprayer should be set at the absolute minimum to reduce overspray.

The stippling brush is primarily used as a tool for stenciling. A technique that works very well with linoleum stencils is as follows: Cut the pattern so that the soft side of the linoleum is up. Align the stencil into position on the scenery. Lightly spray the paint through the stencil pattern with an aerosol sprayer such as a Pre-valve®. Do not use a pneumatic

the stamp so that the orientation of the stamp is comprehensible at a glance.

In some cases, a multicolor pattern can be created using a paint stamp if the pattern is composed of areas of color that are not directly adjacent to one another. The entire pattern can be cut into one paint stamp and then each area can be charged by hand using brushes.

Stencils and Templates

A *stencil* is an intricate painting mask made of flat material with the negative area of a design or pattern cut out (see Figure 9.51). Paint is applied through the stencil. Like the paint stamp, a multicolored design can be created with a stencil by drafting out the color separation on separate stencils and registering them all in the same manner. Registration, color separations, and pattern reconciliation need to be cartooned

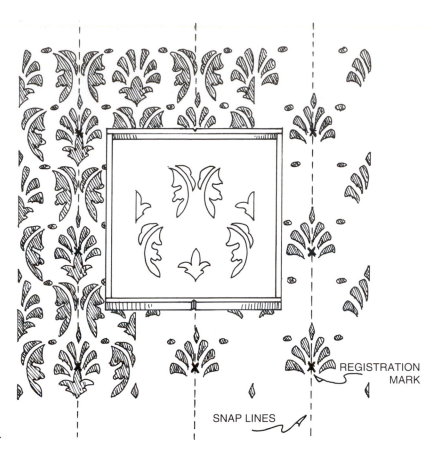

Figure 9.51
Stencil registration and repetition.

REGISTRATION MARK

SNAP LINES

sprayer as the flow of paint is too hard to control. Before removing the stencil, dab at the pattern with a large stencil brush to even out the paint. This method has many advantages. First, once you get a feel for the amount of spray to apply, you never have to stop and clean the stencil off or let it dry out. Second, because the stippling spreads the paint out so thinly, the stencil can usually be repositioned directly adjacent to the last repletion without smearing, even if it partly overlaps it. Because of these advantages

Figure 9.52
A stencil is in place and ready for painting of this drop used in *St. Louis Woman*. Scenic Art Studios, New York.

over spraying, a scenic artist using this method can stencil quickly without having to deal with the compressor hose and noise. Also, several scenic artists can work with multiple color patterns at the same time.

Rollers also work very well with stencils. When working with rollers, it is easy to work with two or more colors. Another advantage of rollers is the texture that they leave works well with some common stencil applications. A dry roller technique is convincing in creating the appearance of velvet wallpaper. Large brick stencils, often cut from a 4′ × 8′ piece of tin or large pieces of linoleum, work well with rollers. The rollers cover the area quickly, and by blending two or more colors across the stencil, a good start is made on the color variation in bricks.

To clean the stencil between repeated uses, carefully wipe off excess paint and set it against a fan to dry. If the stencil is netted, set it on a moist towel or rag and carefully dab it off with a damp sponge. Do not let paint build up on the bobbinet. Make multiple copies of the stencil if the pattern repeats a lot. While one stencil is used for two or three repeated instances, the other stencils can be getting cleaned and dried. Stencils should be completely dry before they are used again.

> What paint should be used with stencils? Any water-based paint can be used with a stencil. Solvent-based paints can also be used, but paint buildup on the stencil may be a problem. The viscosity of the paint depends on the paint technique used. Do not rush work with a stencil. It is a slow process and if there is much to do, it will take time. Concentrate on doing a clean and thorough job rather to avoid having a lot of touch-up work to do on the scenery afterward.

Stencil Registration

Stencils in a repetitive pattern need registration marks, grooves, or diamonds cut into them that correspond to marks on the scenery. If different stencils are used for color separation, the registration marks must be in the same place on all stencils. Registration marks on the scenic units are made along guidelines laid on the scenery prior to stenciling. The guidelines should not be inked in or in any way permanent. If the pattern has a stripe or a border, it may be painted prior to stenciling and used as a guideline for registration.

Carefully think through the registration marks on a stencil so that the stencil can be placed easily and accurately (see Figure 9.50).

When preparing to apply the stencil to the scenery, think through the actual work. Make sure your paint tools and air hose are placed so you can avoid tiptoeing over or dragging the hose through freshly stenciled areas. When placing the registration marks, think about what side of the stencil you will be on when you apply it. Also consider whether you need to do every other repeat and then return to do the missing patterns so the stencil need never rest on a wet area.

When deciding on the steps involved in painting the scenery, it is important to consider at what point the stenciling is to be done. Normally, stenciling should be painted as early as possible so other painting, such as cutting in moldings, toning, and cast shadows, is placed over the pattern. Similarly, with hard scenery, all three-dimensional elements need to be applied after the stenciling has been done so that the stencil can lay flat.

Templates and Spray Masking

Templates are similar to stencils in that they create a mask for painting, but templates are painted around rather than through, and issues of registration are not as critical. A leaf template or various patterns of templates can be used to spray leaf patterns. Spray masking comes into play when an area of scenery needs to be isolated from another for contrasting techniques. Spray masking allows the scenic artist to

> I have found that if careful thought is given to the way painted treatments are layered on top and adjacent to one another, masking may be kept to a minimum. Masking can be a very time-consuming process, and for the sake of alacrity, it should be avoided whenever there is another option. By carefully considering the strategy of adjacent paint treatments, masking out specific areas may be done away with altogether. For instance, by choosing to tone the side of a building from the front edge to the back rather than from the back to the front, the adjacent sky may not have to be masked off. By completing the toning on the side of the building before basing in the front, masking can also be avoided on its edge.

work on a misty, distant sky next to a more crisply painted building by placing a mask or template over the building. Several contours in a complex city scene might need toning along straight edges. Most paint shops keep several lengths of one-foot-wide lauan around to be used for masking sprays. If two scenic artists work as a team, one person can place the masking and move it as necessary while the other sprays. This way several colors can be worked through the scenery at the same time.

Some shapes are small enough to be masked with one or two widths of tape, such as windows in a city scene. If you have hundreds of small windows to mask out on a city drop, carry a putty knife with you to use as a guide to tear the tape off in a straight line. Masking tape can be a very effective template, although time consuming if the forms are round. Tape templates can be cut out right on the scenery, which will speed up work on curving shapes. Lay the tape over the contour to be cut out, overlapping the cartoon and each strip of tape only as much as necessary. You should be able to see the cartoon through the tape. Cut through the tape with a fresh razor blade along the contour. Be careful to apply only enough pressure to score the tape and not cut through to the muslin underneath. The muslin will give just slightly, so the right pressure will score the more ridged tape and not the muslin. Practice on something small and inexpensive first. If you are working on a 30-foot piece of seamless goods, this can be terrifying—it was for me. Once you develop the touch, this method of cutting contour masking will be a very useful technique.

Spray Masking Using Particulates

Soft shapes like clouds are difficult to create with hard-edged masking material such as visquene or fabric because the edges will be too sharp. Instead, particulates such as perlite and vermiculite may be used to effect mask-out sprays intended to create soft-edged shapes. For instance, if a sky is first based white and the shape of the clouds is lightly cartooned with chalk, particulate masking can be sprinkled into the areas that are to remain white. After the blue sky colors have been sprayed and are completely dry, the particulate can be carefully swept and vacuumed up, revealing the white underneath.

For this technique, it is a good idea to match the color of the particulate to the background color if possible. Perlite works best for a cloud effect because it is white. Vermiculite works best for more earthy-colored backgrounds. Sand and sawdust are not usually good choices for this technique because they tend to be dirty and have very fine grains and chips mixed in, which may be messy to clean up.

The preferable method of spraying used in this technique is with a garden sprayer. The psi of a pneumatic sprayer is so strong that it will blow the particulates out of place as perlite and vermiculite are both very light weight.

Spraying Patterns and Masking with Fabric

Erosion cloth, burlap, lace, extruded plastic fencing, and anything else you can think of may be used as a spray pattern of sorts. A piece of the cloth can be laid over scenery that has been base coated and another color sprayed over it. The pattern left behind, depending on the fabric used, will be distinguishable from some distance away. In this way, one piece of cloth can be used to paint a texture on an entire set.

In some cases, a piece of fabric can be used for masking a spray. It may be rather time consuming to mask a long gentle curve with visquene and tape. But a long piece of muslin can be positioned quickly and moved easily into position for another spray. As with any type of masking, be careful that the material doesn't become too saturated with paint and that you don't smear paint on areas that are suppose to stay clean. Wads of cloth or even newspaper may also be held in one hand while spraying around the edges for soft organic shapes. By holding the wad a few inches above the surface while spraying, the edges of the pattern will blur and soften.

TROMPE L'OEIL PAINTING TECHNIQUE

Trompe l'oeil, a French term that means "deceive the eye," is a means of painting any surface employing the pictorial devices of perspective and foreshortening combined with the painting techniques of chiaroscuro and cast shadows. The result is to trick observers into believing they see three-dimensional objects on a two-dimensional plane. Successful trompe l'oeil technique results in stunning results of illusion perfectly suited for the theatre.

The techniques of trompe l'oeil were developed and widely practiced during the Italian Rococo period as a way of satisfying the increasing demand for sumptuous and fantastical interior decoration, reaching a state of perfection in the grand palaces and theatres of Europe. This increasing use of trompe l'oeil coincided with the development of theatrical design and painting. The two grew together, and trompe l'oeil became synonymous with scenic illusion itself. The wing and drop staging of European theatre served as a perfect vehicle for the scenic artist expert in the technique of trompe l'oeil. Illusion of elaborate and exotic locales portrayed in stunning trompe l'oeil techniques became the standard for over 300 years. The history chapters of this book concentrate fully on this development, but here the technique is explained for the painter.

The 300 years of use instilled sound understanding of trompe l'oeil practices in scenic artists working in England, France, and Italy. These practices remain in use today as standard procedure for many scenic designers and scenic artists. Trompe l'oeil technique is the correct combination of many individual techniques, some of which already have been discussed in this book. Foreshortening forms and drawing in linear perspective are discussed in Chapter 8. Both skills are intrinsic aspects of trompe l'oeil.

The Theory of Practice of Trompe l'Oeil

There are three overall aspects to making a successful trompe l'oeil illusion:

1. Create a complete and accurate cartoon.
2. Paint convincing representations of real surfaces and materials like wood, stone, or printed fabric.
3. Model the form with carefully applied light and shadow, sometimes known as *chiaroscuro*, to create the illusion of three dimensions on a two dimensional surface.

Chiaroscuro, meaning "light-dark" in Italian, is the technique of modeling form by gradations of value relating to a specific light source. This "light-dark" describes the shape of the object. Camille Pissarro, the French postimpressionist, further analyzed the relationship of form and its relationship to light. Pissarro observed that four fundamental geometric forms are the basis to all shapes, both human-made and organic: the sphere, cube, hollow cylinder, and pyramid. Pissarro asserted that an artist could adeptly model any form based on combinations of these four elemental forms.

Modeling the shape of each object is where the method of trompe l'oeil begins. Each individual form contained in a composition must be treated separately. Later in the process of trompe l'oeil, these forms are treated as an overall, unified picture with lighting and shadowing. Certainly, trompe l'oeil scene painting is done systematically. Random execution of these steps leads to nothing but confusion. Cartooning, texturing, modeling, and lighting are the way to build the image. One reason for this is that if more than one artist works on a project, all the artists should share a common visual vocabulary, so the work of any one artist is indiscernible from another. Another reason is that, with so much area to cover, only a systematic approach will get you through the process.

A description of a basic system of painting trompe l'oeil follows. As you become familiar with

Figure 9.53 First of three illustrations of a trompe l'oeil drape in progress. Establishing an accurate shape and contrast in one stenciling step on a textured base coat. *42nd Street.* Scenic Art Studios, New York.

Figure 9.54
The next illustration shows initial descriptions of high- and lowlights with added shapes to begin forming the contours. *42nd Street.* Scenic Art Studios, New York.

the technique of trompe l'oeil, you may wish to complete the steps in a different order than they are presented here. Earlier in this book we mentioned the areas of study a scenic artist should be familiar with, fine arts being among the many disciples mentioned. Studying the work of the master artists will help you polish your trompe l'oeil skills. But the main skill involved in trompe l'oeil is that of seeing. You cannot paint an illusion of a thing unless you understand the real life elements that you are trying to paint a representation of. Seeing is one of the most important skills of a scenic artist. Learn how to see the world

not just passively look at it. As you hone your skills as a scenic artist, the entire world will become your instructor. Every form, vista, and edifice will have something to teach you about structure and the effect of light upon it.

Remember that the terms for some of these basic steps of trompe l'oeil may vary from region to region. Being clear on the definitions of terms is important, but mastering the technique is paramount. This basic structure has room for finesse and variation. Some possible variations are discussed, others you will discover on your own as you employ and perfect your technique. The following description of trompe l'oeil technique is predicated on using theatrical scene paint. If you are painting trompe l'oeil with dyes, then all of the steps will be built up out of transparent layers. To some extent the highlight will have to be left clear or painted with a lighter color and throughout before the base color is applied. Casein-based paint works very well for painting highlights on scenery painted with dye.

Color Theory of Trompe l'Oeil

Proper technique in the application of trompe l'oeil technique is only part of the precision and brilliance of this method. By manipulating the color in trompe l'oeil technique, the modeled surfaces in the image can be finessed to improve the illusion of depth. A standard rule in the application of color for trompe l'oeil is warm highlight, cool shadows, or cool

Figure 9.55 More pronounced highlights, cast shadows, and a bit of color help finish the image. *42nd Street.* Scenic Art Studios, New York.

Figure 9.56
Beautiful trompe l'oeil work done on the frescos at the Museo dell'Academia, Florence, Italy.

highlight, warm shadows. If you play the compliments of the colors off of one another, the results will be more interesting as well as apparent. The use of complementary colors accentuates the modeling of the chiaroscuro by creating the impression of cooler-hued surfaces receding into the distance from their warmer counterparts. In compositions where the quality of light is cool—moonlight, for instance—darker slightly warmer shadows will recede from the lighter, more chromatic cool highlights. In general, shades, lowlights, and cast shadows should not be more chromatic than the local color or these areas will not optically recede or pull back. Cast shadow is most effective if it is a deeper value and the complement of the color of light illuminating the scene.

Shade

Identifying the light source or sources within an image is absolutely essential to painting trompe l'oeil. The scenic artist must be fully aware, from the first step, where the light is and where the objects are in relationship to it. In reality, nothing is visible without light.

Begin with the correct placement of shade. The term *shade* refers to the part of a form not facing light. The shadow projected from the object is dealt with later. The color of shade is a step down in value from the base, or local, color of a form. In conventional theatrical trompe l'oeil, the shade is an opaque paint. This helps establish shade as a part of the form itself, not its cast shadow. The color mixed for the

shade usually is a modification of the primary base color. This color should be a step down in both value and neutrality. The shade should not be more chromatic than the base coat. Mixing shades for multicolored base coats may be a little tricky. In this circumstance, it may be necessary to mix a shade that

Figure 9.57   Placement of shade on Pissarro shapes.

is a translucent glaze so that the color and value of the base coat are proportionally deepened by the shade color. Before applying the shade color, lay a swatch of it next to the base color and look at it through squinted eyes. It should "read" as a shaded version of the base.

This first step, the shade, determines the placement of all the steps that are to follow. The shade is brushed in those areas of the form that do not receive direct light. Each of the forms in the picture plane should be treated separately from the others when determining where the shades are located. The object is to model the form—do not be concerned yet with whether the form has a shadow cast across its surface (see Figure 9.57).

Any plane that faces or drops away from the light source will receive a shade. The placement of shade on a square form is the most obvious. Any given plane is either in shade or not. If you are having difficulty deciding whether a plane would be shaded or not, try drawing a sketch of that form in a ground plan view that includes the placement of the light source. By projecting lines from the light source, you will see which planes receive direct light. All that remains is to determine whether the form is above, below, or level with the light source.

The placement of shades on rounded forms can be trickier to figure out. A diagram of a ground plan view also can help with forms such as cylinders (see Figure 9.58). One trap of describing rounded forms occurs when the shade and local color areas are an even half and half. In this case, the form may begin to look square rather than round. The classic approach to modeling a cylinder is to divide it more or less into thirds. One third of the cylinder would be in shade. This is by no means a hard and fast rule, but it is a good place to start when creating the illusion of a rounded form. In the case of a sphere or a cylinder, this theatrical cheat can be used to help round out the forms even more.

On the lighted side of both forms, you may notice a sliver of shade along the edge facing the light. This contrivance is a subtle trick that furthers

the illusion of a rounded form. When placing the shade on more complex forms, compartmentalize the form so that you are only dealing with one section at a time. The shade on each half round, quarter round, convex, and concave surface should be dealt with independently of all the surfaces around them, only taking care that the proportions are equidistant throughout the form. For instance, if you are applying shades to an ornate vase and the shade is applied to one-third of the surface area, be sure to use that one-third proportion throughout.

Bear in mind when dealing with spherical forms that, as the edge of shade approaches the center of the form, the contour will become less pronounced because it is viewed on edge. Imagine cutting an orange in half. Then, holding one half in front of you, rotate it so that the center of the orange becomes an ellipse. This ellipse will become ever shallower until you have just an edge view of the orange half. The same thing happens to the contoured edge of shade as it progresses around a spherical form. When a rounded form also is contoured, as in a capital base or vase, the shade and following lowlight must follow the contour of the form. These are the areas of the lowest light.

When the shades are finished, step back for a moment, and look at the picture through squinted eyes. Squinting your eyes diffuses the image, which helps you see the shift of values more completely and objectively without focusing on specific details. At this point, the shape of the forms should be clearly, not dramatically, defined. Plan the shading of all forms carefully and execute it consistently.

Lowlight

The *lowlight* is a step down in value and neutrality from the shade and should be of a color related to the shade. There should be a natural progression in value and neutrality from the base to the shade and then to the lowlight. Once again, make a swatch of the lowlight and, through squinted eyes, look at the swatch on top of the shade to see the relationship of

Figure 9.58
Sections of curved forms.

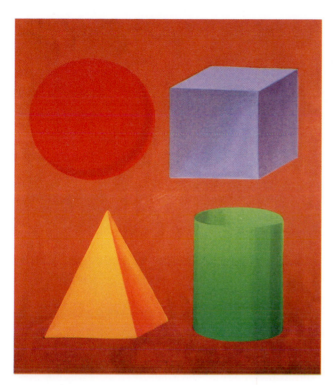

Figure 9.59 Placement of lowlight on Pissarro shapes.

the two colors objectively (see Figure 9.59). Like the shade, the lowlight is conventionally an opaque color.

The lowlight is placed in shaded areas on the planes or curves of the form that receive no direct or ambient light. In the case of the cylinder or the sphere, you may notice a contrivance, the trick of putting the sliver of shade on the lighted side of the forms. Also, by leaving a sliver of the light showing on the shade side of the forms, the illusion of a curved surface is more complete. This is called a *creeping light*. This contrivance should not be used on bas-relief where it should be very clear that the form is connected to the background.

The trick of doing shades in thirds on curved forms can be applied to the proportion of shade to lowlight areas. Generally, the lowlight should occupy about one-third of the area of the shade. Lowlights should be applied only in shaded areas. If there is a creeping light on the form, the lowlight may be backed off from the edge of the form so that a thin sliver of the shade is visible on the lowlight side.

The lowlight, like the shade, is used only to model the forms. It should not be placed in areas of the form that could receive direct light from the light

source because it is in the shadow of another form. Once the lowlight is done, you should be able to look at the forms through squinted eyes and see a crisp illusion of dimension. If some forms are not "reading" as intended at this point, you may wish to rethink the shades and lowlights before continuing.

On larger rounded forms, the shades and lowlights may be softened by blending the edges with water or prewetting the surface so that the edges of the color bleed and soften on their own. On very large forms, the shades and lowlights may even be sprayed on.

Highlights

When you begin painting *highlights*, the illusion of dimensional form and their relationship to one another should be evident in the painting. Highlights should not be necessary for this illusion but rather enhance it. Conventionally, a highlight may be simply a higher value version of the local color of a form. However, the color of the highlight also may serve as a description of the light striking the form. Cool or warm, soft or bright, light resonates with the color and placement of a highlight. If the value difference between the highlight and the local color is subtle, it will give the appearance of a soft light source, such as candlelight. A broad difference in value between the highlight and the local color will give the appearance of a strong light source, such as sunlight. If the surface of the form is a flat finish, the edges of the highlight will be soft and blend into the local color. If the surface of the form is textured, the highlight will accentuate that texture. Highlights also describe the surface of the form. If the surface of the form is shiny, then the highlight will be sharp edged. Very shiny surfaces may even have sharp highlights that reflect the multiple light sources in the composition.

Highlights may be placed on either a plane or the forward edge where two planes join together. Often, two different values of highlights are used, so that the first value is painted on the plane of the object as the primary highlight, and an even higher value highlight is used on the edges as a secondary, brighter highlight (see Figures 9.60 and 9.61).

The placement of highlights on spheres and cylinders is very important. If the highlight is not

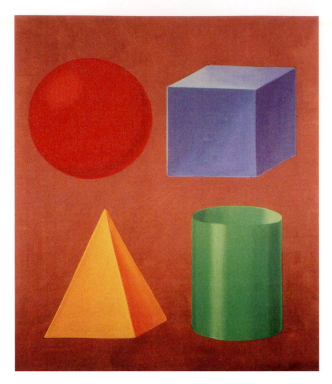

Figure 9.60 Placement of primary highlight on Pissarro shapes.

The paint used for a highlight is opaque to stand out against the local color. Some acrylic-based paints may not stand out against the background. If an acrylic-based paint or dye is being used on the scenery, it may be necessary to switch to a latex or casein for the highlight work to stand out.

Cut Lines

Cut lines are dark accentuation lines that delineate the change of planes or an edge. They should be placed primarily along the joint between receding planes. Cut lines should not be placed on edges that are intended to receive a highlight. Generally there will be a cut line on the side of any form that receives a cast shadow. Beyond this, cut lines should be used minimally to describe the contour of the forms.

The cut line should be the darkest value in the picture, but if too dark, it may look cartoonish. Frequently, the cut lines for the scenic units in the same scene are the same color throughout the entire composition. While the shading and lowlights need to be predicated on the local color of a form, the

placed in the proper relationship to the shade and lowlight, these shapes may look warped. If the highlights are too close to the edge, the sphere or cylinder will look flat; if the highlights are too close to the middle, the shapes will look pointed or squared off. As with the shade and lowlight, a good general rule is to place the highlight about one-third the distance in from the lighted edge of the shape. When dealing with round forms, such as capital bases or vases, the highlight must follow the contour of the form in the same manner as shade and lowlights. Also, different colors of highlights may be positioned slightly different from one another to indicate multiple light sources.

Highlights should be applied very sparingly. Too much highlight will flatten an image and render the dimensioning meaningless. Look at highlights glancing off surfaces in the real world. They actually are very minimal. Even after you exaggerate these highlights for the stage, they are still modest in proportion to the surface area of the form. The highlights do not need to be applied along the entire length of an edge or form. Often, highlights will only glance and skip along an edge or a plane.

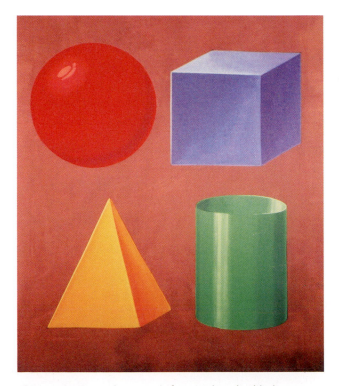

Figure 9.61 Placement of secondary highlight on Pissarro shapes.

process of unifying the composition begins with the cut line, which is another reason it may be the same color in the context of a scene or a backdrop. The paint for cut lines should be opaque.

Cut lines are not a cartoon. If the cut lines are applied like a cartoon along every profile, they will flatten rather then enhance the illusion. Never fully outline an object. Keep in mind that less is more effective. A complete cut line should not be placed along the profile of a form that does not join another plane. For instance, a freestanding column may have a dash of a cut line that strikes up from the bottom and down from the top, particularly on the shade side, but no solid cut line. However, a pilaster would have a solid cut line along the entire length of the shade side of the form where it joins the wall. The cut line on the lighted side of the pilaster may be dashed or broken as necessary to accentuate the joint in the planes. A sphere sitting on the ground would have only a dash of a cut line on the shadow side of the form. On the other hand, a half sphere in a bas-relief would have a cut line that would go nearly all the way around the form, breaking on the highlighted side (see Figure 9.62).

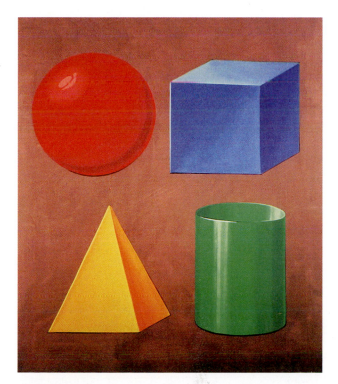

Figure 9.62 Placement of cut lines on Pissarro shapes.

Cast Shadow

Cast shadow truly establishes the depth of field in trompe l'oeil. The cast shadows unify all the various planes and surfaces in the picture plane by placing them in the same light at the same moment of time. A single light source cast very specific shadows. They have a clear direction and indicate the relation of the object to the light. The light has character itself. It may be bright or dim, cool or warm, and so on. The light reveals the texture and shape of objects in the painting. Scenic artists are excellent observers of light; most have a fascination with the different effects of natural and artificial light. Look closely at how shadows of complex forms project on a wall and how colors are affected by shadow. Try to understand cast shadows in interior lighting, as they are almost always from multiple sources. Through close observation of light you will be able to discern when light is depicted correctly in a painting. In trompe l'oeil, the light and shadow play two key roles. First, they are used to define the form of individual objects in relation to the light source as described in this section. Second, light illuminates the whole scene and projects cast shadows, bounces off surfaces, and further describes the dimension of the objects in relationship to one another.

A cast shadow may be placed on the sides of forms as well as in the shade areas of forms. It may also be placed only in the shadowed areas across a surface that would normally receive light if it were not blocked. A normal convention is to do the latter in interior scenes and the former in exterior scenes, where light is harsher and shade areas appear to be deeper in value. In some cases, the light is soft and indirect—perhaps filtered through clouds—however, it will still be necessary to spray or brush soft shadows into the shade areas of forms. If the light source is soft, the cast shadow color should be lighter in value. If the appearance of a strong light source is desired, then a darker cast shadow should be used. Some compositions have multiple light sources. A lighter or different color of cast shadow color can be applied for the secondary and tertiary light sources. These will frequently overlap one another.

Because cast shadow describes only the quality of light and must work with all the surfaces represented, the paint used for the shadow must be transparent. A field of snow on a sunny day is an excellent example of how a cast shadow describes the quality of light. This is a very distinct cast shadow color: the color of the sky. All that one sees is the sky reflecting off the snow where the direct sunlight is blocked. Cast shadow paint should be thinned to the desired value. Do not add white to a cast shadow color. Some deep colors in more economical brands of scene paint have white filler in them that settles out once the paint is thinned. These colors should be avoided when mixing cast shadows. It may be necessary to mix the cast shadow out of a higher-quality line of paint to obtain the desired transparency (see Figures 9.63 and 9.64).

Reflective or Bounce Light

Reflective highlights, also called *bounce light*, describe colors reflected on a form from other lighted surfaces. A general distinction between the two is that reflective light is usually soft edged whereas bounce light is usually a hard-edged dot or streak of color. A highly reflective surface will reflect back not only a light source but the color of other surfaces and forms around it as well. Watch people walking on a very light cement sidewalk on a sunny day around noon. The strong top light of the sun bounces off the pavement and acts like a footlight illuminating the face from below. This is reflective light. If the reflective light is bouncing of a different colored surface, a red ball sitting on a blue surface, for instance, the reflective light will take on the characteristic of the surface it is bouncing off of. The bottom of the ball might be suffused with a blue glow. If the ball is shiny, it may have hard-edged bounce lights reflecting the blue surface below. The shinier an object is, the more it is apt to pick up reflective and bounce lights from other surfaces in the composition. Reflective highlights need not be painted only in the highlight areas but may be placed anywhere on the form, including the shade and lowlight areas (see Figure 9.65).

Figure 9.63 Placement of cast shadows on Pissarro shapes.

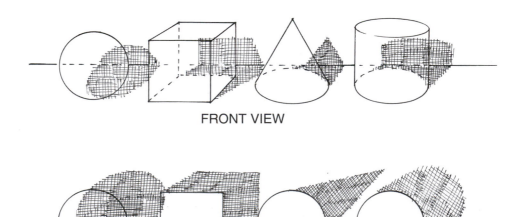

Figure 9.64
Projection of cast shadows on Pissarro shapes.

FRONT VIEW

TOP VIEW

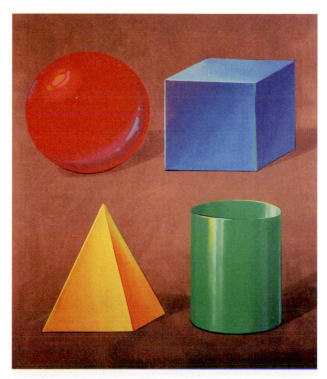

Figure 9.65 Placement of reflective and bounce light on Pissarro shapes.

Like highlights, reflective and bounce lights can be very useful for modeling the form of objects, particularly rounded forms. Reflective highlights should not be applied over the whole length of an edge or plane. One convention is to apply reflective highlights in approximately oval-shaped areas. These ovals tend to be on an angle, creating the impression of a slash of light reflecting across a form. Across the length of a wall paneling, there may be two or three of these oval areas of each reflective highlight. Across a large surface or a flat plane, the reflective highlight color can be sprayed over a section to create an oval or a slash of color. This may be done before any of the other steps of trompe l'oeil.

Reflective highlights may be several different colors. If a surface is highly reflective, such as glass or metal, as many as five or six colors may overlap one another. Some colors of reflective highlights may reflect off one side or another of the form specifically, while others may reflect from underneath. These colors may be related to the color of the stage deck. To offset these areas of high concentration, there may be areas with no reflective highlights at all. The more reflective highlights and bounce lights used, the shinier the surface will appear.

Reflective highlights may be related or complementary to the local color. In most cases, the reflective highlights are related to the local color of other forms in the composition. However, some surfaces work very well with certain colors of reflective light; for example, gold or gilt surfaces work well with turquoise and orange reflective highlights or bounce lights. These highlights are often more chromatic than the local color of the form. In some cases, a more neutral color may be used for reflective color as a means of integrating the form into the composition by means of reflective light.

Bounce lights, like primary highlights, should be opaque so that they "pop." They should be mixed from the more opaque mediums, vinyl or casein. In some cases, the reflective light may be a glaze coat that is used to give areas of the form a wash of color, once again as a means of integrating the form into the composition.

Application Techniques

There are several ways to apply trompe l'oeil. The chosen style may depend on the size of the theater the scenery is going to and the style of the painting. An operatic approach to this technique is the method of applying paint very broadly with little effort made to blend the steps into one another. If a broad operatic style is desired, the trompe l'oeil is applied directly with a brush, making no attempt to soften the edges of the individual colors. If a realistic style is desired, the edges of the shades, lowlights, and highlights may be softened by dry brushing, with water, or by spraying in the color with a pneumatic sprayer. Rounded forms require the most finesse if a more realistic trompe l'oeil is desired. For a photographic appearance, the steps of trompe l'oeil may be applied entirely with pneumatic spray guns and airbrushes.

When working on trompe l'oeil, each step should be completed across all the units laid out before going on. For instance, if several pieces of scenery laid out simultaneously have various gold or gilded details, then the shade will be worked up on all the elements of gold detail at the same time rather than have each element treated individually. This is to save time and to integrate the technique on all elements of the composition.

Finishing and Toning

The final step is to view the composition as a whole. The composition of every painting has areas of focus. Stage scenery does as well. Once the units of scenery

Figure 9.66
Detail of trompe l'oeil gold detail.

are in their configuration on stage, it may be necessary for some corner of the scenery to recede. Backing units may be sprayed down so that they are not a higher value or more chromatic than the primary scenic units. Backdrops or the sides of scenic units in cast shadows may need to be sprayed down so they, too, retreat into the shadows. The edges of drops may need to be sprayed down with a deeper color or with the cast shadow to focus attention on the composition. A good scenic artist is capable of predicting and carrying out much of the overall toning that must be done on the scenery in the shop before the scenery is transported to the theatre.

What scenic artists must remember is that these separate and, sometimes, disparate parts are the rudiments of a whole picture. As all the separate elements are painted, scenic artists must envision them as parts of the whole stage picture. As each component of scenery is painted, it is important to visualize how it fits in with the other components of the scene design. The scenic designer envisioned the entire composition while generating the paint elevations or the model, but the scenic artist works on the actual set pieces. Thus, it is important to understand why the designer deepened the value of the stage deck toward the edges or subtlety varied the hues in the base color of the flattage so that the painting would look as the designer envisioned it.

This process of visualizing is complicated by the fact that these elements will have to be treated as a whole even if they are painted in different parts of the paint shop days apart. As noted above, as pieces are painted, consider how they fit into the entire stage picture. Should an edge be toned down?

Figure 9.67
Detail of trompe l'oeil done on the Video Ballroom Mural at the Public Museum of Grand Rapids, Michigan. Painted by Crabtree Scenic.

Should an entire unit have a few more reflective lights across it because it is in the area of focus? Should a ground row be sprayed down so that it will relate better to the backdrop? Scenic artists should understand how the scenic designer wants the separate pieces of scenery to relate to one another and continually compare these units to one another. This is usually done by memory because much of the scenery will be stacked against the wall or folded up and in the bins waiting to be transported to the theatre.

Figure 9.68
Trompe l'oeil detail of balustrade on a
distressed drop, painted by Susan Crabtree.

A

Figure 9.69 Four examples of backdrops painted using trompe l'oeil technique. (**A**) The library for *Music Man*, designed by Gregory Hill, (Courtesy of Kenmark, Inc., Overland Park, Kansas), painted by Susan Crabtree and Angelique Powers.

B

Figure 9.69
(**B**) Flying over London, *Peter Pan*, designed by Gregory Hill (Courtesy of Kenmark, Inc., Overland Park, Kansas), painted by Susan Crabtree and Ashley Smith.

C

Figure 9.69
(**C**) Stock ballroom backdrop (Courtesy of Kenmark, Inc., Overland Park, Kansas) painted by Susan Crabtree and Angelique Powers.

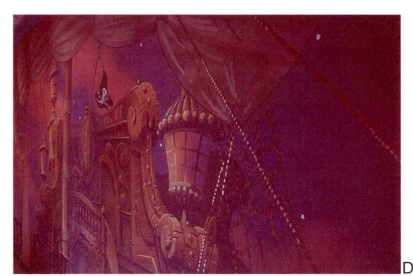

D

Figure 9.69
(**D**) Captain Hook's, *Peter Pan*, designed by Gregory Hill (Courtesy of Kenmark, Inc., Overland Park, Kansas) painted by Susan Crabtree and Ashley Smith.

Figure 9-70   Four examples of exquisite trompe l'oeil technique from the Lyric Opera of Chicago/Northern Illinois University Historical Scenic Collection (Courtesy of The School of Theatre and Dance, Northern Illinois University, Alexander Aducci, Curator).

Figure 9-70   (Continued).

Chapter 10

Creating Aging, Decorative, and Faux Finishes Using Multiple Mediums

This chapter addresses some of the newer techniques of scenic painting—called *multimedium techniques*—many of which have developed in the last century with the advent of new painting and finishing substances. Other techniques are only relatively new to theatre but have developed over the centuries, including faux finish techniques, aging and staining techniques, and some texturing effects. This chapter also discusses a wide range of unconventional paint products that scenic artists occasionally encounter.

We use the term *multimedium* because many contemporary faux techniques rely on mixing paint mediums to purposely contrast finishes or textures for more realistic results. In many other instances, the ability of one product to repel another is used to create wonderfully accurate aging effects. Not all scenic painting follows the traditional paint-on-canvas routine. Modern scenic artists must have a broad knowledge of the many unusual combinations of mediums they can use to get the look they desire, and they must be willing to experiment a little to discover new approaches. It is obvious that not all paint or texture techniques have been discovered, nor are all the solutions to covering and painting scenic materials already known. Hundreds of products have been adapted for scenic uses that were never intended for the stage at all. For example, this chapter discusses many techniques that use organic chemical solvents, toxic dusts, and toxic mediums. (Note that proper safety precautions and protection must be used whenever toxic materials are involved. See Chapter 4, the section "Safety and Health Regulations," for more information.)

THE LAYERING PROCESS: GLAZES AND RESISTS

Many painting techniques, theatrical or otherwise, use paint in thin built-up layers. This is because only through layering relatively transparent paints can some deep, rich, and vibrant colors be achieved. As discussed in the last chapter, scenic paints may be thinned down and used in layers, called *glazes*. Several glazes of flat-finish paint provide a deeper color, due to the layers of paint. When pigment or colorant is suspended in a medium such as a polymer or shellac and applied in successive layers, the result is a strikingly rich color and glowing surface. The actual mediums used to suspend the pigment may vary widely, but the primary technique is consistent throughout all glazing processes.

Glazes with Pigment or Dye and Finish Mediums

The combination of a pigment or dye and a transparent medium creates a useful painting tool for faux finishes. In the years before the appearance of modern polymer mediums, solvent-based mediums were the mainstay for such layering or glazing techniques. *French enamel varnish (FEV)* is one such traditional approach. An FEV is a solution of shellac that is thinned with solvent alcohol and tinted with alcohol-soluble aniline dye. Amber or orange shellac with no added pigment is a useful glaze in itself, particularly with wood finishes, and it may be thinned with solvent alcohol to use as an FEV. An FEV works well for layers of color or as a finish coat in glaze applications on faux woods and marbles. It will slightly cloud reflective and transparent surfaces, so it is a good technique for aging mirror or glass. An advantage of working with shellac is that it may be redissolved with later applications of solvent alcohol to further alter the glaze or even remove it. The FEV can be given a cloudy or gouache appearance by adding white pigmented shellac to it.

The tint in an FEV typically comes from alcohol-soluble aniline dye. The aniline dye provides brilliant color without clouding the shellac, but not all aniline dyes are soluble in the alcohol solvent. Japan colors and some universal tinting colors are soluble in alcohol and shellac to some extent; they may be purchased or ordered through commercial and theatrical paint suppliers. These colorants will result in a cloudy glaze color when mixed with shellac. Always try a sample of colorant with the shellac and alcohol for compatibility before mixing a full bucket.

A substitute for FEV can be made by combining colorant with clear acrylic, latex binder, or PVA. However, these water-based glazes do not penetrate porous surfaces, such as wood or muslin, as deeply as solvent-based mediums, so the finish may not be as rich. These water-based mediums may be tinted with water-based paint, aniline dyes, and colorants, which make them easier to use. They can be used straight or thinned considerably with water or acrylic-based floor wax.

A shellac-based FEV glaze dries to a semigloss finish that increases in sheen as more layers are painted. Glazes made with satin or semigloss urethanes and flat acrylics also will develop a sheen after several layers, but it will not be as pronounced.

Additional glaze mediums are sold specifically for faux-finish work, particularly at paint suppliers that specialize in interior decoration. These mediums have a high viscosity so that they "set up" well on vertical surfaces without sagging or running. Glazing mediums that are oil-based take 4 to 12 hours to set or become dry to the touch. Such slow drying may make it difficult to use these mediums for application in the theatre. Glazing mediums dry to an eggshell finish and may be covered with alkyd finish if a glossier sheen is desired. Water-based glazing mediums are available through most paint and theatrical suppliers. Water-based glazing mediums perform in much the same way as oil-based mediums do, but they dry faster and are safer to use. These mediums contain drying retardants so they remain workable for 30 minutes to an hour and take 4 hours to dry completely.

Finishes

All clear mediums used as a finish over an FEV or glaze may be tinted to add an extra dimension to the treatment. Finishes are available in a variety of sheens ranging from high gloss, gloss, satin, and flat. White shellac and solvent-based urethanes dry with a faint yellowish tint that, in addition to sheen, adds depth to a painted surface. Amber or orange shellac can be used as the final finish for a deep warm tint. As discussed before, shellac may be tinted only with alcohol-soluble dyes and tints. Colorants added to water- or oil-based finishes serve to "pull together" a paint treatment, faux wood, or faux marble, like the application of stain on fine wood. These finishes may be brushed, rolled, or sprayed on.

Resists

A *resist* is a paint process using two or more mediums that repel or slide off of one another. A glaze or finish applied to a flat medium, such as scenic paint, normally will cover it smoothly. However, a resist entails wiping the glaze medium or finish off the base surface to create a texture or grain pattern. This is one form of a resist. It is difficult to separate the finish medium from a flat-finish base coat. If the finish of the base coat is a satin or a gloss sheen, any glaze medium can be wiped or combed off easily. If the base coat was done with a flat-finish scenic paint, it can be covered with a clear coat finish of gloss medium before doing the resist technique.

CREATING FAUX FINISHES

The word *faux* is French for "false, forged, or imitated." A faux-paint technique is the realistic imitation of a specific material, such as marble or

Figure 10.1
Sleigh bed for *Egene Onegin*, Colorado Opera Company, Denver Colorado, scenic design by Bruno Schwegl, painted by Susan Crabtree.

wood, onto a less expensive surface. Faux finishes are very popular interior decoration techniques for obvious places like doors and walls; and they are found, with a postmodern touch of ironic wit, on improbable objects like computers and telephones. The techniques of faux finish have many applications in the theatre, particularly in the painting of properties. (See Figure 10.1.)

Faux treatments are created through a process usually involving anywhere from two to several steps. Once the process is established, it must be carefully followed to maintain consistency. The process may be a simple one-step application of mixed mediums or carefully applied successive paint layers. Any artist creating a faux treatment should first closely examine the material to be mimicked to understand how that material was created. For example, is it a serpentine marble or a wood veneer? The artist should then determine, by doing samples, how best to create the faux finish. Many of the techniques discussed in this chapter in association with faux treatments are similar to the scenic paint treatments discussed earlier in this book. The difference in application of these treatments is that they must be applied with more skill, understanding of the materials being mimicked, and with the finesse brought about by artistic observation. Whenever you are creating a faux treatment you should have a clear understanding of the material being emulated. Books such as Judy Juracek's *Surfaces* are an indispensable aid when creating faux treatments.

The techniques used to create faux finishes are standard painting techniques of wet blend, glazes, dry brushing, graining, and others that have been discussed in Chapter 9. The mediums used for faux finishes vary greatly, depending on desired qualities of transparency and permanence. Standard scenic paint may be used as a base coat or to tint some of these mediums, but rarely is a faux finish executed satisfactorily when it is made up entirely of flat opaque mediums.

Wood

Most experienced scenic artists focus their painting technique on creating the appearance of a specific type of wood, such as oak or walnut, rather than a generic wood grain. In determining how to emulate a specific wood grain, you first must understand the pattern of wood as it is cut from a tree. As discussed in Chapter 9 tree rings are formed as the tree trunk widens over years of growth. When a tree is harvested and cut into board or veneer, these rings become the grain of the wood. If a board is cut along the length of a fairly straight tree trunk, the board will be composed primarily of a straight, parallel grain. Oblong and elliptical grains are created from crosscuts of the tree rings. Knots in the grain come from where branches sprouted from the trunk. Veneers are made by shearing a thin sheet from around a section of the trunk in a continuous spiral, yielding a soft marble-like grain. Some trees, such as pines and poplars, tend to grow with very straight trunks.

Consequently, the boards they yield have a great deal of straight grain. Other trees, such as oak and walnut, which often have curved trunks, yield boards with more crosscut grains. Because mahoganies yield a supple fine-grained wood, they are often used as veneer wood. With proper technique and graining tools, all of these variations can be produced in faux wood. In addition to the proper tools, layers of transparent color in glossy or satin mediums create a depth of color akin to stained or oiled wood.

Wood Graining

A faux wood grain is done by initially painting a base coat that is the hue of the lightest grain of the wood either in a single color or a wet blend. The finish of the base coat will affect how much of the top glaze can be squeegeed or combed off with a graining tool. If the finish of the base coat is slick and smooth, a subsequent coat of glaze will come away very cleanly. This means that surfaces given a faux wood treatment must be very carefully prepared and sanded (see Figure 10.2).

The dark grain of faux wood is created by tinting a transparent medium that then dries to the desired deeper hue. Although not as common, for some light-colored woods, it can be effective to tint the graining color to a lighter hue than the base coat. In either case, the grain is created when a top coat is painted over the base coat in a streaky grain pattern or covered completely with the glaze medium and squeegeed off with a rocker or comb before it dries. Any clear medium can be used for the glaze medium, but shellacs and solvent-based finishes do not work as well for wood grain because of their tendency to spread out once applied. Commercial faux mediums sold specifically for graining and overglaze techniques work very well because they are highly viscous. For large-volume theatrical applications, clear acrylics, latex, PVA, and water-based urethanes work well and are more affordable.

Rockers, graining pads, and tube-style grainers are used to create crosscut grains. Grainers of this sort come in a variety of patterns for different types of grain or variations within a grain. Tube grainers sometimes are sold with a wire handle and wooden dowel for holding and manipulating the grainer. Many scenic artists prefer simply to hold this grainer from either end so that it can be bent and curved for more diversity in the grain patterns. In addition to rocking or rolling the grainers as they are pulled through the medium, they also may be twisted from one edge to the other to vary grain widths. Combs for graining are available in rubber and steel with different widths of teeth. These are used to comb off a straight grain and usually are used in combination with the pattern grainers. Homemade combs can be

Figure 10.2
Various faux wood graining techniques and tools: rocker grainers, tube grainers, combs, and rubber pad grainers.

made from many different materials, such as rubber tread, carpet scraps, a torn edge of cardboard, or wadded newspaper. The advantage in using homemade combs is that irregular patterns can be cut into these to produce more realistic random patterns than their commercial counterparts.

Commercial grainers, combs, and patterns used exclusively to paint a wood grain technique leave a distinctly even and regular grain pattern. When used in combination with commercial tools, homemade tools add a dimension to the technique that lends a hint of realism. When preparing a wood graining project, consider what tools can be made from materials found around the shop to augment commercial grainers and combs. You should become adept at using commercial and homemade graining tools, blending the paint swaths together, and twisting the tools while etching the medium to manipulate the grain realistically.

Checker rollers are interesting devices used to create the short choppy straight grain that speckles the surface of some woods. This type of grain is very common in oak and some mahoganies. The medium used with the checker roller must be fairly viscous or it will drip off the roller. When the roller is passed across a surface, it may splatter a little as well as leave the short choppy grain it was designed to do. If the spatters are not desirable, they can be brushed out in the direction of the grain with a dry brush. An even coarser short grain can be achieved by simply spattering over a base coat with the grain color and dragging through the wet paint with a dry brush.

Brushed graining can be done in lieu of the grainers or to augment them. Grain can be painted on with a small brush and dragged through with a larger brush to soften it. Combing can be done to create a simple straight grain through and in addition to a crosscut grain. A crosscut grain also can be created by combing. By tilting the brush from one edge to the other while it is being pulled through the stroke, it will feather out from one edge to the other. Once you become accustomed to this technique, you can create a broad feathery crosscut grain quickly.

If faux wood grain must look very realistic because of the proximity of the audience, soften it by patting it all over with the flat of a brush. This technique is called *flogging*. Some paint stores and suppliers sell very long-bristled brushes called *flogging brushes* to be used for this technique. This technique works best with glaze mediums that are manufactured for faux finish work. Begin at one end of the

grained surface and pat it gently and repeatedly with the brush in the direction of the grain. Move the brush in the direction of the handle, pulling it gently toward you as you flog the grain. After some practice you will be able to achieve a very realistic faux wood finish using this technique in combination with glazed mediums.

After graining has been completed, it may be necessary and desirable to soften, tone, or deepen it with layers of glazes so that areas of the grain appear to sink into the surface of the wood or darken towards the edges of a panel. These glazes may go over partial areas or the entire surface. Generally, it is best if the glazes are deeper in value. In some instances, particularly in the case of light-grained woods, a lighter glaze made with white pigment is effective. Finally, a gloss or satin finish over the completed faux wood will add depth to its appearance.

Marble

To create faux marble, you must first understand how marble is formed. Just as with wood grain, understanding the structure of the material in question, not just the image, will help you create more realistic effects. Marble is formed by compression, heating, and upheaval, singly or in combination. One of the most common marble types is drift marble. Drift marble is formed by layers of silt settling together and hardening under compression over thousands of years (see Figure 10.3). The solid mass is colored by the various shades of silt, which we see as veins. The veins intertwining through the stone may be either feathery or well defined. Serpentine marble forms with stone pieces broken up into various sized nuggets. This rubble is then filled in with molten rock or silt. When this hardened mass is sliced open, it results in a dramatic multitoned marble. Luminous crystalline marbles are formed by the intense heating of minerals, resulting in layers of dazzling crystals and ribs of color, as found in malachite marbles.

Faux marble, like faux wood, may be the application of several separate layers or a one-step process. A challenge in creating faux marble is to replicate the chaotic nature of a specific marble grain and finish with out creating a repetitious pattern. Unlike treatments painted for faux wood, there is not a large range of specialized tools for painting faux marble. The artist must rely on their powers of observation, and skill and knowledge of available tools and medium. The techniques and tools used in the process may help to ensure that results look natural rather than contrived. In addition to brushwork tools, techniques frequently used in faux marble that add to its depth and character include wet blending, feathering, sponging, spattering, and glazing.

The grain pattern in painted marble is often its most conspicuous component. If a faux marble is poorly done, the grain usually is what gives it away. A poorly executed marble grain tends to look somewhat like tree limbs or repetitious diamond patterns. When painting the grain in a faux marble, keep in mind that a marble veneer or object was cut from a larger marble block and so the grain may pass down into the depth of the stone or up into a cutaway layer. The grain in drift marbles generally is directional, like wood. Some varieties of marble also have a cross grain that is nearly perpendicular to the primary grain. Marble used on floors or walls sometimes is cut in successive sheets and laid as cut off the block: face to face and back to back. The faces are

finished and laid adjacent to one another on the site so that the sheets mirror one another along the seam.

The surface to be painted with faux marble technique should be carefully prepared: all seams must be filled and sanded, any grain covered, and material edges filled and sanded. This is particularly important if the faux marble is seen close up. It is somewhat difficult to separate the various stages and steps to painting faux marble. The order in which these steps are done may be grouped together and executed in a wet-on-wet sequential technique or done in individual, careful steps allowing each application to dry before the next one is applied. Glazes may be blended together over the top of the finish for color variation, or the base coat may be blended for this same purpose, or both may be necessary. As with faux wood, doing a sample first and comparing it to a picture of the marble being mimicked is a good idea.

The first step in a marble finish is the base coat. The base coat may be one color or a blend of several colors. This wet blend may be done in various ways, as best suits the planned marble. The blend may be very soft and well blended, or loosely blended on a damp or fully wet surface so the colors mix of their own accord. The colors simply may be laid in next to one another so that very little mixing occurs. It may or may not be necessary for the base coat to dry before successive steps are done. Depending on the faux marble pattern, you may want to spatter, grain, or sponge directly into the wet base coat so that the paint seeps and mixes together. Working paint this way, wet into wet, may be fast, but it is not very controlled. The use of brushed graining, spattering, and sponge work may be better controlled by allowing each application to dry completely before beginning the next step. An application may be softened by first dampening a surface with water or spraying the still-wet paint with water. Any application may be further softened by working over the still-wet paint with a damp sponge.

The grain of drift marble usually is brushed on. It is natural when painting a grain over a large area to unconsciously develop a pattern. Scenic artists must be continually aware of this as they work. Nearly every text written on faux finishes will discuss the use of a feather for creating marble grain, a method that is not as useful for theatrical applications. Over a large scale, feather graining would be too time-consuming. Occasionally, a feather duster may be used instead of a single feather to effect

Figure 10.3 Faux marble, for the "Furniture Colonnade," Public Museum of Grand Rapids, Michigan, painted by Crabtree Scenic.

marble grain over a large area, but generally this technique does not afford enough control for faux treatments. Graining over a large flat area also may be done with the edge of a three-inch roller, but this method does not work over moldings and three-dimensional surfaces. A serpentine marble has a strongly defined grain, which can be done with careful brushwork. It also may be done by laying down a base of the primary marble finish and then masking out everything but the grain. The masking can be made from torn-up sheets and bits of newspaper or kraft paper. The grain color can be sprayed or spattered over the top of the masking. Once it is dry and the masking has been removed, the grain can be enhanced with some brushwork. Once again, over a large area, this masking approach to a serpentine marble, discussed in many books on faux techniques, may be too time-consuming for theatrical applications. In his interview at the end of Chapter 8, Howard Jones explained a technique for creating the veins of serpentine marble playfully referred to as "Swiss cheese." In this technique, holes were cut into pieces of velour so that what remained was a pattern similar to the veins of the marble. This pieces of velour were then dipped into paint, wrung-out, and then twirlled onto the a prepainted surface to imprint the pattern of the veins. Also, as discussed in Chapter 9, a large paint stamp cut into the pattern of the base marble in a serpentine or grain can be used to quickly cover large areas with a serpentine pattern. In addition to the stamp, the grain may be refined with some brushwork. This technique will not stand up to close observation but may be fine for viewing from a distance.

After the base has been done and graining completed, it may be necessary to break up the surface with some transparent glaze work, which will enhance the natural appearance of the faux marble. One of the prized qualities of marble is its soft, translucent crystalline base. Because of this translucency, it seems as if one can see into the stone. Glaze work adds the necessary variation and depth to the surface by breaking up brushstrokes and opaque color. Glazes may be applied over the entire surface or over partial areas for more variation. Glazes may simply be thinned paint or they can be suspended in a water-based medium, such as PVA or water-based urethanes. Commercial faux-finish glazes work very well for layering color. But, as mentioned previously, consideration must be given to the amount of drying time involved in using these mediums.

The glazes can be brushed, spattered, sponged, or sprayed on, as best suits the marble finish being mimicked. Particularly in lighter-colored marbles, a great deal of depth may be added by applying partially opaque or cloudy glaze work over a higher contrast base and graining. Glazes made from pearlescent paint or interference color will be very transparent but catch or play with the light over the surface of the stone. Interference colors and pearlescent paint are available from Golden Artists Color, Inc and in some lines of scenic paint. As well as being used as over-glazes, these may be used directly as the base coat, and in some cases they may work well as one of the graining colors. Pearlescent and interference glaze colors work best on lighter colors of marble and can be very effective. Bronzing powders are available in a wide range of neutral and saturated colors and may be used minimally in glazes and grains to the same effect. However, because most bronzing powders are very reflective, care must be taken not to over do it.

The finish coat over faux marble adds great depth to its faux-marble surface and gives it the appearance of being polished. A finish for work seen at very close range should be sprayed on in several layers until it is glossy. If the finish is brushed or rolled on, the brush or roller grain will be discernible to the viewer. If the faux marble is meant to be seen only from a distance, as in a theatre, brushed or rolled-on finish will suffice. If desired, the finish can be tinted to add depth by subtly changing the hue of the faux marble.

Even though there may be a great deal of variation in creating faux marble, all the steps must be carefully noted and followed. Before beginning a complex faux-marble process, work through the process by doing samples until you find a satisfactory approach. Complete the sample all the way through to the finish to see how that final step affects the color of the marble.

Metal

Real metallic surfaces and finishes are generally too expensive or heavy to be used in theatrical applications. The scenic artist is called on to replicate a wide range of metals, from common to rare, on a regular basis. Architectural and decorative details such as gold filigree are replicated by gilding or painting with bronzing powder mixed into a medium. Large surfaces of industrial or commercial materials, such as stainless steel or aluminum, also can be replicated in paint but through a longer process.

Figure 10.4
A metallic surface created in paint. Scenic Art Studios, New York.

Gilding

The term *gilding* means overlaying a surface with a metallic leaf. This is done to give the surface a grand or rarefied appearance. The metal used in gilding is gold, copper, or silver leaf. The leaves usually are three to four inches square and sold booked between layers of tissue paper, which holds them until the gilder is ready to use them. Metallic leaves have been hammered and rolled until they are tissue thin. This is all that is necessary to coat the surface with the precious metal. Because the leaves are so thin and delicate, they must be handled with special care and tools.

True metallic leaves cannot be handled with the fingers because the oils on the skin are enough to snag and tear the leaf. Out of necessity, a system of tools has been developed for handling and applying the leaf (see Chapter 5 for a description of these tools). Gilding also must be done in a very stable environment. Drafts and dust will make the work difficult or impossible. The surface to be gilded first is given a coat of a gilding medium. This is a binder that sets up a tacky surface that adheres the metallic leaf. When in place, the leaves are pressed down into the medium with a gilder's mop. This soft, full-bristle brush is used to press the leaf onto the medium and work the leaf into the details. Burnishing tools then are used to fully adhere the metallic leaf to the medium and further work the leaf into all the nooks and crannies of the object. Burnishing is important, as it also adds a significant shine to the leaf.

It usually is unnecessary to use real gold and silver leaf for the theatre. First of all, the expense is prohibitive. Second, working with genuine gold leaf requires time and an undisturbed environment, two conditions in short supply in the theatre. So rarely is true gold leaf used in theatrical work that acquiring these specialized tools may be necessary only for the most discriminating of property painters. However, the knowledge of these tools and the tools of any craft that the scenic artist may need to represent is always helpful.

Composite gold leaf, sometimes called Dutch gold, is much less expensive and much easier to handle because the leaves are not nearly as thin. Dutch gold, commonly used in theatrical work, actually can be handled and placed with clean dry hands. Even though the leaf is easier to handle, this work still should be done on a clean surface with little or no air draft. Metallic leaf adhesive size is glue formulated to use in the gilding process and can be appropriate for some theatrical use. The size is applied to the surfaces that are to be gilded. Once dry, it remains tacky so the leaf will adhere to the surface. Dutch gold also may be placed on freshly applied shellac while tacky.

Bronzing Powders

Bronzing powders are particulates of dry metallic flake. They can be mixed with a broad range of mediums and applied with a brush or sprayer.

These powders mix directly into shellac, oil-based urethanes, and lacquers. They may need to be pulped with solvent alcohol before being mixed into water-based mediums, such as PVA, water-based urethane, clear acrylic, or clear latex. All bronzing powders are very lightweight, particularly the silvers, which are made with aluminum. The dust from mixing these paints will permeate the air. It is best to mix the bronzing powders in a spray booth or hood, where the dust can be vented off. No one not wearing respiratory protection should be in the vicinity while bronzing powders are being mixed (see Chapter 4, the section "Health and Safety Regulations"). Because of the industrial hazards of manufacturing, using, and shipping dry bronzing powders, many manufacturers are now providing premixed metallic paints using mica as the pigment. In many respects these paints handle as well or better for the techniques discussed here and are available in a wide range of colors.

Premixed metallic paints are available at theatrical suppliers, fine arts suppliers, sign painting suppliers, and retail paint stores. Bronzing powders are available from theatrical supply houses. The selection in these lines covers a broad range of metallic finishes. For instance, there are many different qualities of gold: pale gold, bright gold, rich gold, and Roman gold, to name a few. The silvers come in varying shades of aluminum, silver, and stainless steel.

Bronzing powders also are available in a wide spectrum of colors, such as purple, green, red, and various shades of bronze, brass, copper, and deep brown

statuary hues. If a color of bronzing powder must be altered, the powders can be mixed with one another to create a desired hue. These paints also may be tinted with aniline dyes, colorants, and universal tinting colors. That universal tinting colors and colorants will dull the gleam of the metallic paint, depending on how much tint is added to the paint.

Bronzing brushes may be used to apply bronzing powder mixed in medium. These specialty brushes are used by faux-finish artists and furniture decorators. It is not necessary to use these brushes with bronzing powders. In theatrical applications, nearly any soft bristle brush will suffice.

Bronzing powders will develop a grain depending on how they are brushed on. It may be necessary to be meticulous about the direction of your brush strokes when working with these paints.

Graphite

When bronzing powders are applied to a surface, they can be quite lovely, but they are not a thoroughly convincing metallic finish. One explanation for this is that the particles of bronzing powders have a random alignment once applied. The finish of a surface coated with bronzing powder is glittery and the highlights are soft due to this randomness. Real metallic structures, sheets, and leaf are made through combinations of heating and extrusion, rolling, or polishing. The result of these processes is that the molecular structure of metallic surfaces is organized so the

Figure 10.5
Removing excess glitter with a vacuum.
The glitter has been applied with adhesives.
Scenic Art Studios, New York.

surface of metal takes on the deeper glimmering sheen that we equate with well-polished metal.

Gilded gold and silver surfaces can be burnished and polished until they shine, but bronzing powders cannot be polished. They can, however, be coated with a gloss finish that will help give them the appearance of polished gold, silver, or brass. Faux finishes of stainless steel or aluminum made with bronzing powders alone never will have that gleam. Graphite powder can be used with bronzing powders to create a more convincing dull silver of a polished steel metallic surface. The molecules of graphite can be aligned after it is applied through polishing and friction so the surface takes on the distinctive appearance of polished steel.

There are two ways to use graphite in a paint treatment. One technique is to polish a surface with graphite once it has been painted with aluminum bronzing powder. This surface must be well primed and sanded prior to painting. The graphite is mixed into a transparent glaze of lacquer or a solvent- or water-based urethane. Two or three layers of this glaze should be applied to the surface and each allowed to dry thoroughly. After these have dried, they can be hand-sanded with very fine sandpaper or buffed until the surface forms a sheen. A buffing pad used on an electric drill or a machine buffer will create a more convincing dull silver sheen of polished graphite.

Another method of working with graphite is to mix it directly into a silver paint, which, once it is dry, can be buffed to a high sheen. This method is effective for large surface areas that need to have the appearance of sheet metal or stainless steel.

The medium for the graphite must not be too elastic. Water-based urethane, solvent-based lacquer, or oil-based paints work best. Acrylic, PVA, and latex-based paints do not work well because they cannot be sanded or polished as easily. When preparing a metallic treatment of considerable quantity, it is more economical to start mixing the paint from commercial brands of silver paint rather than fabricating it completely from dry bronzing powders. Add about one pound of powdered graphite per gallon of metallic paint. Silver bronzing powder may then be added to the paint to adjust the color or if the graphite darkens it too much. This paint should be applied to a surface that has been carefully spackled, sanded, primed, and sanded again so no trace of a wood grain or seam is visible. Apply this graphite-treated paint with a sprayer rather than a brush or roller to avoid visible brushstrokes. Two to three solid layers should be sprayed. After the graphite paint is thoroughly dry, it can be lightly sanded with a fine sandpaper or buffed to a high sheen.

Imitating Commercial Decorative Materials

Frequently, a scenic artist is asked to mimic modern synthetic materials through a paint process. It may sound strange to say faux linoleum or faux Formica®, but this often is called for in realistic dramas. Many distinctive patterns of these commercial finishes are no longer available, so it is up to the scenic artist to replicate them. All of these faux treatments can be created with water-based paint and finished with water-based or solvent-based urethane of any sheen. These finishes can be tinted with umber, ocher, or even white colorant to age or create the appearance of a yellow or cloudy wax buildup on the surface.

Linoleum Flooring

The earliest linoleum floor patterns often replicated carpeting patterns. These can be mimicked easily enough by laying down a two- to three-color sponged base and stenciling on top of it. The pattern will remain feathery by dabbing with a coarse sponge through a stencil. More contemporary extruded plastic linoleum with abstract patterns can be painted with a base of the dominant color and spattered with the other colors that run through the linoleum. The spatter is blocked while still wet to draw it out. If a long strip of linoleum is being done, a board with an upright handle attached to it may be drawn through the entire length of linoleum. If a very wide area is being painted, do it in two to three-foot-wide sections.

Linoleum tiles usually are laid in alternating directions. Assuming the floor is painted onto 4' × 8' sheet stock, cartoon the tile grid after the base coat. Cut a board the width of the tile so that each tile can be boarded without disturbing the tile next to it. For more exacting work, it may be necessary to individually mask every other tile. Masking may be done for extremely fine detail or if the deck is in forced perspective. Once the complete process is done and dry for the tiles going in one direction, the completed tiles are masked out and the alternating tiles are painted. For further realism, the seams between the tiles can be scored with a sharp awl guided along a metal straight edge. Full 4′ × 8′ sheets of Masonite® may also be treated all over with the linoleum pattern running in one direction the entire length of the sheet and cut into one-foot squares and laid in alternating directions, just like real linoleum tiles. Individual tiles can be cut from quarter-inch Masonite® squares that have rounded edged for greater realism. A convincing octagon tile pattern can be created by incising the pattern of the grout with a cut-awl into the surface of Masonite® after it has been painted and finished with the appropriate sheen.

Of course, real linoleum tiling can be used if it is available in the pattern specified by the scenic designer. After the carpentry staff has installed the tiles, it may be up to the scenic artist to age the floor, covering it with a glaze of grime in the corners and creating a sense of traffic patterns.

Plastic Laminates and Ceramic Tile

Plastic laminate surfaces, like countertops, are treated much like linoleum surfaces. The pattern may be an intricate intermingling of finely drawn shapes, like the famous boomerang design of the 1950s. These patterns can be recreated with stencils or paint stamps. More abstract speckled patterns may be done simply with sponging or spattering. As with linoleum, plastic laminates can be bought and installed as needed. A pattern can be added and the laminate aged as needed. Laminates or faux laminates may need to be sanded afterwards to give the appearance of worn areas, such as found on a diner counter, for instance. When creating a faux laminate for a circumstance such as this, consider what color will need to be apparent when the top layer of paint is sanded off.

Ceramic tile may be painted on using stencils or paint stamps and enhanced with two-dimensional texture techniques and trompe l'oeil for highlights and lowlights. Ceramic tile often is painted on pressed board tile paneling, which helps render the tile pattern. These panels are not very convincing, so you may need to do some glaze work with shellacs or water-based urethane for variation. Individual tiles can be cut from quarter-inch Masonite for greater realism. These tiles are primed with a shellac or oil-based primer. Spraying the primer and base coat may be the most efficient method of handling all the edges of the individual tiles. The base coat, any pattern, and texture techniques can be done with water-based paint. After the tiles have been painted, they can be given the desired sheen with water-based urethanes. Then the tiles are installed with ceramic or linoleum tile adhesive. If the tiles need to look truly realistic, they can be grouted with tile grout or a mixture of drywall compound and fine silicate sand.

PAINTING ON MISCELLANEOUS MATERIALS

There is no apparent end to the variety of materials used to create stage scenery. New materials are adopted constantly by ingenious designers and technicians. Scenic artists must learn the qualities of these materials so they may be painted and their true identity disguised. Some materials may be used in new combinations, requiring new approaches to preparation.

Substitute Glass and Plexiglas

Actual glass rarely is used on stage because it is hazardous. Bobbinet and window screen sometimes are used to suggest glass panes, but in most contemporary productions, Plexiglas is used as a glass substitute. Frequently, scenic artists are called on to paint signage on Plexiglas or give it the appearance of antique rolled glass or stained glass. Fortunately, Plexiglas bonds well with water-, solvent-, and oil-based urethanes, lacquers, polymer-based glues, and shellac.

To create the effect of rolled or antique glass, solvent-based gloss urethane can be rolled over one or both sides of the Plexiglas. When dry, the gloss urethane will not cloud the Plexiglas. Satin urethane does cloud Plexiglas somewhat, which may be desirable.

The effect of thick bottle glass can be simulated by coating Plexiglas with polymer glue in any pattern desired. The glue can be poured on in circles, so that when it dries it thickens toward the edges or the center, like bottle glass. It also may be rolled over the Plexiglas to create a very uneven surface. The polymer glue can be tinted with aniline dyes or colorants.

Tinted shellac, amber shellac, or FEV tinted with dye can be used to simulate stained glass, although an FEV will cloud Plexiglas. Shellacs can be tinted with dyes or universal tinting colors.

Lacquers adhere well to Plexiglas. Lacquers can be mixed to custom colors at the paint store or tinted in the shop with universal tinting colors. Also, most sign painting suppliers and catalogue companies offer a large range of paints designed to adhere to different surfaces. Clear lacquers can be tinted with universal tinting colors and Japan colors for transparent colors.

Water-based gloss urethanes dry to a smooth, transparent finish that does not cloud Plexiglas at all. Water-based urethanes can be tinted with colorants or aniline dyes. These urethanes bond well to the glass and are excellent for simulating stained glass and painting signage. Water-based urethanes may be thinned with acrylic floor wax for glaze techniques.

If a cartoon must be laid out on uncovered Plexiglas, the cartoon should be executed on a piece of kraft or butcher paper that is then taped to the back of the transparent Plexiglas. Then, the Plexiglas may be painted from the front in the same manner as a scrim, while it lays over the cartoon (see Chapter 8 for more discussion of cartooning signage).

It is difficult to get even coverage of a medium on Plexiglas when working with a brush. Windows often are lit from behind, making any irregularities in coverage apparent. Spraying the paint medium across a cut frisket masking is the best way to achieve a smooth coverage. Spray the medium on in two or three even coats. The protective paper covering on Plexiglas may be cartooned, cut, and peeled in the appropriate areas for spray techniques. If the paper masking has already been removed from the Plexiglas

and you must cut your own out of masking tape and paper or adhesive backed shelf lining, it is important to spray the medium on in several very light layers to avoid paint seeping underneath the masking.

If you are working with Plexiglas that, given a tight budget, must be saved for use in future productions, tints can be mixed into vegetable oil soap or dish detergent. This mixture of tint and detergent can be sprayed or brushed on in the same manner as paint then washed off after it has served its purpose. Spraying glass with straight soap is excellent for clouding mirrors or glass. Commercial glass frosting also may be purchased at paint suppliers. An interesting winter-like glass frosting can be made by letting Epsom salts dissolve in puddles of beer on the glass. The frosting will form as this dries. Plexiglas may also be frosted by sanding its surface with fine grit sand paper. Also, commercial glass frosting and glazing products are sold at most hobby supply stores. These products will work better on vertical surfaces and in situations where the scenery has already been installed.

Using Caulk on Plexiglas for Texture

Some texture may need to be applied like a drawing as a raised pattern or delineation between colors in a design, such as in stained glass. Over small areas or

Figure 10.6
Painting lettering onto Plexiglas. Scenic Art Studios, New York.

for delicate patterns, hot glue can be used. Paintable latex caulking can be used for larger areas of raised texture. Latex caulk is available in a great variety of colors from lumberyards, hardware stores, and home improvement centers. This caulking can be purchased by the tube or by the case for large jobs. When simulating stained glass, caulking can be purchased in colors that will give the effect of leading, such as gray, brown, graphite, and black. This caulking adheres well to Plexiglas. This technique may also be done with a texture compound mixed up to the consistency of cake frosting. Drywall compound mixed with PVA can be tinted with almost any color and applied with a pastry bag.

The pattern for the leading first should be cartooned on a piece of kraft paper. The plexiglas, stripped of its paper cover, should be laid on top of the pattern. Caulk must be applied using a caulking gun. As you work with the caulking gun or pastry bag, you will become adept at squeezing it with just the right amount of pressure to get a steady, even flow of caulking or texture compound onto the glass. It is very difficult to lay down a straight line of caulk or texture compound while squeezing the gun or bag, so any straight line should be laid on using a jig as a guide. The jig can be as simple as two spring clamps and a board. If straight lines break up the glass in two directions, only one direction should be done at a time, because the caulk or texture compound may take several hours or a full day to dry. For instance, all the horizontal lines of leading should be done on each pane of glass one day and all the vertical lines should be done the next. If freehand work is to be done with the caulking gun or pastry bag, take the time to practice on an extra piece of Plexiglas before starting on the set pieces. After the caulk or texture compound has dried, the stained glass tints, urethanes, or polymers can be applied. Gray weather proofing stripping, as narrow as one-half-inch wide is sold at home improvement stores. This product is adhesive backed and already gray or black in color, so it is very useful for creating quick and dirty glass leading.

Metal

The metals used in scenic construction generally are steel or aluminum. Steel stock usually is coated with oil at the mill where it is manufactured so that it will not rust while in stock at the steelyard. Before steel can be painted, it should be washed down with mineral spirits or a degreaser to clean off the residue.

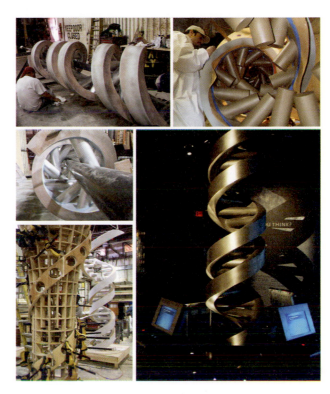

Figure 10.7 Genomic Revolution: DNA in progress. Designed by Tim Nissen, AMNH Exhibition Design Department, Showman Fabricators, Inc.

After a steel or aluminum frame has been welded together, all the joints must be cleaned with a steel brush. To paint the steel, use a solvent-based paint or primer; either alkyd- or shellac-based paints work well. Epoxy-based metal primers have also recently become available.

Frequently the finish desired by the scenic designer is the metal itself. It may be the scenic artist's job to sand the metal surface down to a bright finish of the desired grain with a sanding pad, orbital sander, or grinding wheel and then preserve that finish. Steel sanded down to a bright finish must be protected so that it will not rust or corrode back to a dull finish. Clear lacquer, white shellac, or solvent-based urethane can be sprayed or brushed on to protect a bright steel finish.

Aluminum need not be cleaned off before it is painted. However, like steel, it must be primed with epoxy or solvent-based paint or primers. Once welded together, the joints of the aluminum frame

Figure 10.8
Surfboards made at Showman Fabricators, Inc.

must be cleaned with a steel brush. If a bright aluminum finish is desired, it can be polished with a sanding pad on a grinder or orbital sander. Once polished, aluminum will keep its finish for many months. If the finish must hold indefinitely, it can be sealed with clear solvent-based finishes. Always use proper precautions when sanding or grinding metal or using solvent-based paints (see Chapter 4, the section "Safety and Health Regulations").

Foam Rubber

Foam rubber is a very useful sculpting material. It wraps around almost any form and can be carved or adhered to soft goods with contact cement. Foam rubber can be painted to a certain extent by spraying it with scenic paint or latex just as it is. However, if it is seamed with glue or there is a change in material, the paint emphasizes the change in the surface. To avoid this problem, foam elements should be coated to create an even texture throughout. The foam can be skinned with fabric, either cheesecloth or cotton scrim. It also may be covered with a heavy, flexible primer. Some theatrical suppliers sell a foam coat product that can be used on foam rubber as well as polystyrene foam. Commercial polymer-based sculpture coats will work as well.

Latex-based roof patching is a less-expensive alternative to these products. A homemade foam coat can be made of drywall compound mixed in even proportions with either water-based contact cement or polymer-based glue. The most important quality these foam coatings have in common is that they must be flexible.

Carpeting

It is not uncommon to paint or stencil a pattern onto carpet. This works best with short pile carpet. Regular scenic paint can be sprayed or stippled through a stencil on synthetic carpet fibers. Extra binder should be added to the paint used on ground cloths and carpets because of the foot traffic. French enamel varnishes also may be used on synthetic fiber carpets and rugs.

Aniline dye is the best for wool carpets. Because the aniline dye does not set up, care must be taken to keep any carpet painted with dye completely dry. But in this circumstance, be certain that the carpet will only come in contact with the performers' shoes, and dark colored shoes at that. If an actor must fall, sit, crawl, or lay on the carpet, aniline dye by itself must not be used because of the risk of it transferring the performer's skin or costume. In the cases where a pattern is being applied to a carpet, a stencil can be cut out of linoleum. After the paint has been sprayed through the stencil, lightly tap the paint through the paint into the carpet with a stiff bristled scrub brush before removing the stencil to penetrate the fibers more thoroughly.

When an entire carpet must be toned down, the challenge is to coat the fibers thoroughly so the original color of the carpet is not revealed when the nap is brushed. An FEV works well for toning carpets. The color should be sprayed on in even passes and then worked in with a push broom. The color should be thinned and applied in two or three coats. Several light layers of color help ensure even coverage.

Upholstery

Occasionally, a scenic artist has to tone upholstery fabric. Modern upholstery fabrics often are treated with stain guards. Because the stain guards will repel paint, it is necessary to work out the intensity and medium of the toner on a sample of the upholstery fabric first. If working with a water-based paint, add extra binder to it for better adhesion. If the water-based paint does not adhere to the fabric, an FEV should be used. Never tone down upholstery with aniline dye, as it may transfer to the costumes or the performers' hands. If water-based paint does not adhere to the fabric, then FEV mixed with Japan colors should be used. If the fabric can be stretched and treated before it is tacked on the furniture, it can be sprayed down easily. If an upholstered piece must be toned down, the fabric should be sprayed with several layers of thin color.

Dried Plants

When dried plants, grasses, and foliage are used on stage, one of the main concerns is to ensure they have been treated with flame retardant. Suppliers of flame retardant should be consulted to determine what product is best suited to these materials. Dried materials should be dipped in a flame retardant for complete coverage. Dried foliage too large to dip should be sprayed with flame retardant from two or three sides. After flame retardant has been applied, dried foliage can be painted with water-based paints, stained with aniline dyes, or toned with an FEV. The simplest ways to paint dried foliage are by using a pneumatic or garden sprayer or by dipping the foliage in the paint and letting it drip dry. Remember it is the responsibility of the shop to send samples of any cellulostic materials that have been treated with flame retardant in house to a licensed lab for certification.

AGING TECHNIQUES AND MEDIUMS

Aging refers to any technique or combination of techniques used to render the appearance of age and weathering. The most important goal is to realistically simulate the effects that the years and weather have had on real materials. For instance, barn wood will bleach out in the weather while the nails that hold the barn together may rust and stain the wood. Wallpaper in old buildings may be stained by watermarks. The underside of limestone cornices and lintels on the exterior of an old building may be stained and streaked with soot.

Paint

Any surface can be given the appearance of age by using glazes made from Payne's gray, black, umbers, ochers, and light gray hues. Some materials darken and yellow as they get older, others become grayed and washed out. When the colors are washed on porous materials such as unprimed wood, they will penetrate the wood somewhat and alter the surface color. Glazes made from aniline dyes may also be used to age or enhance the color of raw wood. If the glaze needs to be durable or have a slight shine, the glaze paint can be mixed into or the binder reinforced with a flat-finish acrylic- or water-based urethane.

Peeling and Cracked Paint

The most obvious way to make a painted surface look aged is to give the paint a cracked appearance. There are a few ways to make fresh paint actually crack or to give it a cracked appearance.

Sodium Silicate

Sodium silicate is sold at some theatrical supply houses by the gallon. It is also available through chemical suppliers in bulk quantities of 55-gallon drums. When sodium silicate is mixed with polymer binders, particularly acrylics, the two mediums react chemically, causing a dramatic resistance that cracks the paint (see Figure 10.7). The surface to which the silicate mixture is applied first should be painted with the hue that is to show through the cracked finish coat. This undercoat should be covered with shellac. The shellac undercoat will accomplish two things. It will give the sodium silicate mixture a smooth surface to slide off and the alcohol in the shellac will accelerate the evaporation of the mixture.

The sodium silicate should be mixed in equal proportion with the desired hue of paint. The two mediums should be mixed together just before they are to be used. Because they are not compatible, the mixture has a very short shelf life. Always use all appropriate safety equipment when using these materials. While the shellac on the undercoat is still tacky, the sodium silicate mixture should be brushed or sprayed on with a pneumatic sprayer. While the sodium silicate mixture is setting up, spraying it with solvent alcohol from a garden sprayer will accelerate the drying time and cause the cracks to be more dramatic. A second application of shellac and sodium silicate mixture, after the first one has set up, will result in more profound cracking and aging.

The cracks caused by sodium silicate may look somewhat unnatural because the mixture tends to separate on diagonals while weathered paint tends to crack on verticals, horizontals, or in the direction in which the paint most commonly was applied on that surface. The sodium silicate mixture can be encouraged to crack in a more uniform way by combing it with a wire brush or paint scraper while it is setting up and being sprayed down with the solvent alcohol.

When straight sodium silicate is used as an undercoat, the paint used as a topcoat will crack more subtlety and also sag if applied while the surface is vertical. After the topcoat has dried, the sagging can be accentuated by spraying it with water or a dirty water glaze.

Glue Base

Polymer-based paints are not stable on an undercoating of dry animal glue. The paint or polymer varnish will separate and crack on this base. The cracks caused by this technique are very regular and natural looking, but the glue base that is revealed by the cracks will be shiny. This sheen may be eye-catching and unnatural looking. If the surface is vertical while the paint or varnish is drying, it will sag too.

One way to control the size of crack with this medium is by how thickly the glue is applied. The sagging may be desirable in some circumstances, but one of the drawbacks of this technique is that the sagging is very difficult to control.

Boarding

The technique of boarding can be used to give the appearance of chipped paint. Several layers of closely related colors spattered on the desired background color and smeared with a board can have a very effective appearance. This technique is particularly useful if a large area is to be treated or in combination with one of the cracking techniques described earlier.

Figure 10.9 Paint cracking samples: sodium silicate (top), animal glue undercoat (bottom two).

Wood

Wood on the side of structures, such as houses, out-buildings, and city buildings, ages quickly due to the effects of pollution, weather, and the sun. Aged wood tends to simultaneously deepen in color and bleach out. The result is that the exposed wood turns varying shades of gray. The wood under overhangs, protected from the elements, will age more slowly and become darker from mold, moisture, and pollution. The color of the wood in these areas tends to deepen in color and bleach out less. The wood exposed to the elements will lighten and bleach out considerably.

Wood Pickling

To alter and deepen the actual color of the wood, it must be oxidized. This process can be emulated through *pickling* which is a rapid chemical aging process. Pickling speeds up the oxidation process in woods so that cedar planks straight from the saw mill can be given the appearance of having stood out in the weather for a decade in the course of a few days. Pickling is, however, not instantaneous. The color of the wood will not fully deepen for nearly eight hours. If the wood is being treated out-of-doors, sunlight will accelerate the process.

A few different washes can be used to pickle wood. One solution is made from steel wool and vinegar. First, immerse the steel wool in water and set it aside to rust. Repeat this once or twice until it is thoroughly rusted. Then, drop the steel wool in a bucket of vinegar and let it sit overnight. The next day, strain the remaining fragments of steel wool out of the solution. This is your pickling solution. When sprayed or brushed on most woods, it will cause them to oxidize. Denser woods, such as oak, will not absorb or deepen as much as coarser grained woods, such as pine and cedar. Always test the pickling solution on a sample to ascertain its strength and how it will affect the wood being treated. If too strong, it can be cut with water.

Pickling solution also can be made from iron sulfite. The iron sulfite can be mixed into water and sprayed or brushed on the wood. This pickling solution is unpredictable, oxidizing coarser grained woods more darkly. This works very well with cedar. Iron sulfite, also called *copperas*, a soil additive, can be purchased at garden-supply stores.

Wood and Metal Patinas

A *patina* is the pleasing result of corrosion that occurs when metal surfaces are exposed to air and weather. Artists and architects rely on this when they specify bronzes or copper in their work. The sepia, deep greens, and cerulean blues are the result of exposure of these metals to the elements.

Oxidizing Patina Mediums

Products can be purchased through paint supply stores that specialize in faux-finish products that accelerate the oxidizing of many metals. These corrosive solutions also oxidize wood. The solutions are formulated differently so the resulting patina is of a desired color, such as blue, green, black, and burgundy. These different patina solutions will result in slightly different colors on woods as well. Because these solutions are somewhat costly, they may not be the first choice for large-scale projects. These products work on composites of gold and silver leaf and bronzing powders. The patina will form on the metal as the solution dries. If a deeper patina is desired, the solution may be applied again. The patina finish will be fragile and easily wiped off, so if the scenic units or props are to be handled frequently, the units should be sealed by spraying them with water-based urethanes.

Paints or tinted glazes reinforced with water-based urethanes may also be used to simulate patinas. These glazes can be sprayed, brushed, sponged, or ragged on for the desired appearance and sheen.

Rust

Whenever there are steel nails in wood or iron fixtures on the side of a building, exterior rust will streak down the side of the boards or stone below them. If the rust stain has deepened over the course of many years, it will be a darkish brown. This effect can be achieved with paint.

On the metal itself, the rust may corrode the surface until it has a distinct texture. This texture may be created by sponging on tinted texture compound. If a more dramatic texture is desired to indicate profound neglect, fine sand or plastic flakes can be mixed in with the texture compound. Once the texture compound is dry it can be painted with black, browns, and the more acidic colors of orange and ochers to give the appearance of rust blooming on a metal surface.

Distressing

In scenic painting, the term *distressing* means giving a material the appearance of age, wear, and grime such as a dirty glaze coat. Any technique that contributes to this effect can be termed distressing. The peeling and cracking techniques just described are two forms of distressing. The key to convincing distressing is to observe how various materials age and understand the nature of the wear on these materials as they are subjected to use, age, and weather. For instance, how does rust from nails or support brackets streak down the side of wood planks or a brick wall?

Fabrics

As fabric ages, its color fades in areas exposed to light. This fading can be simulated with a spray of a light opaque glaze. Dust and grime in the atmosphere yellow fabric over time. A dirty-water spray of umber and yellow ocher can accomplish this. When spraying fabric with a glaze, it is best to use a very watery glaze applied in two or three passes and allowed to dry between each application so that there are no hot spots. If the fabric to be aged is upholstered on a piece of furniture that is to look tattered, the arms and seat can be worn down with an orbital sander or frayed with a rasp.

Dirt and Soot

Dirt on an exterior usually is the soot and dust that has accumulated in corners and under overhangs that has not been washed off by rain or weather. In productions that are set in eras and areas where coal was used for heating and in industry, the collection of soot will be especially heavy and dark. Soot collects on the sides of building below overhangs where it is less apt to be washed of by the weather. Soot streaks may be very dark after many years of being exposed to polluted city air.

When distressing interiors, most of the dirt collects and spreads through contact with people and inept attempts to clean. Dirt will collect in the corners. Smoke will yellow ceilings, and soot will streak the walls and ceiling above wood- and coal-burning stoves and fireplaces. Grime will accumulate around the corners of walls, along chair rails, and around doorknobs. A peculiar thing happens around frequently touched areas such as doorknobs and drawer handles. The dirt build-up will "halo" around these areas. Because of the constant contact with human hands it will keep getting cleaned off on the surface adjacent to the knob or handle.

Asphaltum

Asphaltum is a tar-based resin. When thinned with turpentine, the resin will yield a deep sepia-colored glaze that makes a very convincing patina of age and grime. Use proper safety precautions when working with turpentine; it is one of the most toxic solvents commonly used (see Chapter 4, the section "Safety and Health Regulations").

Transparent mediums such as flat clear acrylic may also be tinted and used in the same way as asphaltum for that deep grimy look. The advantage is that they are nontoxic. The disadvantage is that they have a faster drying time so they are not as easy to work with. The drying time can be slowed down by mixing clear acrylic with a water-based glazing medium.

WALLPAPER

Stencils or stamps can be used to simulate wallpaper. However, if the designer desires very complex patterns or the naturalistic appearance that can come only from actual wallpaper, it will be more time- and cost-effective to select a wallpaper pattern (see Figure 10.8).

Conventional Wallpaper

There is not much difference between hanging wallpaper in an actual room and on a set. Wallpaper comes in differing widths; 21 inches up to 30 inches is standard. When ordering wallpaper, you must include enough extra in the order to cover the linear footage lost when matching the patterns on each seam. The catalogue should state how much extra length must be added per panel of wallpaper.

It is simpler to hang the paper on an assembled set in the shop or on stage. If the units are laid out on the shop floor or paint deck, the lap joints of the flattage must be carefully measured and cartooned so that the seams of the paper will match when the set is assembled. When actually hanging the wallpaper, a long worktable should be set up in the middle of

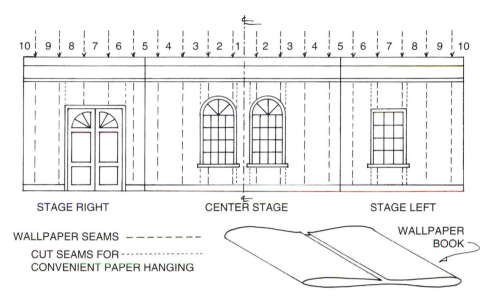

STAGE RIGHT   CENTER STAGE   STAGE LEFT

WALLPAPER SEAMS ─ ─ ─ ─ ─ ─
CUT SEAMS FOR ··············
CONVENIENT PAPER HANGING

WALLPAPER
BOOK

Figure 10.10
Wallpaper layout.

the set or shop. The tools necessary for the job include sponges, a bucket of water, a metal ruler, a ruler with levels on it, a nine-inch roller and roller tray, a straw wallpaper brush, and a hundred count box of razor blades. Because the wallpaper will be wet with wallpaper paste when it is cut to a width, a fresh blade should be used for each cut. Used blades will have dried paste that can snag the paper. Tape each blade before disposing of it or collect them in a paint can that can be sealed and thrown away.

For centuries, wheat paste was used for pasting up wallpaper. In the later part of the 20th century, vinyl wall paste became the new standard for installing wallpaper. Because the paper will expand from the moisture in the paste, it must sit for a time after the back has been rolled with paste. Once you have measured and cut the length, including extra for pattern alignment, and applied paste to the back of the wallpaper, carefully fold the paper both ends to the middle, and then fold it once again in the center. This is called a *book*. Let the book of wallpaper sit for five minutes while the paper expands. Some wallpaper actually must be soaked in water before it is pasted. Manufacturers usually include instructions on how to handle wallpaper.

All surfaces to be papered should be primed. When hanging wallpaper in a room, first choose the focal point of the room and center the first book of wallpaper on that surface. Successive books should be pasted up on alternating sides so that the paste has

a chance to set up before the next book is pasted up alongside of it. The same is true of wall papering a set. First choose the focal point of the set and, using a ruler with levels in it, measure and mark out the vertical the placement registration lines of the successive widths of wallpaper. To hang a book of paper, keep it folded until you are at the top of the ladder or scaffolding. Unfold only the top of the book and position the paper. Once it is in place, brush the paper down from the top and out from the center, being careful to keep the edge lined up on your registration marks. After the top half of the paper is positioned correctly, unfold the bottom of the book and brush the rest of the paper into place. Trim the paper flush to the molding and sponge the excess paste off the molding and the paper before it dries. When working on a set, it may be possible to install the moldings after the wallpaper has been hung.

In a home, the paper must be carefully measured and trimmed around doors and windows. On a set, an additional vertical seam can be added at the corners of door and window casements to speed up the process. The additional vertical seam will not be noticed by the audience. Measure and cut the vertical seam in a book of paper using a straight edge. After the first section of the book has been pasted into place along the edge of the casement, the second section can be matched along the new seam and trimmed at the top and the bottom of the casements.

Raised Pattern Paper

Wallpapers with raised patterns and vinyl-based ornamental details frequently are used on sets. When glazed to bring out the detail or viewed with down-lighting or side-lighting, these intricate patterns enhance the architectural setting. These patterns are available only in their natural white or off-white color. After the patterns have been installed, they can be painted and glazed as desired.

Raised pattern paper installed in commercial and residential interiors must be adhered with a clay-based wallpaper adhesive, usually available through the same manufacturer as the paper. The clay-based adhesive fills and reinforces the pattern of the paper so that it is not easily dented or crushed during day-to-day wear. When installed in the less permanent situation of a stage setting, regular wallpaper paste may be used to hang the paper. Heavier paper borders and vinyl-backed decorative details also may be installed with wallpaper paste or water-based contact cement in the case of heavier molded vinyl borders and details.

Laminate Papers

Laminate wallpaper such as Mylar is made to be used on very smooth commercial wall surfaces. These laminates come in a wide range of finishes and colors and are available from theatrical suppliers. Some of these plastic finishes are adhesive backed, others are paper backed. The adhesive-backed coverings must be applied to a very clean, well-sanded surface. The covering is quite thin and its reflective surface will highlight every imperfection in the surface below it. Air bubbles trapped in thin plastic laminates can be smoothed down by carefully pricking the surface with a pin to release the air. The paper-backed plastic coverings are thicker and so are somewhat more forgiving of the surface. However, the seams and dents in the surface still should be patched and sanded before the covering is applied. The paper-backed coverings can be applied with vinyl wallpaper paste. However, the plastic coverings cannot be booked tight and folded along the edge like wallpaper because the crease caused by folding will remain. Suppliers of the plastic coverings will include recommendations on the brand or type of adhesive that should be used.

As this chapter has shown, scenic artists are called on to work with many different materials and mediums. If you ever encounter a material with which you are unfamiliar, do not hesitate to call the manufacturer to request information or guidelines for its use and application.

Part Four
The History of Scenic Art

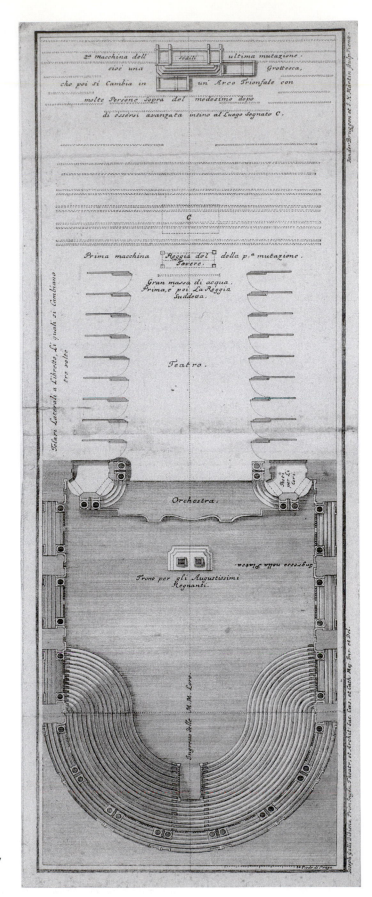

Section of the Teatro Farnese by Pietro Paolo Coccetti, drawn in 1726. The Tobin Collection of the McNay Museum, San Antonio, Texas.

Chapter 11

Ancient Classical Theatre to Medieval Performances: 500 B.C. to 1400 A.D.

The painter's art has enhanced theatre performance and production during virtually all ages of theatre. Painting seems to transform common materials into magical and mysterious objects, like the alchemy of creating gold from base elements. Stage painting did more than fool the eye by clever device. Painting also created powerful images of the unknown. The terrifying specter of hell was created by unknown artists for liturgical dramas and pageants of the pre-Renaissance Christian west. These sorts of scenic elements were possibly the principal way in which most people witnessed profoundly important suggestions of their afterlife. Through scenic art we see expressed theology and entertainment, leaving us a remarkable understanding of life in that time. It is curious that scenic art has remained remarkably intact throughout history. It is true that theatrical performance is much more technically sophisticated than at any other time in the past; however, the art of scenic painting itself is much the same.

Stage painting most likely was a part of early western drama in the Greek theatre of Aeschylus and Sophocles. From Roman accounts of Greek theatre, we know that the stage had painted decoration to augment a scene of a play. We also know that these decorations could change throughout the course of a performance. The description we have of Greek dramatic painting suggests a sophisticated illusionistic style, like perspective or trompe l'oeil. Unfortunately, we have no authoritative record of what painting was like in Greek and Roman theatre. This we do know: once scenic painting entered the stage for theatrical purposes, it remained a significant decorative and dramatic element throughout nearly all of Western theatrical history. As stage decoration progressed through the centuries, it consistently explored the exotic, fantastic, and wondrous stage image through painting. Theatre building styles and stage technology evolved greatly in the 2,400-year interval from classical Greece to the present, but the fundamental visual relationship between the audience, actors, and painted backgrounds remains.

GREECE: 500 TO 250 B.C.

"The ancients required realistic pictures of real things."[1] These are the words of the Roman architect Marcus Vitruvius Pollio, written during the first century B.C. Vitruvius' work is the oldest surviving written record with any reference to architectural practice related to the theatre building and decoration. This book possibly influenced generations of architects in the Roman Empire, but certainly its rediscovery early in the Italian Renaissance was one of the most profound discoveries in the history of art.

---

[1]Vitruvius, Book V, Chapter VI, p. 69, 1999.

361

Vitruvius' 10 books on architecture are the only contemporary description on the practice as well as the aesthetics of Roman and Greek architecture.

Vitruvius reveals much of what we know about the classical Greek and Roman theatre through his book, *De Architetura*. He describes the site of a theatre, acoustical considerations, foundations, harmonics, use and construction of theatres, and the differences between the Greek and Roman styles. He also describes painted scenery and stage equipment. However, these descriptions were made over 400 years after the time of Aeschylus, Euripides, and Socrates. We cannot be certain of the exact time that the elements he describes were introduced, but we can assume that the Greek theatre used moveable and changeable scenic devices at least in the later Hellenistic theatres. We can also assume from documentation that these devices were painted.

The Greek Theatre Building

The first large-scale permanent theatres were built in the 5th century B.C. during the classical period of ancient Greece (see Figure 11.1). These theatre spaces were formal structures placed in very prominent and meaningful sites within a city. Some theatres accommodated thousands of spectators with a good view of the stage and clear hearing of the actor. The earliest of these formal Greek theatres were placed in carefully chosen locations for two reasons: as a

sloping site to aid the seating and acoustics and to situate the view of the audience toward an expansive natural vista behind the area where performers stood. Nature, in effect, provided the first backdrops.

An elevated stage platform developed in the Athenian theatres later in the classical period. It was placed at the back of the orchestra, the large circular area at the foot of the seating. This stage structure, called a *skene*, created an architectural context for entrances and exits and elevated the actor to a more visually prominent position relative to the audience. The *skene* was low at first, connected with steps to the orchestra. The height of the *skene* increased and it became an isolated platform for performance, no longer connected to the orchestra. The *skene* also, eventually, had a back wall that was decorated with architectural refinement based on Greek style. Temporary decorations were added to it for individual play performances. These decorations were certainly painted, but no examples remain of this early scenic art. We must rely on a few written descriptions and the long historical lineage of the form itself. The classical Greek theatre was copied by the Roman Empire and then revived in the Italian Renaissance. It may be true that the Roman stage decorators were influenced by the Greeks, as the architects clearly were. Any knowledge we have of the Greek theatre comes from the Roman interpretation and their records of it left in Vitruvius.

Figure 11.1
A model of a Classical Greek Theatre.

Greek Stage Decoration

Greek theatres are thoroughly documented to have had three essential parts: audience, orchestra, and skene. Of those three, it was the skene, a modest structure, which was the point of focus for an architectural backdrop supporting scenic embellishments. The audience was the spectator area and the orchestra was an architecturally neutral area for actors, often the chorus.

The *Skene* The *skene* possibly was built to allow for entrances and to create dressing and offstage areas for the actors. By virtue of its placement, the *skene* became an architectural background to the stage area and lessened the impact of the landscape as the background. Actors performed in front of the *skene*. The façade of the *skene* was large enough to have doors that served as decoration, as well as for use in the action of the play. The door to a palace, for example, easily could be provided using the *skene*. Vitruvius[2] describes this very arrangement: "In the center are double-doors, decorated like those of a royal palace. At the right and the left are the doors of the guest chambers."

Painted Decoration The *skene* apparently was decorated with temporary and changeable painted pieces. Two types of painted scenic elements, *periaktoi* and *pinakes*, are documented by Vitruvius and Pollux (a Roman architect who described theatres in a book written some 200 years after Vitruvius). *Periaktoi* were triangular columns, like tall vertical prisms, that could rotate to present three different faces, thus allowing the possibility of on-stage scene changes. Exactly where the *periaktoi* were placed on the skene is unknown. Some theories place the *periaktoi* within the open doors; others state that they sat on either side of them. Each face of the *periaktoi* could be painted to represent a different scene. In fact, Vitruvius described three kinds of scenes—the tragic, the comic, and the satyric—which would easily correspond to the three faces of the *periaktoi*.

Pinakes were simple flat panels, possibly painted with just color or formal designs[3] and used to change the face of the skene for particular performances. These *pinakes* probably were placed on the front of the *skene*, between columns, and used like flats are today.

From these written descriptions, it is certain the Greeks used a method of painted decoration. Vitruvius states that Aeschylus invented painted scenery. Aristotle gives the credit, however, to Sophocles. Vitruvius describes a document of scenic painting, written by the painter Agatharchos of Samos, that:

> led Democritus and Anaxagoras to write on the same subject [painting], showing how, given a center in a definite place, the lines should naturally correspond with due regard to the point of sight and the divergence of the visual rays, so that by this deception a faithful representation of the buildings might be given in painted scenery, and so that, though all is drawn on a vertical flat façade, some parts may seem to be withdrawing into the background, and others to be standing out in front.[4]

Agatharchos was a painter who apparently worked for the theatre. His work dates from the second half of the 5th century B.C. At that time, there was an understanding that perspective methods of drawing produced effects of depth and contributed to more realistic painting. Furthermore, this indicates a recognition of the role of perspective illusion for the stage. This sort of technique was to have profound importance on the craft of theatrical painting and decoration much later in the Renaissance. It is unknown when these practices actually began, however. The Greek term for scenic painting, *skenographia*, has remained as the modern term for a theatrical designer, *scenographer*.

ROME: 250 B.C. to 550 A.D.

The Roman Empire spread from the Italian peninsula to eventually subsume much of Europe, eastern Asia, and northern Africa. The city-states of Greece were one of Rome's most significant early conquests, as it spread outward from the Italian peninsula. The Romans borrowed from Greece an aesthetic sensibility that served as an artistic cornerstone of the prolific empire to come. The theatre was no exception. The written record of Vitruvius underscores the absolute respect Rome had for the arts of Greece. Rome studiously imitated Greek forms of theatre and theatrical building. In this manner, the essential Greek format of auditorium, orchestra, and skene remained and served as the basis for further development and elaboration.

---

[2]1999, Book V, Chapter VI, p. 70.
[3]Nicoll, 1966, p. 12.

[4]1999, Book VII.

The Roman Theatre and the *Scaenae Frons*

Rome built theatres in most of its large cities, recognizing that theatre was an important part of cultural life. Their theatres were located close to the center of the city, and they were in constant use. The building resembled the Greek model on many levels; however, Rome brought the building closer to a self-contained architectural unit. The seating was restricted to a half-circle and the orchestra was diminished in size and dramatic importance. The *skene* was replaced by a more elaborate architectural background, called the *scaenae frons* (see Figure 11.2). The *scaenae frons* played a significant role in the decoration and function of the theatre and became the dominant decorative unit. Nearly a building in itself, it was a two- or three-story wall, richly decorated with columns, niches, and statuary. It retained the three doors of the Greek *skene* and sometimes had two more, added for more entrances, particularly as the size of the theatre grew. The stage remained squarely in front of the *scaenae frons*. It became deeper and wider, giving the actor greater freedom of movement.

The impact of the *scaenae frons* was tremendous to the building as a whole. The height of it obliterated most views to the natural surroundings of the location. This allowed theatres to be placed at will in the city, no longer dependent on ideal topography for an appropriate background. The audience seating was built to a height matching the top of the scaenae frons. This meant that the entire building was wrapped in a continuous wall. Effectively, the theatre became an architectural whole, lacking only a roof to completely isolate it from the outdoors. The eventual use of an awning (*velarium*) to cover the audience from the sun virtually created an interior theatre space. The height of the *scaenae frons* allowed two sorts of decorative curtains to be employed in the stage area. One was the *aulaeum*, which functioned as a front curtain. This could be dropped to the orchestra level or raised up to reveal or conceal the stage at will. Another was the *siparium*, which served as a backdrop, concealing the *scaenae frons* and providing a decorative surface. Both curtains easily could have served as painted decoration.

Roman Stage Decoration

There is no question that Roman architects used many types of painted decoration. The remains of Pompeii prove the extent to which painted frescoes were found in the buildings and homes of the Roman Empire. Mosaics also flourished as a major decorative force to a degree never witnessed before this time. Although no scenery exists from this period, it is safe to assume that stages were completed with the presence of painted scenic elements. Frescoes from Pompeii illustrate full

Figure 11.2
A model of a Roman theatre and *scaenae frons*.

stage settings and use of the *aulaeum* and *siparium*. The Romans used all the stage machinery known to the Greeks as well. The *periaktoi* and *pinakes* that Vitruvius recorded would have provided Roman stage painters with ample vehicles for their artistic input. Surviving paintings of Roman stages indicate that the *scaenae frons* could be further embellished with statuary, paintings, and objects to help delineate a scene.

Vitruvius describes the three kinds of scenes in Book V, Chapter VI, which falls immediately before the chapter on Greek theatres. Perhaps Vitruvius recognized that these scenes are of Roman invention. The description is as follows:

> There are three kinds of scenes, one called tragic, second, the comic, third, the satyric. Their decorations are different and unlike each other in scheme. Tragic scenes are delineated with columns, pediments and statues and other objects suited to the kings; comic scenes exhibit private dwellings, with balconies and views representing rows of windows, after the manner of ordinary dwelling; satyric scenes are decorated with trees, caverns, mountains, and other rustic objects delineated in landscape style.[5]

Roman painting explored the world of perspective as a means to represent the real world. Vitruvius' quotation from earlier in this section reflects the demand for real things depicted realistically. Vitruvius noted a degradation of painting away from realism to fantasy. Certainly, in the centuries after Vitruvius to the decline of Rome, there were hundreds upon hundreds of painted embellishments for theatrical productions. Unfortunately, none survive, and we may only speculate as to their content.

THE MIDDLE AGES: 550 TO 1400 A.D.

The Roman Empire dissolved slowly under repeated attacks of the northern tribes, generally called barbarians. The Roman Emperor Constantine split the Roman Empire in two halves around 330 A.D. He left the Western empire centered at Rome and created a new Eastern capitol in Byzantium, renamed Constantinople. The city of Rome began to diminish as a cultural and political force from this point forward. Theatre did persist in Rome beyond Constantine. However, after 568, there is no record of further theatrical performances in the city of Rome. The many theatres of the empire fell into disuse, at least for their original purpose, and many of these buildings were dismantled.

Important arts, crafts, and skills relevant to theatre were abandoned and forgotten from generations of inactivity. The books of Vitruvius were ignored and the precise meaning of the classical orders of architecture submerged into distant memory. New architectural styles developed that now relied on observation and a naive imitation of the past. This allowed for a completely new aesthetic, one that would reflect the sensibilities of each location. French, German, Italian, and English styles were to come as the world approached the first millennium after Christ.

The transition took centuries. Scores of generations passed from the time of great cultural activity in Rome to the calming of European tribal wars and the first establishment of medieval cities around 1100. There were few bright spots in theatrical art, or any arts during this epoch. Charlemagne's creation of the Holy Roman Empire and a self-conscious Roman renaissance took place around 800 A.D. His effort to amass the scholars of the known world at the capitol of the Empire in Aix-la-Chapelle (Aachen, at the intersection of modern Belgium, Germany, and the Netherlands) was successful, for a brief period. Within two generations of Charlemagne's death, however, Europe returned to bitter warfare, as small groups struggled for domination.

Warfare, disease, and poverty limited artistic growth in Europe during the centuries after the fall of Rome. This is the time of the so-called "Dark Ages" before the bold achievement of the French and English Gothic and, later, the Italian Renaissance. The term "Dark Age" itself is a modern misnomer and obscures many significant artistic accomplishments during the evolution of Europe. Yet it is true that theatre was sporadic at best and generally limited to religious spectacle during this long period. The development of the theatre building stopped. No theatres were built in Europe for scores of generations. The art of stage decoration and painting, as the ancient cultures knew, ended. The ability to paint Vitruvius' realism, by means of perspective, was lost. Painting, of course, did not cease, and a new sense of "realism" was to evolve in the Middle Ages.

The Remnants of Classical Traditions

Christianity was by far the most prominent political and artistic force in medieval Europe. Politically and

---

[5] 1999, Book V, Chapter VI, p. 69.

culturally as well as by religious influence, Catholicism brought structure to Europe after the fall of the Roman Empire. The harshness of existence during this epoch left little time or place for theatrical activity. The Church was one of the few enduring features of the time. It was an intrinsic part of life in the Middle Ages. The act of the mass was in itself a drama, and the Church became the source of newer forms of drama, which chiefly revolved around the liturgy. The dramatic literature of Greece and Rome had no place in Catholic theology and naturally fell into disuse. Thus, the entire form and content of theatrical art completely changed and a powerful discontinuity further separated dramatic artists from their classical ancestors.

However, one might see the Catholic celebration of the mass itself as a final living remnant of Roman culture. The celebration of the mass developed in Rome, particularly rapidly once Constantine officially recognized Christianity in Rome in 332 A.D. The Church installed its head official, the Pope, in Rome, underlining the enduring importance of the Eternal City. The Church took over many existing buildings of the Roman Empire for use as houses of worship. The common basilica, normally a meeting hall for the Romans, became a church for many early Christians. These basilicas were large, rectangular open spaces, well suited to large gatherings. These Romans, after converting to Christianity, celebrated mass in Roman basilicas. Many Roman mannerisms of ceremonial dress and formality transferred naturally to the Christian inhabitants of Rome. These traits remained for centuries, as only in the second half of the 20th century was the Catholic mass finally conducted in a language other than Latin. The mass certainly is a form of drama in itself, and the church would eventually serve as the principal host of dramatic performances.

Liturgical Drama

The Catholic Church had no interest in preserving the performing arts or literature that the Romans knew. Instead, the Church became the inspiration of and patron for a new phase in European theatre. Christianity used drama to explain more clearly the teachings of Christ through dramatic performance. Churches staged liturgical dramas in conjunction with the two great Christian festivals: Christmas and Easter, the birth and death of Christ. This dramatic storytelling took place in the church itself as a part of the mass. These dramas became popular as good

entertainment on their own and attracted enough spectators that the entertainment moved outdoors to satisfy the demand. Ironically, the Church itself finally created what it had suppressed for so long: theatre.

The Outdoor Stage   The move to the outdoors was tremendously significant for the production and the theatre. Indoor dramas had a natural stage in the church itself and needed little visual help. Outdoor performances meant construction of a stage or stages to depict the locations of the drama. After a gap of nearly 900 years, theatrical stages were to be built again. Twelfth-century texts describe the presence of many locales, called *loci*, which are stages or sets constructed for outdoor liturgical drama. The crucifix, the sepulcher, a prison, hell, heaven, and several other locales are described in the 12th century French text for *Resurrection*. Each locale appears to be contained in a small stage or mansion. A description of the Anglo-Norman production of *Adam* indicates that paradise was depicted with actors nearly hidden behind curtains and silks, that fragrant flowers and leaves were scattered, and fruit-filled trees completed the scene. These dramas were performed in sequential order, requiring the audience to move from stage to stage. In fact, they were very much like the 14 stations of the cross common to Catholic churches then and now. In these, the worshipper moves from station to station to observe the 14 dramatic steps of Christ's imprisonment and crucifixion.

Mystery Plays, Cycles, and Pageants

By the late 13th century, these religious dramas appeared in many locations in Europe. Their popularity was immense, and the dramas grew to staggering proportions of detail and spectacle. The growth of liturgical dramas demanded intense activity and effort for their production. Guilds and fraternities were established to produce the dramas. Entire towns devoted weeks of effort to prepare for them. These productions became so elaborate that it took up to four days for the performance of one play. These dramas became known as *mystery plays* or *cycles*. The term *mystery play* is very appropriate to the drama as every attempt was made to realistically stage the mysteries of the liturgy in frightening detail. These mystery plays put remarkable emphasis on theatrical production, which created a need for a unique group of skilled artisans. The chiefly anonymous participants in these productions revived, or created, skills of the theatrical arts that were to become crucial to the revival of theatre in the Renaissance.

The plays, or cycles, primarily had two formats. One form is a stationary presentation, where all the scenic elements are dispersed around an open area, such as a town square. The second form is the pageant. In this form, the scenic elements are moved to the spectators on wheels. This latter form was more common in England, whereas the former style was common in Europe. In both cases, the stages were elaborate, self-contained units, generally called *mansions*. The audience was to focus on the mansion while it was in use and ignore everything surrounding it.

Mystery Play Production   Mystery plays served to inspire wonderment and awe in the viewers. Their very existence was to serve religious purposes. We should recognize, too, that these plays were the sole entertainment available for most people. Texts and production notes have survived from some mystery plays in France. We can see from these how the plays grew in scale and spectacle in the 15th and 16th centuries. The mystery play at Villingen shows that the town square became filled with 22 individual stages or mansions, including hell, the garden of Gethsemane, Mount Olivet, the pillar of scourging, the palace of Herod, the court of Pilate, the last supper, Christ's cross, the thieves' crosses, graves, the holy sepulcher, and heaven. The mystery of the passion at Valenciennes in 1547 used 63 actors. At Bourges, the mystery of the acts of the apostles included 494 characters and required 14 days of performance. The 22 mansions constructed at Rouen were prepared over a period of 18 years.

These mystery plays and cycles were immense community undertakings. Evidently, their popularity was great, as many thousands of people attended these presentations, justifying the tremendous expenses and investments in time. From this work, too, came the revival of the craft of theatre. These mystery plays were loaded with intricate devices to create effects of fire, smoke, explosions, torture, and executions. Clearly, individuals with great skills and talent worked in the creation of these complex presentations. The pageants were popular throughout much of northern and central Europe as well. France, Germany, the Netherlands, England, and Belgium all saw many of these productions. Through these great liturgical dramas, the actual practice of theatre and

great invention in theatrical production spread in Europe. Later, as new kinds of drama emerged in the Renaissance, there would be the knowledge and skills to support the continued growth of theatre and production.

The Scenic Elements of Mystery Plays   The drawings of Lucerne and Valenciennes and records from the pageant at Mons and other productions show us how increasingly complex the scenic elements became. Heaven and hell were paramount in importance. At Mons, heaven required complex pulley and winch systems to allow the apostles to rise up. Heaven itself was concealed with painted clouds, and the sky behind heaven was filled with stars. Hell was often the huge, fearsome mouth of a fantastic creature. From this awful mouth came flames, smoke, sparks, thunder, dragons, serpents, and the devil. The manuscript at Mons describes hell as a gigantic "mask of a toad face." It took a stone mason and two assistants three days to form it. Then, it was covered in canvas and painted.

The stage at Mons was immense, and the play called for 67 different mansions, or settings. The records show that five painters were on salary for the production for a considerable length of time. They used all pigments available, varnish, gold leaf, and silver powder. They were called on to paint the sky of heaven and the mask of hell as well as a cloth with the sun and moon, imitation draperies, and architecture. Painting was an extremely integral part of these productions.

Tournaments and Processionals

Stagecraft eventually was kept active by the needs of state, particularly in France and England. The tournament contests often incorporated painted castles for the games. Knights entered on disguised chariots, painted to look like ships at sea or amidst a grove of trees and wild beasts. The visit of a king or queen, a coronation, or a royal wedding demanded elaborate decorations. More painted castles, triumphal arches, gateways, and other embellishments would be erected for these notable events.

The scenic artists and scenic designers of this time mostly were anonymous artists. Their work for theatre was done largely as an outside interest. We have no records of any individual who devoted a career to the visual part of theatre. What their techniques or practices were, we do not know.

Certainly the crossover between fine arts, fresco painting, and theatrical decoration was important. Few took theatre as an important and ongoing profession, but simply as an adjunct to other crafts. The "designing" of the era was the effort to create living allegories and make paintings come to life. It would take a broad cultural revolution to restore scenic decoration to the theatre.

AN INTERVIEW WITH MICHAEL HAGEN, MH HAGEN STUDIO

Susan Crabtree: Could you tell me a little about your shop here, Michael Hagen Incorporated?

Michael Hagen: After over 30 years in this business, it was my long intent to have my own shop. So we built our own shop, designed from experience, for our own specific needs. The shop has a size that suits the work that we do for our clients—it is a 100-foot-wide, 135-foot-long, column-free paint space. That allows us to put any scenery in any combination on the floor and paint it in an efficient manner.

SC: It is a wonderful space. What is the focus of the work that you do?

MH: The majority of our work is painting sets for opera and ballet productions. The last 14 years we have been in the United States; before that we were in Montreal for 25 years. In Montreal we had our first permanent shop, which was big enough to do very large productions. When our lease was up for renewal, they asked us to move to the eighth floor. The new space had one little handicap and that was that it only had a 12-foot freight elevator. Of course, if you are dealing with 24-foot scenery, it's not feasible to get that into a 12-foot freight elevator. We painted the scenery in the construction shop that built the sets; we filled our own shop with backdrops. That is how we ended up being a full-time backdrop shop. In our shop now we can accommodate anything. It makes it more convenient for everybody because we can paint everything in one location.

SC: How long have you been a scenic artist and where did you get your training?

MH: I got my training as an apprentice in the paint shop at the Deutsche Opera in Berlin, Germany. The apprenticeship required that I work in the paint shop four days a week; the fifth day was theory class to acquire the knowledge necessary for the trade. I enjoyed this aspect of the apprenticeship as it gave me great insight into the profession. In a training situation like that, you are surrounded by professionals who have many years of experience and they push you in the right direction to make you learn what you need to learn. By the time I left my training three years later and I was suddenly on my own, I would constantly ask myself, "How would they have done this in Berlin?" because still, in spite of all that scenery training, I was still uncertain in matters concerning the running of a scenery business. I appreciated how much I had learned from this training, but you have to learn to figure a lot out on your own; once you do that, then you can build on the training. People expect to paint scenery and there is so much to learn and so much to know before you get to a level that is acceptable.

SC: It sounds like it was a very formal apprenticeship program.

MH: Some of it was rather informal too, but yes, it was overall a formal thing. First we learned the basic stuff, tacking on backdrops and that sort of thing. It took a while before they ever let you basecoat a backdrop because the shop created all professional scenery that was going to end up on stage and they didn't want you to make a mistake. As a matter of fact, you never really got to work independently on the professional scenery. There was always some sort of guide so that if you made a mess of it, it could always be fixed. You got a lot of opportunities to paint test pieces, paint little backdrops, and then they all stood around and told you what was wrong with it, which is a very good thing, as it gets you going.

SC: How did you decide to become a scenic artist?

MH: I grew up in a musical household but my musical capabilities were not quite as sufficient as most of the students of my father's that were coming through the house, so I needed something that was going to give me an edge, that put me in a different direction. So I took up painting. I did a lot of it from age 15 on. I never went to art school, but I painted up a storm. Once I was finished with my regular schooling I was looking for a way to keep on painting, and one thing I really liked was large-scale painting. I liked large painting and I liked theatre and I liked opera and I liked ballet. So I applied for a painting apprenticeship at the Deutsche Opera, where I got a comprehensive education in the scenery business.

When I finished my apprenticeship, I could have gone to some small theatre in Germany, but a designer who had worked in Canada said I should consider Canada for opportunities. I went to

Montreal in 1966, hardly spoke any English and I did not have any contacts, but I came around rather quickly; during my first year in Canada, I had a wonderful time, met many people, and got work experience in some interesting places: I did a season at Stratford; I did some freelance work for theatres in Montreal. I worked for the Les Grands Ballets Canadiens that year, and I'm still their resident scenic artist after all these years. I worked for the Opera de Quebec (now Opera de Montreal) a few years later. In the next few years, I was painting 10 to 12 shows a year; I also painted movie sets.

I eventually had to give up the film work as I couldn't run a studio and be on film locations at the same time. Things really started to take off in 1974, and I took the unusual step, for a scenic artist, of incorporating the business. Our first American work in 1978 was painting the sets in Montreal for the productions of "La Gioconda" and " Don Carlo" for the Greater Miami Opera (now Florida Opera). In 1979 I took the scary step of renting a permanent paint space; the volume of work for that year increased substantially.

To have your own paint shop, I feel the first thing you need is column-free space. You do not need a lot of people painting scenery but you do need to have a lot of space to paint. If you have space for only one drop on the floor you can, within half an hour, make a drop so wet that you can't step on it. If this is the only space you've got you would have to wait and return later to get more of the work done. I knew that I did not want to paint that way in my permanent studio. So I decided to have a shop floor

that could handle six full-size backdrops. That's how we ended up with a paint floor of 13,500 square feet. We have four scenic painters. That's all it takes because they can be working on six backdrops in a day, and we can paint scenery more efficiently when the scenery is completely laid out.

I run the scene shop as a business; therefore, I have to make it efficient. Efficiency in painting is not the only priority, but when you paint as much scenery as we do, it is important.

SC: Tell me a little bit about your training in Berlin because it was obviously quite different from the training people are used to here in North America.

MH: In Europe, excluding Britain, we paint backdrops on the floor; in England they paint them upright on a paint frame. Painting on the floor eliminates many of the technical problems with using paint frames. You just need a lot of space and you work on everything on the floor. We use lightweight, long-handled brushes and equipment designed for floor painting, which enables the artist to paint in a standing position. I think nowadays this is the most common method of scene painting. The brushes work extremely well once you get used to this style of painting.

SC: Could you continue to explain some of the differences in your training? You were trained fully with dry pigments and you continue to use them, correct?

MH: It was one of the methods of the shop. Before painters always used to make paint using pigment. That's where the term "paint kitchen" comes from, which nowadays has nothing to do with the kitchen

Figure 11.3
The shop floor at Michael Hagen, Inc.

because you don't cook anything in there. But in those days, the main equipment of the paint kitchen was the cookers for fish glue or bone glue being used. To bind the pigment, glue had to be hot at all times in order to work because when it gets cold the glue hardens and you can't use it anymore. So the intent was to keep the paint warm, to have a workable supply of paint on hand. There is an advantage that is quite interesting when you use paint that is bound with warm glue. The line drawn with the brush was incredible—no latex or acrylic can compare. The line would be so smooth and so long—you could draw a sixty-foot line with one fill of the brush.

The other difference was that it was common to paint drops on linen. Linen is too expensive now, and although it is a wonderful material, it is rarely used for backdrops in North America. In those days, linen drops were relatively more expensive than the labor; painters are much more expensive today. Back then, to reuse the linen, they would scrub the linen drops with warm water and you would have a wonderfully smooth canvas you could paint another backdrop on.

We don't use fish glue and rabbit skin glue anymore, but we still use pigment. We bind the pigment with acrylic—that is not very common in North America in scene shops for various reasons—but it creates beautiful clear colors that do not contain fillers, and do not have to be pushed up with dye to make them brilliant. These pure pigments have handicaps—some don't mix very easily, etc.—but each pigment has its own characteristics and it's quite fascinating when working with them. It gives you wonderful effects and makes a big difference.

We have 72 different colors in stock at any given time; all the main colors, all the brilliant colors. Each pigment has to dispersed in water and bound with acrylic to turn it into paint. An advantage is that if you store pigments in dry form they will last for a very long time.

SC: What is your approach when you talk to a designer about the backdrops or the scenery you are going to paint for them? Do you have key questions you like to ask designers to try to get inside their head and make sure you are of one mind?

MH: The key point that you just made is to get into their head; this is really what it is all about. When you work with designers that you have worked with before, you have a much easier time communicating, you can relate things to past shows and you have worked out how they feel about things. Every designer has a way of working, every designer is an individual, and you have to get out of them what it is that they are really after. Sometimes it is not the sketch that is going to tell you the whole story. Every designer has their preferences, how they would like to have things done, that is what you need to work out. That should happen before you do the first brushstroke.

Another thing that is important to remember is that every designer, especially when they design a big show, puts his reputation on the line. If the show doesn't work out, he is the one that gets the bad review. A designer puts his reputation and his livelihood on the line, and the scenic artist has to be trusted to make the design look like it should. So you need to get the designer to feel comfortable with you; you must inspire enough trust that the designer has confidence that you can execute the design in the right way.

SC: Do you have any key questions that you ask designers?

MH: It varies greatly from designer to designer, but if the design is not totally clear and apparent, asking the right questions definitely helps. Sometimes it's not possible to get the right answers, so you have to figure things out on your own. But you always have to think. Too many scenic artists say, "Here is the sketch or the indications that I got and here is what I am going to do." But designers have a way of confusing scenic artists, on occasion, with contradictory instructions about the design. Generally it boils down to every designer wanting to see his designs on stage. If you're in doubt, go back to the original design. Use all that information that you received, but go back to what the designer originally put on paper. Ultimately, the only thing that counts is what is on stage and whether it looks right; nobody cares what is said in between.

SC: What type of training do you think that someone who wants to be a scenic artist should have?

MH: If you want to be a scenic artist, besides the capability of painting, you also have to have a good knowledge about the technical aspects of the profession, and about the style and history of the shows that you are painting. You need to be able to interpret historical designs and understand how occasionally a design has been deliberately distorted through the design process. An interesting component of a scenic artist's work is that you always encounter things that you haven't experienced before. I still do even after all these years. The learning process never stops and that's a good thing.

SC: Looking back over your career, what would you say are some of the most difficult or elusive skills you learned as a scenic artist?

MH: I started out as a one-man operation, and remained that way for several years. Then I had people working for me, and it turned into a business. Basically for me, the most difficult thing to learn, the thing that took the longest, was to actually let go. Because for many years I had the attitude that if you are not going to do it exactly the way I wanted it done, then I would do it myself. I learned along the way that everybody in painting does things differently. Our principle is to not let anything out of the shop that isn't right, so you need to know what works and what doesn't. Other scenic artists might have done it differently, and there is nothing wrong with that. As long as it's a job well done.

SC: Do you think that the scene painting industry has been impacted by digital painting and mechanical reproduction, and do you think that this will have any impact on the way you do things?

MH: I get that question quite often and people ask whether we can do this all on the computer nowadays. At this point in time, the digital printing process is much more expensive than hand-painted scenery. Also, in order to have digital scene painting you have to have a perfect design. Having said that, there are designers who are moving in that direction and are using digital technology for some elements of their work.

In our shop, we use computer technology for communicating with the designers and clients; for example, receiving sketches, updating them with photos of work-in-progress. We also have a website (www.scenepainting.com), which is invaluable for publicity and marketing.

SC: What do you enjoy the most about scenic artistry?

MH: What I like the most about it is when it really works, when it really comes together nicely and when it all comes out, it's a lovely design and it works on stage. I really like when the painting that we have done really works well on stage. I think that is the most rewarding aspect of it.

SC: Do you have any special stories about scenic painting that you would like to relate?

MH: From my earlier days, I have a hysterical story, but I'm going to leave the name of the show out of it. This goes back quite a few years. We were just setting up a new shop, moving from one location to the next, and we had received some exquisite designs a few days earlier in a cardboard box. My business partner and I were transporting things back and forth between the shops. I brought the design sketches in and I put them in what I thought was a clean spot in the shop. We had several guys from Manpower helping us clean the new shop out and there was a lot of cardboard involved. Suddenly my partner called me back at the other location where I was picking up paints and says, "The sketches are gone! One of the kids must have accidentally thrown them into the garbage." The new location was in a huge building and I had no idea what the garbage situation was in that place, so I drove to the trash facility, and I rushed to the loading docks and saw 20 emptied dumpsters standing around a 25-foot container with a compactor in front. The operator asked, "What do you need?" I told him that there is a brown cardboard envelope with designs that I needed. He asked if I could get new ones. I explained that they were original designs and the designer had worked for over a year on them. The operator called the company and they told him how to disconnect the compactor and we got flashlights and got into the container. Everything was cardboard in that garbage compactor. I thought for sure the designs were going to be all crushed up and trashed. We turned over every cardboard box that was in there and took it all outside, sorted it out, and halfway through the container, on the bottom, there was the envelope and only one corner of a sketch was sticking out of the envelope; it had not been crushed. At that moment, the garbage container was the most beautiful spot I had ever been in. It had slid along on the bottom and it was totally intact. I knew if that had not been the case, we would not be talking here right now because that would have terminated my career as a scenic artist. It was all intact, nothing was bent, and nothing was damaged. We painted the entire show and it was a complete success. But it could have all ended right there.

Chapter 12

The Renaissance Theatre and the Baroque Theatre: 1400 to 1800

THE 15th AND 16th CENTURIES: THE RENAISSANCE

Drama and performance were among the many classical art forms revived by the powerful humanist ideals of the Renaissance. Secular plays based on classical texts were examined and staged, and later entirely new dramas came into being. Music drama also came into being later in the Renaissance out of another means to animate Classical Greek dramatic arts based on contemporary and Roman descriptions of it. This experimentation eventually evolved into opera.

All of these works of theatrical art included stage decoration as part of performance, and the decoration itself, like the first texts, was based on an interpretation of classical stage décor. Medieval liturgical dramas gradually were superseded by classical dramas and forms of popular entertainment as secular theatre became viable. In this time, the English theatre went from court pageants and obscure interludes to the works of Shakespeare. The first permanent theatre in Europe since the Roman Empire was built in Italy. Italian artists and architects explored the use of perspective through drawing, painting, and actual building as means to decorate theatrical stages in a new way. Stage decoration itself became a prolific art form of the Renaissance as well as a significant aspect of most theatrical performance.

As the design and construction of theatres was also revived in the Renaissance, the need for artists to decorate stages became present. The stage decorator, a specialist in perspective and painting, is in essence a product of the Italian Renaissance. This evolution is further underscored by the publication of the first book addressing theatrical architecture and design since Vitruvius. In this book by Sebastiano Serlio, the role of specialized painting is clearly recognized in its importance to the theatre and creation of stage scenery. The use of perspective, itself a major discovery of the Renaissance, clearly is the key element in successful stage décor as theatrical performance and spectacle moved from outdoor pageant wagons or churches to indoor stages.

Italy

The renaissance of the classical civilizations of Greece and Rome began in Italy. This is when the theatrical arts of designing and painting that we recognize today also began. Italian artists created the styles of theatrical decoration that were to become common across most of Europe, as secular drama began to compete with the liturgical dramas of the Middle Ages. The Italian style and technique would become the standard that nearly all other countries would emulate as secular theatrical performance spread in Europe.

The Classical Revival and the Rediscovery of Perspective

Many aspects of Greek and Roman classical culture were revived in Italy during the 14th and 15th centuries, including the arts and philosophy. Italy was the natural place for such study as it had been the center of the Roman Empire and still bore many remnants of the civilization that had died out almost a thousand years before. Influential, wealthy families such as the Medicis of Florence supported interest in art and history, humanist thought, and creative individuals. Architecture, literature, and theatre were some of the fields for which interest was renewed. The growth of study and intellectual exploration, the beginning of scientific, methodical analysis of nature, art, and civilization was to have a great impact on the arts, and it affected the theatre for several reasons:

1. Classical literature was revived for theatrical performance, necessitating a shift away from the many hundreds of years of only religious or liturgical drama, as other subjects were opened to performance.
2. A tolerance of theatre and performance by the Church allowed, at least in Italy, the theatre as entertainment to grow. As this secular theatre grew in popularity in Italy, it began to spread to the rest of Europe and eventually displaced liturgical drama altogether.
3. The revival of Roman architecture inspired interest in theatre buildings, stages, and ultimately stage decoration.
4. The rediscovery and subsequent refinement of perspective drawing created a device to create two- and three-dimensional indoor stage pictures with much greater impact, requiring a specialist to create them. The primary skill of the scenic designer of the Italian Renaissance was to understand perspective drawing and apply that knowledge to the stage.

Two significant events of the 15th century, both of which took place in Italy, are the foundations of Renaissance stage designing. First, the Florentine artist and architect Filippo Brunelleschi discovered the principles and practice of linear perspective in 1425.[1] Brunelleschi's discoveries gave artists a system

---

[1]Edgerton, 1975.

with which the visual world could be scientifically measured and drawn. This new technique had a profound effect on all art, much like photography would 450 years later. Second, the Roman architect Vitruvius' *The Ten Books on Architecture* were translated and printed for the first time in 1486. The recent invention of the moveable-type printing press allowed rapid proliferation of this influential work. The *Ten Books* contain evocative references to scenery and perspective painting of the Roman era. Coupled with the new understanding of seeing through perspective, these books provided an inspirational guide for early Renaissance stage decoration.

Early Renaissance Perspective Scenery

Roman theatrical literature and performance had been explored since the 14th century. The printing press allowed greater exchange of information, including performance. The 1486 edition of Vitruvius carries an illustration of recent performances of classical works. An edition of the plays by Terrence, published in Lyons in 1493, features stage pictures, complete with actors and settings. In it, the medieval mansion was still in use but with a small stage in front and a framing device around the edge of the setting.

Performances of *La Calandria* in Urbino and Rome, during 1513–1514, featured a new element. Most likely the first full-stage perspective setting, the design was by Baldassare Peruzzi, the artist apparently also responsible for executing the design. Peruzzi was an architect and painter as well as a set designer and had been greatly influenced by the work of Vitruvius. The design for *La Calandria* was a significant departure from the medieval style of individual mansions. This was a seamless full-stage composition. Houses were grouped together on a center street leading to a distant archway. The four downstage houses apparently were three-dimensional structures; the background was a simple painted backdrop. This may be the first true perspective backdrop in the theatre. The entire composition relies on much greater stage width than medieval style ever permitted. The depth is not astounding in itself but greatly enhanced by the perspective drawing of the background. The scenery demonstrates the ability to unify a stage composition of three- and two-dimensional objects with a background and illustrates the potential of perspective to suggest visual depth.

Sebastiano Serlio and the First Book on Scenic Design

Sebastiano Serlio's *Architettura*, published in 1545, was the first book to discuss stage design since Vitruvius. *Architettura* actually is a seven-volume commentary on architecture, published over several years. The second of the seven books focuses principally on theatre architecture and stage decoration.

Sebastiano Serlio was an architect and architectural decorator as well. At the age of 50, he began study with Baldassare Peruzzi, which is when he probably became influenced by Vitruvius' theories of theatrical designing. Serlio moved to France in 1541 to work for François I and died in Paris in 1551. Though Serlio spent his final decade of life in France, he did not have as profound an effect on stage decoration there as in Italy. It would be the cultural influences of Catherine de Medici's court that would have a much more profound effect on French stage decoration a few decades later.

However, Serlio's *Architettura* is a landmark of Renaissance art and stage design. The book describes the use of perspective scenery based on the Roman model of the tragic, comic, and satyric settings. Serlio illustrated this scenery in an ideal theatre based on Roman form. His proposed theatre was an indoor performance space with semicircular seating. It had no proscenium arch; however, a small, semicircular orchestra separated the stage from the seats. The stage was wide and shallow and raised up. At the rear of the stage was a steeply raked platform holding the perspective scenic units. At the rear of that was a painted backdrop. The vivid perspective was enhanced by the use of a grid drawn on the floor, which diminished to an upstage vanishing point. The composition depended on perspective construction and painting for an illusion of depth.

The scenery itself, of course, was much closer to the work of Peruzzi than anything Serlio may have known of actual Roman scenery, even though the book attempts to revive classical architecture and theatres. There is clearly a similarity between Serlio's proposed stage and a typical Roman theatre in that symmetrical, classical architecture serves as the decoration of the stage. However, the Roman *scaenae frons* was completely absent, replaced by the wide, full Renaissance vistas more similar to what Peruzzi had created for *La Calandria*. Serlio's book, by virtue of its wide publication, created a standard theatre and scenery format that was imitated for decades.

The book was later published and available in English by 1611.[2]

The Teatro Olympico That the Olympic Academy of Vicenza aimed to build a theatre at all was significant in itself. No permanent indoor theatre had been constructed in Europe for over 1,100 years, since the fall of the Roman Empire. The academy sought to create a replica of a Roman theatre for staging classical plays. It selected the accomplished architect Andrea Palladio, who planned and began a theatre building in 1580. Palladio died after three months of construction, and Vincenzo Scamozzi completed the building. The theatre is still standing, including the original stage, which is built mostly of wood.

The Teatro Olympico has an indoor stage that mimics the Roman *scaenae frons* and audience layout. The seating arrangement is a semi-ellipse backed by a colonnade with statuary, and the entire assembly is under a curved ceiling painted with clouds. It is as if an outdoor Roman theatre was reduced and placed into a museum diorama. The elaborate *scaenae frons* includes curious and extensive permanent scenery. Each of the five doors of the *scaenae frons* has arched openings that lead to a three-dimensional urban setting of streets and buildings. The streets appear to converge on the stage itself, like streets running to a town square. Beyond all the streets and buildings is a painted domed sky. It is a most amazing example of highly "forced" perspective architecture and sculpture. The perspective is so greatly exaggerated that walking into the townscape-scenery streets is almost physically impossible as these streets rise steeply away from the floor. The buildings are radically distorted if seen close-up, but from the audience one experiences a convincing stage picture. This remarkable scenery is the work of Scamozzi.

The Teatro Olympico certainly is a landmark work. It was the first true theatre built after over a thousand years. That it still stands certainly qualifies it as containing the oldest existing scenery in the world. Yet of all the stage decoration of the Italian Renaissance, the Teatro Olympico was perhaps the least adventurous. It is static and clearly intended to emulate ancient classical style. Two more remarkable innovations in this period illustrate an exploration into the dynamic and pictorial possibilities of stage decoration.

---

[2]Rosenfeld, 1973.

The Introduction of the Proscenium Frame and Moving Scenery

The stage designs of Peruzzi, Scamozzi, and Serlio essentially were views of a city square. We see this image copied during the Renaissance in the work of others. The design by Bartolommeo Neroni (Il Riccio) for *L'Ortensio*, in Siena in 1561, shows us essentially the Serlian tragic scene. The addition of a large frame of formal architecture to this is most notable. Even earlier, a sketch by Antonio San Gallo the Younger, executed between 1515 and 1530, notes a traditional city square, also surrounded by the frame. These have a suggestion of the formal framing device that became the proscenium frame. San Gallo's sketch also indicates *triangulare machina* on the edges of the paper, and plan views of *periaktoi* are evident. San Gallo may have been sketching an idea of moving the scenery in the fashion that Vitruvius referred to but left incompletely described in his books.

The later work of Bernardo Buontalenti incorporated moving scenery. Buontalenti was commissioned by the Medici family to stage an entertainment in the Uffizi at Florence in 1585. The entertainment was *intermezzi*, which are lighthearted pieces first developed as diversions between presentations of classical dramas. The *intermezzi* took place between acts of the drama and had nothing to do with it. They became so popular that entire evenings were devoted solely to their production, such as this one that Buontalenti was to have created. It appears that Buontalenti integrated changing stage pictures in this production. Written accounts of the spectacle indicate that, instead of the usual single setting, the audience saw:

> [a] continual series of ever-changing and ever startling scenic displays before their wondering eyes. This display featured many scenes. It began with a perspective view of Florence. Then a heavenlike cloud machine with angelic characters followed by a hellish 'horrible cavern full of the most terrible flames and dark vapours.' Then a winter scene transformed into spring. A seascape and another heavenly scene concluding with a vast plain of trees, grottos and caverns.[3]

Buontalenti's sketches of individual scenes survive, but we do not know how these scenic changes were achieved. We do know that *periaktoi* were used in the 16th century Italian stage. That in itself is significant, because to use the *periaktoi*, the three-dimensional

scenery of Serlio and Scamozzi would have to have been completely translated to the two-dimensional flat surface of the *periaktoi*. This transition must have happened in stages throughout the century. Two-dimensional work had been present in backdrops since even Peruzzi's designs in 1514. Toward the end of the century, moving two-dimensional pieces were common. These were either on the three-sided *periaktoi*, two-sided rotating panels, or one-sided sliding shutters.

France

The renaissance of classical theatre and decoration came to France several decades after it had begun in Italy. It came through the work of Italian designers like Peruzzi and others. Catherine de Medici, who wed into the monarchy of France, brought Italian artists to Paris and elsewhere in France. The influence of Italian Renaissance theatre was less powerful in France at first because of the immense popularity of the liturgical dramas and passion plays that were so remarkably well produced. These liturgical dramas were more popular and prominent in France than they had been in Italy. The scenic units, or mansions, were the primary scenic element of theatrical performance in France, and it was natural that they should be adopted for indoor use as permanent theatres were constructed. It would take time for linear perspective to have an influence in France and transform the medieval scenic style. Thus, the 16th century was truly a transitional period for the theatre in France, caught somewhere between medieval pageantry and staging and the new Italian perspective style.

On November 17, 1548, the Parliament of Paris banned the popular and highly sophisticated mystery pageants due to religious unrest. Similar statutes were written in other French cities soon thereafter. Although not strictly applied, the ban led to a degeneration of this medieval tradition and allowed secular drama to fill in the vacuum created by the absence of the mystery plays. The same year, Catherine de Medici traveled to France for the first time and brought with her the first example of Italian perspective scenery. This took place in Lyons as *La Calandria* with decorations by Nannocio. That performance did not immediately alter French theatrical production, however, and it was a long time before the Italian style became wholly accepted in France. A new theatre was built in Paris, also in 1548, at the

[3]Nicoll, 1966, p. 85.

site of L'Hôtel de Bourgogne, which was to become the theatrical center of France in this period.

The medieval tradition was deeply engrained in the French theatre, despite the ban in Paris, and that scenic decorative style remained a great influence, modifying the Italian influence. Vitruvius' books became available in French in 1547, at about the same time Sebastiano Serlio was working for François I at Fontainbleau. Serlio, however, lost the patronage of the crown at the death of François I in 1547 and did not receive significant commissions or exposure to the French. Italian staging techniques were brought to Paris by Catherine de Medici when she appointed Baldassarino de Belgiojoso director of all court festivities in 1577. This appointment provided the royalty with some exposure to a new kind of theatrical art, but the general population was entertained more or less by street performances, whose scenic embellishments were few. The royalty continued theatrical entertainment within the confines of their palaces off and on during the reign of Henry IV and Louis XIII. It was for the young Louis XIV that Italian opera made its debut in France in 1645.

L'Hôtel de Bourgogne L'Hôtel de Bourgogne was the center of public Parisian and French theatre at that time. From the year of the ban of religious plays in 1548, the Confrères de la Passion, who had exclusive right to stage the great mystery plays in Paris, were allowed to continue performing there, although the emphasis was on classical plays and ballads. An Italian troupe was installed in the 1599 season, and by 1600, another French troupe took their place and the name, Comédiens Royaux. Eventually they were to become the Comédie Française and the performers of the plays of Molière. This was a traveling troupe that recognized the need for scenic decoration, with a Monsieur Belleroche who played comic roles and worked on painting the decorations of the plays.[4] This troupe inherited the theatre and its permanent stock of scenery and stayed for a run of nearly 35 years.

The *Mémoire de Laurent Mahelot* is a remarkable testament of the period and one of the best documents of the theatre of the time. Laurent Mahelot, who kept this journal, was director, designer, painter, stagehand, prop master and, happily, diarist of L'Hôtel de Bourgogne. His book records the scenic development of the period through

his own work as a designer-painter as well as the work of Georges Bouffequin and his son, Denis. Mahelot describes the repertoire of the company in the 1630s, and apparently the influence of the medieval mansion was still present. Settings reflected the simultaneous method of presentation common in mystery plays, where several locales are present on the stage at once and the action moves from one locale to the next. Perspective was employed within the settings to achieve the compression of space necessary if the scenic units, essentially the medieval mansions, were to be placed on an indoor stage. The imagery of the scenic units still was essentially of medieval origin and sensibility. Mahelot describes a style that was a miniaturization of the medieval space through perspective, resulting in a unique mixture of the two approaches. Later, native French designers would realize their own version of intricate perspective scenery.

England

Theatrical performance in England during the Renaissance was primarily a continuation of medieval traditions. The rich spectacle of tournaments, street pageants, and miracle plays remained vital in this period until nearly 1600. Other spectacular productions, celebrating royal weddings, coronations, royal entries, and other significant moments of the monarch's reign, also were common.

English theatre did not absorb any of the Italian Renaissance style until the work of the architect Inigo Jones, in the early 17th century. The 16th century was dominated by Shakespeare, the professional actor, and the Elizabethan stage. This stage was decorated relatively simply, relying more on poetry and actor than visual spectacle.

English Medieval Theatre Tradition

The presence of the medieval pageants continued in England as well as a greater tolerance of secular performance. Certainly, the crown enjoyed both. There are accounts of preparations for royal weddings, such as the wedding of Arthur and Catherine of Aragon in 1501 in Westminster Hall. It "exhibited a castle drawn on by artificial beasts which held ladies and singers, a pageant ship bearing Hope and Desire, a mount of love from which the knights assaulted the castle, a tabernacle and an arbour."[5] King Henry VIII

---

[4]Decugis and Reymond, 1953.

[5]Rosenfeld, 1973, p. 4.

was known to participate in royal banquets that included music, masquerades, dancing, and spectacle. Later these were known simply as *masques*.

The Professional Theatre and the Professional Actor

The rise of Protestantism in England reduced interest in the miracle plays. In fact, they were formally suppressed in the 1570s. By 1576, the professional actor was legally recognized, and the growth of professional theatre began. By the end of the century, many professional stages could be found in London. The Theatre, the Globe, and the Fortune arose in a form very different from the Italian Renaissance stage. These were open-air theatres with a simple permanent architectural stage and minimal backgrounds. The theatres are very well documented in a wide variety of books, and no doubt are familiar to the reader.

The permanent backgrounds of these theatres incorporated Italian Renaissance architectural details, but were nothing like Italian Renaissance theatres. The stages were small architectural units, having no inclusion of perspective. They provided entrances, exits, and clear exposure to the surrounding seating. The theatre was dominated by a large, nearly square, raised platform. There were entrances at the back and a balcony for overhead scenes. It is generally assumed that very little space was left for additional decoration of any sort, except for an occasional cloth hanging in the doorway. This stage was visible almost all the way around, and the center of the building was exposed to the sky overhead.

Conclusion

The Renaissance was widely varied in terms of theatrical decorative style and techniques across Europe. In Italy, artists explored the use of perspective for the stage and applied knowledge of classical tradition to create a unified and somewhat realistic stage picture. The knowledge of Vitruvius was spread throughout Europe, and Sebastiano Serlio wrote an important commentary on scenic design, truly the first of its kind. The resulting Italian Renaissance scenic style had stage compositions chiefly of symmetrical architectural vistas. The scenery was arranged on a steeply raked, relatively shallow stage floor. The scenic units themselves first were three-dimensional buildings, as seen in the Teatro Olympico, and later were translated to two-dimensional shutters (what we call *flats*) through perspective drawing. This allowed the stage

picture to be unified into a single, large picture containing many related features. The actual style of painting probably was a minimal application of color in washes over the intricately drawn perspective.

In France and England, however, the medieval tradition remained strong. It was combined with perspective to some degree as French indoor theatres were built. England remained fascinated with outdoor and indoor medieval entertainment in many forms.

The important bond in all these widely varied activities is that the craft of theatre became practiced even more than ever. Clearly, painters, designers, managers, and effects specialists adapted their knowledge to the theatre, contributing to a growing body of skills, knowledge, and talent. This source of expertise was necessary for the remarkable growth that would follow in the coming two centuries. Popular theatre was tolerated by the Church for the first time, and ultimately the popularity and impact of liturgical dramas of the medieval period would be usurped by new texts.

THE 17th AND 18th CENTURIES: THE BAROQUE

The Italian Renaissance had seen the development of perspective vistas for the stage through the revival of Roman architectural practice. Peruzzi, Scamozzi, and Serlio found the means to reproduce realistic locales on stage with two- and three-dimensional scenic pieces. The record of Buontalenti's designs at the end of the 16th century suggests that scenery had become a significant part of the spectacle of theatre. The stage decoration ideas of the Renaissance were expanded upon in the Italian Baroque period. Stage designing, stage painting, and stage machinery all matured in a dazzling burst of creative growth in Baroque Italy. The rapid development then spread outward to other European countries, particularly England and France, reaching as far south as Portugal and Spain and as far north and east as Russia and Scandinavia. It did so largely because Italian architects and designers exported their work. Italy so dominated stage decoration in Europe that in France the baroque illusionistic style of scenery is still called *scène à l'Italienne*.

The transformation in stage design in the Baroque was one of increasing use of complex perspective imagery combined with new technical solutions for on-stage movement of the scenery. The painted world on the stage became awesome and mysterious, as artists explored the potential of perspective painting. Italian Baroque architectural and sculptural style, such as in the work of Bernini and Borromini, was exotic, emotional, and exuberant, thus ideal for the stage and new types of performance like opera and ballet.

The stage offered an important new forum for architects and painters of the time because the compositions made for the stage were free from the practical restrictions of architecture. A stage designer could explore fully the bizarre form of Baroque unencumbered by the reality of stone and structure. The architecture of stage design was realized in paint on flat panels, so it could become almost any imaginable form. The rationality and symmetrical compositions of Renaissance architecture were swept away by Baroque excess and splendor. The canvas that is a stage, with its great height, depth, and artificial light, was the perfect place for the dynamic vision of the Baroque. The theatre became such a vigorous outlet for architects and painters that individual specialists devoted their careers to theatrical designing and painting.

Italian Baroque Stage Decoration

New ideas and practice in theatre placed new demands on stage decoration in the Baroque. First, a new type of performing art developed at the beginning of the 17th century. It began as an attempt to understand the mysterious reference to music in the classical Greek theatre, mixing poetic text with music. The result was opera, a performance that united drama and lyric music. The true importance for stage decoration is that operas demanded new types of settings for their drama and created even more public interest in theatre. The formal Renaissance stage compositions of Serlio were inadequate for the more complex dramas that incorporated ballets and masques as part of the overall structure.

The second influence is that classical dramas themselves became less popular than the more entertaining *intermezzi* or operas. The *intermezzi* and the operas both demanded much more elaborate and fantastic dramatic settings than previously known, and these settings needed to change during the course of performance. Changeable scenery was introduced in Florence in the late 16th century through the work of Buontalenti.

Third, there was recognition that the ability to move scenery and present new scenes would be appreciated and accepted by the audience. This development of mechanized scenic movement led to the fourth influence, the expansion of the theatre building itself. As scenery grew in size and complexity, theatres enlarged the stage area to accommodate it and enlarged the audience area based on the growing popularity of theatre. The final influence in the art of stage decoration and painting is the overwhelming domination in this field by the artists of Italy. All aspects of stage decoration were rooted in Italian effort. Painting, machinery, the operas themselves, the theatres, and the written analysis of the art of stage design came first from the Italian peninsula.

The Use of Perspective in Stage Scenery

A form of "realism" on stage has been pursued in almost every century of theatrical activity, although each era defines realism on its own terms. Even Vitruvius referred to stage painting as "realism." We also know Vitruvius saw perspective as the key to realism, although modern eyes see the Roman style as rather clumsy and decidedly nonrealistic. In Italy, the rediscovery of perspective in the Renaissance allowed seemingly real images to appear in a lifelike scale on stage. In the Baroque, increasingly complex perspective drawing remained the key to creating illusion on the stage. The understanding of perspective improved greatly in the late 16th century through several important scientific studies, some of which were specifically for theatre use. This greatly aided the development of multiple settings during the 17th century.

The earliest stage scenery of the Renaissance, like that at the Teatro Olympico, was three-dimensional. Paradoxically, the Baroque rejected three-dimensional units for the seemingly less realistic two-dimensional scenery. This paradox is explained quite easily. With a greater understanding of the science of perspective, the two-dimensional image was every bit as visually effective as a three-dimensional one. The practical advantages of two-dimensional stage units are obvious. Two-dimensional scenery is far easier to move around on stage than three-dimensional objects and is simpler to construct. It is as true now as it was in the 17th century. The only aspect of two-dimensional stage scenery that is not easier than three-dimensional scenery is that it requires greater skill to paint.

Obviously, this trend toward two-dimensional scenery was made acceptable to the increasingly sophisticated audience only because of the availability of highly skilled painters.

The growing interest in perspective and two-dimensional scenery is reflected in the scientific writing on the subject. In 1545, the French scholar Philander prophetically interpreted Vitruvian scenic pieces as *scaena ductillis*, or flat panels. Guido Ubaldus specifically studied stage scenery and perspective in *Perspectivae Libri Sex*, published in 1600.[6] Giovanni Battista Aleotti was known to employ flat painted scenic panels in 1606 at Ferrara. The famous English designer Inigo Jones relied heavily on flat scenery in his stagings slightly later in the 17th century. A French theorist, Jean Dubrueil, illustrated a simple and straightforward application of flat scenery in perspective *Practique*, published in 1649. Further works followed, such as *Paradossi per Practicare la Prospettiva senza Saperla* by Giulio Troili in 1672, *De Perspectiva Pictorum et Architectorum* by Andrea Pozzo in 1693 and 1700, and *L'architettura Civile Preparata sulla Geometria e Ridotta alla Prospettiva* by Ferdinando Galli-Bibiena in 1711. The practical application of perspective for stage scenery was studied extensively in Italy during the 17th century and practiced widely shortly thereafter.

Permanent theatre buildings reflected the change in staging techniques through their own architectural development during the 17th century. The Renaissance stage was wide and shallow, reflecting the Roman theatre model. The Baroque theatre and stage achieved a radically different shape when the stage became framed by a permanent proscenium arch, visually separating the stage from the audience and isolating the stage picture. The proscenium was considerably taller than what was known before, as theatres grew upward to allow banks of seating boxes to accommodate a growing public. The stage also grew to an immense size, sometimes so much that the total stage space was almost as large as the audience area. The stage became deeper to allow scenery greater depth and, with it, a more convincing illusion. The stage also grew larger to accommodate multiple scenes.

Comparing two ground plans of Inigo Jones's work shows clearly the importance of flat scenery and its development in this era. The plan of *Florimène* in 1635 features four pairs of stationary angled shutters in perspective alignment. The background optimizes flat panels with a system of four pairs of shutters that can close to fill the background, thus providing four separate backings. The design for *Salmacida Spolia* in 1640 illustrates changing Baroque stage technique and Jones' transition. The pairs of angled shutters are replaced by four pairs of bays, each bay with four flat shutters. These shutters can slide out in groups, so the entire stage can change four times, not just the background.

The Teatro Della Pergola in Florence   The Teatro Della Pergola was built in Florence in 1656 by Ferdinando Tacca. The plan of this theatre is startlingly different from the Renaissance format devised by Serlio. It shows us several significant changes in the understanding of perspective through the design of the stage area. The depth of the stage is increased nearly three times over that of Jones' plans from the previous decade. This depth was required to enhance the sense of depth of the scene. Without real depth, the perspective depth had to be forced into a shallower space, making the stage itself totally unusable to the actors. A step into the perspective image would destroy the illusion. The Pergola stage allowed for greater flexibility in entrances and action with its enormous size. This deep stage was to become the standard for the Baroque.

The new approach to placement of the scenery bays on stage at the Pergola demonstrated a further sophisticated approach to perspective. The bays were angled slightly toward the viewer at the front. The angling diminished toward the rear of the stage. That aspect of the Pergola stage was not widely adapted by other theatres, however.

Italian Stage Decorators

Italian Baroque stage scenery was created by highly skilled, specialized artists who relied on a thorough understanding of the application of perspective to the theatre. Many of these artists were skilled in architecture, design, and painting. Therefore, they might design a theatre entirely or a set of scenery for a theatre, as well as participating in the actual painting of the scenery. The act of laying-out, or plotting, perspective was recognized as a skill separate from painting. The art of perspective was generally of much greater value than was painting. The descriptions we have from the Bibiena family and others reflect the deep pride these artists had in their

---

[6]Nicoll, 1966.

command of perspective as well as recognition of its importance.

The sheer popularity of theatre demanded a growing number of theatre specialists. The scenic painter was one such specialist, and many of them came from Italy, as did the designers and architects. Theatre specialists became somewhat popular in their own right, like many artists of the Renaissance and Baroque. Perhaps due to the relatively rapid production process in theatre, some specialists were sought out and central to the popularity of a theatre. The sheer spectacle of theatre reached previously unknown heights in the Baroque, and more often that not, this spectacle left a lasting imprint on the public.

Giovanni Battista Aleotti Giovanni Battista Aleotti (1546–1636) was an important figure in the transitional period from the Renaissance theatres to the Baroque stage. Aleotti was the architect of the famous Teatro Farnese built in 1628 in Parma. This theatre introduced many of the physical aspects of Baroque theatre in a permanent structure. The building is a large, narrow rectangle divided roughly into two halves, one for the stage area and the balance for the audience. The audience seating is a deep U-shaped arrangement of benches. The shape of the seating was novel at the time and became a format that Baroque theatres followed during the 17th and 18th centuries.

The interior of this theatre clearly was influenced by Renaissance decoration surrounding the seating. A sober two-tiered colonnade of Roman arches is topped with statuary, suggesting the wall of the Roman Coliseum. However, the stage itself is a profound departure from classical precedent. In it, a permanent proscenium arch divides the audience and the stage. It is decorated with giant two-story Corinthian columns. Statuary also is present but is placed into niches and perched precariously on small ledges. Within the proscenium frame is a startlingly deep stage. Here, Aleotti continued the use of two-dimensional illusionistic scenery he began a decade earlier. The deeper stage and narrow opening of the proscenium were more effective for the perspective imagery.

Giacomo Torelli Giacomo Torelli (1608–1678), nicknamed *Il Gran Stregone* (the great sorcerer), was one of the most famous and influential theatrical artists of all time. Torelli's use of perspective stage design took the art form of theatrical designing into a totally new realm of dramatic power. Torelli, a student of Aleotti, exploited the increased space offered by theatres based on the Teatro Farnese model. His work, based chiefly in Venice, reflected the architecture and painting of Venice for stronger realistic identity. Torelli designed the scenery for the first publicly performed operas, introducing to the world a method of visualizing the heroic struggles depicted in the new art form. Torelli also created new technical means for moving scenery that allowed highly efficient scenic changes and encouraged scenic changes in full view of the audience. He had a significant influence in France as well, spending 17 years there at the height of his career and effectively transforming the French stage from the quasi-medieval style to the Baroque.

Torelli explored the use of perspective in the deep stages typical of the Italian Baroque. The compositions he created for the stage relied on a rhythmic movement of the eye within the individual stage pictures. Torelli's stage pictures were significantly more complex than his predecessors' as the number of individual units increased and compositions strongly contrasted from one scene to another. Rhythm was established in the alternation of compositions, contrasting the symmetrical repetition common in the Renaissance. Architectural façades alternated their compositional axes, and garden or natural settings used the area above the stage as part of the overall picture. This way, the composition could alternate between vertical and horizontal orientation. Rhythm was established in the image from scene to scene as well as in the tempo of the scenic changes. Opera demanded an increase in settings from classical drama, and the rhythm of the changes was linked to the dynamics of the music itself.

Torelli's innovations included a radical new concept in the use of stage machinery for the movement of the stage picture as well as his mastery of perspective and composition. He perfected a system of moving wings or shutters in unison on the stage, known as the *chariot and pole system*. The side shutters typically had been placed in grooves on the stage floor and slid on or off stage as needed for each scene. An individual was required at each shutter, possibly 12 or more people, and considerable coordination of all hands was needed to change just one scene. Torelli's system put the shutters on carriages that went through a slot cut through the floor to a room below the stage. These carriages were on rollers to move

Figure 12.1
Giacomo Torelli, Italian, 1608–1678. Scene design for *The Elysian Fields*, Act III, Scene 5, from Venere Gellosa, 1643. Collection of the Tobin Endowment, Courtesy of the McNay Art Museum.

easily, and each carriage was tied to a central winch. When the winch rotated, the on-stage carriages were pulled off and the off-stage carriages came on stage, all perfectly coordinated. This giant stage machine could be operated easily by one individual because the carriages were counterweighted. In this manner, the performance could move forward without interruption by the scenic elements, and scenic changes would be so rapid that they appeared to be magic. The shutters or wings on the carriage then could be replaced and prepared for the next scene change. Torelli's invention allowed a proliferation of settings within a performance without relying on the curtain to mask each change.

Torelli's work as a designer brought significant change to the stage imagery as well as its function. As he progressed in his career, he made a distinct shift away from the emphasis on side shutters in front of a backdrop. The overhead space filled with fantastic imagery of clouds, grottos, heavens, and gods. The imagery of scenic design moved further toward the fantasy through the work of Torelli, suggesting not just real places but exploring the exotic and grandiose in a convincingly realistic style.

The Duke of Parma sent Torelli to Paris in 1645 to satisfy the request for a stage designer made by Queen Anne of France. He arrived in June and by December had his first performance in L'Hôtel du Petit Bourbon, which he had renovated to accommodate his carriage system. The performance was the opera *La Finza Pazza*, described later in this chapter. Through this sojourn to Paris and the lengthy period he remained, Torelli changed scenic production and design in France as effectively as he had in Italy. By the close of the 17th century, the major countries of Europe had all adapted Italian scenic style, invented by Torelli, as the standard mode of operatic stage design.

Giacomo Torelli returned to Italy in 1661, after his proposed design for Molière's *Les Fâcheux* was rejected by a young Louis XIV. He continued to work in Italy until his death.

The Bibiena Family

Giovanni Maria Galli (1619–1665) added to his name the town of his birth, Bibiena. He was the first of the Bibienas to create stage scenery and would be followed by a long line of descendants who dominated theatre design as well as stage design throughout Italy and Europe from the mid-17th century until the closing decades of the 18th century. The family's influence was so great that the name Bibiena has become synonymous with Italian Baroque stage design and painting itself. The Bibiena family designed in every major Italian city for many generations and became widely sought after in the major cities of Europe. Their influence is such that the Bibiena family probably is responsible for the tremendous continuity of Baroque style in stage design throughout the world.

The extensive output of the Bibienas has left a well-documented history of Baroque Italian stage design. The family itself was large: Giovanni had two sons who were designers, Ferdinando Galli (1657–1743) and Francesco (1659–1739). His grandsons, Antonio Galli (1700–1774), Giuseppe Galli (1696–1757), Alessandro (1687–1769), and Giovanni Maria Galli (1739–1769) and his great-grandson Carlo (1725–1787) carried on the tradition. The family's career spanned more than 130 years in a time period when theatre, opera, and dance became enormously popular entertainment forms. The transformation the theatre had undergone in the 75 years before Giovanni Maria Galli Bibiena was extensive, for the Teatro Olympico was not yet quite 40 years old at his birth. Opera had only begun to be performed in his youth, and the spectacle of scenery was very much in its infancy. The Bibienas took the innovations of Aleotti and Torelli worldwide, as the demand for lavish theatre production grew in nearly every major city in Europe and beyond.

The Bibienas were accomplished architects, and they brought the Italian scenic style to Europe through their theatres and the scenery they designed for them. Their style perhaps was the most pervasive force in scenic design in the 17th and 18th centuries. The large output of the Bibiena family further underscored the sheer importance and appeal of stage scenery throughout Europe. In short, scenery itself was growing in importance as an element of theatre performance. The Bibienas continued the richly decorative and exotic style of previous designers like Torelli and brought their own influence to the stage picture.

One of the most significant advances the Bibienas created for the stage was a significant sophistication of the use of perspective. An unavoidable aspect of stage designs based on perspective, from the Renaissance to this time, had been the obvious center vanishing point. Stage pictures were developed around the center and often completely symmetrical. For example, Torelli's stage pictures soared upward, exploiting the space above the stage in new ways, but always remained rather rigid as a line of ordered elements pointed to a central vanishing point beyond. Stage compositions of the Renaissance and Baroque often had a tunnel-like effect due to the almost necessary placement of panels in pairs on either side of the stage.

The Bibienas broke this symmetry with dynamic and more dramatic diagonal views of interiors and exteriors that swept across the stage. The scenic image became composed of layers of architectural units through which the audience looked to the distant and mysterious background. The actors were given actual arches and passageways to walk through and around. Through this technique, stage decoration took a step toward a lifelike representation of the world.

The Role of the Scenic Artist and Scenic Painting Tradition in the Italian Baroque

The Italian Baroque produced a scenic style for European theatre that was to remain for nearly 200 years. The inventions of Aleotti, Torelli, and the Bibienas became the standard operating practices for stage designers. As theatres were built across Europe and scenery was designed to fill them, a need arose for a particular style of painting specific to the stage. In many instances, the theatre architect or stage designer executed the painting. There is no record from any scenic painters of the time, but some scenic designers wrote of the craft of painting. Reading *L'Architettura Civile Preperata Su La Geometria E Ridotta Alle Prospettive* by Ferdinando Galli Bibiena reveals much about the practice of painting scenery.

Figure 12.2 Giuseppe Galli Bibiena, Italian, 1696–1757. *Gallery of Mirrors*. Collection of the Tobin Endowment, Courtesy of the McNay Art Museum.

L'Architettura Civile was published in Parma in 1711, when Ferdinando Galli Bibiena was 54.[7] It is a general description of the techniques of a stage designer and his popularity in the "principal Italian cities."[8] In it, he criticizes mediocre design practices and shoddy techniques. The book is exhaustive in its descriptions of the use of perspective for the stage: methods of how to construct scenes at angles, how to draw scenes on oblique wings, and so on. It clarifies the role of the stage painter as compared to an easel painter, particularly in the application of perspective. Bibiena insists that the mastery of perspective is the most essential ingredient to high-quality work by the stage decorator. Stage designs are not so much painted as beautifully drawn in perspective. The references to painting as we know it are very slight, only offhand references to how painting can correct a visual flaw or weak transition of planes.

It also is clear that Ferdinando Galli Bibiena saw himself, without modesty, as a consummate master of the science of perspective. He was meticulous in the application of this scientific method of visualization. He is critical of contemporaries whose perspective work is flawed or unimaginative. Bibiena, in *L'Architettura Civile*, credits himself with devising the method of creating scenes viewed at an angle, a method that was key to breaking the symmetrical rigidity of earlier Baroque designs, as discussed earlier.

The Scenic Artist in the Baroque

Bibiena writes at length about how a stage design is drawn in perspective. Perspective drawing for the stage may have been the most fundamental skill for a stage designer of the Baroque. The drawing process clearly is separated from the painting process and given greater emphasis in the written descriptions from the designers. How did the painting process differ from traditional studio painting? Was there recognition that painting scenery had different considerations and techniques? Aleotti, Torelli, Bibiena—actually none of the scenic designers discusses scenic painting at any appreciable length, not at least scenic painting that we might recognize. All of these men were painters themselves, but they were designers and architects as well, and their own view of stage decoration indicates a lesser emphasis on painting it than drawing it. For these artists of the

Baroque, scenic painting is not distinguished in the way we know. To these Baroque stage decorators, it appears that manipulating perspective in three-dimensional stage space was the most important skill for stage decoration. Ferdinando Galli Bibiena clearly sees himself somewhere between an architect and a perspective painter.[9]

The ability to accurately create immense perspective architectural fantasies was a difficult labor that seems to have required the participation of, or at least supervision by, these designers. Work handed off to assistants and apprentices was more than likely the preparation of the scenery and its final coloration. These designers likely went to work like scenic artists and designers do today, in large studios working on huge canvases. The task of laying out perspective for a stage picture requires large amounts of space and well-prepared scale drawings. The scenic designer was expected to oversee the development of the perspective drawing onto the actual scenery, so in this sense they were working much like today's charge artist overseeing a big drop. The emphasis was not yet on beautifully rendered color pictures. It was still the realm of the well-drafted architectural imagery, cleverly knit together in a seamless vista on stage by the master artist, the stage designer. The role of color was secondary to the drawing, or it seems so through the writing of these early designers. Bibiena states in his later *Direzioni della prospettiva teorica* (published in Bologna in 1732) that, when one paints and colors, it is according to the rules of art.[10] However, Bibiena does not elaborate further what those rules are.

Baldassare Orsini and Scenic Painting The writing of Baldassare Orsini (1732–1810), a stage designer and painter, shows a more detailed and expanded recognition of the role of color and, presumably, painting. Orsini's career flourished at a time shortly after the tremendous influence of the Bibiena family and as stage design was developing even newer styles elsewhere in Europe. In Orsini's time, one can begin to see a transition from the architectonic stage pictures typical of the Bibiena family toward a more painterly environment, emphasizing atmospheric effects.

Orsini wrote several books. *Della goemetria e Prospettiva Practica* (published in Rome in 1771–1773)

[7] Ogden translation, 1978.
[8] Ibid.
[9] Ibid.
[10] Ibid.

included a chapter on scene design. Later, *Le scene del nuovo Teatro del Vezaro di Perugia* (published in Perugia in 1785) detailed his work as scenic consultant for the new theatre of Perugia, which officially opened in 1781. These books record the methods and thoughts of a modestly successful Italian designer in an age when Italian designers were in demand. Orsini illuminated the working world of a designer and painter in the last decades of the 18th century. The inventions of Torelli and the Bibienas had been fully assimilated by stage designers at this time. Orsini appears to understand the complex rules of perspective construction used to create scenes with great depth, scenes viewed at an angle, scenes of circular buildings, and other complex stage pictures.

Orsini addressed scenic painting in a manner that none of the Italian stage decorators had done before. That he addresses it at all is significant and indicates the rising role of color as a means to enhance the architectural stage picture. Orsini returns to Vitruvius' text as a guide to the role of painting. Orsini and Vitruvius state the same goal of "truthfulness" in the depiction of images on stage. Orsini echoes Vitruvius' recognition that different scenes must be portrayed differently, "Having to simulate a temple, a chamber or a dungeon is certainly not the same thing, and an open or charming dwelling place is likewise to be distinguished from a solitary, closed, horrid place."[11] For Orsini, the pursuit of the character of the scene came through painting and color as much as through architecture. He writes that,

> Therefore, the contrasts, the areas of shadow, the diagonal passages of the light, and the coloring are not indifferent matters for a perspectivist. I would propose that the whole scene be defined in three grades of chiaroscuro: that the things which extend from view and occupy the third grade (background) be soft and gentle in their pigments, containing violet; that the pigments which contain greenish and reddish hues be reserved for the middle grade (middle ground); and that those things which are placed in front be of yellow pigment.[12]

Baldassare Orsini also clearly recognized the important role of artificial light in the theatre. He insisted that the work be seen with the effects of lighting so that, "The diminishing effect should originate from the chiaroscuro and from the strength of the brush strokes that are determined by the perspectivist."[13]

Lighting was not a consideration of the theatre of the ancients, whom he often invoked as the source of inspiration for the theatre of his day. But Orsini admitted that it takes greater skill to paint a scene intended to be seen under artificial light. From Orsini we see, perhaps, the first recognition that theatrical painting is like no other, because of its physical size and depth, the need to visually emphasize space through shading and color, the need to suggest a mood, and the presence of artificial lighting.

Torelli and the Bibienas were master perspectivists, and their stage work grew out of the skillful manipulation of architecture in perspective. Orsini clearly was skilled in these arts, but his writing continually reveals an awareness of equally skilled, and unique, painting abilities. He identified the Bibienas as the reformers of scene design and explained that the work previous to the Bibienas relied very little on color and shading. Orsini stressed the importance of painting, echoing Vitruvius, but detailed the process as no other writer had before this. Certainly, perspective drawing was as important to Orsini as to the Bibienas, but Orsini tended to reject the formal treatises on perspective and advised his students to put them away, for they "in truth only frighten studious people."[14] He advocated a simpler understanding and teaching method for perspective and devoted a third of his second book to painting techniques. Orsini's book easily may be the first to instruct scenic painting principles and techniques.

The writing of Baldassare Orsini draws a link between stage decoration and a specific painting technique, scene painting. The stage decorators of the Italian Baroque more often referred to the importance of perspective drawing. Painting received less attention than perspective in the texts before Orsini. It can be seen that stage decorators needed to fully understand perspective drawing and the role that painting plays to support perspective in the artificial lighting of the theatre. The stage decorator of the Baroque could be architect, perspectivist, theatre machinist, and scenic painter together. From the time of Orsini, it appears that painting began to receive increasing emphasis. We know as well that perspective would diminish in importance, particularly in the modern era. In reading Orsini, it seems that his comments on scenic painting are more relevant to the modern scenic artist or scenic designer, whereas the

---

[11]from Geometria, III, Ogden translation, 1978. p. 137.
[12]Ibid, p. 166.

[13]Ibid, p. 185.
[14]Ibid p. 182.

references to perspective have less immediacy to his modern counterparts. Perhaps, at this point, the role of the scenic artist as we know it began.

France

In the Baroque age, France became one of the most influential artistic centers of the world. The resources of the state treasury put toward the development of the arts by the last three Bourbon kings—Louis XIV, Louis XV, and Louis XVI—are part of the reason for this shift. Not that this expenditure was done for any reason other than to express the absolute greatness of the French state, which was the monarch himself, of course. The creation of the French Royal Academies also aided the development of the arts by centralizing talent and resources. Whatever the cause, the effect was 150 years of remarkable achievement in the fine and decorative arts, of which theatre was certainly a part. France was on the ascendancy in wealth, power, and as an artistic magnet for the world. Although Italy clearly was the originator of Baroque stage design, France would adopt and expand on this style, eventually developing some of the finest theatrical literature of the period around the new decorative techniques.

Patronage of the Monarchy

In 1548, Henri II de Valois was celebrated with a triumphal entry into Paris featuring a masquerade on the theme of Orpheus. Unfortunately, Henri was mortally wounded during the festivities, but he might have been somewhat comforted in knowing that the Italian *intermezzi* had made their first appearance in France in his honor. These festivities began a long tradition of extravagant theatrical entertainment for the monarchy in France, in which many highly talented stage decorators emerged. Through exclusive patronage of the monarchy, scenic arts would continue to flourish through the reign of Louis XVI and the French monarchy's demise in 1793.

In 1610, the Florentine stage decorator Francini began a 10-year stay in Paris, working for Marie de Medici. By this time, the art of ballet had taken a stronghold in the Parisian life of the monarchy, and Francini was brought in to design comic and tragic ballets. For the ballet *Alcine*, performed at the Louvre, Francini created a vast forest painted on cloth that was magically transformed with the appearance of an enchanted castle in the form of an amphitheater, ornamented with several columns, doorways, niches, and antique statues. Clearly, Francini was aware of the innovations of Buontalenti and Aleotti. He impressed the crowd with pivoting scenery in a 1617 production, and by 1619, he had put rolling wings to use. All of this was done without the support of a real theatre space. The French fascination with ballet was such that, in 1651, the young King Louis XIV danced in three productions, which possibly reinforced his own love of the theatre. This was highly auspicious for the theatre in France, as Louis was to remain king for another 64 years.

Cardinal Richelieu was well versed in theatrical literature and an author himself. His play *Mirame* premiered in 1641, a year before his death. It featured scenery by Georges Buffequin, the same individual chronicled by Laurent de Mahelot, and seems to have been done in the manner of the late Italian Renaissance—that is, parallel sliding wings with a painted backdrop. The scenery was "classical, influenced by the Italian, but modified by French taste with French innovations; a curtain that opened in the middle and clever lighting device that evoked daylight, moonlight and shadows."[15] With the production of *Mirame*, France was clearly very capable of developing skillful theatrical productions on a level similar to that of Italy.

Italian Stage Decorators in France

On December 14, 1645, opera was first performed in France. *La Finta Pazza* was imported to France by Cardinal Mazarin, then regent. It was performed before the child Louis XIV and the entire royal court at the Salle Royale in the Petit Bourbon Palace in Paris. The scenery was by the great Torelli. Mazarin requested Torelli's appearance and his scenery; Torelli did not disappoint. The prologue of the opera was a virtuoso scenic display from a grove of poplar trees to wagons crossing the Pont Neuf, the statue of Henry IV on the Pont Neuf, Sainte-Chapelle and then Notre-Dame, all before entering the port of Samros, where the action of the story begins. Torelli left the audience awestruck. La Gazette reported that "all present were no less than in raves over ... the scenic decoration and the stage machines, none of which was known in France at that time."[16]

---

[15]Decugis and Reymond, 1953, p. 59.
[16]Ibid, p. 61.

Torelli brought the most advanced Italian Baroque scenery to France, along with opera itself in *La Finta Pazza*. His work inaugurated in the monarchy a passion for great theatrical display and also for a French opera. Torelli spent 16 years in France and produced several other operas, all with generally great success. After his departure, Mazarin continued using Italian stage decorators with Gaspard Vigarani and his son Charles. Mazarin allowed them the use of the pavilion of the Tuileries garden, which they converted into a theatre known as the *Hall of Machines*. Mazarin died in 1661, and Louis XIV began his own long reign as king. Louis moved to Versailles and brought his love of opera, dance, and theatre to a palace that had no theatre. Undaunted, in 1664, Louis celebrated at Versailles with seven consecutive nights of performances, including dance, works by Molière, fireworks, and opera, all designed by the Vigaranis. This festival, however, would signify the diminishing of Italian influence in stage decoration. Louis was more nationalistic than Mazarin, and he sought to have a true French theatre with French designers. There would be no more royal patronage of the Italians in France after the beginning of the reign of Louis XIV. From the time of *La Calandria* in Lyons over 120 years earlier, the Italians had played a great part in the French theatre. Most important, they had brought the knowledge of Baroque stage decoration techniques to France. Now they no longer were wanted. Louis looked to his own country for stage decorators.

Jean Berain I and Jean Berain II

Jean Berain I (1640–1711) was the first significant French stage designer, filling the void left when the Italians lost favor with the monarchy. Berain was an assistant to the architect of Versailles, Charles LeBrun, and a remarkable interior designer himself. He designed the painted interior of the Galerie d'Apollon in the Louvre, where the French crown jewels are currently displayed, as well as the decoration for Louis's private apartments at Versailles. Berain's theatrical career was equally remarkable. He designed over 50 operas in his long tenure as director of the Royal Academy of Music and Dance, which had been created by Louis XIV in 1668. The academy is a government-sponsored institute in which the performing arts—dance, opera, theatre design, and decoration—were studied and practiced.

Jean Berain fully assimilated the staging techniques of Torelli and the Vigarani. He understood the processes of perspective drawing and worked in a format similar to that of Torelli, creating the designs of grottos, palaces, and gardens found on the Italian stage. Yet, his work reflects a greater degree of formality and symmetry typical of the French classical Baroque architectural style and reflecting Berain's long career as an interior decorator. Berain's designs employed the statuary, arabesques, drapery, and large cartouches common to the furniture and wall decoration of the time. Berain was a prolific designer and inventive technician. He created many pieces of intricate stage machinery for flying illusions and other effects.

Jean Berain II (1674–1726) was brought into the academy by his father at the age of 16. He took over the academy at the death of his father in 1711 and remained its head until his own death in 1726. Both Berains encouraged the participation in stage design for opera and ballet of such well-known French artists as Watteau and Boucher.

Jean-Nicholas Servandoni

The flamboyant Jean-Nicholas Servandoni (1695–1766) was perhaps the greatest of all the French designers in the Baroque age. Servandoni was born in Florence, where he was trained as an artist under Giovanni Pannini. He studied theatrical design in Rome and traveled to Portugal and England. He received considerable notoriety in London for his work as a scenic designer for operas. Following these experiences, he went to Paris and offered his services to the academy. He would not have an opportunity for two years, until asked to design Act I of the opera *Pyrame et Thisbé*, which was performed in 1726. Servandoni demonstrated his tremendous talent from that start in *Pyrame et Thisbé*, which was very well received; and several months later, in the design for *Prosperine*, his genius began to emerge. Servandoni was a consummate master of theatrical effects as well as a brilliant painter. His *Prosperine* was described as terrifying and overwhelming in its unending string of beautiful images.

In his 40 years in Parisian theatre, he employed the most sophisticated Italian techniques of perspective. Diagonal compositions, asymmetrical images, circular and oval buildings—all were commonly seen in his work. But Servandoni understood light and illusion better than perhaps any stage decorator up to this point did. He studied lighting and the techniques for creating shadows, moonlight, and strong and faint light. He used local light sources, candelabras, and torches extensively. He imitated sunrise, sunset, and moonlit effects with remarkable accuracy.

Servandoni was famed for his ability to recreate in paint sophisticated materials with almost scientific perfection. His ability to paint marble, stone, and precious metals effectively and in accordance with a specific style of light was one of his gifts. He clearly understood the nuances of perspective and intricacies of stage machinery; moreover, Servandoni's painting technique brought a new aspect to scenic decoration. Servandoni was able to take techniques used by easel painters and expand them to the scale of the stage.

Servandoni represents the apex in French design before the Revolution. He brought to French theatre a fresh style of scenery combined with radically new effects and techniques. Servandoni's world was the world of the painter combined with the perspective techniques common to the Italian Baroque theatre. His style was a harbinger of the trends that stage painting would follow in the 19th century, when perspective image, dramatic painting, machinery, and lighting would fuse into even more compelling and "realistic" stage pictures. He employed painting techniques in a way that Italian Baroque decorators did not. Both were concerned with effective illusion, but Servandoni's style relied on painting over perspective. He may have been the first decorator known for his theatrical painting. He was known as a master of illusionistic painting and an innovator in lighting and machinery. His styles and techniques were to become more imitated in the 19th century. Perhaps Servandoni's career indicates the diminishment of Italian style. With Servandoni, as with Torelli and the Bibienas, spectators attended the theatre to see his work.

England

England, as in France, absorbed the Italian style of stage decoration and used it as a starting point for the development of stage painting. A unique English style was, however, to develop more rapidly than in France in the 17th and 18th centuries before the full flowering of English stage painting in the 19th century.

Inigo Jones

The work of Inigo Jones (1573–1652) thoroughly overshadows all other theatrical contributors during the early Baroque period of stage design in England.

Jones was an architect, painter, stage and costume designer, and the first English designer to bring the Italian technique of perspective scenery to the English theatre. Jones saw the development of perspective scenery in Italy from the earliest steps of the technological movement. He visited the Teatro Olympico shortly after its construction and no doubt was fully aware of the *intermezzi* designed for the Medici family by Buontalenti in the late 1580s.

In 1605, Jones first produced a masque for the court of the English monarch that fully employed the perspective scenery he had seen in his two visits to Italy. During the first decade of the 1600s, Jones moved closer to the adaptation of a proscenium by framing the masques with giant statues, each holding a curtain flanking the stage. Jones was enthralled with stage machinery as well, using stage traps, elevators, cloud machines, and turntables in his stage designs.

Jones's stage decorations came closer and closer to the Italian Renaissance model of Serlio, using fixed side wings with a changing background of shutters. The plan of *Florimène* clearly indicates this fundamental approach to changeable perspective scenery. In his last masque, *Salmacida Spolia*, staged in 1638, Jones adopted fully moving side wings placed flat to the audience. This innovation provided a complete change of four sets of wings and borders and three changeable backdrops.[17]

In a career of 33 years of creating masques for the entertainment of the English throne, Jones brought Italian perspective scenery to England. He also managed to move from the Renaissance technique of perspective scenery to the more complex and moveable forms of the Italian Baroque stage. Jones was truly a visionary artist on the same scale as an Aleotti or Torelli. But, it is significant that the techniques that Jones brought to Great Britain essentially were Italian methods of perspective, which further acknowledges the worldwide impact of the Italian concept of stage scenery.

Scenic development was limited throughout the better part of the 17th century in England for two significant reasons. The Elizabethan stage of Shakespeare's time remained as the more durable format for staging in the popular theatre. No new theatres were built in England to accommodate Italiante scenery until much later in the century. The Elizabethan theatres relied on far less scenery

---

[17]Rosenfeld, 1973.

and in no way could they support the perspective styles that Jones had brought to the court. The court spectacles were eliminated, of course, during the Puritan domination of England and the exile of the monarchy. Only after the restoration of the monarchy would there be a return to elaborate staging of any description in England.

The English Restoration

The return of the English monarchy through Charles II also brought a renewed interest in theatre. Charles II had spent part of his exile in Paris, where he witnessed the works that Torelli staged for Louis XIV and other productions. Charles encouraged the development of the theatre, and he and his successor, James II, were vigorous patrons of public theatre. Their patronage encouraged a theatre for the general public as opposed to the royal theatre and elaborate masques staged previous to the restoration. The Italian techniques practiced by Inigo Jones were continued in these public theatres.

In the latter half of the 17th century, a handful of new or renovated theatres opened in London, all of which were built to accommodate the Italian perspective style of stage scenery. The Lincoln's-Inn-Fields theatre was adapted for regular performances with full scenic accompaniment by 1661. In 1663, the Theatre Royal opened in London, the first theatre built in England that architecturally supported the Italian form of staging. Later, the Dorset Garden Theatre and Drury Lane Theatre were built, both of which were made so that the stage had a full compliment of machinery to support perspective scenery as well as for the elevators, cloud machines, and other effects Inigo Jones introduced earlier in the century. By the end of the 17th century, Italian scenic style was common in London and in competition with the older Elizabethan-style theatres for paying customers. The Italian techniques of the Baroque, such as deep perspective vistas and circular perspectives, became common to English audiences. Little documentation survives from that time, and no designer rose up to the stature of Inigo Jones, nor did scenery change much beyond Jones's style. But clearly, the Italian influence took hold and became the standard for the stage.

The English Painting Tradition

During the Restoration, several individuals became recognized for their abilities as scenic artists. These were not architects or perspectivists in the tradition of Italy, but chiefly decorative painters whose talents were applied to the theatre. Robert Streeter, Issac Fuller, Thomas Stephenson, and Robert Aggas[18] are recorded as being decorative and scenic painters during the last half of the 17th century. Streeter, in fact, was servant-painter to King James II. Their background as decorators and not as perspectivists shows some unique characteristics of the English theatre. One is that the English were far less rigid in the application of perspective than the Italians, who took perspective drawing as a science. In Italy, perspective was the very core of the designers' and painters' art for the theatre. In England, the role of the painter as a decorator developed in this era. Second, English architecture and interior design would continue to demonstrate a greater love of things painted than in most other countries, as that field developed during the 17th and into the 18th centuries. Ultimately, this trend became very significant for the development of the scenic artist. The lush romantic landscapes of the 19th century that are the hallmark of the accomplished scenic artist would arise from this painterly tradition.

The Georgian Period The 18th century, the Georgian age, was a decisive period for stage decoration and painting in England. At that time, scenic art took a turn away from the Italian style to develop its own sensibilities. The English style that developed during this period matured later in the 19th century into a form that we are much more familiar with today. The English Georgian form is the foundation for American scenic painters of the 18th century. English and American style developed quite differently from Italian style. The Georgian period is an important transitional phase as well as one where familiar plays and performance styles also emerged. In this time, the decorative sense that we saw in the previous century would become the dominant force in England, despite the overwhelming presence of the Bibiena family on the European continent.

Italian Influence in England

Both Italian and French painters were working in England for very long periods of time early in the 18th century, but the predominant group was the Italians.

---

[18]Ibid.

The Italians brought two important ingredients: the Italian Baroque style of design and opera. Opera grew in popularity worldwide, and with opera normally came the Italian scenic artists to design and paint the scenery. The Italians were recognized as specialists and masters in the field of design and painting.

Operas, by nature, are very lavish productions. Combined with the absolute necessity to provide brand new scenery for the operas (no stock scenery could possibly suffice), this created a rather large infusion of energy in building and painting scenery for the theatre in England. Sybil Rosenfeld's (1981) wonderful account of Georgian scenic painters takes note of the theatres that boasted foreign scenic artists. The King's Theatre in London listed Marco Ricci, G.A. Pelligrini, Roberto Clerici, Jacopo Amigoni, Antonio Jolli, the famous Giovanni Servandoni, and many other Italian artists in service through the century. The rather large number of Italian artists gives us a good indication of the extent to which Italian Baroque scenery had been established as a worldwide standard of beauty. These artists were evidently bringing the techniques of perspectivist scenery with their brushes, and the apprenticeship possibilities for native English artists began.

The English Painters To fill the growing demand for scenic decoration, some scenery was also brought in from overseas normally requiring a scenic artist to touch up the wings and drops after they came off the ship. Occasionally, scenery would fall off the dock and require extensive drying and repainting to eliminate the resulting salt stains. Often, the scenery had been used for several performances and was a little worse for wear. This practice had potential for providing less than first-rate work. It became obvious to theatre-goers that English versions of the foreign style of scenery were every bit as good as, if not better than, the originals. At least English scenery would not have saltwater stains. Italian and French scenic artists gradually were replaced by their English counterparts during the course of the 18th century.

The first English scenic artists to be permanent employees of a theatre were John Harvey and George Lambert[19] around 1725. From this point on, the number of native scenic artists working in theatres in Great Britain grew quickly. By the middle of the century, there are records of families of scenic artists, the profession being handed down from father to son. Scenic artists in Great Britain as in many countries often were architectural decorative painters or doubled as theatre decorators where they worked. But the number of them grew steadily. Covent Garden listed two scenic painters and four assistants in 1767–1768, and by 1794–1795 the number had increased to 27 scenic artists.[20] Drury Lane had as many as 10 scenic painters working toward the end of the century.

Opera received the bulk of the effort of new scenery and new scenic invention during the Georgian era. Plays often got by with stock scenery recycled from an earlier production or season. This may help explain why so few actual designs, let alone scenery, survive from this period in England. Settings for plays often were combinations of generalized places: tombs, gardens, palaces, walls and gates, prisons, rural settings, and so on. Brand new pieces might be found on stage in the same scene with older ones. Scenery was built to be in service for a considerable period of time, some pieces lasting up to 50 years. Scenic artists thus spent a good part of their time repainting or refurbishing older units.

Scenic artists began to receive recognition for their work in the Georgian era. Program credit normally was given to the artist responsible for painting a particular scene, and the difference between designing scenery and painting it is not totally clear. Philip de Loutherbourg is credited for establishing the practice of recognizing the scenic artist toward the end of the century. De Loutherbourg is the first stage decorator to delineate between designer and painter. Program credit was given to the designer and the executant separately. De Loutherbourg generally was a designer, but that appears to be the exception to the rest of working scenic artists. Certainly, scenic artists were credited as designers when needed, but it was not the overall practice that a person either designed or painted. A sought-after scenic painter might design one work that would be executed by another yet later that same season, and be himself painting the stage design of another designer. Scenic designer and scenic artist were not viewed as different trades, merely subdivisions within the umbrella of stage decorator and decorative painting.

---

[19]Ibid.

[20]Ibid.

Emergence of English Style: Philip de Loutherbourg

Philip de Loutherbourg (1740–1812), a native of Alsace in France, was the most accomplished and recognized English stage decorator of the Georgian period. De Loutherbourg was brought to England and the Drury Lane Theatre by David Garrick and spent much of his career there. De Loutherbourg may have been the most influential theatre artist of the Georgian period, both in style and technique. In his work, one most easily can see a trend to totally new styles, departing radically from the Italian influence. De Loutherbourg also experimented with lighting and new materials to produce more vivid atmospheric stage images and eventually developed a miniature theatre for viewing his most sophisticated stage techniques.

When de Loutherbourg came to the theatre, the Italian style was still common in England. However, he was to represent most clearly the shift in English style away from the Italian imagery to the far more romantic and turbulent landscape more familiar to the English eye. De Loutherbourg was a romantic and a realist. The trend on the English stage during the Georgian period had been toward a greater sense of historical accuracy for costuming, particularly in the performance of Shakespeare. De Loutherbourg would take strides in the same direction for stage scenery. There also was a growing trend in easel painting for "English" landscapes: the sort of dark, misty, mysterious countryside familiar to the English, which bore little relationship to the clear, sunlit Latin skies of the Italian school of painting.

De Loutherbourg most fully realized a trend in the use of scenery on the stage that differed greatly from the Italian Baroque style. Simply put, the English stage was decorated with freely placed flats in asymmetrical compositions, relying less on the symmetrical wings that Italian stage machinery required. These flats provided a means to break the arrangement used in perspective Italian Baroque decoration yet still produce realistic illusions. It was the first significant challenge to the Italian technique of stage design and ultimately would come to replace it in England and later in the United States. De Loutherbourg had not created the technique; one could point to Servandoni's work in Paris as early as 1728 as perhaps the first practitioner of this new style. But de Loutherbourg's work and the English stage would take this new format and exploit it to its full potential. The physical difference allowed the painter much more flexibility in creating the moody English landscape that was to become the far more common image of the late Georgian period and continue well into the Victorian era.

De Loutherbourg was a multitalented artist as well as a gifted scenic painter. Like Servandoni, he experimented extensively with stage machinery and lighting techniques. He differentiated between scenic artist and scenic designer in practice and in public perception. He was a star performer at Drury Lane, and he made sure that he received notice for his work, which assured the scenic artists following him that they would receive similar credit. In short, Philip de Loutherbourg put English scenic painters in the public eye. His mastery of the craft of scenic

Figure 12.3
Philip de Loutherberg, *Forest and Park Model*, Victoria and Albert Museum, London.

painting created new types of wondrous illusion, reliant on a mix of painting and careful lighting. He was to pave the way for generations of English and American scenic artists to become popular artists in their own field.

De Loutherbourg experimented with pure theatrical painting effects off stage in his own model theatre, the *Eidophusikon*, exhibited in the 1780s. In its small six-foot-wide and eight-foot-deep stage, he experimented with transparencies, translucency, shifting colors, and moving backgrounds. All of his techniques in the Eidophusikon became standards of the stage of the 19th century.

Landscapes and Topographical Scenery

Two stylistic trends began during the Georgian era that would fuel the creation of new scenic pieces for specific events and plays. The interest in topographical scenery, the literal and realistic depiction of familiar places, became a unique English trend during this century. The wonder of seeing a recognizable English site on stage became popular for many theatre-goers in the Georgian period, which certainly has continued well into our own time. The beginning of historical accuracy also was seen in this time and became a major force in the 19th century.

Two major London theatres, Drury Lane and Covent Garden, were rebuilt in the closing decade of the 18th century. Both expanded. Drury Lane became the largest theatre in Europe. It held 4,000 spectators and its proscenium was 43′ × 38′—nearly square. The backstage was a cavernous 83′ × 92′ with 102 feet of

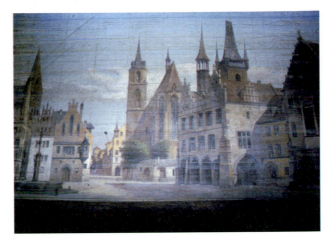

Figure 12.4 *A Northern European Town*, The Lyric Opera of Chicago/Northern Illinois University Scene Collection (Courtesy of The School of Theatre and Dance, Northern Illinois University, Alexander Adduci, Curator).

fly space. These theatres needed new scenery made for their immense stages. The result was a resounding acceptance of the English methods and styles that had emerged during the Georgian period. William Capon's designs for Drury Lane featured historical accuracy in their reproduction of Gothic, Tudor, and medieval locations. Historically accurate scenes arranged freely on the stage were the standard in England at the close of the Georgian period. The scenery was still thoroughly two-dimensional and the work of gifted specialists, called scenic artists.

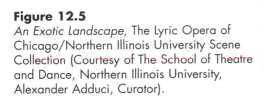

Figure 12.5
An Exotic Landscape, The Lyric Opera of Chicago/Northern Illinois University Scene Collection (Courtesy of The School of Theatre and Dance, Northern Illinois University, Alexander Adduci, Curator).

These two new movements perhaps were the greatest legacy of the Georgian stage. Topographical scenery and historicism were essentially English pursuits, having little to do with the Italian Baroque movement, which was at its peak. The English theatre was the mold that formed the American stage and perhaps is why the great scenic inventions of the Italians have always seemed somewhat irrelevant to our stages. America's theatre also began during this Georgian period, chiefly on English exports. Therefore, the history of American scenic painting begins halfway through a story already well underway. In America, we jump ahead to the newer trends of the English approach to theatre as we enter the golden century of scenic artists—the 19th century.

Chapter 13

The Romantic Theatre and the Modern Theatre: 1800 to the Present

All the trades that make up the theatrical arts—architecture, acting, costuming, designing, directing, painting, writing, and producing—attained new stature and profited from unparalleled popularity during the 19th century. In many ways, it was a golden age of theatre, which became a worldwide phenomenon, achieving a broader social acceptance than ever. Famous actors like Kean and Booth worked the stage and raised the status and popularity of the acting profession. The work of scenic artists reached an apex of public recognition due, in part, to advances in painting techniques and increased demand for stunning visual entertainment.

Technical advances, particularly the more widespread use of controlled lighting, further contributed to increasingly convincing scenic effects. Scenic artists themselves were as famous as actors and it became common for a play or opera to be popular because of the scenery. Certain types of elaborate scenic spectacles developed using no actors at all, making the designer and painters famous. Scenic artists worked in greater concentration than ever before, or possibly since, due to growing demand for scenic decoration in the theatre and related entertainment. By the end of the 19th century, the scenic arts became an industry, dispersing the scenic artist's product throughout the world by railway and sea. By the beginning of the 20th century, the practitioners of scenic art garnered enough political power to successfully unionize in some countries.

Dramatic literary style changed significantly during the 19th century, and scenic artistry changed with it. The popularity of Italian wing and drop scenery, the bread and butter of European theatre, waned as scenic artists explored asymmetrical stage compositions and the more emotionally striking romantic landscapes. Over the course of the century, new ideas of historical accuracy and realism in the theatre emerged, creating interest in new formats of visual theatrical expression and rendering the Italianate style even less relevant, although Italian style scenery maintained a presence in some theatrical and operatic performances. The craft of scenic painting grew more complex and demanding in the late 19th and early 20th centuries, as lighting and other special effects became common in theatres. Through it all, scenic painting itself remained intensely vital. The forms and format of stage scenery changed, but the love of the painted, two-dimensional image was as strong as ever.

Scenic artistry changed even more drastically during the 20th century with the modern movement. The roles of scenic designer and scenic artist were separated from one another formally by unionization in America and England, reflecting a division in duties recognized around the world. The scenic designer's role emerged as the artistic creator of stage scenery, thus diminishing the scenic artist's role to simply the executor of the vision, not the visionary.

The physical form of scenery changed radically as well. If Italianate style was gradually replaced in the previous century, we witness a more rapid rejection of it, as well as all previous styles, at the beginning of the 20th century. The scenic revolution at the turn of the century rejected illusionistic, two-dimensional painted scenery, replacing it with a newer, more plastic three-dimensional scenic structure. In a matter of a couple of decades, from 1880 to 1900, traditional painted scenery became characterized as a burden to "real" dramatic action: dishonest, shoddy, and very old-fashioned.

Moreover, new generations of modern scenic designers sought texture and volume as their media, not just a flat painted image. Traditional scenic artistry was abruptly condemned by the new generation as a meaningless gimmick. Clearly the theorists of that time were totally accurate in observing the dichotomy between flat, painted scenery pretending to be a room or a garden and the actor's effort at verisimilitude. The prolific 19th century of scenic art generally was rejected and decried by professional designers and theorists in the 20th century.

Unfortunately, as a result, many skills common to scenic artists of the past few centuries were nearly lost from lack of use. The intricate geometry of perspective scenery, once the chief skill of the Italian Baroque masters, was lost to all but a few curious individuals. Certainly, stage design has been elevated in the 20th century by probing the emotional, intellectual, and spiritual core of theatrical literature, and many brilliant stage designers have opened new paths through their visionary work. But the craft and art of scenic painting that were commonplace 100 years ago now are sustained by a much smaller number of scenic artists than previously.

The 20th century brought significant changes to how a scenic artist actually paints. Electric lighting, at first largely unwelcome by scenic artists, unmasked poor painting techniques and placed even greater demands on painters. New materials, tools, and techniques have greatly altered exactly what a scenic artist can do on a day-to-day basis, bringing greater ease and convenience to the studio. It is true that painting is still painting. However, modern scenic artists generally must have command of a wider range of skills than their predecessors, as they may spend as much time sculpting or smearing thick texture pastes as actually putting color on canvas. Traditional painting

still exists and is widely used worldwide, but we invariably recognize traditional scenic painting as a specialization.

The proliferation in use of digital and mechanical image reproduction further changed the way scenic artists work. Machines that paint entire backdrops automatically and rapidly are available to the designer and producer. These eliminate the scenic artist entirely. They are expensive and indeed mechanical, but they are in their own infancy and will become far more common, placing a further pressure on traditional painting.

THE 19th CENTURY

At no other time has the art of painting been so celebrated and refined in the theatre than in the 19th century. England and France, and to some degree Italy and the United States, were environments in which the scenic arts flourished. The mechanical stage schemes of the Baroque were perfected, theatre stages became larger than ever, and scores of painters were employed to fill these stages with their imaginary landscapes and architecture. Scenic artists recognized the effect of lighting and color, and through this achieved stage imagery that entranced and captivated audiences. This was an era of magnificence in the art form, though it was also a time in which the very presence of this painted scenery on the stage was put into question. The 19th century was the height and perhaps the end of an era of stage painting.

Technical Innovations of the 19th Century

To speak of new technology in the field of painting may seem highly incongruous at first. The actual technology of painting has changed very little in 2,000 years: we still apply color to canvas with brushes. No new steam-powered binder-infuser was invented in the Victorian age to speed the work of the painter. However, the technology in the theatre changed enough that the painter's art adapted to new potential.

Lighting and Painting Techniques

Philip de Loutherbourg and Jean-Nicholas Servandoni, the leading innovative scenic artists of the 18th century, brought extensive awareness of the potential of controlled lighting to the theatre. De Loutherbourg reworked the lighting system at the Drury Lane Theatre, specifically taking advantage of the newly developed Argand gas lamp to allow for greater illusionistic effects on stage through carefully controlled light. Both de Loutherbourg and Servandoni created dynamic daylight effects with cast shadows, moonlight, clouds passing in front of the moon, sunsets, and variety in time of day or night represented on stage by controlling light. Both designers used colored light, in the form of colored transparent silks, to achieve these effects.

De Loutherbourg is credited with the first use of gauze for translucent effects on stage, much as we use scrim today. He also created a moving backdrop in his Eidophusikon (a scenic device created in the 18th century and described in Chapter 12) to show clouds passing in the sky by slowly unrolling a very long backdrop on a series of rollers. He created an effective moonrise by fitting an Argand lamp to a bow covered with the painted orb.[1] With the work of de Loutherbourg, Servandoni, and their successors, the controlled use of light became an important tool of the scenic artist and scenic designer.

In the 19th century, the techniques of the scenic artist changed considerably from the time of the Baroque. Many techniques familiar to us now became common in this time. The Baroque painting style was essentially a well-colored line drawing. Color was used carefully to support perspective, as bolder colors were placed in front, tints and shades toward the rear. Late in the 18th century, through artists like Servandoni, more illusionistic painting skills developed. Paint imitating marble, metals, and wood became an aspect of the scenic arts. De Loutherbourg and other English scenic artists in the 18th and 19th centuries also explored color layering with paint for improved depth and sense of realism. Paint was applied to the canvas in thin, translucent layers with this technique. The result is a more lively and lifelike surface, much like the effect of watercolor. The understanding of light on a painted surface and the response of painted colors to colored light is part of the knowledge gained in the 19th century. This layering technique and the translucent qualities of paint respond more favorably to artificial light as well.

---

[1]Rosenfeld, 1981.

Panoramas and Dioramas

Scottish artist Robert Barker invented the *panorama* in 1787. A large and highly realistic painting, it was designed originally to be placed around the interior of a circular building. Panoramas typically depicted great landscapes or cityscapes in striking detail and realism. They were curiously photographic in nature, arriving decades before photography itself. The more effectively realistic *diorama* appeared in 1822 in Paris, a creation of Louis J.M. Daguerre and Charles Bouton. The diorama used transparencies and layers of painted surfaces for even more realistic imagery than the panorama. The diorama either moved itself or occasionally moved its viewers around for a real sensation of movement of place. These were complex scenic devices that became popular in their own right as entertainment.

The panorama and diorama launched scenic artists into a totally new phase of their craft, one that was tremendously popular in the 19th century. The panorama scarcely could have been adapted to a stage because of the specific placement of the viewer. However, the diorama was ideally suited for the theatre, and it became a great entertainment. By 1820, the Grieves had perfected a more dynamic diorama for the Covent Garden pantomimes. Their work consisted of a long painting wrapped around rollers and unrolled so that its image appeared to move from one place to another, much as de Loutherbourg had done on a small scale with his Eidophusikon. The audience was taken on a journey by the device of a diorama. The Grieves' device worked splendidly, was enthusiastically reviewed, and assured the diorama a secure place on the English stage for decades. From this point on, no theatre owner would dare present the holiday pantomimes without a diorama.

The 19th century was a period of extensive British colonization, great exploration, and scientific inquiry. The dioramas played a significant role in reporting back to the English public what the world looked like. They were remarkably realistic paintings of tropical scenes, playing the same popular role that newsreels did a century later and travel-oriented television specials do now. The diorama brought the savage and wondrous world to the public, thanks completely to the skill and imagination of the scenic artist. A diorama's subject matter varied from newsworthy to merely geographical in interest, but the aim was to invoke realism. The dioramas also made their creators, the scenic artists, famous. People went to the theatre strictly for the visual delight of the diorama, and that work was always attributed to the scenic artist. The scenic artist generally was the sole researcher, designer, and executant (with assistants) of the dioramas.

Dioramas were popular for years, staying part of English theatre until at least 1977![2] They depicted news events, such as Napoleon's conquest of Egypt or the battle at Moscow. Warfare was popular, particularly naval battles, which were virtually restaged complete with explosions, burning ships, storms, and daring rescues. Travel was another common theme for the diorama. There are references to travel-oriented dioramas to Niagara Falls; up the Nile; to Belgium, France, and Ireland by sea; from Constantinople to St. Petersburg; on polar expeditions; into Africa; and to the top of glacial mountains. The Grieves produced a sensational moving diorama that took the audience on a balloon journey from London to Paris, including the ascent of the craft, aerial views of the entire journey, and a descent into the Tuileries gardens.

The dioramas included many of the techniques explored by de Loutherbourg's Eidophusikon in the previous century. Transparent and translucent materials for greater atmospheric accuracy, cutout two-dimensional miniatures to enhance depth, backlighting, colored lighting, even fog and mists were now in use. All these devices were in the hands of the scenic artist for use in depicting the known world as realistically as possible.

Phantasmagoria and Optical Illusion

First displayed in 1798 in Paris, *phantasmagoria* were akin to magic lanterns and the forerunners of today's scenic projectors. They consisted of a rolling lantern and a transparency, usually a painted-on glass image that was projected onto a thin screen from behind. The projector was moveable so that the image could shrink or loom large during the display as needed. Images could be made to move by combining slides, and a system of dissolves from one to another was created with two projectors and a synchronized shutter. The eerie images must have dazzled audiences of the time, as the specter-like pictures shown in a very dark theatre had a somewhat lifelike quality. They were revolutionary for the time, although limited

in their theatrical use, as they required near-total darkness to be visible. These phantasmagoria were another theatrical entertainment totally dependent on the scenic artist. The slides were carefully painted miniature panoramas and necessitated particularly skilled theatrical artists to paint them.

Scenic Studios and Working Conditions in the 19th Century

Studios built solely for the scenic arts appeared during the 19th century, first in Paris, then later throughout Europe, and eventually in America. Some were very large, open studios with dozens of individuals at work preparing and painting scenery. These studios probably would look familiar to us because the basic, essential tools have changed very little. Some studios were small adjuncts to a theatre building that serviced the theatre itself. In some instances, scenic artists simply worked on stage at night after a performance. What is different from our time to the recent past is the sheer quantity of scenic artists and assistants employed, for the theatre was far greater in the 19th century. Scenic studios today tend to be adjuncts to the carpentry shop and staffed by a much smaller team of painters than in the past.

In the 19th century, the scenic artist also was what we know today as the scenic designer. But these artists worked much differently than today's designers. A 19th-century scenic artist was expected to imagine and create delightful illustrations for the background of a play's performance. Little thought was given to the unified expression of a play's meaning through the scenery in the way it is understood today. It was common practice that several scenic artists would work on one play or opera, each creating in their own style without regard to the overall style.

Scenic artists were meant to provide wonderment and delight in a painted medium, often one piece at a time. They were expected to be thoroughly knowledgeable of architecture, history, mythology, and the exotic, to be better prepared to decorate a play. Top scenic artists were walking encyclopedias of history and styles and could call on that knowledge to create stunning dramatic images meant to be viewed under peculiar lighting. This is not so far off from a description of a truly talented scenic artist of today, but in the 19th century, scenic painters were given free rein to create the scenery at will, based on some rough sketches. As noted above, a 19th-century theatrical production might feature several large scenic pieces,

[2]Rosenfeld, 1981.

each from a different artist. The variety itself may have been desirable to the audiences of the time.

ENGLAND IN THE 19th CENTURY

Perhaps in no other place and time in history has the scenic artist gained such status as in the English theatre of the 19th century. Scores of brilliantly talented scenic artists were known exclusively for their work in the theatre. They were placed prominently in the advertising of plays and reviewed along with the actors. These scenic artists were attached to specific theatres, sometimes for decades, and their departure could mean financial disaster for the unfortunate manager. Theatre had become an extensive entertainment business in England, and the scenery or visual aspects of any performance were a very important selling point.

The English Romantic Painting Style

The romantic scenic style that developed in the English theatre gradually supplanted Italian Baroque scenic style in worldwide acceptance. Romanticism began in the late 18th century and was to flower during the 19th century, particularly in England. It was a crucial step toward the realistic movement

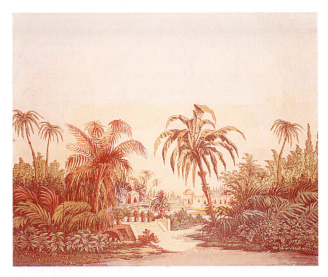

Figure 13.1   The Grieve Family, set design for *Oberon*, Victoria and Albert Museum, London.

of the latter 19th century because many precepts of Romanticism were to be useful in realistic style. Romantic style came to embrace historical accuracy, topographical interest, and more sensitively reflected England itself. The interest in travel and exploration was reflected in the romantic depiction of heroic efforts on the fringes of civilization. Romanticism created a more identifiable heroic figure for English audiences of the time than the abstract classical heroes of the Baroque. Scenery was perhaps more interesting to the viewer at large when it portrayed real places in an engaging way.

The sheer vigor of the popular theatre in London gave fuel to the popularity of scenic spectacle. Theatre was the primary source for entertainment. There was no competition from other media, so theatre was newsteller, storyteller, travel partner, entertainer, and magician. The 19th-century mind sought the distant, exotic, dramatic, and curious. The theatre and its scenic artists brought all that to the stage, from natural disasters to war to many brilliant plays themselves.

The Victorian Style: Romantic Realism and Spectacle

The middle and latter 19th century, known as the *Victorian Age*, saw subtle shifting in the overall romantic spirit. The pursuit of historical accuracy in stage productions grew considerably. Scenic artists were prevailed on to reproduce known places with accuracy and detail. It was by no means the realism we know from the turn of the century, but a curious blend of the real and the romantic. Stages were infused with even greater atmospheric spectacle, as moonlight, storms, wind, fire, rain, turbulent cloudy skies, and other meteorological phenomena became commonplace as a means to express the mood of a play as well as to accurately depict realistic imagery. The Victorian stage saw its first attempt at literal place description in the form of a box setting in 1832. This led to a continuing style of seemingly real dramatic settings. Scenic artists and producers went to increasingly great lengths to mimic the recognizable for the stage. This formula proved to be as popular as the more generic settings of the past.

The emphasis was on spectacle through all styles of the 19th century in England. Romanticism brought rugged, tempestuous landscapes, full of lifelike atmosphere. The popular panoramas brought the remote parts of the world to the stage with convincing illusion. The interest in history and historically accurate

Figure 13.2
The entry of Bolingbroke's into London, from Charles Kean's production of Shakespeare's *Richard II*, by Thomas Grieves (1799–1882), Victoria and Albert Museum, London.

productions, particularly of Shakespeare, allowed for considerable application of research and knowledge to stage scenery. Whatever the role of the design itself, it is clear that Victorian romantic scenic artistry was at a level of remarkable expertise and had fully displaced the Italian Baroque format and style. The technological advances of the late Georgian and early Romantic eras brought many more tools to the scenic artists' disposal. The theatre was still the realm of the painter, but the science of perspective had now given way to a more complex marriage of color, light, motion, and painting technique. The few that could successfully control all of these elements were highly regarded artists for their time. They ensured that scenery itself was a primary attraction of the theatre.

English Scenic Artists and Theatres

Philip de Loutherbourg, without question, was the first leading scenic artist of the Romantic era and one of the first star scenic artists of the English stage. His influence reverberates through the entire 19th century because of the techniques and effects he devised, both on stage and with his Eidophusikon. De Loutherbourg was an accomplished easel painter, too; another profound contribution to the English theatre was his popularizing of the English landscape style. These contributions, both artistic and technical, became standard practice for scenic artists that followed him. The numbers of steadily working scenic artists grew with the theatre in this century in England. With its commercial success came increasing demand for scenic artists and these unique skills.

De Loutherbourg died in 1812. Shortly before his death, two of the four major theatres in London burned again, Covent Garden in 1808 and Drury Lane in 1809. The rebuilt theatres competed with each other for audiences, and both relied on scenic

Figure 13.3 Charles Kean's production of Merchant of Venice, Victoria and Albert Museum, London.

spectacle as a drawing card. Both theatres entered into a prolonged period of great scenic art, employing the finest scenic artists of the era.

Covent Garden was the most popular London theatre in the 19th century. The scenic artists for Covent Garden, for the first half of the century, came principally from the Grieve family. John Henderson Grieve (1770–1845) began work in 1806, his sons Thomas in 1817 and William in 1819. The Grieves became the leading scenic artists at Covent Garden by the 1820s. The family split up in 1829, when William went to the King's Theatre and Thomas followed soon after. J.H. Grieve stayed at Covent Garden as the principal scenic artist until 1843, with only a four-year hiatus elsewhere.

The staff at Covent Garden numbered 11 full-time scenic artists in this era, with additional painters brought in as needed. The Grieve family elevated Covent Garden to a high standard of quality in scenic artistry as well as earning the artists and the theatre excellent reviews from journalists and writers of the time. Covent Garden reached its status as the preeminent theatre of London at that time, chiefly due to their work. The Grieves created settings for melodrama, pantomimes, and operas. In 1820, they introduced the panorama to Covent Garden, further increasing the popularity of the theatre and their own good name. J.H. Grieve is reported to have introduced a paint technique (like Servandoni's) of layering transparent glazes, as in watercolor, providing far superior depth and richness over the solid colors used before this.

The Drury Lane Theatre was a close rival of Covent Garden, although it emphasized melodrama and Shakespeare over the spectacles at Covent Garden. Still, it employed nine full-time scenic artists by its reopening after the 1809 fire. These included William Capon and Thomas Greenwood. However, hiring David Roberts and Clarkson Stanfield in 1822 brought even greater attention to Drury Lane and its scenic artists. The work of these two together began to rival that of the Grieves. A description of a diorama for the melodrama *Zoroaster* in 1824 describes a 482-foot-long moving backdrop, depicting several periods of the day. This enormous backdrop included:

> [a] desert with Arab tents at twilight, a caravan of merchants crossing the desert in the morning, the sphinx and the great pyramids, the ruins of the temple at Apollinopolis Magna, the Colossus of Rhodes, the bay of Naples by sunset, Vesuvius by moonlight, the effects of an eruption with obscure skies suddenly dispersing to present an allegorical vista, a momentary glimpse of Home Sweet Home, the falls of Tivoli, and the Hanging Gardens and the city of Babylon.[3]

The spectacle also included other scenery, such as interiors of the tomb of Cheops, the palace of Gebir at Memphis, a temple of light, and the abode of Isis. The entire production was painted by Roberts and Stanfield with Gaetano Marinari and six assistants. The design of the diorama, however, was entirely the work of Clarkson Stanfield.

The scenic artists at Drury Lane and Covent Garden often were in direct competition, due to the management electing to offer identical plays or spectacles in the same season. Contemporary critics and audiences had the benefit of seeing the finest scenic artists of all time in a constant whirl of bravura and one-upmanship. The great scenic artists would take research voyages to sketch foreign landscapes in preparation for the next great work. Great coronation dramas—in which actual coronation scenes were recreated, fully depicting all the famous cathedrals of England and France—were very popular and a great test of the architectural skills of a scenic artist. Scenic painters commonly were known for superiority in either architecture or landscape painting. William Capon, Gaetano Marinari, and Clarkson Stanfield all were considered exquisite architectural painters, although Stanfield often is described as the best of the group.

Clarkson Stanfield was perhaps the finest English scenic artist since the great de Loutherbourg. His panoramas and dioramas were considered stunning examples of landscape painting. He remained at Drury Lane throughout his entire career. David Roberts had left by 1827 to work with J.H. Grieve at Covent Garden. Stanfield's work did not suffer in the least from the end of this partnership; perhaps his greatness stood out even more boldly. A contemporary description of a single wing of his scenic painting is revealing:

> part of a fisherman's cottage, and there was a group of oars, masts, tackle, baskets and blocks, beautifully painted, and in the same delightfully chaste manner. What first struck me was the absence of that offensive strong yellow which is so common in the work of scene painters. At the bottom of the wing, on the left hand side, a small portion of the priming of the canvas was bare and I saw how carefully the drawing of all the objects had been made out upon it. The details of the baskets were expressed in the most charming way, and so clear and firm that the markings still

---

[3]Rosenfeld, 1981, p. 105.

showed through, after a couch [glaze] of semi-opaque colour had been passed over them. I observed also that all the positive shadows were put on them with transparent colours, while the great masses of half-tint were laid on with half-opaque tints, and the lights of course, solid and firm.[4]

This quotation was from the account of a scenic artist who was well trained in the technique of the profession. Clearly, Stanfield relied on the newer transparent wash effects that J.H. Grieve also was using. Stanfield was honored with a silver wine cooler from the owners of the Drury Lane for "his genius and skill in the scenic department" in 1826. He retired from the theatre in 1834 with few exceptional commissions after that date. He died in 1867.

Scenic Studios in 19th Century England

The Grieves and Clarkson Stanfield were the most renowned scenic artists of the 19th-century English theatre. It is no accident that they were regularly employed at the largest of London theatres, Covent Garden and Drury Lane. Together these two theatres probably employed 20 full-time painters each season, with an additional large number of assistants. London alone housed an additional dozen or so major theatres, which would employ another 50 painters and dozens of assistants.

Often the work was done in a room attached to the theatre itself, the scene-painting room. David Roberts, a painter who started at Drury Lane with Clarkson Stanfield, complained of working conditions at the Edinburgh Pantheon. He was forced to work on stage late at night, when the theatre was closed, because there was no special room for painting scenery. Scenic shops did not appear to have the presence in England as they had in France. Roberts was the subject of a biography in 1866[5] in which his financial success was traced. Roberts was paid weekly £1 10d in his early days to £2 at the Edinburgh Royal, but he had to pay his own color boy from that. At the Drury Lane, he reached a peak of £10 for two to six hours of work a day. An engagement in Dublin earned him £100 for 14 views (backdrops) for a pantomime, which he executed in 14 days. The Grieves were well paid at Covent Garden, well enough that

J.H. Grieve eventually set up his own studio and the scenery was transferred to the theatre by wagon.

English painters generally worked in the eastern technique with the drop stretched on a frame. Alternately, a drop could be hung from a batten and attached at the foot to a roller. It would then be rolled up as sections were completed and dried. A watercolor of Michel Angelo Rooker at work in the 1790s shows an artist alone at work at a paint frame that slips into the floor. The room is well lighted and tall, but narrow. Paint frames are on both long walls, no more than 16 feet apart. Paint and glue are stored in clay pots, some of which are kept on a rolling cart near the painter's side. Rooker uses a small brush and a hand rest and wears a hat while working.

FRANCE IN THE 19th CENTURY

The brilliantly innovative late 18th century theatrical painting of Nicholas Servandoni did not immediately carry forward as the trauma of the French Revolution and the chaotic time of Napoleon made difficult the artistic transition for French theatre into the 19th century. The Royal Academy of Music and Dance did survive the Revolution, except for the "Royal" reference in the title that was eliminated for obvious reasons. Theatre and opera continued performance throughout the Revolution as well as into the conservative neoclassical phase that swept through French art and architecture with the rise of Napoleonic authority. French stage decoration generally pursued the traditional scène à l'Italienne, but also a romantic stylistic approach emerged as is clearly seen in the work of Watteau and François Boucher, both of whom also executed theatrical decor for the Paris Opéra. The French style of those painters is delicate and whimsical, particularly seen in relation to the picturesque of the English school.

The French romantic style of stage decoration would continue to evolve considerably throughout the 19th century, as would the industry of stage decoration itself. French, particularly Parisian theatre, became as important and influential a place for the development of scenic art as was England in this time—if not even more so. Paris itself was home to dozens of major scenic studios every bit as large as a modern scenic studio, themselves an invention of the era in France. Paris was also home to scores of gifted scenic artists. The continued presence of the formerly "Royal" theatres such as the Opéra, the

[4]Rosenfeld, 1981, p. 107.
[5]Rosenfeld, 1981.

Comédie-Française, and what became the Odéon created only a fraction of the demand for stage scenery. There were several score of major commercial theatres presenting historical, lyrical, and dramatic theatre in competition with the national theatres mentioned above. The national Opéra was constantly in demand of scenic decoration for their busy repertory. The Opéra performed in a number of different theatres in Paris before building the famous Salle Garnier, with its enormous stage, opening in 1875. The stages of Montansier, Le Peletier, Favart, Porte Saint Martin, and the Palais-Royal were all used by the Opéra during this century and were some of the 27 major theatres in Paris in demand for stage decoration before the opening of Garnier's Opéra.

For the de Loutherbergs, Grieves, and Stanfields in London, there were their rivals, if not superiors, in Paris by the names of Cicéri, Cambon, and Chaperon. Opera performance was a vital part of Parisian culture and society and there was an intensive repertory performance schedule at the major opera house, especially the national Opéra. It was not uncommon to have 10 to 12 full opera sets stored at the theatre itself to provide for a performance schedule. The production of new and revived operas was so demanding that the Opéra saw fit to maintain a staff of scenic artists to meet the demands of production as well as employing scores of additional artists for new productions.

Paris was a crucible of remarkable scientific and artistic activity in the 19th century. This was the century in which photography came to being and where the realistic movement in theatre began. These two events were to have a profound effect on the art and being of stage painting by the end of the century. Between 1800 and 1900, many significant developments took place in the art of stage painting, resulting in important evolutionary changes in visual style in the theatre. The rapid and revolutionary changes in art that took place in France in this century had an effect on theatrical painting, though not as intensely or rapidly as in the fine arts.

French Stage Decorators

The scène à l'Italienne that was so dominant in Europe through the end of the 18th century was no less so in France. The Italian-born Ingnazio Degotti was one of the principle artists working for the national Opéra at the end of the 18th century, as was his primary rival Jean-Constantin Protain. The artist Jean-Baptiste Isabey was a favorite miniaturist for Marie Antoinette as well as stage decorator for the opera and theatre. His work is undeniably in the scène à l'Italienne as well. Isabey was a pupil of the painter David and the neoclassical style of his work is evident in some of the work of Isabey. It was the successor of Isabey, the great artist Charles Cicéri, who began the transformation of French stage painting in the first decade of the 19th century.

French Scene Shops

The scenic studio of which we are familiar seems to be an invention of the 19th-century Parisian theatrical system. There were many such studios in the city and close suburbs throughout the century as well as some capacity for painting at theatres themselves. But unlike the English system where most painting took place at the theatre, the French scenic artist of the 19th century worked away from the theatre. It further appears that these studios were exclusively for painting. Construction of the scenery took place elsewhere and was brought to the studio by carts. The Opéra National, for example, had a large construction and storage facility on the rue Richer in the 9th arrondissement of Paris, about a mile from the new opera house and closer to many of the other theatres the Opéra occupied throughout the century. Scenic units were framed at this facility, which had been used to create royal festivities in the previous century.

There were at least two dozen major scenic studios in close proximity to each other in Paris, clustered around the 9th, 11th, and 19th arrondissements. These were independent commercial enterprises. A typical scenic studio would employ up to 45 individuals, most of them the scenic artists themselves with apprentices and assistants. An 1896 journal about the studio of Marcel Jambon and Alexandre Bailly describes the physical space as being a cavernous 325 × 65 feet in floor space.[6] Jambon and Bailly's staff worked almost entirely in the continental style, which was predominant in Paris at this time. Among the staff were specialists in several types of painting: architecture, foliage and landscapes, clouds and skies, or cartooning.

The Opéra itself employed 10 artists at the beginning of the 19th century to produce their own scenery.

---

[6]La Revue Illustre, Paris, 1896.

These 10 included one cartoonist, three architectural painters, one apprentice in architecture, one specialist in human figures and an apprentice, two landscape specialists, and one ornamental painter.

Scenery was painted for hire and the costs were based on the surface area being painted. The established rate scale in 1874 indicates five grades of possible cost of scenery depending on style. The five were 1) Landscape, 2) Landscape with Garden Architecture, 3) Regular Architecture, 4) Elaborate Architecture, and 5) Fantastical Architecture.

Charles Cicéri

Pierre-Luc Charles Cicéri was by far the most prolific and most influential stage decorator in Paris in the first half of the 19th century. He was associated with the Paris Opéra from 1806 until close to his death in 1868. As the chief painter for 32 years of this period at the Opéra National, he created more stage decoration for the Opéra than any other artist in history. In Cicéri's painting style as well as in his approach to the physical distribution of scenery on the stage, there is a significant and obvious departure from the work of Isabey and the Italian style that had completely dominated European stage décor. Cicéri's romantic approach is evident in the asymmetric landscapes liberated from distinct linear perspective drawing. Charles Cicéri's painting style was remarkably broad and versatile. He is clearly capable of emulating traditional scène à l'Italienne style as well as creating décor that appears far more humble and realistic.

Cicéri's style encompassed a wide range, including the romantic landscape, a kind of primitive realism, historically accurate locales, highly atmospheric topographies, and the fantastical. In Cicéri's work one can see elegant integration of light, haze, and clouds, all possible elements in the technology of the era. This indicates the awareness that stage decorators of the 19th century had of the potential of light on stage, several decades before the visionary theories of Adolphe Appia.

Cicéri's influence on the art of stage painting was broad. He trained a number of tremendously talented artists in his own atelier, most notably Charles Cambon, Edouard Despléchin, Leon Fuchère, René Philastre, Auguste Rubé, and Charles Séchan. Cicéri also toured the Untied States later in his life and brought a significant body of knowledge with him.

Charles Cambon and the Mid-19th Century

Charles Cambon and other pupils of Cicéri, including Séchan and Fuchère, separated themselves commercially and stylistically from Cicéri in the third decade of the 19th century. This signals a significant evolution of the Romantic movement in France and the end of the scène à l'Italienne. This period of the 19th century was artistically dominated by the evocative writing of Victor Hugo, whose influence is seen in the stage decoration of the period. It is an era of heroic romanticism in which intense contrasts of light and dark become part of stage compositions. Aided by the understanding of the use of light on the

Figure 13.4
This watercolor of Charles Cicéri is for
Ali Baba and the Forty Thieves. Bibliothèque-
Musée de l'Opéra National de Paris.

Figure 13.5
This is an unidentified sepia work of Charles Cicéri with an exotic theme. Bibliothèque-Musée de l'Opéra National de Paris.

stage, decorators in France at this time experiment with far more shadowy and evocative imagery.

Charles Cambon was one of the most prolific of the Parisian stage painters of this time. He created works for the Opéra and a number of theatres in the Paris region and worked frequently to create the architectural decoration of theatre interiors themselves. Cambon proposed much of the technology that was to equip the huge stage of the new Opéra that further underscores his technical knowledge and achievements.

Charles Cambon's painting style is as remarkable as his technical knowledge and commercial success. His works are suffused with dramatic light and shadow. In Cambon's work, one sees modernist stage design techniques in use. Many of Cambon's designs are architecturally suggestive, not the more literal approach common to his predecessors or the work of the English painters. Cambon is very clearly well informed in architecture, thus his work is accurate, not generic as was common in the scène à l'Italienne approach. Yet Cambon allows freedom within the

Figure 13.6
This is a rendering for Act III of *Robert Bruce* designed by Charles Cambon at the Paris Opera. Bibliothèque-Musée de l'Opéra National de Paris.

Figure 13.7
This interior set by Charles Cambon is not identified but is a clear departure from operatic style. Bibliothèque-Musée de l'Opéra National de Paris.

architectural landscape to express it in his own terms. Cambon's work is unmistakable and personal. Cicéri appeared to have a wide variety of styles in his work, yet Cambon has only one style.

Charles Cambon died the year the new Paris Opéra opened in 1875. This theatre has been described as one of the most beautiful buildings in the world, and it is certainly one of the largest stages ever constructed up to this time. It was so much larger than any existing space in Paris that all new scenery was required to fill the surface and volume of the stage. Scenic studios in Paris filled the demand for the decoration in the year 1874–75 during one of the most intensive periods of stage painting to take place in that century, perhaps the culmination of the 19th century itself. The new Paris Opéra was enormous,

Figure 13.8
Use of sepia and gouache is typical in the work of Charles Cambon. Bibliothèque-Musée de l'Opéra National de Paris.

Figure 13.9
Charles Cambon executed many pastel studies for *Armide,* which was never produced. Bibliothèque-Musée de l'Opéra National de Paris.

surpassing the stage size of the Vienna opera and requiring vast sizes and quantities of scenery for it. Scenery was priced by surface area, thus the accounting records of the Opéra National from 1874–75 reveal the overwhelming statistical accomplishments of creating 12 new complete opera settings, each averaging approximately 10,000 square meters. The largest was the new production of *Don Giovanni,* which required 15,000 square meters (162,000 square feet).

The last third of the 19th century in Paris was a time when, among other events, the experiments and theories that guided the artistic revolution in theatre at the beginning of the 20th century came into being. Stage realism and naturalism in the writings of Emile Zola and play productions of André Antoine took place in the 1880s. The artistic movement of naturalism was supplanted by impressionism and post-impressionism at the Parisian salon exhibitions and the more radical counterexhibits. Artists experimented with technology and vice versa as photography became more commonplace, the electric light became available, the ability to travel via rail was within grasp of most, and the great optimistic international exhibits celebrated the potential of the future. The great Parisian Exhibition of 1889, for

Figure 13.10
Don Giovanni, Act I, Scene 1. Charles Cambon's style of sepia and gouache is used to create focus. Bibliothèque-Musée de l'Opéra National de Paris.

which the Eiffel Tower was constructed, included the work of stage painters featuring an immense diorama of the Trocadero and Champs des Mars where the Tower was built.

Auguste Rubé and Phillipe Chaperon

Phillipe Chaperon and Auguste Rubé were perhaps the most recognized of the many dozens of stage painters in Paris at this time. Rubé's career was remarkably lengthy, from his young apprenticeship with Charles Cicéri at the age of 12 or 14 (1829 or 1831) to the end of his life in 1899. Rubé was Cicéri's immediate successor as head painter at the Opéra and was a successful independent businessman operating a large studio with his partner Phillipe Chaperon. He worked more in dramatic theatre than he did the opera, and there is little that remains from his prodigious career.

Phillipe Chaperon was profoundly interwoven with the operatic stage and was a significant contributor for the new scenery created for the new Paris Opéra of 1875. It was Chaperon who designed the main curtain for the new opera house, which has been replaced by the famous 19th-century style painted fire curtain. Chaperon was trained at L'Académie des Beaux-Arts and was winner of the Prix de Rome. His style is meticulous and unmistakable; virtually all of his work is executed in gouache. His work for the stage incorporates many innovations referred to already, such as the extensive use of atmospheric backgrounds and lighting and reliance on a sound knowledge of architectural history. He was responsible for the first production of many of the major operas of the time, including *Aïda*, *Le Cid*, *Henri VIII of Camille Saint-Saëns*, part two of Hector Berlioz's *Les Troyens*, and the first performance in France of Verdi's *Othello* and *Rigoletto*, as well as Wagner's *Tannhäuser*.

Chaperon's work is extremely precise and rich, yet his work appears far less personal than that of Cambon and Rubé. In some ways, Chaperon is more like Cicéri of the earlier part of the century. Chaperon died in 1906, shortly after the publications by Adolphe Appia and Edward Gordon Craig that were to modernize scenic design. With the passing of Chaperon was also the passing of an era. The *Ballets Russes* would shortly appear in Paris to further hasten the decline of the 19th century style.

THE SCENIC ARTS IN THE UNITED STATES

It took less than 200 years for the theatre to develop into a powerful art form and vigorous business enterprise in the United States. What is remarkable is that it started in a most inauspicious and tentative manner with no foundation or tradition to draw upon and guide it.

Figure 13.11
Edouard Déspléchin created some of the décor for the premiere of *Aïda* in Cairo in 1871, Bibliothèque-Musée de l'Opéra National de Paris.

The Beginning Years

Theatre grew hesitantly in America throughout the 17th century. The Puritanical spirit at the foundation of the country generally resisted the urge to put on plays, let alone decorate them. The first theatre building in America was constructed in 1718 in Williamsburg, Virginia. There is no record from it of scenic decoration. New York City had its first playhouse in 1732 and Philadelphia in 1752. Boston, the center of Puritanism, did not see even a play until 1792.

The early playhouses were simple buildings unable to support the scenic conventions current in Europe at that time. Not until 1785 do we hear of any substantial scenic accompaniment to plays, this happening first in New York. John Henry and Lewis Hallam's productions at the John Street Theatre in New York in February 1787 may best reflect the state of scenery at that time. A notice in the New York Advertiser stated:

> Tho' we do not look for a theatre here conducted in so regular a manner as those in Europe, or the decorations so expensive and elegant, yet a proper respect to the audience, and decent and proper scenery, is and ought to be expected ... frequently where the author intended a handsom street or a beautiful landscape, we only see a dirty piece of canvas ... nor is it uncommon to see the back of a stage represent a street, while the side scenes represent a wood.[7]

In the first phase of scenic development, stage scenery was physically brought to America. Lewis Hallam imported scenery from London, probably used scenery, to build a stock from which he would assemble a set. He chose the work of the best scenic artists of Drury Lane and Covent Garden, but the condition of the scenery probably had deteriorated by the time it arrived. American audiences became familiar with the work of French and English scenic artists such as Charles Cicéri (who emigrated to the United States), John Inigo Richards, and Nicholas Thomas Dall through this system. Sign painters, ship painters, house painters, and similar craftsmen were employed to touch up the work or add more pieces to the set. Little scenic construction or invention took place during this early period, certainly nothing on the scale of the European theatre.

[7]Hughes, 1951, p. 42.

The Freelance American Scenic Artist of the 19th Century

Native scenic artists emerged in force during the 19th century in America. The huge success of the theatre as a business during the course of this century fueled the demand for scenery as the country grew westward. Theatre was good business, and eventually awareness grew that scenery made the theatre even more appealing, hence, more successful. Theatres were built in cities across the country as a sort of great civilizing force. Cities put up theatre houses in short order, much as the Roman civilization made a theatre the cornerstone of many cities it built. Often these theatres or opera houses required intricate painted interior decoration as well as actual scenery for the stage. This construction boom created a need for scenic artists. Scenic artists would immigrate from Europe, which provided the first direct exposure to contemporary painting techniques and styles. Many famous European actors found great profit in tours of America and created a direct conduit for the theatrical styles to migrate from Europe, particularly England, to the United States and Canada. These forces and the great popularity of dioramas eventually made scenic artistry a vigorous commercial enterprise.

Scenic artists in America came to have many outlets for their work. Nearly every city in America had an opera house or theatre for entertainment. Of course, the major cities like New York, Philadelphia, Boston, and Baltimore had many theatres operating successfully. Museums often were theatres in their own right, like the museums P.T. Barnum established in New York, based more on sensationalism than science. Cycloramas, dioramas, and panoramas—all were popular entertainment in 19th century American life and relied completely on skilled scenic artistry. Even the Masonic Temples and their practice of Scottish rites demanded large amounts of fantastic scenic invention made by scenic artists.

Scenic Artists at Work for Actor-Managers

The actor-manager arose as a pivotal figure in America, seeming to produce plays for profit, plays that required scenery. Independent actor-managers served as today's producers, as the theatre grew into a healthy business across America. The actor-managers were familiar names from the American stage like

Edwin Booth, Joseph Jefferson, and Edwin Forrest. The actor-manager might be permanently installed in a theatre in a major city or the head of a touring ensemble bringing shows to smaller towns. In either case, these enterprising businessmen discovered a market for a new product, the theatre.

Some actor-managers put a greater emphasis on the quality of production than had been seen in the past, initiating the need for high-quality original scenery, and audiences witnessed an improving stage picture. The actor-manager generally maintained a company of actors and a scenic artist, or more, to paint and maintain the scenic decoration. Harry Isherwood was a scenic artist recorded as painting for Joseph Jefferson from 1830 to 1845. Jefferson, who was a member of David Garrick's troupe in London, was the son of Thomas Jefferson. He was an early pioneer in theatre outside of the East Coast cities and brought theatre to the West and Southwest as America expanded. Isherwood's work has not survived, but he is one of the few individuals to be credited with having a career solely as a scenic artist during this time.

Another such artist was Russell Smith, a landscape painter brought to the theatre by a Pittsburgh producer in 1833. Smith worked until 1884 and recorded his thoughts in his unpublished "Autobiographical Recollections," one of the very few documents describing scenic artists in America in the 19th century. Smith revealed that it was common practice for scenic artists of the time to copy readily available engravings, down to the cross-hatching, for stage pictures. He described a popular impression of the uneven state of the craft:

> I was often made conscious that scene painting in the eyes of many who ought to know better is but a coarse kind of daubing, indeed an inferior trade: and no doubt much of it deserves no higher position with its want of nature and extreme exaggeration of colors.[8]

Smith was a perfectionist who created original work as a designer and scenic artist, which in itself tells us something of the state of the art at the time he was working. He described much stage painting of his contemporaries as unoriginal and derivative. The influence of the producer put pressure on the scenic artist to work quickly and cheaply. According to Smith, originality and quality went unrewarded by producers.

Smith's career spanned a crucial period in American scenic painting. When he began scenic art in the 1830s, the theatre was relatively new to the country.

The theatre grew considerably and, along with it, the demand for stage scenery. It was a time of hectic activity and expansion. The realization that the theatre was highly profitable put a new sort of pressure on the scenic artist by the time of Smith's retirement in the 1880s. By then, the theatre was an established entertainment industry. Actor-managers were being replaced by more powerful producers, seeking higher profit margins. The complaints that Smith revealed in his autobiography, of poor materials and artisanship in the field as a result of greedy and uncaring producers, would be echoed more loudly by the turn of the century, as the theatre in America faced the crisis of labor organization.

The best-known and best-documented freelance scenic artist of the 19th century in America easily may have been Charles W. Witham (1842–1926). Witham's life span went from the end of the era of the actor-manager through the powerful producing syndicates at the turn of the century and well into the birth of the craft unions and the development of the scenic designer. Witham's work reflects the dominant styles of scenic painting at that time.

Witham began his career in Boston in the 1860s, painting for the actor-manager Edwin Forrest. In that decade he moved to New York to work for the Booth Theatre. He stayed in New York until shortly before his 1909 retirement in Boston. Witham was trained as an artist and made a living as a landscape painter before moving to the theatre. His stage work indicates a great awareness of architectural history, particularly in the Shakespearean revivals of the 1870s staged by Augustin Daly. The preoccupation in historicism was a dominant feature in the design and painting of Witham for Daly. Witham would incorporate familiar paintings as the basis for stage pictures of his Shakespearean designs, creating massive living tableaus for the stage.

Witham also brought an early sense of realism through his depiction of New York City locales for a series of comedies about the various immigrants of the city. Witham brought scenic advances to the Booth Theatre as well. He eliminated the English-style wing and groove system and removed the raked deck, creating a flat stage floor on which scenery could be placed freely.

The Diorama in America

The diorama played a large role in the United States, as it did in Europe. Diorama displays were common

---

[8]Larson, 1989, p. 129.

by the 1840s in America, particularly as a device to describe the wild western frontier to the larger eastern cities. An immense and popular work by John Banvard was set up in St. Louis in 1846. Described as the "biggest painting in the world," it was a moving painted strip of canvas that presented a journey down the Mississippi from the confluence of the Mississippi and the Missouri to the Delta. It was accompanied by a lecture, given by the artist, describing his own journey making the sketches for the painting. Dioramas described the far-flung corners of the country to eager audiences but rarely made it to the stage as a part of the action of a play.

Cycloramas emerged later in the century. They were similar to the dioramas in Europe, remarkably lifelike assemblages of paintings and three-dimensional decoration. Cycloramas were static paintings that covered all or a major part of the inside of a building. The special buildings were circular, allowing for a 360° surround painting. The roofs of the buildings had skylights so the interior lighting could be controlled to some degree. Spectators stood in the middle of the painting to view the cyclorama. The cyclorama combined realistic painting with real objects like trees, rocks, carts, models, and statues for remarkably realistic effects. The Civil War became a very popular topic of these cycloramas, as famous battles were described in full detail, complete with severed limbs of dead soldiers. One of the largest Civil War cycloramas has been restored and reopened to the public. Located in Grant Park in Atlanta, it is one of the few remnants of this American scenic phenomenon.

Fraternal Organizations

It was reported that, in 1896, America had some 300 fraternal organizations, or secret societies, with six million members. Some of these organizations, such as the Scottish Rites of Freemasonry, used scenery extensively in their rituals. Initiation ceremonies in particular required elaborate allegorical presentations, which required very elaborate scenery and costuming. Masonic temples spread across the country much like theatres, and nearly every city had at least one temple or lodge. The scenic demands were nearly as great as in a new theatre, and the scenery itself was very lavish. The 19th-century fascination with archeology and the life of ancient civilizations certainly contributed important imagery to these rites. In any case, it provided further opportunities for the growth of the scenic artist as an important member of any community.

In America, the scenic artists of the 19th century never achieved the fame that their British, Italian, and French counterparts had in Europe. Production values were lower in America than in Europe, with the exception of a few remarkable producers, like Forrest, the Booths, and Daly. Theatre buildings were generally less elaborate in America than in

A

Figure 13.12
(A) Tomb, 5th Degree (ca. 1920, Don Carlos Dubois, artist) Great Western Stage Equipment Company Collection (courtesy Performing Arts Archives, University of Minnesota Libraries, St. Paul, Minnesota).

Figure 13.12
(**B**) Tent Encampment, Sosman and Landis
Scenic Studio, Chicago. Holak Collection
(Courtesy Performing Arts Archives,
University of Minnesota Libraries, St. Paul,
Minnesota).

B

Europe, with a few exceptions, until the end of the 19th century. Scenic art was practiced by a number of talented individuals across the country, but for every good painter, there were several mediocre ones willing to work for less money.

However, the need for scenery was large and growing. The expansion of the theatre as a business; the growth of cities and population at a tremendous rate; the popularity of cycloramas, panoramas, and museums; and the popularity of fraternal organizations all relied on scenic decoration. The growth of the business of the theatre was crucial to the next phase of development. As the theatre grew, more producers entered the field for the pursuit of profit over art, which forced an obvious reaction to building and painting scenery—at least, obvious to anyone who has tried to do a big-budget show for less money. Producers cut corners to save money, and scenery was one of the first targets for savings. Economic reality forced scenic artists to band together in commercial ventures, called *scenic studios*, to provide good scenery at a lower cost, keeping a large part of the market. Out of this need came the American scenic studio.

The American Scenic Studio

If the scenic artist was generally an anonymous figure in the American theatre scene in this century, the scenic studio was to become better known than any individual within it. In England and France, individual artists in the theatre became popular and recognized.

In America, the scenic studio became the workshop where relatively unknown artists churned out yards of scenic decoration for a rapidly growing business. The studios consolidated the finest scenic artists into centralized locations and raised the overall level of quality in American scenic painting. The studios provided a large enough workforce that an apprentice system would emerge to provide the labor to assist the master painters. Eventually, the scenic artists working in the studios would become powerful enough to join together in a labor union and create the rules for working conditions that we have inherited. America certainly did not invent the scenic studio; they were quite common in France, Germany, and Italy. But, in America, studios grew so quickly in response to the exploding population of the country and the need for entertainment that they became an industry in their own right by the turn of the century.

Scenic Studios in New York City

New York City was clearly the capital of the American theatre by the latter half of the 19th century. The growth of the theatre syndicates cemented that even further. In 1896, a syndicate of producers formed in New York controlled nearly all the theatres in the United States. They controlled bookings, actors, managers, and the profits. The actor-manager was very nearly squeezed out of business. The business of making and painting scenery centralized itself in New York City, where the producers were and the business was to be had. New York had the greatest

Figure 13.13
English town perspective,
Twin City Scenic Collection
(used with the permission of
the Performing Arts Archives,
University of Minnesota
Libraries, St. Paul, Minnesota).

concentration of scenic artists in the country. At least 30 major scenic artists were working in New York at the time, many of them in their own studios. This included Sidney Chidley, Homer F. Emens, George Gros, Lee Lash, Harley Merry, Russell Smith, Charles W. Witham, and Robert Marston.[9] This small group represented the past, Smith and Witham, and the future, as Chidley, Emens, and Merry would be instrumental in the formation of a union.

Robert Marston was an English scenic artist who came to America with the tour of a European actor and stayed in New York for the rest of his career. He was interviewed at length in 1894, producing a rather dismal view of the state of scenic art at that time.[10] Marston described a very different scene than the one in his home country when Clarkson Stanfield was awarded a silver wine cooler! He blamed the economy and greedy producers:

> First and foremost is cost, artistic quality is second. Get the artists to do it cheapest. The materials are bought wholesale, to the disadvantage of the competing artist. Cheap colours are used instead of the more expensive ones. Certain colours have qualities for which there are no substitutes and no matter how skilled the hand that uses them, the work will be inferior.

Marston found weakness in the studios themselves. These were run by unscrupulous owners who reused stencils, patterns, and designs in any combination they saw fit, if only to make the job cheaper. Marston found no pride in the work or originality from the studios. He stated, "The result of all this is that the best artistic talent in America will either leave the scenic profession or the country."[11] Marston also described terrible working conditions, including poorly lit paint frames and paint bridges 65 feet in the air with no safety considerations.

Edward G. Unitt and Homer Emens, both interviewed about a decade later, related that the conditions had improved but that the role of the scenic artist was still impoverished.[12] Unitt explained:

> The scene painter is not part of a theatrical staff. He is an employee of a firm. He is required to produce as rapidly as possible the scenery for perhaps twenty plays. The greatest number of these will be failures and others must be ready to take their place. This means a large plant and more rapid work. He has absolutely no opportunity toward individuality and naturally does not take the same interest as he did in that atmosphere engendered when he was a member of the staff of a theatre.

Homer Emens was more specific as to the actual work of a scenic artist:

> The scene painter often does not see a play at all. The stage manager brings him a plot. That is all he knows. He carries out what he is expected to do, the scenery is finished and perhaps he never sees it afterwards. Frequently a scene will

---

[9]Larson, 1989.
[10]"Art in the Theatre," 1894, p. 28.

[11]Ibid, p. 37.
[12]"Stage Scenery and the Men Who Paint It," 1908, p. 87.

Figure 13.14
Garden scene backdrop, Armbruster Scenic
Studios, Columbus, Ohio. Courtesy of Dale Seeds,
College of Wooster, Wooster, Ohio.

consist of forty pieces, all being painted at once and the scene painter must carry the tone in his mind for each of these pieces in order to preserve the unity of the scene. Or perhaps there are several plays underway at the same time, each relating to different country and different periods. These, in all their details, must be kept distinct in mind. In fact a scene painter must be a cyclopedia of architectural styles. Persia, Greece, Rome, Ireland and Siberia, Italian gardens and Western plains must all be at his command. He must know periods and epochs. He must be an authority on matters of appropriate decoration and ornamentation for there is no time for research and deliberation.

Scenic studios were staffed by four types of personnel: owners, scenic artists, assistant scenic artists, and paint boys.[13] The owner often had been a scenic artist but concentrated on the financial and contracting end of the business. These owners occasionally might paint, but the majority of the work was done by the scenic artists they employed. The scenic artists designed the setting, made a model of it, and painted what they designed. Sometimes, several scenic artists would work on the settings for a single, large production, sharing the designing duties by act or by scene. The scenic assistants prepared the drops, mixed paints, did large initial washes, cartooned the drops, and assisted the scenic artist. The last group, the paint boys, did the washing, brush cleaning, transported drawings around the city, and helped wherever possible. These were low-paid positions, but they were an effective way to gain an apprenticeship.

Scenic Studios Outside New York City

Chicago was a railroad hub and became the center of the scenic industry outside of New York City.

Major studios like Sosman and Landis, Silko Scenery, and Daniel's Scenic Studio were located in Chicago by the turn of the century. They provided the scenery for theatres, schools, lodges, and opera houses just like Armbruster in Columbus. Many jobs were available in the area. Sosman and Landis itself employed 12 to 20 full-time scenic artists, and the Chicago Grand Opera had five scenic artists on staff, directed by Peter Dunigan.[14]

Many other cities had large scenic studios by the turn of the century, including Kansas City Scenic, Toomey and Volland in St. Louis, and the Twin Cities Scenic Studio in Minneapolis.[15]

The Twin Cities Scenic Studio has been superbly catalogued and documented by C. Lance Brockman and the University of Minnesota Museum of Art. Brockman's book provides us with an excellent insight into the workings of a scenic studio of the time. Twin Cities began as part of the Bijou Opera House in Minneapolis in 1890. The studio moved to a freestanding location in 1905, as business was booming. The new shop had 14 moveable paint frames with narrow bridges between them. Scenic artists worked with a full palette of dry pigments that they combined with water or denatured alcohol for a small amount of paste-like paint, called pulp, as they went along. The paint shop had a full carpentry shop attached to it as well as a drapery shop that was a large part of their business. The scenic artists worked with the assistants as described previously, letting the assistants and paint boys prepare the drops for final painting. It would take a scenic artist no more than one or two days to fully complete all but the most complicated drops.

---

[13]Wischmeier, 1978.

[14]Wischmeier, 1978.
[15]Brockman, 1987.

Figure 13.15
Paint elevation of drapery, Armbruster Scenic Studios, Columbus, Ohio (Courtesy of the Lee Lash Institute, Ohio State University).

Armbruster Scenic Studios

Scenic studios profited from the new railroad network developing in America. A theatre in Menomonie, Wisconsin, could order its scenery from Minneapolis, Minnesota, with ease. The theatre could avoid the cost of having a scenic shop, and the scenic studio could profit from the business. The Armbruster Scenic Studios was the first studio to establish a mail-order business. Mathias Armbruster was a German immigrant scenic artist who worked in Cincinnati as an art-glass painter. After working as a portrait artist after the end of the Civil War, he opened a scenic studio in Columbus, Ohio, in 1875. Armbruster Studios were contracted by a traveling minstrel show to supply backdrops and Armbruster grew, by 1904, the studio came to be the second-largest scenic studio in the country, a remarkable feat considering the location. From Ohio, Armbruster provided scenic decoration for theatres, vaudeville, schools, Masonic temples, and the Broadway stage. Most of the work was ordered from a catalog, and the designs were essentially generic. Armbruster proved that a scenic studio in nearly any location could be a profitable venture. The studio operated until 1958.

The Armbruster Studios established the profitability of a scenic studio that could work inexpensively at a distance from the client. This format was to be widely copied in the United States at that time and provide employment to hundreds of scenic artists, assistants, and sales representatives.

The Unionization of Scenic Artists

The collective force of scenic artists was great enough that, between 1892 and 1918, they would form a representative union for their own craft. This powerful organization today still determines the working conditions, pay scale, and benefits for all member painters in the country.

In July 1892, the American Society of Scenic Painters registered its existence in New York. It was an alliance of New York–based scenic artists. Little is known about the effect of this group, but in April 1896, the group was renamed The Protective Alliance of Scenic Painters and became a national organization with corresponding secretaries in San Francisco, Cincinnati, Boston, Milwaukee, Chicago, and Philadelphia. The union was dedicated to working in harmony with the National Alliance of Stage Employees (later renamed the International Alliance of Theatrical Stage Employees, or IATSE). This working alliance itself forced several members to break off into The Scenic Art League, to distance themselves from the actual labor union that was the National Alliance of Stage Employees. The idea of labor intervention was distasteful and the goal of the league was to protect "the dignity of scenic art as a profession."[16]

In 1912, the alliance re-formed into the United Scenic Artists' Association. Its clear goal was the betterment of working conditions, wages, and job security within the New York City scenic studios.

[16]Wischmeier, 1978.

Figure 13.16 American scenic art was strongly influenced by European technique. The Lyric Opera of Chicago/Northern Illinois University Historical Scenic Collection (Courtesy of the school of Theatre and Dance, Northern Illinois University, Alan Adducci, Curator).

United Scenic Artists' Association represented over 600 scenic artists working for some 22 scenic studios in the metropolitan New York area. In 1918, the association staged a lengthy strike against the studios, forcing the studios to hire "regular artists" to paint the scenery for the upcoming Broadway season. The strike failed its stated goals of specific pay scales and hourly restrictions, but it gained the establishment of an arbitration committee recognized by the studio owners.

Prior to the strike itself, the association gained an autonomous subcharter within the Brotherhood of Painters, Decorators and Paperhangers union. The name of the association was changed to the United Scenic Artists of America (USAA). Only recently was the name shortened to the United Scenic Artists (USA). USA has established itself as the sole union voice for stage designers, costume designers, lighting designers, scenic artists, art directors, mural artists, and allied crafts in the United States. It has successfully set the standard for working conditions and wages in the profession. One must remember that the union, which today is often called the designer's union, began as a collection of scenic artists seeking a better way of life in the work they love.

American Scenic Style

19th-century scenic styles in America were unique derivations from the European masters. Scenic artists from Europe brought with them the Romantic, Baroque, or classical landscapes that they knew from their homes, but the styles seemed to change when they landed on the American shore. Theatres in America were different from the European theatres. There was no historical theatrical background to draw on in the construction or rigging of theatres. They tended to be simpler structures without complex stage machinery.

The Italian Baroque painting style rarely was seen on the stages of the American theatre. It was the Romantic English landscape painting style that best adapted to the American image. The more rugged Western American landscape came to be idealized by native scenic artists throughout the century. Many theatres invested in stock, generic scenery meant for virtually any production. An all-purpose landscape, European cities, prison, palace, village, mountain pass, and forest were common sets available to theatres and opera houses. Often, a theatre might boast a single new drop, oleo, or act curtain as an enticement to patrons.

The oleo was a versatile drop for any sort of entertainment, such as a song, a pantomime, a lecture, or a skit. The oleo drop often hung in the *in-one* position, subdividing the stage into a shallower depth that was more appropriate for a brief interlude. The act curtain or drop curtain functioned as today's main drape, the decorative divider wall between audience and stage. Often, it was the most elaborate piece a theatre owned and was painted to harmonize with the interior decorations of the theatre itself.[17]

Stylistic and technological inventions were reserved mostly for the New York City theatres or found in the complex dioramas or cycloramas. The new interest in historicism of the London theatre was imported with the Shakespearean revivals of Charles Kean and later Augustin Daly. However, fully mounted productions in that style remained in New York. The tours that many European acting companies took across America had to rely on simplified versions of the original scenery so that the production easily

---

[17]Brockman, 1987.

could be adapted to the many diverse theatres it would find on tour.

The new pursuit of realism, with room-like box settings and fully dimensional architecture, was seen on the New York stage in the 1880s. David Belasco is best known for his ultra-realistic melodramas of the turn of the century. He and his chief scenic artist, George Gros, created meticulously detailed interiors, realistic exteriors, and stunning atmospheric effects. Belasco and Gros produced some of the most memorable scenic inventions of the American theatre and certainly some of the finest realistic scenery of the theatre worldwide up to their time. But Belasco and Gros' memorable scenic achievements usually were for less than memorable plays, and ironically, their work was timed for the eve of the revolution that would displace them. As Czar Nicholas II and Louis XVI may be remembered chiefly as unlucky monarchs who were swept away because they could not decipher the powerful mood of their unhappy subjects, David Belasco's studiously perfect realism also became a victim of dramatically bad timing. His laborious scenic and lighting techniques were seen by the avant-garde as the embodiment of every ill of the stage and were severely ridiculed by history.

Realism was but a passing style like Romanticism and the Italian Baroque styles seen before them. The 20th century would bring the scenic designer an entirely new aesthetic for the world of the theatre. As movies replaced theatre's popularity, an international aesthetic weighed in against painted scenery, scenic studios began to shrink, and scenic artists began to disappear. The modern theatre saw traditional painting in a new, harshly critical light. The golden age of scenic painting of the 19th century rapidly turned to a much more fragmented 20th century, as theatre styles changed radically and eventually the theatre lost popularity to movies and television.

THE 20th CENTURY

The 20th century is called the century of revolution by theatre historians.[18] It is the time when all theatrical arts were remade into completely new forms from the conventions that evolved from the Renaissance. The visual world of theatre profoundly changed at the turn of the century. Radical visionaries, such as

Adolphe Appia and Edward Gordon Craig, proclaimed illusionistic painted scenery of the past to be inadequate, worthless. They, and others, saw the stage stripped bare of the painted, two-dimensional artifice of the past. The stage was to become the world of the sculptor, a molded, plastic topography ruled no longer by artists as Clarkson Stanfield and George Gros. The stage now was the realm of the scenic designer, an artist invented for the occasion, a hero to lead the theatre out of the cluttered attic of 19th century romanticism into the crystalline visions of a "real" artist.

Appia and Craig had reason to despise painted scenery. Most of it was probably mediocrity itself. The scenery they despised represented an entire style of theatrical performance, including the self-indulgent, declamatory actor milking Shakespeare for all his worth or the inept company of actors unable to pay any attention to each other on stage for fear of missing the chance to please an adoring audience. Appia and Craig sought a unified, passionate performance style that spoke directly to the soul of the audience. The theatre they envisioned sought truth, meaning, poetry, and relevance. They worshipped the text and music of the theatre and felt, particularly Appia, that the scenery should only evoke imagery not dictate it, for the betterment of drama. Their solution was radical and uncompromising. No illusionistic painting was permitted in their brave new world. The new stage was truthful, a real space for the actor to live in. The scenery could not conflict or compete with the actor's voice, movement, and presence.

Appia and Craig did not remove 19th-century scenic painting from the theatre by themselves. They were part of a larger philosophical movement that advocated scientific inquiry into the human condition and respected the artist's power of imagination. The theatre was a part of an international artistic revolution, including painting, music, architecture, literature, and dance—in short, all the elements of theatre. It was inevitable that the theatre would change to reflect the lives and spirits of the audiences that attended it, not just to entertain these people with diversions. The revolution allowed scenic design to mature into a unique art form and to integrate new technology into theatrical production.

The 19th-century scenic artist was the victim of this revolution, that is certain. The stature, skills, and techniques of scenic artists have atrophied since 1900. The nature of the profession of scenic artistry has changed with the theatre; the scope of the job is far broader than ever. Perhaps the skills of the Bibienas,

[18]Brockett.

de Loutherbourg, Servandoni, and Stanfield no longer are relevant. However, we have seen architecture turn its back to the Renaissance during this century and later return to "rediscover" classicism in the postmodern age. The so-called antique skills of the scenic artist should not be forgotten.

Technology and Scenic Art

In the 20th century, technology had a far greater impact on the scenic artist than in any previous time. The process of painting is much as it has been for centuries, but the materials available to the scenic artist are radically different now from the beginning of the century. Electric lighting in the theatre forced scenic artists to adapt their painting techniques to new effects and increased visibility. The impact of photography as a means of perception and image reproduction has affected the sort of painting a scenic artist might be called upon to execute. Digital imaging and xerography have put powerful new tools in the hands of the scenic designer, even replacing the scenic artist through projected images, photographic collages, and mechanically painted scenic units.

Paint and Painting Tools

Much of the discussion of Chapter 5 is the history of this century's tools for the scenic artist. It is worthwhile to review how many of the tools common to us now are new.

Paint itself has changed tremendously in the last 100 years. For centuries, scenic artists used ground dry pigments as the base for paint. They mixed the pigment with heated animal glue, water, and solvent to make a batch of paint as they went. Maintaining the glue pot was a primary chore of a paint boy or assistant scenic artist. The process is time-consuming and the product is rather perishable. Painting in warm climates is terrific for drop drying, but encourages odd growths in the paint bucket left too long in the sun. Paint mixed from pigment is a little finicky, as it needs continual stirring to prevent settling. The glue to pigment to water ratios are delicate. Too little glue (binder), and the paint will flake off; too much, and the paint is difficult to use or the finish will crack.

Scenic paint was made available in premixed form by the 1940s. American scenic paint manufacturers like Iddings and Gothic took the standard pigments and mixed them with casein as a binder, producing the thick, paste-like paint common today. This has simplified the painting job to a great degree. The several hours of preparing dry pigment into paint for a drop was made unnecessary.

Aniline dyes were widely used during most of the 20th century but are found less commonly now, due to concerns about their toxicity and the availability

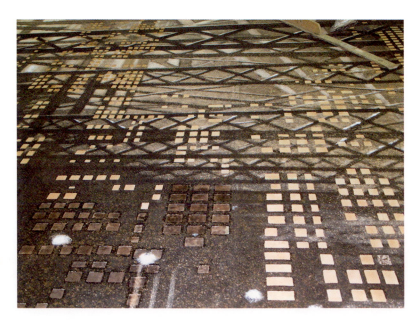

Figure 13.17
A backdrop for the American Ballet Theatre on the floor at Showman Fabricators, Inc. Here we see abstraction and 19th-century techniques together.

of modern highly saturated paints. These dyes are chemically created powdered color. They are mixed in small amounts with water and denatured alcohol to create watercolor-like dye. The vibrancy of the color, even when significantly diluted, made aniline dyes well suited for loose, watercolor painting techniques, washes, scrim work, working whenever transparency was desired, and wonderful cast shadows.

Highly saturated acrylic-based paints are now common and widely available. Their ease of use and cleanup make them very attractive to the scenic artist. Acrylics are flexible enough for painting on traditional scenic materials like canvas and are excellent paints over properly treated wood, metal, and compound textures.

Many tools common to the scenic artist are new to the 20th century. Brushes have changed little, except perhaps that good brushes are harder to find and very expensive when available. Paint spraying tools were made possible with finer metalworking techniques, which allowed mass production of the small parts required for a sprayer. Sprayers are common now in hand-pump, compressed air, and airless varieties, all of which were unknown to the scenic artist of the 19th century.

Stage Lighting

The electrification of stage lighting greatly affected the way the work of the scenic artist was seen on the stage. Most scenic artists of the time preferred gaslight over electric. The gaslight was a softer, dimmer light than electric. Homer Emens had this reaction to electric light:

> Nor do we owe much that is good to electric light. Nothing is better than gas for stage lighting, it is softer. It contributes more to the atmosphere of the stage than electric light. The real advantage of electric light is that it is more readily handled and since it is found in every village, one-night stands have all the effects of light that city stages can have.[19]

Electric light had so many advantages for play production that its presence was unavoidable. Once adapted for the stage, there was no turning back. Electric lighting facilitated translucency effects and it also made possible radical color shifts on the scenery on stage. New scenic designers of the early 20th century, particularly Joseph Urban, quickly grasped the profound shift in the relationship of painting and the new flexible lighting that would illuminate it. Urban employed a "broken color" system that allowed a painted drop, for example, to respond to different colors of light with subtlety. Instead of red light making a drop turn all red, the broken color system layered underpainting of one overall palette with overpainting of another. The color actually broke through in places and the underpainted colors, perhaps cool tones, responded to cooler light. The upper layers of color were geared to the warmer lights of amber and red. In this way drops could be painted to respond atmospherically to the changing light.[20]

Xerography and Digital Imaging

The ability to copy and create images electronically or digitally has been the most radical influence of technology on the scenic artist in the late 20th century. Photography altered audiences' and artists' sense of perception in the 19th century by creating the definitive "realistic" image. Film turned the photograph into a moving image, and the movie industry made that into an entertainment form. The presence of all of these challenged the stage picture and the scenic artist's ability to portray reality. It was inevitable that the photographic image would work its way onto the stage as a tool for the scenic designer.

The result for the scenic artist is an increased amount of copy work as a painter. Designers use the literal qualities of a photograph and the starkness of black- and -white photography as an important part of modern stage design. This requires that the scenic artist paint mechanically or have a machine print the image to be used, applied like wallpaper to the scenery. The quality of halftone images that we see in newspapers is one that a scenic designer may often employ in a design. To reproduce that quality, the scenic artist must carefully reproduce stage versions of the dot screens used to dither the black and white dots of the image.

A scenic designer can more easily photocopy than paint, in color or black and white, nearly any image and incorporate it into a stage design. The proliferation of "borrowed" images, collage designs, and outright copying has placed further pressures on scenic artists. Often, scenic designers will do the photocopying and

---

[19]"Stage Scenery and the Men Who Paint It," 1908, p. 88.

[20]Brockman, 1997.

the assemblage of the copied pieces as a substitute for traditional paint elevations. The scenic artist is invited to sort out the details of copying the style.

By the 1980s, mechanical painting machines were available to make full-stage drops. These machines took the paint elevations of a scenic designer and converted the images into digital information, which then guides the painting mechanism. These machines are large enough to paint goods measuring 28′ × 60′ and can paint onto a variety of materials, including muslin, vinyl, and Plexiglas. Paint is applied by a four-color gun that moves over the material. The paint used is not scenic paint but a solvent-based paint more appropriate for use in the delicate paint guns. The quality of the painting is not unlike that of an inkjet color printer, which may be appropriate for stage use, particularly under certain stylistic conditions. Depending on the material that was painted, the painting may be modified by a scenic artist after it has left the machine. Certainly the image quality will improve in the future and the undeniable economic

benefits of these automated painting devices will draw considerable business away from scenic artists.

This painting machine is an expensive process at the moment but not totally cost-prohibitive. It is certain to become increasingly competitive with the cost of using human scenic artists. This poses interesting questions as to the value of handmade painted imagery and the role of the scenic artist. For those of us who appreciate the living quality of the painter's craft and the simple expression of the artist's gesture, such a machine may seem abhorrent at first. The argument in favor of such a machine is very persuasive, and the presence of such devices, as with electric lighting, is not likely to disappear.

The 20th Century Scenic Artist

The development of the scenic designer in the 20th century is very well documented. It bears no new examination on these pages other than to accept the existence of the scenic designer and to remind the reader that the scenic designer came from the ranks of the scenic artists. How, then, has the role of the scenic artist changed?

Scenic Studios

By the turn of the century, the scenic studio was a strong presence in the major theatre countries of the world—Austria, England, France, and Germany—as it was in the United States. In Europe, the studio had the effect of standardization of scenery, just as it had in America. Fewer and fewer theatres could maintain full-time scenic shops of their own, so the studio fulfilled the need for scenery. The theatre was a growing business in Europe, too, so the quantity of scenery generated around the turn of the century was quite great. Studios increased efficiency and profits but discouraged the individual star painter.

Scenic painting was learned only by apprenticeship. The skills were handed down from one generation to the next in a very closed society of artists. The increasing business of the theatre put tremendous pressure on this society simply to produce. Scenic artists at the turn of the century were not only painters but businessmen as well. Their concerns were with running the studios, acquiring work, and finishing on schedule. Artistic integrity was beginning to slip from the profession.

The studios isolated the scenic artist from the world. This isolation may be seen no place more

Figure 13.18 This portrait was executed for the television series *Legend*. Created by Xuzheng He.

profoundly than in Paris, where the art of painting had been embroiled in revolution from the beginning of the impressionist movement in the 1860s. The radical and famous new styles of painting, publicly displayed at length, had little or no effect on the scenic artists of the time. The closed world of the scenic artist did not embrace any sense of the change in artistic direction.

Perhaps the existence of the studios and the popularity of the theatre made this change impossible. Studios responded to the growing demand for scenic decoration by creating more and more scenery. Ready-made scenery was common in Europe by 1900, as in the United States. The weight of effort to create drops, keep scenery available, and stay competitive with other studios did not foster an atmosphere of experimentation and change. The success of business consumed the possibility of variation from accepted traditional forms.

The Scenic Designer

The scenic artist had been creator and executor of the stage picture for 400 years of development. The revolution of the 20th century would tear those two roles apart from one another, putting the scenic artist in the supporting role of executant. The scenic designer would determine the style; the scenic artist would make it happen. This new relationship finally would alter the scenic studio's relationship to current artistic trends by bringing a new artist, the scenic designer, into the studio.

New Forms of Stage Scenery

A modern revolution in theatre began in Europe and spread to England, Scandinavia, Eastern Europe, Russia, and the United States. By the early 20th century, theatre had been thoroughly changed in its literature, acting styles, directing, and designing. The first visible change was a naturalistic stage picture of the world as it truly is, in great detail. The naturalistic style first brought to the stage by André Antoine's Théâtre Libre in Paris was famously characterized at the time as a "slice of life" placed on the stage.

Naturalism and realism gave way quickly to symbolism, exoticism, expressionism, idealism, and many forms of nonrealistic stage design. The two primary elements of stage design from the Renaissance to the end of the 19th century, painted scenes and illusionistic scenes, suddenly disappeared.

Scenic designers worked three-dimensionally as well as two-dimensionally from this point forward. The scenic artist was faced with very new forms and challenges to work with. Sculpting and texturing became new skills for the scenic artists. Painting styles changed with every new design and scenic designer. The fundamental shift for the scenic artist from creator to replicator had a profound impact on the job. The scenic artist became stylistically anonymous, transparent. This artist's job was to replicate the style of the scenic designer and rarely would one work with the same designer for extended periods.

The ability to emulate the style of another is perhaps the greatest asset of a modern scenic artist. The chameleon-like skill of shifting from one designer's taut, detailed style to another's loose cartoonish style is a common demand on the painter of today. The scenic artist has been removed from top billing to a secondary role, yet the work is as difficult as ever, if not more so. The work of the great early scenic designers of the 20th century was realized by scenic artists who had to learn new skills to achieve the work. Robert Edmund Jones' dense atmospheric settings would only be illustrations in a book if Robert Bergman had not attempted pouring paint right from the bucket. Even Leon Bakst and Pablo Picasso, two of the most painterly scenic designers of the 20th century, had their work done by another: Vladimir Polunin.

Scenic Artists and Scenic Designers in America

In this century, theatre in the United States reached its height in popularity and impact. New York City remained the center of theatre in America. Most of the significant scenic studios in the United States were in the metropolitan New York area for most of this century. Many still are, and most of the members of United Scenic Artists are New York City residents.

The union that began around 1896 had grown to have nearly 900 members by 1941 in the New York City area alone.[21] Of those members, 213 were scenic artists, almost one and a half times the number of scenic designers. Close to 30 scenic studios were operating in the New York area at that time.

Scenic designers and scenic artists in America comprised both Americans and Europeans. Many scenic

---

[21]Larson, 1989.

Figure 13.19
Modern scenic art puts a wide variety of demands on the artist.

artists came from Europe during the first half of the century, as theatre boomed and well-paying jobs were available. One of the earliest scenic designers of the modern era, Joseph Urban, brought an entire team of scenic artists from Vienna with him to America. That team brought the continental style of painting with them and introduced it to New York at the beginning of contemporary design. The team eventually created Triangle Studios, one of the largest and most respected scenic studios in America.

The first professional American scenic designers, such as Jones, Lee Simonson, Jo Mielziner, and Donald Oenslager, relied on their own expressive style of painting in their designs. Painting was still a dominant force in design, but it was a simpler and more personal style. The challenge to the scenic artist was to recreate the work of the scenic designer accurately and sensitively with ultimate regard for the style. Such painters as Robert Bergman and Raymond Sovey of Lee Lash Studios incorporated the continental style of Triangle Studios with the personal styles of the new designers and invented unorthodox techniques to get the job done. This newest generation of scenic artists was willing to use any tool or technique to achieve what the designer intended. Here, the break from the old system, where designer and painter were one person, is most distinct. The scenic designer is free to imagine anything appropriate to the stage picture he or she seeks. The scenic artist becomes the

magician who can solve the riddle of how to achieve the design.

The Impact of the Film Industry

It is ironic that movies have also preserved 19th-century illusionistic painting. The irony is doubled when one realizes that the presence of the movies had such a profoundly negative effect on the theatre's business after the 1930s. Certainly, the film industry attracted scenic artists in great numbers, as film established itself as a major industry during the early part of the 20th century. In the early days, most film scenery was like old-fashioned theatrical scenery with painted dimension and shadows. The camera lens was fooled more easily than the eye.

Modern filmmaking relies heavily on illusionistic painting, although usually in miniature. Most special effects scenes are shot in layers that are assembled in postproduction. Exaggerated, remote, dangerous, or physically impossible backgrounds normally are created by skilled matte artists and layered onto film behind the actors during postproduction after the action is shot. Film production relies more and more heavily on successful illusionistic painting for backgrounds because they are cost-effective and visually perfect. Most audiences are unaware that nearly all stunt shots take place in front of paintings.

The Current Scene

United Scenic Artists merged its locals (New York, Chicago, Florida, and Los Angeles) into one single union during the early 1990s. The membership of the union has grown with the adoption of the two-track examination process. Major scenic studios have emerged in Florida and Nevada to support the explosion of entertainment theme parks and casinos. Broadway theatre has undergone a significant upsurge of popularity through the mega-musical format of such works as *The Phantom of the Opera* and *Sunset Boulevard*, both of which rely extensively on what might appear to be 19th-century styles of scenic grandeur. The film industry continues to rely on skilled muralists, matte painters, and digital artists to create in two dimensions what is too expensive or too dangerous to film on location. There is no doubt that the art of scenic painting will continue throughout the world and that talented painters, who command the art of illusion, will continue to be in demand.

CONCLUSION

The craft of scenic artistry came from distant beginnings in the Greek and Roman theatre. During the Italian Renaissance, scenic designing first was scientifically explored and practiced by some of the greatest talents and minds of the time, particularly Aleotti, Serlio, and Torelli. Italy thoroughly dominated the field of stage painting, creating a systematic approach to decorating the stage that was copied worldwide, often under the supervision of Italian artists. The Bibiena family of scenic artists was at the apex of the Italian style for over 150 years, several decades into the 19th century. The Italians created a stunning world of illusion and motion.

Gradually, the rigid Italian format was replaced by a less symmetrical array of scenic units on the stage, particularly in England. Painting techniques changed in the English style also, as a more romantic and atmospheric landscape filled the stage. The French painter Servandoni and the English painter de Loutherbourg explored evocative lighting effects, transparency, and more subtle means of moving scenery combined with masterful illusionistic painting techniques. Their innovations were fully exploited worldwide during the 19th century by artists such as J.H. Grieve and Clarkson Stanfield in England and Charles Cicéri in France, who became some of the most famous scenic artists in history. The illusionism they and others practiced made the theatre extremely popular and gave rise to other entertainment, panoramas and dioramas, based totally scenic spectacle.

These arts were imported to the United States at the beginning of the 19th century. By the end of the

Figure 13.20
Doug Schmidt's design for *Into the Woods* depended on excellent technique. Scenic Art Studios, New York.

century, America had developed its own scenic artists and an important scenic studio system to produce high volumes of scenery for a growing theatre business. Scenic studios became a major force in Europe as well as America by 1900 and have remained so ever since.

The 20th century completely changed the role of the scenic artist, as the new figure of the scenic designer emerged. The film industry also eroded the importance of theatre in society, and scenic artists drifted to films as an outlet for their skills. With the shrinking of theatrical production and the radical change in theatrical production styles from the 19th century to the 20th century, scenic artistry began to lose grasp of the older techniques of illusion and perspective. Some of these skills are now so far out of favor and practice that few scenic artists or designers fully understand the rules of perspective.

Scenic artists rose in recognition to become famous in the eyes of the public during the 19th century. The modern theatre world turned so rapidly from the techniques scenic artists had practiced for 300 years that those who had been famous in the 19th century became the subject of ridicule by modern scenic designers. The modern scenic artist generally is much more anonymous than his or her predecessors. However, the reliance on scenic artists in theatre and film continues and is likely to continue for centuries to come. There are magical things that only a brush, paint, and talent can describe.

Bibliography

"Art in the Theatre: The Decline of Scenic Art in America." *Magazine of Art* (April 1894).

Ashworth, Bradford. *Notes on Scene Painting*. New Haven, CT: Whitlock's, 1952, 1956.

Association of Theatrical Artists and Craftspeople. *The New York Source Book*. New York: Source Book Press, 1997.

Auletti, Toni. "The Use of a Computer Painting Machine for Theatrical Applications." Masters Thesis, University of Michigan, 1995.

Bablet, Denis, *Revolutions in Stage Design of the XXth Century*. New York–Paris: Leon Amiel, 1977.

———. *Esthétique Générale du Décor de Théâtre de 1870 à 1914*. Paris: Centre National de la Recherche Scientifique, 1975.

Brockett, Oscar G. and Findlay, Robert R., *Century of Innovation*. New Jersey: Prentice-Hall, 1973.

Brockman, Lance. "Revisiting the Twin Cities Scenic Collection." *Theatre Design and Technology* (Winter 1997).

———. *Theatre of the Fraternity*. Jackson, Mississippi: University Press of Mississippi, 1996.

———. *The Twin Cities Scenic Collection*. Minneapolis: University Art Museum, University of Minnesota, 1987.

Burris-Meyer, Harold, and Edward Cole. *Scenery for the Theatre*. Boston: Little, Brown and Co., 1938.

Cambell, Lily B. *Scenes and Machines on the English Stage*. Cambridge, MA: Cambridge University Press, 1923.

Cole, Rex Vicat. *Perspective for the Artist*. New York: Dover Publications, 1976.

Coquiot, Gustave. *Nouveau Manuel Complet de Peintres-Decorateurs de Théâtre*. Paris: Roret, 1910.

Decugis, Nicole, and Suzanne Reymond. *Le Décor de Théâtre en France du Moyen Age à 1925*. Paris: Compagnie Française des Arts Graphiques, 1953.

De Grandis, Luigina. *Theory and Use of Color*. New York: Harry N. Abrams, 1984.

Edgerton, Samuel Y., Jr. *The Renaissance Rediscovery of Linear Perspective*. New York: Harper & Row, 1975.

Fontanesi, Francesco. Illustrazioni Teatrali. Casalecchio di Reno, Bologna, 1988.

Galli Bibiena, *Ferdinando. L'architettura*, Trans. Dunbar H. Ogden. Berkeley: University of California Press, 1978.

———. *Direzioni*, Trans. Dunbar H. Ogden. Berkeley: University of California Press, 1978.

Gregory, Ralph. *Sign Painting Techniques*. Cincinnati, OH: Signs of the Times Publishing, 1973.

"Guys and Dolls," *TCI* (Theatre Crafts International), Volume 26, Number 7 (August–September 1992)

Hughes, Glenn. *A History of the American Theatre 1700–1950*. London: Samuel French, 1951.

Itten, Johannes. *The Art of Color*. Trans., Ernst van Haagen. New York: Reinhold, 1961.

Joseph, Stephen. *Scene Painting and Design*. London: Pitman and Sons, 1964.

Lancaster, Henry Carrington. *Laurent et d'autres décorateurs de l'Hôtel de Bourgogne*, Trans. Mémoire de Mahelot. Paris: Champion, 1920.

Larson, Orville K. *Scene Design in the American Theatre from 1915 to 1960*. Fayetteville, AR: University of Arkansas Press, 1989.

Lucie-Smith, Edward. *Dictionary of Art Terms*. London: Thames and Hudson, 1984.

Mancini, Franco. *Scenographia Italiano del Rinascimento al'eta Romantica*. Rome: Fratelli Fabbri Editori, 1966.

Mayer, Ralph. *The Artist's Handbook of Materials and Techniques*. New York: Viking Press, 1940.

McCann, Michael. *Artist Beware*. New York: Watson-Guptill, 1979.

Moynet, Georges. *La Machinerie Théâtrale Trucs et Décors*, Geneva, Minkoff, 1973

Moynet, Jean. *French Theatrical Production in the Nineteenth Century*, Trans. Allan Jackson. Binghamton, NY: Center for Modern Theatre Research, 1976.

Nicoll, Allardyce. *The Development of the Theatre*. New York: Harcourt, Brace and World, 1966.

Ogden, Dunbar H. *The Italian Baroque Stage*. Berkeley: University of California Press, 1978.

Orsini, Baldassare. *Geometria*, Trans. Dunbar H. Ogden. Berkeley: University of California Press, 1978.

———. *Le Scene*, Trans. Dunbar H. Ogden. Berkeley: University of California Press, 1978.

Pecktal, Lynn. *Designing and Painting for the Theatre*. New York: Holt, Rinehart, Winston, 1975.

Polakov, Lester. *We Live to Paint Again*. New York: Logbooks Press, 1993.

Polunin, Vladimir. *The Continental Method of Scene Painting*. London: Dance Books Ltd., [1927] 1980.

Pozzo, Andrea. *Prospettiva*, Trans. Dunbar H. Ogden. Berkeley: University of California Press, 1978.

Rose, A. *Scenes for Scene Painters*. London: George Routledge and Sons, 1925.

Rosenfeld, Sybil. *Georgian Scene Painters and Scene Painting*. Cambridge, MA: Cambridge University Press, 1981.

———. *A Short History of Scene Design in Great Britain*. Totowa, NJ: Rowman and Littlefield, 1973.

Rossol, Monona. *The Artist's Complete Health and Safety Guide*. NY: Allworth Press, 1994.

———. *Stage Fright*. New York: ACTS, 1987.

Scholz, János, Ed. *Baroque and Romantic Stage Design*. New York: E.P. Dutton, 1962.

Simonson, Lee. *The Stage Is Set*. New York: Theatre Arts Books, 1970.

———, Ed. *Theatre Art*. New York: W.W. Norton, 1934.

Smith, Ray. *The Artist's Handbook*. New York: Alfred A. Knopf, 1987.

Southern, Richard. *The Seven Ages of Theatre*. New York: Hill and Wang, 1971.

———. *Changeable Scenery*. London: Faber and Faber, 1951.

"Stage Scenery and the Men Who Paint It." *Theatre Magazine* **16** (August 1908).

TCI. Buyers Guide. New York: Intertec Publishing, 1997.

Troili, Giulio. *Paradossi*, Trans. Dunbar H. Ogden. Berkeley: University of California Press, 1978.

"USITT Scenic Design and Technical Production Graphic Standards." *T, D & T Magazine* (Spring 1993).

Vitruvius. *The Ten Books on Architecture*, Trans. Ingrid D. Rowland. Cambridge: Cambridge University Press, 1999.

Wagman, Howard M. "Bristle and Its Importance to the American Paint Brush Industry." Masters Thesis, Graduate Division of the Wharton School, University of Pennsylvania, 1952.

Wischmeier, Randolph Jay. "A History of the United Scenic Artists, Local Union 829 and Local Union 350," Masters Thesis, University of Texas–Austin, 1978.

Wolcott, John R. "The Scene Painter's Palette: 1750–1835." *Theatre Journal* 33, no.4 (December 1981).

Index